CONTROLLING MARKET POWER IN TELECOMMUNICATIONS

ANTITRUST VS SECTOR-SPECIFIC REGULATION

Controlling Market Power in Telecommunications

Antitrust vs Sector-specific Regulation

DAMIEN GERADIN

MICHEL KERF

OXFORD
UNIVERSITY PRESS

OXFORD
UNIVERSITY PRESS

Great Clarendon Street, Oxford OX2 6DP

Oxford University Press is a department of the University of Oxford.
It furthers the University's objective of excellence in research, scholarship,
and education by publishing worldwide in

Oxford New York

Auckland Bangkok Buenos Aires Cape Town Chennai
Dar es Salaam Delhi Hong Kong Istanbul Karachi Kolkata
Kuala Lumpur Madrid Melbourne Mexico City Mumbai Nairobi
São Paulo Shanghai Taipei Tokyo Toronto

Oxford is a registered trade mark of Oxford University Press
in the UK and in certain other countries

Published in the United States
by Oxford University Press Inc., New York

© Damien Geradin and Michel Kerf 2003

The moral rights of the authors have been asserted
Database right Oxford University Press (maker)

First published 2003

British Library Cataloguing in Publication Data

Data available

Library of Congress Cataloging in Publication Data

Geradin, Damien
Controlling market power in telecommunications: striking the right balance between antitrust
and sector-specific rules and institutions / Damien Geradin, Michel Kerf.
p. cm.
Includes bibliographical references.
1. Telecommunication–Law and legislation. 2. Antitrust law. 3. Competition. I. Kerf, Michel,
1965- II. Title
K4305 .C66 2002
343.09'94–dc21
2002038135

ISBN 0-19-924243-7

1 3 5 7 9 10 8 6 4 2

Typeset by Kolam
Printed in Great Britain
on acid-free paper by
Biddles Ltd, Guildford and King's Lynn

Acknowledgements

As is almost always the case, the authors benefited greatly from interactions with a number of professors, mentors, and colleagues. In this respect, we owe a special debt to Warrick Smith—Manager of the Private Provision of Public Services Group at the World Bank—who shared with us some of his early work on the relationship between antitrust authorities and sector-specific regulators in infrastructure and heightened our interest in the topic. We are very grateful also to Michael Brunton, Chris Doyle, Rob Frieden, Timothy Irwin, Colin Long, Jose Ricardo Melo, Colin Scott, and Douglas Webb, who shared information and commented on various parts of the manuscript.

We would also like to thank Pablo Cabral, Diana Sendagorta, Sorayut Srisuma, Moira Nealon, Miranda Morozzo, Soniya Mitra and Adam Brenneman who each worked for two to three months as Knowledge Interns at the World Bank and provided excellent research assistance. We would like, in particular, to highlight the contributions of Sorayut, who collected much useful information for the study of the various country models; of Miranda, who researched some of the topics discussed in Chapter 3; and of Adam, who did a truly outstanding job compiling the data on price comparisons between the five countries and preparing the Annex.

Finally, this book would not have been written without the support of our respective institutions. Our thanks go in particular to Paul Demaret, Director of the Institute for European Legal Studies of the University of Liège, and to Nemat Shafik, Vice-President, Private Sector Development and Infrastructure at the World Bank, for their constant encouragements.

Our efforts have been financially supported by the Pôles d'Attraction Inter-Universitaire, a research project initiated by the Belgian State, Prime Minister's Office, Science Policy Programming, and by the World Bank, which granted a three–month sabbatical to one of the authors to start work on this project.

The opinions presented here are those of the authors; they do not necessarily reflect the views of the World Bank's Board of Directors or of the governments that they represent.

DAMIEN GERADIN
MICHEL KERF
Liège and Washington, DC
March 2002

Acknowledgements

Contents

1

Introduction

For much of the twentieth century, competition between different operators was very much the exception rather than the rule in the telecommunications industry. In many cases, the private operators which first launched telecommunications services were subsequently nationalized and, in the period following the Second World War, telecommunications operators—whether public or private—enjoyed legal or de facto monopolies over most segments of the telecommunications market in almost all countries.[1]

In order to prevent these operators from abusing their monopoly power, a series of controls was put in place. Such controls were, for the most part, specific to the telecommunications industry and focused, to a large extent, on the prices which could be imposed on end-users as well as on the minimum service standards which operators had to meet to fulfil their so-called universal service obligations. The instruments used to control the behaviour of telecommunications operators included formal agreements between the companies and public authorities as well as more informal mechanisms when public authorities owned and directly managed the telecommunications operators.

The situation started to change in the 1980s when some countries proceeded to liberalize their telecommunications markets and to take steps—including privatization—to ensure that telecommunications companies would be operated at arm's length from the Government. These reforms have been pursued in earnest up to the present time. Over the past two decades, an increasing number of countries have opened their telecommunications markets to competition. While less than twenty countries had opened the provision of any fixed basic telecommunications services to competition by the mid-1990s, 40 per cent of all countries had done so by the year 2000, including about seventy countries which had allowed competition in basic local services. A very large number of countries —80 per cent or more—have allowed competition in the provision of cellular and Internet services. And by the end of 2000, about one hundred incumbent operators had been privatized, slightly more than the number of incumbent carriers remaining in public hands.[2]

---

[1] See, for example, Bjorn Wellenius and Peter A Stern (eds), *Implementing Reforms in the Telecommunications Sector, Lessons from Experience* (Washington, DC: The World Bank, 1994) 2–3.

[2] See ITU, *Trends in Telecommunication Reform—Interconnection Regulation* (Geneva: International Telecommunications Union, 3rd edn 2000–2001) 1–5.

The need for regulatory oversight of telecommunications activities has not disappeared with the implementation of those reforms. But the nature of that oversight has changed for two main types of reasons. First, the privatization of an increasing number of incumbent operators and the entry of new operators into the telecommunications market mean that regulatory oversight cannot anymore be exercised informally through direct control of the companies by the State. It requires, instead, that formal rules and implementation mechanisms be established. Second, while the ultimate objective of regulation remains to ensure that users are provided with the range and quality of services which they need at the lowest possible prices, competitive pressures are now being relied upon to promote those outcomes. Accordingly, one main function of regulatory frameworks is to establish a level playing field between competitors and to ensure that competitive pressures remain sufficiently intense.

This evolution of regulatory requirements clearly warrants a reassessment of the respective roles of sector-specific rules and implementing institutions on the one hand, and of economy-wide antitrust rules and institutions on the other. One could argue, for example, that as the focus of regulation shifts away from imposing specific price controls upon monopolistic incumbents and toward enhancing competitive pressures between multiple operators, antitrust instruments are bound to replace sector-specific ones. One could also argue, however, that creating and maintaining a competitive environment in an industry as complex as telecommunications is going to require the application of very specific rules by authorities with specialized expertise in telecommunications.

Discussing the merits of these claims and attempting to determine the appropriate scope of sector-specific and economy-wide regulatory instruments in liberalized telecommunications environments is precisely the object of the present book. We will attempt to shed some light on this topic by studying the experiences of five countries which have fully liberalized all segments of their telecommunications sectors, which have each accumulated several years of experience regulating these fully liberalized markets, and which have chosen different mixes of sector-specific and economy-wide instruments for doing so. These five countries are: Australia, Chile, New Zealand, the United Kingdom and the United States.

Chapter 2, which follows the present Introduction, summarises the main factors which prompted governments to introduce competition in telecommunications, discusses the main characteristics of the sector-specific and economy-wide rules and institutions which can be used to implement the economic regulation of telecommunications, and presents seven specific criteria or objectives which can be used to evaluate different regulatory frameworks.

Chapter 3 discusses key issues of economic regulation in telecommunications, which will be touched upon throughout the book. Such issues include the pricing of retail and wholesale telecommunications services, the merits of facilities-based competition versus resale and unbundled access, the allocation of scarce resources such as the radio-electric spectrum for example, the organization of a universal service regime compatible with competitive markets, the merits of imposing vertical separation between different segments of the telecommunications market, the regulatory implications of convergence, and the extent to which one can rely on international comparisons of telecommunications prices to assess the efficiency of different regulatory frameworks.

Chapters 4 to 8 review the experiences of each of the five countries mentioned above. In each case, we discuss the origins and the characteristics of the present regulatory framework, we review the main regulatory decisions which have been taken under that framework, and we try to analyse the extent to which the regulatory framework meets the seven objectives identified in Chapter 2.

Chapter 9 compares how the five frameworks fare vis-à-vis those seven objectives and attempts to identify some lessons of experience or best practices. Finally, we present our conclusions in Chapter 10.

2

Conceptual Framework

This chapter will briefly summarize the shift of paradigm which is taking place with respect to issues of market structure in telecommunications. It discusses the main types of rules and institutions which can be used to control market power in the telecommunications sector. And, finally, it presents seven criteria which can be used to evaluate different regulatory frameworks for telecommunications.

A. Market power and telecommunications

This section will present the reasons which are prompting policy-makers to open telecommunications markets to competition, and discuss the continuing need for intervention by public authorities in that context.

1. From Public Monopolies to Competitive Markets

Telecommunications sectors have until recently been organised in many countries around a dominant, or even a monopolistic, operator. This market organization was justified on the basis of four main types of rationales. First, it was argued that the establishment of telecommunications networks involved large fixed costs and that a single enterprise would therefore be able to provide services at lower costs than would two or more different enterprises (the 'natural monopoly' argument).[1] Second, some have argued that network externalities justified organizing the telecommunications sector on a monopoly basis.[2] Network externalities are present in the area of telecommunications since the value of a

---

[1] There is a rich body of academic literature on the regulation of 'natural monopolies'. For the main works, see William W Sharkey, *The Theory of Natural Monopoly* (Cambridge: Cambridge University Press, 1982); Christopher Foster, *Privatization, Public Ownership and Regulation of Natural Monopoly* (Oxford: Basil Blackwell, 1993); Richard A Posner, *Natural Monopoly and Its Regulation* (30th edn, Washington, DC: Cato Institute, 1999).

[2] For a good discussion of the concept of 'network externalities' see Mark A Lemley and David McGowan, 'Legal Implications of Network Economic Effects' (1998) 86 *California L Rev* 479; Nicholas Economides, 'The Economics of Networks' (1996) 16 *Intl J of Industrial Organization* 673; Michael L Katz and Carl Shapiro, 'Network Externalities, Competition, and Compatibility' (1985) 75 *American Economic Rev* 424. A large list of published articles on network externalities is available at <http://www.stern.nyu.edu/networks/biblio_hframe.html>.

network increases, for each user, with the number of network subscribers.[3] As a result, for a given total number of subscribers, the value of a single network is much greater than the total value of several smaller unconnected networks. Third, monopolistic structures were deemed necessary to enable cross-subsidies between different services or users—ie to enable an enterprise to compensate for losses incurred because of some activities or users (such as rural telephony or local service for example) with the excess profits gained with some other activities or users (such as urban telephony or international services for example).[4] Opening the market to competition would prompt entry into the segments where excess profits are made ('cream-skimming' effect), therefore wiping out the revenues required to operate the cross-subsidies.[5] A fourth argument was that strategic or security concerns dictated that the provision of telecommunications services be reserved to a particular enterprise often controlled by the State.

In many countries, those arguments justified the award of exclusive rights to dominant telecommunications operators. It was clear, however, that if those operators were left free to exploit their market power, well-known negative consequences would be likely to ensue.[6] First, a monopolist can impose quality and price levels, which deprive the users from much of the welfare gains associated with the provision of the goods or services.[7] Those gains can be captured by the monopolist or transferred, in totality or in part, by the monopolist to others in exchange for obtaining or maintaining the monopoly position. Second, if a monopolist does not have the ability to discriminate perfectly between users, it will also limit the amount of goods or services provided below socially optimal levels. Finally, the absence of competition will reduce the incentives of a monopolist to innovate and to operate efficiently. Consequently, regulatory controls were imposed upon the operators in an attempt to keep the volume, quality, and price of services at welfare maximising level and to promote efficiency and innovation.[8] Such controls were often imposed through direct ownership of telecommunications enterprises by the State, with the sector ministry typically

[3] See Mark Amstrong, 'Competition in Telecommunications' (1997) 13 *Oxford Rev of Economic Policy* 64–65.

[4] Nicolas Curien, 'The Theory and Measure of Cross-Subsidies: An Application to the Telecommunications Industry' (1991) 9 *Intl J of Industrial Organization* 73.

[5] On the issue of cream-skimming, see Peter Smith, 'Subscribing to Monopoly, The Telecom Monopolist's Lexicon—Revisited', *Public Policy for the Private Sector*, The World Bank, Note No 53, September 1995, 3.

[6] See N Gregory Mankiw, *Principles of Economics* (Fort Worth, Tex., Dryden Press, 1998) 308 et seq; Richard A Posner, *Antitrust Law: An Economic Perspective* (Chicago: University of Chicago Press, 1978) 8 et seq; Stephen Breyer, *Regulation and Its Reform* (Cambridge, Mass.: Harvard University Press, 1982) 13 et seq.

[7] Simon Bishop and Mike Walker, *The Economics of EC Competition Law* (London: Sweet & Maxwell, 1999) 21.

[8] Alfred A Kahn, *The Economics of Regulation—Principles and Institutions* (Boston, Mass., and London: MIT Press, 1998) vol 2, 220; Tony Prosser, *Law and The Regulator* (Oxford: Clarendon Press, 1997) 5.

performing policy, ownership, as well as regulatory functions (the so-called 'PTT model').[9]

In the last two decades, however, the wisdom of relying on regulated public monopolies for the provision of telecommunications services was increasingly put into question.[10] The first and arguably most important reason is that the performance of those operators proved disappointing. Various studies demonstrated that publicly owned companies, in general, tended to be less efficient than private ones, and that telecommunications markets open to competition tended to perform much better than those which were not.[11] In addition, it quickly became clear that regulation—especially when exercised through public ownership by a sector ministry—suffered many drawbacks.[12] Regulators often lacked the technical skills required to effectively regulate the incumbent operator, short-term political considerations tended to distort the regulatory process, and regulatory capture by the managers of the public monopoly was frequent. In those conditions, it was argued that reliance on competition, even in markets where competition was imperfect, might yield better outcomes than reliance on regulated monopolies. Furthermore, even when competition could not replace regulation, it could reduce the scope for political or industry capture, yield useful information to regulators, and therefore facilitate the regulatory process.

In parallel, the arguments that had been advanced to justify the creation of telecommunications monopolies appeared relatively weak in the first place. Technological evolution, for example, reduces the scope of telecommunications activities that present natural monopoly features.[13] For instance, as the price of mobile communications decreases, mobile networks, which present few if any natural monopoly features, become cheaper to deploy than fixed networks in regions which are not very densely populated.[14] In addition, as will be seen in

---

[9] For a discussion of the PTT model, see Rob Frieden, *Managing Internet Driven Change in International Telecommunications* (Boston, Mass. and London: Artech House, 2001) 54 et seq.

[10] Colin Scott, 'Institutional Competition and Coordination in the Process of Telecommunications Liberalisation' in Joseph McCahery et al, *International Regulatory Competition and Regulatory Coordination: Perspectives on Economic Regulation in Europe and the United States* (Oxford: Clarendon Press, 1996) 383.

[11] See, for example, Ahmed Galal et al, *Welfare Consequences of Selling Public Enterprises—An Empirical Analysis* (Oxford: Oxford University Press, 1994) which examines in detail twelve specific cases of privatization (including three cases in the telecommunications sector) in Chile, Malaysia, Mexico and the United Kingdom; see also Bjorn Wellenius and Peter A Stern (eds), *Implementing Reforms in the Telecommunications Sector—Lessons from Experience* (Washington, DC: The World Bank, 1994) which discusses the international experience of telecommunications sector reform, covering a wide range of issues and countries.

[12] See David M Newbery, *Privatisation, Restructuring, and Regulation of Network Utilities* (Cambridge, Mass.: MIT Press, 2000) 134.

[13] See James Bond, 'Telecommunications is Dead, Long Live Networking', *Public Policy for the Private Sector*, Note 119, The World Bank, July 1997.

[14] It is the fixed line local network that is most often mentiond as presenting natural monopoly features because of the high fixed costs of setting up the network and the low marginal cost of adding an extra consumer, which together entail decreasing average costs. Thus, a single firm will have lower unit costs than two or more smaller firms.

Chapter 3, the development of alternative networks could also be facilitated by the process of convergence that is taking place in the communications sector. Finally, while some telecommunications activities may still retain natural monopoly characteristics, exclusive rights need not necessarily be granted for this reason. If a segment of the sector does indeed constitute a natural monopoly, a single provider should emerge in that sector whether it enjoys a legal monopoly or not. It is only when the competitive process leading to the eventual selection of the single service provider would be considered too disruptive that a real rationale emerges for granting exclusive rights to a single firm from the start.[15] Even then, potential advantages must be weighed against the risk of selecting a monopoly provider that has not been tested by competition and might therefore not be the most efficient. If exclusive rights are granted, there are also serious risks that they might encompass some potentially competitive activities, thereby eliminating competition where it could have taken place. Relying on market forces rather than on administrative decisions to determine which activities constitute natural monopolies presents distinct advantages in a sector like the rapidly changing telecommunications sector.

Network externalities can, for their part, be preserved in a market open to competition provided the various networks can be interconnected. As to the social objectives pursued through cross-subsidy schemes, they can be achieved by means that do not require that a monopoly be maintained in the sector. For example, a fund can be set up through general taxation or through fees levied on all telecommunications operators, and can be used to subsidize some particular services or users.[16] Finally, a range of technical solutions exist to address strategic or security concerns adequately without having to rely on public ownership and restrict market entry.

For these reasons, a large number of countries have now totally or partially privatized their dominant telecommunications operator, and have taken a wide range of measures to promote competition.[17]

2. The Continuing Need for Intervention by Public Authorities

The disappointing performance of public monopolies, a greater awareness of the potential drawbacks of regulation, the weakness of most traditional arguments in favour of monopolistic arrangements, and technical changes which reduced

---

[15] Competition between different providers of infrastructure services, such as telecommunications, might, for example, lead to wide price fluctuations that could be seen as disruptive. In activities such as the provision of local loop services, which are characterized by high fixed costs and low marginal costs, prices might be driven down to marginal costs during periods of intense competition between different network operators and might rise above total average costs when a firm is able to exercise some degree of market power.

[16] See Werner Neu and Ulrich Stumpf, 'Evaluating Compensation Requirements by Telecommunications Universal Service Providers: A New Challenge to Regulators' (1997) 26 *Communications and Strategies* 165.

[17] See Colin D Long, *Telecommunications Law and Practice* (2nd edn, London: Sweet & Maxwell, 1995).

fixed costs in many segments of the markets and facilitated the emergence of a plurality of networks and service providers constitute powerful arguments for relying on competition to foster efficiency in telecommunications and ensure that efficiency gains are passed on to the users. Such benefits cannot be reaped, however, without adequate intervention by public authorities. For example:

—The structure of the market might need to be modified in order to promote competition.[18] For example, in addition to eliminating exclusive rights and other explicit barriers to entry into the various segments of the telecommunications market, it might also be advisable to introduce a degree of vertical separation between different activities in order to reduce the risks of anti-competitive practices and facilitate access to essential facilities.[19]

—In order to be able to provide telecommunications services new entrants must gain access to the networks of the incumbents. This is true even when new entrants build their own facilities, as different networks need to be interconnected.[20] Some measures will usually need to be taken to ensure that interconnection agreements between operators can be concluded under equitable conditions.

—Additional steps might be needed to ensure non-discriminatory access by all competitors to scarce resources, such as telephone numbers, radio spectrum, etc.

—Users are unlikely to switch from one service provider to another if this means they have to change their own telephone number or if they need to dial longer numbers when they place a call. In order to maintain a level playing field between the incumbent and its competitors, steps may thus need to be taken to ensure number portability[21] or dialling parity[22] for example.

---

[18] See Newbery (n 12 above) 135.

[19] An essential facility is a facility which cannot economically be replicated by new entrants but to which new entrants must have access in order to be able to compete with the incumbent in a given market. When an integrated incumbent competes in that market with other operators and, at the same time, controls access to the essential facility, the incumbent might have an incentive to restrict the other operators' access to the facility in order to gain an advantage in the competitive market. In those conditions, preventing a single company from controlling access to the essential facility and also from operating in the competitive market—ie imposing a structural separation between the two activities—might be the best way to remove the 'gate-keeper's' incentives to discriminate between the various operators which require access to the essential facility. For a recent review of the essential facilities doctrine, see Abbott B Lipsky and Gregory J Sidak, 'Essential Facilities' (1999) 51 *Stanford L Rev* 1187. See also Philip Areeda's seminal article, 'Essential Facilities: An Epithet in Need of Limiting Principles' (1990) 58 *Antitrust L J* 841.

[20] The interconnection problem is generally independent of the number of access points to the end-user. The end-user will indeed adhere to a unique network and a service provider will be compelled to interconnect with this network. The presence of network competition should, however, facilitate the negotiation of interconnection agreements among operators. See Damien Geradin and Christophe Humpe, 'Regulatory Issues in Establishment and Management of Communications Infrastructure: The Impact of Network Convergence' (2002) 3 *J of Network Industries*, 99.

[21] Ensuring number portability means ensuring that users are able to keep the same telephone number when switching from one telecommunications operator to another.

[22] Ensuring dial parity means ensuring that users do not have to dial additional numbers when they choose certain telecommunications operators rather than others.

—Cross-subsidies built into the rate structure of incumbent operators are incompatible with competition as new operators can enter the profitable segments of the market and compete away the profits on which the incumbent relies to subsidize the non-profitable services. When authorities decide that some services should remain subsidized, new mechanisms need to be designed to fund such subsidieize in a competitive environment.

—It might also be necessary to sever the links which exist between the incumbent on the one hand and political or regulatory authorities on the other hand, in order to ensure a level playing field between the incumbent and new competitors. This might entail eliminating any direct or indirect anti-competitive subsidies that the incumbent might be receiving, taking steps to require the incumbent to operate as any other commercial entity, or even privatizing the incumbent.

—Once competition has been introduced, it is necessary to take steps to maintain it, for example by preventing agreements or mergers that would stifle competition.

—Finally, in spite of the pro-competition measures listed above, some segments of the telecommunications sector might remain, at least for some time, dominated by an operator able to exercise a substantial degree of market power. This will be the case, for example, in market segments which do retain natural monopoly characteristics and which are also non-contestable (the fixed local loop is often mentioned as an example).[23] Therefore, while effective competition cannot be relied upon to put competitive pressure on operators in all segments of the telecommunications sector, direct controls over the price and quality of the services provided by monopolistic operators might still be required to enhance efficiency and prevent abuses of market power.[24]

The rules and institutions which can be used to promote or protect competition and directly to control the behaviour of operators when competition cannot be relied upon to reduce their market power sufficiently are summarily described below.

---

[23] A market is perfectly contestable when entry into the market and exit from it involve no cost (for example because the facilities which need to be deployed to operate in the market can be sold easily or transferred to other markets). In such a case, the incumbent—even if it is in a monopolistic situation—is unable to exercise market power because of the threat of entry by potential competitors. When entry and exit are costly, however, competitors might then refrain from attempting to challenge an incumbent, thus leaving the latter with substantial market power. This is arguably still the case in the fixed local segment of the telecommunications market as long as alternative modes of communications remain more expensive. Many of the costs of developing a fixed local network would not be recovered by an enterprise forced to exit the market, and an incumbent for which the costs of building such a network are sunk could be expected to remain in the market as long as it could cover its marginal cost (likely to be lower than the average costs because of the existence of the fixed costs). In such conditions, other operators might understandably be reluctant to challenge the monopolistic position of the incumbent. For an exposition of the 'contestability theory', see William J Baumol et al, *Contestable Markets and the Theory of Industry Structure* (New York: Harcourt Brace Jovanovich, 1982).

[24] See W Kip Viscusi et al, *Economics of Regulation and Antitrust* (2nd edn, Cambridge, Mass., and London: MIT Press, 1998) 377 et seq.

B. RULES

The rules which can be used to facilitate or maintain competition in the telecommunications sector or to prevent telecommunications operators from abusing their market power when that power cannot be taken away from them fall broadly into two categories: antitrust rules and telecommunications-specific rules. The exact characteristics of each type of rules will of course differ to a certain extent from country to country. The description presented below focuses only on the main features of these rules and would hold true in most contexts. However, what matters for the purposes of our discussion, is not so much to describe faithfully what are commonly referred to as antitrust or telecommunications-specific rules, but rather to identify the different characteristics of the various rules—whatever their names—which can be used to control market power in telecommunications, in order to discuss which characteristics appear best suited to achieve certain objectives in specific contexts.

1. Antitrust Rules

A very large number of countries have adopted a set of rules that are applicable to most economic activities (including telecommunications and other network industries), unless specific exemptions are granted.[25] Given their wide scope of application, such rules tend to prohibit relatively broad categories of behaviours and to leave a relatively wide degree of discretion to enforcing authorities. Antitrust rules do, however, generally focus on one relatively specific objective, which is to foster economic efficiency, so as to maximize consumer welfare, through the promotion of competition.[26]

Three main types of antitrust rules can be identified.[27] The first type of rules prevents the conclusion of anti-competitive agreements between operators. Prohibited behaviours will usually include agreements aimed at fixing purchase or selling prices, limiting or controlling production or investments, sharing markets or sources of supply or bid rigging. Such rules usually recognise, however, that some agreements between operators might be competitively beneficial: they may foster efficiencies, help create new products or services or methods of

---

[25] See, generally, R Shyam Khemani, 'Competition Law—Some Guidelines for Implementation', FPD Note No 14, The World Bank, July 1994. For a discussion of antitrust laws in the United States and other industrialized nations, see Frederic M Scherer, *Competition Policies for an Integrated World Economy* (Washington, DC: Institute for International Economics, 1994) 17 et seq. See also G Bruce Doern and Stephen Wilks, *Comparative Competition Policy: National Institutions in a Global Market* (Oxford: Clarendon Press, 1996).

[26] It should be noted, however, that, in some jurisdictions, competition law seeks to achieve a range of other policy goals under the rubric of public interest, including fairness, regional development, promotion of employment, and pluralism or diffusion of economic power through promotion of small and medium-size businesses. See Khemani (n 25 above).

[27] For a good discussion of the application of such rules in the telecommunications sector, see Roger G Noll, 'The Role of Antitrust in Telecommunications' (Fall 1995) *Antitrust Bulletin* 501.

distribution, or improve information flow and, thus, facilitate the functioning of the market.[28] This might be the case, for example, when competitors conduct together research and development that none could have carried out independently, jointly purchase supplies or distribute products and thereby reduce their costs, or form a trade association that gathers statistics and other data that each can use to make their operations more efficient. In some legal systems, a notification mechanism has been set up to enable operators to obtain authorizations from the antitrust authorities prior to concluding or implementing an agreement. In others, controls are exercised a posteriori only.

The second type of rules deals with firms which enjoy substantial market power.[29] Their objective is to prevent those firms from abusing their dominant or monopoly position vis-à-vis end-users or other operators. Examples of prohibited behaviours might include, for instance, limiting production, refusing to deal with particular buyers or sellers, imposing excessive or predatory prices, raising rivals' costs, imposing discriminatory prices to different buyers for the provision of similar services under similar conditions, and conditioning the sale of a product to the purchase of another unrelated one (ie tying).

The third type of rules prohibits mergers which would 'substantially lessen competition'.[30] Given the difficulty of unscrambling merged companies once they have operated together, most legal systems which contain rules in this regard provide for *ex ante* controls of proposed agreements. At the end of their enquiry, antitrust authorities will have to take one of the following decisions: clearing the merger in its entirety, prohibiting the merger in its entirety, requiring a partial divestiture of assets or operations sufficient to eliminate the anti-competitive effects while allowing the underlying transaction to proceed; or imposing a range of conditions designed to regulate the conduct of the merged firm so as to prevent anti-competitive effects.[31]

2. Telecommunications-Specific Rules

In addition to general antitrust rules, most countries have also adopted laws or regulations to deal with market power specifically in the telecommunications sector.[32] Typically, such rules are relatively precise; they tend to leave less discretion to enforcing authorities than antitrust rules.

---

[28] World Bank and OECD, *A Framework for the Design and Implementation of Competition Law and Policy* (Washington, DC, and Paris, 1998) 19.

[29] Several factors will generally be used to determine that a firm holds 'market power' in a given market: a high market share, the presence of barriers to entry, the holding of an essential facility, a strong vertical integration, etc. For a good discussion of the concept of market power, see Simon Bishop and Mike Walker, *The Economics of EC Competition Law* (London: Sweet & Maxwell, 1999) § 2.25 et seq.

[30] The precise criterion may vary from one jurisdiction to the other, but a strong negative impact on competition is generally required to prevent a merger from taking place.

[31] See World Bank and OECD (n 28 above) 53.

[32] For an excellent overview of such laws and regulations, see Long (n 17 above)

Like antitrust rules, telecommunications-specific rules may be classified into three broad types. The first type of rules are primarily designed to promote or preserve competition. They might, for example:

(i)   identify the segments of the telecommunications sector where the entry of new operators is permitted;

(ii) define the entry process to be followed by those new operators;

(iii) set technical, procedural, and pricing conditions pertaining to interconnection agreements in order to ensure that all competing operators seeking access to an essential facility are granted access to that essential facility under the same conditions;

(iv) impose some type of separation between the entities controlling access to an essential facility and the entities which operate in competitive markets and seek access to that facility, in order to eliminate the incentives which those who control the essential facility might have to discriminate among those seeking access to it;

(v)   determine conditions for number allocation, number portability, and dialling parity;

(vi) determine how frequencies are to be allocated; and

(vii) prohibit the transfer of public resources or the granting of other advantages to certain publicly owned companies to maintain a level playing field between those companies and their private counterparts.

Other rules are aimed primarily at preventing abuses of market power by firms which do possess a dominant position in some segments of the market. Some of those rules are designed to prevent abuses vis-à-vis other operators: for example, interconnection rules designed to prevent those who control an essential facility from overcharging the operators seeking access to that facility. Other rules are designed to prevent abuses vis-à-vis end-users: for example, price and quality requirements for various types of telecommunications services provided to end-users in markets which are not competitive. Other rules are designed to prevent abuses vis-à-vis end-users: for example, interconnection rules designed to prevent those who control an essential facility from overcharging the operators seeking access to that facility.

Finally, an additional category of sector-specific rules comprises the rules designed to ensure that various public service obligations are being met. Such obligations may comprise, for example, minimum geographical coverage requirements for certain types of services at pre-specified prices, as well as free access to certain emergency numbers and directory services.

C. Institutions

Institutions are needed to interpret, apply and enforce the rules described in Section B above.[33] Given the complexity of the issues to be addressed, an increasing number of countries have opted to establish specialized institutions to perform some or all of those functions. Such specialized institutions are mainly of two kinds: antitrust authorities[34] and telecommunications regulatory agencies.[35] This section presents a brief description of the main features of those institutions. Once again, specific characteristics of each type of institutions will vary from country to country and once again, what matters most is not to focus on the name given to various institutions but on the different ways in which such institutions can be designed and on the main strengths and weaknesses of such designs.

One should emphasize, however, that even when antitrust authorities or telecommunications regulators have been set up, other entities do generally retain important functions regarding the promotion of competition or the prevention of abuses of market power in the telecommunications sector. Political authorities, for example, will usually retain final decision-making powers on some important matters. These might include, for example, market structure reforms (including the identification of activities which are open or closed to competition and the imposition of horizontal or vertical separations between various segments of the market), privatization of the incumbent, establishment of the overall structure of the price regime, public investment, the scope of universal service, and in some cases award and withdrawal of licences or concessions. The courts will also retain an important role. In some systems, for example, antitrust authorities gather evidence and present cases to the courts and it is the courts which decide upon the merits of those cases. The courts will also usually be the final arbiters when parties contest the decisions taken by antitrust authorities or telecommunications regulators. In such cases, courts might retain the authority to judge both substantive and legal aspects of the issues, or they might be empowered to review decisions on legal grounds only and examine, for example, whether procedural requirements have been met or whether antitrust authorities or telecommunications regulators have exceeded their powers.

1. Antitrust Authorities

Antitrust authorities are generally entrusted with the task of promoting competition or controlling the use of monopoly power in all or in most sectors of the

---

[33] See generally OECD, *Relationship between Regulators and Competition Authorities* (hereafter, 'Relationship') (Paris, June 1999) 26.

[34] A list of the national antitrust authorities can be found on the OECD competition policy homepage. See <http://www.oecd.org/daf/clp/LINKS.HTM>.

[35] A list of the national telecommunications regulatory authorities can be found on the OFTEL website. See <http://www.oftel.gov.uk/internat/links.htm#NRA>.

economy. They tend to focus on implementing the antitrust rules presented in Section B above but they might, in some cases, also be in charge of implementing sector-specific rules such as the telecommunications laws or regulations discussed in Section B. They can be entrusted with various types of responsibilities including:

(i) initiating investigations of—or reviewing—potentially anti-competitive behaviours or transactions;

(ii) prosecuting such behaviours; and

(iii) in some cases, passing judgment and imposing sanctions upon parties convicted of having committed anti-competitive actions.

Given the number of firms that fall within their sphere of competency, antitrust authorities tend to act on a case-by-case basis when needed, rather than to closely regulate enterprises on a permanent basis. There are, however, several important areas where competition authorities seem to act on a more permanent, regulatory mode rather than in a case-by-case fashion. This is notably the case where such authorities adopt self-binding guidelines which function much like regulations, supervise access to certain essential facilities, monitor prices that are found to be so high or so low that they amount to abuses of a dominant position, and resort to negotiated consent agreements.[36] Antitrust authorities also usually intervene *ex post* to determine whether a conduct which has already taken place is lawful or not. There are, however, exceptions to this *ex post* feature also. For instance, proposed mergers are normally reviewed by antitrust authorities before they take place and in many regimes, antitrust rules enable operators to seek clearance from antitrust authorities before they conclude certain types of agreements with other operators.

As one of the main objectives pursued through the establishment of an antitrust authority is to ensure that an entity possesses the technical capacity required to decide complex matters in the competition field, antitrust authorities will usually seek to attract highly qualified professionals in the legal and economic spheres. In addition, antitrust authorities are often granted some degree of protection from political interventions in their day-to-day activities: they are usually set up by law as autonomous or independent entities; appointment processes might be designed to prevent partisan nominations at the top echelons of the entity; and measures might be adopted to prevent arbitrary removals. Some measures are usually adopted as well to ensure the independence of the antitrust authority from the enterprises that come under its scrutiny. The most common measure is to require an antitrust regulator to refrain from intervening in cases involving firms with which the regulator has financial or other links.

---

[36] See OECD, 'Relationship' (n 33 above) 212. See also Douglas Melamed, 'Antitrust: The New Regulation' (1995) 10 *Antitrust* 13 (arguing that consent agreements tend to move antitrust enforcement away from law enforcement towards regulation).

2. Telecommunications Regulatory Agencies

Implementing the types of telecommunications-specific rules discussed in Section B above typically constitutes a core part of the responsibilities of telecommunications regulatory agencies. Their functions might include:

   (i) selecting new operators;
  (ii) preparing and granting operating licences;
 (iii) regulating tariffs;
  (iv) administering quality and technical standards;
   (v) administering the rules applicable to number portability and to the allocation of frequency;
  (vi) administering the interconnection regime;
 (vii) resolving disputes between operators and between operators and users;
(viii) administering the universal service obligations regime;
  (ix) monitoring the activities of the operators to ensure that they comply with their obligations, including accounting separation requirements, price and quality requirements, and universal service obligations;
   (x) in some cases, imposing sanctions upon the operators when necessary; and
  (xi) providing advice to the government on telecommunications matters.[37]

They might, in some cases, also have a role in implementing antitrust rules in the telecommunications sector.

Telecommunications regulatory agencies are competent in the telecommunications sector only. In some cases, however, utility regulatory agencies might be set up with competencies across several communications industries (telecommunications, cable, broadcasting, and postal services) or even across several utility sectors (telecommunications, cable, electricity, gas, water).[38] Like antitrust authorities, telecommunications regulatory agencies seek to promote competition and control abuses of market power on the part of the incumbent. However, telecommunications agencies are usually required to take into account a wider set of concerns rooted in redistributive issues.[39] Moreover, unlike antitrust authorities, telecommunications regulatory agencies tend to regulate a small number of enterprises closely, on a quasi-permanent basis. This continuous supervision and the relatively detailed nature of the sector-specific rules that telecommunications regulatory agencies have to apply, means that telecommunications regulators tend to request a greater amount of information from the regulated industry than antitrust authorities. Because of the redistributive functions that some telecommunications regulators have to perform, they

---

[37] For a discussion of the role of telecommunications regulatory authorities, see Damien Geradin, 'Institutional Aspects of EU Regulatory Reforms in the Telecommunications Sector: An Analysis of the Role of National Regulatory Authorities' (2000) 1 *J of Network Industries* 5, at 16–18.

[38] This is, for instance, the case of the public utility commissions in the United States that oversee several industries at the state level.

[39] See OECD, 'Relationship' (n 33 above) 187.

might also require a greater variety of information than antitrust authorities. Finally, unlike antitrust authorities, telecommunications regulators tend to intervene *ex ante*, but once again, there are exceptions to this general rule. For example, regulators might disallow some investments, *ex post*, under rate-of-return regulation,[40] and regulatory sanctions are of course imposed *ex post* as well.

As is the case for antitrust authorities, the objective of ensuring that an entity possesses the technical capacity necessary to perform complex regulatory tasks explains in part why a relatively large number of countries have now established telecommunications regulatory agencies. Some argue that a sector-specific regulator is better able to develop the expertise required to tackle difficult telecommunications issues than infrastructure-wide regulators and, a fortiori, than economy-wide bodies such as antitrust authorities. On the other hand, however, an economy-wide agency might benefit from the experience gained in a plurality of sectors, and could, for example, establish a telecommunications-specific department to give some staff the possibility to specialize in telecommunications-specific issues.[41] Moreover, as will be seen in Chapter 3, economy-wide institutions seem better adapted to a context of convergence characterized by the progressive blurring of the boundaries between traditionally separate sectors.

Telecommunications regulatory agencies, like antitrust authorities, will often enjoy some degree of autonomy from political authorities and be independent from the enterprises that they regulate.[42] Those features tend in fact to be even more apparent for telecommunications regulatory agencies than for antitrust authorities.[43] Telecommunications regulators will often benefit from strong legal protection against arbitrary removal and it is not rare to see telecommunications regulatory boards or commissions whose members have staggered terms in order to prevent a single government from presiding over the renewal of the whole regulatory body. In addition, telecommunications regulators are usually required to sever all the links which they might have with the regulated enterprises, rather than simply to refrain from intervening when a conflict of interests arises.

These greater efforts at protecting telecommunications regulators from undue pressures may well reflect the greater risks that they run in that respect.[44] Telecommunications is a public service and the conditions under

---

[40] See Chapter 3 for a brief presentation of rate-of-return regulation and an explanation of the process of disallowing investments.

[41] See Warrick Smith, 'Utility Regulators—Roles and Responsibilities', *Viewpoint*, No 128, The World Bank, October 1997, 1.

[42] See Warrick Smith, 'Utility Regulators—The Independence Debate', *Viewpoint*, No 127, The World Bank, October 1997.

[43] William H Melody, 'On the Meaning and Importance of "Independence" in Telecom Reform' (1997) 21 *Telecommunications Policy* 195.

[44] Warrick Smith, *Regulatory Institutions for Utilities and Competition*, Mimeo, The World Bank, Private Sector Development, February 1998, 3.

which telecommunications services are provided remain politically sensitive in many countries, thereby increasing the temptation for governments to intervene with respect to tariffs or other aspects of the service.[45] In addition, because it regulates issues such as prices and quality of service, a telecommunications regulatory agency often has a stronger impact on the profitability of the operators that it regulates than an antitrust authority. As mentioned above, exiting the market might be costly in telecommunications, investments might need to be recovered over several years, and close regulation of tariffs or quality standards, for example, are therefore likely to determine to a very large extent the profitability of telecommunications operators. Those operators are thus also likely to use their (usually vast) resources to put pressure on the regulator.[46] Furthermore, sector-specific entities are likely to maintain closer contacts with the sector Ministry and with a very small group of enterprises than would infrastructure-wide or, a fortiori, economy-wide bodies.[47] Telecommunications-specific regulators are therefore arguably more at risk from industry or government capture.[48] In those conditions, in order to attract private investment in the sector, it is extremely important to protect the regulator—particularly if it is sector-specific—from undue industry or government interventions.

D. Seven criteria for evaluating different frameworks for the economic regulation of telecommunications

Given the existence of the different types of rules and institutions summarily described above, governments which seek to control market power in telecommunications have a choice of options. They can choose to put emphasis on general antitrust rules or on more detailed sector-specific rules, they can entrust antitrust authorities with the task of administering all the rules designed to control market power in telecommunications, they can entrust such responsibility exclusively to telecommunications-specific or infrastructure-wide regulators, or they can split responsibilities between the two types of institutions. As will be seen in Chapters 4, 5, 6, 7 and 8 below, the United States, New Zealand, the United Kingdom, Chile and Australia, for example, have chosen very different options.

The relative efficiency of various regulatory models which put different emphasis on antitrust and telecommunications-specific rules and institutions can be

---

[45] See OECD, 'Relationship' (n 33 above) 22.

[46] See Antony Dnes, 'Post-Privatization Performance—Regulating Telecommunications in the UK', *Viewpoint*, The World Bank, October 1995, 1.

[47] See OECD, 'Relationship' (n 33 above) 28.

[48] On the problem of capture, see Georges Stigler, 'The Theory of Economic Regulation' (1971) 2 *Bell J of Economic Regulation* 3; Richard A Posner, 'Theories of Economic Regulation' (1974) 5 *Bell J of Economic Regulation* 335; Sam Peltzman, 'Toward a More General Theory of Regulation' (1976) 19 *J of L and Economics* 211.

evaluated with respect to many different possible criteria.[49] We chose seven of them. These seven criteria cannot constitute an exhaustive list, but we believe that they canvass what are, arguably, many of the most important features which regulatory models in telecommunications should present.

1. Competition and Other Incentives to Generate and Share Efficiency Gains

One key objective of the regulatory framework is to provide operators with incentives to meet users' demands. One option is to generate competition *in* the market. This might require, for example: eliminating legal barriers to entry into various segments of the telecommunications market; ensuring interconnection and access to unbundled services under reasonable conditions, as well as number portability and dial parity; and in some cases, imposing accounting separation, or even the establishment of separate companies, for the pursuit of different activities in order to prevent various anti-competitive practices. Competition *for* the market, on the other hand, might be used to allocate some scarce resources—for example, radio spectrum or public subsidies intended to cover some of the costs of providing telecommunications access to poor and remote areas—to the most efficient operators and to transfer some of the welfare gains associated with service provision to the Treasury (eg when spectrum rights are allocated to the highest bidder) or to the users (eg when public subsidies are allocated to the providers charging the lowest prices to the users). Finally, direct controls might be imposed on the prices and quality of various telecommunications services to protect users from potential abuses of dominant position by monopolistic operators. Various tools of economic regulation which can be used to introduce a degree of competition in the market, or for the market, as well as to control the prices of various telecommunications services, are discussed in the next chapter.

2. Specificity versus Coherence

The telecommunications sector does retain certain characteristics that tend to differentiate it from other industries. For example, it exhibits both natural monopoly features for some activities and network externalities. It also presents some technical issues, such as numbering for example, which do not have an exact equivalent in other sectors. Such characteristics could, arguably, justify the adoption of telecommunications-specific rules and the establishment of telecommunications-specific regulatory authorities. However, ensuring that cross-sector rules and institutions are used to regulate telecommunications would also bring benefits, such as lower risks of distortion between different activities for

---

[49] On the difficulty of selecting a set of criteria as benchmarks for assessing regulatory regimes, see Robert Baldwin and Martin Cave, *Understanding Regulation: Theory, Strategy, and Practice* (Oxford: University Press, 1999) 82–84.

example.[50] As already noted, it would also seem justified by the growing convergence that is observed between telecommunications and other sectors.[51] A discussion of what convergence exactly means, and of its main regulatory implications, will be found in the next chapter.

An adequate balance has, thus, to be struck between addressing the specifics of the telecommunications sector and ensuring sufficient coherence of the regulatory framework as a whole: a number of choices are possible with differing emphasis on economy-wide, infrastructure-wide, communication-wide or purely telecommunications-specific rules and institutions. The choice will depend, in part, on the extent to which the telecommunications sector is similar to, or different from, other sectors of the economy in a particular country. For example, the greater the degree of openness and liberalization of the telecommunications sector, the larger the scope for the application in telecommunications of cross-sector rules applicable to competitive activities in general.

In all situations, there are good reasons, however, to entrust antitrust authorities with the task of reviewing sector-specific rules in order to determine whether such rules are still needed. Indeed, antitrust authorities, which are competent across the economy as a whole and generally focus on the implementation of economy-wide rules, should have no difficulty acknowledging that competition has become sufficiently intense in the telecommunications sector to justify moving away from an emphasis on sector-specific regulation and toward the implementation of economy-wide rules. Telecommunications regulators, who are competent in the telecommunications sector only, might be more reluctant to come to such conclusions in order to preserve their own jobs.

3. Flexibility versus Certainty

As mentioned above, antitrust rules tend to be relatively general while telecommunications rules tend to be more precise. The former therefore grants implementing authorities a wider degree of discretion, giving them more room to tailor individual decisions to particular circumstances. In a sector that evolves as fast as telecommunications, this flexibility undoubtedly has some advantages. On the other hand, rules which are more precise and more difficult to change (for example because their adoption requires co-operation between the executive and legislative branches of government rather than a unilateral decision by a minister or because they are contained in licences which can only be modified pursuant to a long and complex procedure) provide for greater regulatory certainty. Such certainty reduces the risks of litigation and the resulting delays

---

[50] See Henry Ergas, 'Competition Policy in Deregulated Industries' (July/August 1995) *Intl Business Lawyer* 305.

[51] OECD, 'Relationship' (n 33 above) 32.

and costs. It may also be an advantage when it comes to convincing private investors to sink large investments in politically sensitive sectors.[52]

Trade-offs between flexibility and certainty also exist at the institutional level. For instance, the fact that sector-specific regulators tend to intervene *ex ante*, while competition authorities tend to intervene *ex post* means that the intervention of telecommunications agencies tends to provide a greater degree of certainty to operators than the intervention of antitrust agencies. Moreover, the fact that telecommunications regulators are generally in charge of applying more specific rules than competition authorities makes their decisions subject to greater deference from courts than the decisions of competition authorities, hence increasing the degree of certainty offered by such decisions. On the other hand, when economy-wide regulators are in place, operators may be better able to forecast what to expect in their sector from the observation of how the regulatory framework is applied in other sectors.

The right balance between flexibility and certainty will depend, once again, upon the characteristics of the telecommunications sector in the relevant jurisdiction. A key factor, in particular, will be the degree of confidence that the authorities in charge of adopting and of implementing the rules enjoy: more discretion can certainly be granted to those authorities if they are trusted by stakeholders than if they are not.

4. Regulatory Competence and Ability to Resist Undue Pressure

Given the technical complexity of regulatory issues in telecommunications, ensuring that the regulator possesses sufficient competency is one of the main challenges of any regulatory model. Both sector-specific regulatory agencies (which permit a high degree of specialization) and cross-sector bodies (which promote learning across sectors) present some advantages in that respect. In addition, given the scope for political as well as industry pressure on regulatory matters, adequate measures to promote the autonomy of the regulator of the kind mentioned in Section C above are of the utmost importance. As mentioned in that same section, such measures are particularly important for sector-specific regulatory agencies which tend, in general, to be subjected to stronger pressures from politicians and operators than infrastructure-wide regulators and, a fortiori, than economy-wide regulators such as antitrust authorities.

The level of competence required from the regulators can be somewhat reduced by relying to the maximum possible extent on competition to prompt operators to increase efficiency and by designing rules which are relatively easy

---

[52] For a discussion of this issue, see Roger G Noll, 'Telecommunications Reforms in Developing Countries', AEI–Brookings Joint Center for Regulatory Studies, Working Paper 99–10, November 1999, 43 et seq.

to implement. Also, less than perfect regulatory autonomy will be less of an issue when the discretionary powers of regulatory authorities are very limited than when they are particularly large. No amount of regulatory engineering will, however, completely eliminate the need for competent and relatively autonomous regulators able to solve, in an impartial way, the complex regulatory problems that are bound to arise.

5. Regulatory Accountability and Stakeholder Participation

Autonomy needs to be combined with accountability in order to ensure the legitimacy of the regulatory process.[53] Some of the main measures which can be taken to promote regulatory accountability include: establishing procedures whereby the performance of regulators is assessed by public audit offices; ensuring that regulators publish reports of their activities and of the way in which they use their financial resources; promoting the transparency of regulatory processes, inter alia by requiring that the regulatory decisions themselves, as well as the rationale for those decisions, be published; establishing procedures to enable interested parties to present their views before final regulatory decisions are taken; devising processes for handling users' complaints; and providing for appeal mechanisms against the decisions of the regulator (without, however, unnecessarily undercutting the authority of this body).[54]

6. Regulatory Costs

While designing a regulatory framework, one should also aim at limiting the costs of regulation. The costs of regulation include, first, the costs of setting up regulatory agencies. Setting up a single cross-sector agency is usually more cost-effective than setting up several distinct sector-specific agencies, as it avoids, for example, duplication of a certain number of administrative departments. Secondly, there are the compliance costs imposed upon industry participants. These costs tend, on average, to increase with the complexity of the rules. Thirdly, there are costs associated with the potential inefficiencies of the regulatory regime. For example, when disputes are frequent and take a long time to be resolved, procedural costs might be high for the parties, and beneficial reforms might be postponed. Very important costs might also be incurred when regulatory mistakes are made. As regulation is imperfect and the risk of costly mistakes can never be completely eliminated, it is crucial to weigh the potential benefits of regulation against its potential costs. This trade-off needs to be fully taken into

---

[53] On the importance of regulatory accountability, see Colin Scott, 'Accountability and the Regulatory State' (2000) 27 *J of L and Society* 38. See also, Anthony Ogus, *Regulation: Legal Form and Economic Theory* (Oxford: Clarendon Press, 1994) ch 6; Robert Hahn, *Improving Regulatory Accountability* (Washington, DC: AEI Press, 1996); Baldwin and Cave (n 49 above) ch 21.

[54] Martin C Stewart-Smith, 'Industry Structure and Regulation', Policy Research Working Paper, No 1419, February 1995, The World Bank, 32.

account when discussing, in particular, the merits of establishing detailed regulatory rules and specialized regulatory institutions in the telecommunications sector.

7. Allocation of Regulatory Responsibilities

One additional important objective is to allocate regulatory responsibilities efficiently. Some pitfalls need to be avoided in that respect. When several institutions intervene in telecommunications regulation, their respective competencies should be defined clearly to avoid creating uncertainty. Different institutions, for example, should not be given the same level of responsibility to tackle the same issues if inconsistent decisions are to be avoided. It is important also to entrust institutions with the functions which they are best designed to perform and, at the same time, to provide these institutions with the capacity and powers required to perform those functions effectively. Finally, one should not lose sight of the interrelations that exist between different regulatory issues when allocating regulatory responsibilities. Setting performance standards for telecommunications operators, for example, will have a direct impact on their costs and will therefore determine the price at which they can be expected to earn an adequate return. Failing to entrust the task of administering performance and pricing rules to the same institution, or to provide at least for close coordination between the institutions in charge of those matters, would substantially increase uncertainty for the investors.

3

Key Issues of Economic Regulation in Telecommunications

In this chapter, we briefly review some of the key issues of economic regulation in telecommunications. Most of these issues arise in each of the countries which are successively reviewed in Chapters 4-8. Hence, the objective of this chapter is to summarize these issues and present the main relevant arguments, in order to help inform the country-specific analysis.

This chapter will focus, in turn, on:

   (i) the regulation of end-user prices (Section A);
  (ii) the regulation of interconnection prices (Section B);
 (iii) linkages between price regulation and operators' strategic behaviours (Section C);
 (iv) facilities-based competition, resale, or unbundled access (Section D);
  (v) the allocation of scarce resources (Section E);
 (vi) the main auction methods and issues (Section F);
(vii) competition and universal service obligations (Section G);
(viii) vertical separation or vertical integration (Section H);
 (ix) the implications of the process of convergence on the preceding regulatory issues (Section I); and finally
  (x) international benchmarking of telecommunications prices (Section J).

A. PRICE REGULATION OF SERVICES PROVIDED TO END-USERS

Price regulation of end-user services can come under a variety of guises, from general antitrust rules aimed at preventing abusive practices such as excessive, discriminatory or predatory pricing to specific rules designed to define more or less precisely the prices to be paid by the users. We will present here the two main types of specific pricing rules (rate-of-return regulation and price-cap regulation), we will discuss the factors which mitigate, in practice, the differences between these two types of rules, and finally we will discuss the respective merits of metered and unmetered pricing regimes.

1. Rate-of-Return Regulation

In its 'pure' form, rate-of-return regulation enables the regulated firm to charge prices which cover its operating costs and provide a pre-determined return on the capital committed to its operations (see Figure 3.1 below).[1] Rate-of-return pricing is therefore a cost-based method of setting prices. In practice, costs that can unambiguously be allocated to a given service are included in the price of that service and costs that are common to several services are allocated according to some accounting principles to those services. When costs are no longer covered by the regulated prices, the firm can ask for a review to determine a new set of prices.[2]

The main advantages of the rate-of-return system are the following:

(i) Rate-of-return provides security to investors and therefore lowers the cost of capital, since the company is assured that its expenses will be reimbursed and the specified rate-of-return on its investments achieved.

(ii) It ensures that the firm will not make undue profits, which might be particularly desirable when very high profits would be hard to justify politically.

(iii) It provides good incentives to maintain quality since the costs incurred to ensure that quality is maintained are covered by the prices which the firm can charge.

(iv) It reduces risks of regulatory capture by political or industry players since rate-of-return regulation leaves little discretion to the regulators.

FIGURE 3.1. Rate-of-return regulation.

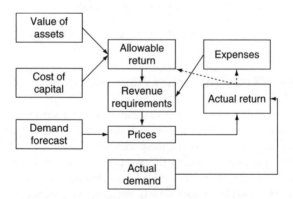

Source: Michel Kerf et al, 'Concessions for Infrastructure—A Guide to their Design and Award', World Bank Technical Paper No 399, Finance, Private Sector, and Infrastructure Network (1998) 38.

---

[1] See generally, David M Newbery, *Privatization, Restructuring and Regulation of Network Utilities*, (Cambridge, Mass., and London: MIT Press, 2000) 38; Robert Baldwin and Martin Cave, *Understanding Regulation: Theory, Strategy, and Practice* (Oxford: Oxford University Press, 1999) 224.

[2] See Jean-Jacques Laffont and Jean Tirole, *Competition in Telecommunications* (Cambridge, Mass., and London: MIT Press, 2000) 84–85.

On the other hand, rate-of-return regulation presents the following main disadvantages:

(i) It provides weak incentives for cost controls, since all costs are covered by the prices.

(ii) It might provide incentives for overinvestment, to the extent that the regulated returns are higher or more secure than alternative investments (a problem known as 'gold-plating').[3]

(iii) It engenders economic inefficiency because prices are purely cost-based and do not reflect demand considerations (see Box 3.1 below).

(iv) It has a relatively high degree of complexity, since regulators must obtain very detailed estimates of the firm's costs.

2. Price-Cap Regulation

Instead of directly regulating the return which the regulated firm is allowed to make on its investment, regulators might impose a cap on the prices which the firm might charge.[4] Price caps are usually imposed upon baskets of prices, ie it is a weighted average of these prices which cannot exceed the cap. The pricing formula generally enables the regulated firm to pass on to users cost increases outside of its control (such as inflation or other exogenous costs).[5] It would also reflect the scope for efficiency gains which the firm is expected to be able to implement. Price caps are supposed to be left unchanged for relatively long periods of time (typically three to five years) during which the firm fully bears its costs and is free to try to maximize its profits.

The advantages and disadvantages of the 'pure' price-cap system described above are very much the opposite of those of the 'pure' rate-of-return system. The main advantages of price-cap regulation are the following:

(i) Price cap regulation provides strong incentives to reduce costs since the firm retains the benefits of lower than expected costs for the period during which prices are fixed.

(ii) It gives the firm flexibility to respond to changing market conditions. As caps are usually imposed upon baskets of prices, the firm remains able—without having to obtain any regulatory authorisation—to change the prices of individual services. This is an important advantage in a sector which evolves fast.

(iii) It minimizes the economic distortions associated with pricing above marginal costs. The flexibility mentioned above enables the firm to raise the price of those services for which demand is relatively inelastic (ie raise prices

---

[3] See Harvey Averch and Leland L Johnson, 'Behaviour of the Firm under Regulatory Constraint' (1962) 92 *American Economic Rev* 1052.

[4] See generally Mark Amstrong et al, *Regulatory Reform: Economic Analysis and British Experience* (Cambridge, Mass., and London: MIT Press, 1994) 165. See also Baldwin and Cave (n 1 above) 226.

[5] See Amstrong et al (n 4 above) 170.

without losing too many customers) and to keep prices lower where demand is more elastic, in order to maximize its profits. This tends to minimize the economic distortion caused by the fact that, in order to break even in an industry characterized by high fixed costs and therefore increasing returns to scale, prices have to be set above marginal costs (see Box 3.1 below).

(iv) It presents a lower degree of complexity than rate-of-return regulation, because the regulators need less detailed information about the firm's costs.

Box 3.1: *Rate-of-Return, Price Caps, and Ramsey–Boiteux Pricing*

Marginal cost pricing—which would maximize overall social welfare and be conducive to an efficient allocation of economic resources in the absence of externalities—yields prices which are insufficient to cover total costs in industries characterized by high fixed costs. Ramsey–Boiteux prices are the prices which would enable a firm selling different services to break even while minimizing the economic distortions created by the existence of price mark-ups above marginal costs.

When demands for the different services are independent of each other, Ramsey–Boiteux prices are such that the mark-up above marginal cost for a given service is inversely proportional to the elasticity of demand for that service. The intuition behind this result is relatively straightforward: imposing higher mark-ups on services with inelastic demand ensures that the overall consumption pattern remains close to the pattern obtained when prices are equal to marginal costs. When demands for different services are interdependent, the cross-elasticities must also be taken into account. In that case, the least distorting way to enable the firm to break even will be to lower the price of a service below the level which would have been chosen with independent demands, when doing so increases demand for a *complementary* service on which the firm charges a mark-up. Conversely, the price of a service should be raised above the level which would have been chosen with independent demands, when doing so increases demand for a *substitute* service on which the firm charges a mark-up.

When allowed to do so, a firm will, in fact, impose prices whose structure conforms to the structure of Ramsey–Boiteux prices. Indeed a firm maximizes its profit by imposing high mark-ups on services with inelastic demand and by taking into account, in the way described above, the impact which a price change on one service has on demand for other services. Rate-of-return regulation, which fixes the prices of individual services on the basis of cost considerations only, is unlikely to yield Ramsey–Boiteux price structures. Price-cap regulation imposed upon baskets of prices, on the other hand, enables the firm to adjust the prices of individual services to take elasticities and cross-elasticities into account and therefore promotes the 'automatic' adoption of Ramsey–Boiteux price structures, provided that the weight

(continuous)

(continued)

attributed to each price in the basket reflects the volume of the corresponding service actually sold by the firm. This latter condition imposes substantial information requirements on regulators, however, as information on the demand for different services (including demand elasticities) must be known.

Source: Jean-Jacques Laffont and Jean Tirole, *Competition, in Telecommunications* (Cambridge, Mass., and London: MIT Press, 2000) 60–65; Eli M Noam, *Interconnecting the Network of Networks* (Cambridge, Mass., and London: MIT Press, 2001) 81.

Price-cap regulation does, however, present the following main disadvantages:

(i) It entails higher risks to investors and therefore it raises the cost of capital. With prices set for long periods of time, the firm may benefit from unexpected cost reductions but may also suffer from unexpected cost increases.

(ii) Under a given set of price caps, the firm might be able to reap very high profits, which might constitute a political liability for public authorities.

(iii) It provides lower incentives to maintain quality since the firm might benefit from cost reductions which would jeopardize quality (this risk is higher in industries where quality is difficult to observe or where customers do not have a choice of suppliers, so that lower quality does not necessarily translate into lower sales).[6]

(iv) It creates relatively high risks of regulatory capture as the regulators are given relatively wide discretionary powers.

(v) It might induce the firm to lower the price of a given service below marginal costs—and ration consumers of that service to limit its losses on sales of that service—in order to be able to raise substantially the price of other services—and make large profits on those—while still complying with the overall requirements of the price-cap.[7]

(vi) The pricing flexibility associated with price-cap regulation might yield 'anti-social' prices. Imposing higher mark-ups on services whose demand is more inelastic maximizes overall social welfare as it maximizes the sum of consumer net surpluses (which reflect the difference between what consumers are willing to pay and what they actually pay for the services which they purchase) and of the firm's net surpluses (which reflect the difference between the firm's marginal costs and the prices at which it sells its services). This way of measuring social welfare gives, however, the same social value to surpluses derived by rich and poor users or by firms. As a result, higher mark-ups will be imposed on the prices of services consumed by poor users, when poor users have a more inelastic demand for a given service than rich users (because the latter have more options, for example).[8]

---

[6] See Amstrong et al (n 4 above) 173; Baldwin and Cave (n 1 above) 252.

[7] Laffont and Tirole (n 2 above) 88.

[8] ibid 73.

3. Factors Mitigating the Differences Between Rate-of-Return and Price-Cap Regulation

In practice, rate-of-return and price-cap regulation are never implemented in the 'pure' or most extreme forms presented above and the differences between the two modes of regulation are far less stark than they are made to appear in the preceding paragraphs. For example:

(i) Under rate-of-return regulation, regulators often allow the firm to earn its allowed return on new investments only if they judge that such investments are justified. This mitigates the overinvestment bias of rate-of-return regulation. On the other hand, it also increases the risks of the system for investors as well as the risks of regulatory capture as it increases the discretionary powers of the regulators.

(ii) Revising prices to take cost changes into account is often a relatively lengthy process under rate-of-return regulation. This regulatory lag introduces some incentives for cost minimization as the firm keeps the benefits of unexpected cost decreases until new prices are set.

(iii) As indicated above, price-cap formulas might enable the regulated firm to pass on exogenous costs to users. As long as these costs are truly exogenous, the incentive properties of the price-cap system are not undermined; in practice, however, distinction between endogenous and exogenous costs is rarely perfectly clear.[9]

(iv) Under price-cap regulation, regulators who review prices every three to five years use all the information available about the firm at the time of the review, including information about the unexpected cost-cutting which the firm managed to achieve during the previous period. While this information should not be used to claw back some of the profits made during the previous period, it does provide an indication about the rate at which the firm might be expected to improve efficiency in the future. Unexpectedly large cost-cutting during one period will therefore usually result in more stringent caps over the next period. This so-called 'ratchet effect' reduces the firm's incentives to decrease costs aggressively.

(v) As indicated in the previous point, regulators do study costs under price-cap regulation, and they do try to set the caps so as to enable a reasonably efficient firm to make a 'normal' return over the period for which the caps are set. This means that price-cap regulation is not necessarily much less complex than rate-of-return regulation.

(vi) In practice, higher than expected profits might be politically unsustainable and regulators operating under a price-cap system might feel compelled to intervene to change the caps before the end of the three- to five-year

---

[9] Michel Kerf et al, 'Concessions for Infrastructure: A Guide to their Design and Award', World Bank Technical Paper No 399 (Washington, DC: The World Bank, 1998) 41.

period.[10] This also reduces the firm's incentives to become 'too successful' at minimizing costs.

(vii) The risk that a firm operating under a price-cap system might price some service below marginal cost and ration the provision of that service to reap large profits on other services can be mitigated by imposing a ban on rationing and/or on pricing at levels below marginal costs; regulators are also usually responsible for imposing universal service obligations which mitigate any risk of anti-social pricing.

(viii) Finally, so-called 'sliding scale rules' can be designed to provide for profit or loss sharing between the government and the regulated firm. Such rules are, in many ways, hybrids between 'pure' rate-of-return and 'pure' price-cap systems—rules which enable the firm to keep a larger (smaller) share of unexpected profits will more closely resemble a 'pure' price-cap (rate-of-return) system.

4. Metered versus Unmetered Local Call Regimes

In most countries, users of local phone services are charged according to the duration of their communications, ie a metered local call regime is in place. In some countries however—including three of the five countries studied in this book—unmetered regimes exist, under which users are charged a flat monthly fee which is independent of the amount of time during which they use the local network. The debate on the pros and cons of these two approaches has gained in importance with the recent boom in Internet access by individual dial-up users who connect with their local Internet Service Provider (ISP) through a call over the local telecommunications network.

The main advantages of an unmetered regime are the following:

(i) Unmetered local call regimes clearly encourage the use of the Internet since users do not feel constrained about the amount of time they spend online.[11] This in turn promotes faster Internet growth, as demonstrated by a recent OECD study which shows that penetration of Internet hosts and secure servers is substantially higher in unmetered than in metered markets.[12]

(ii) No tracking of individual calls is required under an unmetered regime, which reduces monitoring and accounting costs.

---

[10] Baldwin and Cave (n 1 above) 238.

[11] On Internet pricing, see, generally, Gerald Falhauber, 'Pricing Internet: The Efficient Subsidy' in Brian Kahin (ed), *Building Information Infrastructure* (New York: McGraw-Hill, 1992); William Lehr and Martin Weiss, 'The Political Economy of Congestion Charges and Settlements in Packet Networks' (1996) 20 *Telecommunications Policy* 219; Jeffrey MacKie-Mason and Hal R Varian, 'Pricing the Internet' in Brian Kahin and James Keller, *Public Access to the Internet* (Cambridge, Mass.: MIT Press, 1995) 269; Jeffrey MacKie-Mason and Hal Varian, 'Pricing Congestible Network Resources' (1995) 13 *IEEE J* 1141.

[12] OECD, Local Access Pricing and E-Commerce, DSTI/ICCP/TISP(2000)1/FINAL, 27 July 2000.

(iii) Direct usage costs are negligible compared with the fixed costs associated with setting up and maintaining the network infrastructure. An unmetered regime under which users pay a flat fee every month does therefore match relatively well the structure of the costs actually incurred by the local telecommunications service provider.[13]

The main argument against unmetered local call regimes is that they do not provide any incentives to economize on the use of the network. Internet users, in particular, might be tempted to stay online for very long periods of time, thereby creating congestion problems.

While this drawback is real, several qualifications are important. First, designing a price regime which adequately captures the costs of congestion and sends the right economic signals to both users and providers of services is far from easy. With direct usage costs basically equal to zero, the price of usage should be zero as long as the network remains uncongested, and should only become positive when congestion develops. In these conditions, adopting a metered price regime which distinguishes between peak and off-peak periods might be a step in the right direction, but tariff regimes designed to match patterns of usage of telephony will likely need to be reviewed as patterns of Internet usage tend to be markedly different. Alternatively, metering could be applied not to time but to the number of uploaded or downloaded Mbytes, on the assumption that the best way to limit congestion is to provide users with incentives to limit the volume of information which they send or ask to receive. In order to ensure that prices do reflect closely actual congestion levels, more complex schemes would be required however, such as the real-time Vickrey auctions proposed by MacKie-Mason and Varian, or the so-called 'Paris Metro Pricing' option proposed by Andrew Odlyzko (see Box 3.2 below).

Box 3.2: Pricing Schemes Aimed at Addressing Internet-Related Congestion

The Internet uses packet-switching technology. This refers to the fact that the data stream from a given computer is broken into packets (of about 200 bytes on average) which are then sent out onto the network. Each packet contains a header with information necessary for routing the packet from origination to destination. It is possible for packets from a single session to take different routes to destination and conversely, packets from different sources can share the same line. Currently, packets are generally accepted onto the network on a first-come, first-served basis. If the network becomes overloaded, packets are queued and delayed or even discarded.

One tool which could be used to relieve such congestion is a type of auction called 'real-time Vickrey auction'. Under a real-time Vickrey auction, packets would not be processed on a first-come, first-served basis but would be
(continuous)

---

[13] Jeffrey K MacKie-Mason and Hal R Varian, *Economic FAQs About the Internet* (1994) 12 available at <http://www.virtualschool.edu/mon/Economics/VarianInternetEconomics.html>.

(continued)

prioritized on the basis of the value that the user puts on getting the packet through quickly. Users would thus assign to packets bids indicating their willingness to pay for immediate servicing. On congested routes, packets would be prioritized based on willingness to pay. Users would not be charged a price equal to their own willingness to pay, however, but the packet price of the lowest priority packet that is admitted on the network. This price structure would provide the right incentives for truthful revelation and would ensure that packets with the highest cost of delay get served first. If all congestion revenues are reinvested in capacity, it would also ensure that capacity is expanded to the point where its marginal value is equal to its marginal cost. The main drawback of this scheme is its complexity: the requirement that a bid be attached to every packet imposes large burdens on the users and—already congested—transmission infrastructure.

An alternative would be to partition a network into separate sub-networks and to apply different usage charges to each sub-network. On average, sub-networks charging higher prices will be less congested. The scheme is based on the system which was used some time ago in the Paris Metro, whereby the only difference between first and second class carriages was the price charged: both types of carriages were identical, but the pricing scheme ensured that first class carriages were less crowded. While such a scheme would be simpler to implement than Vickrey auctions, it does not ensure that congestion revenues provide an accurate measure of congestion costs for the users since the price structure is set *ex ante* and does not necessarily reflect users' valuations as closely as individual bids.

Source: Jeffrey K MacKie-Mason and Hal Varian, *Economic FAQs About the Internet* (1994) 18; Martin Cave and Robin Mason, *The Economics and Regulation of the Internet* (10 April 2001) 28; and Andrew M Odlyzko, 'Paris Metro Pricing for the Internet', Proc ACM Conference on Electronic Commerce (EC'99), ACM, 1999 140–147.

Second, even in the absence of a metered regime for local calls, users will still have incentives to limit their use of the local network for Internet connections if the ISPs impose a metered price regime. The extent to which congestion-sensitive price signals are also given to the operator responsible for maintaining and investing in the local network—as this operator might well be different from the user's ISP—will then depend upon the access regime which is in place between the ISP and the local network operator (once again, prices—in this case the access prices to be paid by the ISPs—could be based on time of day, number of Mbytes uploaded and downloaded, or Vickrey auctions, for example).

Third, while it is true that users' incentives to economize on network use disappear under a flat price regime for both local calls and Internet service provision,[14] the access regime between the ISPs and the local network operator

---

[14] And flat-rate pricing regimes are being offered by a growing number of ISPs: ibid 45.

might still be designed, as pointed out above, to send congestion-sensitive price signals to the latter.

Finally, beyond the price considerations discussed above, the existence of alternatives to dial-up Internet access will play a crucial role in helping solve Internet-related congestion problems on the local telecommunications network. For example, if Internet users have the opportunity to get uncongested Internet access at competitive prices through alternative networks—such as cable networks, for instance—congestion problems on the local loop are likely to be 'automatically' addressed, to a certain extent, as some Internet users will opt to access the Internet through these alternative networks. Note, however, that in the absence of adequate price mechanisms, alternative networks might be built when it would have been cheaper to solve congestion problems by upgrading the existing local network.

B. Price regulation of interconnection

The challenge of interconnection pricing is to attempt to strike the right balance between the following main interrelated objectives:

(i) to promote competition between different operators;
(ii) to preserve the incentives of the provider of interconnection (hereafter the 'incumbent') to maintain and upgrade its network;
(iii) to ensure that the incumbent has incentives to limit the actual (as opposed to the opportunity) costs of providing interconnection;
(iv) to design interconnection prices which maximize overall social welfare; and
(v) to limit regulatory costs (both for the regulator and for the operators) as well as the risk of regulatory mistake or capture in the pricing process.

As is the case for end-user prices, interconnection prices can be regulated through general antitrust rules or through more specific rules. We will focus here on five main types of specific pricing rules and discuss the extent to which such rules do meet the objectives mentioned above.

1. Backward-Looking Cost-Based Pricing

According to this methodology, the interconnection price includes the costs which are specifically attributable to the provision of interconnection services (ie the incremental costs) plus a share of the common costs which cannot be attributed to any specific services. All costs are normally evaluated through historic cost accounting (ie by computing costs actually incurred when the relevant equipment was purchased, as reflected in the company's accounts).

Common costs are typically allocated according to a 'fully distributed' approach.[15]

The main advantages of this model are as follows:

(i) As the incumbent is compensated for the costs it actually incurs, but not for the profits it might make when it uses its own facilities to serve users in a downstream market, this methodology promotes competition in the downstream market. Indeed, competitors which only pay the actual (as opposed to the opportunity) costs of interconnection to the incumbents are likely to find that they can underprice the incumbent in a downstream market where the latter is reaping substantial profits.

(ii) To the extent that historic costs do accurately reflect the costs actually incurred (see point (iii) under disadvantages, below), this methodology ensures that the incumbent recoups its investments, including fixed costs and is thus able to maintain and invest in the network.

(iii) Since accounting data is usually readily available and understood, this methodology may facilitate negotiations between access seekers and access providers.

The main disadvantages are the following:

(i) As the incumbent receives no compensation for the profits which it might lose if new entrants use the incumbent's facilities to 'steal' some of its customers in the downstream market, it is therefore likely to lose money on the provision of interconnection. The incumbent thus has incentives to restrict the new entrants' access to its facilities by using all the non-price exclusionary practices at its disposal.[16]

(ii) Cost-based pricing enables inefficient entry: if the incumbent makes monopoly profits in the downstream market, a firm with higher costs than the incumbent might still enter the market if it accepts lower profits than the incumbent.

(iii) Historic-cost accounting may well present a distorted picture of the costs actually incurred by the service provider (eg inflation might not be taken

---

[15] Fully distributed costing (of each service of a multi-service firm) is computed by allocating to a given service the identifiable costs directly caused by the provision of that service plus a share of the common costs (this share is usually proportional to the volume of service produced or to the marginal cost of producing the service).

[16] Such exclusionary practices might, for example, include: refusing to provide interconnection or delaying the provision of interconnection by invoking technical constraints; raising competitors' costs by forcing rivals to purchase elements or functionalities which they do not need or by making technological choices with respect to network configuration, interface equipment, etc which favour the incumbent over its competitors; and lowering demand for access from competitors' networks by refusing to provide number portability, imposing cumbersome access codes, or skimping on network maintenance. See Jean-Jacques Laffont and Jean Tirole, *Competition in Telecommunications* (Cambridge, Mass., and London: MIT Press, 2000) 165.

into account and depreciation policies adopted for accounting purposes might not always reflect the useful life of the equipment). There is therefore no foolproof guarantee that the incumbent will be able to recoup its investments.

(iv) As the price of interconnection is based on the incumbent's actual costs, the incumbent has little incentive to reduce costs.

(v) When backward-looking cost-based pricing is used to regulate interconnection prices while the downstream, competitive market is left unregulated, the incumbent has incentives to engage in accounting cross-subsidization (ie the transfer of costs from unregulated activities, where the firm benefits from reduced costs, to activities regulated on a cost-plus basis) and/or in managerial cross-subsidization (ie the allocation of the best human resources or equipment to unregulated activities and the allocation of under-performing staff and equipment to activities where the firm is not penalized for lower efficiency). Indeed the firm gains by transferring costs from the downstream market to the essential facility segment where high costs of providing interconnection can be reflected in the interconnection price (since the incumbent is compensated for the costs it actually incurs in providing interconnection). Both accounting and managerial cross-subsidies introduce economic distortions in the process of resource allocation between different activities and while accounting cross-subsidies might be prevented through the implementation of appropriate accounting rules monitored by regulators, there is very little which regulators can do to prevent a firm which has the incentives to do so, from engaging in managerial cross-subsidies, since the allocation of resources across activities is a business decision which must be left to the firm.

(vi) Whether the price of interconnection will, to some extent, reflect Ramsey–Boiteux pricing structures depends upon whether demand considerations are taken into account in the allocation of the fixed or common costs to different services. In general, under backward-looking cost-based methodology it is not the case (since costs are distributed on the basis of volume or cost considerations rather than on the basis of demand elasticity considerations) and the resulting price structure is therefore sub-optimal.

(vii) While historic-cost accounting is usually well understood, it might not always be straightforward to allocate booked costs to interconnection facilities and services, as historic costs might not necessarily be desegregated enough to enable easy identification of the costs caused by interconnection.

2. Forward-Looking Long-Run Incremental Cost (LRIC)

A variety of pricing methods are based on the evaluation of forward-looking long-run incremental costs. While these methods do vary to some extent, the basic approach is the same—we describe this basic approach below as the 'LRIC model'.[17] The LRIC model considers the incremental costs incurred in the long run, which are causally related to the provision of interconnection, and which would be incurred by an incumbent using the most efficient current technology to provide such interconnection.

The main advantages of the model are the following:

(i) As is the case for backward-looking cost-based pricing, LRIC promotes competition by new entrants in the downstream market since it does not compensate the incumbent for the profits it might forgo in providing interconnection.

(ii) As costs are to be considered under a long-run time frame, all costs causally related to the provision of the service—including those costs which would be considered as fixed under shorter time frames—are treated as variable costs and must therefore be taken into account. Under a strict approach to LRIC pricing, only the truly incremental costs of interconnection—ie the costs which would be avoided if the benchmark efficient firm stopped providing interconnection—should be taken into account. In that scenario, the only fixed costs which would be taken into account would be the interconnection-specific fixed costs. Most LRIC methods, however, do, in addition, include in the interconnection price part of the common costs related to the provision of interconnection—ie those costs which would not be avoided if the benchmark efficient firm stopped providing interconnection (because they need to be incurred to supply other services which the firm provides as well) but which would need to be incurred if the firm were to provide interconnection on a stand-alone basis.[18] The interconnection price thus provides for the remuneration of the various fixed costs which would be incurred by a benchmark efficient firm in the provision of interconnection.

(iii) As the compensation of the incumbent is based—at least in theory—not on its actual costs but on the costs of a benchmark efficient firm, the incumbent has incentives to be efficient and reduce the actual costs that it incurs in providing interconnection.

(iv) Contrary to backward-looking cost-based pricing, LRIC does not provide incentives for accounting and/or managerial cross-subsidization when the downstream, competitive market is left unregulated. As the interconnection price is not based on the costs which the incumbent actually incurs (but on the cost of a benchmark efficient firm), the incumbent would not gain by shifting costs from the competitive to the regulated segment of the market.

---

[17] For an excellent presentation of the different variants of LRIC-type pricing methods, see Hank Intven (ed), *Telecommunications Regulation Handbook* (Washington, DC: The World Bank, 2000) B-14–B-18.

[18] See, for example, Christian M Dippon, 'Local Loop Unbundling: Flaws of the Cost Proxy Model' (2001) 3 *Info* 159, 164.

The LRIC presents, however, a number of disadvantages:[19]

(i) As is the case under backward-looking cost-based pricing, under LRIC the incumbent receives no compensation for the profits which it might lose if new entrants use the incumbent's facilities to 'steal' some of its customers in the downstream market. As the incumbent is therefore likely to lose money on the provision of interconnection, it has incentives to restrict the new entrants' access to its facilities.

(ii) Like backward-looking cost-based pricing, LRIC enables inefficient entry.

(iii) As the actual costs of the incumbent might well be higher than those of the efficient benchmark firm chosen under LRIC, the incumbent might be unable to recoup its investments.[20]

(iv) As is the case for backward-looking cost-based pricing, whether the price of interconnection will, to some extent, reflect Ramsey-Boiteux pricing structures depends upon whether demand considerations are taken into account in the allocation of the common costs to different services. Once again, in general, it is not the case (under most LRIC methodologies, the mark-up over the truly incremental cost of interconnection reflects the relative importance of common versus incremental costs, rather than demand considerations)[21] and the resulting price structure is therefore sub-optimal.

(v) Determining the forward-looking costs of a complex network is a very difficult exercise which requires, inter alia, good information on the current cost of the equipment used to provide interconnection (in order to estimate the investment costs which would be incurred by a benchmark efficient firm), on the cost of capital of an efficient benchmark firm (which depends, inter alia, upon an estimate of the risks that usage of the interconnection facilities may be lower than expected)[22] and on the future rate of technological progress (which is crucial to set an appropriate depreciation rate for the firm's investments: rapid technological progress will reduce the cost of providing interconnection for an efficient firm in the future, which in turn requires a rapid depreciation schedule to enable the interconnection pro-

---

[19] For a very detailed analysis of the shortcomings of LRIC, see J Gregory Sidak and Daniel F Spulber, *Deregulatory Takings and the Regulatory Contract: The Competitive Transformation of Competitive Industries in the United States* (Cambridge: Cambridge University Press, 1997) 403–427.

[20] This can, for example, be the case when LRIC prices are set without taking into account regulatory requirements which may constrain the depreciation formulas or the investment choices of the operators. See Eli M Noam, *Interconnecting the Network of Networks* (Cambridge, Mass., and London: MIT Press, 2001) 100–101.

[21] See Intven (n 17 above) B-18.

[22] Some authors have argued that regulators applying LRIC methodology often fail to remunerate the incumbent properly for the risks taken in building and improving its networks. In other words, these authors argue that regulators often underestimate the risk that demand might not materialize and that the investment might be unsuccessful. As a result, if the investment succeeds competitors gain access to it at a price which is too low, and if the investment fails the incumbent has to bear, alone, the cost of the unsuccessful investment. See, for example, Thomas M Jorde et al, 'Innovation, Investment and Unbundling' (2000) 17 *Yale J on Regulation* 1, 16.

vider to recoup the cost of today's investments before tomorrow's reduction of the LRIC-mandated interconnection price).[23]

(vi) In addition to being complex, LRIC methodology leaves a wide degree of discretion to the regulator, which increases the risk of regulatory capture.

3. The Efficient Component Pricing Rule (ECPR)

The ECPR model requires the incumbent to charge an interconnection price which covers the actual costs of providing interconnection plus the opportunity cost of (or profit forgone in) providing interconnection. Similarly, assuming that each call being handled by the new entrant would otherwise have been handled by the incumbent firm, the interconnection price under ECPR equals the price at which the incumbent would sell a service to a given end-user in the downstream market minus the costs which it avoids when the new entrant shoulders some of the costs of providing this service to the end-user.[24]

The ECPR's main advantages are the following:

(i) Entry has no direct impact on the profit of the incumbent since the incumbent is compensated for the opportunity cost of providing interconnection.[25] Consequently, the incumbent has no incentives to resort to exclusionary practices against its competitors.

(ii) The ECPR ensures that only efficient entry can take place, ie competitors will enter the market only if they are more efficient than the incumbent.[26]

(iii) As the interconnection price under ECPR preserves the profits of the incumbent, it might therefore contribute to cover the incumbent's fixed costs.

[23] Some authors argue that, for long-lived equipment in particular, depreciation rates are often set too low to enable operators to recoup their investment under LRIC methodology in sectors such as telecommunications where rates of technological change—and associated price reductions—are particularly rapid. See for example, Jorde et al (n 22 above) 16.

[24] Imagine, for example, that a long-distance service provider, which has built its own long-distance network, needs access to the incumbent's local loop to compete with the incumbent in the market for the provision of long-distance services to end-users. Let c_0 be the cost of conveying a call on the local loop, whether the call is placed by one of the incumbent or one of the new entrant's long-distance subscribers. Let c_1 be the cost for the incumbent of conveying a call on its own long-distance network. And let p be the price which the incumbent charges to its long-distance subscribers for conveying one of their calls (over both its local loop and its long-distance network). Under the ECPR, the interconnection charge should be the cost for the incumbent of providing access (c_0) plus the opportunity cost of providing access ($p - [c_0 + c_1]$) which is equal to $p - c_1$, ie the price which the incumbent charges for a long-distance call minus its avoided costs (ie the cost of conveying the call over its long-distance network, which is avoided when it is the new entrant which conveys the call over its own long-distance network).

[25] Indeed, in the example developed in the previous note, the incumbent makes a profit of $p - c_0 - c_1$ when it provides long-distance services itself. When it is the new entrant which provides the service, the incumbent's profit equals the interconnection price ($p - c_1$) minus the cost of access (c_0), ie $p - c_0 - c_1$.

[26] In the example described above, the cost for the competitor of providing long-distance services to one of its subscribers is the interconnection price ($p - c_1$) plus the cost of conveying the call over its long-distance network (say c_2), which is therefore equal to $p - c_1 + c_2$. If $c_2 > c_1$, ie if the competitor is less efficient than the incumbent, the competitor's price will need to be higher than p if it is to cover its costs and the competitor will therefore be unable to enter the market profitably.

(iv) Under ECPR, the interconnection price does not directly reflect the actual costs of providing interconnection (as mentioned above, assuming that each call handled by the new entrant is diverted from the incumbent, the interconnection price equals the price at which the incumbent would sell a service to end-users in the downstream market minus the costs which the incumbent avoids when a competitor shoulders some of the costs of providing that service).[27] The incumbent does not, therefore, receive compensation if the actual costs of providing interconnection increase, which gives the incumbent incentives to reduce the actual costs that it incurs in providing interconnection. Note, however, that if the incumbent is able to reflect increases in its actual costs of providing interconnection in the retail price, the interconnection price is affected by these cost increases and the incumbent might thus lose its incentives to keep these costs down.[28] The incumbent might also lose incentives to limit its actual costs of providing interconnection if increasing these costs enables the incumbent to reduce its costs in the competitive downstream market (see the fourth drawback of ECPR below).

(v) To the extent that the incumbent is able to take demand elasticities into account to determine its prices in the downstream market (as will be the case if the potentially competitive downstream market is left unregulated), the interconnection price will itself reflect those demand elasticities (since the interconnection charge covers the incumbent's forgone profits, which is a function of the price which the incumbent is able to charge in the downstream market). This in turn means that, to some extent, the interconnection price should reflect welfare-enhancing Ramsey–Boiteux principles.[29]

The ECPR presents, however, the following main drawbacks:

(i) If the incumbent is able to earn excess profits in the downstream market, the ECPR does little to correct the situation: retail prices might be somewhat lower once interconnection is granted to new entrants but only to the extent that new entrants are more efficient than the incumbent and pass these efficiency gains on to end-users. The incumbent is, for its part, compensated for its whole forgone profits.

---

[27] The actual cost of providing interconnection (ie c_0 in the notation adopted above) does not affect the interconnection price, since the actual cost of interconnection washes out in the calculation of the incumbent's opportunity cost $(c_0 + p - [c_0 + c_1]) = p - c_1$, as indicated in n 24 above.

[28] In other words, using the notation adopted above, if an increase of the actual costs of providing interconnection (c_0) translates into a similar increase of the retail price (p), the interconnection price ($p - c_1$) increases by the same amount and the incumbent is therefore compensated for the increase of its costs.

[29] Such interconnection prices would, however, reflect Ramsey–Boiteux principles only very imperfectly for a number of reasons. For example, as the incumbent is providing two distinct types of services—interconnection services to new entrants, and services to end-users—the mark-up on each of these services should reflect demand considerations relevant for each of them. Not only the demand elasticity of services provided to end-users, but also the elasticity of the demand of new entrants for interconnection services would therefore need to be taken into account.

(ii) Conversely, if the incumbent is forced, because of price regulation for example, to provide services in the downstream market below costs, the ECPR does not correct the situation. The opportunity cost of providing interconnection is negative and the interconnection price does not therefore cover the incumbent's costs of providing interconnection.[30]

(iii) As mentioned above, the determination of the interconnection price is based on the assumption that each call handled by the new entrant is traffic diverted from the incumbent. However, to the extent that the new entrant lowers charges or provides better services, it may expand the total number of calls. In that case, the incumbent's opportunity cost of providing interconnection may be zero (if there is excess network capacity) and calculating the ECPR as the incumbent's retail price minus the so-called avoided costs would overstate the incumbent's compensation (at least as long as retail prices are not set below costs).[31]

(iv) As the interconnection price equals the price at which the incumbent would sell a service to end-users in the downstream market minus the costs which the incumbent avoids when a competitor shoulders some of the costs of providing that service, the incumbent has incentives to engage in managerial or accounting cross-subsidization in order to shift costs from the downstream market to the bottleneck segment, as this enables the incumbent to increase the interconnection price (indeed, it reduces the avoided costs which the incumbent must subtract from the end-user price to calculate the interconnection price).[32]

(v) The ECPR is a relatively complex and heavy-handed regulatory process, as it requires constant monitoring of the incumbent's costs and profits, and revisions of the interconnection price when changes occur.

4. Peering Arrangements

Under peering—also called 'bill and keep'—arrangements, parties typically provide each other with free access to their networks. Such arrangements are relatively common between Internet service or Internet backbone providers. Unlike previous interconnection pricing methodologies, peering arrangements imply reciprocity between operators.

The main advantages of peering arrangements are the following:

(i) Peering arrangements will promote competition in the downstream market when they are favourable to new entrants. This will be the case if a new entrant causes more traffic to flow to the incumbent's network than vice

---

[30] In the notation adopted above, this situation means that $p < c_0 + c_1$. Therefore, the interconnection charge, $p - c_1$, is smaller than c_0.

[31] See Eli M Noam, *Interconnecting the Network of Networks* (Cambridge, Mass., and London: MIT Press, 2001) 89.

[32] In other words, following the notation adopted above, reducing the avoided costs (c_1) increases the interconnection price ($p - c_1$).

versa. This, in turn, will often be the case if the incumbent's network is more developed than that of the new entrant so that Internet activity by the new entrant's subscribers, for example, will often require the use of the incumbent's network while the incumbent's subscribers will less often need access to the facilities of the new entrant.

(ii) As a 'bill and keep' formula does not provide compensation for the costs actually incurred in providing interconnection, the operators have strong incentives to reduce the costs incurred in providing interconnection.

(iii) As there is no compensation for the cost of providing interconnection, there are no incentives for the type of accounting and/or managerial cross-subsidization described above.

(iv) Peering arrangements make for very simple pricing rules indeed. In addition, they do not require any measurement of traffic flows and therefore provide for the saving of measurement costs.

On the other hand, peering arrangements suffer from serious drawbacks:

(i) As the operators receive no compensation either for the actual or for the opportunity costs of providing interconnection, they have strong incentives to restrict access to their facilities.

(ii) Peering arrangements also enable inefficient entry when traffic flows between networks are unbalanced in favour of the new entrants.

(iii) If traffic flows are unbalanced, the free access policy does not reflect the economic costs incurred by the different operators.[33]

(iv) As the operator which uses the network of another does not internalize the costs which it imposes upon that other operator, it has incentives to try to use the other operator's network rather than its own even when it is not optimal to do so. This is the so-called 'hot potato' problem.[34] While significant free riding by one operator can be relatively easily detected between networks of similar sizes with generally balanced traffic flows, the situation is very different when one network handles much higher volumes of traffic than another one, as free riding on the part of the smallest operator might well remain undetected by the largest.[35]

5. The Global Price Cap

The global price-cap methodology, proposed by Laffont and Tirole,[36] consists of imposing a global cap on a basket of prices comprising both the price of

---

[33] Mobile operators, for example, often favour 'bill and keep' arrangements because mobile users typically make many more calls than they receive. See Noam (n 31 above) 77.

[34] See Noam (n 31 above) 76.

[35] See Henry Ergas, *Internet Peering: A Case Study of the ACCC's Use of its Power Under Part XIB of the Trade Practices Act 1974*, Mimeo, 8 May 1999, 14.

[36] See Jean-Jacques Laffont and Jean Tirole, 'Creating Competition Through Interconnection: Theory and Practice' (1996) 10 *J of Regulatory Economics* 227; and Jean-Jacques Laffont and Jean Timole 'Access Pricing and Competition' (1994) 38 *European Economic Rev* 1673.

interconnection and the prices of final services in the downstream market. The weights used in the computation of the price-cap are exogenously determined and are proportional to the forecasted quantities of services sold. The objective is to set the cap at a level which would enable the incumbent to cover all the actual costs incurred in providing interconnection. As is typical of price-cap regulation, the cap is supposed to be set for a relatively long period after which a review process takes place and a new cap is set for a period of similar duration.

A global price-cap presents the following advantages:

(i) A global price-cap enables the incumbent to price both interconnection and sales on the downstream market in a way which maximizes its overall profits, provided that the chosen prices conform to the overall cap. This may limit, to some extent, the incumbent's incentives to restrict the access of other operators to its facilities, as the provision of interconnection may turn out to be a profitable activity.

(ii) Provided the global price-cap is indeed set at a level which enables the incumbent to cover all the actual costs of providing interconnection, this pricing methodology ensures the sustainability of the incumbent's provision of interconnection services.

(iii) As the cap remains fixed for a long period of time, the incumbent has incentives to reduce the actual costs that it incurs in providing interconnection, as this will increase its profitability until the next price review.

(iv) As the cap—at least between price reviews—does not vary with the costs actually incurred by the incumbent, and as it applies to both the provision of interconnection and to the sale of services in the downstream market, the incumbent has no incentive to engage in accounting and/or managerial cross-subsidization between its different activities.

(v) The incumbent is able to take demand elasticities into account to determine both its interconnection and its downstream prices, which means that the price structure that it will choose should reflect welfare-enhancing Ramsey–Boiteux principles.[37]

The disadvantages of a global price-cap are as follows:

(i) While giving the incumbent a degree of flexibility in determining prices in the markets for interconnection as well as for end-user services might limit its incentives to restrict other operators' access to its facilities, it does not necessarily eliminate such incentives. The incumbent could, for example, decide to price interconnection very high and end-user services very low (in a way which would be consistent with the global cap) in an effort to drive its

---

[37] Contrary to the situation under ECPR, where the incumbent has incentives to take into account the elasticity of the demand for end-user services but not the elasticity of the demand for interconnection services, the global price-cap, which includes both interconnection prices and end-user prices, gives the incumbent incentives to take all relevant demand elasticities into account; see Jean-Jacques Laffont and Jean Tirole, *Competition in Telecommunications* (Cambridge, Mass., and London: MIT Press, 2000) 170.

competitors out of the market. Such a price structure would of course be unfavourable to the incumbent as well, but the incumbent might still select that strategy if it believes that its superior financial resources will enable it to outlive its competitors and that the losses it is likely to make under this price structure will convince the regulator to relax the cap at the next price review. An alternative strategy would be to price interconnection very low in order to be able to price end-user services very high and restrict competitors' access through non-price exclusionary practices.[38]

(ii) There is no guarantee that a global price-cap will prevent inefficient entry. If, for example, demand is less elastic in the downstream market than in the market for interconnection services, the incumbent could be expected to recoup most of its fixed costs through a mark-up on the prices of end-user services, in accordance with Ramsey–Boiteux principles. Under a global price-cap, this would imply keeping interconnection prices low (to 'compensate' for high end-user prices), which in turn could enable inefficient entry.

(iii) A global price-cap can induce an operator to adopt a price structure which exactly conforms to Ramsey–Boiteux prices only if the weights attached to the different prices in the price-cap formula are exactly proportional to the realized consumption quantities of the different services.[39] Knowledge of realized consumption quantities is also required to set the cap at a level which will enable the incumbent to just cover the actual costs of providing interconnection. Such perfect foresight on the part of the regulator is clearly an unrealistic objective. The best one can hope for is a reasonable forecast, is a which will permit the adoption of weights leading to an actual price structure which does not stray too far from cost-covering Ramsey-Boiteux prices. And even that is a very steep regulatory challenge as it requires good knowledge of the incumbent's costs and of the shape of the demand curve for both interconnection and end-user services.

6. A Brief Assessment

Two points clearly stand out from the above analysis. First, while each of the methods described above has specific characteristics and a particular set of advantages and disadvantages, final results depend, in practice, upon the way these methods are implemented (eg whether an incumbent operator will be able to recoup its investment under LRIC pricing will depend, inter alia, upon whether the interconnection price provides for the remuneration of common

---

[38] Laffont and Tirole suggest that the first type of exclusionary practice could be prevented by requiring the incumbent to price interconnection no higher than at ECPR levels. In order to prevent the second exclusionary strategy, they suggest that a price floor on interconnection prices could be imposed on the incumbent—and the level of the floor could conceivably be set by the other operators which have an incentive to avoid exclusion. See Laffont and Tirole (n 37 above) 174 and 178.

[39] ibid 170.

costs or whether the allowed depreciation rate reflects the rate of technological progress in the industry).

Second, however they are applied, each method has its pros and cons and one cannot identify a single 'best' or 'preferred' methodology. It all depends upon which policy goals are given priority. Thus, for example, if the overriding objective is to devise a rule that maximizes competitive pressures, LRIC will often be preferred to ECPR. On the other hand, if it is more important to prevent inefficient entry and to minimise the incumbent's resistance to new entry, the reverse choice will generally be made. Finally, the policy goals which are being given priority will be determined, in turn, by the specifics of individual situations—for example, the degree of market power which the incumbent is able to exercise, the level of regulatory capacity, or the extent to which the incumbent is operating efficiently. Operators' incentives to resist or accommodate interconnection requests by competitors will, in particular, determine to some extent whether the active promotion of new entry needs to be a key regulatory objective. These incentives are discussed in some detail in Section C below.[40]

C. Linkages between Price Regulation and Operators' Strategic Behaviours

The way in which end-user and interconnection prices are regulated will, of course, affect the strategies of competing telecommunications operators and such strategies, for their part, need to be taken into account when designing an appropriate framework of price regulation. We will discuss here two types of issues: (i) operators' incentives to cross-subsidize different activities when such activities are regulated in different ways; and (ii) some strategic considerations which apply when operators need to use each others' networks to complete some of their calls (ie typically, when different operators have established not only long-distance but also local networks and therefore need access to each others' networks in order to complete calls from their subscribers to their competitors' subscribers).[41]

1. Price Regulation and the Cross-Subsidization of Different Activities

While, in practice, the regulation of end-user as well as interconnection prices is likely to blend to a certain extent the properties of cost-based and non-cost-based methods, different rules might still provide the regulated firms with very different incentives. Thus, the incentives for cost cutting, for example, will vary

---

[40] For some additional discussion of the types of considerations which should guide the choice of interconnection rules, see Eli M Noam, *Interconnecting the Network of Networks* (Cambridge, Mass., and London: MIT Press, 2001) 113–116.

[41] Many of the arguments presented in this section are discussed in Laffont and Tirole, *Competition in Telecommunications* (Cambridge, Mass., and London: MIT Press, 2000) 52–54 and 189–212.

with the extent to which the regulated firm is allowed to keep the benefits of its efficiency-enhancing efforts. As a result, applying different regulatory systems to different services produced by the firm is likely to induce the firm to engage in accounting or managerial cross-subsidization between the different services, which distorts the process of resource-allocation between different activities as pointed out above.[42]

2. Strategic Considerations of Competing Operators

Two competing operators which need to use each other's network face two basic conflicting incentives with respect to the level at which they would wish to set the interconnection price which they impose on each other. On the one hand, a high interconnection price will reduce the competitiveness of their competitor, forcing it to raise its prices in the retail market. In fact, imposing high interconnection prices on each other can constitute a form of collusion between the competitors since it forces them to raise their prices in the retail market without having to enter into any formal agreement in that regard. On the other hand, however, operators might wish to limit the interconnection price which they impose on their competitor, in order to lower the intensity of competition for market share. Indeed, when interconnection prices are high, it is much cheaper for an operator to convey a call between two of its own subscribers (which does not involve interconnection) than to convey a call between one of its subscribers and one of its competitor's subscribers. Competitors then have strong incentives to maximize the number of calls which originate and end within their own network, ie to compete fiercely for market share.

Similar sets of conflicting incentives operate with respect to the determination of retail prices. On the one hand, high retail prices might increase operators' profits and might be used by one operator as a signalling device to indicate a desire to avoid price wars with competitors. In order to be able to impose high prices, a new entrant might also decide to limit the coverage of its network so that the incumbent faces competition in a small part of its geographic market only. The incumbent—if it cannot offer different prices to its customers depending upon where they are located—is thus likely to keep its prices high in order to extract maximum profit from its captive customers. This in turn would enable the new entrant to impose relatively high prices also, while still being competitive with the incumbent. On the other hand, under different sets of circumstances, competitors might seek to maximize profits through the adoption of relatively low prices aimed at capturing a substantial share of the market or might reduce retail prices to signal their will to maintain their market share and reduce the appetite of their competitors for a fight for market share.

Which types of incentives will prevail depends upon a multitude of factors. For example:

---

[42] See B.1 end, above.

(i) Strong substitutability between the services offered by the incumbent and by its competitors (eg because those services are basically the same, because the incumbent does not have a strong brand name, etc.) will tend to increase incentives to compete for market share, since small price cuts in the retail market might induce large numbers of users to switch from one service provider to the other. When substitutability is high, an incumbent might therefore be tempted to limit both its interconnection and its retail prices (in an effort to reduce its competitors' incentives to fight for market share).

(ii) The ability to impose non-linear pricing in the retail market (and thus distinguish, for example, between a connection charge and a per minute charge) might also tend to increase incentives to compete for market share. Indeed, under linear pricing, a competitor which decreases its retail prices in order to gain market share also induces its subscribers to increase their volume of calls and therefore increase the interconnection payments it must make to its competitors. With non-linear pricing, however, a competitor might try to increase its market share through low connection charge, while discouraging high volumes of calls by charging high per-minute prices. Adoption of non-linear pricing by its competitors might thus induce an incumbent to offer better interconnection conditions to reduce the intensity of competition for market share.

(iii) On the other hand, a competitor without the means to deploy quickly its network to connect new users might be content under a regime of high interconnection prices and high retail prices.

(iv) An incumbent with deep pockets and the ability to reduce prices suddenly in the retail market (for example under price-cap regulation) might also deter competitors from attempting to capture large parts of the retail market and induce them to accept relatively high interconnection and retail prices.

(v) Also, it is easier for operators to collude through high interconnection prices and/or high retail prices when the number of competitors is limited.

Different approaches to the regulation of interconnection and retail prices will, in turn, be warranted, depending upon the types of incentives which are likely to prevail in a specific market environment. For example, when new entrants can mount a strong challenge to the incumbent because their services are close substitutes to those of the incumbent, because they can adopt non-linear pricing, because they have the resources required to expand their network quickly, because they face an incumbent unable to reduce retail prices quickly and/or because they are numerous, it might be argued, in theory, that imposing strict limits on interconnection and retail prices need not be a top regulatory priority. Indeed, faced with very strong competitors, the incumbent is likely to decide that offering fair interconnection conditions and keeping its retail prices low (in order to limit the appetite of its competitors to fight for market share) might be its best option. And if the incumbent's interconnection offer were still deemed unacceptable by its competitors, the latter would, in any case, be able to deploy their own facilities. A market environment with opposite characteristics would, in general, call for stricter regulation of both interconnection and retail prices.

D. Facilities-based competition, resale, or unbundled access?

Under a regime of facilities-based competition, different networks, operated by different operators, can be interconnected and when an operator provides interconnection services to a second operator, the first operator assumes responsibility for carrying, over its own network, calls or data which did not originate on its network. When, on the other hand, an operator provides resale services to a second operator, the second operator—which may or may not operate a different network—is able to rely on the first operator's network to carry calls or data over it. Unbundling enables the second operator to choose the specific components of the first operator's network which it wants to be able to use, and to combine these components with components of its own in order to provide services to end-users. The network components which a new entrant may use under an unbundled access regime may include both physical network facilities (such as the copper wire linking customers' premises to local switches; the local switches; transmission facilities between different switches; and transmission towers) and non-physical features and services (such as directory information databases; operator services; and subscriber listings in telephone directories).[43]

We review below the main advantages and disadvantages that an unbundled access regime has with respect to a regime of facilities-based competition. We also mention, where appropriate, the extent to which the main advantages and disadvantages of an unbundled access regime differ from those of resale.

The main advantages of unbundling are as follows:

(i) Unbundled access facilitates entry, and therefore competition, by new operators, as it enables those operators to provide services in certain markets without having to establish their own networks in those markets. For this reason, granting unbundled access is seen as a particularly promising way to introduce competition in market segments characterized by high barriers to entry such as the fixed local market. The same is true of resale. Note that interconnection, by contrast, enables competition only within market segments where new entrants have their own networks (eg a new entrant which established its own long-distance network can compete for the provision of long-distance services to end-users with an incumbent present in both the local and long-distance market provided that the new entrant is granted interconnection to the incumbent's local facilities).

---

[43] See Hank Intven (ed), *Telecommunications Regulation Handbook* (Washington, DC: The World Bank, 2000 3–39, 3–40.

(ii) Provided that the price at which unbundled access is granted reflects the true economic value of that access (and provided that non-price exclusionary practices can be prevented), unbundled access avoids unnecessary duplication of network components. Once again, the same is true of resale.

(iii) Unbundled access also promotes innovation as new entrants, by combining components from the incumbent's network with their own, might offer services which the incumbent did not offer (eg high-speed data services, which can be provided over the existing copper wires provided that the new entrant can connect the required pieces of equipment to the local loop). This, in turn, might prompt the incumbent to offer those services as well, thereby creating competition for the provision of innovative services. Resale, for its part, does not promote innovation to the same extent, as the new entrant is forced to use the incumbent's facilities as they are.

On the other hand, unbundling presents the following main disadvantages:

(i) The pricing issues which are associated with the provision of unbundled access—as well as with resale—are conceptually similar to those associated with interconnection. As we have seen, it is thus exceedingly difficult to design a price regime which promotes competition, preserves the incumbent's incentives to invest in its network and limit access prices, reflects welfare maximization principles, and limits regulatory costs as well as the risk of regulatory mistake or capture. Unbundled access pricing is arguably particularly difficult since, unlike resale or interconnection pricing, it requires that an appropriate price be established for access to each specific network component.

(ii) Precisely defining the individual network components to which access must be granted is also a very difficult regulatory task, which is specific to a regime of unbundled access.

(iii) Unbundled access also requires a high degree of technical co-ordination between the different operators (much higher than under a resale or interconnection regime) to ensure the smooth connection of different network components. This, in turn, is likely to entail high transaction costs.

(iv) The necessary technical co-ordination mentioned above, may also facilitate collusion between the different operators.

(v) Since under an unbundled access regime new entrants establish a new network by combining some network components of the incumbent's network and some network components of their own, they may be in a much stronger position than under a resale or facilities-based regime to prevent the incumbent from modernizing its network without their assent.[44]

---

[44] See Alfred E Kahn, *Whom the Gods Would Destroy or How Not to Deregulate* (Washington, DC: AEI–Brookings Joint Center for Regulatory Studies, 2001) 63.

E. ALLOCATION OF SCARCE RESOURCES

Scarce resources which may need to be allocated to operators in the telecommunications sector include, for example, the radio-electric spectrum. Public subsidies—which certainly constitute a limited resource as well—may also need to be allocated to operators to enable them to meet non-commercially viable universal service obligations.

Such scarce resources can be allocated in a variety of ways. Four main methods are summarily described below.[45]

1. Administrative Processes

Allocation of the resources is made through some ad hoc administrative processes or through formally constituted hearings. One advantage of administrative processes is flexibility. The Government can impose whatever decision criteria it chooses and, thus, use this method to achieve specific policy goals. Administrative processes tend to have some serious drawbacks, however. First, they are usually slow and cumbersome. Second, they might lack transparency and it might be difficult for the operators and the public to judge whether the award was made fairly. Third, given the difficulty for bureaucrats to evaluate the price of the resources offered or the merits of the various applicants, there is a risk that such resources might be given for less than their full value and to operators which might not be the most efficient, nor those who value the resources most highly. Finally, given the degree of discretion which is left to those in charge of the process and the significant economic interests at stake, there is a risk that applicants will seek to influence the decision process through lobbying or bribery.

2. Lotteries

Lotteries are an assignment of public resources through a random drawing. Lotteries are attractive because they are usually quick and easy to administer, and because they are perceived as fair since every applicant has an equal chance of winning. But they also have drawbacks. As is the case with administrative processes, there are no guarantees that resources will be allocated to the operators best able to use them at a price which reflects the value which such operators would place on the resources. Lotteries tend, in fact, to attract frivolous applicants and speculators without the technical competence and the financial means to use the resources efficiently.

---

[45] The analysis which follows draws heavily on Valeen Afualo and John McMillan, 'Auctions of Rights to Public Property', in Peter Newman, *The New Palgrave Dictionary of Economics and the Law*, vol 1 (London: Macmillan, 1998), 125.

3. A First-Come, First-Served Regime

A first-come, first-served regime, like a lottery, presents the advantage of working quickly and cheaply, but it has the same random character and inefficient outcomes as a lottery. Depending upon the designated queuing mechanism, a first-come, first-served regime can be perceived as more or less fair. For example, queuing mechanisms which give an advantage to incumbents (because they are already in place) tend to consolidate dominant positions in the market. Another problem with this method is that since the applicants most willing to wait are generally those which have the lowest opportunity costs, queuing actually favours those with access to few alternative resources and those operators are generally very unlikely to be the most efficient.

4. Auctions

In light of the limitations of other allocation methods, auctions have been recognized by many governments as the best way to allocate scarce resources.[46] Auctions are generally seen as an objective and transparent way to allocate resources. They are efficiency-enhancing in that they tend to allocate the resources to the operators which value them the most and they let those best placed to do so—ie the operators—pass judgement on the value of the resources to be allocated. Some observers have argued, however, that auctions have led some operators to pay such high sums to acquire certain resources—in particular spectrum appropriate for the provision of 3G services—that those operators will be forced to impose high consumer prices and may be left without the resources required to implement speedy network roll-outs.

Such arguments are rather weak, however. The auction price, once paid, is a sunk cost for the operator.[47] When deciding how to set its prices, a firm will rationally only take into account its forward-looking costs and revenues, as well as the likely behaviour of other firms.[48] Future service price levels will thus depend to a large extent on the level of competition prevailing in the industry. Similarly, the pace of roll-out of networks and services will be affected by competition. Other things being equal, an operator which pays a substantial sum for the use of radio frequencies will wish to roll out services and maximize its commercial return as quickly as possible.

It is true, of course, that a winning bidder may overvalue the resources on offer and pay 'too much' for them. This may worsen the operator's financial position

---

[46] Generally on auctions, see Preston McAfee and John McMillan, 'Auctions and Bidding' (1987) 25 *J of Economic Literature* 699; John McMillan, 'Selling Spectrum Rights' (1994) 8 *J of Economic Perspectives* 145.

[47] Martin Cave and Tommaso Valletti, 'Are Spectrum Auctions Ruining our Grandchildren's Future?' (2000) 2 *Info* 349.

[48] ibid.

and make it more costly or more difficult for that operator to secure the financing required to provide services to end-users. This could indeed affect the operator's forward-looking costs and therefore affect its prices and investment decisions. However, as mentioned above, no one is better placed than the operators themselves to judge the value of the resources which are being auctioned and relying on non-competitive means of allocating such resources would greatly increase the risks that the resources might be allocated to operators which are not the most efficient at extracting, from the use of the resources, the maximum possible value. Finally, auctions can be designed to minimize, to some extent, the risk of overvaluation by the winning bidder. The specific advantages and disadvantages of various auction methods are discussed below.

F. MAIN AUCTION METHODS AND ISSUES

We review below the pros and cons of various methods which can be used to create competition for the market (to facilitate exposition of the arguments, we will refer below to the winning bidder as the bidder making the *highest* offer, whether it is the one offering the highest sum to the Government or the one requiring the lowest public subsidies to undertake some specific tasks).[49] We will also discuss the main factors influencing the length of the period for which resources should be auctioned as well as the different measures which can be taken to maximize the competitiveness of auctions.

1. First Price or Second Price Auctions

Under a first price auction, the winning bidder pays an amount which corresponds to its bid. Under a second price auction, the winning bidder pays the amount corresponding to the second-highest bid. The main advantages and disadvantages of first and second price auctions are the following:

(i) First price auctions tend to yield higher revenues to the Government.
(ii) When there is a large difference between the first and the second bid, second price auctions might yield results that are politically unsustainable (unless the value of the highest bid can be kept secret from the public).
(iii) On the other hand, in first price auctions, bidders need to guess how their rivals will bid (instead of bidding exactly how much it values the resources on offer, the most efficient firm should try to guess how much the second most efficient firm values those resources in order to place a bid which is only slightly above that of its nearest rival). In second price auctions firms

---

[49] The material in this section is taken, mainly, from Michael Klein, 'Designing Auctions for Concessions—Guessing the Right Value to Bid and the Winner's Curse', *Public Policy for the Private Sector*, Note 160, The World Bank, 1998; and Michael Klein, 'Bidding for Concessions—The Impact of Contract Design', *Public Policy for the Private Sector*, Note 158, The World Bank, 1998.

do not need to think about their competitors' valuations and can make an offer which reflects their own valuations. As a result, first price auctions make bidding more complex for bidders and increase the risk that the firm with the best bidding strategy, rather than the firm which is the most efficient, win.

(iv) In addition, second price auctions reduce the risk that the winning bidder fall prey to the 'winner's curse'. In any auction, there is a risk that the most optimistic, rather than the most efficient, bidder will win and that the offer made by the winning bidder will prove unsustainable thereby creating pressures for renegotiations. A second price auction thus reduces to a certain extent the risk that the winning bidder will be forced to pay a price which proves unsustainably high.

2. Sealed or Open Bid Auctions

In a sealed bid auction, bidders submit their offers in sealed envelopes, which are opened at the same time. In open bid auctions, bidders raise their bids in multiple rounds, in response to what others are bidding, until only the winner is left. The winner pays the last price which it has offered. The main advantages and disadvantages of sealed and open bid auctions are as follows:

(i) Sealed bid auctions might offer better protection against collusion among bidders. Indeed, in open auctions, each bidder can generally observe how the others are bidding. It is therefore easier to identify who might be breaking an agreement and to take immediate retaliatory action by bidding more aggressively. Some measures can however be implemented to make it easier for bidders to break collusion agreements under open bidding. Bidders could, for example, bid remotely and their identity could be kept secret.

(ii) Open bid auctions, on the other hand, yield offers which are very close to the second-highest offers since bidders tend to raise their bids slowly, round after round, and the winning bidder therefore usually bids only slightly more than its nearest rival. Like second price auctions, open auctions tend therefore to offer some protection against the winner's curse.

(iii) While they resemble second price auctions, open bid auctions tend to be more politically sustainable since the winning bidder does not need to reveal how high it was really willing to bid.

(iv) A second reason why open bid auctions offer protection against the winner's curse is that open bidding offers more information about how much other firms value the resources on offer. When it sees that its competitors are beginning to drop out, an over-optimistic bidder might revise its valuation downward.

(v) Because they offer more information than sealed bid auctions, open bid auctions among prudent bidders should also, however, yield higher offers than sealed bid auctions. Under sealed bid auctions, prudent bidders will tend to make conservative offers so as not to be victim of the winner's curse. Under open bid auctions, with better information, they will tend to revise their estimations upward if they see that most of their competitors keep bidding.

3. Sequential or Simultaneous Bid Auctions

When different sets of resources, for example different spectrum bands, have to be auctioned, one can choose to auction each set sequentially or to auction all of them simultaneously. The respective advantages and disadvantages of the two methods are as follows:

(i) The main advantage of sequential bid auctions is that they tend to be simpler to organize.
(ii) Sequential bid auctions also offer some flexibility. They can be designed as open or sealed bid auctions to best suit the specific requirements of a particular situation. Simultaneous bid auctions, on the other hand, should only be open since the objective is to enable bidders to adjust their bids for a particular set of resources in response to whether they are winning or losing their bids for other sets of resources.
(iii) The fact that bidders under simultaneous bid auctions are able to adjust their bidding strategies to take into account the way in which different bidding processes for different sets of resources are developing is a clear advantage when the value of a particular set of resources depends, for a bidder, upon whether or not it can get another set. For example, the value of a spectrum band might be much higher for a bidder if it can get an adjacent band as well when this enables the deployment of technologies which could not be used within a single band. Bidders who compete for the right to provide universal services in a given geographical area might also want to reflect in their bidding strategy the economies of scale or scope which they would derive from serving more than a single area. In such situations, simultaneous bid auctions yield more information to bidders than sequential bid auctions. It therefore enables bidders to better tailor their bids and to bid more aggressively.

4. Length of the Period for which Resources are Auctioned

The main risk associated with awarding resources for a long period of time, is that while the winning bidder might have been the most efficient operator at the time the auction was held, there is no guarantee that it will remain the most efficient several months or years later. One way to address the issue is to re-auction the rights at regular intervals. This option also has some drawbacks however. First, it raises transaction costs. Second, when the winner of the second auction 'inherits' installations built by the winner of the first auction (eg the network of public phones installed by the operator selected as the universal service provider in a given area), the latter might have incentives to skimp on maintenance during the months immediately preceding the second auction (unless it is confident it will receive adequate compensation for the non-amortized value of its investments, or unless it can take part in the second auction and is confident it will win again). This problem occurs more frequently when rebidding takes place at frequent intervals.

In order to award resources for long periods while maintaining strong incentives for efficiency, one possibility is to ensure some degree of in-market competition. This can be done, for example, by allocating different spectrum bands to different bidders who then compete in providing the same types of cellular services to end-users, or, as discussed below, by indicating that the right to provide universal service in a given area is granted to the winning bidder on a non-exclusive basis. The efficiency-enhancing impact of competition in the market has to be balanced against the fact that bidders are likely to submit lower offers when they do have to face in-market competition. Another possibility to maintain incentives for efficiency without having to organize frequent auctions is to give the winning bidder maximum flexibility with regard to the technology which it can use (ie to focus regulatory efforts on defining the ends to be met by the bidders rather than the means to be used to meet those ends) and to enable the winning bidder to sell the rights which it has acquired to other operators. In those conditions, if a more efficient operator emerges in the future (eg an operator more efficient at deploying a new technology better suited to extracting value from the resources acquired by the winning bidder), that operator should place a higher value than the winning bidder on the resources which the latter has acquired and both parties should thus be able to conclude a mutually profitable transaction which would transfer the resources to the operator which values them most.

5. Maximizing the Competitiveness of the Auction

Several measures can be taken to induce a sufficient number of operators to bid aggressively against each other. It has already been pointed out that sealed bid auctions make collusion more difficult than open bid auctions and that open and simultaneous bid auctions reveal more information to bidders than sealed and sequential auctions and therefore induce prudent bidders to bid more aggressively. Implementing pre-qualification processes (which reduce the number of bidders and therefore increase the likelihood of winning for each of them) and reimbursing (some) bidders for (some of) the costs incurred in preparing their bids might also increase bidders' interest in the auction and make for more aggressive bidding.[50] Finally, when bidders know that they will operate

---

[50] Michel Kerf et al, 'Concessions for Infrastructure: A Guide to their Design and Award', World Bank Technical Paper No 399 (Washington, DC: The World Bank, 1998) 72 and 82.

under a rate-of-return type of regulation, they will typically bid more aggressively than when they are to operate under a price-cap type of arrangement. The reason is that the possibility of passing costs on to users—which is greater under rate-of-return than under price-cap—reduces the competitive advantage of the most efficient firms, thereby forcing them to bid more aggressively. This benefit of more aggressive bidding needs of course to be balanced against the drawbacks of rate-of-return (such as lower incentives to control costs).

G. COMPETITION AND UNIVERSAL SERVICE OBLIGATIONS

As mentioned in Chapter 2, cross-subsidies between different categories of telecommunications users have commonly been used to subsidize the provision of services deemed essential but not commercially viable. As pointed out in the same chapter, however, such cross-subsidization is incompatible with a regime of open competition between operators and needs to be replaced, in liberalized markets, by a system whereby subsidies are not integrated into the prices of telecommunications services sold to some users.

In order to be fully compatible with a regime of undistorted competition, the subsidy system needs to ensure that it does not give an unfair advantage to any competing operator—an advantage which could stem either from the way subsidies are being collected or from the way they are being allocated. As far as collecting the required revenues is concerned, several options are compatible with a regime of undistorted competition. Collecting revenues from general taxation is one such option. Collecting such revenues through a levy imposed upon all telecommunications operators and proportional to the turnover of these operators is generally regarded as competitively neutral as well (under such a regime, an unduly expensive system of universal service obligations might, however, have a negative impact upon the overall level of competition in the telecommunications market as it would require that high levies be imposed upon the operators which in turn might discourage entry into the market).

On the allocation front, one would generally want to ensure: (i) that the operators which provide universal services receive subsidies which are just sufficient to cover the costs which they incur; and (ii) that the costs, thus covered, are those of efficient operators. An effective way of meeting the above two objectives is to award, through a competitive auction, the right to provide a pre-specified set of services in a given area to the operator which requires the smallest subsidy to complement the price that can be charged to end-users.[51] Alternatively, the value of the subsidy might be fixed in advance. In that case, a competitive auction might be used to select the operator willing to provide the services for the lowest end-user charge. When that charge is also fixed in advance, the

---

[51] See Dennis Weller, 'Auctions for Universal Service Obligations' (1999) 23 *Telecommunications Policy* 645.

auction can be held to select the operator willing to provide the most comprehensive services. In all cases, the system provides for an accurate estimate of the costs of providing the services since the operators themselves—which are best placed to do so—are made to reveal either the overall tariff level which they need or the level of services which they can provide. The system also ensures that the most efficient operator is selected.

The winning bidder might be given an exclusive or a non-exclusive right to provide the services. An exclusive right might raise the value of the auctioned right for the winning bidder and therefore lead the bidders to submit more ambitious offers. If several exclusive rights are granted to different operators for different services or in different geographical areas, some degree of yardstick competition might be possible as well.[52] On the other hand, granting a non-exclusive right to the winning bidder means that, while it has the advantage of having received the subsidies, the selected operator might still face competition in those parts of the market where services can be provided on a fully commercial basis. This is likely to reduce the value of the auctioned right for the bidders, but allowing for a degree of competition in the market (as opposed to competition for the market) might impose stronger competitive pressures upon the winning bidder and therefore further promote efficiency and adequate service quality.

An alternative possibility is to eschew competitive auctions altogether and indicate instead that a specific amount of subsidy will be given to any operator providing a particular service (eg x dollars per additional connected user in a given territory). If the user charge is not fixed in advance, competition in the market should ensure that the sum of the user charge plus subsidy reflects the cost of providing the service for an efficient operator. If the user charge is fixed in advance, competitive pressures should, at least to some extent, help to ensure that service quality levels reflect the overall tariff level. In both cases, as every operator has the opportunity to compete for the subsidies and since the available subsidies are not awarded at the start to a single operator, all operators are put on an equal footing and competition in the market can be more intense than under the previous approaches.

H. Vertical separation or vertical integration?

Vertical separation is typically considered between activities carried out in a monopolistic segment of the market and activities carried out in a—potentially or actually— competitive segment of the market, when the firms operating in the competitive segment need access to the services provided in the monopolistic

---

[52] 'Yardstick competition' refers to the possibility of comparing the performance of operators which do not directly compete with each other in the same market. Publishing comparisons of performance might be enough to prompt less efficient operators to improve their operations. Such comparisons of performance can also be used by regulators to adjust the performance standards and other requirements which they impose upon regulated firms.

segment. The main objective of vertical separation is to prevent the operator of the monopolistic facilities from distorting competition in the competitive segment by discriminating in favour of its own facilities in that segment. Vertical separation can take different forms, from a mere separation of accounts, to complete separation of ownership, and the extent to which it can eliminate the incentives or the ability of the monopolistic operator to engage in discriminating practices depends upon the form of vertical separation which is implemented, as described in Table 3.1 below.

TABLE 3.1. Types of vertical separation and their respective impacts

Type of separation	Description	Effects on incentives to discriminate against non-integrated rivals	Effects on ability to discriminate against non-integrated rivals
Accounting	The preparation of separate accounts, on some pre-defined basis, for some specific functions or services	None	Very little without significant regulatory oversight
Functional	The separation of different services into different divisions of the same firm, possibly with different management and information systems and prohibitions on the flow of business-sensitive information between them	None	Very little without significant regulatory oversight
Corporate	The separation of different services into different corporations, although owned by the same company	None	Very little without significant regulatory oversight
Operational	Putting the operation—but not the ownership—of the non-competitive component under the control of an independent entity	None for the owners but might eliminate incentives to discriminate on the part of the operator (depending on governance of operating entity)	Ability to discriminate remains but incentives to discriminate might have been eliminated (as mentioned in previous column)

TABLE 3.1. (*continued*)

Joint ownership	Each competitive firm owns a share of the non-competitive component	Each owner has incentives to discriminate against the other owners and against new competitors	Ability to discriminate between owners is much reduced as the different incentives tend to cancel each other out; ability of owners to discriminate jointly against new competitors might remain
Ownership	Separate owners of the competitive and non-competitive components	Eliminates incentives to discriminate	Ability to discriminate remains but incentives to discriminate have been eliminated (as mentioned in previous column)

Source: Based on Sally Van Siclen, 'Privatization and Deregulation of Regulated Industries, and Competition Policy', Paper prepared for the 5th International Workshop on Competition Policy, Seoul, Korea, 8 November 2000, 6.

The benefits which can be derived from undistorted competition in the potentially competitive segment will depend in turn upon the cost structure of the industry. For example, when important costs are incurred in the competitive segment of the market, the cost savings which could be brought about by undistorted competition in that segment might be important, thus arguing in favour of vertical separation. When, on the other hand, relatively few costs are incurred in the competitive segment, vertical separation is less likely to bring substantial benefits. In addition, the scope for competitive pressure will depend upon the extent to which economies of scale might exist in the competitive segment. When such economies of scale do exist, the number of competitors which the market can support might be limited and so might therefore be the gains which can be expected from promoting unfettered competition in that market.

The main drawbacks of vertical separation are the following:

(i) Vertical separation might entail the loss of economies of scope.
(ii) Vertical separation might increase transaction costs, as agreements which could easily be concluded within a single entity might become more difficult—and therefore more costly—between vertically separated entities.[53]
(iii) When the vertically separated entity operating in the potentially competitive segment retains substantial market power, vertical separation might lead to 'double marginalization' whereby monopolistic profits are extracted in both

[53] On the impact of the existence of transaction costs on the optimal size of firms, see the seminal article by Ronald H Coase, 'The Nature of the Firm' (1937) *Economica* 386–405.

segments of the market, thus resulting in prices in the downstream market which are further from the social optimum than would be the case if a single vertically integrated monopolistic firm operated in both segments.[54]

(iv) Independently of cost considerations, users might have a preference for a vertically integrated one-stop-shop meeting all their telecommunications needs in the various segments of the market.

A crucial factor to consider when weighing the pros and cons of vertical separation is the relative strengths or weaknesses of the incumbent operator and of the regulatory authorities. It is clear that the most far-reaching forms of vertical separation, which eliminate the operator's incentives to distort competition in the competitive segment, can compensate for the inability of the regulator to preserve competition in a vertically integrated setting. On the other hand, when the regulator is able effectively to control the behaviour of a vertically integrated incumbent, or when the market power which the incumbent possesses in one market segment and can leverage in the other is relatively weak, vertical separation might not be required.

I. REGULATORY IMPLICATIONS OF CONVERGENCE

Many of the regulatory issues discussed above are likely to be affected by the so-called process of 'convergence'.[55] The notion of convergence is commonly used to refer to the progressive disappearance of the traditionally defined boundaries *within* the communications sector (telecommunications, cable television, and broadcasting), and *between* the communications sector and the information/content industry and the information technology industry.[56] This process is essentially driven by digitization, which provides a common format allowing for network substitutability. Convergence is not, however, only taking place at the network level, but also at the level of services (with, for example, the creation of new, hybrid services, such as interactive video, video-on-demand, digital games, etc) and markets (with, for example, telecommunications companies investing in cable and vice versa).[57]

Among the main impacts of convergence on regulatory regimes and institutions are the following:[58]

---

[54] John Vickers and Michael Waterson, 'Vertical Relationships: An Introduction' (1991) 39 *J of Industrial Economics* 445, 446.

[55] For an extensive study of the convergence process, see Thomas F Baldwin et al, *Convergence: Integrating Media, Information and Communication* (Thousand Oaks, Cal.: Sage Publications, 1996).

[56] See Dimitry Ypsilanti and Patrick Xavier, 'Towards Next Generation Regulation' (1998) 22 *Telecommunications Policy* 643, 644.

[57] See Damien Geradin, 'Regulatory Issues Raised by Network Convergence: The Case of Multi-Utilities' (2001) 2 *J of Network Industries* 113.

[58] The paragraphs which follow are largely based on Ypsilanti and Xavier (n 56 above).

(i) Convergence should facilitate and accelerate the streamlining of sector-specific regulatory regimes. Convergence widens the technology platforms available to access customers and thus acts to eliminate the access bottleneck. In a situation of fully-fledged convergence where several networks compete for the provision of local access, mandatory requirements on the incumbents to grant interconnection and unbundled access to their competitors might become unnecessary and even undesirable.[59] Network competition should also stimulate competition at the service level and thus reduce the need for other forms of regulation, such as price controls.

(ii) Convergence increases the importance of the requirements of regulatory symmetry and competitive neutrality. Convergence is a process which requires a certain amount of experimentation to find out which technology and infrastructure are more appropriate for which service. The outcome of this process should not be arbitrarily distorted by regulatory asymmetry whereby certain network operators (and, thus, certain technological choices) are privileged in comparison with others.

(iii) Convergence-induced competition in local access should decrease the risks to competition created by traditional forms of vertical integration. For instance, in a situation of fully-fledged convergence with different operators using different technologies and infrastructures to gain direct access to end-users, there seems to be no justification left for preventing local exchange operators from providing long-distance services. However, as convergence progresses, new forms of horizontal and vertical integration across infra-structures, services and content will take place and create new risks for the competitive process.

(iv) Finally, convergence increases the need for consistency in the regulatory treatment of alternative networks and services. It strengthens the case for greater reliance on economy-wide rules and institutions as the prime regulatory instruments for the communications sector.

J. International benchmarking of telecommunications prices

Before turning to the discussion of the regulatory framework adopted in each of the five countries under study in the present book, it is important to sound a note of caution regarding the interpretation of comparisons between telecommunications prices in different countries. The discussion of the different types of regulatory arrangements for the telecommunications sector, which we are about to carry out is aimed at informing the policy debate about what appears

---

[59] See Damien Geradin and Christophe Humpe, 'Regulatory Issues in Establishment and Management of Communications Infrastructure: The Impact of Network Convergence' (2002) 3, *J of Network Industries* 99.

to work best and what does not. And the level of telecommunications prices in a given country is undoubtedly an important element to take into consideration when trying to determine whether the regulatory arrangements implemented in that country appear to be successful or not. We will, for that reason, make use of price comparisons in the following chapters. We will rely, in particular, on price comparisons which we computed on the basis of November 2001 data for the five countries which are the focus of our analysis (the results of these comparisons are presented in the Annex). It is, however, essential to keep in mind that establishing the exact extent to which differences between telecommunications prices are due to the quality of the regulatory framework (and in particular to the more or less successful combination of economy-wide and sector-specific regulatory instruments) is fraught with difficulties.

Some of the main factors which make the interpretation of international benchmarking of telecommunications prices particularly challenging are listed below:

(i) Specific services included in the various baskets may not always be easily comparable across countries. For example, the concept of local calls may refer to calls within areas of very different sizes, thereby reducing the validity of the price comparisons. Also, baskets of international services are never exactly the same for different countries since the country of origin is a different one in each case.

(ii) The selected baskets and prices may not be equally representative of the competitiveness of telecommunications offerings in the different countries. For example, as calling patterns differ from country to country, the chosen basket may correspond more closely to actual patterns in one country than in another, which may impact the relative level of competition between operators to provide this mix of services. Also, as it has become impossible to identify all possible pricing plans proposed by all operators in each country, comparisons are usually based on the best, broadly available offer by the main telecommunications company in each country. Once again, this offer may be more representative in some countries than in others.

(iii) Differences in input prices faced by telecommunications operators in different countries—unrelated to the quality of the telecommunications regulatory framework—might explain some of the differences in telecommunications prices. These differences may to some extent be corrected by using Power Purchasing Parities (PPPs) to convert the prices of telecommunications services into a common unit of account. However, available PPP-based prices correct for the differences in the price levels of a broad range of goods and services between different countries. This difference may or may not be a good proxy for the differences in the price levels of the inputs consumed by telecommunications operators.[60]

---

[60] For a good description of the rationale for using PPP-based prices rather than prices at current exchange rates, see Michelle A Vachris and James Thomas, 'International Price Comparisons Based on Power Purchasing Parity' (Oct 1999) *Monthly Labor Rev* 3–12.

(iv) Geography, climate, and other natural factors may also affect the cost of providing telecommunications services. Urbanization patterns in particular, have an impact on the density of telecommunications networks and therefore on their costs. A few studies have attempted to quantify this impact for some of the countries of interest here. They used engineering models developed in the United States which identify the main factors—including population densities and average number of lines per person—that determine the average costs of providing basic local telephone services. Results differed somewhat according to the model used and to the levels of regional aggregation of the available data but, on the whole, it is clear that denser networks tend to be cheaper to install. One study estimates that the costs of fixed local services in Australia and New Zealand are more expensive than in the United States by 10–14 per cent and 15–20 per cent respectively, while they are 19–22 per cent less expensive in the United Kingdom than in the United States.[61] Another study confirms that local networks are more costly in Australia and in New Zealand than in the United States, but it estimates that costs are somewhat higher in Australia than in New Zealand.[62]

(v) A range of government interventions, unrelated to the quality of the regulatory tools used to control market power in telecommunications, may also affect the prices of telecommunications services. Macro-economic policies, to take just one example, may certainly affect the prices of telecommunications services. Low telecommunications prices in some market segments may also reflect direct price controls rather than a more efficient regulatory framework overall. This may, for example, well be the case for fixed local calls whose prices are kept below costs in some countries, thereby making price comparisons focused only on those calls difficult to interpret.

On the whole, it is clear, however, that price discrepancies between telecommunications prices in different countries cannot, generally, be attributed exclusively to the factors mentioned above. A careful comparison between telecommunications prices in different countries can therefore provide some useful information about the effectiveness of the regulatory framework—but one must recognize that the causal links between prices and regulatory arrangements are far from straightforward and that prices are affected by numerous factors whose exact impacts are often impossible to ascertain with absolute precision.

[61] See Dan Alger and Joanne Leung, *The Relative Costs of Local Telephony Across Five Countries*, New Zealand Institute for the Study of Competition and Regulation (NZISCR), Wellington, New Zealand (March 1999) 6.
[62] See Peter Cribbett, *Population Distribution and Telecommunication Costs*, Productivity Commission Staff Research Paper (Canberra: AusInfo, August 2000) 27.

4

United States

The regulatory framework in the United States puts heavy emphasis on sector-specific features. Detailed sector-specific rules have been adopted on a number of issues and a powerful sector-specific regulator has been established. An analysis of the US model is therefore well suited to discuss the pros and cons of the sector-specific regulatory option.

A. Origins of the Present Regulatory Framework

In February 1996, Congress adopted the Telecommunications Act of 1996.[1] This Act provided the first major overhaul of the 1934 Communications Act, which regulated the telecommunications industry for more than sixty years.[2] During these sixty years, changes in the political climate and the telecommunications industry necessitated a revision of the regulatory framework.

The Communications Act of 1934 (the '1934 Act') was adopted during the Great Depression with a view to protect the American consumers against AT&T which, through an aggressive policy of acquiring independent telephone companies,[3] had gained a virtual monopoly over all segments of the

---

[1] Telecommunications Act of 1996, Pub L No 104-104, 110 Stat 56. A great number of articles detail the content of this law. See, for instance, Thomas G Krattenmaker, 'The Telecommunications Act of 1996' (1996) 29 *Connecticut L Rev* 123; Michael I Meyerson, 'Ideas of the Marketplace: A Guide to the 1996 Telecommunications Act' (1997) 49 *Federal Communications L J* 252; Robert M Frieden, 'The Telecommunications Act of 1996: Predicting the Winners and Losers' (1997) 20 *Hastings Communications and Entertainment L J* 11.

[2] Communications Act of 1934, Ch 652, 48 Stat 1064 (amended 1996).

[3] In the late part of the 19th century and the early part of the 20th century, competition between local exchange operators flourished. Many cities were served by two or more operators, usually a Bell company and one or several independent companies. However, many companies did not interconnect with each other. This gave an advantage to the local Bell companies that usually had a larger customer base. In addition, AT&T, the company created by the Bell Company to connect local exchanges, used its control over the inter-city network as leverage to gain control over independent companies, by denying them the right to interconnect with that network for long-distance calls. See Jeffrey Blumenfeld and Christy C Kunin, 'United States' in Colin Long (ed), *Telecommunications Law and Practice* (London: Sweet & Maxwell, 1995) 649, 652. AT&T's consolidation policy based on leveraging market power led the DoJ to file a suit against the Bell system to prevent it from acquiring additional independent companies. This suit was settled in 1913 by a written commitment of AT&T vice-president Nathan Kingsbury (known as the 'Kingsbury commitment') in which AT&T agreed to stop acquiring independent companies, as well as to offer interconnection with its intercity network to the remaining independent local operators. However, AT&T convinced Congress to override part

telecommunications industry. AT&T was the only company to offer long-distance services and, through its Bell Operating Companies (BOCs), it provided most of the local exchange services in the country. With its subsidiary Western Electric Company, AT&T also dominated the manufacturing and distribution of telephone equipment as the Bell system bought almost exclusively from Western Electric. Telephone service as a whole was viewed as a natural monopoly that needed to be regulated for the benefits of all users.[4]

With this objective in mind, the 1934 Act provided for the creation of the Federal Communications Commission ('FCC') and entrusted it with the mission of regulating interstate telephone service. Specifically, the Commission controlled entry, regulated prices (through a system of 'rate-of-return' regulation), and took other regulatory decisions that it considered in the public interest. Pursuant to the 1934 Act, the FCC also had sole authority to review mergers and acquisitions between telephone companies.[5] While the FCC had jurisdiction to regulate interstate services, intrastate telephone services continued to be regulated by the state utility commissions created by the states at the turn of the century.[6] In many instances, states granted franchised monopolies to local exchange companies, most of them BOCs.

As the telephone industry developed in the 1950s and 1960s, many began to challenge the basic premise that telephone service was a natural monopoly.[7] Potential competitors sued the FCC and AT&T in order to loosen AT&T's monopoly grasp on the manufacture and distribution of telecommunications equipment[8] and the provision of long-distance services.[9] After gaining entry into such markets, these competitors began to allege that they could not compete fairly because AT&T was leveraging its monopoly power over local

---

of the Kingsbury commitment by adopting the Willis–Graham Act, which exempted AT&T from the antitrust laws when acquiring additional companies. See Willis–Graham Act of 1921, Ch 20, 42 Stat 27, repealed by Communications Act of 1934, Ch 652, 48 Stat 1064, 1102.

[4] Peter H Huber et al, *Federal Telecommunications Law* (2nd edn, New York: Aspen Law & Business, 1999) 21.

[5] See the 1934 Act, s 221(a).

[6] The 1934 Act, s 1 gives the FCC authority over 'interstate and foreign commerce in wire and radiotelecommunications'. Section 2(b) limits the scope of FCC power by explicitly denying the FCC jurisdiction 'with respect to charges, classifications, practices, service facilities, or regulation for or in connection with intrastate communication service by wire or radio carrier'. Taken together, these provisions give the FCC authority over all interstate communications but reserve authority over intrastate communications to the states.

[7] Huber et al (n 4 above) 32.

[8] In 1956, the DC Circuit reversed an FCC decision prohibiting customers from attaching a 'Hush-a-Phone' to their handset for increased privacy. See *Hush-a-Phone Corp* 20 FCC 391 (1955), reversed, 238 F 2d 266 (DC Cir 1956). In addition, a decade later, the FCC ruled that a 'Carterfone', a device permitting direct communication between a mobile radio and a landline network, would be permitted because the Bell system had failed to demonstrate 'harm to the network'. See *Use of the Carterfone Device in Message Toll Telephone Services* 13 FCC 2d 420 (1968).

[9] See *In re Applications of Microwave Communications, Inc (MCI)* 18 FCC 2d 953 (1969) (allowing, despite AT&T's protestations, Microwave Communications, Inc to provide microwave service in St Louis, Chicago, and nine intermediate locations).

exchanges to maintain its market share in services that were increasingly open to competition.[10]

In 1974, the Department of Justice ('DoJ') started an antitrust suit against AT&T. The core of the DoJ's case was that AT&T was granting competitors interconnection to its local exchange network only on discriminatory terms, and that AT&T was cross-subsidizing its own inter-city services with revenues from the monopoly local exchange services. In 1982, AT&T and the DoJ announced they had entered into a consent decree designed to end the litigation.[11] This consent decree, also known as the Modified Final Judgement (MFJ),[12] was approved by Judge Greene of the US District Court for the District of Columbia.

Pursuant to the MFJ, AT&T agreed to divest its twenty-two BOCs into seven independent local exchange carriers,[13] in exchange for being permitted to enter into other lines of business (eg data services) and compete with virtually no restrictions in long-distance (inter-LATA) services (see Box 4.1 below). The BOCs, for their part, were restricted to providing only local (intra-LATA) telephone services.[14] They were specifically prohibited from entering into certain lines of business, including long-distance services, information services and telecommunications equipment manufacturing.[15] In addition, they were bound to provide all competing long-distance carriers non-discriminatory access to their local exchange network.[16] A cumbersome waiver and triennial review process was set up, giving Judge Greene decision-making responsibility over whether or not to let, in the future, the BOCs enter into new lines of business.[17]

---

[10] Huber et al (n 4 above) 39.

[11] See *United States v AT&T Co* 552 F Supp 131 (DDC 1982), aff'd sub nom *Maryland v United States* 460 US 1001 (1983). There is an abundant academic literature on this case. See, for example, Timothy J Brennan, 'Regulated Firms in Unregulated Markets: Understanding the Divestiture in US v. AT&T' (1987) 32 *Antitrust Bulletin* 741; Paul W MacAvoy and Kenneth Robinson, 'Winning by Losing: The AT&T Settlement and its Impact on Telecommunications' (1983) 1 *Yale J on Regulation* 1.

[12] This decree is known as the Modified Final Judgement because it modifies a previous decree, known as the Final Judgement (FJ), which settled an antitrust suit brought by the DoJ in 1949 against AT&T for an alleged conspiracy between AT&T and Western Electric to monopolize the manufacture and distribution of telecommunications equipment. Pursuant to the FJ, AT&T was allowed to retain ownership of Western Electric, in return for agreeing to grant non-exclusive licences for all existing and future patents and to stay out of any business other than the furnishing of common carrier communications services.

[13] These comprised Ameritech, Bell Atlantic, BellSouth, NYNEX, Pacific Telesis, SBC Communications, and US WEST. In recent years, some of these companies have merged.

[14] RBOCs could also provide wireless services, which were not part of the line-of-business restrictions imposed on them following the MFJ.

[15] See *United States v AT&T* 552 F Supp 186–194. On these restrictions, see Mark C Rosenblum, 'The Antitrust Rationale for the MFJ's Line-of-Business Restrictions and a Policy Proposal for Removing Them' (1996) 25 *Southwestern U L Rev* 605.

[16] See *United States v AT&T* 552 F Supp 197–200.

[17] For an excellent account of Judge Greene's administration of the MFJ, see Joseph D Kearney, 'From the Fall of the Bell System to the Telecommunications Act: Regulation of Telecommunications Under Judge Greene' (1999) 50 *Hastings L J* 1395.

Box 4.1: Local Access Transport Areas

As a result of the MFJ, the United States was divided into 184 areas known as Local Access Transport Areas (LATAs), with an average population of 500,000 per LATA.

In most LATAs, the majority of inter-city calls within LATA (intra-LATA) are handled by the BOC of the LATA. Of the original 184 LATAs, 156 were served by BOCs and 28 by independent local exchange carriers (such as GTE). The MFJ required calls between LATAs (inter-LATA) to be served only by an inter-exchange carrier (IEC).

Each LATA has established one or more points of access (POPs) for connection to the IECs for long-distance between LATAs. A call destined for a different LATA is sent by the local switch in the originating LATA to the IEC's POP. At the POP, responsibility for handling the phone call transfers from the Local Exchange Carrier (LEC) to the IEC. The IEC's own switches then direct the call across its network to the destination LATA, at which point it hands off the call to the receiver's LEC, which completes the call. For assistance on both ends of completing a long-distance phone call, IECs pay LECs 'access charges'.

Intrastate access charges (access charges for a long-distance (inter-LATA) call, but remaining with the caller's state) are regulated by the state PUCs. Interstate access charges (access charges for a long-distance (inter-LATA) call, but destined outside the caller's state) are regulated by the FCC.

Source: Marion Cole, *Introduction to Telecommunications—Voice, Data, and the Internet* (Upper Saddle River, NJ: Prentice-Hall, 2000).

In a second set of proceedings, collectively called 'computer enquiries',[18] the FCC adopted several rulings addressing the competitive risks arising from vertically integrated telephone operators engaging in competitive activities (such as the provision of 'enhanced' or information services) that were dependent on facilities and services over which they enjoyed a monopoly (on the concept of 'enhanced' services, see Box 4.2 below).[19] The risks in question—leveraging monopoly power in one sector to maintain or extend dominance in other sectors through cross-subsidization or discriminatory access to the network—were similar to those involved in the MFJ. However, while the MFJ addressed these risks by restricting companies (through divestiture) to the provision of either competitive or monopoly services, the FCC adopted a set of rules that would permit companies to provide both competitive and monopoly services. In its *Computer II*

---

[18] For a discussion of these enquiries, see Robert M Frieden, 'The Computer Inquiries: Mapping the Communications/Information Processing Terrain' (1981) 33 *Federal Communications L J* 55; Robert M Frieden, 'The Third Computer Inquiry: A Deregulatory Dilemma' (1987) 38 *Federal Communications L J* 383.

[19] This paragraph is based on Jeffrey Blumenfeld and Christy C Kunin, 'United States' in Colin Long (ed), *Telecommunications Law and Practice* (London: Sweet & Maxwell, 1995) 655.

decision adopted in 1984, the FCC required the companies to establish separate subsidiaries for their competitive and monopoly enterprises.[20] However, two years later, in its *Computer III* decision,[21] the FCC abolished the separate subsidiary requirements and replaced it with a model based on non-structural safeguards, such as accounting safeguards.

Box 4.2: Basic versus Enhanced Services

One interesting issue examined in the computer enquiries by the FCC was whether computer data processing service providers were subject to Title II of the Communications Act which contains common carrier regulation.

After examining the record developed through its inquiry, the FCC determined in its *Computer I* decision that the public interest would not be served by regulation of data processing services. Thus, computer services were 'unregulated' from the outset, permitting the data industry to develop innovative services exempt from the numerous common carrier requirements of Title II of the Communications Act.

In *Computer II*, the Commission focused on the need to develop a workable categorical definition of both regulated telecommunications services and unregulated data services. The result was the creation of the distinction between 'basic' and 'enhanced' services. Present-day examples of unregulated enhanced services include voice messaging, protocol processing, alarm monitoring and electronic publishing, as well as Internet access services.

Source: Jason Oxman, 'The FCC and the Unregulation of the Internet', OPP Working Paper No 31 (Federal Communications Commission, July 1999).

The period following the MFJ witnessed growing competition between long-distance carriers and a progressive erosion of AT&T's market share. In 1994, AT&T's share of revenues of the long-distance market was down to 55.2 per cent (from 90.1 per cent in 1984).[22] As a result, in 1995, the FCC re-classified AT&T as a 'non-dominant' carrier with the consequence that its long-distance telephone rates stopped being regulated.[23] In the following year, AT&T was deemed non-dominant for international telephone service as well.[24]

---

[20] Amendment of s 64.702 of the Commission's Rules and Regulations, Second Computer Enquiry, Final Decision, 77 FCC 2d 384, modified on recons, 84 FCC 2d 50 (1980), further modified on recons, 88 FCC 2d 512 (1981), aff'd sub nom *Computer and Communications Indus Assn v FCC* 693 F 2d 198 (DC Cir 1982), cert denied, 461 US 938 (1983), aff'd on second further recons, FCC 84–190 (4 May 1984).

[21] Amendment of s 64.702 of the Commission's Rules and Regulations, Report and Order, 104 FCC 2d 958 (1986).

[22] See FCC, *Trends in Telephone Service* (March 2000).

[23] See *Motion of AT&T Corp to be Reclassified as a Non-Dominant Carrier* 11 FCC Rcd 3271 (1995).

[24] See *Motion of AT&T to be Declared Non-Dominant for International Service* 11 FCC Rcd 17963 (1996).

By the 1990s, the burdensome character of the MFJ's review process, as well as major shifts in technology and outlook,[25] began forcing Congress to reconsider the basic premises of the telecommunications regulatory framework.[26] First, the legally sanctioned market sharing between the BOCs and long-distance operators was no longer tenable. On the one hand, the BOCs wanted to enter the long-distance market, but they were prevented from doing so by the MFJ.[27] On the other hand, Congress considered that competition in local exchange services was largely insufficient. Moreover, the growing convergence between different segments of the communications sector rendered other forms of legally imposed entry barriers—such as, for instance, the prohibition imposed upon cable television operators and local telephone companies to enter each other's markets—increasingly unacceptable.

In that context, the main objective of the Telecommunications Act of 1996 was to bring down all barriers to competition in the telecommunications sector.[28] Indeed, Congress declared in the opening sentence of its Conference report that the 1996 Act was adopted to provide for 'a competitive, deregulatory national policy framework designed to accelerate rapidly private sector deployment of advanced telecommunications and information technologies and services to all Americans by opening all telecommunications markets to competition'.[29]

B. THE MAIN RULES

In this section, we will successively review the sector-specific rules governing the economic regulation of telecommunications and the general antitrust regulations.

1. Telecommunications-Specific Rules

The sector-specific framework for the economic regulation of telecommunications is found in the 1934 Communications Act, as amended by the 1996

---

[25] See Joseph A Klein, 'Antitrust Law as a Regulator of the Rapidly Transforming Telecommunications Market' (1998) 23 *Communications & Strategies* 209, 212 (arguing that 'the MFJ's key premise of divisible local exchange monopoly and competitive markets was being overtaken by technological; regulatory and market developments').

[26] See Daniel F Spulber, 'Deregulating Telecommunications' (1995) 12 *Yale J on Regulation* 25.

[27] See Robert E Litan and Roger G Noll, 'Unleashing Telecommunications: The Case for Competition', Policy Brief No 39, The Brookings Institution (November 1998) 1 ('despite their state-regulated monopolies, the RBOCs were unhappy with the line-of-business restrictions, and persistently pushed courts, regulators, and elected officials to enter competitive markets').

[28] See 'An Interview with William E. Kennard' (October 1998) *Global Competition Rev* 11 ('The theory of the (1996) Act was that local companies would compete in long distance, long-distance companies would compete in the local market, cable television would get into the telephone business, and there would be much more competitive activity on the part of existing players').

[29] S REP NO 104–230, at 1 (1996).

Telecommunications Act. Four key aspects of this framework will be examined hereafter:

(i) the market-opening rules of the 1996 Act;
(ii) the rules applicable to wireless telephony;
(iii) the universal service system set up by the 1996 Act; and
(iv) the pricing rules applicable to telecommunications carriers.

1.1 The Market-Opening Rules of the 1996 Act

Three aspects of the 1996 Telecommunications Act will be examined hereafter: (i) the removal of all legal, economic and operational barriers to entry into the local telephone market; (ii) the authorization granted to the BOCs to enter into the long-distance telephone market upon satisfying fourteen competitive safeguards and certain conditions; and (iii) the elimination of the ban imposed upon cable and telephone operators from entering each other's market.

Local competition provisions

Section 253 of the Act removes all legal and regulatory barriers to entry on the local markets by prohibiting all state statutes or regulations impeding the ability of 'any entity to provide any interstate or intrastate telecommunications'. This provision strikes down all franchised monopolies that were given by the states to local exchange companies.

Congress considered, however, that the removal of legal and regulatory obstacles was not sufficient to ensure effective competition in the local telecommunications market since such competition could still be impeded by important economic and operational barriers, such as refusal to interconnect or discriminatory interconnection conditions. In order to overcome such obstacles, s 251 of the 1996 Act imposes a series of duties on telecommunications carriers involved in local exchange. Section 251 requires each 'telecommunications carrier' to interconnect with other carriers.[30] In addition to interconnection, all LECs are barred from either prohibiting or imposing discriminatory conditions on the resale of telecommunications services.[31] They are also required to provide 'number portability' and 'dialling parity',[32] as well as access to their poles, conduits and other rights of ways to competing providers of telecommunications services.[33]

Additional obligations are imposed on Incumbent Local Exchange Carriers (ILECs).[34] In addition to all of the duties listed in the preceding paragraph, these ILECs are required to provide, at just and reasonable rates, interconnection 'at

---

[30] Section 251 defines 'telecommunications carriers' to include incumbents and new local exchange carriers. 47 USC § 251(a)(1).

[31] 47 USC § 251(b)(1).

[32] ibid § 251(b)(2) and (3).

[33] ibid § 251(b)(4).

[34] 'Incumbent Local Exchange Carriers' denote the local carriers in existence when the Act was adopted.

any technically feasible point with the carrier's network'.[35] They must also provide competitors with 'unbundled' network elements upon request.[36] In addition, the Act requires ILECs to offer for resale 'at wholesale rates any telecommunications service that the carrier provides at retail to subscribers'.[37] Finally, they must permit firms seeking interconnection to locate their equipment on their ILEC premises.[38]

Section 252 of the Act establishes a three-step procedure for completing or litigating interconnection agreements. Under this section, an ILEC receiving a request for interconnection, services, or network elements may negotiate and enter into a binding agreement with the requesting carrier without regard to the statutory duties assigned to it by s 251.[39] This agreement must be approved by the state utility commission.[40] If the parties are unable to come to an agreement on their own, either party may request that the state utility commission participate in the negotiation and mediate any differences.[41] If an agreement has not been completed on the 135th day after the initial interconnection request, either party to the negotiation may ask the state commission to arbitrate any open issue and issue binding rules on the parties.[42] If a state commission does not perform its responsibilities under s 252, the FCC may take over and pre-empt the state commission's powers under that section.[43] Finally, a carrier unhappy with the state commission's arbitration decision may appeal it, but only to a local federal district court which will determine whether the decision meets the requirements of the 1996 Act.[44]

BOCs' entry into the long-distance market

Sections 271 and 272 of the Telecommunications Act deal with the issue of the BOCs' entry into the long-distance market.[45] Section 271 allows the BOCs to provide long-distance services to their own customers provided three conditions

---

[35] 47 USC § 251(c)(2)(B). In practice, this means that incumbents must interconnect with all carriers upon request, at the locations they specify, while other carriers may interconnect with each other indirectly, ie by each carrier connecting to the incumbent.

[36] 47 USC § 251(c)(3). 'Unbundled access' means the availability of access to distinct parts of the incumbent's network, at an appropriately lower cost than access to all elements of the network. Thus, a competitor can purchase only those network components and functions that it needs to offer its services.

[37] 47 USC § 251(c)(4)(a).

[38] ibid § 251(c)(6).

[39] The minimum requirements for the agreement are that it includes a 'detailed schedule of itemised charges for interconnection and each service or network element included in the agreement': 47 USC § 251(a)(1).

[40] For figures on the number of interconnection agreements reached, see Peter H Huber et al, *Federal Telecommunications Law* (2nd edn, New York: Aspen Law & Business, 1999) 485.

[41] 47 USC § 252(a)(2).

[42] ibid § 252(b)(1).

[43] ibid § 252(5).

[44] ibid § 252(e)(6). For an illustration, see *GTE South, Inc* 6 F Supp 2d 517 (ED Va 1998).

[45] Generally on s 271, see Tim Sloan, 'Creating Better Incentives through Regulation: Section 271 of the Communications Act of 1934 and the Promotion of Local Exchange Competition' (1998) 50 *Federal Communications L J* 312.

are met.[46] First, the BOC must have concluded, with one or more competitors, interconnection agreements that satisfy the requirements of s 271(c)(2)(B), the so-called fourteen-point 'competitive checklist'.[47] The requirements contained in this list essentially relate to the interconnection obligations imposed in s 251. The BOCs' ability to offer long-distance services is thus conditioned on meeting their interconnection obligations, thereby giving them an incentive to open their local service areas to competitors. Second, s 271(d)(3)(C) states that the FCC may not approve a BOC's application unless it determines that 'the requested authorization is consistent with the public interest, commerce and necessity'.[48] Third, even with the competitive checklist in place, s 272 requires that a BOC create a separate affiliate to provide long-distance services.[49] This separate affiliate must operate independently from its BOC parent,[50] keeping separate books and records and having separate offices, directors and employees.[51] In order to prevent illegitimate subsidies, all transactions between an affiliate and its BOC parent must be 'on an arm's length basis'.[52]

End of ban on competition between cable television and local telephone service providers

The 1996 Act also eliminates the regulatory barriers preventing cable television operators and local telephone companies from entering each other's markets. First, the 1996 Act repeals a 1984 statute prohibiting telephone companies from offering cable television services directly to subscribers in their service areas.[53] It provides for a system where telephone companies (or anyone else) are authorized to offer cable television and may choose from a menu of options as to how they will be regulated.[54] Likewise, the 1996 Act clears away the rules that kept cable operators from providing local telephone service.[55]

The only major restriction that is maintained by the 1996 Telecommunications Act is the limitation on mergers and buy-outs between cable companies and local telephone companies within their respective areas. The 1996 Act contains parallel prohibitions: a local telephone company cannot acquire more than 10 per cent of a cable company offering services in its local area and vice versa.[56]

---

[46] Because of the lack of a similar danger of unfair competition, BOCs are free to offer long-distance services to those customers not within their local service areas immediately; see 47 USC § 271(b)(2).

[47] 47 USC § 271(c)(2)(B). Alternatively, if a BOC has not received a qualifying interconnection request within a designated period of time, the BOC can satisfy this requirement by providing a statement of generally available terms and conditions that complies with the competition checklist and that 'has been approved or permitted to take effect by the (relevant) state commission': ibid.

[48] For a discussion of this relatively obscure standard see David Turestky, 'Bell Operating Company Interlata Entry Under Section 271 of the Telecommunications Act 1996: Some Thoughts', Remarks before the Communications Committee NARUC Summer Meeting, 22 July 1996, available at <http://www.usdoj.gov/atr/public/speeches/turetsky796.html>.

[49] 47 USC § 272(a)(1).   [50] ibid.   [51] 47 USC § 272(b)(2) and (3).

[52] ibid § 272(b)(5).   [53] ibid § 533(b), now repealed.   [54] ibid § 571(a)(2)-(4).

[55] ibid § 253(a).   [56] ibid § 652(a)(b).

Not only are direct mergers prohibited, but joint ventures between cable operators and telephone companies in the same market are also proscribed by the 1996 Act.[57]

1.2 Wireless Telephony

While the 1996 Act marks a significant turning point in the legislation of wireline communications, it contains few new requirements addressing wireless services.[58] The only new regulation introduced by the 1996 Act with regard to the wireless industry was the imposition of 'reciprocal imposition' on wireless–wireline interconnection, a measure that allowed wireless companies to enjoy the same interconnection rates as the new competitive local access providers. Otherwise, wireless companies are essentially exempt from the unbundling, resale and other regulatory requirements that apply to wireline carriers.

A significant piece of legislation with respect to wireless services is the Omnibus Budget Reconciliation Act of 1993 that authorized the FCC to start awarding new cellular licences through competitive bidding.[59] Until then, the FCC had experimented with various approaches to the licensing problem—from comparative hearings to lotteries.

1.3 Universal Service

Section 254 of the 1996 Act provides for a new regime of universal service.[60] Before the passage of the 1996 Act, universal service was promoted through a patchwork quilt of indirect and hidden subsidies at both state and federal levels (see Box 4.3 below).[61] Recognizing the vulnerability of these implicit subsidies,[62] the Act directs the FCC and the states to restructure their universal support mechanisms to ensure delivery of affordable telecommunications to all Ameri-

---

[57] ibid § 652(c).

[58] See Robert G Kirk, 'Wireless Mobile Communications' in Leon T Knauer et al (eds), *Beyond the Telecommunications Act—A Domestic and International Perspective for Business* (Rockville, Mld.: Government Institutes, 1998) 74.

[59] As part of the Omnibus Budget Reconciliation Act of 1993, Pub L No 103-66, § 6002, 107 Stat 312, 387–392), Congress added s 309(j) to the Communications Act authorizing the FCC to award licences for rights to use the radio spectrum through competitive bidding.

[60] See, generally, Eli M Noam, 'Will Universal Service and Common Carriage Survive the Telecommunications Act of 1996' (1997) 97 *Columbia L Rev* 955, 960; Nicole M Millard, 'Universal Service, Section 254 of the Telecommunications Act of 1996: A Hidden Tax?' (1997) 50 *Federal Communications L J* 265; Allen S Hammond, 'Universal Service in the Digital Age: The Telecommunications Act of 1996: Codifying the Digital Divide' (1997) 50 *Federal Communications L J* 179; Angela J Campbell, 'Universal Service Provisions: The "Ugly Duckling" of the 1996 Act' (1996) 29 *Connecticut L Rev* 187; Mackenzy Lapointe, 'Universal Service and the Digital Revolution: Beyond the Telecommunications Act of 1996' (1999) 25 *Rutgers Computer and Technology L J* 61.

[61] Generally on universal service, see Milton Mueller, *Universal Service: Competition, Interconnection and Monopoly in the Making of the American System* (Washington, DC: AEI Press, 1997).

[62] Because the most profitable services, such as business service, attract the most new entrants, competition decreases the profit margin on services typically used to subsidize universal service. As incumbents are forced to sell their previously profitable services at more competitive prices, their ability to cross-subsidize diminishes.

cans in an increasingly competitive marketplace.[63] Another objective of the 1996 Act was to extend the scope of universal service so as to facilitate access by schools, libraries and rural health care providers to advanced telecommunications services, including the Internet.

Box 4.3: *Universal Service*

Historically, universal service was achieved through a number of implicit mechanisms designed to shift costs from rural to urban areas, from residential to business customers, and from local to long-distance services.

The *urban-to-rural* subsidy has been mainly accomplished through geographic rate averaging, as a result of which high-density (urban) areas—where costs are typically lower—subsidize low-density (rural) areas.

State pricing rules have also generally created a *business-to-residential* subsidy. For example, most states have established local rate levels whereby businesses pay more on a per-line basis than do residential customers, whereas the costs of providing business and residential lines are usually similar.

Finally, interstate and intrastate access charges—the charges paid by long-distance carriers to LECs in compensation for the originating or terminating services they provide—have been set at a level that is higher than the real costs of originating or terminating calls. Since these charges are then recovered through high prices for long-distance services, they amount to a long distance-to-local subsidy.

Of the three implicit subsidy mechanisms, only the interstate access charge system has been regulated by the FCC, the two other mechanisms being regulated by state utility commissions.

Following the 1996 Act, the FCC has overhauled its interstate access charge system so as to make support to universal service explicit (see Section D below).

Source: Universal Service Order, *First Report & Order*, 12 FCC rcd 8776 (1997).

Pursuant to the 1996 Act, universal service obligations are defined by a Federal–State Joint Board set up by the FCC.[64] The Joint Board must take into account a number of principles, including that rates be 'just, reasonable and affordable', that access to advanced telecommunications and information services should be provided in all regions of the nation, and that such services be available to all consumers including low-income consumers and those in rural, insular, and high-cost areas.[65]

---

[63] See Gregory L Rosston and Bradley S Wimmer, 'The ABC's of Universal Service: Arbitrage, Big Bucks, and Competition' (1999) 50 *Hastings L J* 1585, 1586 ('The Telecommunications Act of 1996 recognizes the effect competition will have on the current system and requires regulators to overhaul it').

[64] 47 USC § 254(a).   [65] ibid § 254(b).

The actual mechanism for ensuring the funding of universal service is to be decided by the FCC (see Section D below). However, the Act indicates that universal service support should be 'explicit', and that all providers of interstate telecommunications services must contribute to this mechanism on an equitable and non-discriminatory basis.[66] These contributions will then go to 'eligible telecommunications carriers'—those carriers that offer and advertise the components of universal service throughout a designated area.[67] In order to encourage competition, the Act provides that, in non-rural areas, the state commissions must designate more than one carrier as eligible if multiple carriers request the designation and meet the statutory requirements.[68]

In order to prevent anti-competitive forms of cross-subsidization, the Act states that eligible carriers may only use universal service support for the provision, maintenance, and upgrading of facilities and services related to the provision of universal service.[69] For interstate services, the FCC must establish whatever cost allocation rules and accounting safeguards are necessary to ensure that universal services bear no more than a reasonable share of the costs of the facilities providing all services.[70] The states have the same responsibility for intrastate services.[71]

1.4 Pricing Rules

In the United States, power to regulate telecommunications prices is divided between the FCC and the state utility commissions. While the FCC has the power to regulate the prices of interstate long-distance telecommunications services and international services, the state utility commissions have the power to regulate intrastate long-distance and local services.

As we have seen, the FCC no longer regulates the prices of long-distance and international services. The FCC continues, however, to regulate the interstate component of the access charges that the IECs pay to the LECs to originate or terminate long-distance calls. By contrast, state utility commissions continue to regulate the rates of intrastate telephony, both local and long-distance. In recent years, a majority of the states have abandoned rate-of-return regulation and opted for price-cap methodologies.[72]

---

[66] ibid § 254(d).   [67] ibid § 254(e).

[68] ibid § 214(e)(2). For rural areas, the decision whether to designate more than one carrier is left to the discretion of the state utility commission.

[69] ibid § 214(e).

[70] ibid § 254(k).

[71] ibid.

[72] John AK Huntley et al, 'Laboratories of De-Regulation? Implications for Europe of American State Telecommunications Policy' 1997 (1) *J of Information, L and Technology*, available at <http://elj.warwick.ac.uk/jilt/telecoms/97_1hunt/default.htm>.

2. Antitrust Rules

In addition to the above regulatory requirements, antitrust laws remain applicable to telecommunications operators.[73] The two major federal antitrust laws in the United States are the Sherman Act[74] and the Clayton Act,[75] adopted in 1890 and 1914 respectively.[76]

The substantive provisions of the Sherman Act are contained in its first two sections. Section 1 outlaws all contracts, combinations, and conspiracies that unreasonably restrain interstate commerce.[77] Section 2 also outlaws any attempt to monopolize or conspire to monopolize any part of interstate commerce. Pursuant to s 2, monopolies are not, per se, illegal. Unlawful monopolization exists when a firm has become the only supplier not because its product or service is superior to others, but by suppressing competition through anti-competitive conduct. Similarly, the Clayton Act outlaws a number of business practices where the effect of the practice might be to reduce competition substantially or to create a monopoly.[78]

The prohibitions contained in these statutes, as interpreted by federal courts,[79] are of central relevance in the telecommunications field. Section 2 of the Sherman Act can be used by the DoJ or private litigants to prevent dominant undertakings, typically ILECs, from adopting abusive behaviours vis-à-vis new

[73] Georges J Alexander, 'Antitrust and the Telephone Industry after the Telecommunications Act of 1996' (1996) 12 *Santa Clara Computer and High Technology L J* 227, 244 (arguing that the Telecommunications Act does not provide for antitrust immunity). For a review of antitrust cases in the telecommunications field, see Peter H Huber et al, *Federal Telecommunications Law* (2nd edn, New York: Aspen Law & Business, 1999) 351 et seq.

[74] 15 USC §§ 1–2.

[75] ibid § 12.

[76] On US antitrust law and policy, see generally Herbert Hovenkamp, *Federal Antitrust Policy: The Law of Competition and its Practice* (St Paul, Minn.: West Publishing, 1994).

[77] 15 USC § 1. Section 1 therefore prevents all forms of collusion between telecommunications operators. Agreements to set prices or divide markets or anti-competitive group boycotts are, per se, violations of s 1. Antitrust enforcers may also decide to examine under s 1 the numerous joint ventures or strategic alliances that are concluded on an almost daily basis between telecommunications operators. See generally, Thomas A Piraino, 'A Proposed Antitrust Analysis of Telecommunications Joint Ventures' (1997) *Wisconsin L Rev* 639. The examination would aim at ensuring that such ventures or alliances bring efficiency gains that exceed their restrictive impact on competition and are therefore in the interests of the consumers. See ibid.

[78] The most important sections of the Clayton Act are s 2, which deals with price discrimination (as amended by the Robinson–Patman Act of 1936); s 3, which deals with tying and exclusive dealing contracts; and s 7, which deals with mergers and joint ventures (as amended by the Celler–Kefauver Act of 1950).

[79] One of the central characteristics of these statutes is that they are crafted in very broad terms, thereby giving federal judges a pivotal role in defining the scope of the statutes' prohibitions. See Ernest Gellhorn and William E Kovacic, *Antitrust Law and Economics in a Nutshell* (4th edn, St Paul, Minn.: West Publishing, 1994) 31 (arguing that '(n)o scheme of federal economic regulation grants judges comparable discretion to determine litigation outcomes through their interpretations of legislative commands').

entrants. Pursuant to the so-called 'essential facilities' doctrine,[80] a dominant undertaking that controls an essential element of infrastructure must grant its competitors access to it under non-discriminatory terms.[81] The essential facilities doctrine could thus provide an alternative avenue for new entrants that seek to obtain access to the incumbents' networks and facilities.[82]

Finally, antitrust rules apply to mergers and acquisitions between telecommunications operators. Under the Communications Act of 1934, s 221(a), mergers and acquisitions between telephone companies were immune from the full application of antitrust laws if approved by the FCC. The 1996 Act, s 601(b), however, repeals that provision. Mergers and acquisitions are thus now subject to the full scope of the Clayton Act, s 7, which prohibits the acquisition of stock or assets by any 'person' where 'the effect of such acquisition may be to substantially lessen competition, or to create a monopoly'.

C. The main institutions

The above regulatory framework is essentially implemented by five separate bodies (or sets of bodies): the FCC, the various state utility commissions, the DoJ, the Federal Trade Commission and the federal courts.[83]

1. The Federal Communications Commission

The FCC is a large bureaucracy comprising more than 2100 employees.[84] It is divided into several operational bureaux and offices organized by substantive

---

[80] The doctrine originated in the Supreme Court decision *United States v Terminal Road Assn of St Louis*, in which the Court required joint owners of a railroad switching junction to afford competing railways access to the junction 'upon such just and reasonable terms and regulations as will . . . place every such company upon nearly an equal plane as may be with respect to expenses and charges as that occupied by the proprietary companies': 224 US 383 (1912). On this doctrine see, eg, Philip E Areeda, 'Essential Facilities: An Epithet in Need of Limiting Principles' (1990) 58 *Antitrust L J* 841, 851; Allen Kezsbom and Alan Goldman, 'No Shortcut to Antitrust Analysis: The Twisted Journey of the "Essential Facilities" Doctrine' (1996) *Columbia Business L Rev* 1.

[81] In *MCI v AT&T*, the Court of Appeals of the Seventh Circuit ruled that AT&T's refusal to grant MCI access to its local telecommunications network constituted an 'act of monopolization'. The Seventh Circuit set the essential facilities test as follows: '(1) control of the essential facility by a monopolist; (ii) a competitor's inability practicably or reasonably to duplicate the facility; (3) the denial of the use of the essential facility to a competitor; and (4) the feasibility of providing the facility': *MCI Communications v AT&T* 708 F 2d 1081, 1132 (7th Cir, 1982).

[82] See Joseph A Klein, 'Antitrust Law as a Regulator of the Rapidly Transforming Telecommunications Market' (1998) 23 *Communications & Strategies* 209.

[83] In addition to these bodies, a brief reference should also be made to the National Telecommunications and Infrastructure Administration (NTIA) which undertakes studies and makes recommendations to the President, Congress and the FCC on telecommunications policy issues, and manages the federal Government's use of spectrum.

[84] For a good discussion of the structure and workings of the FCC see Gerald W Brock, *Telecommunication Policy for the Information Age* (Cambridge, Mass., and London: Harvard University Press, 1994) 53.

FIGURE 4.1. FCC organizational chart

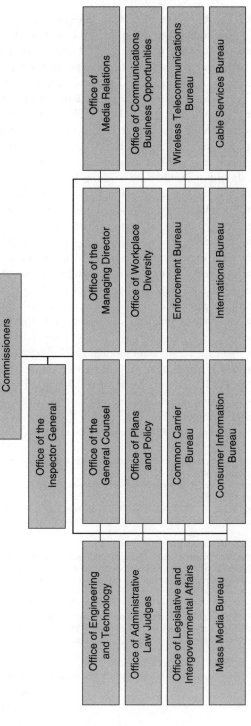

Source: <http://www.fcc.gov/fccorgchart.html>.

areas (see Figure 4.1 above).[85] The FCC is an 'independent agency', meaning that it is not an executive branch agency headed by a cabinet officer but rather a creation of Congress accountable to Congress.[86] Congress decides the size of the FCC's budget each year through its fiscal appropriation process. Budget decisions are made after hearings are held. The total budget for 1998 amounted to $186,514,000.[87] Various committees within the Congress also have responsibility for 'overseeing' the activities of the FCC.[88] When a legislator on such a committee has concerns about a particular FCC action or proposed action, he may convene a hearing to question the regulators. At these hearings, as well as at budget hearings, explicit and implicit messages are often delivered about the directions the FCC should or should not be taking.[89]

The FCC is governed by five commissioners, no more than three of the same political party, nominated by the President and confirmed by the Senate.[90] The commissioners serve a five-year term, which is subject to renewal at the discretion of the President. The terms are staggered so that no more than one commissioner's term expires each year. The commissioners are usually highly qualified professionals.[91] The President designates one of the commissioners to serve as Chair; he may change the commissioner designated as Chairperson, but may not remove a commissioner, except for cause.[92] None of the commissioners can have a financial interest in any Commission-related business.[93]

The FCC regulates so-called 'interstate services', including recovery of part of the cost of local access facilities that are used to originate and/or terminate interstate traffic. The FCC is also in charge of regulating all wireless services, ie it allocates radio spectrum, issues licences, and determines the policies within which wireless carriers compete. The FCC is also the 'primary arbiter' of the 1996 Act.[94] As we have seen, the 1996 Act calls on the FCC to adopt the detailed

[85] A list of FCC bureaux and offices, as well as a description of their functions can be found at <http://www.fcc.gov/aboutus.html>.

[86] See Thomas G Krattenmaker, *Telecommunications Law and Policy* (2nd edn, Durham, NC: Carolina Academic Press, 1998) 20.

[87] See *FCC Budget of $ 212,977,000 Proposed for Fiscal Year 1999*, Federal Communication Commission News, available at <http://www.fcc.gov/Bureaus/Miscellaneous/News_Releases/1998/nrmc8011.html>.

[88] See Gerald W Brock (n 84 above) 57.

[89] See Mark D Director, *Restructuring and Expanding National Telecommunications Markets: A Primer on Competition, Regulation and Development for East and Central European Regulators* (The Annenberg Washington Program) ch 2 available at <http://www.annenberg.nwu.edu/pubs/telmar/telmar02.htm>.

[90] 47 USC § 4.

[91] At the end of 2001, the FCC board of commissioners comprised a former Chief of Staff of the Antitrust Division of the DoJ, a former high level official in the US Department of Commerce and two telecommunications lawyers with expertise in both private and public sectors.

[92] 47 USC § 5(a).

[93] ibid § 5(b)(2)(A)(i).

[94] NERA, *Costs of Telecommunications Competition Policies*, report prepared for Telecom New Zealand, 9 May 2000.

rules and standards necessary to implement s 251, and to ensure compliance thereafter with the requirements of that provision.[95] In addition, the FCC has the final authority to rule on a BOC's s 271 applications. Together with the DoJ, the FCC has authority to review mergers and acquisitions between telecommunications operators pursuant to a 'public interest' standard.[96] Finally, it plays a key role in the implementation of the Act's new universal service provisions, through its regulation of the access charges that long-distance companies pay to the local companies which originate or terminate long-distance calls. The FCC does also co-ordinate with a Federal State Joint Board comprising state and federal commissioners specially set up to implement the 1996 Act's universal service provisions.

The FCC is required to act in accordance with an elaborate process that ensures public participation in decision-making.[97] The Administrative Procedures Act (APA), which governs this process, requires the FCC—and other federal agencies—to give public notice of matters to be acted upon and an opportunity to comment. It also requires the FCC to make reasoned decisions, explained in writing, based upon the evidence submitted to them.[98] All final FCC actions are subject to review by the federal courts, which have jurisdiction to reverse Commission decisions that do not comply with the requirements of the APA. When reviewing FCC decisions, courts are not free to substitute their own judgement on matters of substance, but can overturn Commission actions that fail to meet the standards and practices of federal administrative law.[99]

2. State Utility Commissions

As mentioned above, the state utility commissions have the power to regulate the prices of intrastate long-distance and local services. The state utility commissions also play an important role in the implementation of the 1996 Act. These commissions usually comprise several commissioners appointed by the governor and confirmed by the state legislature.[100] Contrary to the FCC, which only deals with telecommunications, the state commissions commonly oversee other industries, including, most commonly, the energy utilities and transport companies, and thus have cross-sector responsibilities. With some exceptions, state commissions have relatively small staffs and are therefore selective in choosing

---

[95] 47 USC § 251(g).

[96] See Section B above.

[97] See Director (n 89 above).

[98] This Act is codified at 5 USC §§ 551–559.

[99] See Thomas G Krattenmaker, *Telecommunications Law and Policy* (2nd edn, Durham, NC: Carolina Academic Press, 1998) 20.

[100] These commissioners are often state politicians who are closely influenced by local political considerations. State utility commissions thus offer fewer guarantees of independence than the FCC. See John AK Huntley, 'Competition and the Provision of a Universal Telecommunications Service' (1994) 17 *World Competition* 7, 14.

the issues in which they get involved.[101] In the telecommunications field, state commissions have traditionally concentrated their efforts on rate regulation and consumer protection.[102]

While the 1996 Act requires state commissions to carry out various functions,[103] they have particularly important duties in the area of interconnection. Under s 252, state commissions approve the interconnection agreements negotiated between ILECs and new entrants.[104] They also play a role of mediator and arbitrator when the operators are unable to reach an agreement.[105] Once a dispute reaches arbitration, state commissions may set the prices at which interconnection must be granted to the new entrants.[106]

One of the most obscure parts of the Telecommunications Act relates to the division of responsibilities between the FCC and the state utility commissions with respect to the implementation of the local competition provisions.[107] To some extent, the Act alters the traditional jurisdictional separation between regulation of interstate and intrastate services by allowing the FCC to issue regulations designed to encourage competition in the *local* exchange market.[108] The scope of the FCC rule-making power is, however, rather uncertain. For instance, the Act does not clearly indicate whether the FCC has authority to mandate state commissions to follow its pricing guidelines when it arbitrates interconnection disputes. As will be seen below, this issue was litigated before federal courts.[109]

3. The Department of Justice, Antitrust Division

The third key institutional player with respect to the economic regulation of telecommunications is the Antitrust Division of the DoJ.[110] This Division is in charge of implementing antitrust laws.[111] It is headed by a politically appointed

---

[101] The total staffs of these commissions range from less than 50 in sparsely populated states (eg, 24 in Delaware and 46 in Montana) to several hundreds in the larger states (eg, 725 in New York and 1,024 in California). See Joseph F Schuler, 'Will the Sun Set on PUCs?' *Public Utilities Fortnightly* (15 July 1998) 28, 29.

[102] See Jeffrey Blumenfeld and Christy C Kunin, 'United States' in Colin Long (ed), *Telecommunications Law and Practice* (London: Sweet & Maxwell, 1995).

[103] See, for instance, ss 214 and 254 (universal service) and 271 (review of BOCs' application to enter the long-distance market).

[104] 47 USC § 252(a)(1).

[105] ibid §§ 252(a)(2) and (b).

[106] ibid § 252(c)(2).

[107] See Duane McLaughlin, 'FCC Jurisdiction Over Local Telephone Under the 1996 Act: Fenced Off?' (1997) 97 *Columbia L Rev* 2210.

[108] ibid 2229.

[109] See text accompanying nn 139 et seq below.

[110] For a description of the Division's structure, see Antitrust Division Manual, ch 1, Organization of the Department of Justice and the Antitrust Division, available at <http://www.usdoj.gov/atr/foia/divisionmanual/ch1.htm>.

[111] Antitrust laws are also implemented by the Federal Trade Commission (FTC), a body that was established in 1914 as a result of the passage of the Clayton Antitrust Act and its companion Federal Trade Commission Act. See text accompanying nn 118–125.

Assistant Attorney-General, and as such is an integral part of the legal arm of the Federal Government. The Antitrust Division does not therefore have the same degree of independence vis-à-vis the Executive as does the FCC. The Division prosecutes cases of antitrust law violations, such as restrictive practices between competitors or abuses of a dominant position, and it frequently files both civil and criminal actions simultaneously. Most civil antitrust actions initiated by the Division terminate in a settlement that is filed with the court and incorporated in a judicial order known as a 'consent decree'.[112] Successful criminal actions may, on the other hand, lead to the adoption of severe penalties, such as substantial fines or imprisonment.[113]

The Antitrust Division of the DoJ also investigates mergers and acquisitions for compliance with federal antitrust laws, and has the authority to file suits to prevent a transaction. As we have seen, the 1996 Telecommunications Act repeals the FCC's authority to immunize telecommunications company mergers from antitrust scrutiny.[114] In practice, the FCC and the DoJ thus have concurrent jurisdiction to review mergers between carriers, but under different statutory provisions. While the FCC's jurisdiction is based on the 1934 Act, ss 214 and 310(d) (unamended by the 1996 Act), which grants that agency authority to review mergers under a 'public interest' standard, the DoJ's statutory authority is found in the Clayton Act, s 7, which prohibits transactions which may 'substantially lessen competition'.[115]

In addition to the above enforcement duties, there are also areas where the DoJ plays an important advisory role. As we have seen, s 271 gives ultimate authority for BOCs' application approval to the FCC. As part of the approval process, the FCC, however, must consult with the DoJ and give the DoJ's evaluation 'substantial weight',[116] even though the FCC is not bound by the DoJ's assessment. Likewise, the DoJ is not bound to an evaluation of the competition checklist of s 271(c)(2)(B). Instead, the Act states that the DoJ may use any standard that it determines appropriate. The general standard which the DoJ uses to determine whether s 271 approval should be granted is whether the relevant local exchange market is 'fully and irremediably open to competition'.[117]

---

[112] See Philip Areeda, *Antitrust Analysis—Problems, Text and Cases* (Boston, Mass., Toronto and London: Little Brown and Co, 1981) 64.

[113] The Sherman Act sets a maximum fine of $10 million for corporate defendants, and antitrust felonies also can result in corporate fines equal to twice the company's pecuniary gain or twice the pecuniary loss by victims, whichever is the greatest: 15 USC § 1. Individuals may be punished by fines of up to $350,000 and by jail sentences as long as three years: ibid.

[114] See Section B above.

[115] See 15 USC § 18.

[116] 47 USC § 271(d)(2)(A).

[117] See 'The State of Competition in the Telecommunications Marketplace Three Years after Enactment of the Telecommunications Act of 1996': Before the Subcommittee on Antitrust, Business Rights, and Competition, Senate Judiciary Committee, 106th Cong (25 February 1999) (statement of Joel Klein, Assistant Attorney-General, US Department of Justice), available at <http://www.usdoj.gov/atr/public/testimony/2264.htm>.

4. The Federal Trade Commission

Besides the FCC and the Antitrust Division of the DoJ, the Federal Trade Commission (hereafter, the 'FTC') is another federal body playing a role in the telecommunications field.

Like the FCC, the FTC is an independent agency headed by five commissioners, nominated by the President and confirmed by the Senate. Each commissioner serves a seven-year term and the President chooses one of the commissioners to act as Chairperson. No more than three commissioners can be of the same political party. In 2000, the FTC employed about 1000 staff.[118] It comprised three bureaux (the Bureau of Consumer Protection, the Bureau of Competition and the Bureau of Economics), as well as seven regional offices.[119] For the year 2000, the FTC's total budget authority amounted to $126 million.[120]

The FTC is the only federal agency that is active in both the antitrust and consumer protection areas as it is entrusted with the enforcement of a variety of federal laws in these two areas. The FTC describes its mission as 'to ensure that the nation's markets function competitively, and are vigorous, efficient, and free of undue restrictions'.[121]

As far as antitrust enforcement is concerned, the FTC is involved in both merger and non-merger investigations.[122] The Clayton Act, s 11 and the FTC Act, s 5 bar the FTC from exercising jurisdiction over common carriers. The FTC has, however, investigated a variety of mergers in the cable and entertainment industries. It has, in particular, played a leading role in the AOL–Time Warner merger, which is discussed below.[123]

Regarding consumer protection, the FTC describes its current priority areas as Internet fraud, identity theft, the law enforcement challenges posed by the global electronic marketplace, and the marketing of violent entertainment products.[124] As far as telecommunications are concerned, the FTC has taken various initiatives to prevent unfair trade practices, such as 900 number and international telephone number scams.[125]

5. Federal Courts

Finally, the important role played by federal courts in the implementation of the telecommunications regulatory framework needs to be mentioned. First, federal

---

[118] See FTC, 'Fiscal Year 2002 Congressional Justification Budget Summary' (hereafter, 'Budget Summary'), available at <http://www.ftc.gov/ftc/oed/fmo/budgetsum2002.htm>.

[119] See FTC, 'Offices and Bureaux', available at <http://www.ftc.gov/ftc/history1.htm>.

[120] See FTC, 'Budget Authority', available at <http://www.ftc.gov/ftc/oed/fmo/budgetauth.htm>.

[121] See FTC, 'Vision, Mission & Goals', available at <http://www.ftc.gov/ftc/mission.htm>.

[122] For a summary of its recent activities, see ABA Antitrust Section Spring Meeting, 'Summary of Bureau of Competition Activity Fiscal Year 1996 Through 31 March 2000', available at <http://www.ftc.gov/bc/abafy96thru00.pdf>.

[123] ibid.

[124] See 'Budget Summary' (n 118 above).

[125] See FTC, 'Consumer Protection—Telephone Services', available at <http://www.ftc.gov/bcp/menu-call.htm>.

courts are expected and empowered to review the constitutionality of the laws, including telecommunications legislation. This is a crucially important task given the conflicts of competence that may occur between institutions involved in the economic regulation of telecommunications. Federal courts also determine whether regulatory agencies, such as the FCC, have complied with the Administrative Procedures Act, eg to ensure that promulgated rules are reasonable and that appropriate procedures were followed. Courts routinely hear and decide antitrust cases brought by the DoJ or individuals, including those involving telecommunications carriers. Federal courts also enforce compliance with the terms of consent decrees adopted to settle civil antitrust actions.

Prior to the adoption of the Telecommunications Act of 1996, the degree to which federal courts should use their powers to influence national telecommunications policy was a matter of controversy.[126] Some observers denounced the fact that Judge Greene had used his powers to administer the MFJ to shape US telecommunications policy. According to these critics, it should not be the task of a federal judge to decide, for example, whether to prohibit BOCs from entering various businesses. Such a decision, which has a profound impact on the US telecommunications market, should be made by the FCC and the Congress. More fundamentally, as will be argued below, it is not clear that, in general, a federal judge will have the technical competence to deal with complex and fast-evolving telecommunications issues. By striking down the MFJ and adopting regulatory requirements to be implemented by the FCC, the 1996 Telecommunications Act aimed at decreasing the influence played by the judiciary on telecommunications policy issues.

D. IMPLEMENTATION OF THE REGULATORY FRAMEWORK

Numerous developments have taken place in the United States over the last few years and, in particular, since the adoption of the 1996 Telecommunications Act. Such developments include:

(i) the adoption of the Local Competition Order and the legal battles that followed to determine whether the FCC was competent to adopt such Order,

(ii) the adoption of the Universal Service and Access Charges Reform Orders,

(iii) the initial rejection of the BOCs' applications to enter the long-distance market,

---

[126] See Mark D Director, *Restructuring and Expanding National Telecommunications Markets: A Primer on Competition, Regulation and Development for East and Central European Regulators* (The Annenberg Washington Program) ch 2, available at <http://www.annenberg.nwu.edu/pubs/telmar/telmar02.htm>.

(iv) the numerous mergers that took place between telecommunications operators,

(v) the debate over cable open access,

(vi) the use of auctions to allocate spectrum,

(vii) the use of peering arrangements between Internet backbone networks, and

(viii) the proposals for structural separation of BOCs.

1. Adoption of the Local Competition Order

The 1996 Telecommunications Act mandated the FCC to establish, within six months of the adoption of the Act, the regulations necessary to implement s 251.[127] On 6 August 1996, the FCC released the First Report and Order containing the FCC's findings with regard to the implementation of the policy principles contained in s 251.[128] This document, which totals 683 pages, addresses three paths of entry into the local telephone market: full facilities-based entry, purchase of unbundled network elements from the incumbent local exchange carriers, and resale of the incumbent's retail services. The FCC prescribed certain rules to permit competing carriers to choose efficient points at which to interconnect with the ILEC's network. It also determined which network elements ILECs had to make available to their competitors on an unbundled basis (see Box 4.4 below). In addition, the FCC set forth a methodology to be used by state utility commissions in establishing rates for interconnection between competitors which have each established their own facilities and for the purchase of unbundled elements (when one competitor has not established fully-fledged facilities). The Order concludes that this pricing methodology must be based on the incumbent's Total Element Long-Run Incremental Cost (TELRIC). The TELRIC methodology, as defined by the FCC, is a form of forward-looking long-run incremental costs methodology,[129] requiring that access prices be based upon the costs of an efficient benchmark firm.[130] With respect to resale of the incumbent's retail services, on the other hand, the pricing methodology is basically that of the ECPR.[131] Here, the price is not established by evaluating the cost of each individual element, but by establishing a list of costs which are presumed avoidable and which must be deducted from the ILECs' retail prices to obtain the access price.[132]

However, the FCC's First Order was immediately challenged by a group of ILECs and state regulators. The plaintiffs' core argument was primarily

---

[127] 47 USC § 251(D)(1).

[128] See *Implementation of the Local Competition Provisions in the Telecommunications Act of 1996*, FCC Docket No 96–98, First Report and Order, 11 FCC Rcd 15,499 (1996).

[129] See Chapter 3, Section B.2 above.

[130] See J Gregory Sidak and Daniel Spulber, *Deregulatory Takings and the Regulatory Contract: The Competitive Transformation of Network Industries in the United States* (Cambridge: Cambridge University Press, 1997) 420.

[131] See Chapter 3, Section B.3 above.

[132] See First Report and Order (n 128 above) § 863 et seq.

Box 4.4: Network Elements to be Unbundled

The Telecommunications Act 1996, s 251(c)(3) imposes a duty on ILECs to provide competitors with 'non-discriminatory access to network elements on an unbundled basis at any technically feasible point on rates, terms and conditions that are just, reasonable and non-discriminatory...'. In its Local Competition Order, the FCC interpreted s 251 to mean that ILECs must make available, on an unbundled basis, the following network elements:

(1) local loops;
(2) network interface devices;
(3) local switching;
(4) interoffice transmission facilities;
(5) signalling networks and call-related databases;
(6) operations support systems; and
(7) operator services and directory assistance.

Source: 'Implementation of the Local Competition Provisions in the Telecommunications Act of 1996', FCC Docket No 96–98, First Report and Order, 11 FCC Rcd 15,499 (1996).

jurisdictional. They argued that primary authority to promulgate rules governing pricing belonged to the states rather than the FCC. They also argued that, even if it had the authority to regulate pricing, the pricing formula chosen by the FCC for interconnection and unbundled access would accomplish an uncompensated taking of property in violation of the Fifth Amendment.[133] In October 1996, the Court of Appeals for the Eighth Circuit granted a motion to stay the FCC's pricing rules for local competition,[134] holding there was sufficient likelihood that the FCC lacked authority to determine just and reasonable fees for local services, including the prices for the use of elements of the incumbents' local exchange networks. Later, the Eighth Circuit confirmed that the FCC lacked jurisdiction to issue pricing rules.[135] The FCC appealed and, on 25 January 1999, the Supreme Court overturned this judgement,[136] ruling that the FCC had general jurisdiction to implement the 1996 Act's local competition

---

[133] US Constitution, Amendment V ('(N)or shall private property be taken for public use, without just compensation'). For a discussion of this argument, see E Sanderson Hoe and Stephen Ruscus, 'Taking Aim at the Takings Argument: Using Forward-Looking Pricing Methodologies to Price Unbundled Network Elements' (1997) 5 *Comm Law Conspectus* 231; David Gabel and David I Rosenbaum, 'Who's Taking Whom?: Some Comments and Evidence on the Constitutionality of TELRIC' (2000) 52 *Federal Communications L J* 239.

[134] *Iowa Utils Bd v FCC* 108 F 3d 418 (8th Cir, 1996).

[135] See *Iowa Utils Bd v FCC* 120 F 3d 753 (8th Cir, 1997). On this case, see generally, Jim Chen, 'TELRIC in Turmoil, Telecommunications in Transition: A Note on The Iowa Board Litigation' (1998) 33 *Wake Forest L Rev* 51; Wang Su, 'FCC Preemption Power' (1998) 13 *Berkeley Technology L J* 435.

[136] *AT&T Corp et al v Iowa Utils Bd et al* 25 January 1999. On this case, see Michael L Gallo, 'AT&T Corp v. Iowa Utilities Board' (2000) 15 *Berkeley Technology L J* 417.

provisions and that the FCC's rules governing unbundled access were consistent with the 1996 Act as well.

The FCC's Supreme Court victory was only partial. Indeed, the Court ruled that, while drawing the list of unbundled network elements that ILECs had to make available to their competitors (see Box 4.4 above), the FCC did not adequately consider the s 251(d)(2) 'necessary and impair' standards and ordered the FCC to provide a more adequate justification for its action.[137] In response to the Court, the FCC released on 5 November 1999 a Third Report and Order promulgating interpretations of the 'necessary' and 'impair' standards of s 251(d)(2).[138] This ruling addressed the FCC's concerns by removing operator services and directory assistance, as well as the switching for customers with four or more lines in certain high density areas from the list of unbundled elements that had to be provided by ILECs to their competitors. On the other hand, the new Order required greater unbundling of the local loop by mandating that ILECs provide access to subloops or portions of loops, and dark fibre optic loops and transport.[139]

2. Adoption of the Universal Service and Access Charge Reform Orders

On 7 May 1997, the FCC adopted two additional orders designed to implement the Telecommunications Act's provisions. In conformity with the Act, these orders seek to adapt existing universal service and access charges mechanisms to a competitive marketplace.

The first Order deals with a host of issues critical to the implementation of the new universal provisions of the 1996 Act (the 'Universal Service Order').[140] This Order defines the services that will be supported by federal universal service support mechanisms.[141] It also defines who contributes to such mechanisms, as well as the methodology for assessing the contributions. Consistent with the principle that universal service must be competitively neutral, the FCC empha-

---

[137] *In re Implementation of the Local Competition Provisions of the Telecommunications Act of 1996*, Third Report and Fourth Further Notice of Proposed Rulemaking, FCC Docket No 99-238.

[138] Although the 1996 Act imposes a duty on ILECs to make certain network elements available on an unbundled basis, this duty is not unfettered. Instead, the FCC must determine, at minimum, whether: (a) access to such network elements as are proprietary in nature is necessary, and (b) the failure to provide access to such network element would impair the ability of the telecommunications carrier seeking access to provide the services that it seeks to offer: 47 USC § 251(d)(2).

[139] For a discussion of this Third Report, see Timothy J Tardiff, 'New Technologies and Convergence of Markets: Implications for Telecommunications Regulation' (2000) 1 *J of Network Industries* 447, 452–453.

[140] Federal–State Joint Board on Universal Service, Report and Order, 12 FCCR 8776. This report only provides for a Federal universal service plan. States may also establish their own universal service support mechanisms. See Mark P Trinchero and Holly Rachel Smith, 'Federal Preemption of State Universal Service Regulations Under the Telecommunications Act of 1996' (1998) 51 *Federal Communications L J* 303.

[141] ibid § 61. These services include: (i) voice graded access to the public switched network, with the ability to place and receive calls; (ii) Dual Tone Multifrequency (DMTF) signalling or its functional equivalent, also known as touch-tone service; (iii) single-party service; (iv) access to emergency

sized that all carriers—including, for instance, wireless providers—must make contributions[142] and are entitled to universal service support irrespective of the specific technology used to serve end customers.[143] As far as the allocation of universal service subsidies is concerned, the FCC provides for different methods depending on the type of services to be supported.

With respect to the support to be provided to consumers located in high-cost areas, the FCC set up a system whereby a carrier that offers services to a customer located in such an area receives an administratively set subsidy based on the forward-looking cost of providing the service reduced by a nation-wide revenue benchmark calculated on the basis of an average revenue per line.[144] Such subsidies must be 'portable' so that competing carriers can assess the profitability of serving subsidized end-users and pocket the subsidy upon per-suading an end-user to switch carrier.[145] The FCC, however, recognizes that there are many potential advantages to defining universal service support levels for rural, insular, and high-cost areas through the use of a competitive bidding mechanism. For the Commission, competitive bidding 'could supplement an-other forward-looking economic cost methodology in determining the universal service support levels because a properly structured bidding system requires competitors to reveal expected revenue opportunities'.[146]

Besides high-cost areas, the FCC also determines the mechanisms to be put in place to provide support to low-income customers, as well as schools, libraries, clinics and hospitals. As far as schools and libraries are concerned, the FCC provides for a system whereby these institutions can seek to obtain low prices on all commercially available services through a system of competitive bidding.[147] Specifically, schools and libraries have to make the list of services they need known to the operators that are then given a period of time to bid for such services. Once the bidding period has lapsed, the school or library in question must sign a contract with the service provider that put forward the best offer. Price must be the primary consideration in choosing a provider, although other criteria may be included, such as service quality, prior experience, personnel qualifications, management capability, and schedule compliance, thus leading to the most cost-effective solution.[148]

The second Order seeks to adapt the existing system of interstate access to the new pro-competition philosophy of the 1996 Act (the 'Access Charge Reform Order').[149] As pointed out above, the system put in place prior to the Act

---

services, including 911 and Enhanced 911; (v) access to operator services; (vi) access to interexchange services; (vi) access to directory assistance; and (vii) Lifeline and Link Up Services for qualifying low-income consumers.

[142] Contributions are to be based on retail, end-user telecommunications revenue: ibid § 843.
[143] ibid § 134.
[144] ibid § 199 et seq.
[145] ibid § 15.
[146] ibid § 207.
[147] ibid § 30.
[148] ibid § 481.
[149] Access Charge Reform Order, First Report and Order, 12 FCCR 15,982.

embodied implicit subsidies and support flows that are not sustainable in a competitive environment.[150] Specifically, the Order reforms the current rate structure to bring it into line with cost-causation principles, phasing out significant implicit subsidies from one category to the other.[151] Non-traffic sensitive costs (eg common line costs) are to be recovered through flat charges, whereas traffic-sensitive costs (eg switching and transport charges) are to be recovered through usage-based, or per-minute, charges.[152] The pricing methodology chosen by the FCC is once again that of forward-looking long-run incremental costs. This reform led to an immediate reduction of the access charges paid by long-distance carriers to LECs and an increase in charges borne by subscribers.[153] Since adoption of the second Order, the access charges have been further reduced by several billion dollars, which has translated into lower consumer prices.[154]

An important aspect of the Access Charge Reform Order is that it confirmed the FCC's traditional approach of treating Internet Service Providers (ISPs) as local phone customers. Thus, rather than paying higher access charges, ISPs simply purchase phone lines from the local phone company as any local business would do. Despite complaints of local carriers, the FCC has always refused to allow access charges being imposed on ISPs on the ground that such charges would slow down the pace of development of the Internet and other related services.[155] In its Order, the FCC did, however, raise the ceiling on the monthly subscriber-line charge local phone companies may collect on second (and additional) residential phone lines.[156] Thus, local carriers would receive incremental revenues from Internet usage through higher demand for second lines of consumers.[157]

3. The Rejection of the BOCs' s 271 Applications

During the 1996–2001 period,[158] the FCC received nineteen s 271 applications submitted by the BOCs (see Table 4.1 below).The FCC rejected the first five

[150] ibid § 32.

[151] ibid § 35.

[152] ibid §§ 44–49.

[153] The Access Charge Order has not necessarily, however, made long-distance providers better off since their overall contribution to universal service has in fact increased. See A Michael Noll, 'The Costs of Competition—The FCC Telecommunications Orders of 1997' (1998) 22 *Telecommunications Policy* 47.

[154] See FCC News, 'FCC Reduces Access Charges by $ 3.2 Billion; Reductions Total $6.4 Billion Since 1996 Telecommunications Act', available at <http://www.fcc.gov/Bureaus/Common_Carrier/News_Releases/2000/nrcc0029.html>.

[155] See Access Charge Reform Order (n 149 above) §§ 344–345 ('We think it is possible that had access charges applied to ISPs over the last 14 years, the pace of development of the Internet and other services may not have been so rapid. Maintaining the existing price structure for these services avoids disrupting the still-evolving information services industry').

[156] ibid § 345.

[157] See Federal–State Joint Board on Universal Service, Report to Congress, 13 FCC Rec 11,501, 11,530, § 60 (1998).

[158] It should be noted that the legality of s 271 has been challenged in court by SBC Communications, one of the BOCs. On 31 December 1997, a federal district court in Wichita Falls, Texas, ruled that s 271's restrictions over BOCs' access to the long-distance market were unconstitutional: *SBC*

applications on the ground they failed to comply with s 271 requirements and, in particular, the fourteen-point 'competitive checklist'.[159] In each of these cases, the DoJ, which the FCC must consult before taking a final decision had also rendered a negative opinion.[160] While the Act does not set out a specific standard that the DoJ must use in making its evaluation of the Bell's application, the DoJ adopted a standard that required showing that the Bell's local market in the state for which long-distance approval is sought is fully and irreversibly open to

TABLE 4.1. BOC applications to provide in-region long-distance services

State	Company	Status
New Jersey	Verizon	Pending
Rhode Island	Verizon	Pending
Georgia/Louisiana	BellSouth	Withdrawn
Arkansas/Missouri	SBC	Approved
Pennsylvania	Verizon	Approved
Connecticut	Verizon	Approved
Missouri	SBC	Withdrawn
Massachusetts	Verizon	Approved
Kansas/Oklahoma	SBC	Approved
Massachusetts	Verizon	Withdrawn
Texas	SBC	Approved
Texas	SBC	Withdrawn
New York	Verizon	Approved
Louisiana	BellSouth	Denied
Louisiana	BellSouth	Denied
South Carolina	BellSouth	Denied
Michigan	Ameritech	Denied
Oklahoma	SBC	Denied
Michigan	Ameritech	Withdrawn

Source: Federal Communications Commission, 'RBOC Applications to Provide In-Region, InterLATA Services Under § 271' (2001).

Communications, Inc v FCC 981 F Supp 996 (ND Tex, 1997). Specifically, the Court found that these restrictions, insofar as they apply only to certain named operators—the BOCs—constituted a 'bill of attainder' prohibited by the US Constitution. This judgment was, however, subsequently overturned by the Court of Appeals of the Fifth Circuit: *SBC Communications v FCC* 23 September 1998, Docket 98-10140. On this issue, see Thomas A Buckley, '*SBC Communications, Inc. v. FCC*: Does Section 271 of the Telecommunications Act of 1996 Constitute a Bill of Attainder Against the Bell Operating Companies?' (1998) 6 *Communications L Conspectus* 225.

[159] See FCC, *Local Telecommunications Competition—A Chronology: 'Baby Bells' Section 271 Long Distance Applications*, available at <http://www.fcc.gov/Bureaus/Common_Carrier/News_ Releases/1999/nrc9101a.htm>.

[160] The DoJ evaluations are available at <http://www.usdoj.gov/atr/public/comments/sec271/ sec271.htm>.

competition.[161] The DoJ considered that none of the first five BOCs' applications met this standard.

Several subsequent BOC applications were, however, successful. On 22 December 1999, the FCC authorized Bell Atlantic to provide long-distance service in New York.[162] In its decision, the FCC observed that '(t)he well established pro-competitive regulatory environment in New York in conjunction with recent measures to achieve Section 271 compliance has, in general, created a thriving market for the provision of local exchange and exchange access service. Competitors are able to enter the local market using all three entry paths provided under the Act'.[163] This decision was almost immediately challenged by AT&T in the US Court of Appeals for the District of Columbia. AT&T argued that Bell Atlantic had not opened its network enough and was discriminating against competing carriers. On 1 August 2000, the Court of Appeals rejected AT&T's application finding that the FCC's decision allowing Bell Atlantic to offer long-distance service was in conformity with s 271.[164] Since then, six additional applications were approved by the FCC, while two (Verizon in New Jersey and Rhode Island) were still pending at the time of writing.

4. Mergers between Operators

Perhaps the most spectacular development which occurred over the period which followed the adoption of the Telecommunications Act 1996 relates to the flurry of mergers between telecommunications operators.[165] These mergers are being fostered not only by changes in the regulatory framework, but also by the advent of new technologies and other dramatic developments—eg increased globalization—taking place in the telecommunications market. They include mergers between:

  (i) BOCs (eg the mergers between Bell Atlantic and NYNEX, SBC and Pacific Telesys, and SBC and Ameritech);

  (ii) BOCs and non-BOC local exchange carriers (eg the mergers between SBC and SNET and Bell Atlantic and GTE);

  (iii) long-distance operators (eg the merger between WorldCom and MCI and the failed merger between MCI–WorldCom and Sprint);

---

[161] See Marius Schwartz, 'Conditioning the Bells' Entry Into Long Distance: Anticompetitive Regulation or Promoting Competition?', paper presented at the Robert Schuman Center of the European University Institute, Florence, 9 September 1999.

[162] See 'FCC Authorises Bell Atlantic To Provide Long Distance Service in New York', 22 December 1999, available at <http://www.fcc.gov/Bureaus/Common_Carrier/News_Releases/1999/nrcc9101.html>.

[163] ibid.

[164] See *AT&T v FCC* 1 August 2000, Docket No 99-1538.

[165] Statement of Joel I Klein before the House Committee on the Judiciary concerning consolidation in the telecommunications industry, Washington, DC, 24 June 1998. Document available at <http://www.usdoj.gov/atr/public/testimony/1806.htm>.

(iv) long-distance operators and cable companies (eg the merger between AT&T and TCI, and AT&T and Mediaone);

(v) long-distance operators and competitive local access providers (eg the merger between AT&T and Teleport);

(vi) wireless carriers (eg the merger between Airtouch and Vodafone);

(vii) a BOC and a long-distance operator (eg the merger between US West and Qwest); and

(viii) a cable network/content provider and an ISP (the merger between Time Warner and AOL).[166]

The FCC and the DoJ cleared most of these transactions. The most notorious exception is, however, the planned merger between MCI–WorldCom and Sprint that was announced in October 1999.[167] On 27 June 2000, the DoJ announced its decision to start legal proceedings to block the merger between the two long-distance operators because 'the deal would reduce competition in many of the nation's most important telecommunications services and would result in higher prices for millions of consumers and businesses'.[168] Following this announcement, which was applauded by the FCC Chairman,[169] the parties decided to call off the transaction.

Most of the transactions were cleared provided that the parties accepted to comply with conditions, both of a 'structural' and 'behavioural' nature. For instance, in June 2000, the FCC approved the Bell Atlantic–GTE merger,[170] subject to the obligation for the merged company to transfer substantially all of GTE's Internet business into a separate public company.[171] The merged entity also had to comply with twenty-five merger conditions designed to enhance local phone competition in the markets in which Bell Atlantic or GTE is the incumbent local exchange carrier (ILEC), strengthen the merged company's incentives to enter local phone markets outside of its territories, and promote equitable and efficient advanced services deployment.[172] As will be seen in the next sub-section,

---

[166] For a discussion of some of these mergers, see 'No Sign of Let-Up as Wannabes Follow in Worldcom's Wake' *Financial Times*, 17 May 1999.

[167] See Laura M Holson and Seth Schiesel, 'MCI Worldcom to Acquire Sprint in Stock Swap Valued at $108 Billion' *New York Times*, 5 October 1999.

[168] See 'Justice Department Sues to Block Worldcom's Acquisition of Sprint', document available at <http://www.usdoj.gov/opa/pr/2000/June/368at.htm>.

[169] See 'Statement of FCC Chairman William E Kennard Regarding US Department of Justice Action on Proposed Worldcom–Sprint Merger', document available at <http://www.fcc.gov/Speeches/Kennard/Statements/2000/stwek055.html>.

[170] See 'Federal Communications Commission Approves Bell Atlantic–GTE Merger With Conditions', document available at <http://www.fcc.gov/Bureaus/Common_Carrier/ News_Releases/2000/nrcc0031.txt>.

[171] This condition was necessary to guarantee compliance with s 271 which forbids a BOC company, such as Bell Atlantic, from providing long-distance voice or data services to customers in its service territory before it demonstrates that its local market is open to competition. At the time the transaction was cleared, Bell Atlantic has only received authorization to offer long-distance services in New York State.

[172] For a summary of these conditions, see <http://www.fcc.gov/ba_gte_merger/conditions.txt>.

significant conditions were also imposed by the FTC and the FCC in the recent AOL–Time Warner merger.[173]

5. The Debate over Cable Open Access

In recent years, a debate has raged in communications policy circles as to whether cable operators should be subject to 'open access' rules.[174] Most cable television companies require their Internet subscribers to purchase service from their affiliated ISP.[175] Under open access rules, cable companies would be mandated to also provide access to unaffiliated ISPs.[176] Open access has become a crucially important issue at a time when, as will be seen below, cable modem is seen as the prime technology to bring broadband services to households.

Associations of ISPs have lobbied the FCC to adopt rules requiring open access on the ground that in the absence of such rules the policy followed by cable operators of linking cable modem service to the use of their affiliated ISP would eliminate competition among ISPs in the broadband market with resulting price increases and harm to innovation. By contrast, cable operators have been opposed to open access on the ground that ISP exclusivity would be necessary to recoup the investments to be made to upgrade their networks so as to make them available for broadband access.[177]

While the FCC failed to rule on this matter,[178] the FTC took significant steps to promote cable open access when, in December 2000, it authorized the AOL–Time Warner merger subject to the condition that the merged entity make available to subscribers at least one non-affiliated cable broadband ISP service on Time Warner's cable system before AOL itself begins offering service, followed by two other non-affiliated ISPs within 90 days and a requirement to negotiate in good faith with others after that.[179] The FTC consent decree applies only to the AOL–Time Warner deal and not to other cable owners, thereby

---

[173] We have seen that, although it is legally barred from reviewing mergers between common carriers, the FTC is competent to investigate mergers in the cable and entertainment sectors.

[174] For arguments in favour of open access, see Mark A Lemley and Lawrence Lessig, 'The End of End-to-End: Preserving the Architecture of the Internet in the Broadband Era' (2001) 48 *UCLA L Rev* 925; Mark A Lemley and Lawrence Lessig, 'Open Access to Cable Modems' (2000) 22 *Whittier L Rev* 3. For arguments against open access, see James B Speta, 'The Vertical Dimension of Cable Open Access' (hereafter, 'The Vertical Dimension') (2000) 71 *U of Colorado L Rev* 975; James B Speta, 'Handicapping the Race for the Last Mile?: A Critique of Open Access Rules for Broadband Platforms' (2000) 17 *Yale J on Regulation* 39.

[175] For a discussion of such practices, see Jerry A Hausman et al, 'Cable Modem and DSL: Broadband Internet Access for Residential Customers' (2001) 91 *AEA Papers and Proceedings* 302, 305.

[176] See Hugh Carter Donahue, 'Opening the Broadband Cable Market: A New Kingsbury Commitment' (2001) 3 *Info* 111.

[177] For a discussion of this argument, see Speta, 'The Vertical Dimension' (n 174 above) 995.

[178] For a discussion of the 'wait and see' approach of the FCC, see Donahue (n 176 above) 121.

[179] See FTC, 'FTC Approves AOL/Time Warner Merger with Conditions', press release, available at <http://www.ftc.gov/opa/2000/12/aol.htm>.

limiting the impact of the decree. However, observers suggest that the compromise hammered out in the decree will have a significant influence on the open access debate.[180]

6. Spectrum Auctions

The Omnibus Budget Reconciliation Act of 1993 mandated the FCC to issue rules to implement its competitive bidding authority by 8 March 1994. On that date, the FCC adopted its initial regulations governing general auction structure.[181] Since then, the Commission has adopted specific rules for competitive bidding tailored for distinct services and conducted auctions for those services. As far as the design of auctions is concerned, the FCC generally opted for a system of simultaneous multi-round auctions.[182]

In the period 1994–97, the FCC conducted fourteen auctions and awarded more than 4300 PCS licences (and other licences) to auction winners.[183] Each of these licences covers exclusive rights for a particular slice of the radio spectrum over a geographic area. During that period, winning net bids totalled $23 billion. Given this success, Congress decided in 1997 to extend the FCC's auction authority to the year 2007.[184]

On 9 November 2000, the FCC adopted a policy statement and a Notice of Proposed Rulemaking (NPRM) pertaining to taking steps towards allowing secondary markets in wireless spectrum rights.[185] Current rules over the transfer of spectrum rights between companies are often criticized as excessively rigid[186] and preventing the development of such secondary markets.[187] The Policy Statement identifies three key areas on which the FCC will focus on in its efforts to foster the development of secondary markets: (i) remove, relax or modify its

---

[180] See Corey Grice and Evan Hansen, 'FTC Decision: A Broadband Portent', *ZDNet News*, 14 December 2000. For a different view, see Seth Schiesel, 'Rules for AOL–Time Warner Have a Narrow Impact' *New York Times*, 18 December 2000.

[181] See 'Implementation of Section 309(j) of the Communications Act—Competitive Bidding', Docket No 93-253, Second Report and Order, 9 FCC Rcd 2348 (1994).

[182] See Wireless Communications Bureau, 'FCC Report to Congress on Spectrum Auctions' (hereafter, the 'FCC Report on spectrum auctions'), FCC 97-353, 18 Oct 1997.

[183] See 'FCC Report to Congress on Spectrum Auctions' 1.

[184] See Balanced Budget Act of 1997, Pub L No 105-33, §§ 3002–3004, 111 Stat 251, 258–268 (1997).

[185] See Federal Communication Commission, 'Principles for Promoting the Efficient Use of Spectrum by Encouraging the Development of Secondary Markets' (hereafter 'Principles for Secondary Markets'), FCC 00-401, 9 November 2000.

[186] At the moment, licensees may seek to transfer their licences to others, but the FCC must approve these transfers. The licence transfer can take up to 18 months, and involve complex regulatory proceedings during which the FCC may demand concessions, which are sometimes unrelated to the use of the licence. These lengthy proceedings prevent the development of secondary markets in spectrum with the consequence that a substantial part of the allocated spectrum remains unused. For a criticism of the current procedure, see 'Comments of 37 Concerned Economists', comments submitted to the Federal Communications Commission, 7 February 2001.

[187] US economists have for a very long time pleaded for ensuring greater fluidity in the transfer of spectrum rights. See, eg, Ronald H Coase, 'The Federal Communications Commission' (1959) 2 *J of L and Economics* 1; Douglas W Webbink, 'Frequency Spectrum Deregulation Alternatives', Federal

rules and procedures to eliminate unnecessary barriers to the operation of secondary market processes and to promote flexibility in the use of spectrum; (ii) encourage advances in equipment that will facilitate use of available spectrum for a broad range of services; and (iii) encourage mechanisms, including information sources, spectrum exchanges and brokers, that bring together buyers and sellers and effect transfers of spectrum in a timely manner.[188]

In their reply comments to the policy statement, some parties urged the FCC to promote spectrum secondary markets through the creation of a system of 'Band Guard Managers'.[189] Pursuant to such an approach, which has already been followed by the FCC for the allocation of the 746–806 MHz bands,[190] band guard managers act as a kind of spectrum 'clearinghouse' by subdividing the spectrum they acquire at auctions and leasing it for value to third parties.

7. Peering Arrangements between Internet Backbone Networks

In order to provide end-users with universal connectivity, Internet backbones must interconnect with one another to exchange traffic destined for each other's end-users.[191] Currently, Internet backbone providers are not governed by any industry-specific interconnection regulations, unlike telecommunications carriers. Instead, each backbone provider will base its decisions on whether, how, and where to interconnect by weighing the benefits and costs of each interconnection.[192]

Until 1997, the major backbones and ISPs operated under 'peering' agreements, under which they exchanged traffic at no charge.[193] In May 1997, WorldCom/UUNET broke ranks and started charging smaller ISPs and back-

---

Communications Commission (1980) 2 OPP Working Paper No 1; Gregory L Rosston and Jeffrey S Steinberg, 'Using Market-Based Spectrum Policy to Promote the Public Interest' (1997) 50 *Federal Communications L J* 1; Pablo Spiller and Carlo Cardilli, 'Towards a Property Rights Approach to Communications Spectrum' (1999) 16 *Yale J on Regulation* 1; Howard Shelansky and Peter H Huber, 'Administrative Creation of Property Rights to Radio Spectrum' (1998) 41 *J of L and Economics* 581.

[188] See 'Principles for Secondary Markets' (n 185 above) §§ 25 et seq.

[189] See 'Reply Comments of the Industrial Telecommunications Association', comments submitted to the Federal Communications Commission, 9 March 2001.

[190] The FCC recently adopted rules allowing leasing of spectrum through band manager licensees in allocating the 'guard band' frequencies of the 746–806 MHz commercial bands. The Guard Band Manager is defined as a commercial licensee that has the ability to lease access to its licence spectrum to other eligible users. See FCC News, 'FCC Adopts Rules for Guard Band Manager Auction', available at <http://www.fcc.gov/Bureaus/Wireless/News_Releases/2000/nrw1009.html>.

[191] For an excellent discussion of the role played by peering agreements between backbone providers, see Michael Kende, 'The Digital Handshake: Connecting Internet Backbones', OPP Working Paper No 32, Federal Communications Commission, September 2000. For further analysis on the subject, see Robert M Frieden, 'Does a Hierarchical Internet Necessitate Multilateral Intervention?' (2001) 26 *North Carolina J of Intl L and Commercial Regulation* 361; Robert M Frieden, 'Last Days of the Free Ride? The Consequences of Settlement-Based Interconnection for the Internet' (1999) 1 *Info* 225.

[192] ibid.

[193] This paragraph draws heavily on Peter H Huber et al, *Federal Telecommunications Law* (2nd edn, New York: Aspen Law & Business, 1999) 168.

bone operators for interconnection. Only ISPs that could 'route traffic on a bilateral and equitable basis' to and from WorldCom/UUNET would be offered free interconnection. Despite complaints from smaller backbones, other large Internet backbones decided to follow suit and started charging smaller operators.

As a result, from the community of backbone providers emerged an elite, self-selected group of true 'peers' (usually referred to as 'top-tier backbones'). These became the dominant suppliers of the true Internet Backbone, the other players becoming their customers.[194] Because of the non-disclosure agreements that govern interconnection between backbones, it is difficult to state with accuracy the number of top-tier backbones. However, according to a recent FCC study, there are currently five: Cable&Wireless, WorldCom, Sprint, AT&T, and Genuity (formerly GTE Internet working).[195]

8. Proposals for Structural Separation of BOCs

Frustrated by the slow implementation of the unbundling provisions of the 1996 Act and the resulting lack of local competition, competitive local exchange companies brought forward the idea that BOCs should be split into a wholesale company (often referred to as 'LoopCo'), that would provide local network services to all local operators, and a retail company that would operate as one of those local operators (see Figure 4.2 below).[196] They argue that an independent wholesale company would lose any incentives to discriminate between retail operators and impede competition from taking place.[197]

Picking up this idea, the Pennsylvania Public Utility Commission (hereafter, the 'PPUC'), on 22 March 2001, ordered Verizon Pennsylvania to implement a 'functional structural' separation between its wholesale and retail activities.[198] Under such a functional separation, Verizon would continue to operate as one company but the retail and wholesale divisions would be required to operate at arm's length, pursuant to a code of conduct. This decision was criticized by Verizon's competitors which regretted the PPUC did not mandate a full structural separation whereby wholesale and retail operations would be carried out by two companies acting under separate ownership.[199]

[194] ibid 169.

[195] See Kende (n 191 above).

[196] See Roy L Morris, 'A Proposal to Promote Telephone Competition: The LoopCo Plan' CCH Power and Telecom L (January/February 1998) at 35.

[197] See Competitive Telecommunications Association, 'Structural Incentives: The Simpler, More Efficient Path to Local Competition', paper presented at the National Association of Regulatory Utility Commissioners Summer Meeting, Seattle, Washington, 14 July 2001.

[198] Pennsylvania Public Utility Commission, 'Re: Structural Separation of Bell Atlantic–Pennsylvania, Inc Retail and Wholesale Operations', Opinion and Order, Docket Number M-00001353, 22 March 2001. This Order seeks to implement the structural separation of Verizon Pennsylvania prescribed by the PPUC's 1999 Global Order on Local Phone Competition.

[199] See, eg, Alex Daniels, 'Competitors Hope to Take Verizon to the Chopping Block', *Techway Washington*, 15 October 2001, document available at <http://washtech.com/washtechway/2_20/techcap/12957–1.html>.

FIGURE 4.2. LoopCo restructuring

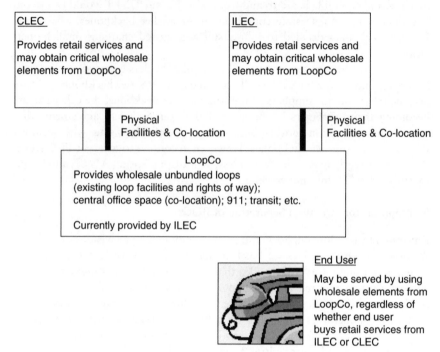

Source: Morris, n 196 above.

Similar structural reforms are currently contemplated in several other states and in August 2001 Senator Hollings introduced a Bill in the US Senate (S 1364 entitled 'Telecommunications Fair Competition Enforcement Act 2001'), which inter alia would only authorize BOCs to provide retail service 'through a division that is legally separate from the part of the Bell operating company that provides wholesale services' and 'in a manner that is consistent with a code of conduct designed to ensure these divisions deal at arms-length with each other'.[200]

E. A CRITICAL APPRAISAL OF THE REGULATORY FRAMEWORK

As noted at the beginning of the chapter, the central feature of the American model for the economic regulation of telecommunications is that it relies, to an unusually high degree, upon the implementation of detailed regulatory requirements,[201] rather than upon general antitrust rules, to prevent abuses of

---

[200] 107th Congress, 1st Session, S 1364, submitted on 3 August 2001.

[201] As pointed out by Roger Noll, the 1996 Act, which forms the basis of the American model, is the 'single most regulatory statute about an economic regulatory regime that has ever been passed'. See Roger Noll, Remarks in the Panel 'Unleashing True Competition in Telecommunications' at the Brookings Institution's National Issues Forum (23 November 1998), available at <http://www.brook.edu/comm/transcripts/19981120.htm>.

market power.[202] The American regulatory model thus offers a good benchmark of how the seven criteria identified in Chapter 2 above can be met through the application of detailed, pro-competition regulatory requirements.

1. Competition and Other Incentives to Generate and Share Efficiency Gains

In order to promote competition in the local market, the 1996 Act contains a series of measures aimed at enabling competitors to use the local companies' infrastructure to provide local services. Thus, for example, s 251 requires incumbent local operators to interconnect with other carriers,[203] to ensure number portability and dialling parity,[204] and to provide competitors unbundled access to their network.[205] The FCC determined that prices for interconnection under facilities-based competition and for the purchase of unbundled network elements should be based on the incumbent's Total Element Long-Run Incremental Cost (TELRIC), while prices for the resale of the incumbent's retail services should be calculated according to a retail-minus method similar to the ECPR methodology described in Chapter 3.[206] Section 252 establishes a specific procedure for resolving interconnection disputes through intervention of the infrastructure-wide regulators established at the state level, the state utility commissions. Finally, ss 271 et seq allow BOCs to offer long-distance services to their own customers provided, inter alia, they meet their interconnection obligations under s 251 and create a separate affiliate to provide long-distance services.

The design of these various measures raises several important issues. A first set of concerns relate to the unbundling of the local loop strategy promoted by the 1996 Act and implemented via several FCC orders. First, some commentators consider that it is wrong to 'mandate' incumbents to provide their competitors with unbundled network elements under the conditions established by law as competition would be more intense if competitors were forced to build their own facilities.[207] Yet, despite technological progress, some network elements remain very difficult to duplicate and, in a market still largely dominated by ILECs, local loop unbundling might be an essential tool to stimulate local competition. According to a recent study, at the end of 2000, about one third of competitive local exchange operators relied on unbundled network elements to provide their

---

[202] It is also a major regulatory effort to promote entry of new competitors in the local exchange market.

[203] 47 USC § 251(a)(1).

[204] ibid § 251(b)(2) and (3).

[205] ibid § 251(c)(3).

[206] See Local Competition Order, n 128 above.

[207] See, eg, Adam Thierer, 'A 10-Point Agenda for Comprehensive Telecom Reform' (2001) 63 *Cato Institute Briefing Papers* 5 ('Genuine head-to-head, facilities-based competition will not develop so long as regulators are proposing technology and network sharing as the universal cure-all for America's communications woes').

service.[208] Many companies also rely on the unbundled network elements to provide DSL services in competition with the incumbents.[209] In a country such as the United States where the local incumbents continue to dominate local access, unbundling of the local loop may thus a be valid strategy to stimulate competition and innovation at least in some cases. A key issue, however, is whether access conditions—and in particular the prices of unbundled elements—are set in an adequate manner.

Some of the disadvantages of the LRIC methodology identified in Chapter 3 are stressed by several authors who criticize the use of the TELRIC pricing methodology devised by the FCC to calculate the price of unbundled elements.[210] Those authors mention, for example, that incumbents might be unable to recoup their investments because:

(i) it may be unrealistic to assume that they will be able to contain their costs by constantly using the current most efficient technology;[211]
(ii) the FCC formula might fail to take into account the speed at which technological progress reduces the cost of providing interconnection (and would therefore set a depreciation rate which would be too low);[212] and
(iii) the FCC formula might fail to remunerate the incumbents properly for the risk they took in setting up their networks in the first place.[213]

In addition, it appears that, from a legal standpoint, the FCC's hypothetical network standard is contrary to the language of the 1996 Act and thus illegal as has been recently confirmed by a judgment of the Court of Appeals of the Eighth Circuit.[214]

Besides local access, a second type of issues raised with respect to the local competition provisions of the 1996 Act relates to the incentives devised to ensure

---

[208] See Robert W Crandall, 'An Assessment of the Competitive Local Exchange Carriers Five Years After the Passage of the Telecommunications Act' (June 2001), available at <http://www.usta.org/on_the_ hill/HR1542/crandall.pdf>.

[209] ibid.

[210] See, generally, J Gregory Sidak and Daniel F Spulber, 'Givings, Takings and the Fallacy of Forward-Looking Costs', 72 *New York U L Rev* 1068; J Gregory Sidak and Daniel F Spulber, 'The Tragedy of the Telecommons: Government Pricing of Unbundled Network Elements Under the Telecommunications Act of 1996' (1997) 97 *Columbia L Rev* 1081.

[211] See Statement of Alfred E Kahn on FCC's Proposed Reforms of Carrier Access Charges, 14 February 1997 7 ('In a world of continuous technological progress, it would be irrational for firms constantly to update their facilities in order completely to incorporate today's lowest-cost technology, as though starting from scratch, the moment those costs fell below prevailing market prices: investments made today, totally embodying today's modern technology, would instantaneously be outdated tomorrow and, in consequence, never earn a return sufficient to justify the investment in the first place').

[212] See Thomas M Jorde et al, 'Innovation, Investment and Unbundling' (2000) 17 *Yale J on Regulation* 1, 16.

[213] ibid.

[214] See *Iowa Utilities Board v FCC* No 96-3321, 18 July 2000 (indicating that it was clear from the language of the 1996 Act that Congress intended the price of unbundled network elements to be based on the cost of providing such elements and 'not on the cost some imaginary carrier would incur by providing the newest, most efficient, and least cost substitute for the actual item or element which will be furnished by the existing ILEC pursuant to Congress's mandate for sharing').

the effective implementation of those provisions. Section 271—which conditions the BOCs' ability to offer long-distance services on meeting their interconnection duties under s 251—is based on the assumption that the prospect of entering the long-distance market is a sufficiently attractive carrot to entice the BOCs to open their local networks. Conversely, it was assumed that long-distance companies would strive to enter the local market even if by doing so they would, in effect, help the BOCs establish that effective competition had been introduced in their markets and that they should therefore be authorized to provide long-distance services. Some observers have argued that these assumptions were in fact mistaken. On the one hand, the BOCs seem to have made only a half-hearted effort to enter the long-distance market (where, as will be seen below, revenues have been shrinking)[215] and have instead focused on maintaining their local monopoly,[216] while, on the other hand, long-distance providers might have been reluctant to enter the local exchange market for fear that this may allow in turn the BOCs to enter the core of their business.[217] Linking BOCs' entry to the long-distance market to compliance with the Act's market opening provisions was a risky strategy that might eventually have led some telecommunications carriers to adopt a behaviour which is the opposite of the one that was initially sought by Congress.[218]

On the other hand, if local and long-distance companies do enter each others' markets, an additional concern might emerge. A degree of vertical integration would, in effect, be re-introduced into the telecommunications sector, with the associated risks of preferential treatment or other anti-competitive behaviours which can arise in that context. The fact that the BOCs are required to establish separate affiliates to provide long-distance services alleviates this concern to a certain extent. However, the same obligation is not imposed upon long-distance companies entering the local market, nor do ILECs have to separate wholesale from retail sales ventures. In any case, regulatory requirements notwithstanding,

---

[215] See Seth Schiesel, 'For Local Phone Users, Choice Isn't an Option' *New York Times*, 21 November 2000 ('Most recently, revenue has begun evaporating in the long-distance telephone business, potentially reducing the Bell companies' enthusiasm for that market and undermining the formula—letting local carriers into the long-distance business once they open their local networks—on which the Telecommunications Act has relied'.)

[216] See Nicholas Economides, 'The Telecommunications Act of 1996 and Its Impact', September 1998, available at <http://raven.stern.nyu.edu/networks/telco96.html>. Commentators have argued that a key factor driving recent mergers between BOCs was their desire to consolidate their position in the local market. See, for instance, Richard Waters, 'New Communications Industry Takes Shape', *FT Telecoms, Financial Times Survey*, 9 June 1999, at C11 (arguing that few RBOCs were prepared to take the risk of opening their local market to gain access to the long-distance market, and that they chose instead 'to extend their "footprint" through merger, turning themselves into formidable giants').

[217] However, given the fact that there are three main long-distance operators in the US—AT&T, MCI and Sprint—each might actually end up trying to enter the local market, thinking that the others would do so anyway. See Jean-Jacques Laffont and Jean Tirole, *Competition in Telecommunications* (Cambridge, Mass., and London: MIT Press, 2000) 27.

[218] For a more positive assessment of s 271, see Marius Schwartz, 'The Economic Logic for Conditioning Bell Entry into Long Distance on the Prior Opening of Local Markets', AEI–Brookings Joint Center for Regulatory Studies, Working Paper 00-4, April 2000.

the establishment of a separate affiliate might not necessarily guarantee full arm's length relationships between a long-distance affiliate and its BOC parent. The reality of such risks can be shown by the two following illustrations. First, as has been seen above, almost immediately after it had received its s 271 authorization, Bell Atlantic (now Verizon) was found by the FCC Enforcement Bureau to have engaged in strategic, anti-competitive conduct against its rivals. More generally, a 1999 study which compared access arrangements with the Bell Operating Companies (which, with the exceptions of Bell Atlantic in New York and SBC in Texas, are vertically separated) and GTE (then, a vertically integrated, rival telecommunications company) found that access negotiations with integrated GTE took longer and were less likely to be successful.[219] GTE's negotiating stance was systematically more aggressive than that of the Bells and, despite the access regulatory regimes, entry was systematically lower in regions serviced by GTE.

Thus, while the long-distance market is competitive, regional local markets are still de facto monopolized by the BOCs, and with monopolistic operators in one segment of the market the risks of vertical integration should not be underestimated. These risks need, however, to be weighted against the potential efficiency benefits which might be reaped by allowing operators to provide services across the different segments of the telecommunications market. And some particular features of the US market might, in fact, somewhat reduce the risks associated with vertical integration. First, after close to twenty years of regional segmentation of the local markets and vertical separation between the local and long-distance markets, several strong, independent companies, with well-known brands, have emerged. This means that in the United States, more than in many other countries, various operators—some of them with direct experience in the provision of local services—might eventually be in a position to challenge local incumbents. The degree of potential rivalry in the local market has, however, been reduced by the successive mergers which took place between BOCs,[220] although the FCC has sought to enhance the merged companies' incentives to enter the local phone markets outside their territories through 'voluntary agreements'.[221] Second, the scope and breadth of the US market makes it a particularly fertile ground for the deployment of new technologies, which might in time sufficiently reduce the costs of installing new local facilities to further reduce the scope for abuses of dominant position in the local market.

It is still too early to pass final judgement on the efficacy of the local competition provisions of the Act. So far, it is hard to argue that they have had much impact on the level of competition in the local segment of the market as the

[219] See Frederico Mini, 'The Role and Incentives for Opening Monopoly Markets: Comparing GTE and RBOC Cooperation with Local Entrants', Georgetown University, Department of Economics, Working Paper 00-09, July 1999.

[220] As a result of these successive mergers, two entities (Bell Atlantic, now Verizon and SBC) each control one third of all local phone lines in the United States.

[221] For a critique of such agreements, see Bryan N Tramont, 'Too Much Power, Too Little Restraint: How the FCC Expands Its Reach through Unenforceable and Unwieldy "Voluntary Agreements"' (2000) 53 *Federal Communications L J* 49.

BOCs and the other ILECs still very largely dominate the local exchange market.[222] As indicated above, these provisions have led to many legal challenges that have considerably delayed their implementation. As a result, four years after the 1996 Act's passage, the FCC's unbundling efforts have still failed to bear fruit.[223] Section 271 may also have given a disincentive to long-distance operators to enter the local market because of the fear that this may allow the BOCs to become competitors in long-distance. The local service rate structure may have been an additional factor that has prevented competition from taking hold. The rates for residential basic service have been traditionally maintained artificially low for political reasons and, in recent years, rate rebalancing has been slow.[224]

As a result, the market penetration of competitive local exchange carriers ('CLECs') is slower than anticipated,[225] though some recent FCC data suggests their shares of the market has been growing fast during 2000.[226] According to these figures, as of 31 December 2000, CLECs provided 16.4 million (or 8.5 per cent) of the approximately 194 million nation-wide local telephone service lines to end-user customers. By contrast, CLECs only provided 8.3 million (or 4.4 per cent) of nation-wide local telephone service lines at the end of 1999. This represents a 97 per cent growth in CLEC market share during 2000. The same data shows, however, that, at the end of 2000, about 60 per cent of the CLEC local telephone lines served medium and large business, institutional and government customers. This suggests that while competition for business customers is growing, individual users largely continue to be served by ILECs.

It is also early to assess the impact of provisions aimed at letting BOCs enter the long-distance market as it was only in December 1999 that a BOC was, for the first time, considered to have sufficiently opened its local market to competition to be allowed to provide long-distance services under the provisions of s 271. Since then, six additional BOC applications to provide in-region long-distance services have been approved by the FCC. Unlike local exchange services, the long-distance market was already competitive prior to the adoption of the 1996 Act with several long-distance companies competing against one another (see Table 4.2 below). Prices, already very low in 1996 by international

[222] See Seth Schiesel, 'For Local Phone Users, Choice Isn't an Option' *New York Times*, 21 November 2000.

[223] See Mark Naftel and Lawrence J Spiwak, *The Telecoms Trade War* (Oxford and Portland, Ore.: Hart Publishing, 2000) 206–207.

[224] See Alexander C Larson and Douglas R Mudd, 'The Telecommunications Act of 1996 and Competition Policy: An Economic View in Hindsight' (1999) 4 *Virginia J of L and Technology* 1: 'The reason that competition from alternate suppliers does not take place is most likely because prices have been set so low in the first place, with regulatory sanction. This means that there are no positive profits an entrant can expect to earn in this market. Even if entry is not proscribed by law, at the subsidized retail price the lack of a profit opportunity makes entry rather unlikely to occur'.

[225] See Robert W Crandall and Jerry A Hausman, 'Competition in U.S. Telecommunications Services: Effects of the 1996 Legislation' in Sam Peltzman and Clifford Winston (eds), *Deregulation of Network Industries: What Next?*, AEI–Brookings Joint Center for Regulatory Studies (2000) 73.

[226] FCC, 'Trends in Telephone Service', Industry Analysis Division, Common Carrier Bureau (August 2001) section 9.1.

standards, have been following a downward trend for the last decade that does not appear to have been fundamentally influenced by the adoption of the Act. In fact, recent months have seen ferocious price wars between long-distance companies, which have resulted in shrinking revenues for such companies.[227] The fact that in the price comparisons presented in the Annex, the US long-distance market is only the second cheapest in US dollars based on PPPs (the cheapest market being the United Kingdom) suggests, however, that some further price reductions could be achieved (see Annex, Graph 4b).

In this regard, some observers continue to maintain that the long-distance market will only become truly competitive when the BOCs are entitled to enter this market.[228] BOCs should indeed be able to lure a substantial share of their own local subscribers to their long-distance service.[229] This in turn could set off a much more vigorous general round of long-distance price reductions. This analysis seems to be confirmed by a recent study that finds

TABLE 4.2. Market shares of total toll revenues for US long-distance carriers 1984–2000

Year	AT&T	MCI WorldCom	Sprint	All others
1984	90.1%	4.5%	2.7%	2.6%
1985	86.3%	5.5%	2.6%	5.6%
1986	81.9%	7.6%	4.3%	6.3%
1987	78.6%	8.8%	5.8%	6.8%
1988	74.6%	10.3%	7.2%	8.0%
1989	67.5%	12.3%	8.4%	11.8%
1990	65.0%	14.5%	9.7%	10.8%
1991	63.2%	15.6%	9.9%	11.3%
1992	60.8%	18.1%	9.7%	11.5%
1993	58.1%	19.7%	10.0%	12.3%
1994	55.2%	20.7%	10.1%	14.0%
1995	51.8%	24.6%	9.8%	13.8%
1996	47.9%	25.4%	9.7%	17.0%
1997	43.8%	25.7%	9.5%	19.8%
1998	43.1%	23.5%	8.5%	24.9%
1999	40.5%	23.7%	9.8%	26.0%
2000	38.0%	22.5%	9.0%	30.5%

Source: FCC, 'Trends in Telephone Service' (August 2001).

[227] See Seth Schiesel, 'Phone Mergers that May Help Competition', *New York Times*, 27 November 2000 (arguing that the problem from long-distance companies is that 'market competition is working too well' and that, as a result, 'all of the companies in the long-distance business are beating each other senseless').

[228] See Crandall and Hausman (n 225 above) 102.

[229] See Robert W Crandall and Thomas W Hazlett, 'Telecommunications Policy Reform in the United States and Canada', AEI–Brookings Joint Center for Regulatory Studies Working Paper 00-9, December 2000 13.

statistically significant evidence that s 271-approved BOC entry enabled the average customer to reap a 9 per cent savings on her monthly inter-LATA bill in New York and 23 per cent savings in Texas.[230] The authors of the study also claim to have found statistically significant evidence that CLECs have a substantially higher cumulative share of the local market in states where BOC entry has occurred.[231] In light of these findings, they argue that the costs created by delaying the BOCs' entry into the long-distance market (in terms of forgone welfare gains) clearly outweighed the potential benefits.[232]

International telephone calling has become an increasingly significant segment of the US telecommunications market. According to FCC figures, the number of calls made from the United States to other countries increased from 200 million in 1980 to 5.2 billion in 1999.[233] The market has not only expanded, but has also become more competitive. Since 1985, when MCI began to compete with AT&T for international calls, numerous carriers (56 in 1999) have begun to provide international services by using their own facilities or leased lines from other carriers.[234] A large number of operators are also engaged in resale of other carriers' services. AT&T's share of international telephone service revenues has fallen sharply in recent years (from 82 per cent in 1989 to 46.6 per cent in 1999), mainly to the benefits of MCI WorldCom and Sprint.[235] Competition on the main international routes is tough and the price comparisons presented in the Annex show that the US international telephone services market is the most competitive of the five countries examined (see Annex, Graphs 5a, 5b, 6a, and 6b).

The gradual shift toward price-cap regulation by the state utility commissions, for its part, did, as could be expected, raise concerns in some specific cases with respect to the quality of service. Customers of US West, for example, complained of increased delays after the company laid off many workers in response to a change of regulatory regime aimed at increasing the company's incentives to cut costs.[236] But the shift toward price-cap regulation does contribute to promote greater efficiency on the part of the operators. In addition, this regime reduces the risk of managerial or accounting cross-subsidies between different activities,[237] as it ensures that most telecommunications services— which can potentially be provided by the same companies since adoption of the Telecommunications Act 1996—are regulated in ways which provide similar incentives to cut costs to the operators. The price-cap system imposed upon local

---

[230] See Jerry A Hausman et al, 'The Consumer-Welfare Benefits from Bell Company Entry into Long-Distance Telecommunications: Empirical Evidence from New York and Texas', document available at <http://papers.ssrn.com/sol3/cf_dev/AbsByAuth.cfm?per_id=206474>.

[231] ibid.

[232] ibid.

[233] See FCC, 'Trends in Telephone Service' (n 226 above) section 6.1.

[234] ibid.

[235] See FCC, 'Trends in the International Telecommunications Industry' (April 2001) table 27.

[236] See Jean-Jacques Laffont and Jean Tirole, *Competition in Telecommunications* (Cambridge, Mass. and London: MIT Press, 2000) 5.

[237] See Chapter 3, Section C.

retail prices—unlike a rate-of-return system—prevents a company from passing on undue cost increases to end-users and the same is true of the TELRIC used to regulate various access prices and of the unregulated, competitive regime applicable to the provision of long-distance services. Incentives for cross-subsidization may, however, remain because of the use of the ECPR to set prices for the resale of local services.[238]

As far as wireless telephony is concerned, three remarks should be made. First, the bidding process initiated by the FCC in 1993 is a far more efficient way to allocate spectrum than the administrative hearings or lotteries that were used by the FCC until that time. Auctioning spectrum rights leads to economic efficiency by putting spectrum into the hands of those who value it most highly.[239] It also ensures transfers of some of the welfare gains associated with service provision to the Treasury. As pointed out in Chapter 3, the system of simultaneous auctions for spectrum rights used by the FCC presents substantial informational advantages for the bidders and tends therefore to promote better informed and more aggressive bids. Moreover, the FCC plans to introduce further flexibility into the system by allowing companies controlling frequencies to resell them on a secondary market. Such a secondary market should further increase the efficiency of matching supply and demand for spectrum, and thus lead to lower costs for all services making use of spectrum.[240] It should help maintain the economic efficiency of spectrum allocation even when spectrum rights are originally auctioned for long periods of time.

Second, many of the new operators that won auctions have now started operations and are injecting a higher degree of competition in markets which had been dominated by duopolistic incumbents for more than a decade. According to recent FCC data, 91 per cent of the total US population have access to three or more different operators offering mobile telephone services in the counties in which they live, while 75 per cent of the population live in areas with five or more mobile telephone operators competing to offer service and 47 per cent of the population can choose from at least six different mobile telephone operators.[241] Prices, which had remained relatively high under duopolistic arrangements, have decreased sharply in recent years. According to Crandall and Hazlett, throughout the 1984–95 period real, inflation-adjusted cellular rates had fallen at a rate of 3 or 4 per cent per year.[242] Even more strikingly, between

[238] See Chapter 3, Section B.3.

[239] For an evaluation of the efficiency of the US system of spectrum auctions, see Peter Cramton, 'The Efficiency of FCC Spectrum Auctions' (1998) 41 *J of L and Economics* 727; Peter Cramton, 'The FCC Spectrum Auctions: An Early Assessment' (1997) 6 *J of Economics and Management Strategy* 431.

[240] See Stephen Labaton, 'FCC to Promote a Trading System to Sell Airwaves' *New York Times*, 13 March 2000.

[241] See FCC, 'Sixth Annual Report and Analysis of Competitive Market Conditions With Respect to Commercial Mobile Services' (hereafter, 'Sixth Report on Mobile Services'), FCC 01-192 (17 July 2001) 6.

[242] See Robert W Crandall and Thomas W Hazlett, 'Telecommunications Policy Reform in the United States and Canada', AEI–Brookings Joint Center for Regulatory Studies Working Paper 00-9 28.

1995 and 1999, real cellular rates fell at a rate of 17 per cent per year as PCS service providers offered service at per minute prices less than 50 per cent of prevalent cellular rates.[243] The competitiveness of the US mobile market is confirmed by the price comparisons in the Annex, which shows that this market is the second cheapest of the five countries compared when prices are based on PPPs (see Annex, Graphs 11b and 12b).

Third, in spite of the increasingly competitive nature of the US wireless market, the penetration rate of wireless services (39 per cent nation-wide according to recent FCC data)[244] is not as high as in most other industrialized countries.[245] Several factors may explain why penetration remains low. First, most states continue to keep residential rates low, thereby reducing the incentives for consumers to substitute wireless for wireline services.[246] Second, the United States' failure to implement 'calling-party-pays' tariffs acts as a disincentive for consumers to use wireless phones as a way to receive incoming calls.

Unlike in the wireless sector, the United States can claim to be the country with the highest level of Internet use in the world. According to recent statistics, at the end of the year 2000, the United States had 143 million Internet users or the equivalent of 54 per cent of the American population.[247] Internet penetration in the United States can be largely explained by the fact that users enjoy flat-rate local access charges (the vast majority of users currently rely on dial-up Internet access).[248] Internet use has also been stimulated by the existence of a vibrant market for ISP services[249] with most ISPs providing flat-rate Internet service packages.[250] At the backbone level, competition is also taking place between a range of national and regional backbones connected to each other by peering or transit agreements in the absence of binding interconnection regulation.[251] With prices based on PPPs, the US Internet market appears to be the most competitive among those of the five countries examined in this book (see Annex, Graphs 9b and 10b).

While current pricing schemes have led to a spectacular growth of Internet use, some observers have, however, expressed concern that the combination of

---

[243] ibid.

[244] See 'Sixth Report on Mobile Services' (n 241 above) 6.

[245] See Simon Romero, 'Wireless is Getting a Cool Reception in US' *New York Times*, 29 January 2001.

[246] See Crandall and Hazlett (n 242 above) 30.

[247] See The Big Picture Geographics, 'The World's Online Populations', available at <http://cyberatlas.internet.com/big_picture/article/0,1323,5911_151151,00.html>.

[248] According to a recent survey, 88 per cent of Internet users would continue to rely on dial-up Internet access. See United States General Accounting Office, 'Technological and Regulatory Factors Affecting Consumer Choice of Internet Providers' (hereafter, the 'GAO Report') (October 2000) 12.

[249] At present, there are approximately 7,000 ISPs in the United States and, according to a 1998 study, 92 per cent of American consumers had seven or more ISPs to choose from in their local areas. See the GOA Report (n 248 above) 29.

[250] Flat-rate access packages have been made possible by the fact that, unlike long-distance carriers, ISPs do not pay usage-based access charges to the local exchange operators. ISPs typically connect to LECs through business lines that have no usage charges for receiving calls.

[251] See text accompanying nn 200–204 above.

flat-rate local access and ISP service charges might not be sustainable in the long run as it creates congestion in the local network.[252] Sidak and Spulber observe that '[c]alls on the PSTN to ISP points of presence clearly entail usage costs and make claims on scarce capacity. The pricing of calls to ISP points of presence should reflect these costs'.[253] As we have seen in Chapter 3, usage charges can be placed directly on end-users (by introducing a time sensitive element in the way local access is charged) or on the ISP itself (through the access charges they pay to the local exchange operators). We have seen, however, that designing usage charge regimes is far from easy (because of the difficulty of developing price schemes that do effectively reflect congestion levels) and no proposal to put in place such regimes has been seriously considered yet.

In such circumstances, the best way to address congestion issues is probably to provide an enabling environment for the development of alternatives to dial-up access.[254] Recent data on the rapid growth of the number of broadband connections to the Internet show encouraging signs that such alternatives are being developed in the United States.[255] According to FCC statistics, high-speed lines connecting homes and businesses to the Internet increased by 158 per cent during 2000, to a total of 7.1 million (see Table 4.3 below).[256] As far as residential access is concerned, the majority of such connections are based on cable modem systems, which have thus become the prime source of broadband Internet access in the United States.[257]

TABLE 4.3. High-speed lines

Types of technology	December 1999	June 2000	December 2000	Per cent change	
				Dec 1999–Dec 2000	June 2000–Dec 2000
ADSL	369,792	951,583	1,977,377	435	108
Other wireline	609,909	764,099	1,063,563	74	39
Coaxial cable	1,414,183	2,284,491	3,576,378	153	57
Satellite and fixed wireless	312,204	307,151	376,506	NM	NM
Fibre	50,404	65,615	112,405	NM	NM
Total lines	2,756,492	4,372,939	7,106,229	158	63

Source: FCC, 'Trends in Telephone Service' (2001).

[252] See, eg, Kevin Werbach, 'Digital Tornado: The Internet and Telecommunications Policy' OPP Working Paper No 29 (Federal Communications Commission, March 1997) 58.
[253] See J Gregory Sidak and Daniel F Spulber, 'Cyberjam: The Law and Economics of Internet Congestion of the Telephone Network' (1998) 21 *Harvard J of L and Public Policy* 327, 363.
[254] See Werbach (n 252 above) 66.
[255] See FCC News, 'Federal Communication Commission Releases Data on High-Speed Services for Internet Access', press release, 9 August 2001.
[256] ibid.
[257] See Jerry A Hausman et al, 'The Consumer-Welfare Benefits from Bell Company Entry into Long-Distance Telecommunications: Empirical Evidence from New York and Texas', document available at <http://papers.ssm.com/sol3/cf_dev/AbsByAuth.cfm?per_id=206474>.

As we have seen above, concerns have been raised that exclusivity links between cable operators and affiliated ISPs could hamper competition in the ISP market. While this risk is real,[258] we have seen that it has been partly addressed by the FTC consent decree forcing AOL–Time Warner to offer non-discriminatory access to unaffiliated ISPs.[259]

As far as universal services are concerned, the 1996 Act marks a progress compared to the previous regime, which relied, to a large extent, on indirect and hidden subsidies between services and between operators to finance universal service provision.[260] Section 254 indicates that universal service support should be explicit, which is a first step toward a more competition friendly regime. It also attempts to put all competitors on a level playing field by stating that all telecommunications operators providing long-distance service must contribute to the costs of universal service on an equitable and non-discriminatory basis,[261] and that these contributions must go to all operators that offer components of universal service throughout a designated area, whether these operators be incumbents or new entrants.[262] Transfers from long-distance to local and from urban to rural users do remain, however, and the cost of universal provision might be overestimated in the absence of mechanisms to ensure some degree of competition for the market or in the market for the provision of universal services. In fact, universal service charges amount to a $5 billion tax on long-distance service users and the net cost of universal service obligations represents about 5 per cent of total sector revenues, a figure that is very high by international standards.[263]

Finally, the United States has relied on structural measures to facilitate competition in telecommunications. The rationale for the AT&T divestiture was that, to ensure free, unimpeded competition in long-distance telecommunications, it was necessary to remove the incentives for the local exchange operators to discriminate against long-distance operators by preventing them from providing long-distance services. Although other factors may have played a role, this structural separation certainly helped the development of long-distance competition as, within five years from the divestiture, AT&T's market share for long-distance services decreased from 90.1 per cent (in 1984) to 67.5 per cent (in 1989).

As we have seen, s 271 will, however, allow the BOCs to re-integrate vertically provided that they meet certain conditions designed to further competition in the local market. The fact that few s 271 applications have so far been accepted appears to have less to do with the fear that the BOCs will be given again the ability to leverage their control of the local network to monopolize the

---

258 See text accompanying nn 174–177 above.
259 See text accompanying nn 179–180 above.
260 See text accompanying n 61 above.
261 47 USC at § 254(d).
262 ibid § 254(e).
263 See Bjorn Wellenius, 'Extending Telecommunications Beyond the Market—Toward Universal Service in Competitive Environments' *Viewpoint* Note 206 (The World Bank, March 2000).

long-distance segment, than with the enduring vision within the FCC that s 271 needs to be used as a carrot to induce BOCs to open their local market to competition.

The failure of the 1996 Act to bring competition in the local market has induced some observers, as well as some state regulators and federal policy-makers, to propose that a structural separation be imposed between the whole-sale and retail operations of BOCs. It is subject to question whether the 'func-tional' separation approach that is being implemented (in Pennsylvania) or proposed (in other states or in the US Senate) will have any real impact on local competition. As we have seen in Chapter 3, the imposition of a functional separation does nothing to remove the *incentives* of the monopolistic operator (ie the wholesale company) to discriminate between retailers in order to favour its own parent company. Moreover, it does not generally remove the *ability* of this operator to engage in such discriminatory practices unless there is significant regulatory oversight. In this regard, a full structural separation (including at the ownership level) would offer better guarantees against discrimination.

The potential benefits of breaking up the BOCs should, however, be balanced with the costs that would be incurred. As we have seen in Chapter 3, structural separation might involve transaction costs as well as opportunity costs in terms of loss of economies of scope. It is not easy, however, to evaluate the significance of such costs. For instance, while Verizon Pennsylvania indicated in a testimony that the introduction of a structural separation between its wholesale and retail activities would cost it $1 billion, an economist hired by AT&T contended that such costs should not exceed $41 million.[264] Current stock market trends tend to suggest that the economies of scope between various activities might, in fact, be lower than previously thought. While telecommunications conglomerates, such as MCI WorldCom or AT&T were star performers on the market, Wall Street now seems to favour specialist companies competing horizontally in their field of expertise.[265] Finally, among the costs that should be taken into account before engaging in structural reforms are the risks that such reforms be delayed by years of litigation, a factor that cannot be overlooked in the particularly litigious US system.[266]

2. Specificity versus Coherence

The 1996 Telecommunications Act contains a set of telecommunications-specific requirements that are to be implemented, for the most part, by a telecommuni-cations-specific regulator. This regulatory model is clearly based on the view that

---

[264] See AT&T News Releases, 'Economist Finds Evidence Verizon is Grossly Exaggerating Cost of State-Required Verizon Split' (8 March 2001).

[265] See, eg, 'Ma Bell Does the Split' *The Economist*, 28 October 2001 79–80.

[266] See Pennsylvania Public Utility Commission, 'PUC Orders Functional Structural Separation of Verizon', press release (22 March 2001) (PUC Chairman John Quain indicating that 'a functional structural separation approach should deliver the benefits of competition to customers sooner than a physical break-up because a physical break-up would be followed by years of costly lawsuits').

the application of economy-wide antitrust principles may not be sufficient to control market power in telecommunications.

Sector-specific rules and institutions do have some advantages.[267] However, the rigid regulatory distinctions currently made between telecommunications, cable, and other means of communication seem poorly adapted to a context of convergence. Greater reliance on economy-wide rules, such as antitrust legislation, would seem to present advantages in that regard. By contrast, the structure of the FCC seems, prima facie, to be well-adapted to a context of convergence since the agency regulates both telecommunications and cable. Convergence seems, however, to go beyond the communications sector to cover all network industries.[268] Antitrust authorities or infrastructure-wide regulatory agencies, based on the model of the state utility commissions, would therefore be better positioned to regulate converging industries.

Paradoxically, it can be argued, however, that while too many detailed regulations have been adopted, on the whole, in the US telecommunications sector, there are issues on which additional telecommunications or infrastructure-specific rules do, in fact, appear to be needed. For instance, the general antitrust rules under which the DoJ has to assess mergers (the Clayton Act, s 7) mandate the latter to base its decision on a criterion—whether or not the transaction lessens competition[269]—that is wholly inadequate in industry sectors that are suddenly opened to competition after having been dominated by monopolies.[270] Indeed, the merger between two BOCs does not lessen competition in either Bell's market—because none existed in the first place. This problem could be solved, however, by authorizing the DoJ to use in its review of telecommunications mergers a more flexible criterion than the 'impact on competition' standard it is currently bound to use.

3. Flexibility versus Certainty

One clear advantage of the detailed regulatory framework put in place by the 1996 Telecommunications Act is that it clarifies the respective rights and duties of telecommunications operators, and thus tends to reduce uncertainty in the marketplace. For instance, the 1996 Act imposes on local exchange carriers requirements to provide number portability and dialling parity.[271] This sends a

---

[267] See Chapter 2.

[268] A clear illustration of this is the apparition on the American market of so-called 'telelectric' companies, ie, gas and electric utilities that install fibre-optic lines within their controlled public rights of way, and then use or lease these fibre lines to provide competitive long-distance, high-speed data and video services. See Benjamin Lipschitz, 'Regulatory Treatment of Network Convergence: Opportunities and Challenge in the Digital Era' (1998) 7 *Media L and Policy* 14, at 18.

[269] See 15 USC § 18. See also the US Department of Justice & Federal Trade Commission, Horizontal Merger Guidelines, available at <http://www.usdoj.gov/atr/public/guidelines/horiz_book/hmg1.html>.

[270] See 'William Kennard's Colosseum' *The Economist*, 15 May 1999 75.

[271] See text accompanying n 32 above.

positive signal to potential new entrants and provides a welcome degree of clarification to the operators' responsibilities.

Unfortunately, while the 1996 Act contains precise rules on a series of issues, it is vague on some other key aspects. For instance, the 1996 Act fails to draw a clear line between the respective competencies of the FCC and the state utility commissions with respect to the implementation of its local competition provisions.[272] As we have seen, this led to a three-year legal battle that was extremely costly and seriously impeded the implementation of the Act during its first few years of existence.[273] Arguably, in a complex institutional system such as the United States, one of the key components of any legislative scheme should be to delimit clearly the competencies of the institutions that will get involved in the implementation of its provisions.[274]

On the other hand, the 1996 Act's detailed regulatory requirements over issues such as interconnection or the purchase of unbundled network elements may be excessively rigid and leave too little discretion to the regulatory authorities to tailor appropriate solutions in a constantly evolving marketplace.[275] This problem of rigidity is, however, mitigated in two ways. First, though the FCC is mandated by the 1996 Act to implement a large set of detailed rules, there remains a series of matters for which this body retains large discretionary powers as it is requested to act in the 'public interest', a concept whose definition is rather vague.[276] Second, some provisions of the Act allow the FCC to reduce the regulatory burden that is imposed on telecommunications operators when justified by circumstances. Section 160 of the 1996 Act, entitled 'regulatory flexibility', enables the FCC to forbear from applying provisions of this Act if it determines that forbearance from enforcing those provisions 'will promote competitive market conditions'.[277] Use of s 160 is, however, restricted with

---

[272] See *AT&T Corp et al v Iowa Utilities Board* 25 January 1999, n 136 above. Scalia dissenting ('It would be gross understatement to say that the Telecommunications Act of 1996 is not a model of clarity. It is in many important respects a model of ambiguity or indeed even self-contradiction. That is most unfortunate for a piece of legislation that profoundly affects a crucial segment of the economy worth tens of billions of dollars').

[273] See Aimee M Adler, 'Competition in Telephony: Perception or Reality? Current Barriers to the Telecommunications Act of 1996' (1999) 7 *J of L and Policy* 571, 613.

[274] This is particularly true considering that constitutional challenges to regulation may be the most effective form of action for those wishing to contest the validity of an act. See Joseph D Kearney and Thomas W Merrill, 'The Great Transformation of Regulated Industries Law' (1998) 98 *Columbia L Rev* 1323, 1373.

[275] See Eli M Noam, *Toward a Common Law of Telecom* (1996), available at <http://www.columbia.edu/dlc/wp/citi/citinoam19.html>.

[276] There is a rich body of literature criticizing the vagueness of this criterion and the abuses that may result thereof. See, eg, William H Read and Ronald Alan Weiner, 'FCC Reform: Governing Requires a New Standard' (1998) 49 *Federal Communications L J* 293; Erwin G Krasnow and Jack N Goodman, 'The "Public Interest" Standard: The Search for the Holy Grail' (1998) 50 *Federal Communications L J* 605; William T Mayton, 'The Illegitimacy of the Public Interest Standard at the FCC' (1989) 38 *Emory L J* 715.

[277] 47 USC § 160(b). This provision was, for instance, used by the FCC to detariff domestic long-distance services (Domestic Detariffing Order, 11 FCC Rcd at 20,733) and international exchange services (*In the matter of 2000 Biennial Regulatory Review; Policy and Rules Concerning*

respect to some of the provisions of the Act[278] and it also requires that a series of strict conditions be met.[279] In addition, s 161 of the Act, entitled 'Regulatory Reform' requires the FCC to review, every two years, all of its rules that apply to telecommunications service providers and determine whether any are no longer necessary in the public interest.[280] Section 161 then directs the Commission to repeal or modify unnecessary rules.

4. Regulatory Competence and Ability to Resist Undue Pressure

Although the Telecommunications Act 1996 imposes a number of duties on the state utility commissions and the DoJ, the FCC is the major institutional player as far as implementation of the Act is concerned. The technical capacity of the FCC is generally highly regarded (although, as will be seen below, regulatory mistakes have been made by the FCC) and the Commissioners who head the agency are usually qualified professionals. The 1934 Communications Act, which created the FCC, also contains a series of requirements designed to ensure the independence of the Commissioners vis-à-vis political authorities and market players.[281] For instance, no more than three commissioners (out of a total of five) can be of the same political party, none of the commissioners can have financial interests in any Commission-related business, and commissioners can only be removed for cause.

Another factor that would tend to reduce the risks of 'agency capture' is the presence of detailed regulatory requirements in the 1996 Act. Indeed, the lower the discretion of the regulator, the less industry and political authorities may hope to influence the regulatory process. This line of reasoning is, however, subject to two caveats. First, as noted above, there are certain areas where the FCC does enjoy large discretionary powers. Moreover, while the adoption of detailed regulatory requirements may contribute to reduce the risks of 'agency capture', it may also contribute to 'legislative capture'. Indeed, there is little doubt that Congressional debates over extremely complex and detailed provisions are influenced by armies of lobbyists funded by telecommunications

the International, Interexchange Marketplace, Report and Order, IB Docket No 00-202, FCC 01-93). For a discussion of § 160, see Thomas J Hall, 'The FCC and the Telecom Act of 1996: Necessary Steps to Achieve Substantial Deregulation' (1998) 11 *Harvard J of L and Technology* 797.

[278] The FCC may not forbear from applying the requirements of § 251(c) or 271(a) until it determines that those requirements have been fully implemented. See 47 USC § 160(d).

[279] See 47 USC § 160(a)–(c).

[280] For a discussion of § 161, see Harold W Furchtgott-Roth, 'Report on Implementation of Section 11 by the Federal Communication Commission', 21 December 1998, document available at <http://www.fcc.gov/commissioners/furchtgott-roth/reports/sect11.html>.

[281] Some authors consider that despite their independent status, some FCC commissioners, and in particular former FCC Chairman Reed Hundt, work very closely with the White House. See Randolph J May, 'An Agency for Bill and Al' *Legal Times*, 5 June 2000, 75. More recently, Commissioner Powell has also criticized current FCC Chairman William Kennard for his participation in a 'political trip' to California with President Bill Clinton and fellow FCC Commissioner Gloria Tristani. See FCC News, 'FCC Commissioner Michael M. Powell Criticizes Apparent Politization of Commission Business', document available at <http://www.fcc.gov/Speeches/Powell/Statements/2000/stmkp006.html>.

operators.[282] To some extent, legislative capture may succeed more easily than regulatory capture because politicians offer fewer guarantees of independence than regulators. This is not to say, of course, that regulatory agencies should be given a blank cheque. But one should be aware that the more detailed the legislative provisions, the greater the scope for attempting to influence the legislative process.

5. Regulatory Accountability and Stakeholder Participation

One of the advantages of relying on FCC proceedings is that they offer more room for public intervention than antitrust proceedings. The FCC has to give public notice of matters to be acted upon and an opportunity to comment on such matters. FCC decisions must also be reasoned. They are subject to review before federal courts on legal, but not substantive or factual grounds. A clear downside of some of these processes, however, is that they tend to be extremely burdensome. There is also a danger that certain actors use them—for instance, by filing large comments or by systematically challenging FCC decisions—to slow down the implementation of reforms that go against their interests.

6. Regulatory Costs

One clear drawback of the American regulatory model is that it involves huge regulatory costs. The 1996 Act directs the FCC to make an impressive series of rulings, the elaboration and implementation of which absorb large administrative resources.[283] As we have seen, the FCC is a large bureaucracy with a significant budget. One also needs to add the resources spent on telecommunications regulation at the state level by the state utility commissions. Finally, telecommunications carriers also need to invest massive internal and external legal resources to ensure compliance of their operations with the requirements of the Act. In this regard, it seems fairly obvious that law firms and telecommunications consultants have greatly benefited from the adoption of the 1996 Act.

Finally, one should not overlook the costs of regulatory inefficiencies. As mentioned above, uncertainty regarding the respective responsibilities of the FCC and state commissions has led to very costly judicial proceedings. In addition to the costs of the proceedings, one should take into account the cost, upon the economy at large, of delaying the reform process. The cost of regula-

---

[282] See Stephen Labaton, 'Communications Lobby Puts Full-Court Press on Congress' *New York Times*, 24 October 2000. See also Kearney and Merrill (n 274 above) 1323, 1394, and especially the press articles quoted in their n 329.

[283] As pointed out by Thomas Krattenmaker, the Act's local competition provisions 'impose so many restrictions, and direct the Commission to write so many rules, that one must fear that the regulatory costs of this open access regime will exceed its payoff in reduced rates or improved service quality'. See Thomas G Krattenmaker, 'The Telecommunications Act of 1996' (1996) 29 *Connecticut L Rev* 123.

tory mistakes must also be taken into account. There is cause for concern here as the scope for such mistakes tends to increase with the number and complexity of the rules. It could be argued, for instance, that s 271 might constitute one such mistake. This provision has so far failed to achieve its intended objective and, as noted above, may even have contributed to delay the arrival of competition in the local exchange markets.

7. Allocation of Regulatory Responsibilities

The lack of clarity in the allocation of responsibilities between the FCC and the state utility commissions has already been pointed out.[284] Other issues stem from the peculiar relationship between the FCC and the DoJ, which are requested to cooperate in some areas and have concurrent jurisdiction in others. The Telecommunications Act, s 271 gives final authority to the FCC to rule on BOCs' applications to enter the long-distance market but, before taking a decision, the Commission must consult with the DoJ and give 'substantial weight' to the latter's evaluation.[285] By contrast, in the area of mergers and acquisitions, the FCC and the DoJ have concurrent jurisdiction to review transactions between telecommunications operators. Their review process is entirely separate and based on distinct statutory authority.

The above interactions between the FCC and the DoJ have been praised by a number of authors as a source of synergy between these institutions.[286] It has been argued, for instance, that in the context of the application of s 271, the FCC has much to gain by taking into account the DoJ's opinion over whether a specific BOC has sufficiently opened its market to competition to be entitled to provide long-distance services. Determining whether a given market is (sufficiently) competitive is indeed one of the core competencies of the antitrust division. Similarly, it has been observed that the FCC–DoJ's dual merger review process can yield some real benefits. Because of their different statutory authority, these institutions can examine transactions from different, complementary angles. While the DoJ considers whether the effect of the acquisition may 'substantially lessen competition', the FCC's test is much broader since it includes 'the effect on competition as well as other factors derived from the FCC's public interest obligations under the Communications Act'.[287]

---

[284] See text accompanying nn 143–146 above.

[285] See text accompanying n 121 above.

[286] See, for instance, James F Rill et al, 'Institutional Responsibilities Affecting Competition in the Telecommunications Industry', in Claus Dieter Ehlermann and Louisa Gosling, *European Competition Law Annual 1998: Regulating Communications Markets* (Oxford and Portland, Ore.: Hart Publishing, 2000) 667.

[287] See 'Mergers, Consumers, and the FCC', Remarks of Commissioner Gloria Tristani before the National Association of Regulatory Utility Commissioners, 8 November 1998, available at <http://www.fcc.gov/Speeches/Tristani/spgt813.html>. This view is not necessarily shared by all FCC Commissioners. For instance, Commissioner Furchtgott-Roth has expressed the view that 'for the FCC to conduct antitrust review is to duplicate the efforts of the Antitrust Division' and that, therefore,

The above assessment may be too enthusiastic. It is true that there are a number of good reasons to give the FCC final decision-making powers with respect to s 271. For instance, s 271 requires the BOCs to comply with their interconnection duties under s 251, a provision that the FCC is in charge of implementing. One could also argue that s 271 review requires the making of a policy choice that goes beyond the traditional sphere of competence of an enforcement agency, such as the DoJ.[288] On the other hand, however, it could be argued that, in principle, it is a competition authority such as the DoJ, with experience in assessing the degree of competitiveness of different markets across the economy, which should be entrusted with the task of determining whether the local competition market is sufficiently open to competition.[289]

As for the FCC–DoJ's dual jurisdiction over mergers between telecommunications operators, it certainly presents a series of difficulties. A first obvious problem is the risk that the two bodies adopt inconsistent positions. In the Bell Atlantic/NYNEX merger, for instance, the DoJ did not raise any objections.[290] By contrast, the FCC only allowed the merger after imposing several conditions.[291] This creates uncertainty in the marketplace. Moreover, from a practical standpoint, this dual review process is extremely slow (with parties having to wait sometimes for more than a year to have a transaction cleared by the two reviewing bodies),[292] involves a great deal of duplication (with similar documents having to be sent to two different institutions) and, therefore, is unnecessarily costly.[293]

---

antitrust review should be left to the DoJ. See Remarks of Commissioner Harold W Furchtgott-Roth before the National Association of Broadcasters, 15 October 1998, available at <http://www.fcc.gov/Speeches/Furchtgott_Roth/sphfr815.txt>. For a more recent and more elaborate statement of Commissioner Furchtgott-Roth's position, see Testimony of Federal Communications Commissioner Harold W Furchtgott-Roth before the House of Representatives Committee on the Judiciary, Subcommittee on Commercial and Administrative Law Oversight Hearing, 25 May 1999, Novel Procedures in FCC Licence Transfer Proceedings, available at <http://www.fcc.gov/Speeches/Furchtgott_Roth/Statements/sthfr925.html>.

[288] See James R Weiss and Martin L Stern, 'Serving Two Masters: The Dual Jurisdiction of the FCC and the Justice Department Over Telecommunications Transactions' (1998) 6 *Communications L Conspectus* 195, 198 ('In contrast to the FCC, the Justice Department generally acts as an enforcement agency, rather than a policy-making body').

[289] This was the position taken by the DoJ during the congressional debate over the 1996 Act. See Hearing on Telecommunications Policy Reform Before the Senate Comm On Commerce, Science and Transportation, S REP No 104-218, 25 (1995) (statement of Anne K Bingaman, Assistant Attorney-General, Antitrust Division).

[290] See 'Antitrust Division Statement Regarding Bell Atlantic/NYNEX Merger', US Department of Justice press release, 24 April 1997.

[291] See 'FCC Approves Bell Atlantic/NYNEX Merger Subject to Market-Opening Conditions', Federal Communications Commission press release, 14 August 1997.

[292] Note, however, that some legislation has been proposed in the Senate that would place limits on the time taken by the FCC in reviewing mergers. See Antitrust Merger Review Act, s 467 introduced by Senators Dewine and Kohl on 25 February 1999.

[293] See Testimony of Roy Neel, President and CEO of the United States Telephone Association, Before the Subcommittee on Antitrust, Business Rights and Competition of the Committee on Judiciary, United States Senate, 13 April 1999, available at <http://www.usta.org/releases/rls99-21.html> .

Some observers have suggested that a good way to overcome the above difficulties would be to set up a new merger procedure patterned on s 271.[294] Pursuant to that new system, the FCC would lead the enquiry and the DoJ would file comments on the merger. According to the authors of that proposal, this new system 'would consolidate decision making, allow the industry to reap the efficiency benefits of single rather than dual agency review, and promote consistency in merger evaluation'.[295]

In our opinion, it would be preferable to concentrate merger review in the hands of the DoJ which has the advantage of reviewing mergers across different fields of activity.[296] Our position is not isolated. It is supported by at least one former FCC Commissioner and several influential Congress members. In a series of speeches and articles in the press, former FCC Commissioner Furchtgott-Roth argued that the FCC lacks merger review authority and that, therefore, the review of mergers between telecommunications companies should be left to the DoJ.[297] Similarly, in a bill introduced in Congress in May 1999 (S 1125), Senator McCain seeks to deprive the FCC from any merger review power.[298] Specifically, the bill provides that the FCC would have 'no authority to review a merger... or to impose any term or condition on the assignment or transfer of any license... in the course of a merger... while that merger... is subject to review by either the DoJ or FTC'.[299]

Other bills introduced in the 106th Congress regarding the telecommunications merger review process, such as Senator Dewine's Bill (S 467) or Senator Pickering's Bill (S 1125), do not seek to cut the FCC out of that process, but to accelerate the speed of FCC review by forcing it to act within specified limits.[300] For its part, the FCC announced in January 2000 that it was planning to implement rules with a view to ensure a 'predictable, transparent and streamlined merger review process'.[301]

---

[294] Weiss and Stern (n 288 above) 210.

[295] ibid.

[296] As mentioned above, however, the DoJ would have to be authorized to assess mergers in telecommunications according to a criterion different from the present one that focuses only upon whether or not the transaction lessens competition.

[297] See Testimony of FCC Commissioner Harold W Furchtgott-Roth Before the House Committee on Commerce, SubCommittee on Telecommunications, Trade, and Consumer, 14 March 2000, document available at <http://www.fcc.gov/Speeches/Furchtgott_Roth/2000/sphfr004.html>. See also Harold Furchtgott-Roth, 'The FCC Racket' *The Wall Street Journal*, 5 November 1999.

[298] See Lisa I Fried, 'Curbing FCC Powers: Agency's Role in Telecom Mergers Questioned' 221 *New York L J* 5.

[299] See 'Summary: Bills Pertaining to Telecom Antitrust Merger Reviews', available at <http://www.techlawjournal.com/cong106/atr/Default.htm>.

[300] ibid.

[301] See FCC News, 'FCC Implements Predictable, Transparent and Streamlined Merger Review Process', document available at <http://www.fcc.gov/Bureaus/OGC/News_Releases/2000/nrgc0001.html>.

5

New Zealand

The New Zealand model, unlike that of the United States, has put very heavy emphasis on general antitrust law to be applied by antitrust authorities to control market power in telecommunications. An analysis of the New Zealand model can therefore yield valuable information on the pros and cons of a regulatory framework contrasting sharply with that of the United States.

A. ORIGINS OF THE PRESENT REGULATORY FRAMEWORK

During most of the twentieth century, telecommunications services were provided in New Zealand by the Post Office which was, in addition, responsible for the provision of postal and some banking services. The Post Office, during that period, was operated as a government department with a single centralized decision-making structure overseeing all of its activities and conditions of employment which were those of the civil service. Regulatory functions in the telecommunications sector were shared between the Government and the Post Office itself.[1]

Following Britain's entry into the European Community in 1973 (which limited the access of New Zealand's agricultural products to the British market) and the two oil crises of 1973–74 and 1979, the authorities decided to increase the level of industry protection against international competition, to launch ambitious public projects aimed at reducing the country's dependence on imported oil, to extend an already generous welfare system, and to combine lax monetary policy with direct controls on prices and wages.[2] By the early 1980s, as the public deficit grew, inflation increased, and productivity plummeted, it was clear that those policies were failing.

With the accession to power of a new Labour Government in 1984, radical reforms were rapidly implemented, aimed at increasing reliance on market mechanisms, competition, and private initiative, and at reducing the scope of government intervention in the economy.[3] The Post Office, which held

---

[1] See David Boles de Boer and Lewis Evans, 'The Economic Efficiency of Telecommunications in a Deregulated Market: The Case of New Zealand' *The Economic Record* (March 1996) 25.

[2] On the policies of the New Zealand Government in the early 1980s, see, for example, Allan Bollard and Michael Pickford, *Utility Regulation in New Zealand*, Institute of Economic Affairs, Lectures on Regulation, London (1996) 4–7.

[3] ibid 7–10.

a statutory monopoly in the markets for terminal equipment, as well as for local, national and international telephony, was an obvious candidate for reform. By 1984, it was widely perceived as inefficient and over-regulated. Its total staff of 41,000 made it the largest employer in New Zealand and was considered excessive, waiting lists were long, maintenance poor, and services inadequate.[4]

A Government-commissioned review of the Post Office structure was carried out in 1985–86. It recommended that the Post Office be reorganized into different business units, that operators be entrusted with commercial but not regulatory functions, and that the markets for terminal equipment and for value-added services be opened to competition. Following completion of the review, the Post Office was split, on 1 April 1987, into three autonomous State-owned enterprises: Telecom (in charge of telecommunications); New Zealand Post (in charge of postal services); and Postbank (in charge of banking services). Regulatory and policy functions were transferred to the New Zealand Department of Trade and Industry, which became the New Zealand Ministry of Commerce on 1 December 1988, and was renamed the Ministry of Economic Development in 2000.[5]

The Government then commissioned additional studies on the impact that the introduction of competition would have on the telecommunications sector. In July 1987, a Touche Ross study concluded that deregulation would yield significant economic benefits and the Government then decided to proceed with rapid liberalization of the telecommunications sector. The Telecommunications Act 1987 provided for the phased elimination of all exclusive rights pertaining to users' equipment, and the Telecommunications Amendment Act 1988 imposed a complete opening to competition of all segments of the market from 1 April 1989.[6] In addition, a study by National Economic Research Associates recommended the development of an appropriate legal framework for the creation of tradable property rights to manage and use the radio spectrum. These recommendations were implemented in December 1989 with the adoption of the Radiocommunications Act 1989.[7]

Finally, in September 1990, Telecom was sold to a joint venture between local investors and two large United States telecommunications companies, Bell Atlantic and Ameritech, notwithstanding public opposition to the privatization reportedly running at about 90 per cent. The sale price was NZ$4.25 billion, by

---

[4] See Bell Gully's Communications, Technology and Media Group, *Telecommunications Law and Regulation in New Zealand* (1999/2000 edn, October 1999) 2.

[5] See Dennis Campbell (ed), *International Communications Law* (Washington, DC: BNA International Inc, 2000) NZ/9.

[6] For an analysis of the liberalization process in New Zealand telecommunications from 1987 to 1989, see, for example, Richard A Joseph, 'The Politics of Telecommunications Reform: A Comparative Study of Australia and New Zealand', University of Wollongong, Science and Technology Analysis Research Program, Working Paper No 12, July 1993, 20–27; Eli M Noam, Seisuke Komatsuzaki and Douglas A Conn (eds), *Telecommunications in the Pacific Basin: an Evolutionary Approach* (Oxford: Oxford University Press, 1994).

[7] See Bell Gully's Communications, Technology and Media Group (n 4 above) 3.

far the highest price paid for any New Zealand asset privatized to date. The proceeds were used to retire Government debt. A condition of the sale was that Bell Atlantic and Ameritech would reduce their aggregate ownership in Telecom to no more than 49.9 per cent, in part through offers of shares in the company to the public.[8]

B. The main rules

The regulatory model adopted in New Zealand at the end of the 1980s is often characterised as 'light-handed' regulation. It was established with the objective of relying to a large extent on general antitrust rules and to make very limited use only of telecommunications-specific rules. However, during the year 2000, the Government announced that it intended to overhaul the regulatory framework, and in particular to modify some antitrust rules and to adopt a series of additional telecommunications-specific rules.[9] Many of these changes came into effect in late 2001. These reforms and their rationale are discussed in Sections D and E below. The present Section focuses on the rules in force prior to implementation of those changes, starting with the main antitrust rules and following up with the few existing telecommunications-specific rules.

1. Antitrust Rules

Antitrust legislation is contained in the Commerce Act 1986. It applies to all industries and its stated objective is to promote competition in markets within New Zealand.[10] Part II of the Commerce Act prohibits a range of restrictive trade practices that hinder competition. Thus, s 27 prohibits contracts, arrangements or understandings that have the purpose, or have, or are likely to have, the effect of substantially lessening competition in a market. Section 30 prohibits arrangements that have the effect of fixing, controlling or maintaining the price, discounts, or rebates of goods or services. Section 36, for its part, prohibits use of a dominant position in any market for the purpose of restricting entry to, preventing or deterring competitive conduct in, or eliminating any person from, the market in question or another market.

Part III of the Act deals with the acquisition or strengthening of a dominant position. Section 47 prohibits the acquisition of assets of a business or shares, if this would, or would be likely to, result in any person acquiring or strengthening a dominant position in a market.

---

[8] On the privatization of Telecom, see Rex J Ahdar, 'Battles in New Zealand's Deregulated Telecommunications Industry' (1995) 23 *Australian Business L Rev* 78, and Bell Gully's Communications, Technology and Media Group (n 4 above) 3.

[9] See Hon Paul Swain, Minister of Communications, 'Government Announces "World Leading" Telecommunications Reform', media release, 20 December 2000, available at <http://www.executive.govt.nz/minister/swain/index.html>.

[10] See Bell Gully's Communications, Technology and Media Group (n 4 above) 13.

Part IV of the Act empowers the Government to impose price controls on the supply of goods or services when competition is limited and when these controls are in the interests of users, consumers, or retailers. Price control regulations may be revoked, amended or varied at any time.[11]

Finally, Part V of the Act provides for the granting of authorizations or clearances. Thus, contracts, arrangements, and understandings that fall within the scope of Part II of the Commerce Act can be authorised when it appears that the benefits they would generate to the public exceed any potential disadvantages.[12] Business acquisitions, dealt with under Part III of the Act, can also be authorized when they would benefit the public or cleared when they would not, in fact, create or strengthen a dominant position.[13]

2. Telecommunications-Specific Rules

Telecommunications operators do not need to be licensed in New Zealand and, before the recent reforms, responsibility for a range of technical issues—including interconnection, numbering, carrier pre-selection, and roaming—lay with the operators themselves.[14] A few sector-specific rules did exist, however. The main ones are described below.

2.1 The Kiwi Share

At the time of the privatization of Telecom in 1991, the Government retained one preferential share (the so-called Kiwi Share) in Telecom in order to impose upon the company four main obligations aimed at ensuring the provision of universal services. First, Telecom had to maintain a local free calling option for all residential customers, ie Telecom could impose a line rental charge, but the local calls themselves were free. Second, Telecom had to ensure that the line rental price for residential users in rural areas was no higher than the standard residential line rental price, ie Telecom could not engage in geographical de-averaging. Third, Telecom had to keep the price of a residential line rental at or below its 1 November 1989 level in real terms, unless its profitability was unreasonably impaired. And fourth, Telecom had to continue to make ordinary residential telephone service as widely available as at the date of its privatisation.[15]

2.2 The Disclosure Regulations

Telecommunications Disclosure Regulations were introduced in 1990 in an attempt to remedy, to some extent, the information asymmetries that favour

---

[11] See Commerce Act, ss 52–55.

[12] ibid s 58.

[13] ibid ss 66 and 67.

[14] See Ministry of Economic Development, 'New Zealand Telecommunications 1987–1998', New Zealand Telecommunications Information Publication No 6, December 1998, 7–8.

[15] See Colleen Flood, 'Regulation of Telecommunications in New Zealand—Faith in Competition Law and the Kiwi Share' (1995) 3 *Competition and Consumer L J* 214–218.

Telecom as the incumbent owner of the public switched telephone network. The Disclosure Regulations required Telecom to disclose certain financial, accounting, and pricing information, including standard contract prices, and terms and conditions for the supply of specific goods and services. Telecom had to prepare this information every three months and make it available to the public.[16] The Regulations were amended in December 1993 to force Telecom to disclose all interconnection agreements with other parties, including its own subsidiaries.[17] In August 1999, the Government announced further changes to the disclosure regime, to take effect on 1 January 2000. Under the new regime, Telecom has been required to publish, twice yearly, separate financial statements for its local loop and for its other telecommunications services. Telecom has had to use an avoidable cost methodology (ie an ECPR-type methodology) to calculate the costs of its local loop services. The objective was to provide to Telecom's competitors some information that they could use when negotiating interconnection agreements for access to Telecom's local loop. In addition, Telecom was to calculate Kiwi Share obligations' costs in accordance with a specified set of principles. Telecom has maintained that it was incurring losses in complying with the Kiwi Share obligations and it has imposed interconnection prices that include a contribution to cover such losses. Once again, the objective of the disclosure regime was to provide relevant information to parties negotiating interconnection agreements with Telecom. Finally, some services have been added to the list of services about which Telecom had to disclose specific information, while international calls have been removed from the list.[18]

2.3 Telecom's Undertakings

Telecom, in addition, offered certain pro-competition assurances to the Government in two separate letters of undertakings. In a first letter dated 8 June 1988, Telecom indicated its intention to restructure the company into a holding company, a finance company, and an operating company with distinct subsidiary companies including five separate local telephone companies, a long-distance company and a company operating mobile services. Telecom stated that the subsidiary companies would not be permitted to offer preferential treatment to other Telecom companies and would deal with each other and with competitors on a total arm's length basis.[19] In a second letter of 6 July 1989 Telecom committed, inter alia, to provide interconnection on a fair and reasonable basis, to avoid any discrimination against competitors, and to co-operate fully with the Commerce Commission to assist with the prompt resolution of any complaints.[20]

[16] Telecommunications (Disclosure) Regulations 1990, SR 1990/120.
[17] ibid reg 4(1)(d).
[18] See Ministry of Economic Development, Amendments to the Telecommunications (Disclosure) Regulations 1990, August 1999 1–2.
[19] Letter, Telecom to the Minister of State-Owned Enterprises, 8 June 1988.
[20] Letter, Telecom to the Minister of Commerce, 6 July 1989.

2.4 Radiocommunications Act 1989

The Act introduces a distinction between spectrum management rights and spectrum licences. Management rights are issued by the Government and give the manager the exclusive legal right to manage a particular nationwide band of frequencies for a period of up to twenty years. No radio transmission can, however, be made in any radio spectrum subject to a management right until a licence has been issued by the manager and registered by the Registrar of Radio Frequencies. A key characteristic of management rights is that they are technology-neutral: they do not limit use of the spectrum to any specific telecommunications or broadcasting application. Licences, for their part, are issued by spectrum managers. They give the licensee the right to make use of certain frequencies and list the specific conditions applicable to the use of those frequencies. Licences are granted for periods that cannot exceed the expiry date of the management right under which they are issued. Both management rights and spectrum licences can be freely traded and the Radiocommunications Act specifies that the Commerce Act, s 47 is applicable to the acquisition and disposition of management rights and spectrum licences.[21] The overall objective of the system is to facilitate competitive entry in telecommunications and broadcasting and to promote economic efficiency by enabling market forces to determine which application would extract maximum value from spectrum utilization.[22]

C. The main institutions

As is the case with respect to the rules, the institutional framework applicable to the economic regulation of telecommunications was substantially modified at the end of 2001. These changes, like those pertaining to the substance of the rules, are discussed under Sections D and E below. The present Section reviews the main institutions prior to implementation of those changes.

1. The Commerce Commission

Under the Commerce Act 1986, the Commerce Commission is the main body responsible for monitoring the application of antitrust regulations. The Commission must have three to five members appointed by the Governor General[23] on the recommendation of the Minister of Economic Development. It has an annual budget of about NZ$7.4 million and a staff of about 70.[24] Prior to the

---

[21] See Radiocommunications Act 1989, ss 33, 34, 42, 48, 49, 56, 98, 99, 101 and 138.

[22] See Robert W Crandall, 'New Zealand Spectrum Policy: A Model for the United States?' (1998) XLI *J of L and Economics* 837.

[23] The Governor General is the representative of the Commonwealth in New Zealand. Decisions requiring the signature of the Governor General are, in practice, taken by the Government.

[24] See Commerce Commission's Annual Plan 2000–2001, 36, available at <http://www.comcom. govt.nz/about/annual.cfm>.

recent reforms, only two of these staff were working on telecommunications matters on a full-time basis, with other staff being pulled in if required (see Figure 5.1 below).[25]

The Commission is a body that is formally independent from the legislative and executive branches and it enjoys some protection against undue pressure from the Government. Thus, for example, the Commission's budget is directly determined by Parliament[26] and the causes for which the appointment of a Commission member can be terminated are enumerated in the Commerce Act.[27] Also, the risk that the Government might designate purely political appointees to the Commission is somewhat limited by the fact that Commission members must be chosen on the basis of their knowledge of, or experience in, industry, commerce, economics, law, accountancy, public administration or consumer affairs.[28] The Commission must, however, 'have regards to the economic policies of the Government as transmitted in writing from time to time to the Commission by the Minister (of Economic Development)'.[29] In practice, the Government has communicated few statements of economic policy to the Commission. The process is also relatively transparent as such communications must be published and communicated to Parliament.[30] The independence of the Commission from industry is guaranteed by specific conflicts of interest rules.[31]

FIGURE 5.1. New Zealand Commerce Commission organizational chart

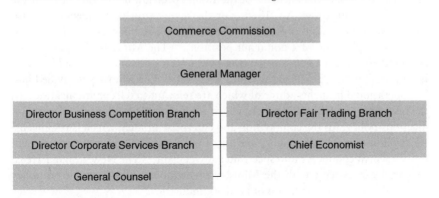

Source: <http://www.comcom.govt.nz/about/org_chart.cfm>.

---

[25] See Ministerial Inquiry into Telecommunications, Final Report (27 September 2000) 35, available at <http://www.teleinquiry.govt.nz> .

[26] See Commerce Act, s 20.

[27] ibid s 13.

[28] ibid ss 9 and 10.

[29] ibid s 26.

[30] See Kerrin M Vautier and Allan E Bollard, 'Competition Policy in New Zealand' in Carl J Green and Douglas E Rosenthal, *Competition Regulation in the Pacific Rim* (New York: Oceana Publications Inc, 1996) 390.

[31] The Commerce Act s 14 requires Commission members to disclose their financial interests in businesses that are the objects of regulatory proceedings before the Commission and to discontinue their participation in such proceedings.

The Commission can issue determinations over a range of issues covered by the Commerce Act.[32] Thus, it is the Commission that, under the Commerce Act, Part V, can authorize contracts, arrangements, and understandings, which fall within the scope of Part II of the Act, or business acquisitions dealt with under Part III. It is also the Commission that can clear business acquisitions that would not create or strengthen a dominant position.[33] Finally, the Commission determines the prices to be charged for the goods or services identified by the Government as requiring price controls under Part IV of the Commerce Act.[34] In the course of its functions, the Commission can serve notice requiring information, search under warrant, or issue confidentiality orders over information obtained. It makes formal written determinations on the outcome of its investigations.[35] Finally, for enforcement purposes (including imposition of penalties), the Commission takes a prosecuting role before the courts when it believes that some provisions of the Commerce Act have been violated.

2. The Minister of Economic Development

The Minister of Economic Development is responsible for the provision of policy advice to the Government on business and consumer issues, including telecommunications issues. The Ministry of Economic Development is, in particular, responsible for the management of the radio spectrum under the terms of the Radio Communications Act 1989 (but the acquisition of frequencies is also subject to the provisions of Part III of the Commerce Act concerning the acquisition or strengthening of a dominant position).[36] The Minister also plays a key role in identifying the goods or services over which price controls would need to be imposed under Part IV of the Commerce Act.[37] The Ministry is divided into five operational branches, three of which are relevant to telecommunications: (i) the resources and network branch, which is responsible for general telecommunications policy; (ii) the competition and enterprise branch, which is responsible for generic competition policy; and (iii) the operations and risk management branch which conducts radio spectrum management.[38] The New Zealand Treasury works in concert with the Ministry of Economic Development on policy issues related to the regulation of network industries.[39]

---

[32] For a fuller discussion of the role of the Commerce Commission, see Peter Allport, *Natural Monopoly Regulation in New Zealand*, Institute of Public Affairs Deregulation Conference, Melbourne, 24 July 1998.

[33] See text accompanying n 13 above.

[34] Commerce Act, s 70.

[35] See Vautier and Bollard (n 30 above) 390.

[36] See Ministry of Economic Development, 'New Zealand Communications 1987–1998', New Zealand Telecommunications Information Publication No 6, December 1998, 7.

[37] See Commerce Act, s 53, which indicates that decisions to subject certain goods or services to price controls are made by the Governor General, who is instructed to do so by the Government on the recommendation of the Minister of Economic Development.

[38] Dennis Campbell (ed), *International Communications Law* (Washington, DC: BNA International Inc, 2000) 32.

[39] See <http://www.treasury.govt.nz/orgstructure/rtp/#tax>.

3. The Courts

Actions introduced on the basis of the Commerce Act are presented before the High Court. Decisions of the High Court can then be appealed to the Court of Appeal, and finally to the Privy Council in Britain which is the highest jurisdiction of New Zealand. The determinations made by the Commission can, for their part, be appealed on factual as well as legal grounds, first to the High Court and then to the Court of Appeal.[40] The Commerce Act provides for an expert lay-member to sit in the High Court on antitrust matters.[41] Only the Courts have the power to impose pecuniary penalties.[42]

As could be expected given the design of the New Zealand regulatory framework, the courts played a major role with respect to many of the issues discussed in the present section. These issues are:

  (i) the scope of the Commerce Commission's competence;
 (ii) interconnection conditions;
(iii) pricing policies in the local market;
 (iv) numbering, pre-selection and roaming issues;
  (v) spectrum allocation;
 (vi) the extent to which an incumbent can try to control the flow of Internet traffic carried by its network (an issue discussed in the I4free v. Telecom case);
(vii) Telecom's commitment to the undertakings which it presented to the Government in the late 1980s; and
(viii) reviews and modifications of the regulatory framework.

1. The Scope of the Commerce Commission's Competence

In November 1991, the Commerce Commission initiated an inquiry about the telecommunications sector to analyse the obstacles that could prevent competition in telecommunications and to determine the effectiveness of the disclosure regime in removing those obstacles.[43] Following publication of the Commission's report, Telecom brought proceedings before the High Court challenging the Commission's authority to conduct such a broad inquiry.[44] The High Court

[40] See Commerce Act, ss 91–97.
[41] ibid ss 77 and 78.
[42] ibid ss 80–87.
[43] Commerce Commission, 'Telecommunications Industry Inquiry Report', Wellington, 23 June 1992.
[44] See *Telecom Corporation of New Zealand Ltd v Commerce Commission* (1991) 4 NZBLC 103,057.

concluded that the Commission could not conduct a formal inquiry and publish a public report unrelated to a particular complaint or transaction constituting the subject of its specific functions under the Commerce Act.[45] The Commerce Commission lodged an appeal against the High Court's judgment that was dismissed by the Court of Appeal.[46] The Court of Appeal presented similar arguments to those of the High Court and added that whether there should be a review of the effectiveness of the regulatory regime for telecommunications and what form it should take were matters for the Government, not the Commission, to decide.[47] Following that decision, the Commerce Commission's role was thus basically limited to enforcing specific provisions of the Commerce Act and adjudicating on authorization applications.

2. Main Interconnection Disputes

2.1 Clear-Telecom—Long-Distance Interconnection

Clear Communications Ltd—a telecommunications consortium made up, at the time, of Bell Canada, Television New Zealand, MCI, Todd Corporation, and New Zealand Rail Group—entered into interconnection negotiations with Telecom in mid-1990 to compete in the long-distance, domestic and international market. Its negotiating position was probably somewhat strengthened by the fact that the Government was unwilling to approve Telecom's privatization until an interconnection agreement had been reached.[48] A Memorandum of Agreement was signed by Clear and Telecom in August 1990, thus paving the way for Telecom's privatization in September.

The final agreement, concluded in March 1991, constituted, from Clear's point of view, an improvement over the standardized interconnection offer that Telecom had published in July 1989.[49] Telecom's standard offer stated that Telecom's competitors would be charged an interconnection price equivalent to the price paid by Telecom's regular business users; the new operators would be required to pay Telecom to be provided with information such as the Automatic Number Identification (ANI) required to enable them to bill their subscribers; and the customers of the new telecommunications operators would have to dial a three- or four-digit access code.[50] Under the terms of the 1991 agreement, on the other hand, interconnection charges were 6 per cent lower than standard business rates, Clear was not required to pay for ANI, and

---

[45] ibid 103,067.

[46] See *Commerce Commission v Telecom Corporation of New Zealand Ltd* (1994) 2 NZLR 421.

[47] ibid 437.

[48] See Milton Mueller, 'On the Frontier of Deregulation: New Zealand Telecommunications and the Problem of Interconnecting Competing Networks' in David Gabel and David F Weiman (eds), *Opening Networks to Competition, The Regulation of Pricing and Access* (Boston, Mass., and Dordrecht: Kluwer Academic Press, 1998) 115.

[49] Telecom Corporation of New Zealand Ltd, *Interconnection Guidebook*, July 1989.

[50] See Milton Mueller (n 48 above) 114.

Telecom agreed to eliminate the access code once Clear's share of the long-distance market exceeded 9 per cent.[51]

However, in 1993, a dispute arose between Clear and Telecom over several interconnection issues and the parties decided to go to arbitration before a retired Court of Appeal judge.[52] Clear argued, inter alia, that Telecom had been late in providing non-code access after the 9 per cent threshold had been reached and that Telecom had charged an unreasonable price for granting non-code access to Clear. With respect to the last point, Clear sought an order from the arbitrator setting a fair price. After a protracted hearing which lasted thirteen weeks and involved a large number of expert witnesses, Clear obtained satisfaction on both counts.[53] The arbitrator ruled that Telecom had been four months late in granting Clear non-code access[54] and he set the charges to be paid by Clear to obtain non-code access at a much lower level than that originally fixed by Telecom.[55]

2.2 BellSouth–Telecom Mobile Interconnection

BellSouth started negotiations on GSM interconnection with Telecom in February 1992 and an agreement was concluded by mid-1993. It proved less advantageous for BellSouth than the agreement Clear had previously secured with regard to long-distance services, BellSouth had to pay slightly more than the standard charge for business users and was required to pay for ANI information. While it did enter into the agreement, BellSouth indicated that it was dissatisfied with several of its terms.[56] Some provisions of the agreement—such as the obligation imposed upon BellSouth to obtain Telecom's authorization prior to concluding agreements on interconnection with third parties—were in fact later dropped because of their obviously anti-competitive nature.[57]

2.3 Clear–Telecom Local Loop Interconnection

The cases that have constituted the main test of New Zealand's regulatory model prior to the 2001 reforms are the cases that opposed Clear Communications and Telecom between 1991 and 1995.[58] Clear, which was already competing with

---

[51] ibid 115–116.

[52] See Sir Duncan McMullin, *Clear Communications Ltd v Telecom Corporation of New Zealand Ltd*, interim award, 26 March 1994.

[53] See Rex J Ahdar, 'Battles in New Zealand's Deregulated Telecommunications Industry' (1995) 23 *Australian Business L Rev* 110–111.

[54] See 'interim award' (n 52 above) 76.

[55] ibid 107.

[56] BellSouth's Managing Director wrote: '(the Government) believed that monopoly minus regulation would equal competition. In fact, monopoly minus regulation equals regulation by monopoly'. See Carl Blanchard, 'Telecommunications Regulation in New Zealand—How Effective is Light-Handed Regulation?' (1994) 18 *Telecommunications Policy* 154, 159.

[57] See Mueller (n 48 above) 118–119.

[58] Numerous articles have been devoted to the analysis of these cases. See, for example, Colleen Flood, 'Regulation of Telecommunications in New Zealand—Faith in Competition Law and the Kiwi Share' (1995) 3 *Competition and Consumer L J* 214; Ahdar (n 53 above); Mueller (n 48 above); William B Tye and Carlos Lapuerta, 'The Economics of Pricing Network Interconnection: Theory and

Telecom in the long-distance telecommunications market in New Zealand, also wanted to provide local telephone services—mainly to business users—in competition with Telecom. The two companies failed to reach an agreement on the conditions of Clear's access to this segment of the market and Clear introduced an action against Telecom before the courts in an effort to secure conditions which Clear would deem satisfactory.

Two issues did not raise much controversy. The judges agreed that Telecom was in breach of the Commerce Act, s 36 insofar as it sought to force Clear's customers to dial an access code.[59] Telecom's initial position that Clear should pay the same interconnection charges as any of Telecom's large customers with their own switchboards was also considered clearly anti-competitive.[60] However, a much more controversial issue emerged during the course of the proceedings before the High Court, when Telecom changed its position and argued that the Efficient Component Pricing Rule (ECPR), better known in New Zealand as the Baumol–Willig rule, should be used to determine the interconnection price.[61] Clear, for its part, argued that the ECPR was contrary to the Commerce Act, s 36 because it would force Clear to underwrite Telecom's monopoly profits.

The High Court recognized that application of the ECPR would enable Telecom to recover its economic costs as well as monopoly profits.[62] It indicated however that the rule would compensate Telecom for having to meet its universal service obligations, while still enabling Clear to enter the market if it were more efficient than Telecom.[63] In that case, according to the Court, Clear would be able to attract users by charging them less than Telecom; Telecom in turn would need to lower its prices and as a result, the profits for which it would have to be compensated under the ECPR would decrease. Applying the rule would thus result in the progressive disappearance of monopoly profits if they existed.[64]

Application to the Market for Telecommunications in New Zealand' (1996) 13 *Yale J on Regulation* 419; Carl Blanchard, 'Telecommunications Regulation in New Zealand—The Court of Appeal's Decision in Clear Communications v. Telecom Corporation' (1994) 18 *Telecommunications Policy* 725; Carl Blanchard, 'Telecommunications Regulation in New Zealand—Light-Handed Regulation and the Privy Council's Judgement' (1995) 19 *Telecommunications Policy* 465; Valentine Korah, 'Charges for Inter-Connection to a Telecommunications Network' (1995) 2 *Competition and Consumer L J* 213; George A Hay, 'Reflections on Clear' (1996) 3 *Competition and Consumer L J* 231; Warren Pengilley, 'The Privy Council Speaks on Essential Facilities Access in New Zealand: What are the Australasian Lessons?' (1995) 3 *Competition and Consumer L J* 28; Michael Carter and Julian Wright, *Bargaining over Interconnection: The Clear-Telecom Dispute*, Center for Research in Network Economics and Communications, University of Auckland, Working Paper No 13, 1997.

[59] See *Clear Communications Ltd v Telecom Corporation of New Zealand Ltd* (1992) 5 TCLR 166.

[60] ibid 188.

[61] On the ECPR, see the seminal article of William J Baumol and J Gregory Sidak, 'The Pricing of Inputs Sold To Competitors' (1994) 11 *Yale J on Regulation* 171, and the response by Alfred E Kahn and William E Taylor, 'The Pricing of Inputs Sold To Competitors: A Comment' (1994) 11 *Yale J on Regulation* 225. See also Mark Armstrong, Chris Doyle and John Vickers, 'The Access Pricing Problem: A Synthesis' (1996) 44 *J of Industrial Economics* 131–150.

[62] See *Clear Communications Ltd v Telecom Corporation of New Zealand Ltd* (n 59 above) 212.

[63] ibid 217.

[64] ibid 215.

Under those conditions, application of the rule would not reveal an anti-competitive purpose and would therefore not violate the Commerce Act, s 36.[65] In its conclusions, the Court did not impose any specific interconnection price on the parties but urged them to resume negotiations and to resolve their differences within the framework provided by the Court.[66]

Clear then lodged an appeal against the decision of the High Court.[67] The Court of Appeal overturned the High Court's ruling. It questioned, on two grounds, the finding of the High Court that application of the ECPR would enable competition to eliminate monopoly profits progressively. First, the Court of Appeal suggested that, instead of engaging in price competition with Clear and seeing its profits progressively disappear, Telecom might prefer to keep its prices high in order to retain its profits through a high interconnection charge, even if that meant that some of its subscribers would be captured by Clear.[68] Second, the Court of Appeal argued that even if Telecom did lower its prices to match Clear's prices, the requirement that frequent price reviews be carried out to reassess the value of the interconnection charge under the ECPR would give rise to continual disputes between the parties and would be incompatible with the Commerce Act.[69] The Court of Appeal concluded that application of the ECPR would amount to imposing upon a new entrant an obligation that it indemnify the monopolist for any loss of profits,[70] that this would put the new entrant at a competitive disadvantage and that, in those conditions, an anti-competitive purpose could be assumed.[71] The Court indicated that the interconnection price should be based on the incremental costs involved in providing interconnection services and a reasonable return on capital.[72] It stated, however, that it could not go as far as to determine a specific interconnection price as it was not a price-fixing authority.[73]

Telecom, then, contested the judgment of the Court of Appeal before the Privy Council.[74] The Privy Council, in turn, rejected the decision of the Court of Appeal and ruled, as the High Court had originally done, that application of the ECPR would not violate the Commerce Act, s 36. To reach that conclusion, the High Court had focused on the purpose pursued by Telecom. The Privy Council focused instead on the concept of use of a dominant position. It considered that in charging Clear its opportunity cost for interconnection with the local loop, Telecom would not be using its dominant position since it would be acting in the same way as firms in a competitive market which also seek to recover the opportunity costs of providing goods or services to competitors.[75]

---

[65] ibid 218.
[66] ibid 220.
[67] See *Clear Communications Ltd v Telecom Corporation of New Zealand Ltd* (1993) 4 NZBLC 103,340.
[68] ibid 103,343.   [69] ibid 103,343.   [70] ibid 103,343.
[71] ibid 103,360–103,361.   [72] ibid 103,363–103,364.   [73] ibid 103,364.
[74] See *Telecom Corporation of New Zealand Ltd v Clear Communications Ltd* (1994) 4 TCLR 138.
[75] ibid 159.

The Privy Council accepted the findings of the High Court that application of the ECPR would enable competition to eliminate monopoly profits progressively if they existed and rejected the Court of Appeal's argument that the need for continuing price reviews would infringe the Commerce Act.[76] The Privy Council added that, in any case, s 36 could only deal with monopoly pricing in an indirect way by ensuring that competition was introduced in the market, as other provisions existed within the Commerce Act, such as those on price control in Part IV, which the Government could use if it wanted to control pricing directly.[77] In the end, the parties were, once again, left with the task of trying to reach a specific agreement that would conform to the Court's judgment.[78]

Various offers and counter-offers were made by Clear and Telecom in the following months. In July 1995, the Government indicated to the parties that it would consider intervening directly if an agreement was not reached within a limited period of time.[79] An agreement was finally signed in March 1996, with interconnection prices below ECPR levels. Since then, interconnection agreements between local networks have been renegotiated and Telecom has concluded with Clear, and with TelstraSaturn, agreements which provide for 'bill and keep' (or 'peering arrangements') when certain conditions are met (in particular when traffic flows are roughly in balance).[80]

3. Price Discrimination in the Local Market

Saturn launched a residential telephone service in the Wellington area in 1998, with a rate of NZ$29.95 per month compared to Telecom's NZ$35.66 (with both companies offering unlimited local calls at no additional cost). Telecom responded by offering an option that reduced the standard residential service price to a level comparable to that offered by Saturn. This option was, however, available only in the areas served by Saturn. The Commerce Commission investigated whether this instance of price discrimination was contrary to s 27 (which prohibits arrangements that lessen competition in a market) or to s 36 (which prohibits abuses of dominant positions) of the Commerce Act. The Commerce Commission stated that if Telecom had reduced prices below costs through cross-subsidization from areas where it was making monopoly profit, the Commerce Act would likely have been breached. In this case, however, the Commerce Commission found no evidence that Telecom had priced services

---

[76] ibid 160.

[77] ibid 160–161.

[78] See 'Clear Seeks Intervention in Communications Row' *Otago Daily Times*, 21 October 1994, 3, where Clear's Chief Executive was quoted as saying: 'The one thing this judgement is not is the final resolution.'

[79] See Malcom Webb and Martyn Taylor, 'Light-Handed Regulation of Telecommunications in New Zealand: Is Generic Competition Law Sufficient?' (Winter 1998/99) 2 *Intl J of Telecommunications L and Policy* 1, 3.

[80] See Ministry of Economic Development, 'New Zealand Communications 1987–2001' (August 2001) 24, available at <http://www.med.govt.nz/pbt/telecom/tip8/tip8.pdf>.

below costs and it considered therefore that the offering of regional price discounts constituted a legal response to competition from Saturn.[81] In January 2001, Telecom announced a new monthly residential rate of NZ$29.95 in both Wellington and Christchurch, just ahead of TelstraSaturn's launch, in March, of a new residential cable service in Christchurch.[82]

4. Numbering, Pre-Selection and Roaming

Prior to the 2001 reforms, not only interconnection, but also a series of other technical issues such as numbering, pre-selection and roaming were left to the parties to negotiate. The New Zealand Telecommunications Numbering Advisory Group (NZTNAG) had been set up to discuss numbering issues and to provide advice to the Minister of Communications on those issues. All significant carriers and representatives from the New Zealand Consumers' Institute and from the Telecommunications Users Association of New Zealand were entitled to join the NZTNAG, which operated by way of consensus.[83]

The NZTNAG agreed that call forwarding would provide an acceptable interim solution for number portability and that commercial and other technical terms relating to number portability were to be determined through negotiated agreements between operators.[84] The Commerce Commission, for its part, warned that parties who would adopt 'unreasonable positions' on number portability and thus delay agreements could potentially be violating the Commerce Act, s 36.[85] In August 1998, as little progress had been made, the Minister of Communications set a deadline of 30 November for the industry to reach agreement on numbering administration and portability issues.[86] In December 1998, five companies signed an agreement called the Number Administration Deed which set out principles for the independent administration of numbers, a process to determine long-term number portability solutions, and binding arbitration to resolve disputes.[87] The parties applied to the Commission for

[81] See Ministerial Inquiry into Telecommunications, 'Issues Paper' (April 2000) 25, available at <http://www.teleinquiry.govt.nz/reports/issues/issues.pdf>. See also Commerce Commission, 'Commission will not intervene in Telecom move to match Saturn's prices', media release 1998/61, available at <http://www.comcom.govt.nz/publications/display_mr.cfm?mr_id=422>.

[82] See 'New Zealand Communications 1987–2001' (n 80 above) 16.

[83] ibid 5; and Webb and Taylor (n 79 above) 11.

[84] Dennis Campbell (ed), *International Communications Law* (Washington, DC: BNA International Inc, 2000) 82.

[85] See Alan Bollard and Rae Ellingham, *Regulation in New Zealand Telecommunications: The Regulatory Body's Perspective*, AIC Conference, Competition, Customer Care and Retention in New Zealand Telecommunications, Stamford Plaza, Auckland, 28 October 1997, 8.

[86] See Ministry of Economic Development (n 80 above) 9.

[87] The five companies that signed the agreement are Newcall Communications Ltd, Teamtalk Ltd, Telecom New Zealand Ltd, Telstra New Zealand Ltd, and Vodafone New Zealand Ltd. Other companies will be able to become signatories under the same terms and conditions. Local telephone numbers are currently being ported using call forwarding. Call forwarding is, however, incompatible with some intelligent network functions such as calling line identification and it introduces a small delay while the call is transferred. This is why the Deed establishes a process to identify more advanced, long-term number portability solutions. See Commerce Commission Media Release

authorization because the Deed might have been in breach of the Commerce Act. That authorization was granted in May 1999.[88] Some additional operators did become parties to the Deed after that date.[89]

Pre-selection for long-distance fixed to fixed calls originating in New Zealand had been negotiated commercially prior to the recent reforms. However, carrier pre-selection for fixed-to-mobile calls did not exist, nor did roaming.[90]

5. Spectrum Allocation

New Zealand has launched an interesting experiment with respect to the allocation of the radio-electric spectrum. Whereas, in most countries, spectrum rights allocated to private operators are precisely defined and specify, for example, the type of technology to be used, the Radiocommunications Act 1989, as pointed out in Section B, above, introduced the concept of technology-neutral, tradable, spectrum management rights, which leave the spectrum manager complete freedom to determine how the spectrum is to be used.[91]

The first three tenders for spectrum allocation were conducted through a sealed-bid, second-price auction; the next three were auctioned by sealed-bid, first-price auctions; and after that, in 1997, the Government decided to shift to simultaneous, ascending, multiple-round auctions.[92] Management rights applicable to frequencies suitable for cellular telephony were auctioned as part of the second tender in 1990 (the other tenders concerned mainly frequencies suitable for television and radio services). This process gave rise to a number of issues.

First, it was feared that Telecom would strengthen its dominant position in the market in violation of the Commerce Act, s 47. The first round of tenders took place in 1990 and concerned three cellular bands: the so-called AMPS-A, TACS-A and TACS-B bands. Telecom, which was already providing cellular services on AMPS-B bands and which owned the public network, won the AMPS-A and TACS-B bands while BellSouth won the TACS-A band. The Commerce Commission refused to clear the acquisition of the AMPS-A band by Telecom because it considered that it would strengthen its dominant position in the mobile telephony market. It further refused to grant an authorization to Telecom because, in its view, the efficiency gains that Telecom could derive from adding the AMPS-A band to the AMPS-B band that it already possessed would be more

1999/64, available at <http://www.comcom.govt.nz/publications/display_mr.cfm?mr_id=544>; and Ministerial Inquiry into Telecommunications (n 81 above) 26.

[88] See Ministry of Economic Development, 'New Zealand Telecommunications 1987–2000', New Zealand Telecommunications Information Publication No 7 (February 2000) 12.

[89] See Ministerial Inquiry into Telecommunications, Final Report (27 September 2000) 72.

[90] ibid 75 and 77.

[91] See text accompanying nn 21–22 above.

[92] See Robert W Crandall, 'New Zealand Spectrum Policy: A Model for the United States?' (1998) XLI *J of L and Economics* 828.

than compensated by the risk that strengthened dominance would increase Telecom's internal inefficiency.[93] Following an appeal by Telecom, the Commerce Commission's decision was confirmed by the High Court on similar grounds.[94]

Acquisition of the TACS-B band was, for its part, cleared by the Commission subject to a commitment by Telecom to divest itself of this band should it win back the AMPS-A band on appeal.[95] The Commission's decision to clear the acquisition of the TACS-B band by Telecom was, however, overturned on appeal. The High Court considered that the Commission had failed to give Broadcast Communications Ltd (BCL) a proper opportunity to be heard when the issue of Telecom's commitment arose.[96] It also stated that the Commission had applied an incorrect test to determine whether the acquisition of the band was likely to strengthen Telecom's market dominance and that application of the correct test would reveal that a strengthening of dominance was, in fact, likely.

Telecom then lodged an appeal against both High Court decisions before the Court of Appeal.[97] The Court of Appeal only ruled on the acquisition of the AMPS-A band, however, because shortly after the High Court decisions were rendered, tenders were reopened for the award of the TACS-B band and this band was eventually sold to Telecom Australia (later to become Telstra).[98] The Court of Appeal, while applying a narrower definition of dominance than the High Court, still concluded that acquisition of the AMPS-A band would enable Telecom to strengthen its dominant position in the mobile market. However, two years had elapsed since the High Court's decision, and this proved beneficial to Telecom. BellSouth's entry into the mobile market was, by then, imminent and a third operator, Telstra, had acquired a cellular licence. Consequently, the Court of Appeal considered that the risk that Telecom's increased dominance would lead to internal inefficiency was minimized because of the competition that Telecom was about to face, while the efficiency gains which Telecom would realize if it obtained the AMPS-A band could enable substantial cost savings.[99] For these reasons, the Court decided to authorize Telecom's acquisition of the AMPS-A band.[100]

A second issue related to the variability of the revenues raised by different auctions. As indicated above, the Government awarded the cellular bands

---

[93] See *Telecom Corporation of New Zealand Ltd/The Crown*, Commerce Commission Decision No 254 (17 October 1990).

[94] See *Telecom Corporation of New Zealand Ltd v Commerce Commission* (1991) 3 NZBLC 102,340.

[95] See Telecom Mobile Radio Ltd/The Crown, Commerce Commission Decision No 256, 30 November 1990.

[96] See *Broadcast Communications Ltd v Commerce Commission* (1991) 3 NZBLC 102,391 and 102,404.

[97] See *Telecom Corporation of New Zealand Ltd v Commerce Commission* (1992) 3 NZLR 429.

[98] See Rex J Ahdar, 'Battles in New Zealand's Deregulated Telecommunications Industry' (1995) 23 *Australian Business L Rev* 78, 89.

[99] ibid 89–92.

[100] See *Telecom Corporation of New Zealand Ltd v Commerce Commission* (n 94 above) 439.

through second-price auctions and while the highest bids for the AMPS-A and TACS-A auctions were close to one another, there was more than a two-fold difference between the second-highest bids which determined the revenues raised by each auction. It is, in part, to avoid this problem that the Government switched to first-price auctions after the first three tenders and then to simultaneous, ascending, multiple-round auctions in 1997.

Finally, a third issue is that users have, so far, failed to make full use of the possibility to resell spectrum rights and switch between different uses that the system was expressly designed to promote. Telstra, for example, kept its TACS-B band for years without making use of it and to this day, only Telecom and Vodafone (which bought BellSouth in August 1998) have been active in the mobile market.[101] In order to inject more competition into the market, the Government initiated, at the end of 2000, an auction for the acquisition of 3G spectrum. It imposed a limit to the portion of the spectrum that any single operator could acquire in order to enable four parties to acquire 3G spectrum.[102] The auction was concluded in January 2001. Telecom, Clear, Vodafone and TelstraSaturn all purchased 3G spectrum.[103]

6. I4free v Telecom

Before the recent negotiation of 'bill and keep' arrangements, the local loop interconnection agreement between Telecom and Clear required each party to pay for the calls which terminated on the other operator's network. While below ECPR levels, the interconnection price was higher than the expenses actually incurred to provide the interconnection service, which gave each operator an incentive to maximize the number of calls terminating on its own network. In order to increase the termination payments it would receive from Telecom, Clear aggressively signed up ISPs, offering to share with them the interconnection payments it would receive from Telecom. Telecom then induced ISPs to adopt a number starting with the 0867 prefix by announcing that it would charge Internet users two cents per minute (after the first ten hours per month) if those users did not use the 0867 prefix. Telecom also offered financial incentives to prompt ISPs to move from Clear to Telecom. Clear fought back by taking advantage of its number portability agreement with Telecom. It convinced some ISPs, such as i4free, to switch from Telecom to Clear while keeping their 0867 number under the number portability agreement, thus ensuring that users would still avoid the two cent surcharge.

---

[101] See Robert W Crandall, 'New Zealand Spectrum Policy: A Model for the United States?' (1998) XLI *J of L and Economics* 837.

[102] See Ministerial Inquiry into Telecommunications, Final Report (27 September 2000) 76, available at <http://www.teleinquiry.govt.nz>.

[103] See Ministry of Economic Development, 'New Zealand Communications 1987–2001' (August 2001) 16.

Telecom claimed that it had introduced the 0867 prefix in order to better manage its network and protect it from network overload. Telecom argued that when an ISP's servers suffered a serious fault and disconnected Internet users, Telecom was besieged by incoming calls because computers are configured to call the ISP back automatically and repeatedly. Telecom stated that the 0867 prefix facilitated identification of Internet traffic and enabled the company to restrict access to a malfunctioning server until the problem was resolved. Telecom said that by migrating to Clear with its 0867 number, i4free undermined the network management system described above and that, in addition, i4free had breached its contract with Telecom which prohibited the ISP from terminating calls on a network other than that of Telecom. For those reasons, Telecom disconnected i4free in April 2000.

Many experts were doubtful about the validity of Telecom's arguments. Most of them considered: that Telecom had failed to provide compelling evidence of significant threat to its network; that if such a threat existed, it was due to underinvestment on Telecom's part; and that, in fact, Telecom introduced the 0867 prefix to stifle competition in the provision of wholesale services to ISPs. The latter claim was based on several grounds: Telecom refused to make termination payments to Clear and its other competitors for 0867 calls; Telecom did not impose the 0867 prefix on its own ISP Xtra (which retained its previous 0873 access code), thereby protecting Xtra's users from the disruption caused by having to use a new prefix; and it provided Xtra with information about traffic to other ISPs which, theoretically, could be used by Xtra for marketing purposes.[104]

The High Court issued an injunction to prevent Telecom from disconnecting i4free.[105] In May 2000, Telecom and Clear reached an agreement under which Internet users will not pay a two-cent per minute charge to call Clear's non-0867 ISPs while Clear will encourage users to utilize the 0867 service.[106] Finally, in August 2000, the Commerce Commission initiated action against Telecom for an alleged breach of the Commerce Act Part II.[107]

7. Telecom's Undertakings

One issue that has resurfaced, recently, concerns Telecom's undertakings. The company has in fact proceeded to amalgamate its different businesses (the regional local telephone companies and the long-distance and mobile companies) contrary to the engagements it had taken in its 1988 letter. It is arguing that the 1988 letter provided information on intended restructuring and other

[104] See Ministerial Inquiry into Telecommunications, 'Issues Paper' (April 2000) 18, available at <http://www.teleinquiry.govt.nz/reports/issues/issues.pdf>.
[105] See New Zealand Herald Online, Court order gets i4free back in 0867 game (4 April 2000), available at <http://www.NewZealandHerald.com>.
[106] See 'New Zealand Communications 1987–2001' (n 103 above) 13.
[107] See 'Final Report' (n 102 above) 97.

matters to Telecom's shareholders but did not and was not intended to constitute legally enforceable commitments.[108] As a result, the usefulness of the Disclosure Regulations was reduced (for example, the interconnection agreement between Telecom and its mobile subsidiary which originally was a public document, is not publicly disclosed any more following the amalgamation of Telecom's various businesses). Clear has initiated proceedings against Telecom for having failed to comply with its obligations and against the Government for having failed to enforce the undertakings.[109]

8. Reviews and Modifications of the Regulatory Framework

Several important reviews of the New Zealand regulatory framework have been conducted over the last decade.

8.1 Government's Report on Access to Natural Monopolies

The long dispute between Clear and Telecom over the conditions of local loop interconnection led the Government to undertake an analysis of the issues associated with access to vertically integrated natural monopolies. In an Officials' Report published in 1996, the Government stated that it would continue for the time being with the current regulatory regime based on the Commerce Act, coupled with the threat of imposing further regulation.[110] The Government also issued a press release, however, which revealed that it had serious concerns with the Privy Council's ruling on the legality of the ECPR. The press release indicated that the Government would be concerned if the rule was applied in the future as it considered that the ECPR had the potential to restrict competition.[111]

8.2 Commerce Act Amendments

Following a consultation process initiated in January 1998 with the publication of a discussion paper on how to strengthen enforcement of the Commerce Act,[112] the Government announced that it would introduce a range of changes to the Commerce Act. Some modifications were made in 1999 to increase the range of price control mechanisms that the Commerce Commission could impose under the Commerce Act, Part IV.[113] In April 2000, the Government

---

[108] Ross Patterson, 'Light-Handed Regulation in New Zealand Ten Years On: Stimulus to Competition or Monopolist's Charter?', paper distributed at the TUANZ Competition Symposium, Wellington, New Zealand, 7–8 April 1998, 27.

[109] See Dennis Campbell (ed), *International Communications Law* (Washington, DC: BNA International Inc, 2000) 29.

[110] See Office of the Ministers of Commerce and Communications, 'Regulation of Access to Natural Monopolies – Officials' Report', June 1996.

[111] See 'Government signals future directions for regulation of telecommunications, electricity and gas', press release, 26 June 1996.

[112] Ministry of Economic Development, 'Penalties, Remedies and Court Processes under the Commerce Act 1986: A Discussion Document' (Wellington, New Zealand, January 1998).

[113] See Commerce (Controlled Goods or Services) Amendment Bill, 295-1, Explanatory Note, at 1, available at <http://www.med.govt.nz/ers/electric/control1999/bill295-1.html#a3>.

announced further changes. Thus the Commerce Act, s 36, has been modified to apply to behaviours which amount to taking advantage of a substantial degree of market power (rather than to the use of a dominant position). The objective is to broaden the scope of application of s 36, after the very narrow interpretation given by the Privy Council to the concept of use of a dominant position in the *Telecom v Clear* case on local interconnection.[114] Section 47 has also been modified to prohibit acquisitions that would have the effect of substantially lessening competition in a market (rather than the acquisitions that result in any person acquiring or strengthening a dominant position). Once again the goal is to broaden the scope of application of the provision. Finally, penalties for breach of the Commerce Act have been increased and companies are prohibited from indemnifying their agents with respect to pecuniary penalties imposed for price fixing arrangements.[115]

8.3 Ministerial Inquiry into Telecommunications

In February 2000, the Government announced the launch of a Ministerial Inquiry into Telecommunications aimed at assessing whether changes to the regulatory environment for telecommunications would be warranted. The Inquiry concluded that New Zealand's policy of heavy reliance on general competition law had fallen short of expectations in some respect and that a number of new sector-specific rules were necessary:

• First, some services should be 'specified' or 'designated' by the Minister of Communications. Providers of specified services would be required to abide by a number of technical conditions in order to ensure that access seekers are provided with the service in a timely and non-discriminatory manner. Providers of designated services would, in addition, have to abide by certain pricing rules when granting access to the service. The Inquiry considered that three services provided by Telecom on its fixed wire network should be designated immediately: (i) interconnection; (ii) leasing of local loop capacity to provide data service to end-users; and (iii) resale of retail services. It stated that access prices should be based on TSLRIC methodology for the first two types of services while a 'retail-minus' method (ie retail prices minus avoidable costs—similar to ECPR) should be used for the resale of retail services. The Inquiry suggested a two-step process to calculate such prices: a first estimation would be based on international benchmarking and would be followed, if one of the parties contested this first estimation, by a final decision based on the application of the relevant pricing methodology to the specific case at issue. The Inquiry recommended, in addition, that number administration and portability be designated on a deferred basis, ie that it be designated if no agreement had been reached by July 2001 under the provisions of the Number Administration

[114] See text accompanying n 75 above.
[115] See Ministry of Economic Development, 'Review of the Competition Thresholds in the Commerce Act 1986 and Related Issues: A Discussion Document' (Wellington, New Zealand, April 1999).

Deed.[116] The Inquiry argued against immediately designating local loop un-bundling but indicated that this designation should be considered in the future if it appeared that Telecom was investing insufficiently in enhanced services (eg xDSL) or hindering the resale of retail services. Specified services, for their part, would include, among others, interconnection and carrier pre-selection on all networks, as well as resale of mobile services and roaming.[117]

- Second, some modifications should be made to the Kiwi Share regime: the Kiwi Share obligations should be better defined and embodied in legislation; Telecom should be required to ensure that ordinary residential services con-tinue to be as widely available as they are today (rather than as they were on 11 September 1990 when the Kiwi Share was created); the concept of ordinary residential services for which Telecom must make a local free-calling option available should include low-speed Internet access; and the price-cap regime imposed upon residential line rentals should be maintained, but Telecom should be released from the obligation to keep the price of rural residential line rentals no higher than that of urban rentals. The Inquiry indicated that, in its view, further investment by Telecom was required to ensure provision of reliable voice service and low-speed data access to residential customers. It stated that Telecom should bear the costs of the Kiwi Share obligations unless it could prove that its overall profitability was unreasonably impaired and it recommended strict monitoring of Telecom's compliance with the Kiwi Share obligations. Finally, the Inquiry argued that organising competitive tenders to determine which operator should be responsible for ensuring that the Kiwi Share obligations are met would be too complex and it considered therefore that Telecom should retain full responsibility in that respect.[118]
- Third, the Minister should be able to require the resale of any radio-spectrum that is not being used.[119]

The Inquiry also argued for significant reforms of the regulatory institutions:

- First, a sector-specific regulator, the Electronic Communication Commissioner (ECC), should be established, with an office of about eight to ten people and a budget of about NZ$1.5 million, funded through an industry levy. The ECC would rule on the access terms of specified and designated services when parties are unable to reach an agreement. The ECC's decisions could be enforced through the Courts by any party to the agreement. Appeals against the decisions of the ECC could be lodged before the High Court, which could review decisions both on factual and legal grounds.[120] The ECC would make recommendations to the Minister regarding the addition or removal of ser-vices from the list of specified or designated services and would monitor Telecom's execution of its obligations.[121]

---

[116] See text accompanying nn 87–89 above.

[117] See Ministerial Inquiry into Telecommunications, Final Report (27 September 2000) 42–81, available at <http://www.teleinquiry.govt.nz>.

[118] ibid 82–91.   [119] ibid 99.   [120] ibid 28–37.   [121] ibid 43–44.

- An Electronic Communications Industry Forum, made up of telecommunications operators, would be established. Its main role would be to develop codes of conduct with respect to specified and designated services at the request of the ECC or on its own initiative. Codes would need to be approved by the ECC before taking effect.[122]
- Before making a final pricing review determination or a recommendation to designate or specify a new service, the ECC would need to hold public hearings.[123]

8.4 *Response to the Telecommunications Inquiry*

On 20 December 2000, the Minister of Communications announced that a number of reforms would be implemented in response to the recommendations of the Inquiry.[124] A Telecommunications Act has been adopted in December 2001. It contains a number of new sector-specific rules:

- The new legislation integrates the concepts of designated and specified services suggested by the Inquiry. The designated and specified services, however, vary, in some respects, from those recommended by the Inquiry. Designated services include: interconnection with Telecom's fixed network (as recommended by the Inquiry); interconnection with other operators' fixed networks (which the Inquiry proposed to specify); resale of retail services (as recommended by the Inquiry); number portability (which the Inquiry had recommended to designate on a deferred basis); and Telecom's fixed network to mobile carrier pre-selection (while the Inquiry had argued for specifying pre-selection on all networks). Specified services for their part include roaming, among others, as recommended by the Inquiry. In line with the Inquiry's recommendations, the Government decided not to designate local loop unbundling for the time being; the Commerce Commission is however required to submit within two years to the Minister of Communications a report on whether or not local loop unbundling should be a designated or a specified service. The pricing methodology to calculate interconnection prices is TSLRIC (as recommended by the Inquiry) or—if the Commerce Commission considers that TSLRIC would not be best to promote competition for the benefit of end-users—either a pure 'bill and keep' method or a combination of TSLRIC and 'bill and keep'. A 'retail-minus' pricing methodology is to be used for the resale of retail services, as recommended by the Inquiry. The Baumol–Willig rule, for its part, is expressly excluded as a potential pricing method. Finally, a two-step pricing methodology has been adopted along the lines of what was suggested by the Inquiry, with an initial determination followed, if a party objects, by a pricing review determination (see Box 5.1 below).[125]

---

[122] ibid 38–41. [123] Appendix 5, Sections 46 and 54.

[124] See Ministry of Economic Development, Government Response to the Telecommunications Inquiry, Telecommunications: Summary of Government Decisions, available at <http://www.med.govt.nz/pbt/telecom/response/index.html>.

[125] See Telecommunications Act 2001, Sch 1 and s 59A.

Box 5.1: *Pricing Methodology Adopted in the Telecommunications Act 2001*

The Telecommunications Act 2001 opts for a two-step process to resolve disputes over pricing principles for a designated service: (i) the Commission bases its initial determination on international benchmarking; (ii) if one of the parties contests the initial determination, the Commissioner issues a pricing review determination based upon a more thorough analysis.

For interconnection with Telecom's fixed network, the initial determination is derived from benchmarking of similar prices in comparable countries that result from the application to networks similar to that of the incumbent of a TSLRIC method, a pure 'bill and keep' method, or a combination of TSLRIC and 'bill and keep' as the case may be. The pricing review determination is based, for its part, on application of the relevant methodology to the specific case at issue.

A similar process is followed with respect to interconnection with networks other than Telecom's, except that at both the initial and final stage, the Commission can choose to rely on a price that it would have determined for interconnection with a network of Telecom's that corresponds closely to the access provider's network.

For resale of retail services, initial determination would be based on Telecom's retail price less a discount set by benchmarking. The pricing review determination would be based on Telecom's retail price minus Telecom's avoided costs.

Source: Telecommunications Act 2001, Sch 1.

- The Kiwi Share regime has been updated by an agreement reached between the Government and Telecom in December 2001. The new regime corresponds to a large extent to the proposals of the Inquiry. For example, network coverage obligations are extended to reflect current coverage levels; the local free-calling option includes standard calls to the Internet as well as fax calls; the price-cap regime imposed upon residential line rentals is maintained but Telecom may offer lower prices, including prices differentiated on a geographical basis if it wishes (which eliminates the 'geographical averaging' previously imposed upon line rental prices); and Telecom must provide reliable data service capability of at least 9.6 kilobits per second to 99 per cent of residential lines and of 14.4 kbps to 95 per cent of residential lines within two years. The monitoring regime is also strengthened and Telecom is required to present, at least annually, an audited report on its performance against a number of service quality measures.[126] Finally, the Government concurred with the

---

[126] See Telecommunications Service Obligations (TSO) Deed for Local Residential Telephone Service, December 2001, s 7, s 21 and Sch Part II, available at <http://www.med. govt.nz/pbt/ telecom/deed/index.html>.

Inquiry that tendering out the Kiwi Share obligations would be highly complex and should not be undertaken for the time being. It announced, however, that it intended to reconsider the issue after a year.[127] On two specific issues, the Government did adopt a position different from that recommended by the Inquiry: (i) it did not see a need to embody the Kiwi Share obligations in legislation given that Telecom agreed to enter into a revised arrangement encompassing the obligations described above; and (ii) it considered that other operators should contribute to the net costs incurred by Telecom because of the Kiwi Share obligations. The Commerce Commission will calculate these costs on an annual basis and allocate them to all network operators which have interconnected with Telecom's network and to Telecom itself. The level of each operator's contributions will be based on that operator's share of relevant telecommunications revenues and payments will be made directly to Telecom rather than indirectly through the interconnection price as was the case before. The Commerce Commission can reduce the revenues to be transferred to Telecom if Telecom has not fulfilled its Kiwi Share obligations.[128]

• Contrary to the Inquiry, the Government considered that it was unnecessary to impose 'use or sell' requirements with respect to the radio spectrum.

The Government also reformed the regulatory institutions. While substantial, these reforms differ, to some extent, from those recommended by the Inquiry:

• A Telecommunications Commissioner is responsible for resolving access disputes, making recommendations to the Minister of Communications on further designations or specifications, and monitoring execution of the Kiwi Share obligations. As recommended by the Inquiry, the cost of carrying out telecommunications-specific regulatory functions is to be covered by an industry levy. Contrary to the recommendations of the Inquiry, however, there is no separate regulatory body for telecommunications. The Telecommunications Commissioner is a specialist Commissioner, with specialist staff, within the Commerce Commission. When making determinations with respect to designated services or with respect to the allocation of universal service costs, the Telecommunications Commissioner must decide jointly with two other Commissioners. When the Telecommunications Commissioner recommends modifications to the list of designated or specified services, its report must include the views of two other members of the Commission. In all other cases, for example, to solve disputes pertaining to specified services, the Telecommunications Commissioner can act alone.[129] The Minister can only accept or reject a recommendation by the Commission to modify the list of designated or specified services—ie the Minister cannot act alone in this area.[130] Finally,

---

[127] See Ministry of Economic Development, 'Government Announces Updated Kiwi Share Obligation' 4, available at <http://www.med.govt.nz/pbt/telecom/minister20011218b.html>.
[128] See Telecommunications Act, ss 73–86.   [129] ibid s 10.   [130] ibid s 64.

appeals against the decisions of the Commission can be lodged before the High Court, but—contrary to the recommendations of the Inquiry—on legal grounds only.[131]

- Industry participants have been invited to set up an Industry Forum. As suggested by the Inquiry, the Forum can develop codes on access principles for designated or specified services at the request of the Commission or on its own initiative, and those codes need to be approved by the Commission before being implemented.[132]
- As recommended by the Inquiry, consultation mechanisms have been strengthened: the Commission needs to consult or hold public hearings before making determinations on access conditions or recommendations to modify the list of designated or specified services.[133]

E. A CRITICAL APPRAISAL OF THE REGULATORY FRAMEWORK

Unlike in the United States, economic regulation of telecommunications in New Zealand has relied to an unusually high degree upon the implementation of general antitrust law by antitrust authorities, rather than on telecommunications-specific rules and institutions. This is why the term 'light-handed regulation' has been applied to the New Zealand regulatory model.[134] In addition, the main features of the New Zealand model as presented above have been in existence for the past ten years, a sufficient period to enable observers to derive some useful lessons of experience. For these two reasons, the New Zealand model provides a particularly valuable test of the extent to which the seven criteria identified in Chapter 2 can be met through an application of general rather than sector-specific rules and institutions.

1. Competition and Other Incentives to Generate and Share Efficiency Gains

As in all the other countries discussed in the present book, formal legal barriers to entry have been removed in all segments of the telecommunications sector in New Zealand. In some respect, New Zealand did in fact push the liberalization process further than the other countries as telecommunications operators are allowed to provide any type of services without having to obtain licences.[135]

---

[131] ibid s 56.

[132] ibid Sch 3.

[133] ibid ss 22, 34, 46 and 64.

[134] See, for example, Ross Patterson, 'Light-Handed Regulation in New Zealand Ten Years On: Stimulus to Competition or Monopolist's Charter?', paper distributed at the TUANZ Competition Symposium, Wellington, New Zealand, 7–8 April 1998, 27; Malcolm Webb and Martyn Taylor, 'Light-Handed Regulation of Telecommunications in New Zealand: Is Generic Competition Law Sufficient?' (Winter 1998/99) 2 *Intl J of Telecommunications L and Policy* 1.

[135] See text accompanying n 14 above.

A number of anti-competitive practices have been dealt with relatively easily in New Zealand. For example, even in the difficult local access cases, the courts unanimously pronounced that Telecom's attempts to impose an access code upon Clear's customers were anti-competitive.[136] Telecom's attempts to impose upon Clear the same access charge as the one it imposed upon large customers were also identified early on as anti-competitive and so was the obligation imposed upon BellSouth to obtain Telecom's authorization prior to concluding interconnection agreements with third parties. The High Court also reacted quickly to prevent Telecom from disconnecting i4free.

It is clear also that the telecommunications market has become increasingly competitive in New Zealand over the last decade. Telecom is slowly losing market share in the telecommunications industry (see Table 5.1 below).

Telecom, TelstraSaturn (which bought Clear in November 2001 and now operates as TelstraClear), Global One, Worldxchange, Telegroup, Compass, and Newcall are all competing in the international market and statistics of the Ministry of Economic Development tracking the price of a basket of domestic long-distance and international services show a sustained price decline over the 1990s with steeper reductions in recent years (see Figure 5.2 below).

Telecom is also beginning to face some degree of competition in the local market through the launch of residential services by Saturn in Wellington and Christchurch. As pointed out above, this has prompted Telecom to offer more competitive residential rates in these areas.[137]

In the mobile market, Telecom's competitor, Vodafone, is rapidly increasing its share of the market and overall penetration rates have improved quite fast over the last two years (see Table 5.2 below). This might well be due to the fact that the two incumbents are gearing up for a more competitive environment following the recent auction of 3G spectrum which might promote the entry of additional competitors into the mobile market.[138] Such competitive pressures

TABLE 5.1. Market revenue shares in the New Zealand telecommunications market

	1996–97	*1997–98*	*1998–99*	*1999–2000*	*2000–2001*
Telecom	72.5%	71.7%	70.6%	67.8%	66.1%
Clear	6.5%	6.2%	5.6%	5.3%	5.5%
TelstraSaturn	1.6%	1.6%	1.7%	2.2%	2.9%
Vodafone	1.2%	2.1%	3.3%	6.8%	7.7%
Others	18.2%	18.4%	18.8%	17.9%	17.8%

Source: *The Evening Post*, Wellington, NZ, 23 November 2000 and Bruce Christian, Incumbent's Concessions Open New Zealand Market, January 2001, available at <http://www.phoneplusinternational.com/articles/111sec4.html>.

---

[136] See text accompanying n 59 above.   [137] See text accompanying nn 81–82 above.
[138] See text accompanying nn 102–103 above.

FIGURE 5.2. Residential long-distance calls: percentage change of price index

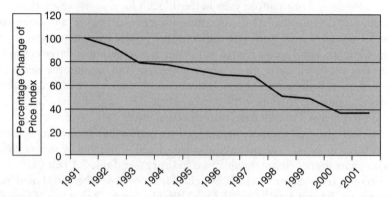

Source: Ministry of Economic Development, *New Zealand Telecommunications 1987–2001*, New Zealand Telecommunications Information Publication No 8, August 2001, 23.

might have contributed in particular to the development of the pre-paid market (on which Vodafone has focused much effort) and to more aggressive marketing and distribution campaigns.[139]

The market for dial-up Internet services appears to exhibit some competitive features as well. Internet penetration is relatively high with 1.3 million Internet users (or about 35 per cent of the population) in 2001.[140] In early 2000, New Zealand had more Internet hosts per 1,000 inhabitants than Australia and the United Kingdom, and more secure servers than the United Kingdom (but slightly less than Australia).[141] While it may contribute to congestion problems in the local loop, the existence of free unmetered local calls certainly helps to limit to some extent the overall price of Internet access and to raise Internet penetration rates.[142] Leased lines can be obtained from various suppliers such as Telecom, TelstraClear, BCL and other firms with microwave transmitting equipment,[143] and this reduces barriers to entry into the ISP market: 36 ISPs have been identified by CyberAtlas in 2001[144] and price competition seems to be increasing between

---

[139] See ABN AMRO, Telecoms Sector Research, *Australian and NZ Mobile Review* (June 2001) 32.

[140] See CyberAtlas, *The World's Online Populations*, available at <http://cyberatlas.internet.com/big_picture/article/0,1323,5911_151151,00.html>.

[141] Boles de Boer, Evans and Howell report two sets of figures—depending on the methodology used—for Internet hosts per 1,000 inhabitants in early 2000: 88.1, 77.3 and 60.3 respectively for New Zealand, Australia and the United Kingdom according to Network Wizards, and 78.6, 60.8 and 40.8 according to Telecordia. The same authors report the following figures for secure servers per one million inhabitants: 119.1, 92.7 and 55.2 respectively for Australia, New Zealand, and the United Kingdom. See David Boles de Boer, Lewis Evans and Bronwyn Howell, *The State of e-New Zealand* (September 2000) 12, 14 and 18, available at <http://www.iscr.org.nz/navigation/research.html>.

[142] Users of local phone services in New Zealand pay a fixed monthly fee but there are no additional charges that are based on the number or duration of local calls.

[143] See David Boles de Boer, Christina Enright and Lewis Evans, *The Internet Service Provider (ISP) Markets of Australia and New Zealand* (May 2000) 6, available at <http://www.iscr.org.nz/navigation/research.html>.

[144] See 'The World's Online Populations' (n 140 above).

TABLE 5.2. Evolution of the cellular market in New Zealand

	1990	1991	1992	1993	1994	1995	1996	1997	1998	1999	June 2000	June 2001
Telecom's cellular connections (in 000s)	29	54	72	100	144	229	340	423	476	609	980	1298
BellSouth/Vodafone's cellular connections[1] (in 000s)	0	0	0	0	2.5	12	38	68	106	182	562	990
BellSouth/Vodafone's market share (%)	0	0	0	0	1.7	5	10	14	18	23	37	43
Penetration rate (%)	0.8	1.6	2.1	2.9	4.1	6.4	9.3	13.6	16.5	21	40	59

[1] BellSouth was sold to Vodafone in November 1998.
Source: Ministry of Economic Development, 'New Zealand Telecommunications 1987–2001', New Zealand Telecommunications Information Publication No 8 (August 2001) 18.

some of these service providers (for example, in 1999, Xtra, the largest ISP, started to offer flat-rate access to the Internet for NZ$39.95 per month after Clear announced that it intended to do the same and, in 2000, it is Clear which lowered its rate to NZ$24.95 after Xtra announced that it would do the same).[145]

Some new entrants have also started to appear in the market for broadband services. The main development in that respect is TelstraSaturn's entry into the residential local loop market in Wellington and Christchurch. The company is offering a package of residential local loop and cable services which supports the provision of cable TV and high-speed Internet access. The service is likely to be available in the other main urban centres in New Zealand over the next three to five years. Telecom is, for its part, offering xDSL services in many urban areas.[146]

Telecom has undoubtedly improved its efficiency over the past decade, as shown in the graph below tracking the number of lines per employee (see Figure 5.3 below).

Finally, in spite of the price-cap imposed upon residential services through the Kiwi Share obligations, quality of service seems to have been maintained, and has even improved recently in some respects (see Table 5.3 below).

While these positive developments are undeniable, it is clear also that interconnection issues proved extremely hard to solve in New Zealand. As mentioned above, until very recently, implementation of the Commerce Act was seen as the main instrument to maintain conditions of effective competition in the telecommunications sector. Additional elements of the regulatory framework were, however, supposed to facilitate freely negotiated commercial agreements

FIGURE 5.3. Telecom's number of lines per employee

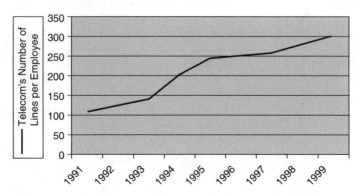

Source: Ministry of Economic Development, *New Zealand Telecommunications 1987–2001*, New Zealand Telecommunications Information Publication No 8, August 2001, 19.

---

[145] See Ministry of Economic Development, 'New Zealand Telecommunications 1987–2001', (August 2001) 10 and 14, available at <http://www.med.govt.nz/pbt/telecom/tip8/tip8.pdf>.

[146] See Ministerial Inquiry into Telecommunications, Final Report (27 September 2000) 92, available at <http://www.teleinquiry.govt.nz>.

TABLE 5.3. New Zealand—Quality of service indicators

	1996	1997	1998	1999	2000
Faults per 100 lines per year	46	43.8	46	39.5	19.3
Percentage of faults cleared within 24 hours	54	59	70	79.5	82.2
Percentage of repair commitments that meet user's request	80	80	84	92.7	91.5
Average directory assistance answering time (seconds)	10.5	11.1	4.8	7.2	6.4

Source: Ministry of Economic Development, 'New Zealand Telecommunications 1987–2001', New Zealand Telecommunications Information Publication No 8 (August 2001) 30.

between parties, in particular, on interconnection. The 1990 Disclosure Regulations were supposed to help Telecom's competitors negotiate more effectively with the incumbent by forcing Telecom to publish certain information.[147] Telecom's undertakings to deal with its own subsidiaries and with competitors on an arm's length basis and to provide interconnection on fair and reasonable terms were also supposed to help new operators reach satisfactory agreements with Telecom.[148] In addition, the Government threatened in several instances to adopt additional regulation if the operators failed to reach pro-competitive agreements.[149] These additional elements proved insufficient, however. The Disclosure Regulations have generally been considered ineffective. As mentioned above, Telecom violated its undertakings and this, in turn, reduced the usefulness of the Disclosure Regulations. Also, the Government's threats proved insufficient to force agreements between operators on the most contentious interconnection issues.

Under these conditions, parties were, in many cases, unable to come to an agreement without going to court first (as in the access to the local loop interconnection cases for example).[150] In other cases, an agreement that had been reached was later contested and modified (as was the case for the Clear–Telecom long-distance interconnection agreement).[151] Even when the parties were able to agree, it generally took a long time and Telecom's competitors often expressed dissatisfaction with the results (as BellSouth did with respect to its mobile interconnection agreement with Telecom).[152]

In those instances when parties had to go to court, judicial proceedings on interconnection tended to be long and expensive.[153] In addition, several

[147] See text accompanying n 18 above.
[148] See text accompanying nn 19–20 above.
[149] On interconnection pricing, for example. See text accompanying n 79 above.
[150] See text accompanying nn 58–80 above.
[151] See text accompanying nn 52–55 above.
[152] See text accompanying nn 56–57 above.
[153] See, for example, n 203 below.

commentators argued that by upholding the legality of the ECPR for interconnection to the local loop, the Privy Council had taken a position which was
very favourable to Telecom and which forced all operators subsequently negotiating interconnection agreements with Telecom to start such negotiations at
a disadvantage, at least until the Baumol–Willig rule was explicitly rejected by
the Telecommunications Act 2001.[154]

As mentioned above, the interconnection price finally negotiated between
Telecom and Clear was lower than ECPR prices and 'bill and keep' arrangements
have recently been negotiated between Telecom and its competitors in the local
market. These latter arrangements, in particular, might indicate that the negotiation process becomes somewhat easier as parties gain experience in dealing
with specific interconnection issues and that the incumbent is willing to agree on
terms which are relatively favourable to its competitors when those competitors
threaten to sign up an increasing number of subscribers to their own networks.
In addition, Telecom's interconnection agreements generally contain a comparability clause which would force Telecom—if it concluded a lower rate in
another agreement—to apply that new rate in similar agreements containing
the comparability clause.[155] It seems fair to say, however, that New Zealand's
light-handed approach to interconnection has been less than satisfactory.

Number portability issues also proved very difficult to tackle in New Zealand.
An agreement has finally been reached between some operators, but the Government had to intervene and the whole process took a very long time (in fact, as
indicated above, an agreement was reached between five operators only in
December 1998, after the Government-imposed deadline of 30 November 1998).

Because of such problems, some authors consider that on the whole, Telecom
has been subjected to insufficient competitive pressures. They point out that,
while real, Telecom's progressive loss of market share has been very gradual and
that while the dispersed population base of New Zealand undoubtedly increases
the costs of some telecommunications infrastructure—especially the cost of fixed
local loop facilities[156]—prices still appear higher than they would be if Telecom
faced more stringent competition. Telecom retains, for example, a very high
share of the local market: it is estimated that Telecom retained about 96 per cent
of fixed line connections as of June 2001.[157] Also, according to the price
comparisons presented in the Annex, PPP-based prices for national long-distance
calls are higher in New Zealand than in the other four countries (they are the
second highest in current US$), and PPP-based prices of international calls are
the second highest (second or third highest in current US$, see Graphs 4a, 4b, 5a,
5b, 6a, and 6b).

In the mobile market, while Vodafone has rapidly improved its market share,
as noted above, this development is very recent. Until 1999, Vodafone's market

---

[154] See 'Final Report' (n 146 above) 62.
[155] See 'New Zealand Communications 1987–2001' (n 145 above) 26.
[156] See Chapter 3 Section J.
[157] See 'New Zealand Communications 1987–2001' (n 145 above) 18.

share remained modest and overall penetration rates of mobile telephony also remained relatively low (see Table 5.2 above). Also, while new entrants might appear in the mobile market following the recent auction of 3G spectrum, only two operators have so far been active in mobile telephony. Prices of mobile services appear to be high, as New Zealand prices are the highest of our sample, both when based on PPPs and when expressed in current US$, and for different volumes of calls (see Annex, Graphs 11a, 11b, 12a and 12b). The fact that roaming was not available until the adoption of the Telecommunications Act 2001 might have contributed to hinder competition and early development of the mobile market.[158]

The variance observed between the different successful bids for cellular frequencies in 1990 was, for its part, clearly due to the form of auction which was used. The Government opted for second price auctions in a market which, given its small size, attracted only a small number of bidders. As a result, there were substantial differences between the first and second bids and the levels of the second highest bids varied greatly from one auction to another. The simultaneous, ascending, multiple-round auction system adopted in 1997 would appear to be better suited to the characteristics of the New Zealand market and should solve this issue.

Another issue concerns the resale of spectrum, which, as mentioned above, has not taken place as expected. This is probably due less to a flaw in the design of the spectrum management rights than to the fact that the New Zealand market is very small. This might impede the development of an efficient secondary market for spectrum rights as well as the development of new equipment required to take full advantage of the possibility to switch between spectrum uses.[159]

In the market for Internet services as well, there are some indications that competitive pressures might be somewhat limited. As noted above, a number of ISPs are operating in New Zealand. However, Xtra, the ISP affiliated with Telecom, holds about 40 per cent of the New Zealand market and while the dial-up Internet prices presented in the Annex appear competitive in current US$, they are the second most expensive, after Chilean prices, when based on PPPs (see Graphs 9a, 9b, 10a and 10b).[160] In addition, while the proponents of facilities-based competition consider that the New Zealand regime has prompted TelstraClear to establish its own local infrastructure in the main urban centres, starting with Wellington and Christchurch, one could argue that if only Telecom is offering xDSL services, it is because the provision of unbundled local services has not been mandated. Finally, unlike local call prices, both

---

[158] See text accompanying n 14 above.

[159] See Robert W Crandall, 'New Zealand Spectrum Policy: A Model for the United States?' (1998) XLI *J of L and Economics* 839.

[160] See David Boles de Boer, Christina Enright and Lewis Evans, 'The Internet Service Providers (ISP) Markets of Australia and New Zealand' (May 2000) 10, available at <http://www.iscn.org.nz/navigation/research.html> and CyberAtlas, 'The World's Online Populations', available at <http://www.cyberatlas.internet.com/big_picture/article/0,1323,5911_151151,00.html>.

Telecom's xDSL and TelstraClear's cable modem services are priced on a metered basis. While this latter price structure might be better suited to help prevent congestion problems, comparisons between various Internet access services by DSL and by cable in OECD countries reveal that Telecom and TelstraClear's offers are among the most expensive.[161] This would tend to suggest that competition remains limited in the market for broadband services.

Finally, the Telecommunications Inquiry estimated that if competition was strengthened through implementation of its proposed designation and specification scheme, the New Zealand economy would gain NZ$44 million each year (pure welfare gain) and the users would gain NZ$328 million (transfer of wealth from Telecom's shareholders to users).[162] These figures were, however, contested by some commentators.[163]

While the evidence presented above is somewhat mixed, and while there are signs that competitive pressures are intensifying in some markets, it seems clear that competition could have been more vigorous, or could have emerged sooner, if clearer rules had been adopted earlier on some issues such us interconnection, numbering, carrier pre-selection, and roaming. In this context, the Telecommunications Act 2001 that designates interconnection, number portability, and Telecom's fixed network to mobile carrier pre-selection, and which specifies roaming should be a step in the right direction. As mentioned above, the Act opts for the TSLRIC methodology to cap interconnection prices unless the Commerce Commission considers that it would not be the best method to promote competition for the benefit of end-users. This priority given to the relatively demanding TSLRIC method might well be justified as long as the competition that Telecom is facing in the local market remains limited.[164] In practice, it is the way in which the rule is applied which will determine whether it strikes the right balance between spurring competition in the market and ensuring that the incumbent retains appropriate incentives to invest in the local infrastructure.

Some positive steps have also been taken with respect to universal service obligations. As mentioned above, the new agreement reached between Telecom and the Government in December 2001 enables Telecom to charge different line rental prices in rural and in urban areas. This recognizes existing cost differentials and might constitute a first step toward increasing the viability of—and therefore the potential for competition in—the provision of some rural services. In addition, calculating each operator's share of the universal service costs and transferring those amounts directly to Telecom, as required by the new agreement, is more transparent than relying on the interconnection payments for that

---

[161] See OECD, Local Access Pricing and E-Commerce, DSTI/ICCP/TISP(2000)1/FINAL, 27 June 2000, 70–71, available at <http://www.olis.oecd.org/olis/2000doc.nsf/linkto/dsti-iccp-tisp(2000) 1-final>.

[162] See 'Final Report', (n 146 above) 69.

[163] See, for example, the NECG News Release of 1 November 2000, 'Inquiry Report Numbers Don't Add Up', available at <http://www.necg.com.au/press_re_enquiraddup.html>.

[164] See Chapter 3, Section C.

purpose. But on the whole, the system remains clearly sub-optimal. Telecom is still designated, *a priori*, as the party responsible for meeting universal service obligations.[165] Telecom has calculated the costs of these obligations, as required by the revised Disclosure Regulations.[166] They were estimated at NZ$166.9 million per annum, in 2000, or a rather substantial 3.85 per cent of total sector revenues.[167] In spite of the specific guidelines which must be followed, both to calculate these costs and to allocate them between the various operators, there is still no guarantee that the compensation that Telecom will receive will cover exactly the intended share of the costs, nor that Telecom is the most efficient provider of universal services, as long as no competitive mechanisms are used to reveal the operators' best estimates of those costs and to identify the operator best able to meet these obligations most efficiently.

Some authors consider that another flaw of the New Zealand model is that structural reforms were not implemented in telecommunications and that this contributed to minimize the competitive pressures imposed upon Telecom. Those who share these views argue that in order to accelerate the introduction of competition in the New Zealand telecommunications market, it would have been advisable to impose strictly upon the incumbent the type of structural reforms envisaged in Telecom's undertakings.[168] Separating cellular from wireline operations or local from long-distance services, for example, would limit the incentives of the incumbent to leverage a dominant position in one market to gain a competitive advantage in another one. Separating the provision of access to the local infrastructure from the provision of local retail services could, for its part, help to strengthen competition in the local retail market. Both forms of separation would increase the number of access agreements. This, in turn, could yield information on access costs and thus facilitate negotiations between access seekers and access providers. Some structural separation between different market segments has in fact been recently adopted in the electricity sector.[169]

Had appropriate disclosure requirements been combined with some degree of vertical separation in the telecommunications sector, this would not only have increased the information available to new operators and thus potentially

---

[165] See text accompanying nn 126–127 above.

[166] See text accompanying n 18 above.

[167] From the estimates of the costs of the Kiwi Share obligations presented in Telecom Corporation of New Zealand Ltd, 'Telecommunications (Information Disclosure) Regulations 1999—Kiwi Share Obligation Loss Estimate' (31 March 2001), available at <http://www2.telecom.co.nz/pdf/kiwishare/summaryfd2.pdf>.

[168] See, for example, Milton Mueller, 'On the Frontier of Deregulation: New Zealand Telecommunications and the Problem of Interconnecting Competing Networks' in David Gabel and David F Weiman (eds), *Opening Networks to Competition, The Regulation of Pricing and Access* (Boston, Mass., and Dordrecht: Kluwer Academic Press, 1998) 126–129.

[169] In order to promote effective competition in the sector, the Electricity Industry Reform Act adopted in July 1998 mandates, inter alia, structural reforms such as a separation of natural monopoly components from competitive activities (transmission and distribution on the one hand and generation and trading on the other), as well as substantially increased information disclosure requirements (see in particular Parts 2–5 of the Act).

facilitated access negotiations between parties, it could also have helped judges by making public a greater number of agreements which could have been used to design specific solutions to new cases. Indeed, the essential facilities doctrine developed in the US[170] has shown that judges applying general antitrust rules to solve issues of access were able to devise specific solutions only when the remedy was to grant access to the plaintiff under the same conditions as those already granted to others, under conditions which the plaintiff itself had already enjoyed before, or under conditions established by a specialized regulator.[171] Judges were unable to come up with specific solutions when access had to be granted for the first time in the absence of a specialized regulator, as was the case in the local loop interconnection dispute in New Zealand.

One could argue, however, that since competition is progressively taking hold for the provision of mobile and long-distance services and since a new interconnection regime has now been adopted, it might not be necessary to impose a separation between the local market and the other telecommunications markets. But while Telecom and its facilities-based competitors in the local market have apparently concluded their latest round of interconnection negotiations relatively easily, Telecom's continued near-total dominance in that segment of the market argues in favour of at least considering the pros and cons of separating the provision of local infrastructure from the provision of local retail services.

2. Specificity versus Coherence

On the one hand, relying on economy-wide rules and institutions to regulate the sector has certainly promoted a coherent treatment of telecommunications and other economic activities. On the other hand, however, it could be argued that the absence of specific rules on interconnection was the main cause of the long delays with which some interconnection disputes were resolved in New Zealand. As mentioned above, the uncertainty generated by the absence of more specific rules on this topic hindered the conclusion of agreements between parties as well as the adoption of precise solutions by the judges. For example, while the courts confirmed the legality of the ECPR, they did not specify how the rule needed to be applied and what the interconnection price should be (the High Court expressly stated that it was not a regulatory agency and that it could not pursue investigations as to whether Telecom earned monopoly rents, possessed excess capacity, or was inefficient).[172] Speedier adoption of specific rules allowing for roaming could also have helped intensify competition sooner in the mobile

---

[170] See Chapter 4, Section B.

[171] See George A Hay, 'Reflections on Clear' (1996) 3 *Competition and Consumer L J* 231, 240, and Warren Pengilley, 'The Privy Council Speaks on Essential Facilities Access in New Zealand: What are the Australasian Lessons?' (1995) 3 *Competition and Consumer L J* 28, 29.

[172] *Clear Telecommunications Ltd v Telecom Corporation of New Zealand Ltd* (1992) 5 TCLR 166 at 217.

market. And specific rules on local loop unbundling might have prompted some operators to compete with Telecom for the provision of xDSL services.[173]

In addition, antitrust rules such as s 36, pertaining to the use of a dominant position, and s 47, pertaining to mergers and acquisitions, are designed to prevent restrictions of competition. As mentioned with respect to the United States, they might therefore be ill-adapted when it comes to introducing competition in markets that were previously monopolized.[174] Observers of the New Zealand experience have pointed out, in addition, that such rules might also lead to inefficient results, from an economic point of view, when they are applied to vertically integrated industries. For example, a monopolist operating a bottleneck facility might be forced, under rules such as s 36, to decrease the price at which it sells goods or services to operators with whom it competes in a downstream market but might be free to price as it wishes when it does not compete in that market. Indeed, in the former case, when it imposes high prices, there is a risk that the monopolist might distort competition in the downstream market in its favour while, in the latter case, all competitors in the downstream market are treated in the same way. As a result of the application of s 36, in order to be able to keep charging high prices, the monopolist might decide to operate only in the bottleneck market and not in the downstream competitive market even if economies of scale or scope would dictate vertical integration.[175]

Finally, the New Zealand experience demonstrates that antitrust law does not necessarily constitute an appropriate instrument to distinguish between rules that can be effectively implemented in a given regulatory environment and those which might not. For example, in the absence of a specialized regulator, assessing the value of interconnection prices under the ECPR would likely have been very difficult in practice since it would have required very detailed information on the incumbent's costs.[176] Having to perform regular reviews to reassess the value of interconnection prices in an effort to progressively eliminate monopoly profits would have presented additional difficulties.[177] Such practical considerations were, however, deemed irrelevant to determine the legality of an ECPR-based interconnection price under s 36 by the Privy Council.[178] Ensuring adoption of a more practical rule would have required more specific regulations than s 36.

As mentioned above, ss 36 and 47 have been amended in an effort to broaden their scope. The extent to which the amendments do effectively enlarge the scope of these provisions is open to question and it seems clear, in addition, that whatever their impact on the scope of ss 36 and 47, these amendments do not directly address the type of issues mentioned above.[179]

---

[173] See text accompanying n 117 above. [174] See Chapter 4, Section E.2.
[175] See Hay (n 171 above) 242–243. [176] See Mueller (n 168 above) 124–125.
[177] See text accompanying n 69 above. [178] See text accompanying n 76 above.
[179] Several commentators have argued that replacing 'use of a dominant position' by 'taking advantage of a substantial degree of market power' in s 36 might broaden its scope of application to the extent that a substantial degree of market power does not necessarily imply a dominant position. However, the test applied by the Privy Council in the local loop interconnection case (ie whether the firm would be acting in the same way as firms in a competitive market) is what reduced

The introduction, under the Telecommunications Act 2001, of a number of sector-specific rules to promote competition in the telecommunications market marks a progress toward a better balance between specificity and coherence. The creation of a specialized Telecommunications Commissioner with specialist staff, within the Commerce Commission, appears to be a promising way of ensuring a sufficient degree of sector-specific expertise while maintaining the overall coherence of economic regulation across the whole economy. Finally, the decision that the initial determination of interconnection prices would be derived from benchmarking of similar prices constitutes a much clearer and more practical rule than those derived earlier from an application of antitrust law by the courts.

3. Flexibility versus Certainty

The New Zealand model, with its heavy reliance on general antitrust rules, has left a wide degree of discretion to judges as long as a binding precedent has not been set by a higher court. In such a system, setting precedents does take time and, in addition, the particular circumstances of a case will often differ in some ways from those of another, so that the scope for discretion is likely to remain for a long period. Besides, even when a precedent has been set, it can be changed by the court that set it or by another court of equal or superior rank. As mentioned above, this has the advantage of allowing for a high degree of flexibility in tailoring appropriate solutions.[180] Conversely, it introduces, however, a high degree of uncertainty for operators and subscribers alike.[181] For example, the concepts of use of a dominant position and of purpose, which are mentioned in s 36, have been the object of conflicting court decisions. More generally, this uncertainty is well illustrated by the several instances where different courts ruled differently on the same facts (for example, with respect to the local loop interconnection cases, and with respect to the acquisition of frequencies cases where circumstances had changed by the time the Court of Appeal reviewed the case).[182]

The New Zealand regime might, in addition, be deemed to have left too much discretion to the Executive. While the price control regime envisaged under Part IV of the Commerce Act has never been used up to now, it leaves a large degree of discretion to political authorities and to the Commerce Commission. The criteria

---

the scope of s 36 and that same test could still be applied under the revised formulation. Similarly, replacing, in s 47, a prohibition 'to acquire or strengthen a dominant position' by a prohibition 'to substantially lessen competition' in a market, would undoubtedly broaden the scope of the section, but it would not address the fact that merger provisions such as s 47 are ill-suited to promote the introduction of competition in markets where none existed before. See Ministerial Inquiry into Telecommunications, Final Report (27 September 2000) 21–23, available at <http://www.teleinquiry.govt.nz>.

[180] See Chapter 2, Section B.
[181] See discussion of the third criteria in Chapter 2, Section D.
[182] See the accompanying n 99 above.

to be used by the Government to identify the goods or services which can be subjected to price controls are vague: as mentioned in Section B.1, price controls can be imposed when competition is limited and when such controls would be in the interests of users or consumers.[183] In addition, no guidance is provided to the Commerce Commission as to how such price controls should be designed and administered.[184] Investors could therefore legitimately be concerned that such broad powers could be misused, thus preventing them from receiving adequate returns on their investments.

As to the Government's threat of imposing more detailed regulation upon the industry, while it might have facilitated the conclusion of some agreements,[185] it failed, as pointed out above, to prevent long and difficult judicial processes with respect to the most contentious issues. Even more importantly perhaps, governments' threats constitute a very informal and therefore rather uncertain regulatory instrument: the willingness of governments to act upon such threats is difficult to estimate and is likely to differ from one government to the next. This is illustrated by the fact that the long-distance interconnection agreement between Clear and Telecom was more favourable than the mobile interconnection agreement concluded between BellSouth and Telecom, in large part, it seems, because there was more pressure on Telecom in the former case, as conclusion of an acceptable agreement had been set by the Government as a pre-condition for the privatization of the company.

Telecom's rate of investment has been falling substantially over the 1990s (see Figure 5.4 below). Some commentators have argued that Telecom, in fact, underinvested in infrastructure over the past decade and that this might, at some point, hinder the further development of e-commerce.[186] This might, in part, reflect the relatively high degree of uncertainty that has existed in the New Zealand telecommunications sector.

The New Zealand model of spectrum allocation also provides substantial flexibility to operators, and this, on the other hand, appears, at least in theory, to constitute a clear improvement upon the more rigid way in which most other countries allocate spectrum rights.

Through the adoption of more specific rules and the strengthening of the Commerce Commission's skills and powers with respect to telecommunications, the new regime adopted in late 2001 contributes, to a large extent, to reduce the level of uncertainty that has existed in the sector.

---

[183] See text accompanying n 11 above.

[184] See Commerce Act, s 70.

[185] Government intervention might have had such an effect, for example, with respect to the interconnection agreements concluded between Clear and Telecom for both long-distance and local services, and with respect to the agreement concluded by some operators on number portability. See text accompanying nn 48, 79 and 86 above.

[186] See Paul Budde Communication Pty Ltd, *Report on the Telecommunications and Information Highways Market in New Zealand 2000/2001* (22 November 2000), available at <http://www.budde.com.au/Static/PressReleases/NZpress.html>.

FIGURE 5.4. Telecom's net capital expansion as a percentage of depreciated asset base

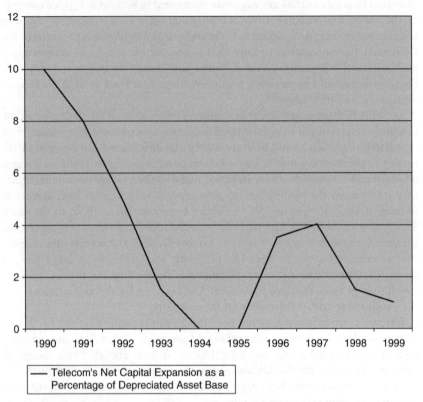

Source: Centre for Research in Network Economics and Communications, University of Auckland, *The Costs and Benefits of Regulating Electronic Communications Services—A Report to the Ministerial Inquiry into Telecommunications in New Zealand*, 27 September 2000, 84.

4. Regulatory Competence and Ability to Resist Undue Pressure

As indicated in Section C, in New Zealand, prior to the adoption of the 2001 reforms, it was the judges who were ultimately in charge of enforcing economic regulation in the telecommunications sector. The Commerce Commission did not, for its part, have the power to set conditions of interconnection, for example, or to impose penalties. It also operated on a limited budget and with very few analysts specialized in network industries.[187] In addition, the Commerce Commission's competency had been interpreted in a narrow manner by

---

[187] John P Small, 'Light Handed Regulation of Network Industries in New Zealand', paper distributed at the TUANZ Competition Symposium, Wellington, New Zealand, 7–8 April 1998, 9.

the courts[188] and its decisions could be overturned by the courts on a legal as well as a factual basis.

This scheme, which gave the major role to judges, offered strong guarantees regarding the autonomy of the regulatory process. Indeed, judges enjoy protection against undue pressures from the Government and are independent from industry, so that the risks of regulatory capture are limited. Members of the Commerce Commission, for their part, also enjoy protection against government pressure, albeit to a more limited extent,[189] and they are independent from industry as well.[190] The fact that both the Commerce Commission and the courts are competent across the whole economy and tend to intervene on a case-by-case basis without getting involved in constant regulatory oversight limits the contacts which those institutions have with any particular sector minister or operator and thus further reduces the risks of regulatory capture by the Government or by the industry.[191]

Serious doubts have been raised about the capacity of non-specialized judges to fully understand complex technical and regulatory matters in spite of the presence of an expert lay-member in the High Court.[192] A review of the case law of the courts does indeed provide some examples of insufficient economic analysis. For instance, in the local loop interconnection cases, the Privy Council considered that, by charging Clear according to the ECPR, Telecom would not be using its dominant position since it would be acting in the same way as firms do in a competitive market when they seek to recover the opportunity costs of providing goods or services to competitors.[193] The Privy Council apparently failed to realize that, from an economic point of view, the comparison was not valid. Indeed, a firm in a dominant position and enjoying monopoly profits would have much higher opportunity costs and a much greater ability to impose a pricing structure ensuring that it recovers those costs than a firm operating in a competitive environment.[194] The level of penalties imposed by the courts for violations of the Commerce Act constitutes another example. Those penalties

[188] See text accompanying nn 43–47 above.

[189] As indicated in Section C, the Commission's budget is determined by Parliament, its members must possess minimum competencies and experience, and they can only be dismissed on grounds restrictively enumerated in the Commerce Act, three elements which somewhat protect the Commission's autonomy vis-à-vis the Executive. On the other hand, other factors might, at times, constitute a threat to the Commission's autonomy: for example, the Executive alone is responsible for designating the Commissioners and the Commission must have regards to the economic policies of the Government.

[190] See text accompanying n 31 above.

[191] See Roger Kerr and Bryce Wilkinson, 'The Regulation of Monopoly in New Zealand', paper distributed at the TUANZ Competition Symposium, Wellington, New Zealand, 7–8 April 1998, at 36–39.

[192] See Susan Lojkine, *Competition Litigation in the High Court*, Materials for the Third Annual Workshop, Competition Law and Policy Institute of New Zealand, vol II (August 1991), 10. See also Malcolm Webb and Martyn Taylor, 'Light-Handed Regulation of Telecommunications in New Zealand: Is Generic Competition Law Sufficient?' (Winter 1998/99) 2 *Intl J of Telecommunications L and Policy* 1, 6–7.

[193] See text accompanying n 75 above.

[194] See Rex J Ahdar, 'Battles in New Zealand's Deregulated Telecommunications Industry' (1995) 23 *Australian Business L Rev* 78, 102, and George A Hay, (n 171 above) 243–244.

appear in some cases to have been insufficient to compensate for the unlawful gains of the violators, thereby failing to deliver the intended deterrence effect.[195]

Courts appear, in addition, ill-equipped to provide the continuous oversight that certain regulatory mechanisms tend to require. For example, once again in the local loop interconnection cases, the High Court and the Privy Council were probably right to maintain that application of the ECPR could result in the progressive elimination of Telecom's monopoly profits, if such profits existed.[196] The reason, as discussed in Chapter 3, Section C.2, is that if Telecom did not match the lower retail prices of a more efficient rival building its own local network, that rival would have an incentive to expand its network and increase its market share in order to ensure that a greater number of calls could be made entirely on its own network, thereby decreasing Telecom's profits.[197] With lower retail prices, Telecom's opportunity cost of providing interconnection services would decrease and this, in turn, should lower the interconnection price under the ECPR, thereby prompting another round of retail price reduction on the part of Telecom's rival. However, as mentioned above, in order to gradually eliminate Telecom's monopoly profits in this way, the interconnection charge would have to be revised at regular intervals,[198] and courts appear to lack the capacity to carry out these regular reviews.

As mentioned above, under the Telecommunications Act 2001, a specialized Telecommunications Commissioner is to join the Commerce Commission. The Commissioner will have a specialist staff, and will be required to make final access pricing decisions jointly with two other Commissioners and to consult two Commissioners before recommending that services be designated or specified. This solution would appear to present many advantages: it will increase the number of telecommunications specialists focusing on regulatory issues in New Zealand while maintaining the cross-fertilization of experience across sectors and the protection against both government and industry capture generally associated with economy-wide regulatory bodies.

5. Regulatory Accountability and Stakeholder Participation

The Commerce Commission publishes, online, an annual report of its activities; its decisions are published and reasoned; appeals against those decisions can be brought before the courts; and the courts are also required to publish their decisions and the reasons explaining those decisions. One potential problem with the regime in place prior to the 2001 reforms was that, in spite of their

---

[195] See Allan Bollard and Michael Pickford, Utility Regulation in New Zealand, Institute of Economic Affairs, Lectures on Regulation, London (1996) 52; see also David Harmer and Grant Hannis, 'The Commerce Act—What Must Change?', paper distributed at the TUANZ Competition Symposium, Wellington, New Zealand, 7–8 April 1998, 3.

[196] See text accompanying nn 64 and 76 above.

[197] Carl Blanchard, 'Telecommunications Regulation in New Zealand—How Effective is Light-Handed Regulation?' (1994) 18 *Telecommunications Policy* 154, 162.

[198] See text accompanying n 69 above.

lack of expertise on complex issues of telecommunications regulation, the courts could review the Commission's decisions not only on legal, but on factual grounds also. Several commentators also argued that users' opinions on issues of telecommunications regulation have not always been heard sufficiently clearly in New Zealand.[199] Both the Commerce Commission and private parties have had the opportunity to bring actions before the courts for breaches of the Commerce Act, but no mechanisms were provided to ensure that consumer representatives, if they were not parties to the dispute, could intervene in the proceedings to present their views.

The 2001 reforms have corrected the first issue by limiting the grounds for appeal to the courts to legal questions only. The new framework also provides for a greater degree of stakeholder involvement. The Industry Forum, for example, promotes industry participation in the regulatory process. Also, specialized regulators—such as the Telecommunications Commissioner—tend to provide more opportunities for user intervention and the new legislation requires the Commerce Commission to consult or hold public hearings before making determinations on access conditions or recommendations to modify the list of designated or specified services.

6. Regulatory Costs

One obvious benefit of the New Zealand regulatory model prior to the 2001 reforms is that it involved very limited direct costs as its regulatory institutions were not expensive to establish and maintain. As mentioned in Section C, the budget of the Commerce Commission, which enforces the Commerce Act across the whole economy, is very modest.[200] In addition, as there were few sector-specific rules, compliance costs for the industry remained small and incentives to spend large sums on lobbying activities were reduced.[201]

However, the parties incurred substantial legal expenses during the protracted litigation that took place in New Zealand.[202] Besides, while very difficult to estimate, other costs were likely to be substantial in New Zealand. First, there were the costs that resulted from the delays incurred in reaching some final decisions, particularly on interconnection. The Clear–Telecom access dispute in the local loop interconnection cases, for example, postponed competition in the local markets by several years, which undoubtedly imposed a cost on the

---

[199] Ministry of Economic Development, 'Penalties, Remedies and Court Processes under the Commerce Act 1986: A Discussion Document' (Wellington, New Zealand, January 1998) 44. See also Richard A Joseph, 'The Politics of Telecommunications Reform: A Comparative Study of Australian and New Zealand', University of Wollongong, Science and Technology Analysis Research Program, Working Paper No 12, July 1993, 32.

[200] See text accompanying n 24 above.

[201] See John Belgrave, Speech on the Regulatory Environment, Economist Conference, 14 March 1995, 6.

[202] Clear estimated that it had spent $NZ 8–10 million for the High Court trial alone of the *Clear v Telecom* local access case. See Ahdar (n 194 above) 106.

New Zealand economy. Second, costs were also incurred if, as argued above, there was insufficient protection against regulatory mistakes in New Zealand.

The 2001 reforms will increase the direct costs of regulation as some telecommunications specialists will join the Commerce Commission together with a new Telecommunications Commissioner. These extra costs are likely to be limited, however, as there will be no new, separate, regulatory agency. Cost savings, for their part, could be substantial if the scheme reduces litigation, accelerates the introduction of competition in some market segments, and lowers the risks of regulatory mistakes.

7. Allocation of Regulatory Responsibilities

When compared with that of most other countries, the framework applicable to the economic regulation of telecommunications prior to the adoption of the Telecommunications Act 2001 was relatively simple in New Zealand and the allocation of regulatory responsibilities appeared to be quite clear.

The main criticism which could be made in this area is that regulatory responsibilities might not have been allocated to those best equipped to handle them. It may seem somewhat paradoxical, for example, that decisions taken by the Commerce Commission, a body which comprises some experts on telecommunications regulatory matters, could be appealed before the High Court, which includes only one economic expert, and that decisions of the High Court could then be appealed before the Court of Appeal, which includes no expert at all on economic issues.[203] In addition, the Commerce Commission's competencies had been interpreted very narrowly while the courts—which tended to lack the required technical capacity—and the Executive—which was susceptible to give priority to short-term political objectives—had arguably been granted excessive powers.

The 2001 reforms are likely to improve the situation as they substantially increase the powers of the Commerce Commission while they limit the role of the courts and reduce the risks that the Executive will exercise undue influence (while the Government does retain some discretionary powers with respect to price controls, the uncertainty associated with the Government's recurrent threats of imposing more detailed regulation upon the industry is likely to recede).

---

[203] See text accompanying nn 28 and 41 above.

6

United Kingdom

The UK telecommunications regime contains some particular features, which distinguish it from the regimes adopted in the other countries considered in this book. For example, while detailed sector-specific rules have been adopted, as in the United States, such rules are, for the most part, included in the licences of the various operators. Also, the sector-specific regulator in charge of implementing those rules is also in a position to exercise unparalleled influence on the implementation of general antitrust provisions, as it possesses basically the same enforcement powers, with respect to those provisions, as the antitrust authorities.

A. ORIGINS OF THE PRESENT REGULATORY FRAMEWORK

The provision of telecommunications services within the United Kingdom started at about the same time as the invention of the telephone itself.[1] Bell Telephony Company began service in 1878 and Edison Telephone Company started its operations in 1879. These companies then merged to form the United Telephone Company, which was subsequently reorganized as the National Telephone Company (NTC). The General Post Office (hereafter, the 'GPO'), however, won an important case in 1880 in which the High Court found that its monopoly over telegraph services should extend to other electrical means of communication, including the telephone.[2] The GPO licensed the NTC to provide the service, but it began to build its own network. The Government subsequently decided to purchase the trunk lines of the NTC and to have the Post Office extend and develop the trunk system. In 1899, new legislation permitted municipal authorities to establish telephone services, and a number of them applied for licences. Except for the City of Kingston-upon-Hull, all subsequently surrendered their licences, and either the NTC or the GPO took over provision of the services. In 1912, the provision of telecommunications services was nationalized and operated together with postal services as part of the GPO. The telephone system of Kingston-upon-hull continued to remain independent, however.

---

[1] See Steven K Vogel, *Freer Market, More Rules—Regulatory Reforms in Advanced Industrial Countries* (Ithaca, NY: Cornell University Press, 1996) 67; Ingo Vogelsang and Bridget M Mitchell, *Telecommunications Competition—The Last Ten Miles* (Washington, DC: The AEI Press and Cambridge, Mass. and London: MIT Press, 1997), 252 et seq.

[2] *A-G v Edison Telephone Co of London* (1880) 6 QBD 244.

Between 1912 and 1980, the UK telecommunications sector operated under full State ownership and in the complete absence of competition. During that period, the only significant reform was the transformation of the GPO from a government department into a public corporation through the 1969 Post Office Act. In 1981, the British Telecommunications Act (hereafter, the '1981 Act') made the postal and telecommunications services of the GPO the responsibility of two different undertakings.[3] Postal services were retained by the Post Office, but the 1981 Act transferred to British Telecommunications (hereafter, 'BT') the exclusive privilege to run the UK network. The 1981 Act, however, granted the Government powers to license competitors in the provision of public telecommunications networks. The Government decided to use this power to authorize one additional competitor to compete with BT and a private joint venture, Mercury Communications Limited (hereafter, 'Mercury'),[4] was established and licensed to operate a new public voice and data system based entirely on digital technology.[5] The 1981 Act also brought to an end BT's monopoly on terminal equipment. The Act empowered the Government to permit persons other than BT to supply and maintain terminal equipment, which it did in 1983. The first telephone set, however, temporarily remained the prerogative of BT.

In November 1983, the Government announced that it did not intend to license operators other than BT and Mercury to provide fixed telephony services both domestically and internationally until November 1990.[6] The alleged objective of this policy was to create and protect a duopoly for a period of time over which Mercury could build its network and progressively gain market share. Mercury built direct links with large companies and competed with BT for residential users' long-distance and international services through access to BT's local network.[7]

Through the 1984 British Telecommunications Act (hereafter, the '1984 Act'), BT was privatized as a public limited company. The UK Government expected that the privatization of BT (and other public utilities such as electricity, gas and water companies) would increase the economic and customer service performance of these companies and would curtail public expenditures.[8] Prime Minister Thatcher and the ruling Conservative Party also sought to promote a culture of 'popular capitalism' whereby an important fraction of the British population

---

[3] See Colin D Long, *Telecommunications Law and Practice* (2nd edn, London: Sweet & Maxwell, 1995) § 2-03.

[4] Mercury is a subsidiary of Cable & Wireless, formerly an international telecommunications carrier focusing on the market of the former UK colonies and privatized in 1981. It is today called Cable & Wireless Communications.

[5] Long (n 3 above) § 2-03.

[6] ibid § 2-05.

[7] See Jean-Jacques Laffont and Jean Tirole, *Competition in Telecommunications* (Cambridge, Mass., and London: MIT Press, 1999) 29.

[8] See Willem Hulsink, *Privatisation and Liberalisation in European Telecommunications—Comparing Britain, the Netherlands and France* (London and New York: Routledge, 1998), 134.

would hold shares in formerly public companies.[9] The incumbent was left intact as a vertically integrated network operator and service provider.[10] The Government also wanted to privatize BT rapidly, and BT's management was strongly opposed to a break-up.[11] The British Government thus chose to emphasize the regulation of conduct rather than of structure in the telecommunications industry.[12] The 1984 Act also abolished BT's exclusive privilege and replaced it by a public telecommunications operator's licence. A core aspect of the Act is that it provided for the creation of an independent sector-specific regulatory authority, the Office of Telecommunications (OFTEL), to be administered by a new officer, the Director General of Telecommunications (hereafter, the 'DGT').

Retail prices have been regulated by OFTEL since 1984 through an RPI – X price-cap applicable to a weighted basket of services. In 1984, the basket included local and domestic long-distance services and covered about half of BT's total sales. International telephone services, private circuits and apparatus, and connection charges were not part of the regulated basket. The X figure was initially set at 3 per cent for a period of five years. An exception was made for line rentals, the price of which could not be increased by more than 2 per cent in any year. In 1989, as BT's profitability indicated that the company was coping very easily with the price-cap, OFTEL set a more stringent cap on BT's regulated prices by changing it to RPI – 4.5 per cent and broadened the basket of regulated services.[13] At the same time, BT also committed itself to offering discounts to subscribers with low calling volumes.

As BT and Mercury were unable to reach agreement on interconnection rates, OFTEL also intervened to set those rates.[14] BT's licence stipulated that access charges should cover the costs of providing interconnection, including relevant overheads and a reasonable rate-of-return on the relevant assets, on the basis of fully distributed costs calculated on a historic basis. OFTEL faced a policy dilemma: if BT was forced (because of the RPI + 2 per cent constraint on the level of rental charges) to cover the fixed costs of local network provision partly out of call charges (ie if BT had an 'access deficit'), and if Mercury was allowed to access BT's local network at marginal usage cost, then this could lead to

[9] See Brian Levy and Pablo Spiller, *Regulation, Institutions and Commitment* (Cambridge: Cambridge University Press, 1996) 93.

[10] It has been reported, however, that many of those involved in shaping the UK regulatory landscape, include Nigel Lawson (Chancellor of the Exchequer), Alan Walters (the Prime Minister's advisor on economic matters) and the Prime Minister herself were initially in favour of breaking BT up along regional lines following the example of the Baby Bells in the United States. See Alison Young, *The Politics of Regulation—Privatised Utilities in Britain* (London: Palgrave, 2001) 10 and 18.

[11] See Mark Amstrong et al, *Regulatory Reform: Economic Analysis and British Experience* (Cambridge, Mass. and London: MIT Press, 1994), 215.

[12] See Ingo Vogelsang and Bridget M Mitchell, *Telecommunications Competition—The Last Ten Miles* (Washington, DC, and Cambridge, Mass., and London: The AEI Press and MIT Press, 1997) 255.

[13] ibid 272.

[14] See Tommaso Valletti, 'The Practice of Access Pricing—Telecommunications in the United Kingdom', Policy Research Working Paper No 2063, The World Bank, Economic Development Institute (February 1999) 5.

inefficient cream-skimming with the result that BT could no longer cover those fixed costs. In order to address this issue, one could insert an access charge contribution into interconnection charges. On the other hand, given BT's overwhelming dominance at the time of privatization, favourable terms of interconnection to the incumbent's network infrastructure might be necessary to stimulate competition.[15]

OFTEL ruled that Mercury should pay for all direct costs of providing access and a per-minute charge for the use of the local network according to time and distance parameters. After their initial determination, the charges were to follow an RPI – 3 per cent formula. OFTEL did not provide any explanation as to the methodology it followed to set interconnection charges.[16] Without information about such methodology, the relationship between these charges and the marginal or average costs of providing interconnection is not easy to establish. According to some authors, the DGT subsequently stated that the 1985 ruling was designed to exempt Mercury from any contribution to BT's alleged access deficit and that Mercury was granted advantageous interconnection with a view to help it enter the market in the face of BT's incumbency advantage.[17]

The duopoly phase achieved disappointing results and was generally misguided.[18] Despite substantial entry assistance, Mercury failed to provide a serious challenge to the incumbent. In fact, Mercury was content with attacking BT in its most vulnerable markets, effectively cream-skimming its most profitable segments.[19] On most segments, the discipline had thus to be imposed by the system of price control administered by OFTEL.[20] Overall, BT easily coped with the price controls to which it was subject as its increasing profitability after privatization suggests.[21] Most observers agree that allowing competition by a single operator, rather than liberalizing the market—especially for a period as

---

[15] Except in relatively rare circumstances where both customers are involved in a call are connected directly to Mercury's network, BT lines will be needed to initiate and/or deliver calls. Thus, BT had a monopoly for a necessary input for Mercury's operation. Amstrong et al (n 11 above) 218.

[16] According to Valletti (n 14 above), one of the reasons for not giving detailed explanations about the determination was that OFTEL feared that parties could thus appeal for judicial review of some aspects of the determination, thereby delaying the process.

[17] See Valletti (n 14 above).

[18] See Martin Cave, 'The Evolution of Telecommunications Regulation in the UK' (1997) 41 *European Economic Rev* 661.

[19] See Martin Cave and Peter Williamson, 'Entry, Competition, and Regulation in UK Telecommunications' (1996) 12 *Oxford Rev of Economic Policy* 113. Several factors, discussed in Chapter 3, might explain why Mercury failed to compete effectively with BT for market shares: relatively low interconnection prices might have reduced the need for Mercury to maximize the number of calls originating or terminating within its network; BT's well-known brand might have meant that Mercury could only capture BT's customers if it accepted it had to implement very deep price cuts; the duopoly structure of the industry might have facilitated some degree of collusion between operators in the retail market; and BT's financial strength and ability to adjust its individual retail prices quickly (and to lower them if necessary) under the price-cap regime might have reduced Mercury's appetite for launching price wars with BT to capture a large section of the retail market.

[20] See Valletti (n 14 above) 4.

[21] Vogelsang and Mitchell (n 12 above) 289.

long as the one chosen by the British Government (ie seven years)—hindered the development of competition in UK telecommunications.[22]

A similar duopoly policy was followed for cellular services with two licences awarded to Cellnet (partly owned by BT) and Vodafone in 1982.[23] Cellnet and Vodafone were only allowed to sell services through service providers.[24] Some of these providers were independent, while others were owned and operated by the duopolists through legally separate entities. The rationale for this approach was twofold. First, it was thought that having intermediaries in the form of service providers would limit the risk that Cellnet and Vodafone take advantage of their market power as duopolists. Second, it was believed that having a competitive intermediate tier would enhance competition in the supply of mobile services, would lead to lower prices, faster diffusion, greater innovation, and customer benefits.

Little of the anticipated competitive rivalry took place during the duopoly period.[25] After a short period of price competition, Cellnet and Vodafone settled down to a regime of parallel pricing, which remained stable from early 1987 to late 1992. The stability and uniformity of wholesale airtime prices spilled over into the retail market, with service providers deviating only marginally from retail tariffs recommended by the network. Reasons for this lack of competition are twofold. First, service providers linked to the networks (through ties of partial or complete ownership) represented a significant share of the retail market.[26] These providers focused their marketing efforts exclusively on airtime from a single network, a factor that reduced inter-brand competition. Second, the nature of the contracts between networks and service providers sought to 'tie' even independent service providers to a single network. For instance, such contracts involved substantial discounts on airtime, as well as additional bonuses related to the achievement of growth targets.[27] Valletti and Cave argue convincingly that '(t)he price stability, together with the similarity of firm's behaviour and the high resulting profits for both, suggests that during the (duopoly) period the incumbent firms tacitly colluded and behaved effectively as a single monopolist in the market'. As in the fixed telephony market, it thus appears that the duopoly approach failed to encourage the development of competition and mainly bene-fited the duopolists.

---

[22] Interview with Chris Doyle (Charles River Associates), 22 June 2000 and Colin Long (Olswang), 23 June 2000.

[23] See Tommaso Valletti and Martin Cave, 'Competition Policy in UK Mobile Communications' (1998) 22 *Telecommunications Policy* 109 and Cave and Williamson (n 19 above) 116–118.

[24] This restriction was later removed when other operators were allowed to enter the market.

[25] Cave and Williamson (n 19 above) 117.

[26] The commercial success of the tied service providers may have been due to the fact that they were cross-subsidized by their respective networks. OFTEL responded by introducing measures requiring tied service providers to comply with certain financial criteria designed to prevent cross-subsidies. OFTEL, 'Fair Competition in Mobile Service Provision: A Statement by the Director General of Telecommunications' (May 1994). Independent service providers complained that the restriction on cross-subsidy was never enforced. See Cave and Williamson (n 19 above) 117.

[27] Valletti and Cave (n 23 above) 115.

In November 1990, the seven-year duopoly period promised by the Government for local and national fixed services finally expired. The same month the Government presented to Parliament a consultative document, 'Competition and Choice: Telecommunications Policy in the 1990s'. Following consultation, the Government published in March 1991 a White Paper in which it announced that it had decided to end the duopoly policy and that it would consider on the merits any application for a licence to offer telecommunications services over fixed lines within the United Kingdom. The duopoly policy was, however, temporarily maintained with respect to international facilities.[28] The duopoly of mobile networks ended in 1993 with two further licenses being issued to Orange and One2One. Finally, the duopoly policy with respect to the international network was abolished in June 1996. At that time, all segments of the UK telecommunications market were thus liberalized.

B. The main rules

In this section, we will successively review the telecommunications-specific rules and the antitrust provisions.

1. Telecommunications-Specific Rules

As mentioned above, the UK telecommunications regulatory framework is essentially composed of the requirements contained in the licences granted to the telecommunications operators.[29] The first part of this section will thus describe the provisions in the 1984 Telecommunications Act governing the licensing process as well as the content of the Public Telecommunications Operator Licence, ie the type of licence granted to the main telecommunications operators. The second part of this section will then briefly discuss the statutory requirements applicable to the allocation of radio spectrum, ie a key input for an increasingly large number of telecommunications services.

1.1 The Licences

The main statutory requirements applicable to licensing are primarily found in the 1984 Act, as well as in the EC Licensing Directive and other relevant EC legislation.

Section 5 of the 1984 Act provides that 'a person who runs a telecommunication system within the UK shall be guilty of an offence unless he is authorised to run the system by a licence granted under section 7'. Section 7 provides that a

---

[28] Colin D Long, *Telecommunications Law and Practice* (2nd edn, London: Sweet & Maxwell, 1995) § 2-12.

[29] On the role of licences in UK utility regulation, see David M Newbery, *Privatization, Restructuring, and Regulation of Network Utilities* (Cambridge, Mass., and London: MIT Press, 2000), 57–59.

telecommunication licence may be granted by the Secretary of State for Trade and Industry (hereafter, the 'SoS') after consultation with the DGT, or by the DGT himself, provided he is so authorized by the SoS.[30] So far, no such authorization has been given.

Licences may be granted to all persons, to persons of a class ('class licences') or to a particular person ('individual licences').[31] The licence sets out conditions under which the operator may run a telecommunications system and provide service over it. These conditions reflect requirements of the 1984 Act and also of a series of European directives applying to the telecommunications sector. Pursuant to the 1984 Act, ss 12 and 13, licence conditions may be modified with the consent of the licensee or, in the absence of consent, following a reference to the Competition Commission.[32] The requirement to obtain written consent is a cumbersome and time-consuming process, particularly when the DGT wishes to modify the licences of a large number of operators.[33] For this reason, the licence modification procedure has been recently modified by the Electronic Communications Act 2000.[34] Under the new procedure, the DGT will be able to modify licences provided that relevant licencees do not formally object to the modification. If the DGT wishes to make a modification despite objections from relevant licensees, he will generally need to refer the matter to the Competition Commission.

The operator of a telecommunications system may be licensed as a Public Telecommunications Operator (hereafter, 'PTO') by the SoS under s 9.1 of the Act.[35] Such classification facilitates acquiring rights of ways and imposes some duties, such as reaching certain penetration levels or providing universal service obligations. In general, the SoS designates as PTO licensees operators installing infrastructure to offer two-way services to a substantial class of customers and those installing long-distance networks.[36] The rest of this section focuses on the licensing of PTOs that represent the most significant operators on the UK market.

---

[30] 1984 Act, s 7(1).

[31] ibid s 7(3).

[32] ibid s 12.

[33] See DTI, 'Licence Modification Procedure: Proposed Changes to the Telecommunications Act 1984', document available at <http://www.dti.gov.uk/telecom/index2.htm#intro>.

[34] Electronic Communications Act 2000, Part III, ch 7, available at <http://www.uk-legislation. hmso.gov.uk/acts/acts2000/20000007.htm#11>.

[35] Section 8 refers to the conditions which may be applied to a person running a public telecommunications system, which may include the conditions requiring that person (in essence): (a) to provide specified telecommunications services; (b) to interconnect its telecommunication system with a telecommunication system run by any other person; (c) to permit the provision of specified telecommunications services by means of the licensed system; (d) not to show undue preference or undue discrimination to or against particular persons with respect to its services; and (e) to publish notice of its charges and other terms and conditions.

[36] Non-PTO licences are easier to get than PTO licences. They apply to private networks, such as telephone networks of utilities, closed user groups such as banks, or simple resale of international private lines. See Ingo Vogelsang and Bridget M Mitchell, *Telecommunications Competition—The Last Ten Miles* (Washington, DC, and Cambridge, Mass., and London: The AEI Press and MIT Press, 1997) 264.

The first and most important PTO licence delivered in the United Kingdom is BT's licence. BT's licence came into force on 5 August 1984, the day before BT became a public limited company and a few months before its flotation the same year.[37] Mercury obtained its licence in 1982 but only really started its operations in 1985.[38] During the period 1990–98, the SoS issued a large number of PTO licences (over 125) for a wide range of domestic and international services.[39] One problem with these licences was that, since they were issued at different times, there were variations between them.[40] This created a system of great complexity and opacity. Moreover, variations between licences were not always objectively justified, with operators providing similar services having to comply with different conditions. Quite clearly, the UK licensing system failed to comply with the criteria of transparency, objectivity, proportionality and non-discrimination that were set in the Directive (EC) 97/13 on Licensing (hereafter, the 'Licensing Directive'), the provisions of which had to be transposed into UK law.[41]

In 1998, the Government decided to modify the existing licences in order to bring them into line with the Licensing Directive. The modification of the existing PTO licences was realised by the Telecommunications (Licence Modification) (Standard Schedules) Regulations 1999[42] and related Regulations which came into force on 27 September 1999.[43] The central plank of the reform was to replace a large number of different PTO licence texts with, so far as possible, a standard PTO licence. For reasons discussed below, tailored versions of the PTO licence were, however, maintained for the two universal service providers (BT and Kingston Telecommunications), the four main mobile operators, and the cable operators. We will analyse hereafter the main aspects of the Standard PTO Licence. Then, we will turn to the BT licence.

The Standard PTO licence contains a set of general conditions that apply to all providers of publicly available telephone services (Conditions 1–36). There are also several sets of special conditions which are triggered only in certain circumstances (Conditions 37–64). For instance, special conditions will apply if the licensee:

---

[37] See Long (n 28 above) § 5.02.

[38] Tommaso Valletti, 'The Practice of Access Pricing—Telecommunications in the United Kingdom' Policy Research Working Paper No 2063, The World Bank, Economic Development Institute (February 1999) 3.

[39] A list of all PTOs can be found on OFTEL's website at <http://www.oftel.gov.uk/oftlic.htm>.

[40] See DTI, 'Implementation of the Licensing Directive: Changes to Existing Licences', Consultation Document (November 1998) (hereafter, 'Implementation of the Licensing Directive'), available on the DTI's website at <http://www.dti.gov.uk/cii/ec_directive.htm>.

[41] Generally on the EC Licensing Directive, Gerald Oberst, 'European Telecommunications Licensing' (1997) 5 *Computer and Telecommunications L Rev* 216.

[42] See the Telecommunications (Licence Modification) (Standard Schedules) Regulations 1999, SI 1999/2450, document available on the DTI's website: <http://www.hmso.gov.uk/si/si199924.htm>.

[43] See the Telecommunications (Licence Modification) (Fixed Voice Telephony and International Facilities Operator Licences) Regulations 1999, SI 1999/2451; the Telecommunications (Licence Modification) (Mobile Public Telecommunications Operators) Regulations 1999, SI 1999/2452; the Telecommunications (Licence Modification) (British Telecommunications) Regulations 1999, SI 1999/2453; the Telecommunications (Licence Modification) (Cable and Local Delivery Operator

(i) provides international telecommunications services;
(ii) is determined by the DGT to have significant market power (SMP) in a particular market in the telecommunications sector (a 25 per cent or more market share raises a presumption of SMP); and/or
(iii) is determined to be a universal service provider.

The general conditions impose a number of social and commercial obligations on operators. They also contain conditions designed to promote fair competition. Among such conditions is a requirement that licensees provide number portability to other operators.[44] Another condition requires that where the licensee has special or exclusive rights for the provision of sectors other than telecommunications and that its annual turnover from its telecommunications activities in the EC exceeds 50 million euros, it must keep separate financial accounts for its telecommunications activities.[45] Finally, the Fair Trading Condition (the 'FTC'), which is based on the EC Treaty, Articles 81 and 82, allows the DGT to take immediate enforcement against anti-competitive agreements and abuses of a dominant position.[46] With the entry into force of the Competition Act 1998 that contains prohibitions similar to those included in Articles 81 and 82 and gives enforcement powers to the DGT, the FTC lost its practical use and ceased to have any effect on 31 July 2001.[47]

Among the special conditions, Conditions 39–42 concern the provision of universal service. Under the regime preceding the licensing reform, only BT and Kingston Telecommunications had been designated as universal service providers (hereafter, 'USPs').[48] The new licensing regime maintains such arrangements. In the tailored licences adopted for BT and Kingston, the above conditions apply automatically. Under the Standard PTO Licence, however, other operators could in the future be determined to be USPs in a particular area or in respect of particular obligations. Pursuant to Condition 38, the DGT can determine an operator to be provider of a specific element of universal service within a specified area. Such a specified area shall not contain less than

Licences) Regulations 1999, SI 1999/2454; and the Telecommunications (Licence Modification) (Kingston Communications (Hull) PLC) Regulations 1999, SI 1999/2455. Documents available on the DTI's website at <http://www.hmso.gov.uk/si/si199924.htm>.

[44] See Condition 28.

[45] See Condition 30. Note that this condition implements the requirement found in Directive (EC) 96/19, Art 8 on the implementation of full competition in telecommunications markets (hereafter, the 'Full Competition Directive').

[46] The FTC was originally introduced into BT's licence coming into force in December 1996. It was later incorporated into the licences of all PTOs. For a discussion of the implications of the FTC, see OFTEL, 'Guidelines on the Operation of the Fair Trading Condition' (March 1997) available at <http://www.oftel.gov.uk/fairtrade/guidelin.htm> and OFTEL, 'Dealing with Anti-competitive Behaviour—An OFTEL Guide', available at <http://www.oftel.gov.uk/publications/1995_98/about_oftel/ac1297.htm>.

[47] See OFTEL, 'The Application of the Competition Act in the Telecommunications Sector' (January 2000) § 4.9, document available at <http://oftel.gov.uk/competition/catc0100.htm>.

[48] See Colin D Long, *Telecommunications Law and Practice* (2nd edn, London: Sweet & Maxwell, 1995) § 5.08–09.

100,000 premises. The factors that the DGT must consider when making such a determination are enumerated in the licence.[49]

A number of special conditions also apply to operators that are determined by the DGT as having 'Significant Market Power' pursuant to EC telecommunications legislation.[50] One such condition provides that SMP Operators have to *meet* all reasonable requests of interconnection to their network (non-SMP operators only have an obligation to *negotiate* interconnection with each other).[51] Interconnection charges will have to be 'reasonably derived from costs'.[52] Pursuant to another condition, SMP Operators have to publish an interconnection offer within three months of having been determined as having Significant Market Power.[53] Finally, there is a requirement on SMP Operators that have an annual turnover in telecommunications activities in the United Kingdom of more than 20 million euros to keep separate accounts for their interconnection activities and their other activities.[54]

As indicated above, tailored versions of the PTO licence have been developed for a series of operators, including BT and Kingston, the main mobile operators and the cable operators. As far as BT and Kingston are concerned, the addition of several obligations to the Standard PTO Licence is mainly due to the fact that both companies share the characteristic of being ex-incumbents.[55] BT is the principal incumbent UK operator and, at the time of the licensing reform, enjoyed a market share of more than 85 per cent of the fixed exchange lines. As a result, BT's licence contains price control formulas, the overall effect of which is to require BT to reduce, or restricts the extent to which it can increase the price of many of its telephone services in the retail or the wholesale market.[56]

BT's licence also includes conditions designed to promote fair competition. One condition imposes a prohibition on unfair cross-subsidies.[57] BT has also to comply with very detailed accounting separation requirements.[58] The Government justified the necessity of these requirements, which go beyond what is

---

[49] These factors include: (a) the relative size of the licensee's business, including the extent, density and resilience of the applicable systems in the provision of telephone services in a particular area compared with other providers of such services in the area under consideration; (b) the relative capacity of the licensee to comply with any or all of the relevant conditions; (c) the likely net cost to the licensee of complying with any or all of the conditions in Part A; (d) the financial stability of the licensee; and (e) the willingness of the licensee to comply with any or all of the conditions in Part A.

[50] See, eg, Art 4.3 on interconnection in telecommunications with regard to ensuring minimal service and interoperability through application of the principles of open network provision (ONP): [1997] OJ L199/32 ('An organisation shall have significant market power when it has a share of more than 25% of a particular telecommunications market in the geographical area within which it is authorised to operate.'). For a discussion of the obligation imposed by EC telecommunications legislation on operators having significant market power, see Pierre Larouche, *Competition Law and Regulation in European Telecommunications* (Oxford: Hart Publishing, 2000), 296–297.

[51] See Conditions 9 and 45.   [52] See Condition 47.1.   [53] See Condition 46.

[54] See Condition 50.

[55] See DTI, 'Implementation of the Licensing Directive', available at <http://www.dti.gov.uk/cii/ec_directive.htm>.

[56] Conditions 69–74.   [57] Condition 75.   [58] Conditions 76–78.

required in the Standard PTO licence, on the ground that a very large number of operators use BT's interconnection services at some point. The interconnection charges represent a major element of their costs.[59] These specific accounting requirements should allow OFTEL to identify separately the network costs appropriate to interconnection charging and to ensure that BT's retail business pays the same for the same use of its network as BT charges other operators.

Finally, BT's licence contains a condition that mandates it to provide unbundled local loop services.[60] Specifically, this condition obliges BT to provide individual telephone lines to other operators, allows co-location of equipment by operators in BT's local exchanges and requires BT to provide the necessary support to enable operators to deliver their service direct to customers using BT lines. The condition also provides that BT must give access to its network facilities at a charge to be agreed with the access seekers or, in default of agreement, to be determined by the DGT. The charges, whether agreed between the parties or determined by the DGT, should be such that they:

(i) shall permit recovery of an appropriate portion of common costs;
(ii) shall permit the recovery of long run incremental costs when these costs have been reasonably and necessarily incurred;
(iii) may reflect different circumstances and does not need to be uniform throughout BT's licence area, provided the differences in charges are objectively justified; and
(iv) shall include a reasonable return on the capital employed.

As far as mobile operators are concerned, special conditions apply to Vodafone and Cellnet under the 'market influence' trigger that is part of their PTO mobile licences.[61] One such condition obliges Vodafone and Cellnet to offer wholesale airtime to independent service providers,[62] an obligation that is not imposed on One2One and Orange on the basis that they do not have market power. Moreover, other conditions require that Vodafone and Cellnet provide separate accounts for various activities,[63] do not show undue preference or undue discrimination in the provision of various services,[64] and publish charges, terms and conditions for services.[65] On the other hand, no price controls are imposed on Vodafone and Cellnet's services.

---

[59] See 'Implementation of the Licensing Directive' (n 55 above).

[60] See OFTEL, 'Legal Framework for Local Loop Unbundling Now in Place', press release 30/00 (28 April 2000) available at <http://www.oftel.gov.uk/press/releases/2000/pr30_00.htm>. See also Chris Watson and Anne M Connaty, 'BT and Unbundling of the Local Loop' (2000) *Computer and Telecommunications L Rev* 7.

[61] See OFTEL, 'Notice of Determinations that Vodafone and BT Cellnet Have Market Influence under Condition 56 of their Respective Licences' (November 1999), available at <http://www.Oftel.gov.uk/competition/mble1099.htm>.

[62] See Condition 56A.

[63] See Condition 56B.

[64] See Condition 57.

[65] See Condition 58.

1.2 Rules Regarding the Management of Radio Spectrum

The Wireless Telegraphy Act makes it a criminal offence to establish or use any station for wireless telegraphy or install or use any apparatus for wireless telegraphy except under the authority of a licence granted by the SoS. Thus, for public telecommunications services that use radio spectrum, a licence is required and issued under the Wireless Telegraphy Act 1949 to complement the licence which is issued by the SoS under the Telecommunications Act 1984 (see preceding section). The licence issued under the 1949 Act contains conditions relating to the use of spectrum, such as approved standards for radio-equipment, maximum signal of interference levels, roll-out requirements, and fees.

Until recently, the Radiocommunications Agency, which is in charge of managing radio spectrum in the United Kingdom, relied solely on administrative decisions to allocate spectrum and the licence fees tended to be set no higher than necessary to recover administrative costs. A more market-oriented approach to spectrum management was, however, introduced by the Wireless Telegraphy Act 1998 (hereafter, the '1998 Act'). The 1998 Act introduced two forms of spectrum pricing: (i) administrative pricing, in which fees are set by regulation on the basis of spectrum management criteria (such criteria include the availability of and demand for the service in question and the desirability of providing spectrum efficiency, economic benefits, innovation and competition) and (ii) auctions in which fees are set directly by the market.

2. Antitrust Rules

The central competition law instrument in the United Kingdom is the Competition Act 1998 (hereafter, the 'Competition Act' or the 'Act').[66] The Act, which entered into force on 1 March 2000, replaces or amends legislation including the Fair Trading Act 1973, the Restrictive Practices Act 1976, the Resale Prices Act 1976, and the majority of the Competition Act 1980. The old legislation was considered 'unduly technical, and did not contain sufficient sanctions against genuinely harmful anti-competitive conduct, while unnecessarily catching innocuous agreements'.[67]

The new legislation introduces two prohibitions. The first is a prohibition on agreements between undertakings, decisions by associations of undertakings or concerted practices which have the object or effect of preventing or distorting competition in the United Kingdom (or a part thereof) and which may affect trade within the United Kingdom (the 'Chapter I prohibition').[68] This prohibition is

[66] Generally, on the Act, see Martin Coleman and Michael Grenfell, *The Competition Act 1998: Law and Practice* (Oxford: Oxford University Press, 1999).

[67] See OFT, 'The Competition Act 1998—The Major Provisions' (hereafter, 'The Major Provisions') § 1.2, document available at <http://www.oft.gov.uk/html/comp-act/technical_guidelines/oft400.html>.

[68] For a discussion of the Chapter I Prohibition, see OFT, 'The Competition Act 1998—The Chapter I Prohibition', OFT 401 (March 1999), document available at <http://www.oft.gov.uk/html/comp-act/technical_guidelines/oft401.html>.

subject to certain exclusions[69] and exceptions.[70] The second is a prohibition of conduct by one or more undertakings which amounts to the abuse of a dominant position, in a market in the United Kingdom (or a part thereof), which may affect trade within the United Kingdom (the 'Chapter II prohibition').[71] There is no possibility of exceptions from the prohibition of abuse of a dominant position. However, this prohibition may be subject to certain exclusions.[72]

The Chapters I and II prohibitions in the Act are based on the EC Treaty, Articles 81 and 82. One of the central objectives of the Competition Act is indeed to 'Europeanize' UK competition law.[73] In order to achieve this objective, the Competition Act does not only model its main prohibitions on EC competition law, but also sets out certain principles with a view to ensuring that the UK authorities handle questions arising under the Act in a manner that is consistent with the treatment of corresponding questions arising under EC law. Specifically, s 60 of the Act places a dual obligation on these authorities in considering and dealing with the application of Chapter I and II prohibitions. First, they must ensure that there is no inconsistency with either the principles laid down in the EC Treaty or the judgments of the European Court of Justice. Second, the UK authorities must have regard to any relevant decision or statement of the European Commission. The formula 'statement of the Commission' is limited to the 'statements' which have the authority of the European Commission as a whole, such as decisions on individual cases under Articles 81 and 82, the Annual Competition Report, and the Commission's two notices on the application of EC competition rules to the telecommunications sector.

While anti-competitive behaviours that have an impact within the United Kingdom will be caught by the Competition Act, EC competition law applies to anti-competitive agreements that may affect trade between Member States.[74] UK telecommunications operators may, therefore, be subject to EC law as well as the prohibitions in the Competition Act. There are provisions in the Act designed to reduce the possibility of investigation of the same issue by both the European Commission and by the Director General: (i) agreements which are exempt from the EC Treaty, Art 81 prohibition benefit from an automatic parallel exemption under the Act; and (ii) an agreement of which the European Commission has been notified is provisionally immune from penalties under the Act, in the same way as it is provisionally immune from the European Commission fines, until the European Commission formally determines the matter or withdraws the immunity.[75]

---

[69] ibid § 4.

[70] ibid § 5.

[71] For a discussion of the Chapter II prohibition, see OFT, 'The Competition Act 1998—The Chapter II Prohibition', OFT 402 (March 1999) document available at <http://www.oft.gov.uk/html/comp-act/technical_guidelines/oft402.html>.

[72] ibid § 2.4.

[73] See Margareth Bloom, 'A UK Perspective on the Europeanisation of National Competition Law', speech delivered at the Conference 'Modernisation and Decentralisation: The New Relationship between Community and National Competition Law', University College, London, 17 September 1999.

[74] See EC Treaty, Arts 81 and 82.   [75] See 'The Major Provisions' (n 67 above) § 6.7.

Complaints alleging breach of the Competition Act may be made to the Director General of Fair Trading or, if appropriate, to a sector-specific regulator (for, instance, the DGT). Where the complaint relates to issues falling within the concurrent jurisdiction of a regulator, the complaint will usually be dealt with by that regulator rather than the Office of Fair Trading (see Section C below). Financial penalties of up to a maximum of 10 per cent of the turnover of an undertaking in the United Kingdom may be imposed for an infringement of Chapter I or Chapter II prohibitions.[76] Third parties who consider that they have suffered a loss as a result of any unlawful agreement or conduct may also make a claim for damages in court.[77]

While the Competition Act seeks to prevent restrictive practices and abuses of a dominant position, it does not apply to mergers and acquisitions.[78] Under Schedule 1 to the Act, an agreement does not fall within the scope of the Chapter I prohibition to the extent that the agreement would result in two companies ceasing to be distinct enterprises for the purposes of the Fair Trading Act, Part V (hereafter, the 'FTA').[79] The aim of the exclusion is to prevent agreements or conducts from being subject to control under both the Competition Act and the merger provisions of the FTA.[80] When an agreement is considered to be a merger, only the provisions of the FTA will be applicable.

Not all merger transactions lead to the opening of an investigation under the FTA.[81] Under this statute, a merger situation qualifies for investigation under the FTA, and thus may be referred to the Competition Commission by the SoS, where the gross value of the world-wide assets being taken over exceeds a certain value (the assets test)[82] or where, as a result of the merger, the merged enterprises together account for more than 25 per cent of the supply or acquisition of goods or services of a particular description in the United Kingdom or a substantial part of it (the share of supply test).[83]

If, at the end of its enquiry, the Competition Commission reports that the merger in question may be expected to operate against the 'public interest',[84] the SoS has the power, but is not bound, to issue an order preventing the merger, attaching conditions to it, or even unscrambling a merger that has already taken

---

[76] ibid § 13.

[77] See OFT, 'The Competition Act—Enforcement' OFT 407 § 5.1, available at <http://www.oft. gov.uk/html/comp-act/technical_guidelines/oft407.html>.

[78] See OFT, 'The Competition Act—Exclusion for Mergers and Ancillary Restrictions' (hereafter, 'Exclusion for Mergers') OFT 416, available at <http://www.oft.gov.uk/html/comp-act/technical_ guidelines/oft416.html>.

[79] ibid § 2.2.

[80] In order to ensure that the exclusion does not have the effect of allowing transactions that significantly restrict competition to escape scrutiny altogether, however, it can be withdrawn in certain limited circumstances. See OFT, 'Exclusion for Mergers' (n 78 above) § 3.

[81] For a good discussion of the workings of the FTA, see Richard Whish, *Competition Law* (London: Butterworths, 1993), 671 et seq.

[82] Currently, £70 million.

[83] See s 64 of the Act.

[84] For a discussion of the factors that the MMC (now the Competition Commission) considers in its determination, see Whish (n 81 above) 692.

place. As noted by Whish, in practice, these formal powers are rarely used.[85] Instead, the SoS, if he decides to accept the recommendation of the Competition Commission, will ask the Director General of Fair Trading to enter into negotiations with the companies concerned in order to secure appropriate undertakings.

In the area of mergers, EC competition law must also be taken into account. Under Council Regulation (EEC) 4064/89 on the control of concentrations between undertakings,[86] the European Commission has exclusive jurisdiction to deal with mergers that involve a 'Community dimension'.[87] The parties to a concentration with a Community dimension must notify the Commission that will assess whether or not the concentration is compatible with the common market.[88] This question will be answered by an analysis of the relevant product and geographic markets and an assessment of the aggregate share of the parties in the affected market.

C. THE MAIN INSTITUTIONS

The above regulatory framework is implemented by the following institutions: the Secretary of State for Trade and Industry, OFTEL, the Office of Fair Trading, the Competition Commission, the Radio Communications Agency, and the courts.

1. The Secretary of State for Trade and Industry

The Secretary of State for Trade and Industry ('SoS') is the Cabinet member in charge of overseeing both telecommunications and competition policies.

As far as telecommunications is concerned, the primary role of the SoS is to take position on strategic issues (eg the speed of liberalization of the market, the opening of the market to foreign competitors etc). The major policy documents, such as the 1991 White Paper, were thus drafted and formally issued by the SoS. The DGT, however, is generally associated with this policy process. Thus, for instance, much of the 1991 White Paper reproduced the DGT's proposals with respect to the control of BT's tariffing, contribution towards the financing of its activities, and the terms on which interconnection between PTOs should be regulated.[89]

---

[85] ibid 690.

[86] [1989] OJ L395/1, as amended by Council Regulation (EC) 1310/97 [1989] OJ L180/1. Generally, on the EC Merger Regulation, see Christopher Jones and Enrique Gonzalez-Diaz, *The EEC Merger Regulation* (London: Sweet & Maxwell, 1992); John Cook and Christopher Kerse, *EC Merger Control* (London: Sweet & Maxwell 2000).

[87] EC Merger Regulation, Art 1.1.

[88] ibid Art 2.1.

[89] See Colin D Long, *Telecommunications Law and Practice* (2nd edn, London: Sweet & Maxwell, 1995) § 3-02.

In addition to its policy-making functions, the SoS holds the power to deliver licences after consultation with the DGT and, thus, to shape the content of the UK telecommunications regulatory framework. It also has the power to appoint the Director General for Telecommunications and retains veto power over the DGT's decisions. As will be seen below, the SoS can instruct the regulator not to make a reference to the Competition Commission or not to make a particular amendment to a licence, though this power has never been used.

Recent reforms have reduced the role of the SoS in the competition policy field.[90] In contrast with the provisions of the previous regime,[91] the new Competition Act provides no role for the SoS with respect to the control of anti-competitive agreements or conducts. One objective of the Act was indeed to shelter the handling of competition cases from political influence. As in the telecommunications sector, the SoS will retain policy-making functions. It also retains the power to appoint the Director General for Fair Trading.

2. OFTEL

The Office of Telecommunications (OFTEL) is the telecommunications-specific regulator in the United Kingdom. OFTEL, which was set up under the Telecommunications Act 1984, is headed by the Director General of Telecommunications (DGT) who is appointed for a fixed term, is independent from ministerial control and cannot be dismissed under normal circumstances (see Figure 6.1 below). OFTEL has about 160 staff, all based in London.[92] Some are from the Civil Service and others are experts with consumer, business and industry backgrounds. OFTEL's gross expenditures for 1999–2000 were £12,634,000.[93] OFTEL's funding is provided by Parliament, but in practice the cost of operating OFTEL is met almost entirely from licence fees.

Under the 1984 Act, the DGT has a number of duties and powers. The duties assigned to the DGT are set in the 1984 Act, s 3. Essentially, the DGT is to exercise his functions so as to secure the provision, as far as practically feasible, of such telecommunications services as are necessary to satisfy all reasonable demands for them, as well as to ensure that the persons providing such services are able to finance them.[94] In addition, the DGT is bound to promote the interests of consumers and to maintain and promote effective competition between persons engaged in telecommunications activities.[95]

---

[90] See Derek Morris, 'A New Dawn for Competition Policy in the UK', IBC Conference, 24 November 1999, available at <http://www.competition-commission.org.uk/inquiries/ibcspeech.htm>.

[91] On the previous regime, see Bruce Doern and Stephen Wilks, *Comparative Competition Policy—National Institutions in a Global Market* (Oxford: Clarendon Press, 1996) ch 6.

[92] On the institutional structure, see <http://www.oftel.gov.uk/about/oftguide.htm>.

[93] See OFTEL's Management Plan for 1999–2000, document available on OFTEL's website at <http://www.oftel.gov.uk/publications/1999/about_oftel/plan599.htm>.

[94] 1984 Act, s 3(1).

[95] ibid s 3(2) (a) and (b).

FIGURE 6.1. OFTEL organizational chart

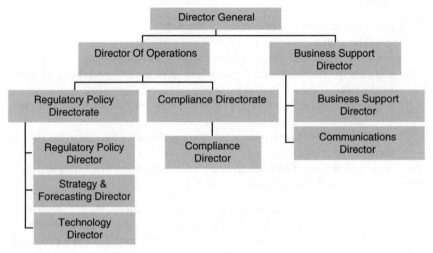

Source: <http://www.oftel.gov.uk/about/org_chart.htm>.

The DGT has extensive powers under the 1984 Act, including the power:

(i) to enforce licence conditions where a telecommunications operator is found to be in breach;

(ii) to make determinations, for example to set out the terms of interconnection between networks when the two operators cannot agree between themselves;

(iii) to propose modifications to licences; and

(iv) to advise the SoS on the granting of new licences.[96]

As will be discussed in the next sub-section, the Competition Act 1998 also entitles OFTEL, as well as the other sector regulators, to enforce the prohibitions of the Act.

3. The Office of Fair Trading

The Office of Fair Trading (OFT) plays a key role in protecting the economic welfare of consumers, and enforcing UK competition policy. Set up in 1973 and headed by the Director General of Fair Trading (hereafter, the 'DGFT'), the OFT is a non-ministerial department of Government. It has a staff of over 400 and its total budget for the 1998–99 financial year was £21,700,000.[97] It is divided into several divisions, one of which has specific responsibility for competition matters. The competition division, which has 130 staff, is divided into seven branches, including a branch dealing specifically with media, sport and information industries.

---

[96] On OFTEL's duties see Long (n 89 above) § 2-07.

[97] See Competition Policy in OECD Countries 1998–99, 'The United Kingdom', 18, document available at <http://www1.oecd.org/daf/clp/Annual_reports/1998–99.htm>.

The DGFT has the power to enforce the Competition Act. Specifically, the DGFT may:

(i)   give guidance on the application of the Act;

(ii) consider complaints about breach of the prohibitions;

(iii) impose interim measures to prevent serious and irreparable damage;

(iv) consider notifications for a decision and issue decisions on the application of the Act;

(v)   grant exemptions from Chapter I prohibitions (subject, where appropriate, to conditions);

(vi) carry out investigations both on the regulator's own initiative and in response to complaints;

(vii) issue and enforce directions to bring an infringement to an end; and

(viii) impose financial penalties in case of infringement.

For a number of industries, including telecommunications, the enforcement of the Competition Act is carried out by the sector regulator concurrently with the DGFT.[98] With some minor exceptions, this means that the DGT enjoys the same enforcement powers as the DGFT.[99] The complex issues raised by the existence of concurrent powers are discussed in Section E below.

4. The Competition Commission

The Competition Commission (hereafter, the 'CC') is a public body which rules on competition issues referred to it by the SoS and (among others) the DGT. The CC replaces the Merger and Monopoly Commission (MMC), which was dissolved by the Competition Act 1998. The CC, which entered into functions on 1 March 2000, has two distinct roles.

First, on the reporting side, the Commission has taken over the functions of the MMC, including the FTA inquiries into mergers and monopolies, and regulatory inquiries involving licence amendments. To carry out these reporting functions, the Commission comprises a full-time Chairman and a number of part-time members drawn from business, academia, trade unions, the law, and other professions. The Commission also has a specialist staff of about ninety. Both the Chairman and the members are appointed by the SoS following a competitive process. Commission members are assigned to a reporting panel or to specialist panels.

---

[98] To carry out this mission, the sector regulators have all the powers of the DGFT to apply and enforce the Act with respect to the activities of the undertakings active in their designated sector. Note that the DGFT alone, however, has powers to issue guidance on penalties and to make and amend the DGFT's procedural rules which set out the procedures to be followed in carrying into effect the provisions of Part I of the Act. In each case, the DGFT is required to consult with the regulators.

[99] See OFT, 'The Competition Act 1998—Concurrent Application to Regulated Industries' (hereafter 'Concurrent Application') OFT 405, at § 2.4, document available at <http://www.oft.gov.uk/html/comp-act/technical_guidelines/oft405.html>.

As far as telecommunications are concerned, the Competition Commission will be called to intervene when the DGT has been unable to amend a licence by agreement with the licensee.[100] In such a case, the DGT must refer the matter to the Commission. Pursuant to this reference process, the Commission is asked to investigate and report on whether the licence condition in question might be expected 'to operate against the public interest' and, if so, whether amendments to the licence could prevent this. The Commission has six months from the date of the reference to complete its enquiry. After considering the evidence, the Commission produces a report with factual information on the industry and the licensee, the views of the interested parties and the Commission conclusions. If the Commission does not find that the existing situation is against the public interest, the regulator cannot change the company's licence. But if it finds that the current situation may be able to operate against the public interest, it will propose amendments that could remedy this, and the regulator is allowed to change the company's licence taking into account the Commission's conclusions. In any event, the SoS retains veto power over the regulator. He can instruct the regulator not to make a reference to the Commission or not to make a particular amendment. As already noted, so far, this power has never been used.

The second role of the Commission is to hear appeals against decisions made by the DGFT or the sector regulators with respect to violations of the prohibitions contained in the Competition Act. A senior lawyer appointed by the SoS after consultation with the Lord Chancellor presides over the Competition Appeals Tribunals. The President must constitute an appeal tribunal to deal with each appeal. Each appeal tribunal so constituted consists of a Chairman, who must be the President or a chairman appointed by the President from the panel of chairmen, and two other members from the appeal panel of the Competition Commission. Members of the appeal panel are appointed by the SoS and come from a variety of backgrounds. The current panel is composed of eight members, all appointed on 1 March 2000 for a three-year term.

5. The Radiocommunications Agency

The Radiocommunications Agency (hereafter, the 'RA') is an executive agency of the Department of Trade and Industry with responsibility for the management of the non-military radio spectrum throughout the United Kingdom. The Chief Executive of the Agency is appointed by the SoS. He reports to a Director General within the Department of Trade and Industry. The Director General is assisted in assessing the performance of the Agency by a Steering Board that he appoints.[101] The RA's headquarters are located in London and the agency also has a network of eight local offices throughout the United Kingdom which provide local customer services. The RA's total staff is around 520 as of

[100] This paragraph draws on Richard Green, 'Checks and Balances in Utility Regulation—The UK Experience' *Public Policy for the Private Sector*, Note No 185, The World Bank (May 1999) 3.

[101] Exchange of e-mails with Mr Anthony Howard, Radiocommunications Office, 31 July 2001.

1 October 2000 and, for the year 2000, the RA's total expenditures amounted to almost £50 million.[102]

6. The Courts

Section 18 of the 1984 Act provides that telecommunications operators which are aggrieved by a final or provisional order of the DGT, and who question its validity on the ground that the action was not within its relevant powers (specified in s 16 of the Act) or was made in a manner that failed to comply with the proper procedure (specified in s 17 of the Act), may lodge an appeal against it before the courts. The appeal body in England, Wales and Northern Ireland is the High Court; in Scotland it is the Court of Session. In its original version, s 18 provided that regulatory decisions could not be challenged by any other legal proceedings than the above judicial review procedure.

In 1998, the Government put forward a proposal to reform s 18.[103] It considered that, besides judicial review, it would be desirable to allow for more extensive appeal rights, especially as to allow errors of *fact* to be considered. In the Government's view, broader appeal rights were necessary to subject decision-making in telecommunications to proper checks and balances. They were also necessary to better implement the relevant requirements of the ONP Framework Directive (EC) 90/387 and the EC Licensing Directive, which require the laying down of certain procedures for appealing against decisions of a national regulatory authority. This proposal was adopted in the Telecommunications (Appeals) Regulations 1999 (hereafter, the 'Appeals Regulations') which entered into force on 20 December 1999.[104]

The new appeal procedure covers decisions regarding the grant or refusal of licences, the inclusion of licence conditions and the enforcement and revocation of licences. It also applies to other decisions which materially affect those providing or seeking to provide telecommunications services.[105] Under the Appeals Regulations, a person aggrieved by a decision covered by the new appeals procedure may appeal against the decision on one or more of the following grounds:

(i) that a material error as to the facts has been made;
(ii) that there was a material procedural error;
(iii) that a material error of law has been made; or
(iv) that there was some other material illegality, including unreasonableness or lack of proportionality.

---

[102] Radiocommunications Agency, Annual Report and Accounts, 2000–2001 58.

[103] DTI, 'New Appeals Mechanism: Consultation Document', document available at <http://www.dti.gov.uk/cii/appealsintro.htm>.

[104] Telecommunications (Appeals) Regulations 1999, SI 1999/3180, available at <http://www.dti.gov.uk/cii/newsi.htm>.

[105] See the new s 46B of the Telecommunications Act 1984 introduced by the Telecommunications (Appeals) Regulations 1999.

The grounds for appeal under the new procedure include grounds on which an appellant might otherwise seek judicial review, but also allow the court to examine the regulator's finding of facts.[106] In England, Wales and Northern Ireland an appeal lies to the High Court, whereas in Scotland it lies to the Court of Session before the Lord Ordinary. The court determining the appeal may either dismiss the appeal or quash the decision. And where the court quashes a decision it may refer the matter to the SoS or the DGT with a direction to reconsider it and reach a decision in accordance with the findings of the court.

Besides judicial review and the new appeal procedure, courts may also be called to apply competition rules. First, third parties which consider that they have suffered a loss as a result of an unlawful agreement or an abusive conduct contrary to the Competition Act have a claim for damages in courts. Second, s 49 of the Competition Act provides that a decision from an Appeal Tribunal of the Competition Commission may be appealed either on a point of law or as to the amount of the penalty. Any such proceedings are to be made before the Court of Appeals for conflicts arising regarding activities taking place in England and Wales, the Court of Session for activities in Scotland, and the Court of Appeals in Northern Ireland for activities in Northern Ireland. Finally, since the EC Treaty, Articles 81 and 82 have direct effect,[107] individuals who believe that an agreement or a conduct violates such provisions can start legal proceedings before the courts in order to have such provisions enforced.[108] UK courts thus have to apply both UK and EC competition law.

D. IMPLEMENTATION OF THE REGULATORY FRAMEWORK

We will review, in this Section, the major developments relating to:

  (i) the regulation of fixed retail services;
  (ii) the regulation of wholesale services;
  (iii) the regulation of mobile services;
  (iv) alternative service provision;
  (v) universal service obligations;
  (vi) the debate over equal access;
  (vii) the implementation of new market-oriented spectrum management tools;
(viii) a third light-handed phase of regulation; and
  (ix) discussions over BT's structure.

---

[106] See, DTI, 'New Appeals Mechanism: Consultation Document' (n 103 above) § 13.

[107] See Case 127/73 *BRT v SABAM* (1974) ECR 51, 62; Case 155/73 *Sacchi* (1974) ECR 409.

[108] See Christopher Bellamy and Graham Child, *Common Market Law of Competition* (3rd edn, London: Sweet & Maxwell, 1993) § 10-004.

1. The Regulation of Fixed Retail Services

The duopoly review in 1991 initiated a new phase of regulation of UK telecommunications characterized by the opening of the market to many additional entrants with an increased degree of interventionism on the part of OFTEL. The duopoly review led to a tightening of the price-cap. The X figure, which had been set at 3 per cent in 1984 and brought to 4.5 per cent in 1989 as mentioned in Section A above, was brought to 6.25 per cent and the range of regulated services which had been enlarged in 1989 was enlarged again to include international calls. In 1993, BT's retail prices were further tightened to RPI – 7.5 per cent for a period of four years (see Table 6.1 below).

During the 1997 price review, the DGT clearly indicated its intention to pull back from regulation as competition advances, and to ensure that *fair* competition takes place.[109] The retail price control for public switched telephony set by OFTEL for the period August 1997 to July 2001 is RPI – 4.5 per cent.[110] This new retail price is measured on the services used by a sub-set of BT's customers that are not likely to benefit from competition. As shown in Table 6.1, this means that the scope of the cap will be considerably reduced from 64 per cent (for the price-cap covering the period 1993–97) to 22 per cent of BT's services (for the period 1997–2001). According to Scott, OFTEL's strategy was to offer the carrot of substantial deregulation of prices to tempt BT to accept a new Fair Trading Condition in its licence.[111] This would allow OFTEL to challenge anti-competitive behaviour, such as excessive or discriminatory pricing, as a competition authority.[112] Since its insertion into the BT licence, the FTC has been used by OFTEL on a number of instances (usually in combination with other Conditions imposing fair trading requirements on BT) to prevent abusive behaviour on the

TABLE 6.1. Control on BT's retail prices

Control period	Control formula	Coverage (in terms of BT's services)
1984–89	RPI-3%	49%
1989–91	RPI-4.5%	55%
1991–93	RPI-6.5%	67%
1993–97	RPI-7.5%	64%
1997–2001	RPI-4.5%	22%

Source: M Cave, 'The Evolution of Telecommunication Regulation in the UK' (1997) 41 *European Economic Rev* 694.

---

[109] OFTEL, 'Pricing of Telecommunications Services from 1997—A Statement Issued by the DGT' (June 1996).
[110] For the same period, BT is also subject to a retail price control of RPI + 0 per cent for private leased circuits.
[111] See Colin Scott, 'The Proceduralization of Telecommunications Law' (1998) 22 *Telecommunications Policy* 243.
[112] ibid.

part of the incumbent. As has been noted above, the rationale for this Condition has now disappeared with the entry into force of the Competition Act of 1998.

In the fall of 2000, OFTEL released the Price Control Review, a policy analysis OFTEL had to carry out given the expiry of the controls imposed for the period 1997–2001.[113] In this document, OFTEL analyses the degree of competition achieved in various segments of the market and the consequences of price controls. As far as the retail market is concerned, OFTEL recognizes that the market is beginning to change significantly with increasing competition from both direct access (ie facilities-based) and indirect access (ie relying on BT's network) operators.[114] Reductions in BT's market shares in the main call markets reflect this increasing competition, though in the residential market its shares remain high. OFTEL also notes that BT's overall level of profitability exceeded what BT requires to cover its full costs and make a reasonable return.[115] OFTEL, however, acknowledges that a series of factors should increase competitive pressures on BT and will impact its market share in 2001 and beyond.[116] In particular, several regulatory developments (eg the implementation of carrier pre-selection and the unbundling of BT's local loop) and increased cable expansion should provide competitive stimulus. However, OFTEL considers that it is difficult at the time of review to assess with an acceptable level of accuracy whether, taken together, the developments will provide sufficient pressure on BT to restrain prices.[117] As a result, OFTEL proposes that BT's licence be modified to extend the current retail controls until July 2002 and that the level of competition be reassessed during the final quarter of 2001.[118] If that assessment suggested that competition had not become fully effective, and appeared unlikely to become so in the near future, OFTEL would consider whether further price control or other measures to stimulate competition were needed.

In July 2001, OFTEL released a detailed review of the market in fixed telephony services.[119] Among the main findings were that:

(i) competition was increasing in all fixed telephony markets but was not yet effective;

(ii) BT would remain dominant in the provision of access for the foreseeable future; and

---

[113] See OFTEL, 'Price Control Review: A Consultative Document Issued by the Director General of Telecommunications on Possible Approaches for Future Retail Price and Network Charge Control' (hereafter, the 'Price Control Review') (October 2000), document available at <http://www.oftel.gov.uk/publications/1995_98/pricing/ncct797.htm>.

[114] ibid § 2.3.

[115] ibid § 2.7.

[116] ibid § 2.8 et seq.

[117] ibid § 2.14.

[118] ibid § 2.29.

[119] OFTEL, 'Competition in the Provision of Fixed Telephony Services—A Consultation Document Issued by the Director General of Telecommunications' (31 July 2001), document available at <http://www.oftel.gov.uk/publications/pricing/pcr0701.htm>.

(iii) the current terms of access to BT's network might not prevent but certainly deter entry from service providers and hence restrict innovation in pricing and products in the calls market.

OFTEL subsequently published a consultation paper, 'Protecting Consumers by Promoting Competition',[120] which contains a set of proposals 'to replace the current retail price controls on BT with a package of measures better designed to encourage competition, while still protecting the most vulnerable consumers in a changing marketplace'.[121] OFTEL's main proposals are:

  (i) to encourage greater market entry by mandating BT to provide a 'wholesale line rental' product;[122]
 (ii) to give service providers and operators using BT's network the ability to offer a 'one bill' service;[123]
(iii) to remove RPI – X control, but only when call prices have fallen sufficiently to signal that clear competition is now the main determinant of these prices (the removal would be automatic when a threshold still to be determined is reached, without further regulatory review); and
(iv) to protect low spending customers by maintaining a safeguard cap, preventing bills from rising in real terms, after the threshold has been reached.

Stakeholders are given a period of three months to comment, following which OFTEL will publish its final conclusions in June 2002.

2. The Regulation of Wholesale Services

The 1991 review, at the end of the duopoly period, led to a reassessment of the interconnection charges set following the 1985 determination. The new charges published by BT in December 1993 required third operators to contribute to BT's access deficit.[124] The access deficit contributions (ADCs) were intended to take into account the losses BT suffered for being unable to raise the price of its line rentals as to fully cover its costs. Payment of these ADCs was waived until an entrant had a market share of 10 per cent or BT's market share

---

[120] OFTEL, 'Protecting Consumers by Promoting Competition—Consultation on OFTEL's Review of the Fixed Telephony Market' (31 January 2002) document available at <http://www.oftel.gov.uk/publications/pricing/2002/pcr0102.htm>.

[121] ibid S 1.

[122] What OFTEL essentially means is 'that existing operators, telecommunications service providers and new entrants from other sectors wanting to enter the fixed telephony market will be able to buy the wholesale line rental product from BT network on non-discriminatory terms': ibid S7.

[123] What OFTEL means is that 'the bill from the alternative supplier would cover the cost of both the line rental and the calls made, rather than there being a separate BT line rental bill. A single bill gives operators the ability to charge in wholly different ways—for example, virtually free calls but a high subscription or no explicit line rental at all and all costs recovered from the costs of calls': ibid.

[124] See Mark Amstrong et al, *Regulatory Reform: Economic Analysis and British Experience* (Cambridge, Mass., and London: MIT Press, 1994) 219.

fell below 85 per cent.[125] The ADC system ended in 1996 when the RPI + 2 per cent constraint on BT's rental charges was abolished.

For the period 1997–2001, OFTEL modified once again its method for calculating interconnection charges. First, OFTEL changed the methodology from fully distributed, historic costs to LRIC (plus a mark-up for common costs). OFTEL justified the change on the ground that the new methodology was 'better reflecting the basis on which commercial businesses in competitive markets make investment decisions and thus providing the industry with more appropriate price signals'.[126] BT argued that the LRIC adjustment would result in it suffering a windfall loss, but it nevertheless accepted the change. Second, under the new access regime, the degree of control imposed on BT's services is inversely related with the degree of competition achieved in such services:

(i) competitive services: these services, which are those where a high degree of competition exists or without barriers to any sort of entrants, are outside of the network price control and BT is free to set its charges;[127]

(ii) prospectively competitive services: these services, which are those that are not competitive by the time of the introduction of the new regime but are expected to become competitive during the control period, are regulated by a safeguard cap (RPI + 0 per cent), so that initial charges do not increase;[128]

(iii) non-competitive services: these services, which are not likely to be subject to a relevant degree of competition during the control period, are subject to basket controls. Three baskets are capped by the RPI−X mechanism. The productivity factor is set at 8 per cent for a four-year period for all three baskets that cover roughly half of BT's network activities. The three baskets are call termination services (local exchange segments), general network services (call origination, local-tandem conveyance, single transit), and connection services (interconnection circuits). Within each basket, individual services are subject to a system of floors (to avoid predation) and ceilings (to avoid exploitation) based respectively on incremental costs and stand-alone costs.

The consultative document on the consequences of price controls, released by OFTEL in the fall of 2000 as mentioned under 1, above, also addresses wholesale market issues.[129] OFTEL believes that the competitive environment for the provision of interconnection services has not changed sufficiently for it to

[125] See Tommaso Valletti, 'The Practice of Access Pricing—Telecommunications in the United Kingdom', Policy Research Working Paper No 2063, The World Bank, Economic Development Institute (February 1999) 8.

[126] See OFTEL, 'Network Charges from 1997', at § 3.13, document available at <http://oftel.gov.uk/publications/1995_1998/pricing/nccjul97.htm>.

[127] In practical terms, only operator assistance services belong to this category.

[128] Services included in this category are inter-tandem conveyance and transit, international direct dial conveyance, international private lease circuits, directory enquiry services, and access to emergency services.

[129] See OFTEL, 'Price Control Review', available at <http://www.oftel.gov.uk/publications/1995_98/pricing/ncct797.htm>.

remove any non-competitive interconnection services from the baskets in which they are presently controlled, nor does it believe that any of the individual safeguard cap controls (RPI + 0 per cent) can be removed.[130] It therefore proposes that, from October 2001, services that are presently deemed to be non-competitive and prospectively competitive respectively will continue to be classed as such unless evidence is brought to suggest the contrary. OFTEL proposes that, from October 2001, prospectively competitive services be subject to individual charge controls set at RPI + 0 per cent and that, from the same date, the baskets of non-competitive interconnection services be subject to charge controls of between RPI − 7.5 per cent to RPI − 11.5 per cent.[131]

Until recently, OFTEL's policy with respect to resellers of BT's services was that such resellers should pay prices based on a 'retail-minus' formula (BT's prices minus any cost saved by not servicing the retail user). In contrast, network operators such as Mercury and Energis can obtain the same services from BT at wholesale prices.[132] In its 2000 Price Control Review, OFTEL, however, proposed a change of policy, which would enable simple resellers to purchase interconnection services from BT at charges based on BT's costs instead of BT's retail prices.[133]

Finally, in recent months, OFTEL took several initiatives that should have a positive impact on the development of Internet use in the United Kingdom. First, in July 1999, OFTEL announced its intention to require BT to unbundle its local loop by July 2000, a regulatory move that had been requested by companies wishing to provide ADSL services over BT's network. OFTEL published in September 2000 guidelines designed to give effect to the requirements for BT to unbundle its local loop.[134] These guidelines were adopted amidst sharp criticisms that OFTEL had taken too much time to take the necessary measures to force BT to allow access to its local loop.[135] They provide a description of the services and information BT needs to supply to other operators, as well as the conditions of supply. In addition, the DGT subsequently issued determinations and directions on a range of important issues for the implementation of local loop unbundling, including a determination on the prices for the use of the local loop itself,[136] a determination on the method for allocating space at BT

---

[130] ibid § 3.9.

[131] ibid §§ 3.10 and 3.12.

[132] As pointed out by Ryan, that is because network operators have been designated as 'relevant connectable systems' under the terms of Condition 13 in BT's licence. Relevant connectable systems can obtain services from BT at a price equal to cost. See Michael Ryan, 'United Kingdom Policy on Equal Access and the Promotion of Network Competition' (1998) *Computer and Telecommunications L Rev* 7.

[133] OFTEL, 'Price Control Review: A Consultative Document Issued by the Director General of Telecommunications on Possible Approaches for Future Retail Price and Network Charge Controls' § 2.24, document available at <http://www.oftel.gov.uk/publications/pricing/pcr0300.htm>.

[134] See OFTEL, 'Access to Network Facilities: Oftel Guidelines on Condition 83 of BT's Licence' (September 2000), available at <http://oftel.gov.uk/competition/llug0900. htm>.

[135] See Dan Roberts, 'Leaving the Opposition Out of the Loop', *Financial Times*, 20 September 2000.

[136] OFTEL, 'Determination Under Condition 83.16 of the Licence of British Telecommunications PLC Relating to the Charges for the Provision of Metallic Path Facilities and Associated

exchanges,[137] a direction on access to BT's exchanges by third parties,[138] and a direction on the price for 'shared access' to the local loop.[139]

Second, on 26 May 2000, OFTEL requested BT to offer a wholesale unmetered Internet access service to other telecommunications operators which request it by no later than 1 June 2000.[140] This decision essentially came as a result of an interconnection dispute between BT and MCI WorldCom (see Box 6.1 below). The service that has to be offered by BT is known as FRIACO (Flat Rate Internet Access Call Origination). It will allow other operators to provide unmetered Internet access to consumers in competition with BT's own unmetered access known as Surftime.

Box 6.1: The BT/MCI WorldCom Dispute over Unmetered Interconnection

In December 1999, MCI WorldCom referred to the DGT an interconnection dispute with BT. In September 1999, MCI WorldCom had requested that BT supply it with an interconnection service providing for flat (unmetered) Internet call origination. BT, however, refused to supply MCI WorldCom with the proposed service. In its submissions to the DGT, BT justified its decision by arguing that existing metered interconnection services available from BT enabled MCI WorldCom to provide unmetered access to its customers.

In its direction, the DGT rejected BT's claim because it considered that if operators wishing to provide unmetered Internet access are forced to purchase interconnection services from BT on a metered basis, they will be exposed to forecasting risk as they will have no certainty about the extent to which their unmetered retail products will be used. If call volumes per customer exceed their forecasts, these operators' payments to BT will increase, but their (flat-rate) income from each customer will remain the same. The lack of an unmetered wholesale call origination product therefore has the potential to create a situation under which an operator offering a retail unmetered service would suffer a margin squeeze.

Source: OFTEL, 'Direction Under Condition 45.2 of the Public Telecommunications Licence granted to British Telecommunications plc and under Regulation 6(6) of the Telecommunications (Interconnection) Regulations 1997'.

Internal Tie Circuits' (December 2000), available at <http://www.oftel.gov.uk/publications/pricing/llup1200.htm>.

[137] OFTEL, 'Local Loop Unbundling: Access to BT's Exchanges by Third Parties' (13 December 2001), available at <http://www.oftel.gov.uk/publications/broadband/llu/escac1201.htm>.

[138] OFTEL, 'Local Loop Unbundling: The Terms of the Access Network Facilities Agreement Statement and Determination' (February 2001) available at <http://www.oftel.gov.uk/publications/broadband/llu/anf0201.htm>.

[139] OFTEL, 'Local Loop Unbundling: Final Charges for Shared Access' (18 October 2001) available at <http://www.oftel.gov.uk/publications/broadband/llu/shac1001.htm>.

[140] OFTEL, 'Direction Under Condition 45.2 of the Public Telecommunications Licence granted to British Telecommunications plc and under Regulation 6(6) of the Telecommunications (Interconnection) Regulations 1997', available at <http://www.oftel.gov.uk/publications/internet/fria0500.htm>.

Third, in December 2000, the DGT published a draft direction requiring BT to offer specified wholesale leased line services to other telecommunications operators on a non-discriminatory basis and at cost-oriented prices.[141] This direction follows the publication of a policy document by OFTEL in August 2000 in which it had found that competition was not effective in the leased lines retail market, resulting in prices higher than they would be in a competitive market.[142] This direction will allow BT's competitors to purchase so-called 'terminating segments' from BT at wholesale prices (rather than at retail prices as has been the case so far).[143] By adding these terminating segments to their 'trunk networks', this will in turn allow competitors to provide retail end-to-end leased line services at a competitive price, thereby increasing the level of competition in this market largely dominated by BT.

3. The Regulation of Mobile Services

As mentioned in Section A above, the arrival of Orange and One2One in the mobile market in 1993 ended the duopoly structure that had previously characterized the market. To the extent that the two former duopolists, Vodafone and Cellnet, continued to possess market power in the market for calls from mobile phones, the specific requirements to provide airtime to service providers remained in their licences, thereby creating an asymmetric regime.

In March 1998, the DGT made two references to the MMC relating to charges for calls made from fixed lines to mobile phones.[144] The DGT considered that Cellnet and Vodafone's termination charges were excessive, and should be regulated so as to be cost reflective. He believed that Cellnet and Vodafone were able to set the charges without significant market pressure, because someone wanting to make a fixed-to-mobile call had no choice but to call the network to which the called party had subscribed.[145] The MMC concluded that, though the mobile industry and technology were evolving rapidly and new competitive pressures may emerge, competitive constraints on termination charges

---

[141] OFTEL, 'National Leased Lines—Statement and draft direction issued by the Director General of Telecommunications' (December 2000), available at <http://www.oftel.gov.uk/publications/pricing/nll1200.htm>.

[142] OFTEL, 'National Leased Lines—Effective Competition Review and Policy Options' (hereafter, 'Effective Competition Review and Policy Options') (August 2000), available at <http://www.oftel.gov.uk/publications/pricing/nll0800.htm>.

[143] One of the main barriers to entry for telecommunications operators into the end-to-end retail leased lines market is the structure of the wholesale market. In general these operators have not built out large networks between the customer and the digital main switching unit (DMSU) and, thus, have to rely on terminating segments from BT in order to offer an end-to-end retail service. These terminating segments are provided at retail prices. BT is, however, able to buy such segments from itself at wholesale prices, thereby gaining a cost advantage over its competitors. See 'Effective Competition Review and Policy Options' (n 142 above) § 3.14.

[144] MMC, 'Cellnet and Vodafone: Reports on references under section 13 of the Telecommunications Act 1984 on the charges made by Cellnet and Vodafone for terminating calls from fixed-line networks', available at <http://www.competition-commission.org.uk/reports/421cellnet.htm>.

[145] ibid § 8.17.

were still inadequate.[146] For the MMC, the only effective means of remedying or preventing the adverse effects created by this lack of competition were to impose a price control on termination charges.[147] It recommended that charges be reduced from 14.83 pence per minute (ppm) to 12.15 ppm and that a price-cap of RPI – 9 per cent be applied to the initial 12.15 ppm for the following three years.[148]

OFTEL conducted reviews of the mobile market in 1999[149] and 2001.[150] In the 2001 Review, OFTEL found that competition was increasing to the benefit of the consumers, but that the market was only 'prospectively competitive'.[151] The main factor that prevented OFTEL from concluding that the mobile sector was now effectively competitive was that some operators (Vodafone and BT Cellnet) were still pricing above the level that would be found in an effectively competitive market and that they, therefore, retained some degree of market power. However, OFTEL expects that competition between the four existing operators should continue to develop and prices should continue to fall.[152] The arrival of a fifth operator (Hutchinson 3G) in the market following the UMTS licence auctions should also further increase competitive rivalry in mobile services in the future. In the light of growing competitive pressures, OFTEL considers that it can start reducing regulation and it therefore proposes to lift the designation of 'market influence' for Vodafone and BT Cellnet.[153] This implies that a series of obligations which specifically apply to these two operators, such as the obligations to offer wholesale airtime to independent service providers on request (see Section 1.1 above), should no longer be imposed.

4. Alternative Service Provision

The end of the duopoly for domestic fixed services in 1991 attracted many new entrants including cable television (hereafter, 'CaTV') operators and other utility companies, such as for instance Energis (then a subsidiary of the National Grid). While the latter could build telecommunications facilities around their infrastructure, the former benefited from economies of scope between television and telecommunications services.[154] Entry of CaTV operators was encouraged by the

---

[146] ibid § 1.6.

[147] ibid § 1.12.

[148] ibid § 1.11.

[149] See OFTEL, 'OFTEL's Review of the Mobile Market: Statement Issued by the Director General of Telecommunications' (hereafter, the 'Mobile Market Review') (July 1999) available at <http://www.oftel.gov.uk/publications/1999/competition/mmrv799.htm>.

[150] OFTEL, 'Effective Competition Review: Mobile—A Statement by the Director General of Telecommunications' (26 September 2001), document available at <http://www.oftel.gov.uk/publications/mobile/mmr0901.htm>.

[151] ibid S 5.

[152] ibid S 9.

[153] ibid S 10.

[154] Tommaso Valletti, 'The Practice of Access Pricing—Telecommunications is the United Kingdom', Policy Research Working Paper No 2063, The World Bank, Economic Development Institute (February 1999) 6.

asymmetric regulatory approach adopted by the Government.[155] While CaTV companies could offer telecommunications services, public telecommunications operators could not offer home entertainment services. The objective was to stimulate competition in local markets (cable systems used to convey television can also be used to carry telecommunications services, thereby providing an alternative to BT's local loop), something that Mercury had largely failed to achieve.[156] Moreover, the fear was that if BT were allowed to enter the television market, the cable companies would not survive as suppliers of either television or telecommunications services.[157]

In 1998, in a policy document entitled 'Broadband Britain', the Government indicated its decision to progressively relax the line of business restrictions imposed on public telecommunications operators.[158] Pursuant to this new approach, national public telecommunications operators were permitted to both convey and provide broadcast entertainment over their networks in areas of the country not yet covered by cable operator franchises, with a commitment to allow national PTOs and others to convey and provide broadcast entertainment throughout the whole territory from 1 January 2001.[159]

5. Universal Service Obligations

Besides price control, OFTEL determined in 1997 the content of universal service obligations for a period of four years (1997–2001).[160] OFTEL placed upon BT and Kingston Communications an obligation to provide: a connection to the fixed network to support voice telephony and low speed data and fax transmission on reasonable request; the option of a more restricted service package at low cost; and reasonable geographic access to public phones across the United Kingdom. Moreover, all customers should be able to access 999/112 services free; receive itemized bills; choose selective call barring and have access to operator assistance and directory information; and be given the option of an outgoing calls barred (OCB) service, together with a repayment plan, as an alternative to disconnection for non-payment. The provision of universal service should be at geographically averaged prices.

As far as the funding of universal service obligations is concerned, OFTEL decided that such obligations would have to be provided by BT and Kingston without any compensation. OFTEL computed that USO costs ranged from

---

[155] See Willem Hulsink, *Privatisation and Liberalisation in European Telecommunications—Comparing Britain, the Netherlands and France* (New York and London: Routledge, 1998) 140.

[156] Valletti (n 154 above) 6.

[157] See Mark Amstrong, 'Competition in Telecommunications' (1997) 13 *Oxford Rev of Economic Policy* 69.

[158] See Department of Trade and Industry, 'Broadband Britain: A Fresh Look at the Broadcast Entertainment Restrictions' (April 1998) available at <http://www.dti.gov.uk/cii/c20/index.html>.

[159] ibid § 31.

[160] OFTEL, 'Universal Telecommunications Services' (July 1997) document available at <http://www.oftel.gov.uk/publications/1995_98/consumer/univ_2.htm>.

£60 to £90 million.[161] OFTEL considered, however, that these costs were in great part compensated by the commercial advantages BT and Kingston could obtain from providing universal service, including enhancement of corporate reputation, marketing and brand recognition, benefits associated with consumers' life-cycles, etc.[162] Net costs, after accounting for benefits, were within the range of £0–£40 million, figures that did not justify the creation of a Universal Service Fund.

Together with its consultative document on the consequences of price control mentioned above, OFTEL also released in the fall of 2000 a consultative document on universal telecommunications services.[163] In this document, OFTEL invites feedback from interested parties on a series of proposals regarding the level of universal telecommunications service and the way such a service is to be funded from September 2001. OFTEL's key proposals are that: (i) the universal service should not, at this stage, be extended to include mobile, data and broadband services but these areas will be kept under review and (ii) BT and Kingston Communications should continue to fund universal service obligations as the costs of such obligations do not represent an unfair burden. Following consultations with all stakeholders, these proposals were confirmed in a statement of the DGT in August 2001.[164]

6. The Debate over Equal Access

A controversial issue in the mid 1990s was whether BT should be forced to grant equal access to its competitors. Until then, BT's customers could have access to services (eg long-distance telephony) provided by another operator via BT's local network by dialling extra digits or following additional procedures. Equal access meant the substitution of such arrangements by one in which there would be a parity in the number of digits to be dialled or other procedures to be followed in order to route a call over either BT's or the second network operator.[165]

In 1996, OFTEL released a policy document in which it expressed doubts about the overall economic benefit of introducing equal access.[166] First, a cost–benefit study by consulting firm NERA suggested that the benefits of mandating equal access (in terms of increased competitive pressure on existing operators)

---

[161] See OFTEL, 'Universal Telecommunications Services—A Consultative Document on Universal Service in the UK from 1997' (December 1995) § 9.4.

[162] ibid § 9.8.

[163] OFTEL, 'Review of Universal Telecommunications Services' (September 2000) document available at <http://www.oftel.gov.uk/publications/consumer/uso0900.htm>.

[164] See OFTEL, 'Universal Service Obligation: A Statement Issued by the Director General of Telecommunications' (30 August 2001) available at <http://www.oftel.gov.uk/publications/consumer/uso0801.htm>.

[165] See 'OFTEL's Policy on Indirect Access, Equal Access and Direct Connection to the Access Network: Statement from the Director General of Telecommunications' (hereafter, 'OFTEL's Policy on Indirect Access') § 9, document available at <http://www.oftel.gov.uk/publications/1995_98/competition/access96.htm>.

[166] ibid § 23.

might be lower than the costs of introducing such a system. OFTEL was also concerned that the introduction of equal access 'could discourage operators from developing alternative access networks if they risked the benefits of their investments to competing operators'.[167] Equal access could thus impede the facilities-based competition strategy promoted so far by OFTEL and the British Government. OFTEL concluded, on balance, that there was no need for directing BT to provide equal access.

A few years later, the United Kingdom was, however, forced to introduce equal access by European legislation. Directive (EC) 98/61 mandated Member States of the European Union to ensure that at least organisations having Significant Market Power (typically the incumbent, such as BT) offer carrier pre-selection to their subscribers by 1 January 2000.[168] A deferment was, however, granted by the European Commission in respect of BT, deferring compliance with the requirements of the carrier pre-selection provisions of Directive (EC) 98/61 until 1 April 2001.[169] At present, an obligation to provide carrier pre-selection services figures in Condition 50A of BT's licence.

7. Implementation of the New Market-Oriented Spectrum Management Tools

As has been seen in Section B above, the Wireless Telegraphy Act 1998 introduced two new market-oriented spectrum management tools, ie administrative pricing and auctions.

Since the entry into force of the Act in June 1998, the Radiocommunications Agency has progressively introduced administrative pricing across a range of spectrum-using sectors.[170] Implementation has been conducted in stages, with pricing applied first in sectors suffering from the worst distortions caused by the previous cost-based regime. Within each sector, transition from old licence fees to the new incentive prices has generally been phased in over four years so that users have an opportunity to adjust.

Auctioning of spectrum licences has also taken place on two different instances. First, in May 2000, the UK Government awarded five licences (A–E) for third generation (hereafter, 3G) mobile telephony.[171] Licences were allocated on the basis of simultaneous multiple-round auctions with ascending bids. Different bandwidths were on offer with the largest licence (Licence A) reserved

---

[167] ibid.

[168] See European Parliament and Council Directive 98/61, Art 1, amending Directive (EC) 97/33 with regard to operator number portability and carrier pre-selection, [1999] OJ L268/37.

[169] See Commission Decision 2000/54 of 22 December 1999 concerning the request by the United Kingdom for a deferment, pursuant to Directive (EC) 97/33, Art 20(2) (the 'Interconnection Directive'), of the obligation to introduce carrier pre-selection: [2000] OJ L19/69.

[170] See Laurence Green, 'The UK Approach to Spectrum Pricing and Auctions', paper presented at the IDEE Telecom Conference, 11 June 1999, available at <http://www.radio.gov.uk/topics/spectrum-price/documents/idee.htm>.

[171] For an explanation of the main features of the auctioning process, see Information Memorandum, 'United Kingdom Spectrum Auction—Third Generation, The Next Generation of Mobile

TABLE 6.2. Results of 3G licences auctions in the United Kingdom

Licence	Winner	Bandwidth allocated	Sum (000)
A	TIW	2 × 15 MHz paired spectrum, plus 5 MHz unpaired spectrum	£4,384,700
B	Vodafone	2 × 15 MHz paired spectrum	£5,964,000
C	BT	2 × 10 MHz paired spectrum, plus 5 MHz unpaired spectrum	£4,030,100
D	One2One	2 × 10 MHz paired spectrum, plus 5 MHz unpaired spectrum	£4,003,600
E	Orange	2 × 10 MHz paired spectrum, plus 5 MHz unpaired spectrum	£4,095,000
Total			£22,477,000

Source: DTI, 2000.

for a new entrant. Licence A was won by TIW UMTS (UK) Ltd, while the four remaining licences were won by the four operators already active in the UK mobile services market (see Table 6.2 above). At the end of the last auction round, total bids exceeded £22 billion, a sum that was higher than the estimates of most observers.

Second, in November 2000, the Agency held an auction of regional licences for the Broadband Fixed Wireless Access Spectrum. The auction was not as successful as that of 3G mobile licences. Only 16 of the 42 available licences were sold, leaving seven regions without any licences sold.[172] Following the auctions, the UK E-Government Minister Patricia Hewitt told the Trade and Industry Committee of the Parliament that the outcome of these auctions suggested that 'there was actually not a commercial case for rolling out high-speed Internet access' in some areas and that 'there is likely to be a need for public intervention'.[173]

The Agency has also been considering the introduction of spectrum trading as an additional market-based spectrum management tool. In 1998, the Agency issued a preliminary consultation paper on spectrum trading and reduction of administrative burden on the transfer of licences.[174] The Government announced on 25 May 1999 that, in light of the favourable response to the consultation, the RA would work closely with industry to develop detailed proposals to introduce spectrum trading, subject to the necessary legislative changes being made.[175]

Communications' (hereafter, 'Next Generation of Mobile Communications') (NM Rotschild & Sons and Radiocommunications Agency, 1 November 1999).

[172] The value of the 16 licences issued was £38,160,000. See RA, Annual Report and Accounts 2000–01 10.

[173] Oral evidence given to Select Committee on Trade and Industry, 13 December 2000.

[174] Radiocommunications Agency, 'Managing Spectrum though the Market' (1998).

[175] See 'Next Generation of Mobile Communications' (n 171 above) 2.2.8.

8. Towards a Third 'Light-Handed' Phase of Regulation

It is generally acknowledged that regulation of UK telecommunications can be divided into three phases: a first duopoly phase (1984–91), a second phase of market opening to new entrants accompanied by a tightening of regulation (1991–97), and a third phase of 'normalization' where telecommunications-specific regulation would be progressively phased out and telecommunications operators would be disciplined by the same rules as the other sectors of the economy.[176]

In its policy paper 'Achieving the Best Deal for Telecoms Consumers', published in January 2000, OFTEL indicated its willingness to relax the regulatory framework and replace regulation with its more general powers to regulate anti-competitive conduct under the Competition Act.[177] In OFTEL's view,

The Strategy will bring a new approach to OFTEL's work which will mean that as competition develops further, and provided that OFTEL is satisfied consumers are adequately protected, telecoms regulation will be progressively reduced. In this way the telecoms market will be governed increasingly by the same legal requirements as are placed on other industries in the economy rather than through telecoms specific regulation. This means that the case for any new regulation will be scrutinised very closely and new regulation will be introduced if it is absolutely necessary for the promotion of competition and for the protection of the consumers, and if these aims cannot be achieved in any other way. Regulation will be as 'light touch as possible'—alternatives to formal regulation such as co-regulation and self-regulation being considered wherever possible. Existing regulation will also be subject to scrutiny to see if it continues to be needed.[178]

The implementation of this new deregulatory strategy can already be felt in some recent OFTEL actions discussed above, such as its proposals to abandon the current price-cap mechanism on retail telephone prices when a given 'trigger' was reached and its decision to lift the designation of 'market influence' for Vodafone and BT Cellnet, thereby lowering the regulatory burden applicable to these operators. This strategy has also recently received support in the Government's White Paper 'A New Future for Communications' (hereafter, the 'Communications White Paper'). This White Paper provides that OFCOM, the new communications regulator the Government suggests to create (see Box 6.2 below),[179] should rely more on its general powers under the Competition Act than on sector-specific rules to promote effective competition in the communications

---

[176] See Martin Cave, 'The Evolution of Telecommunications Regulation in the UK' (1997) 41 *European Economic Rev* 661; Tommaso Valletti, 'The Practice of Access Pricing—Telecommunications in the United Kingdom', Policy Research Working Paper No 2063, The World Bank, Economic Development Institute (February 1999).

[177] OFTEL, 'OFTEL Strategy Statement: Achieving the Best Deal for Telecoms Consumers' (January 2000), available at <http://www.oftel.gov.uk/publications/about_oftel/strat100.htm>.

[178] ibid § 9.

[179] Generally on OFCOM's proposed structure and missions, see David Edmonds, 'OFCOM: What Are We Worried About?' (11 October 2001), available at <http://www.oftel.gov.uk/publications/about_oftel/strat100.htm>.

services sector for the benefit of consumers.[180] Moreover, the White Paper provides that this body should roll back regulation promptly where increasing competition renders it unnecessary,[181] that where new requirements are necessary, it should consider the use of 'sunset' clauses which would remove the regulation if, and when, it is no longer required,[182] and that it should encourage alternative regulatory approaches, such as co-regulation and self-regulation, where these will best achieve the regulatory objectives.[183]

Box 6.2: OFCOM's Proposed Structure and Competencies

In its Communications White Paper, the UK Government proposed to combine the existing functions of OFTEL, the several bodies regulating the broadcasting sector (ie the Broadcasting Standards Commission, the Independent Television Commission, and the Radio Authority) and the Radiocommunications Agency into a single regulatory authority, entitled OFCOM, which would be responsible for the whole communications sector. OFCOM would be governed by a Board composed of executive and non-executive members, rather than a single individual. Members of the Board would be collectively accountable.

OFCOM would be responsible for economic regulation of communications, content regulation, and spectrum management. As in the case of OFTEL, OFCOM would have concurrent powers with the OFT to implement the Competition Act prohibitions in the communications sector.

Source: DTI, White Paper 'A New Future for Communications'.

9. Discussions over BT's Structure

In April 2000, BT announced its intention to separate its wholesale (network) and retail activities.[184] The company indicated subsequently that this vision would be implemented by creating a new network company, NetCo, which would be structurally and managerially separate from the retail activities (see Figure 6.2 below).[185] According to BT, the move 'is pro-competitive and removes any perceived conflicts between Netco and the rest of the company'.[186] Competitors have, however, expressed strong scepticism that NetCo could be trusted to operate independently from the rest of BT. They argue such a structure, pursuant to which both wholesale (ie NetCo) and retail (ie BT Retail)

---

[180] ibid § 2.1.
[181] ibid § 8.11.
[182] ibid § 8.11.2.
[183] ibid § 8.11.1.
[184] See BT press release, 'BT reveals plans to lead the next wave of the communication revolution' (hereafter, 'BT's restructuring plans') (13 April 2000) available at <http://groupbt.com/mediacentre/releases/2000/nr35.htm>.
[185] See BT press release, 'Statement from Sir Peter Bonfield, CEO of BT' (7 November 2000).
[186] See 'BT's restructuring plans' (n 184 above).

FIGURE 6.2. BT's proposed new structure

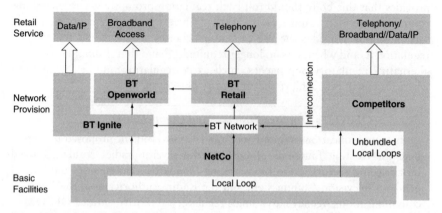

Source: Jonathan Sandbach, 'Levering Open the Local Loop: Shaping BT for Broadband Competition' (2001) 3 *Info* 195.

activities remain part of the same holding, fails to eliminate incentives for NetCo to discriminate in favour of its parent retail company.

More recently, some observers have, however, developed a more radical proposal whereby BT would divest its entire local access network.[187] They consider that, given BT's failure to implement its unbundling commitments in order to protect its own ISDN and ADSL services, such a drastic structural change 'would be the only way to make unbundling work and open competition in the local loop to increase broadband service offerings'.[188] In the summer of 2001, BT received two offers, one for its UK fixed line business for £18 billion from German bank WestLB and one for its local access network from the Earthlease consortium for £8 billion, but it rejected them.[189] BT's financial difficulties combined with increased regulatory pressure to force it to share access to its network might, however, force it to reconsider its position on this matter.

E. A CRITICAL APPRAISAL OF THE REGULATORY FRAMEWORK

As pointed out at the beginning of this chapter, the UK regulatory regime presents a few features which distinguish it from that of other countries discussed in this book: for example, the insertion of many sector-specific rules in the operators' licences and the allocation of important antitrust enforcement powers to the sector-specific regulator. In addition, we have seen that some efforts are

[187] See, for instance, Tom Steinberg, 'Open Networks: A Solution to Britain's Broadband Problems?' (Institute of Economic Affairs, February 2001).

[188] See Michelle Donegan, 'Operators Target BT's Network' *Communications Week Intl*, 21 May 2001.

[189] See Michelle Donegan, 'Telcos Pressured to Split Up' *Communications Week Intl*, 8 October 2001.

being made to increase reliance on antitrust rather than sector-specific instruments. We review below how the UK model is faring against the seven criteria identified in Chapter 2.

1. Competition and Other Incentives to Generate and Share Efficiency Gains

The United Kingdom is generally considered as being a pioneer country in the opening of telecommunications markets to competition, as well as in the development of incentive mechanisms in telecommunications regulation.

One of the key features of the UK regulatory regime is its strong emphasis on encouraging facilities-based competition.[190] In order to sustain this objective, active entry assistance was provided to alternative network operators through asymmetric regulation. Besides the prohibition that prevented BT and Mercury from providing home entertainment services on their telecommunications networks (a prohibition that favoured cable operators), BT and Mercury were not allowed to offer fixed wireless technology except in sparsely populated areas (a prohibition that favoured fixed wireless operators, such as the now-defunct Ionica).

By contrast, several examples show that OFTEL did nothing to encourage non-'pure' facilities-based competition on the local market.[191] First, OFTEL was opposed to both equal access and unbundling of BT's local loop, which it considered as running counter to the UK policy of encouraging the establishment of alternative infrastructures.[192] Similarly, as mentioned above, OFTEL's interconnection pricing strategy was unfavourable to service resellers since they had to pay retail-minus prices for the services they received from BT, while network operators such as Mercury and Energis could obtain the same services at wholesale prices.[193] One implication of this charge system, designed to reward those operators which have built their own facilities, was that resellers were at a cost disadvantage compared to network operators (unlike a cost-based system, retail-minus meant that resellers had to contribute to BT's forgone profits) and, thus, were in a more difficult position to compete.

Facilities-based competition has failed, however, to deliver the expected results (as BT is still largely dominant in the exchange lines market) and recent policy decisions suggest that OFTEL has decided to revisit its strategy of 'pure' facilities-based competition. First, under the pressure of EC legislation, OFTEL has now required BT to provide equal access to competitors and unbundle its local loop, even though OFTEL has been accused by BT's rivals of dragging its

---

[190] See Jean-Jacques Laffont and Jean Tirole, *Competition in Telecommunications* (Cambridge, Mass., and London: MIT Press, 1999) 32.

[191] See Michael Ryan, 'United Kingdom Policy on Equal Access and the Promotion of Network Competition' (1998) *Computer and Telecommunications L Rev* 6.

[192] Statement of the DGT, 'OFTEL's policy on indirect access, equal access and direct connection to the access network' (July 1996).

[193] As pointed out by Ryan, that is because network operators have been designated as 'relevant connectable systems' under the terms of Condition 13 in BT's licence. Relevant connectable systems can obtain services from BT at a price equal to cost. See Ryan (n 191 above) 7.

feet for adopting the necessary measures to ensure access to BT's lines.[194] Moreover, in the 2000 Price Control Review OFTEL also proposed that simple resellers be entitled to purchase interconnection services from BT at charges based on BT's costs instead of BT's retail prices.[195] It is hoped that this will give these operators a competitive boost.

In market segments where competition is insufficient, the UK Government decided to put in place price controls. In this regard, a distinctive feature of the UK regime was its reliance on price caps in order to regulate both retail and, more recently, wholesale markets. The Government's reliance on price caps as a tool to control retail prices as early as 1984 came from its anxiety to avoid the perceived problems of US-style rate-of-return regulation in terms of cost inefficiency, administrative burden and risks of capture.[196] However, as we have seen in Chapter 3, Section A above, there are a number of factors mitigating the differences between rate-of-return and price-cap regulation. In particular, regulators do study costs under price-cap regulation with a view to set the caps so as to enable a reasonably efficient firm to make a 'normal' return over the period for which the caps are set. This could be observed in the United Kingdom. For example, when OFTEL reviewed its price-cap at the end of the 1984–89 period, BT's rate-of-return in current cost terms was apparently a key determinant of the tightening of the efficiency factor to 4.5 per cent.[197] The DGT subsequently stated the efficiency factor was set 'at a level which gives BT an expectation of covering the cost of capital employed for the services under control, and takes account of the risk for BT while providing demanding targets for improvements in customer service and increased efficiency'.[198] Rate-of-return considerations thus seem to have played a role in the price-cap setting.

We have also seen in Chapter 3 that, though price-cap regimes have many virtues, they provide fewer incentives to maintain quality since the regulated firm might benefit from cost reductions that would jeopardize quality. This problem seems to have happened in the United Kingdom. A few years after the introduction of the price-cap regime, BT's service quality had degraded so much that OFTEL was forced to adopt new quality measures to respond to consumers' discontent.[199] Specifically, the DGT decided that BT should resume publication of its quality of service statistics on a six-monthly basis (BT had stopped publishing such statistics after privatization) and should face financial penalties in some form for poor service quality.[200]

As far as interconnection charges are concerned, BT's licence originally stipulated that access charges should cover the costs of providing interconnection,

---

[194] See text accompanying nn 168–169 above.
[195] See text accompanying n 195 above.
[196] See Mark Amstrong et al, *Regulatory Reform: Economic Analysis and British Experience* (Cambridge, Mass., and London: MIT Press, 1994) 216.
[197] ibid 227.
[198] See BT Share Prospectus (November 1991) 26, quoted in Amstrong et al (n 196 above) 227.
[199] See Amstrong et al (n 196 above) 222.
[200] ibid.

including relevant overheads and a reasonable rate-of-return on the relevant assets, on the basis of fully distributed costs calculated on a historic basis. As we have seen, OFTEL set interconnection charges at a level favourable to Mercury. Following the 1991 price review, OFTEL modified its approach and decided to introduce in the charges an access deficit contribution (ADC). This system, which ended in 1996 when BT was allowed to rebalance its line rental charges, drew its inspiration from the ECPR in that the ADC paid by a competitor on a call is proportional to the profitability of that call for BT and so it can be regarded as the opportunity cost element of the ECPR.[201] The practical effect of the system was diminished, however, by OFTEL's discretion to grant ADC waivers. The linkage of waivers to the entrant's market share was criticized by Laffont and Tirole because such a system reduced Mercury's incentives to increase its market share.[202]

For the period 1997–2001, OFTEL modified once again its method for calculating interconnection charges by switching from fully distributed historic costs to TELRIC. The switch to TELRIC—ie a methodology based on the estimation of the marginal costs of a benchmark efficient firms—brings to a certain extent the access charge regime more closely in line with the price control regime imposed upon retail prices, since neither regimes are, in theory,[203] based on actual costs. This might somewhat reduce the incentives of the firm to engage in accounting or managerial cross-subsidies between different activities. Since 1997, non-competitive services are divided into three baskets, each of them subject to a RPI − 8 per cent formula. As pointed out by Valletti, the main rationale for having separate baskets is the fear that BT may recover an excessive proportion of its costs from call termination, which is likely to remain the main bottleneck in place in the future.[204] Thus, dividing up services into separate baskets reduces the ability of the incumbent to cross-subsidize the elements that are more likely to become competitive with those that will remain non-competitive.

In addition to pioneering with the use of price caps, the United Kingdom has been one of the first countries to experiment auctions for 3G licences. Such auctions have drawn harsh criticism by observers from the telecommunications industry on the ground that the huge cost (ranging from £4 to 6 billion for each operator) involved in acquiring a licence through auction will lead to higher consumer prices and reduce the readiness of telecommunications operators to invest in networks.[205] As discussed in Chapter 3, since the licence fees are irrevocable sunk costs, these arguments do not seem to hold with economic theory.[206]

---

[201] See Laffont and Tirole (n 190 above) 168.

[202] ibid 30.

[203] In practice, we have seen, however, that the price-cap regime imposed in the retail market was not as different as might have appeared at first from a cost-based rate-of-return regime. See text accompanying nn 197–198 above.

[204] See Tommaso Valletti, 'The Practice of Access Pricing—Telecommunications in the United Kingdom' Policy Research Working Paper No 2063, The World Bank, Economic Development Institute (February 1999) 13.

[205] See David Harrington, 'Access for All? Spectrum Auctions in the Local Loop' (2000) 2 *Info* 351.

[206] See Chapter 3, Section E.4.

Some observers, however, argue that the huge sums invested in acquiring a licence will have a 'psychological' effect on operators, which, for instance, will feel more vulnerable, and will thus be more reluctant to engage in price wars and more inclined to act collusively. It is difficult to say at this stage whether this prediction will come true. Some operators have already suggested that to recoup the investment made in acquiring 3G licences, tariffs will have to be increased.[207] It seems, however, that the presence of five operators will be a key factor to ensure low prices for consumers. Moreover, with the entry into force of the Competition Act, OFTEL and the OFT appear to be well equipped to prevent restrictive practices between operators.

As far as the competitiveness of the various market segments is concerned, the local market is currently the least competitive. In spite of the Government's strategy of facilities-based competition, BT is still largely dominant in the market for the provision of fixed exchange lines. Table 6.3 below shows that, in June 2001, BT still controlled 81.5 per cent of the exchange lines for residential customers and 88.2 per cent of the lines for business customers. Table 6.3 also shows that the market share of cable operators has decreased between September 2000 and June 2001 in both residential and business markets. This suggests that the penetration of cable operators might have already reached its peak.

Table 6.4 below, however, shows that BT's market shares in the calls market are declining at a faster rate than its share in the exchange lines market. This is due to the presence of non-facilities-based operators that provide a variety of services through BT's network. This Table also shows that BT retains a strong position in the local calls market, both for residential and business customers. The erosion of BT's market share has been stronger in the national (long-distance) and international call markets, particularly for business users. The

TABLE 6.3. Market shares (number of lines)

Market segment	Company	September 1999	September 2000	June 2001
Residential customers	BT	83.0%	80.3%	81.5%
	Cable	16.3%	19.0%	17.9%
	Kingston	0.7%	0.7%	0.6%
Business customers	BT	90.1%	88.5%	88.2%
	Cable	8.2%	9.2%	9.0%
	Kingston	0.5%	0.6%	0.7%
	Others	1.2%	1.7%	2.0%

Source: OFTEL, 'Protecting Customers by Promoting Competition' (January 2002).

---

[207] See Colin Blackman, 'Editorial: Spectrum Auctions—Who's Screwing Whom?' (2000) 2 *Info* 339, 340.

United Kingdom

TABLE 6.4. Summary of BT's market shares for calls (in terms of revenues)

Services	Customer type	BT's share 1996–97	BT's share 1997–98	BT's share 1998–99	BT's share 1999–2000	BT's share 2000–2001
Local calls	Residential	91.2%	86.2%	82.3%	79.4%	75.4%
	Business	87.3%	84.4%	80.3%	74.5%	68.8%
National calls	Residential	88.7%	86.6%	84.4%	79.7%	72.8%
	Business	70.7%	66.0%	60.9%	56.4%	52.1%
International	Residential	77.5%	71.9%	74.7%	69.2%	63.9%
	Business	47.9%	39.0%	37.8%	38.2%	37.6%

Source: OFTEL, 'The UK Telecommunications Industry: Market Information 2000/01' (December 2001).

TABLE 6.5. Mobile revenues by operators

	Vodafone	BT Cellnet	One2One	Orange
2000–2001	36%	23%	17%	23%
1999–2000	40%	27%	15%	18%
1998–99	42%	31%	13%	14%
1997–98	44%	33%	10%	13%

Source: OFTEL, 'Effective Competition Review' (September 2001).

price comparisons provided in the Annex show that, with prices based on PPPs, the UK's long-distance market is the cheapest of those examined in the book, while its international call market is the third cheapest (see Annex, Graphs 4b, 5b, and 6b).

In the mobile market, since the entry of Orange and One2One, the market shares of the two former duopolists, Vodafone and Cellnet, have declined indicating increasing competitive pressures.[208] As shown by Table 6.5 above, Vodafone and BT Cellnet's shares of mobile revenues have declined quite substantially over the last few years, while the shares of new entrants have rapidly increased. Increased competitive pressures have also had a significant impact on prices. During the period 1990–98, prices fell 68 per cent in real terms, the biggest reductions during this period coinciding with the entry into service of One2One and Orange in 1993 and 1994 respectively.[209] Since 1999, prices have continued to fall though at a lower pace. The price comparisons provided in the Annex show that, with prices based on PPPs, the UK mobile market is the cheapest of those examined in this book (see Graphs 11b and 12b). As we

[208] See OFTEL, 'Competition in the Mobile Market: A Consultative Document Issued by the Director General of Telecommunications' (hereafter, 'Competition in the Mobile Market') (February 1999) available at <http://www.oftel.gov.uk/publications/1999/competition/cmm0299.htm>.
[209] See ibid § 1.15.

have seen above, in light of the competitiveness of the market, OFTEL has recently proposed that regulation of mobile services be progressively reduced.

As far as the development of the Internet is concerned, several factors suggest that the UK market for dial-up Internet access is 'effectively competitive'.[210] A large number of ISPs (more than 400 according to the Internet Service Providers Association) provide a variety of dial-up access packages.[211] Prices for ISP services have been driven down by competition with companies, such as Freeserve, offering free ISP services as early as 1999.[212] However, until 2000, metered local charges held back the development of Internet use in the United Kingdom.[213]

In early 2000, the United Kingdom became the first country in Europe where fully unmetered services appeared on the market. On 14 February 2000, Telewest, a major cable operator, launched the first fully unmetered Internet access service in the United Kingdom.[214] Given the attractiveness of unmetered services for Internet users, other companies had to follow suit and offer unmetered Internet packages to consumers. If Telewest was able to be the first company to offer fully unmetered ISP services, it is because it did not have to rely on BT's local loop to have access to the consumers. Other operators faced much greater difficulties in offering unmetered services (eg the conflict between MCI World-Com and BT discussed above), although their position has been improved by the DGT's decision to require BT to offer wholesale flat rate Internet access call origination (FRIACO) to its competitors. Competition has had a downward effect on prices and, according to a recent benchmarking study published by OFTEL, unmetered Internet dial-up access for residential users is now much cheaper in the United Kingdom than in Germany (from £18 per month in the United Kingdom as compared to £39 per month in Germany) and slightly cheaper in the United Kingdom than in California (from £18 per month in the United Kingdom as compared to £19 per month in California).[215] According to the price comparisons provided in the Annex, PPP-based Internet prices in the United Kingdom are only the third cheapest of our sample, however (see Graphs 9b and 10b).

Second, regarding broadband Internet access, it is with considerable delays that BT has started to provide ADSL services to the UK consumers. According to

---

[210] See OFTEL, 'OFTEL's 2000/01 Effective Competition Review of Dial-Up Internet Access' (30 July 2001) available at <http://www.oftel.gov.uk/publications/internet/imr0701.htm>.

[211] For some examples of such packages, see OECD, 'Local Access Pricing and E-Commerce' (hereafter, 'Local Access Pricing'), DSTI/ICCP/TISP(2000)1/FINAL (26 July 2000) 51–52.

[212] When consumers dial up an ISP they are charged at the local call rate. These call charges are then split between the originating operator (BT), the terminating operator, and the ISP. Free ISPs have been able to fund their activities out of their share of call revenues. See OECD, 'Local Access Pricing' (n 211 above) 45.

[213] See OFTEL, 'Pricing of Calls to the Internet: Possible Initiatives to Bring About More Appropriate and Flexible Tariffs' (November 1999) available at <http://www.oftel.gov.uk/publications/1999/info_super/oifp1199.htm>.

[214] See 'Telewest Launches Unlimited Internet Access', press release, 13 December 1999, available at <http://www.telewest.co.uk/ pressreleases/ pr68.html>.

[215] See OFTEL, 'International Benchmarking Study of Dial-Up PSTN Internet Access, Mobile and Fixed Line Services—June 2001', available at <http://www.oftel.gov.uk/publications/research>.

recent OFTEL figures, at the beginning of 2001, only a tiny fraction of BT's telephone lines (approximately 50,000 lines out of 35,000,000) had been upgraded to provide ADSL services.[216] The requirement placed on BT to unbundle its local loop should permit other operators to provide high bandwidth services. However, BT has dragged its feet and, as we have seen above, OFTEL has been sharply criticized for taking too much time to adopt the necessary measures to force the incumbent to allow access to its local loop. As a result, in early 2001, only BT provided an ADSL service to consumers, while about 100 ISPs were selling this service to consumers. This places the United Kingdom near the bottom of the European telecommunications league both with respect to the number of ADSL lines offered to consumers and the total of ADSL lines offered by the incumbent's competitors (which currently amounts to 0 per cent in the United Kingdom).[217]

Some degree of competition in broadband services is, however, brought about by cable operators which have started supplying cable modem broadband Internet access to their consumers. As already noted, cable operators do not need to rely on BT's network to provide such services, which gives them a greater ability than operators relying on BT's infrastructure to undercut the incumbent's prices for broadband services. Cable operators, however, suffer from network coverage limitations (50 per cent of households compared with BT that holds approximately 85 per cent of all telephony lines). It is also expected than additional competition will come from broadband fixed wireless (BFW) access providers, though the failure of the auctioning of the BFW licences in some UK regions suggest that broadband Internet access through this technology will only be provided in some parts of the country in the years to come.

Overall, broadband Internet access is insufficiently provided in the United Kingdom. According to an October 2000 report published by an Internet measurement firm, less than 1 per cent of UK households have a broadband connection.[218] Moreover, insufficient competition has kept broadband Internet access prices high compared with other OECD countries. A recent international benchmarking study of DSL and cable modem services published by OFTEL states that the monthly charge for broadband services is around £40 per month in the United Kingdom compared to £31 in Germany, £32 in the United States, and £37 in France.[219]

The obligation to provide universal service is currently placed on BT and, in Hull, on Kingston Telecommunications. As we have seen, these operators do not receive any compensation for carrying out their universal service obligations for the moment. There is, however, some disagreement between BT and OFTEL over

[216] See OFTEL, 'Local Loop Unbundling Fact Sheet—April 2001', available at <http://www.oftel.gov.uk/publications/local_loop/llufacts/llufacts0401.htm>.

[217] Sarah Parkes, 'Competition in the Last Mile Remains Elusive', *Financial Times Special Survey on Telecoms* (18 July 2000) IV.

[218] See Jane Wakefield, 'UK Slow to Take Up Broadband, Says Report' *ZDUKNet News*, 18 October 2000, available at <http://zdnet.com.com/2100-11-524888.html>.

[219] OFTEL, 'International Benchmarking of DSL and Cable Modem Services' (July 2001) available at <http://www.oftel.gov.uk/publications/research/2001/dslb0101.htm>.

the net costs of carrying out such obligations. The DGT could, as pointed out above, select another operator to be provider of a specific element of universal service within a specified area.[220] According to recent OFTEL policy documents, there is little prospect, however, that an additional designation will be made in the near future.

One advantage of the current British universal service regime is that it does not cost any money to the public purse. On the other hand, it is subject to question whether this regime is fair to BT and Kingston or to the users. While the incumbents' estimates of the costs of USOs are probably exaggerated, it is not entirely clear whether these costs are more than or less than compensated by various commercial advantages. In this regard, one of the merits of establishing a competitive selection of USO providers is that it would provide much more precise information about the true costs of USOs.

Finally, a word should be said about BT's structure. The main structural decision taken by the British Government when it initiated the liberalization of the telecommunications industry was to privatize BT intact, instead of breaking it up vertically along the lines of what happened to AT&T in the United States as a result of the MFJ.[221] As noted above, an important reason for this decision was the desire to privatize BT rapidly.[222] A second reason is that the UK authorities envisaged a regime of facilities-based competition under which it was hoped that BT would lose its near monopoly of the local market and could therefore not use its market power there to distort competition in other segments of the telecommunications sector. The relative failure of facilities-based competition and BT's continued dominance in the local and long-distance markets indicate that it might have been preferable to vertically separate BT at the time of privatization.

More recently, observers have pointed to the need for a different type of structural reform, the objective of which would be to stimulate competition in the local loop. In the middle of 2000, BT made public its intention to create a new wholesale company (ie NetCo), which would be structurally and managerially separate from BT's retail division (ie BT Retail). As we have seen in Chapter 3, such functional separation fails to remove incentives for the bottleneck infrastructure holder to discriminate in favour of its parent retail company. In this regard, critics of the separation model proposed by BT are right to point out that a full separation between BT's local network and its local resale activities would be more effective in terms of preventing discrimination and, thus, strengthening competition in the local loop. The potential benefits of a break-up of BT would of course have to be balanced with the costs that would be incurred.

---

[220] See text accompanying n 220 above.
[221] This sub-section is essentially based on Mark Amstrong et al, *Regulatory Reform: Economic Analysis and British Experience* (Cambridge, Mass., and London: MIT Press, 1994) 206, 215 and 240.
[222] See text accompanying n 11 above.

2. Specificity versus Coherence

Prior to the 1998 reform, the UK competition law framework was considered by many to be weak and ineffective.[223] It is therefore unsurprising that, when it privatized and progressively liberalized telecommunications, the British Government decided to control BT's market power through sector-specific regulation to be implemented by a sector-specific regulator.[224]

One of the core features of the UK system is that, besides the 1984 Telecommunications Act, the bulk of regulation is found in the licence of the operators. Over the years, through its various modifications, BT's licence has become a sophisticated document that contains a large number of substantive conditions, as well as a detailed price control regime. The implementation of these sector-specific rules has been entrusted to OFTEL, a body exclusively in charge of regulating telecommunications.

Sector-specific rules and institutions present advantages. But, as already noted, highly detailed and specific rules appear poorly adapted to a context of growing convergence between communications industries. The setting-up of sector-specific regulators may also be a source of problems. As pointed out by Dieter Helm, inconsistent decisions taken by regulators in the different network industries can lead to distortions in both capital and product markets.[225] Inconsistent regulatory decisions may create distortions in the capital markets, as investors switch between utilities to benefit from the most favourable treatment. Inconsistent decisions over price levels and structure by the individual regulators could also lead to a form of product or service substitution, as variations in pricing strategies might induce users to switch between networks or services.

Several factors, however, tend to suggest that the UK regulatory regime should gain in coherence in the years to come. First, in recent policy documents, OFTEL made clear that it will increasingly rely in the future on the prohibitions in the Competition Act 1998 to control market power in telecommunications.[226] If this new approach materializes (we have seen that the Government supported this approach in its recent Communications White Paper), it should allow the regulator to reduce the density of the regulatory framework progressively by cutting down the length and level of specificity of the operators' licence. OFTEL's new

---

[223] See Colin Long, 'Whether and How to Regulate Convergence' (1999) *Computer and Telecommunications L Rev* 3.

[224] See Margareth Bloom, 'The Impact of the Competition Bill' in Christopher McCrudden (ed), *Regulation and Deregulation: Policy and Practice in the Utilities and Financial Services Industries (Oxford Law Colloquium)* (Oxford: Clarendon Press, 1999) 237.

[225] See Dieter Helm, 'British Utility Regulation: Theory, Practice and Reform' (1994) 10 *Oxford Rev of Economic Policy* 17, 28–29.

[226] See OFTEL, 'OFTEL's Response to the UK Green Paper—Regulating Communications: Approaching Convergence to the Information Age' (hereafter 'OFTEL's Response to the UK Green Paper on Convergence') (January 1999) § 1.22, available at <http://www.oftel.gov.uk/publications/1999/broadcasting/gpia0199.htm>.

competition law 'philosophy' is in conformity with the policy approach suggested by the European Commission in its 1999 Communications Review pursuant to which the arrival of competition in telecommunications markets and the increasing significance of convergence between the telecommunications, audiovisual, and IT sectors should lead to a streamlining of sector-specific regulation and a greater reliance on competition rules and principles.[227] However, what is unusual, or even unique, about the UK approach is that the prohibitions contained in the Competition Act will be jointly enforced by the DGFT and the sector regulators. The issues raised by this concurrent enforcement of competition rules will be discussed in sub-section 7.

Moreover, in its response to the UK Green Paper on Convergence, OFTEL argued that, to the extent some sector-specific rules need to be applied to supplement competition rules,[228] these rules 'should be generic, in order to promote consistency and avoid regulatory obsolescence'.[229] In conformity with the EC Licensing Directive, such rules should be contained in 'general authorizations' set out in legislation that would replace the current system of individual licences.[230] OFTEL also suggests the adoption of the principle of 'forbearance' which would empower regulators to refrain from applying rules where they are unnecessary because agreed objectives are being achieved by market forces or other means.[231] Once again, this policy line is supported in the Government's Communications White Paper.

Finally, the creation of single regulator for the whole communications industry (OFCOM) to replace individual regulators in the telecommunications and broadcasting sectors will be another factor leading to a growing degree of coherence. A similar process of merger between regulators is also observable in other utility sectors: for instance, the formerly separate electricity and gas regulators have recently been merged into a single energy regulatory body (OFGEM).[232]

3. Flexibility versus Certainty

As noted above, one of the distinctive features of the UK telecommunications regime is that the bulk of regulation is found in the operators' licences which

---

[227] See Communication from the Commission to the European Parliament, The Council and the Economic and Social Committee and the Committee of the Regions, 'Towards a New Framework for Electronic Communications Infrastructure and Associated Services—The 1999 Communications Review' COM (1999) 539, § 3.3.3. For a discussion, see Damien Geradin, 'Institutional Aspects of EU Regulatory Reforms in the Telecommunications Sector: An Analysis of the Role of National Regulatory Authorities' (2000) 1 *J of Network Industries* 24.

[228] As pointed out by OFTEL, continued reliance on sector-specific rules will be needed to deal with the 'permanent market failures' in the communications sector (existence of bottlenecks, etc). See 'OFTEL's Response to the UK Green Paper on Convergence' (n 226 above) § 1.23. See also generally, Edward Pitt, 'Telecommunications Regulation: Is It Realistic to Rely on Competition Law to Do the Job?' (1999) *European Competition L Rev* 245.

[229] See 'OFTEL's Response to the UK Green Paper on Convergence' (n 226 above) § 1.22.

[230] ibid § 1.7.   [231] ibid § 1.22.   [232] See <http://www.ofgem.gov.uk/>.

usually contain a large set of substantive requirements, and, in the case of BT, a detailed pricing regime as well. Such detailed licences make clear the respective rights and duties of telecommunications operators and, thus, tend to reduce uncertainty.

Uncertainty is further reduced by the fact that licences can only be modified with the agreement of the operator or, absent such agreement, pursuant to a complex and precisely specified process. One of the key concerns of the British Government when it designed the telecommunications regulatory framework was to ensure that the privatization and liberalization processes could not be reversed by a future Government.[233] Market opening reforms in telecommunications were controversial in the early 1980s and there was a risk that such reforms could be reversed if a Labour Government were to come back to power.[234] 'Hard-to-modify' licences offered a more credible way of conveying commitment to investors than regulatory rules in specific legislation which, in the British system where the Government and the Parliament tend to be dominated by a single political party, might be easily modified by a future Government.[235]

An obvious drawback of the British system is its rigidity. Detailed licences reduce the amount of discretion left to the regulator. Moreover, the difficulty of modifying licences makes it hard for the regulator to adapt the regulatory framework to new market circumstances. As pointed out by OFTEL itself, 'a fast moving market needs a flexible regulatory system capable of adapting [ie changing the rules] equally fast when necessary; the present legislation does not allow for this'.[236]

Several policy and legal developments should, however, introduce a greater degree of flexibility into the British regulatory regime.

First, recent OFTEL policy papers and the Government Communications White Paper advocate increased reliance on new, less intrusive regulatory instruments, such as co-regulation and self-regulation, which should enable the authorities 'to respond quickly and effectively to a rapidly changing market'.[237] Co-regulation is a mode of regulation whereby the regulator and the stakeholders—industry players, consumer groups, etc—work together with, typically, the

---

[233] Brian Levy and Pablo Spiller, *Regulation, Institutions and Commitment* (Cambridge: Cambridge University Press, 1996) 98 et seq.

[234] Clare Hall et al, *Telecommunications Regulation—Culture, Chaos and Interdependence Inside the Regulatory Process* (New York and London: Routledge, 2000) 20.

[235] ibid. See also David M Newbery, *Privatization, Restructuring, and Regulation of Network Utilities* (Cambridge, Mass. and London: MIT Press, 2000) 56–57 ('With a tradition of adversarial politics, and frequent reversals in party control under the "first past the post" system of election, there would be little guarantee of stability of primary legislation given the considerable hostility to privatising network utilities by the then opposition Labour party. Licenses, however, are legally enforceable contracts that will be upheld in the courts by the independent judiciary and cannot be readily changed without the agreement of the license holder.')

[236] See 'OFTEL's Response to the UK Green Paper on Convergence' (n 226 above) § 1.7.

[237] See 'OFTEL, Achieving the Best Deal for Telecoms', § 10, available at <http://www.oftel.gov.uk/publications/about_oftel/strat100.htm>.

regulator setting the framework for stakeholders to work within.[238] In contrast, self-regulation is based on voluntary co-operation by stakeholders without intervention by the regulator.[239] Reliance on these new regulatory approaches should also help to reduce the need for detailed conditions in the licences and, thus, contribute to establishing a more flexible regulatory framework.

Second, OFTEL's increased reliance on its enforcement powers under the Competition Act will add a further degree of flexibility. Contrary to the conditions encapsulated in the licences, the prohibitions of the Competition Act are drafted in a much broader fashion that allows a greater degree of discretion on the part of the regulator. But as will be seen in sub-section 7 below, the existence of concurrent enforcement powers may introduce risks of inconsistency and, thus, uncertainty in the regulatory framework.

4. Regulatory Competence and Ability to Resist Undue Pressure

OFTEL has generally been recognized as a pioneer body that has taken a pro-active stance towards creating competition in telecommunications, although in recent months it has been criticized for its failure to take appropriate measures to ensure that BT unbundles its local networks.[240]

However, as is revealed in a recent study on the functioning of OFTEL, a problem for OFTEL has been the constant changes in its staff.[241] For instance, this study shows that 39 per cent of OFTEL's staff left the organization during 1997.[242] Many OFTEL staff members are on secondment from other public bodies, law firms, and consulting companies and they consider working for OFTEL as just a step in their career. A positive aspect of this staff mobility is that OFTEL's immigrants bring different understandings about operating procedures and ways of working from their different backgrounds. A clear drawback of this 'immigrant and emigrant society', however, is that working relationships tend to be temporary and knowledge is segmented.[243] Another problem facing OFTEL is that it has far less technical, economic, and legal resources than BT, its main 'opponent' in the regulatory process.[244] This resource asymmetry is made particularly serious by the British system of 'regulation by bargaining' that is described below. In a complex negotiation, BT's superior resources give it an advantage that may allow the company to achieve regulatory gains.

---

[238] An example of co-regulation is the development by industry under OFTEL's impulsion of consumer codes of practices that make offerings more transparent. See OFTEL, 'Encouraging Self and Co-Regulation in Telecoms to Benefit Customers' (June 2000) Table 3, available at <http://www.oftel.gov.uk/publications/about_oftel/self0600.htm>.

[239] An example of self-regulation is the creation of LINX (the London Internet Exchange) which promotes efficient interconnectivity between backbone ISPs: ibid.

[240] See *HC Select Committee on Trade and Industry 6th Report*, 2000–01 (HC 90), § 24 et seq (reviewing the evidence it received criticizing OFTEL's handling of local loop unbundling).

[241] See Hall et al (n 234 above) 36. The rest of this paragraph draws on the results of this study.

[242] ibid.   [243] ibid.   [244] ibid 187.

One main goal for the British Government at the time of BT's privatization was to ensure that the regulatory process would not be captured by the incumbent. For example, fear of regulatory capture was one of the reasons that induced the British Government to avoid a multi-person regulatory commission along the lines of federal agencies in the United States. The Government considered that such a structure created 'several possible entry points for industry lobbying' and thus was particularly vulnerable to capture.[245] A further mechanism to reduce the risk of capture was to separate monitoring and enforcement from the granting of licences, as well as to involve the MMC in the licence modification process. The involvement of several actors in the regulatory process built in checks and balances that limit the possibility for the incumbent to dominate the regulatory process.[246]

Far from achieving this objective, the British Government built a system that fails to give adequate protection against the risks of regulatory capture. First, most commentators argue that a single regulator is generally more prone to capture than a commission.[247] A change of government could, for instance, lead to the appointment of a new DGT whose views on key regulatory issues (prices of end-user services, consumer rights, etc) are closer to the ones of the new Government.[248] Second, BT has strong leverage over OFTEL as the regulator cannot modify licences without the operators' agreement.[249] Instead of referring a licence modification opposed by BT to the Competition Commission, a time-consuming, resource-intensive, and uncertain process, OFTEL has usually preferred to negotiate with BT in order to obtain its agreement for the licence modification. Many observers have criticized this system of 'regulation by bargaining' which gives BT 'formal equality with OFTEL in the regulatory structure', whereas representatives of consumers remain at the periphery of this structure.[250]

Lack of enforcement powers is another factor that encouraged OFTEL to find negotiated solutions with BT. As illustrated in Figure 6.3 below, the licence enforcement process is a particularly cumbersome procedure in which OFTEL is totally dependent on the courts to impose formal sanctions. Unlike many regulators in other jurisdictions, OFTEL is unable to impose a fine or other penalties when it considers that an operator is in breach of its licence conditions. Being unable to impose hard penalties, OFTEL has often sought co-operative solutions, thereby giving BT the opportunity to extract further concessions.[251]

OFTEL's new powers under the Competition Act should, however, contribute to diminish BT's influence in the regulatory process. First, at the decision-making level, OFTEL's reliance on the prohibitions contained in the Act to prevent

---

[245] ibid 22.   [246] ibid 103.

[247] See Dieter Helm, 'British Utility Regulation: Theory, Practice and Reform' (1994) 10 *Oxford Rev of Economic Policy* 17, 32.

[248] ibid.

[249] See Colin D Long, *Telecommunications Law and Practice* (2nd edn, London: Sweet & Maxwell, 1995) xiii.

[250] See ibid 14.   [251] See Hall et al (n 234 above) 184.

FIGURE 6.3. Licence enforcement process

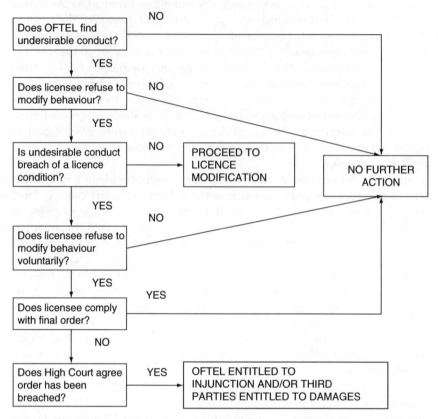

Source: Clare Hall et al, *Telecommunications Regulation: Culture, Chaos and Interdependence Inside the Regulatory Process* (London and New York: Routledge, 2000).

certain conducts might progressively reduce the importance of licence modification as a regulatory tool. Similarly, at the enforcement level, OFTEL's significant powers under the Act (including the possibility to impose heavy fines) would allow it to intervene in a far more effective and independent manner than under the current licence enforcement procedure.

Incidentally, OFTEL's reliance on the Competition Act's prohibitions should also reduce political influence over the regulatory process. While the SoS has the ability to intervene in the licence modification process by vetoing licence modifications agreed upon between the regulator and the regulated operator (on national security grounds) or by referring them to the Competition Commission (on any grounds), it plays no role in the enforcement of the prohibitions contained in the Competition Act.

5. Regulatory Accountability and Stakeholder Participation

During the initial years of its existence, OFTEL was often portrayed as a secretive institution. For instance, the details of OFTEL's 1985 interconnection determination were not made public and, as a general matter, it was difficult to know the reasons that motivated OFTEL's decisions. Subsequently, however, the regulatory process has become more open.[252] Today, for all important regulatory matters, OFTEL issues consultation documents, invites representations on these, calls meetings of representatives from industry and other groups, makes public the representations made, and publishes its advice to the Secretary of State.[253] In addition, since 1995, OFTEL publishes an annual operating plan that discloses objectives, priorities, and a detailed work programme.

Besides public openness, another important component of accountability is the possibility for operators to appeal the regulator's decisions. As has been seen, s 18 allows operators aggrieved by a regulatory decision to have it judicially reviewed. So far, in spite of the large resources that are possessed by BT and its competitors, as well as the substantial financial interests at stake in regulatory decisions, courts have played a modest role in telecommunications regulatory policy.[254] This may be due to the fact that the grounds on which courts are prepared to review the DGT's decisions are limited to illegality and impropriety. Courts will generally avoid reviewing the substance of the decisions.

There may, however, be increasing inclinations to litigate. First, the Telecommunications (Appeals) Regulations 1999 created a broader appeals procedure allowing operators to challenge regulatory decisions on a larger set of grounds than traditional judicial review. Though operators will probably welcome this new procedure, it is not clear whether judges should be given the right to review the substance of regulatory decisions. As pointed out above, judges are ill-equipped to rule on substantive matters and, thus, should arguably be confined to reviewing the legal aspects of the regulator's decisions. Second, the Competition Act 1998 allows persons subject to a decision of the DGFT or a sector regulator to appeal to the Competition Commission.[255] Such a right of appeal also extends to third parties.[256] Decisions of the Competition Commission are in turn subject to appeal to the Court of Appeal on points of law and levels of penalty only.

---

[252] See Robert Baldwin and Martin Cave, *Understanding Regulation: Theory, Strategy and Practice* (Oxford: Oxford University Press, 1999) 320.

[253] All these documents are available on OFTEL's website at <http://www.oftel.gov.uk>.

[254] See Baldwin and Cave (n 252 above) 298.

[255] See OFT, 'The Major Provisions' 21, available at <http://www.oft.gov.uk/html/compact/technical_guidelines/oft401.html>.

[256] See ibid 22.

6. Regulatory Costs

With a budget of only £12,634,000, it seems fair to say that the cost of OFTEL is relatively limited. Of course, to calculate the exact level of regulatory costs, one would have to add to this amount the costs generated by the other institutions involved in the telecommunications regulatory process (ie the DTI and the Competition Commission), a calculation that might not be easy to make since these institutions' involvement in telecommunications regulation is only one of their missions. But even if the total direct costs of telecommunications regulation could be calculated, it would certainly be smaller than the costs of large regulatory agencies, such as the US Federal Communications Commission.

Besides OFTEL's small size, several other features tend to limit telecommunications regulatory expenses in the United Kingdom. First, as has been noted, adoption of detailed regulatory requirements in licences generally reduces uncertainty and, thus, the likelihood of litigation. OFTEL's increased reliance on the more broadly drafted prohibitions of the Competition Act should, however, introduce a greater degree of uncertainty in the marketplace, though the progressive development of competition case law should reduce this inconvenience. Second, the relative lack of intervention of courts in regulatory processes has also limited litigation costs, though, as has been noted in the previous sub-section, there may be greater inclinations to litigate in the future.

In addition to direct regulatory costs, account should be taken of the costs of regulatory inefficiencies. For instance, most observers of the UK telecommunications markets consider that both the British Government and OFTEL made regulatory mistakes. First, as we have seen, the duopoly approach chosen by the Government in 1984 proved detrimental to competition and the interests of consumers. Arguably, a second mistake was the Government's excessive reliance, following the end of the duopoly period, on facilities-based competition that failed to deliver the expected results.

7. The Allocation of Regulatory Responsibilities

The most interesting issue with respect to the allocation of regulatory powers in the United Kingdom relates to the concurrent powers that have been granted to the DGFT and the sector regulators to enforce the prohibitions of the Competition Act 1998. Unsurprisingly, this issue of concurrency was a controversial matter that raised considerable debate in Parliament and elsewhere during the period prior to the Act's adoption. Strong views were expressed both in favour of and against granting competition enforcement powers to the sector regulators.[257]

---

[257] The following paragraphs draw on Margareth Bloom's analysis of the arguments for and against concurrency. See Margareth Bloom, 'The Impact of the Competition Bill' in Christopher McCrudden (ed), *Regulation and Deregulation: Policy and Practice in the Utilities and Financial Services Industries (Oxford Law Colloquium)* (Oxford University Press, 1999).

Among the arguments in favour of concurrent regulation were the following. First, it was argued that the sector regulators have developed considerable specialist expertise in their sectors and that this knowledge would be a valuable asset for the application of the Competition Act's prohibitions. Another argument in favour of concurrent regulation is that it should facilitate the move from sector-specific regulation to competition law. The argument was that in the absence of competition powers the regulators 'would be reluctant to see their roles diminished and hence the move from a regulatory culture to competition would be delayed unnecessarily'.[258]

But strong arguments were also advanced against concurrent regulation. A first argument was that concurrent regulation would lead to a less efficient use of resources because of the risk of duplication of work between sector regulators and the OFT.[259] A related concern was that sector regulators may not be able to have the critical mass of staff with the expertise in law and economics that is needed to apply the prohibitions contained in the Competition Act. A second, more important, argument was that concurrent powers to enforce the Competition Act created a risk of inconsistent and, hence, less predictable application of the Act's prohibitions.[260]

Eventually, the arguments in favour of concurrency triumphed and sector regulators were granted enforcement powers under the Competition Act. The drafters of the Act did not ignore the risk of inconsistency and, thus, there are several provisions in the Act and other arrangements that should contribute to ensure consistency in the implementation of the rules. First, the Act provides for a system of appeals that is common to all cases whether they are handled by the sector regulators or the DGFT. Specifically, the Act provides for full appeals to be heard by Appeals Tribunals of the Competition Commission and for subsequent appeals on a point of law or on the amount of a penalty to be lodged before the Court of Appeal. This common system of appeals should contribute to the 'unification' of the interpretation of the Competition Act. Second, s 60 of the Act makes provision for the interpretation of the prohibitions in a manner that is consistent with the principles and case law which would apply to a like matter under EC law. This clause applies to both the DGFT and the sector regulators. Third, the DGFT and the regulators are bound by the same set of procedural rules to be adopted by the Secretary of State for Trade and Industry on the basis of a proposal of the DGFT.[261] In order to ensure a coherent approach in the application of competition rules, the DGFT has also adopted a series of technical guidelines giving general advice and information on how the prohibitions will be applied and enforced. Both the procedural rules[262] and the guidelines[263] contain specific arrangements for handling concurrent regulation. Finally, the OFT and

---

[258] See n 257 above, 241.   [259] ibid 242.   [260] ibid 243.   [261] See Bloom (n 257 above).

[262] See the Competition Act 1998 (Concurrency) Regulations 2000, SI 2000/260, available at <http://www.hmso.gov.uk/si/si2000/20000260.htm>.

[263] See OFT, 'Concurrent Application to Regulated Industries', FT 405, available at <http://www.oft.gov.uk/Business/Legal+Powers/ca98+publications.htm>.

each sector regulator are represented on the Concurrency Working Party (hereafter, the 'CWP'). The CWP was formed in 1997 to ensure full co-ordination between regulators and the DGFT, to consider the practical working arrangements between them, including ensuring that a single case would not be investigated by more than one authority, to ensure consistency of approach in casework, to co-ordinate the use of concurrent powers, and to prepare the guidelines.[264]

Rather than completely reassuring those concerned with the risks of overlap and inconsistency, however, the above provisions and arrangements illustrate how challenging it will be to ensure cohesion in the application of competition rules across regulated sectors. The drafters of the Act probably started their work under the misguided assumption that each regulated sector was a system on its own that required specific arrangements for the application of competition law. This approach was strongly supported by OFTEL that had sought, since the mid-1990s, to reposition itself within the regulatory space as a competition authority instead of a mere industrial regulator. In OFTEL's view, this was the only way to ensure its survival and to gain stronger enforcement powers against BT.[265] On the other hand, entrusting the OFT with exclusive enforcement powers of the prohibitions of the Competition Act would have meant a progressive reduction of the role played by sector regulators. Though this approach was probably better suited to a context of increased convergence between regulated industries, it was also probably too politically difficult.

[264] ibid § 3.7.
[265] See Clare Hall et al, *Telecommunications Regulation—Culture, Chaos and Interdependence Inside the Regulatory Process* (London and New York: Routledge, 2000) 157.

7

Chile

The Chilean Government decided to promote competition in all segments of the telecommunications market in the early 1980s. During the first few years, sector-specific rules were largely confined to technical standards, monitored by the telecommunications regulator SUBTEL. The regulatory framework was subsequently modified in the late 1980s and in the first half of the 1990s to include further sector-specific rules on pricing, interconnection, and market structure, and to grant additional responsibilities to the regulator. A shift thus progressively occurred from a regulatory framework dominated by economy-wide components (albeit with a sector-specific regulator unlike in New Zealand) to a regulatory framework with more emphasis on sector-specific components (without, however, adopting regulations as detailed as in the US model, and without conferring as much power on SUBTEL as the FCC has). At the same time, however, the scope of price regulation was progressively reduced as competition took hold in various segments of the telecommunications market. The Chilean model of the post-liberalization period constitutes, therefore, a good testing ground to judge the efficacy of various mixes of economy-wide and sector-specific regulatory features in a single country setting.

A. Origins of the Present Regulatory Framework

Telephone services were introduced in Chile in 1880 by the Compañia de Teléfonos de Edison. In 1927, the company was acquired by International Telephone and Telegraph Corp (ITT). At the time, there were about 26,000 telephones in the country and the only inter-city link was between Santiago and Valparaiso.[1]

In 1930, in order to expand coverage and promote integration of the different parts of the country, Chile negotiated an agreement with the company, which led to the creation of the Compañia de Teléfonos de Chile (CTC). The agreement, incorporated in Law 4791/1930, detailed the rights and obligations of the company. CTC was granted a non-exclusive fifty-year concession to provide local and long-distance services. At the end of the concession the Government could compensate the owners for the value of the net fixed assets and acquire the company, or the concession would be extended for a period of thirty years. CTC, for its part, committed to meet specific network expansion targets and was given the right to purchase other telephone companies at prices determined through commercial agreements or estimated by three experts (one appointed by each

---

[1] See Ahmed Galal, 'Regulation and Commitment in the Development of Telecommunications in Chile', Policy Research Working Paper No 1278 (The World Bank, 1994).

party and one by the Government). CTC was allowed a rate-of-return of up to 10 per cent, with excess profits divided equally between the Treasury and the company. Tariffs, which embodied cross-subsidies in favour of local service users, could be revised by the board of directors of the company and implemented within 30 days if the Government had not raised objections during that period. Disputes between the Government and the company over the interpretation of the concession were to be resolved by Supreme Court decisions against which no appeal could be introduced.[2]

While CTC met its initial investment commitments, the pace of network expansion eventually slowed and ITT was accused of inflating its costs. In 1958, the Government reached a new agreement with the company. CTC was granted a rate-of-return of 10 per cent (instead of up to 10 per cent) on revalued capital, and committed, for its part, to an eight-year investment programme.[3] In practice, however, tariffs were often adjusted on political grounds. They frequently failed to keep up with inflation and cross-subsidization was maintained. Investments, on the other hand, remained modest and unmet demand increased.[4]

In the 1960s, the role of the State increased in the economy in general—for example, following an agrarian reform, about 60 per cent of Chile's arable land ended up under the administration of the State—and in the telecommunications sector in particular.[5] In December 1964, the Government created, by Decree 5487, the long-distance service company ENTEL held by the state-holding company CORFO (the Corporación de Fomento de la Producción). ENTEL operated under a general law (Decree Law no 4 of 1959) which governed the electricity and telecommunications sector except for CTC (still subject to Law 4791/1930). The two main provisions of Decree Law no 4 applicable to ENTEL were the requirement imposed upon any provider of telecommunications services to obtain a Government licence and the setting of a 10 per cent rate-of-return on fixed assets.[6] ENTEL's tariffs were determined by a Tariff Commission, composed of the Superintendent for Electric and Gas Services, and representatives of the President, the Ministry of Economy, the National Planning Office, and CORFO.[7] Then, in 1967, the Government reached a new agreement with CTC that committed the company to a new investment programme. The Government also announced, however, a new national policy for telecommunications according to which it would assume primary responsibility for expanding the network and ensuring the provision of efficient national and international telecommunications services. CORFO was to purchase up to 49 per cent of the shares of CTC which would

[2] ibid 4–6.   [3] ibid 6.

[4] See Ahmed Galal et al, *Welfare Consequences of Selling Public Enterprises: An Empirical Analysis* (Oxford: Oxford University Press, 1994) 257.

[5] See Dominique Hachette and Rolph Luders, *Privatisation in Chile: An Economic Appraisal* (Oakland, Cal.: Institute for Contemporary Studies, 1992) 32.

[6] See José Ricardo Melo, 'Liberalisation and Privatisation in Chile' in Bjorn Wellenius and Peter A Stern (eds), *Implementing Reforms in the Telecommunications Sector: Lessons from Experience* (Washington, DC: The World Bank, 1994) 145–146.

[7] See Galal (n 1 above) 7.

focus its activities exclusively on local telephony while ENTEL would provide only long-distance services.[8]

In 1970, the socialist-led Government of Salvador Allende came to power, with a narrow election victory over the right wing coalition led by Jorge Alessandri. The Allende administration started to implement a wave of nationalization and other interventionist policies. For example, while CORFO held an equity stake in 46 companies in 1970, this had increased to 500 companies by 1973. In May 1971, the Government informed ITT that it would initiate steps to nationalize CTC. In September of that year, relying on an old law of 1932 which allowed the President to intervene temporarily in the management of certain industries under vaguely defined conditions, the Government stepped up its involvement in the company by appointing an overseer.[9] Formal nationalization of CTC, however, never occurred under the Allende Government, but during the early 1970s, telecommunications prices were often adjusted below inflation and both CTC and ENTEL lacked resources to expend, modernize, and provide new services.

The 1973 military coup ushered in the military regime of General Pinochet, intent on reversing the policies of the previous administration. In the economic field, a group of Chicago-trained economists took the lead in designing a deregulation and privatization programme aimed primarily at improving economic efficiency and at reducing the budget deficit which had reached about 25 per cent of GDP during the last year of the Allende administration. These policies were, however, not implemented, at first, with respect to some large enterprises, including CTC and ENTEL, which were considered 'of strategic importance for national development'.[10] In fact, in late 1973, Law 4791/1930 was revoked and, in 1974, CTC, now subjected like other telecommunications operators to the provisions of Decree Law no 4 of 1959, was formally transferred to the State through a sale of ITT's remaining shares to CORFO.[11] While neither CTC nor ENTEL was granted exclusive rights, they kept, de facto, the quasi-monopoly that they had enjoyed until then. Cost-rationalization measures and new pricing policies were, however, introduced to increase the efficiency of those strategic enterprises.

While these measures did contribute to increasing substantially the quality of telecommunications services, it became progressively clear that further efficiency gains and additional financial resources were required to keep pace with accelerating technical changes in telecommunications and to satisfy a growing demand for more and better services fuelled by the emergence of a new class of entrepreneurs for whom high-quality telecommunications services were becoming increasingly important. This, plus a desire to lock in the pro-market reforms

[8] ibid 6–8.

[9] ibid 28. See also Walter T Molano, *The Logic of Privatisation: The Case of Telecommunications in the Southern Cone of Latin America* (Westport, Conn.: Greenwood Press, 1997) 42.

[10] See Oscar Munoz (ed), *Despues de las Privatizaciones: Hacia el Estado Regulador* (Santiago de Chile: CIEPLAN, 1993) 81.

[11] See Molano (n 9 above) 42.

which had been implemented and prevent a future civilian government from controlling major state-owned enterprises, account for a shift in policy by the military regime vis-à-vis the telecommunications sector in the late 1970s and in the 1980s.[12]

In 1977, SUBTEL, the Subsecretaría de Telecomunicaciones reporting to the Ministry of Transport and Telecommunications, became the new regulator for telecommunications. Pending further reforms, however, CORFO, as the owner of both CTC and SUBTEL, played a major regulatory role. In addition, SUBTEL's authority was further reduced by the fact that it was headed by a colonel whereas both CTC and ENTEL were headed by generals.[13]

In 1978, the Government adopted a new telecommunications policy: telecommunications services were normally to be provided by private operators; licences, where required, would be granted on the basis of objective criteria; and tariffs would be deregulated except where markets were not competitive.[14] These principles finally became law when they were reflected in the new General Law of Telecommunications (Law 18.168/1982). This legislative framework is examined in the next section.

In addition, in 1986, the Government began selling limited amounts of stock in CTC and ENTEL through the Santiago stock exchange and private sales, and in 1988 a majority of the Government's shares in CTC and ENTEL were transferred to the private sector. By the early 1990s the Chilean Government held no significant ownership in any telecommunications company.[15]

B. The main rules

The main rules applicable to the telecommunications sector in Chile are included in the General Law of Telecommunications. We examine this piece of sector-specific legislation first, and turn to the general antitrust rules afterwards.

1. Telecommunications-Specific Rules

The General Law of Telecommunications no 18.168, of 1982, replaced Decree Law no 4 of 1959 for the telecommunications sector and implemented the pro-market policies that had been announced by the Government in 1978. The law

---

[12] ibid 30. See also ibid 46.

[13] See Ahmed Galal, 'Regulation and Commitment in the Development of Telecommunications in Chile', Policy Research Working Paper No 1278 (The World Bank, 1994) 8–9.

[14] ibid 9.

[15] See Melissa Tomlinson, *Latin American Telecommunications: A Study of Deregulation and Privatisation in Argentina, Chile and Mexico* (Alexandria, Vir.: Telecom Publishing Group, 1995) 68; and Pierre Guislain, *The Privatisation Challenge: A Strategic, Legal and Institutional Analysis of International Experience* (Washington, DC: The World Bank, 1997) 210.

aimed at establishing a pro-competition regime for the provision of all types of telecommunications services. It provided for multiple entries in all market segments without limiting the number of operators except when technical reasons—such as the scarcity of available radio frequencies—required that the number of competitors be capped.[16] Telecommunications operators had to obtain licences to be allowed to provide services to the public. Such licences were awarded by decree, in a non-discriminatory way, and on the basis of a competitive selection process when the number of operators had to be limited.[17] The licences were awarded for renewable periods of thirty years[18]; they were free except for the fees that were due if they entailed the use of the radio-electrical spectrum.[19] No licences were required to provide private and value-added services.[20] The law added that licensees could establish their own facilities or use those of other providers.[21]

The law imposed an obligation upon all providers of public services to grant interconnection to competitors under technical conditions determined by the regulator.[22] Interconnection prices were to be determined by the parties themselves, which could present their case to the antitrust authorities if they failed to reach an agreement.[23] Telecommunications prices, for their part, were to be determined by market forces, except for fixed services if the antitrust regulator considered that markets for the provision of those services were insufficiently competitive.[24] In that case, the law indicated, through relatively vague provisions, that prices were to be set on the basis of the direct and necessary costs of providing the service.[25] The antitrust authorities could, however, at any time, decide that a specific service became sufficiently competitive and that, consequently, its price did not need to be regulated any more.[26]

Telecommunications operators had to abide by technical norms regarding, inter alia, numbering plans, network maintenance and operation, and use of the radio-electric spectrum.[27] Finally, a schedule of sanctions—including warnings, pecuniary penalties, suspension or revocation of licences—was established to punish violations of the law.[28]

Decree Law no 1 of 1987, which modified the 1982 law, established new and much more sophisticated tariff-setting provisions. The 1987 provisions—regrouped under Title V of the Law—set forth, in great detail, the procedures and methodology to be used to determine prices in insufficiently competitive markets. Such procedures and methodology were established to determine the prices of fixed services for which antitrust authorities consider that there is

[16] See Law no 18.168 of 1982, arts 12 and 13.   [17] ibid art 8, paras 1-2, and art 13.
[18] ibid art 8, para 3.   [19] ibid arts 31–36.   [20] ibid art 8, paras 5–6, and art 10.
[21] ibid art 26.   [22] ibid art 25.   [23] See Galal (n 13 above) 9.
[24] See Law no 18.168 of 1982, art 29, para 2.
[25] See Ahmed Galal et al, *Welfare Consequences of Selling Public Enterprises: An Empirical Analysis* (Oxford: Oxford University Press, 1994) 257.
[26] ibid.   [27] See Law no 18.168, at art 24.   [28] ibid arts 36–39.

insufficient competition.[29] The regulated tariff regime is based on the LRIC methodology. The long-run marginal cost of service provision is calculated and tariffs are then increased in order to cover average costs, which include a 'fair' rate-of-return on capital and are above marginal costs in industries characterized by economies of scale. The mark-ups above marginal costs are apportioned via Ramsey pricing.[30] The cost of capital, for its part, is calculated taking into account the risk premium of the activity and the systematic risk of the industry.[31] The prices that are established according to the above parameters are maximum prices only.[32] A more detailed explanation of the price-setting technique is presented in Box 7.1 below.

Box 7.1: Price-Setting Technique for Regulated Telecommunications Services in Chile

1. Demand is first estimated for each service/zone/firm bundle.
2. For each service, the marginal cost of development is then calculated based on the concept of an 'efficient firm'. The law defines the efficient firm as one that starts from scratch and uses only the assets necessary to provide that service.
3. Revenue is then estimated for each service, such that the net present value of providing the service is equal to zero. This revenue equals the marginal cost of development.
4. To move from the marginal cost of development to LRIC prices, efficient marginal tariffs are increased in the least distorting fashion (via Ramsey pricing) so that the firms make a fair rate-of-return.
5. The fair rate-of-return is defined as the sum of the rates of return on the risk-free assets and the risk premium of the activity, weighted by the systematic risk of the industry. That is: $R_i = R_{rf} + B_i (R_p - R_{rf})$, where R_i is the rate-of-return on revalued capital of firm i, R_{rf} is the rate-of-return on risk-free assets, B_i is firm i's systematic risk, and R_p is the rate-of-return on a diversified investment portfolio.

Source: General Law of Telecommunications no 18.168, arts 30–30 K; Ahmed Galal, 'Regulation and Commitment in the Development of Telecommunications in Chile', Policy Research Working Paper No 1278 (The World Bank, 1994) 11.

The different costs, the structure and level of tariffs, and indexation formulas are to be calculated in conformity with the provisions of the law by the operator itself or by experts whom it hires.[33] The operator's proposals are then submitted, through the regulator, to the Ministries of Economy and Telecommunications. This process results in the adoption of a tariff formula that remains in place for the next five years.[34] Tariffs can, however, be readjusted every two months to reflect changes of indexation indices.[35]

---

[29] ibid art 29, para 2.   [30] ibid arts 30 C–30 F.   [31] ibid art 30 B.
[32] ibid art 30 H.   [33] ibid art 30 I.   [34] ibid art 30.
[35] ibid art 30 H.

Decree Law no 1 of 1987 also introduced universal service obligations. Licensees are required to provide service, within two years, to those located within the territory of the licence who ask to be connected to the network, and to those located outside of that territory who are ready to cover the cost of all network extensions required to provide the service to them.[36] To ease the financial burden on the companies, the law stated that licensees could ask for reimbursable financial contributions from those requiring new telephone lines. These contributions could be reimbursed through bonds or shares of the companies or through any other means on which the parties would agree.[37] In addition, given the level of unmet demand that existed in 1987, the law provided for gradual implementation of the above provisions. Operators could indicate that the requirement to provide universal service would initially apply to some parts of the licence territory only, and they were given a ten-year period to progressively extend universal service to the whole territory. Furthermore, during those ten years, new demand had to be met within three years instead of two.[38]

Another major reform of the telecommunications law took place in 1994. Law no 19.302 of 1994 specified that interconnection prices were to be subjected to the detailed tariff setting provisions introduced in 1987 under Title V of the General Telecommunications Law.[39] Regulations were adopted later to authorize telecommunications companies to pass on to their subscribers the access charges which they had to pay to terminate calls on other companies' networks.[40]

Law no 19.302 of 1994 also inserted a new provision in the General Telecommunications Law to require telecommunications operators to implement a multi-carrier system whereby users can choose their long-distance provider through a pre-selection system, as well as through the dialling of appropriate codes on a call-by-call basis. The law states that the various long-distance companies must be granted access to the local network on rigorously equal terms: the number of digits which a user must dial to access different companies must be the same, and the provider of local services cannot discriminate in any way between users because of their choice of long-distance carriers.[41] The law also stated that telecommunications operators had to create legally separate subsidiaries to enter the long-distance markets.[42]

For a transition period of a few years, the law imposed stricter limits on the share of the long-distance market which could be gained or kept by companies operating in both local and long-distance markets than by completely

[36] ibid arts 24 B and 24 C.
[37] ibid art 24 D. This provision was, however, very rarely applied in practice.
[38] See Transitory Provisions of Decree Law no 1 of 1987, art 1.
[39] See Law no 18.168, art 25, para 5.
[40] See SUBTEL, 'Informe de Gestion 1998' 3, available at <http://www.subtel.cl/publicaciones/index.htm>.
[41] See Law no 18.168, art 24 *bis*.
[42] ibid art 26, para 2.

independent companies operating in the long-distance markets only.[43] This provided in fact some temporary protection both to ENTEL and to CTC against competition from the other. Table 7.1 below presents the schedule of market share restrictions imposed upon Chilean companies in the long-distance market. It shows, for example, that in 1995, CTC, which already provided local services, could not gain more than 35 per cent of the domestic long-distance market while a completely separate company could gain (or maintain, in ENTEL's case) an 80 per cent market share. Conversely, in the international market segment, ENTEL's share was limited to 70 per cent in 1995 if it did not have more than a 40 per cent share of the local market, but to 20 per cent only if it did.[44]

In order to increase access to public telephones in rural and low-income urban areas, the Government set up in 1994 a Telecommunications Development Fund.[45] This Fund is financed by the national budget and administered by a Council for the Development of Telecommunications chaired by the Telecommunications Minister, and comprising, in addition, the Ministers of Economy, Public Works, Finance, and Planning and Co-operation (or their representatives) as well as three telecommunications experts designated by the President.[46] The Council decides upon an annual programme of projects eligible for subsidies. These projects typically entail installing at least one public phone in each community within a given territory. They are awarded through competitive bidding to the operators requiring the lowest subsidy. Bidding documents specify service obligations, tariffs, interconnection principles, and the maximum amount of available subsidies, but the choice of technology, network structure, specific location of public telephones, and the option to provide individual connections or other telecommunications services in addition to the required public phones

TABLE 7.1. Market share restrictions in the Chilean long-distance market

	Domestic Long-Distance		International Long-Distance	
	Affiliated Company	Non-Affiliated Company	Affiliated Company (with more than 40% share of local market)	Non-Affiliated Company
1995	35%	80%	20%	70%
1996	45%	70%	30%	65%
1997	55%	60%	40%	60%
1998	60%	60%	Not applicable	Not applicable

Source: Transitory Articles of Law no 19.302, of 1994, art 5; Luis Guasch and Pablo Spiller, *Managing the Regulatory Process: Design, Concepts, Issues and the Latin America and Carribean Story* (Washington, DC: The World Bank, 1999) 119.

[43] See the Transitory Articles of Law no 19.302 of 1994, art 5.
[44] See Luis Guasch and Pablo Spiller, *Managing the Regulatory Process: Design, Concepts, Issues and the Latin America and Caribbean Story* (Washington, DC: The World Bank, 1999) 119.
[45] See Law no 18.168, art 28 A.   [46] ibid art 28 B.

are left to the operators. The licences granted to the winning bidders are non-exclusive.[47] In late 2000, the Telecommunications Law was modified to broaden the objectives to be pursued by the Fund beyond installing public phones in rural and in low income areas: the Telecommunications Development Fund can now be used to facilitate access to any telecommunications services, and in particular to the Internet.[48]

2. Antitrust Rules

In addition to the sector-specific rules discussed above, general antitrust provisions are applicable to the telecommunications sector. Antitrust provisions are contained in Decree Law no 211 of 1973, as subsequently modified by various decree laws. The Law is vague and prohibits any action or agreement that seeks to hinder free competition in economic activities.[49] It presents a non-exhaustive list of anti-competitive actions or agreements which includes: agreements aimed at limiting overall supply or allocating supply quotas to various producers;[50] market sharing or exclusive distribution agreements;[51] price fixing arrangements or imposition of monopolistic prices.[52] There are no provisions dealing specifically with mergers.[53]

The Law does not require that specific types of potentially anti-competitive actions be notified in advance to and be cleared by, antitrust authorities. It does, however, provide for a mechanism to obtain clearance for those actions that are brought to the attention of antitrust authorities.[54] In addition, antitrust authorities are given broad powers to prevent anti-competitive actions from taking place, and nothing would prevent them from indicating that some proposed actions would require prior approval.[55] Finally, the law also states that no individual can be granted exclusive rights to perform any economic activity.[56]

C. The main institutions

The main industry-specific regulator, SUBTEL, carries out most of the technical regulatory work, while various ministries retain final decision-making powers on a wide range of issues. Specialized antitrust entities and the courts play important roles as well.

---

[47] ibid arts 28 E and 28 F. On rural telephony in Chile, see also Bjorn Wellenius, 'Closing the Rural Communication Access Gap: Chile 1995–2002', The World Bank, Draft paper of 24 June 2001, available at <http://www.infodev.org/library/working.htm>.

[48] See Law no 18.168, art 28 D, as modified by Law no 19.724.

[49] See Decree Law no 211 of 1973, art 1.   [50] ibid art 2 a.   [51] ibid art 2 c.

[52] ibid art 2 d.

[53] See Luis Guash and Pablo Spiller (n 44 above) 288.

[54] See Decree Law no 211 of 1973, art 8 b.   [55] ibid art 17 b.   [56] ibid art 4.

1. SUBTEL

SUBTEL, established in 1977, is the main telecommunications-specific regulator in Chile. It is an agency of about 230 people, headed by the Telecommunications Subsecretary (see Figure 7.1 below).[57] SUBTEL is neither financially nor administratively independent: it is a public agency under the authority of the Minister of Transport and Telecommunications and its staff is subject to civil service rules regarding remuneration and other matters.[58] The Subsecretary is designated by the President and can be removed at will by the Executive.[59] No provisions exist to prevent the staff of SUBTEL from taking up positions with regulated companies once they leave the regulatory agency.[60] SUBTEL's total 2000 budget was about $5.5 million.[61]

SUBTEL carries out most of the technical work required for the regulation of the telecommunications sector. For example, SUBTEL is responsible for processing licence requests.[62] SUBTEL also determines the technical conditions under which interconnection must be granted.[63] It prepares various technical plans relating, for example, to numbering, to the operation and maintenance of the networks, and to the use of the radioelectric spectrum,[64] and it provides specific instructions to operators on how to conform to such plans.[65] SUBTEL is also in charge of determining how to calculate the fees to be paid for the use of the radioelectric spectrum.[66] Finally, providers of public telecommunications services cannot initiate service unless their facilities have been approved by SUBTEL as meeting various technical requirements.[67]

It is SUBTEL that determines the technical and economic criteria on the basis of which the licensee must calculate the prices of regulated services. If a disagreement arises between SUBTEL and the licensee regarding those criteria, each party can require that a committee of three experts—one designated by SUBTEL, one by the licensee, and one by mutual agreement—be asked to pronounce on the matter. The final decision belongs, however, to SUBTEL.[68] A committee, formed in the same way, can also be established if public authorities object to the final prices proposed by the operators. Such objections can only be formulated in relation to the technical and economic requirements of the law. In that case, the final decision belongs to the Ministries of Economy and Telecommunications.[69]

---

[57] See SUBTEL, 'Informe de Gestion 2000' 63, available at <http://www.subtel.cl/publicaciones/index.htm>.

[58] See Eduardo Bitrán and Raúl Sáez, 'Privatisation and Regulation in Chile' in Barry P Bosworth et al (eds), *The Chilean Economy: Policy Lessons and Challenges* (Washington, DC: The Brookings Institution, 1994) 365–366.

[59] See Eduardo Bitrán and Pablo Serra, 'Regulation of Privatized Utilities: The Chilean Experience' (1998) 20 *World Development* 960.

[60] ibid.   [61] See 'Informe de Gestion 2000' (n 57 above) 61.

[62] See Law no 18.168, arts 13–15.   [63] ibid art 25.   [64] ibid art 24.

[65] ibid art 24, para 2.   [66] ibid art 34.   [67] ibid art 24 A.   [68] ibid art 30 I.

[69] ibid art 30 J.

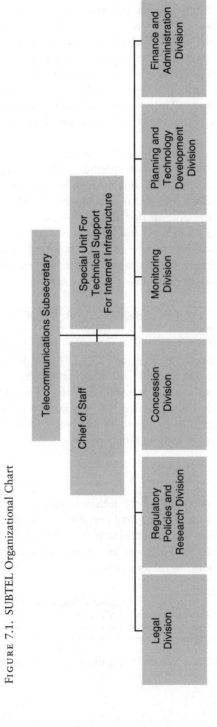

FIGURE 7.1. SUBTEL Organizational Chart

Source: <www.subtel.cl/subtel/organizacion.htm>.

The law authorizes users located outside the territory of any telecommunications licence to build themselves the facilities required to connect them to a telecommunications network. The users can also ask third parties, which do not hold a telecommunications licence, to build such facilities. In both cases, SUBTEL must approve construction of the facilities.[70] As mentioned above, the law also authorizes operators progressively to extend to the whole territory of their licence, over a ten-year period, the zone in which they are required to meet universal service obligations.[71] The schedule according to which various parts of the licence territory are to be added to the universal service zone must be approved by SUBTEL.[72]

SUBTEL also plays a role to ensure effective implementation of the multi-carrier system, inter alia by helping to design the specific rules applicable to the operators in that respect and by allocating through lotteries the various dialling codes identifying the various long-distance companies.[73] SUBTEL is also the Executive Secretariat of the Council that administers the Fund for the development of telecommunications in rural and low-income urban areas.[74] As such, SUBTEL prepares a yearly programme of projects for which bids should be invited, it sets the maximum subsidy which might be required, prepares the bidding documents, manages the bidding process, and designs the operating licences.[75]

SUBTEL monitors the operators' compliance with the regulatory framework, and it processes the complaints which it receives from operators protesting against the behaviour of other operators and from users dissatisfied with the telecommunications services they receive.[76] SUBTEL has the right to require from the telecommunications operators all information which it needs to perform its functions.[77] It can suspend provision of a service for up to thirty days when technical norms are being violated.[78] It can require assistance from the police in the performance of its monitoring functions.[79] Only the courts, however, can impose pecuniary penalties on the operators.

2. The Government

While SUBTEL carries out most of the technical regulatory work, it is the Government which takes most of the final decisions on regulatory matters. In fact, most of these decisions are embodied in presidential decrees, signed by the President and the Minister of Transport and Telecommunications, as well as the Minister of Economy in some cases. This is the case, for example, for the

---

[70] ibid art 24 B.   [71] See text accompanying n 38 above.
[72] See Transitory Provisions of Decree Law no 1 of 1987, art 1.
[73] See Law no 18.168, art 24 *bis*.   [74] ibid art 28 B.   [75] ibid arts 28 B and 28 G.
[76] See, for example, SUBTEL, 'Informe de Gestion 1999' 36–38, available at <http://www.subtel.cl/publicaciones/index.htm>.
[77] See Law no 18.168, art 37, para 2.   [78] ibid art 39.   [79] ibid art 39 *bis*.

granting of licences,[80] the adoption of the technical plans regarding numbering and other technical issues,[81] as well as the adoption, every five years, of the formula which is used to calculate the tariffs of regulated services.[82] It is the Council for the Development of Telecommunications, comprising the Ministers of Telecommunications, Economy, and Finance which formally adopts the yearly programme of projects eligible for subsidies from the Telecommunications Development Fund, and which awards those projects and the associated subsidies to the winning bidders.[83] Finally, it is the Minister of Transport and Telecommunications who has primary responsibility for imposing the sanctions listed in the General Telecommunications Law.[84]

3. The Antitrust Authorities

Four distinct types of institutions are in charge of implementing the provisions of the competition law: the Regional Preventive Commissions; the Central Preventive Commission; the Resolution Commission; and the Office of the National Economic Attorney-General.[85]

The Regional Preventive Commissions comprise four members: the Regional Ministerial Secretary of Economy who chairs; one member appointed by the Governor of the region; one appointed by the Regional Development Council; and one appointed by the presidents of the neighbourhood committees of the capital of the region.[86] The Regional Preventive Commissions are in charge of resolving antitrust issues in their regions. They can, for example: suspend the application of anti-competitive agreements; cap the prices of certain products or services; or require that public authorities with regulatory competencies exercise their functions to prevent anti-competitive behaviours.[87]

The Central Preventive Commission, for its part, comprises: a representative of the Ministry of Economy who chairs; a representative of the Ministry of Finance; two university professors, in the fields of law and business, appointed by the Council of University Rectors; and a representative of the neighbourhood committees of the metropolitan area.[88] It exercises the same functions as the Regional Preventive Commissions for the antitrust issues which concern the metropolitan area or which involve more than one region.[89] Any person may file a complaint before the Central or Regional Preventive Commissions which must then investigate and issue an order.[90]

The Resolutive Commission is made up of five members: a Supreme Court Justice who chairs; a representative of the Ministry of Economy and a representative of the Ministry of Finance, appointed by their respective ministers; as well

---

80 ibid art 15.   81 ibid art 24.   82 ibid art 30 J.   83 ibid art 28 E.
84 ibid art 36.   85 See Decree Law no 211 of 1973, art 6.   86 ibid art 7.
87 ibid art 8.   88 ibid art 10.   89 ibid art 11.
90 See Luis Guash and Pablo Spiller, *Managing the Regulatory Process: Design, Concepts, Issues and the Latin America and Caribbean Story* (Washington, DC: The World Bank, 1999) 296.

as a Law School Dean and an Economics Department Chair randomly selected from universities located in Santiago.[91] The Resolutive Commission investigates, on its own or at the request of the National Economic Attorney-General, all situations which could constitute a violation of the competition law.[92] It is the Resolutive Commission which determines whether the prices of particular telecommunications services need to be regulated.[93] It also pronounces on appeals lodged against decisions of the preventive commissions.[94] Decisions of the Resolutive Commission can be appealed to the Supreme Court only when they impose the modification of the statute of a corporation or the dissolution of that corporation, when they block a person from belonging to a professional association or corporation, and when they impose monetary penalties.[95] Membership in all antitrust commissions is for two years, and is not remunerated.[96]

The National Economic Attorney-General is designated by the President and can be sanctioned or dismissed only upon proposal by the Comptroller General.[97] It is a government agency, subject to the restrictions imposed upon the public sector, with a rather limited budget of about US$ 1 million.[98] The Office of the National Economic Attorney-General must, inter alia: investigate potential violations of antitrust provisions; represent the public interest before the Resolutive Commission, the Supreme Court, and the various tribunals; and require the Resolution and Preventive Commissions to exercise their functions.[99] The National Economic Attorney-General normally asks SUBTEL to research matters and present evidence when the case under investigation concerns the telecommunications sector. SUBTEL, for its part, may refer issues to the National Economic Attorney-General and request rulings on antitrust telecommunications matters.[100]

4. The Courts

The courts and tribunals play an important role in the regulatory process as decisions by SUBTEL or by the Ministers in charge of telecommunications regulation can, as a rule, be appealed before them. The General Telecommunications Law identifies a few specific decisions which can be appealed before the Court of Appeals, such as, for example, the awards of licences and the impos-

---

[91] See Decree Law no 211 of 1973, art 16.   [92] ibid art 17.
[93] See Law no 18.168, art 29, para 2.   [94] See Decree Law no 211 of 1973, art 17.
[95] ibid art 19.   [96] See Guash and Spiller (n 90 above) 295.
[97] See Decree Law no 211 of 1973, art 21.

[98] See Eduardo Bitrán et al, 'Privatizing and Regulating Chile's Utilities, 1974–2000: Successes, Failures, and Outstanding Challenges' in Guillermo Perry and Danny M Leipziger (eds), *Chile: Recent Policy and Emerging Challenges* (Washington, DC: WBI Development Studies, 1999) 340.

[99] Decree Law no 211 of 1973, art 24.

[100] See Raimundo Beca, 'Privatisation, Deregulation, and Beyond: Trends in Telecommunications in Some Latin American Countries', in Meheroo Jussawalla (ed), *Global Telecommunications Policies: The Challenge of Change* (Oakland, Cal.: Greenwood Press, 1993) 134.

ition of monetary penalties.[101] In addition, under general administrative law, all administrative decisions can be appealed on legal as well as substantive grounds. The courts can decide to suspend the contested decisions while they are being reviewed.[102]

D. Implementation of the regulatory framework

Implementation of a pro-competition regime in the telecommunications sector has a particularly long history in Chile since full liberalization occurred as early as 1982. It is also a rich history, to the extent that various adaptations were made to the overall framework, as mentioned above, in an attempt to ensure that competition would not remain merely a theoretical possibility but would become an effective reality in the telecommunications sector. The following developments are examined below:

- (i) implementation of the 1982 General Telecommunications Law;
- (ii) implementation of specific pricing provisions for interconnection and fixed services after 1987;
- (iii) efforts to intensify competition in the long-distance market;
- (iv) spectrum allocation for the provision of mobile services;
- (v) pricing of mobile services;
- (vi) recent efforts at controlling market power in local telephony;
- (vii) implementation of the Telecommunications Development Fund;
- (viii) proposed modifications to the regulatory framework.

1. Implementation of the 1982 General Telecommunications Law

In the early 1980s, a few small private companies were granted licences to provide fixed local telephone service. Some of those licence territories overlapped with CTC's service areas and CTC was required to provide interconnection to the new networks.[103] However, under the 1978 Telecommunications Policy and the 1982 General Telecommunications Law, no formal process had been devised to determine interconnection conditions and the new companies often found it quite difficult to reach a satisfactory agreement with CTC or to ensure that CTC abide by the terms of such agreements.[104] Several antitrust

---

[101] See Law no 18.168, arts 15 and 36 A.

[102] Bjorn Wellenius, 'Regulating the Telecommunications Sector: The Experience of Latin America', Conference on Regulation in Post-Privatization Environment, Buenos Aires, 21–22 May 1998.

[103] See José Ricardo Melo, 'Liberalisation and Privatisation in Chile' in Bjorn Wellenius and Peter A Stern (eds), Implementing Reforms in the Telecommunications Sector: Lessons from Experience (Washington, DC: The World Bank, 1994) 150.

[104] See Ahmed Galal, 'Regulation and Commitment in the Development of Telecommunications in Chile', Policy Research Working Paper No 1278 (Washington, DC: The World Bank, 1994) 23.

complaints were filed by the new companies against CTC. In every case, the antitrust commissions pronounced against CTC, but only after rather long processes.[105]

Retail pricing also proved problematic. After adoption of the 1982 law, the Resolutive Commission ruled that both fixed local and long-distance services were provided in markets which were insufficiently competitive to be left un-regulated. Since both CTC and ENTEL were still publicly owned, and given SUBTEL's lack of clout and experience, tariffs were in fact negotiated between the two companies, SUBTEL, and the Ministry of Economy. Prices were set at economically inefficient levels and cross-subsidization was maintained, in spite of the fact that the law required that prices be established on the basis of costs.[106]

2. The Implementation of the 1987 Pricing Provisions

As indicated above, very specific pricing guidelines were established in 1987 for services provided in markets characterized by insufficient competition. The markets for fixed local and long-distance services were still considered insufficiently competitive to be left unregulated. CTC and ENTEL prepared tariff proposals as requested by the law, and a new tariff structure was adopted in 1989 for the next five years.[107] This new structure, widely seen as an improvement over the previous regime, was designed to eliminate most cross-subsidies between local and long-distance services over a five-year period, with the exception of international rates which were still well above costs.[108]

3. The Introduction of Effective Competition in the Long-Distance Market

Two major antitrust suits which started at the end of the 1980s paved the way—albeit after very long processes—for the introduction of fierce competition in the long-distance market. The first suit raised the issue of whether Telefónica of Spain, which had become shareholder of both CTC (44 per cent) and ENTEL (20 per cent), could keep its participation in both companies. The Preventive Commission, which had been asked to intervene at the request of the National Economic Attorney-General, ruled that Telefónica could not maintain an equity interest in both companies because of the risk that CTC would use its quasi-monopoly in the local market to discriminate against ENTEL's competitors.[109] Telefónica appealed against this ruling and the case was finally settled on 20 April 1993, when Chile's Supreme Court confirmed that Telefónica had to sell its participation in one of the two companies. Telefónica chose to exchange its ENTEL shares for shares of Cointel, the consortium controlling 60 per cent of

---

[105] See Luis Guash and Pablo Spiller, *Managing the Regulatory Process: Design, Concepts, Issues and the Latin America and Caribbean Story* (Washington, DC: The World Bank, 1999) 114.

[106] See Ahmed Galal et al, *Welfare Consequences of Selling Public Enterprises: An Empirical Analysis* (Oxford: Oxford University Press, 1994) 257.

[107] ibid 258.   [108] See Melo (n 103 above) 153.   [109] See Beca (n 100 above) 135.

Telefónica de Argentina.[110] This ruling ensured that CTC and ENTEL would really compete with one another if they were allowed to enter each other's markets, which was precisely the issue tackled by the second lawsuit.

The second suit also went all the way up to the Supreme Court. It started when ENTEL objected to CTC's application for licences to provide long-distance services through satellite links and fibre-optic cables. ENTEL argued that given CTC's quasi-monopoly of the local market, allowing the company to enter the long-distance market would be anti-competitive. ENTEL, for its part, applied for a licence to provide local services in specific business sectors of Santiago. CTC objected to that application, arguing, inter alia, that ENTEL would be able to focus on the most profitable parts of the local market only. SUBTEL referred the matter to the National Economic Attorney-General, requesting a ruling on the following three questions: (i) how would competition be affected by vertical integration?; (ii) can the local and long-distance markets be considered different markets?; and (iii) should local companies be prevented from participating in the long-distance market?

In October 1989, the Preventive Commission ruled that local and long-distance companies could not enter each other's markets. In November 1989, the Resolutive Commission reversed, on appeal, the first ruling and stated that local and long-distance companies could enter each other's market if two conditions were met: (i) a company which decided to enter a new market had to do so via a subsidiary in order to facilitate identification of transfer costs; and (ii) the provider of local services had to provide interconnection to all long-distance providers through a multi-carrier system. ENTEL lodged an appeal against the second ruling before the Supreme Court and in May 1990, the Supreme Court returned the case to the Resolutive Commission, with a request that the Resolutive Commission conduct an in-depth study on the feasibility of the multi-carrier system and on the impact on competition of letting subsidiaries of companies operating in one market enter another market.[111] The Resolutive Commission took three years to study the issue and in 1993, it upheld its prior decision.[112] The Supreme Court settled this suit by confirming the decision of the Resolutive Commission.[113]

As indicated above, Law no 19.302 of May 1994 launched the multi-carrier system whereby users can pre-select their long-distance company and also choose it on a call-by-call basis, it imposed the creation of subsidiaries for providers who wanted to enter the long-distance market, and it specified that SUBTEL was competent to regulate interconnection prices under the provisions of Title V of the General Telecommunications Law.[114] Implementation of the new system did not go entirely without problems. There have been occasional blockages of competitors' dialling codes by the local service provider, as well as

---

[110] See Pierre Guislain, *The Privatisation Challenge: A Strategic, Legal and Institutional Analysis of International Experience* (Washington, DC: The World Bank, 1997) 210.

[111] See Galal (n 104 above) 24. [112] See Guash and Spiller (n 105 above) 119.

[113] See Melo (n 103 above) 159. [114] See text accompanying nn 39–42 above.

delays in connecting dialled calls.[115] However, clear interconnection standards were set and enforced by SUBTEL, and this new policy combined with the option of choosing long-distance providers on a call-by-call basis was remarkably successful at introducing competition in the long-distance market. Such competition prompted a deregulation of long-distance prices in Chile, and thus only interconnection prices and prices of local services remained subjected to regulation after the second rate-setting process which took place in 1994.[116]

4. Spectrum Allocation for the Provision of Mobile Services

In 1988, three licence territories, together covering the whole country, were established for the provision of mobile services and licences were granted in such a way that two companies operated in each territory.[117]

During the first half of the 1990s, CTC and CTC cellular offered their clients a so-called 'super phone'. Super phones automatically re-routed unanswered calls originally directed at the fixed telephone to the subscriber's mobile phone. BellSouth, which competed in the mobile segment, complained to the Resolutive Commission about what it saw as an attempt by CTC to leverage its dominant position in the fixed local market to gain an unfair advantage in the mobile market. The Resolutive Commission imposed a fine upon CTC and asked the Government to introduce regulation requiring that providers of fixed local services carry out mobile operations through distinct subsidiaries supervised by the Securities Commission, as already required for the provision of long-distance services.[118]

In early 1996, VTR and CTC which had two mobile licences each—they both had one licence in the same territory and each operated in one of the other two territories—merged their cellular phone companies and set up a new enterprise, STARTEL, serving the whole country. The Preventive Commission, however, forced STARTEL to sell one of the two licences which it held in the one territory where VTR and CTC had both held one licence.

In November 1996, SUBTEL auctioned three nation-wide licences for mobile telephony using the personal communication system (PCS) standard. This process was delayed by more than a year because of lawsuits filed by CTC and BellSouth. ENTEL was finally awarded two of those licences while the third one went to Chilesat.[119]

At the end of 2000, SUBTEL was in the process of auctioning three additional nation-wide PCS licences as well as a number of wireless local loop licences. In both cases, the Resolutive Commission had intervened to force SUBTEL to modify the award process. As far as the PCS licences were concerned, the

---

[115] See Guash and Spiller (n 105 above) 98.

[116] See Bitrán et al, 'Privatizing and Regulating Chile's Utilities, 1974–2000: Successes, Failures, and Outstanding Challenges' in Guillermo Perry and Danny M Leipziger (eds), *Chile: Recent Policy Lessons and Emerging Challenges* (Washington, DC: WBI Development Studies, 1999) 364.

[117] ibid 372.   [118] ibid 376.   [119] ibid 372–373.

Commission required that a public bidding process be held, contrary to SUB-TEL's original plan.[120] In the wireless local loop market, the Commission forced SUBTEL to increase the number of licences on offer and to reduce the deposit guarantee required from the operators in order to make the award process more competitive and facilitate the entry of new operators in the market for the provision of wireless local loop services.[121]

5. Pricing of Mobile Services

In 1998, the Resolutive Commission forced CTC STARTEL to suspend its 'calling party pays plus' system, under which CTC's fixed local subscribers could call users of STARTEL's mobile phones for the price of a regular fixed call while the recipient of the call on the cellular phone paid no charge.[122] The 'calling party pays plus' system constituted a break from the system in place since the advent of mobile telephony in Chile, whereby a subscriber to the fixed network calling a mobile phone would pay the fixed telephone charge and the recipient of the call would pay a charge as well to cover the operating costs of the mobile network.[123] The antitrust authorities considered that the 'calling party pays plus' system constituted an anti-competitive cross-subsidy from CTC's regulated fixed activities to CTC's unregulated mobile activities.[124]

During the course of 1998, interconnection prices for accessing mobile networks were calculated and in early 1999, a 'calling party pays' system was introduced for all companies, whereby the price of a call originating on a fixed network and terminating on a mobile network is paid exclusively by the person who originates the call, but includes the interconnection charge.[125] This reform, which reduces costs for mobile phone users, makes mobile telephony more attractive and more competitive with respect to fixed telephony.

6. Recent Efforts at Controlling Market Power in Local Telephony

CTC has so far retained a dominant position in the fixed local market and has been found guilty of abuses of monopoly power by the regulatory authorities a number of times. In 1988 and 1989, for example, CTC required payments from

---

[120] Pyramid Research Perspective, *Chile: More Mobile Competitors in the Region's Most Competitive Market?*, 19 January 2001, 1.

[121] Pyramid Research Perspective, *Chile: Revised WLL Bidding Rules and New 3G Frequencies*, 2 October 2000, 1.

[122] See The Economist Intelligence Unit, *Chilean Mobile Market Blown Open with New Competition*, 1999, available at <http://db.eiu.com/search_view.asp?doc_id=DB168669&action=go&to picid=&pubcode=&search=Chilean+Mobile+Market+Blown+Open&date_restrict=&hits=25 &x=54&y=4>.

[123] See SUBTEL, 'Informe de Gestion 1998' 3–4, available at <http://www.subtel.cl/publicaciones/index.htm>.

[124] See Jorge Rosenblut, 'Telecommunications in Chile: Success and Post-Deregulatory Challenges in a Rapidly Emerging Economy' (1998) 51 *J of Intl Affairs* 8.

[125] See 'Informe de Gestion 1998' (n 123 above) 1.

those who had requested a telephone line up to two years before the lines were actually provided. In addition, CTC discriminated between users by announcing that it would register requests for new lines, sold at a high price, up to a given date, and by starting, some time later, a new registration campaign for lines to be sold at a lower rate. The Preventive Commission condemned that conduct but only in 1993 and it judged that, by then, too much time had elapsed since the conduct had taken place to warrant intervention by the National Economic Attorney-General.[126]

On the other hand, when CTC and VTR—a holding controlling various operators providing local, long-distance and cable services—announced merger plans in 1997, the Preventive Commission stated that any merger would require its prior approval and it hinted that a merger between CTC's local operations and VTR's cable services would not be allowed because it would eliminate a promising source of competition in the local market.[127] The two companies apparently decided, then, to shelve their plans for a complete merger and to focus instead on a smaller deal involving the sale of VTR's long-distance operations to CTC. The Resolutive Commission approved the sale of 93.6 per cent of VTR Larga Distancia to CTC in August 1998, overturning an initial negative ruling by the Preventive Commission.[128]

In early 1998, SUBTEL requested that the Resolutive Commission review the list of telecommunications services subject to regulation. The Resolutive Commission ruled that, in the local market, dominant enterprises should remain subject to price regulation. CTC is the only company which is to be regulated except in the south of the country and on the Isla de Pascua where Telefónica del Sur, Telefónica Colhaique, and ENTEL are dominant. The Resolutive Commission also ruled that access to various elements of the local network had to be regulated to promote unbundled access to the local network and therefore foster competition in the local market.[129] The prices of unbundled elements are to be set in accordance with the LRIC methodology described above.

New tariffs were imposed on CTC in 1999, which the company unsuccessfully tried to challenge in the courts.[130] These new tariffs imposed sharp price reductions upon CTC. For example, a 14 per cent reduction in the price of local calls and a 62 per cent reduction in the price which can be charged for the use of the fixed local network to access the Internet. Access charges to be paid by operators which seek to terminate calls on CTC's fixed network have been drastically reduced as well with a 62 per cent reduction and a 97 per cent reduction for

---

[126] See Pablo Serra, 'La Politica de Competencia en Chile' (1995) 10 *Revista de Análisis Económico* 72.

[127] See Bitrán et al (n 116 above) 376–377.

[128] See The Economist Intelligence Unit, *Chile's Antitrust Commission Approves CTC Acquisition of VTR Long Distance*, 1998, available at <http://db.eiu.com/search_view.asp?doc_id=DB44023&action=go&topicid=&pubcode=XC&search=Chile%27s+Antitrust+Commission+approves&date_restrict=&hits=25&x=51&y=13>.

[129] See 'Informe de Gestion 1998' (n 123 above).

[130] See 'Telefónica: Planned Final Dividend to Be Omitted' Financial Times 28 October 1999.

terminating domestic long-distance and international calls respectively.[131] Prices were also set for unbundled services (according to LRIC) as well as for resale services (according to a retail-minus method).[132] Finally, price reductions for end-user and access services were imposed on Telefónica del Sur and Telefónica Colhaique as well in 2000.[133]

Finally, there still is no system, at present, to reassign existing numbers to new service providers in order to enable users to keep the same number, whatever local provider they choose.[134]

7. The Implementation of the Telecommunications Development Fund

As indicated above, in 1994 the Chilean Government set up a Fund, managed by SUBTEL, to increase telecommunications access in rural and poor urban areas. The objective is to provide at least one public telephone per locality, but operators are, however, free to provide additional services if they wish. Seven licensing rounds, for concessions covering just above 6000 localities in total, were conducted from 1994 to 2000. SUBTEL collected requests for payphones from local authorities, telecommunications companies, and the general public. It grouped these requests into projects, typically comprising twenty to fifty localities. Eligible projects were those deemed desirable for the economy at large (ie projects with positive social net present value) but unlikely to be commercially viable (ie projects with negative private net social value). For each eligible project, SUBTEL estimated the maximum amount of available subsidy and the projects exhibiting the highest ratio of social net present value over estimated required subsidy were awarded first.[135]

The concessions were offered, without any exclusivity rights, for a period of thirty years, to the bidders requiring the lowest subsidies. Operating licences authorized the winning bidder to install payphones as well as to provide any additional services included in the bid. The tender documents specified the conditions of service, applicable price regulations, and deadlines to initiate service. Payphones must be available to the public twenty-four hours a day, every day, for ten years. End-user prices of local calls from payphones are capped at a level about 50 per cent higher than the price of calls from urban coin-operated telephones. Long-distance calls from payphones are carried by competing operators. The long-distance charge is unregulated and so is the price of any other services included in the bid. Licensees are, however, required to post both local and long-distance call charges in each public payphone and to inform SUBTEL of any changes. Payphone service is generally required to begin six to twenty months after the licence is granted.[136]

---

[131] See Pyramid Research Perspective, *MTT Approves CTC Tariff Cuts*, 4 May 1999 1–3.
[132] See Decreto No 187, 4 May 1999, s 1.6.
[133] See SUBTEL, 'Informe de Gestion 2000' 24, available at <http://www.subtel.cl/publicaciones/index.htm>.
[134] See Rosenblut (n 124 above) 9.   [135] ibid 4.   [136] ibid 4–5.

New rural companies initially had difficulty concluding interconnection agreements with urban companies. These problems were, however, eventually solved through SUBTEL's regulation of the access charges which rural companies could impose upon urban companies to terminate calls on the rural networks. These charges tend to be much higher than access charges between urban companies because of the higher costs of providing service in rural areas.[137]

In addition, some modifications were made to the regulatory framework to facilitate the activities of the rural companies. Thus, for example, the numbering system was changed to enable companies—as well as individual callers—to identify rural numbers, thereby facilitating calculation and payment of rural access charges. Rural companies were also exempted from some technical standards which unnecessarily increased the cost of rural services.[138] Finally, as mentioned above, the Telecommunications Law was modified in 2000 to broaden the scope of the services which can be subsidized through the Telecommunications Development Fund: auctions for the award of licences to operate private telecentres are to be launched in 2001 following the model established for rural payphone projects.[139]

The tender documents for rural payphone projects were also modified in some respects as lessons started to emerge from the experience of the first rural companies. For example, the subsidy, in current pesos with no adjustment for inflation, was initially paid in a lump sum once the facilities had been built and inspected by SUBTEL. Later on, operators were entitled to receive part of the subsidy after a certain number of phones had been installed, but a substantial part of the subsidy was still withheld until all phones were operational. Also, operators were initially not allowed to change the location of the payphones after licences had been issued, even if better locations were subsequently identified, and they could not close down any payphones before ten years even if usage dwindled due to changes—in demographic or economic conditions, for example—outside of the operators' control. From 1999, changes in location became possible subject to approval by the Council. As the administrative process to request such changes was not specified, however, considerable delays occurred.[140]

8. Proposed Modifications to the Regulatory Framework

Two draft laws which would modify the regulatory framework for telecommunications are currently under discussion. One would require television broadcasters to set up distinct subsidiaries supervised by the Securities Commission in order to provide telecommunications services. As is the case in the other markets where some degree of vertical separation between different activities has been

---

[137] See Bjorn Wellenius, 'Closing the Rural Communication Access Gap: Chile 1995–2002', The World Bank, Draft paper of 24 June 2001, 11, available at <http://www.infodev.org/library/working.htm>.

[138] ibid 16–17.   [139] ibid 20–21.   [140] ibid 16.

required, the objective of this measure would be to facilitate identification of unlawful cross-subsidies or other anti-competitive practices.[141] The second draft law would contain measures enabling users of telecommunications services to participate in the price-setting process.[142]

E. A CRITICAL APPRAISAL OF THE REGULATORY FRAMEWORK

The Chilean model presents a number of interesting features, which heighten the interest of comparing it with the other country models analysed here. First, because Chile was a pioneer in the field of telecommunications liberalization, the workings of the post-liberalization regulatory framework can be analysed over a period of almost two decades. Second, as pointed out at the beginning of this Chapter, the Chilean model represents, in a way, a compromise between the New Zealand and US approaches: throughout the post-liberalization period, the Chilean regulatory framework put, overall, more emphasis on sector-specific components than the New Zealand model but less than the US model. Third, as indicated earlier as well, the design of the regulatory framework changed over the period, which provides therefore an opportunity to judge the efficacy of different regulatory options in a single country setting. Finally, Chile, unlike the other countries examined in this book, is a middle-income, rather than a high-income country. In that context, providing for a sufficient degree of regulatory certainty, promoting regulatory autonomy, mobilizing adequate regulatory capacity, and ensuring adequate telecommunications access to poor and rural areas, for example, present special challenges. A study of the Chilean case provides, therefore, a good opportunity to evaluate how sector-specific and non-sector-specific approaches fare in addressing those particular challenges.

1. Competition and Other Incentives to Generate and Share Efficiency Gains

Chile is clearly one of the countries which has most thoroughly focused on fostering competition in the telecommunications sector in an attempt to ensure that telecommunications services would be efficient and that users would benefit from efficiency gains. Competition did not, however, emerge immediately after implementation, in the early 1980s, of a legal framework allowing for multiple entry into each market segment. In fact, during most of that decade, the telecommunications sector remained dominated by two publicly owned monopolistic operators: CTC in the local market, and ENTEL in the long-distance market.

---

[141] See Chapter 3, Section H.
[142] See SUBTEL, 'Informe de Gestion 1999' 11–12, available at <http://www.subtel.cl/publica ciones/index.htm>.

While the companies were subject to technical standards monitored by SUBTEL, the price regulation regime—deemed necessary because of the lack of competition—left much to be desired. The two companies were, in fact, able to take part in the regulation of their own prices which, contrary to the objectives of the 1982 Telecommunications Law, were established at economically inefficient levels without much regard to the actual costs of providing the services.[143] In addition, CTC was free to negotiate interconnection prices with its would-be competitors whose only recourse was to turn to the antitrust authorities when agreements could not be reached, a slow and expensive process.[144]

The incentive regime under which CTC and ENTEL operated changed substantially during the last years of the 1980s. The 1987 law established a very detailed pricing regime, based on LRIC methodology, which became applicable to fixed local and long-distance services.[145] As described in the law, the pricing methodology applied in Chile presents an advantage over most LRIC-based regimes in that it specifically requires that the mark-up needed, on top of marginal costs to cover average costs be calculated in a way which minimizes economic distortions, ie in accordance with Ramsey–Boiteux principles.

The privatization of CTC and ENTEL, for its part, severed some of the links between the Government and the operators. This helped to establish a clearer separation between operational and regulatory responsibilities and it contributed to ensure a more satisfactory implementation of the price regime than had been the case in the early 1980s. As indicated above, the price schedule implemented in 1989 brought prices closer to costs and promoted a rebalancing between local and long-distance tariffs, with a progressive reduction of long-distance prices.[146] Such price reductions should probably have been faster, however, given the fact that ENTEL enjoyed rates of return of more than 40 per cent in the early 1990s.[147]

As mentioned above, intense competition developed in the long-distance market in the 1990s. It was made possible by a series of factors. The implementation of a detailed, pro-competition pricing regime in 1987 played an important role. The two major antitrust decisions of 1993 which mandated complete separation between CTC and ENTEL and which enabled CTC to enter the long-distance market opened the door for a strong challenge, by CTC, of ENTEL's dominant position in that market. The implementation of the multi-carrier system which enabled users not only to pre-select a long-distance provider, but also to choose such providers on a call-by-call basis, proved particularly effective at drawing multiple competing operators to the long-distance

---

[143] See text accompanying n 106 above.
[144] See text accompanying nn 103–105 above.
[145] See text accompanying nn 29–35 above.
[146] See text accompanying nn 107–108 above.
[147] See Eduardo Bitrán and Raúl Sáez, 'Privatisation and Regulation in Chile' in Barry P Bosworth et al (eds), *The Chilean Economy: Policy Lessons and Challenges* (Washington, DC: The Brookings Institution, 1994) 363.

market. Finally, while interconnection problems did arise early on, extending the application of the tariff provisions of the General Telecommunications Law to interconnection issues ultimately enabled SUBTEL to ensure a successful implementation of the new regime.[148]

By early 1995, ENTEL's share of the long-distance market had already fallen below 50 per cent.[149] By 1997, eight firms were actually competing in that market and by March 2001 there were thirteen long-distance carriers in operation.[150] Price wars between different providers have made the Chilean domestic and international long-distance market very competitive. The impact of competition in the international segment of the long-distance market can be evaluated if one notes that, had the rate-setting formula in place before the introduction of the multi-carrier system remained in force, a call from Chile to the United States would have cost US$2.40 per minute in 1997, while it actually cost US$0.34 per minute at that time.[151] Prices in the long-distance market have continued to decline from 1997 to 2000, by about 9 per cent and 36 per cent in real terms, for domestic long-distance and international calls respectively.[152] The price comparisons presented in the Annex reveal that Chilean national long-distance prices are the lowest in our sample when expressed in current US$ and the third lowest when based on PPPs (see Graphs 4a and 4b). The prices of international calls are competitive as well when expressed in current US$—albeit they are high when based on PPPs (see Graphs 5a, 5b, 6a, 6b, 7a, 7b, 8a, and 8b).

Price wars between the various long-distance operators, combined with restructuring costs to cope with a more competitive environment and with a reduction of receipts from international accounting rates,[153] sharply reduced the rates of return on equity for long-distance service providers, from close to 50 per cent in the early 1990s to less than 10 per cent in 1995. The rates of return for local telephony, on the other hand, remained relatively more stable over the period, fluctuating between 15 and 22.5 per cent (see Figure 7.2 below).

Competition in the mobile market was made possible, in the 1990s, inter alia by the award of multiple licences in the same territories and by the presence of strong operators in that market (among them CTC and ENTEL). Competition

---

[148] See text accompanying nn 114–116 above.

[149] See Luis Guash and Pablo Spiller, *Managing the Regulatory Process: Design, Concepts, Issues and the Latin America and Caribbean Story* (Washington, DC: The World Bank, 1999) 120.

[150] See SUBTEL, 'Informe de Estadisticas Basicas del Sector de las Telecomunicaciones en Chile', Informe No 2, April 2001 (hereafter, 'Estadisticas Basicas del Sector de las Telecommunicaciones—April 2001') 11, available at <http://www.subtel.cl/publicaciones/index.htm>.

[151] See Luis Guash and Pablo Spiller, *Managing the Regulatory Process: Design, Concepts, Issues and the Latin America and Caribbean Story* (Washington, DC: The World Bank, 1999) 120.

[152] See 'Estadisticas Basicas del Sector de las Telecommunicaciones—April 2001' (n 150 above) 40–41.

[153] International carriers charge each other so-called accounting rates to terminate international calls. Such accounting rates are actually much higher than the cost of terminating the calls so that an operator handling more incoming that outgoing calls receives significant revenues from foreign operators. As Chile's international rates went down, the imbalance between its outgoing and incoming international calls—which had traditionally favoured its national operators—started to decrease. See Guash and Spiller (n 151 above) 121.

FIGURE 7.2. Return on equity of CTC and ENTEL 1990–1995

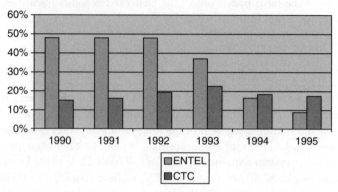

Source: Luis Guash and Pablo Spiller, *Managing the Regulatory Process: Design, Concepts, Issues and the Latin America and Caribbean Story* (Washington, DC: The World Bank, 1999) 118.

considerably intensified in particular when ENTEL's PCS network became operational, prompting mobile telephone companies to lower their rates by 50 per cent in 1998. In addition, the application of detailed price rules to interconnection proved essential to determine the cost of interconnection between fixed and mobile networks and enable implementation of the 'calling party pays' regime.[154] Chilean prices are currently the lowest of our sample in current US$ (albeit the second highest when based on PPPs—see the Annex, Graphs 11a, 11b, 12a, and 12b).

There are now six mobile operators in the market and competition has prompted an expansion of the mobile segment of the telecommunications market which is truly remarkable, as shown in Figure 7.3 below.[155] With more than 3.4 million subscribers at the end of 2000 (or 22.2 subscribers per 100 inhabitants), the number of mobile users now exceeds the number of fixed telephone users and the 'calling party pays' regime should further stimulate the development of the mobile market.

In the fixed local market, competition remains limited. CTC still has about 82 per cent of lines in service.[156] Excluding the concessions awarded for rural telephony, CTC remained, at the end of 2000, the only provider of fixed local services in eight regions (out of twenty-four) and it competes with only one other operator in another nine regions.[157] One obstacle to competition was the absence, until the last rate-setting process in 1999, of any specific rules on the pricing of unbundled elements and of resale services. As a result, would-be competitors found it very difficult to reach agreements on unbundling and

---

[154] See text accompanying n 125 above.

[155] See 'Estadisticas Basicas del Sector de las Telecommunicaciones—April 2001' (n 150 above) 3, 12.

[156] CTC Chile, *Memoria Anual 2000* 19.

[157] See 'Estadisticas Basicas del Sector de las Telecommunicaciones–April 2001' (n 150 above) 8.

FIGURE 7.3. Expansion of the Chilean cellular market 1992–2001

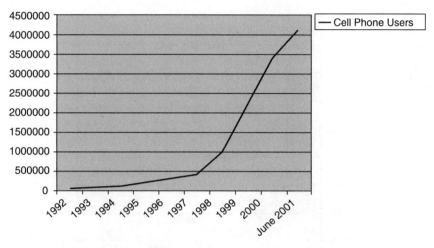

Source: SUBTEL, 'Informe de Estadisticas del Sector de las Telecomunicaciones en Chile', Informe No 3 (December 2001) 8.

resale with CTC and had to build their own infrastructure instead.[158] In fact, unbundling and resale obligations still remain today, for the most part, to be implemented adequately. The absence of number portability still hinders competition as well. In addition, CTC's monopoly position in the local market undoubtedly makes price regulation more difficult as the absence of comparable firms in the market limits the information available to the regulator and complicates the evaluation of the cost structure of a benchmark efficient firm.[159]

Competition does, however, appear to be emerging slowly. For example, over the year 2000, the number of CTC's competitors has increased in four regions and no less than six companies are operating in the Santiago metropolitan area.[160] In addition, the price of local telephony has decreased in recent years: over the period 1993–2000, the reductions were 16.5 and 13.5 per cent for the fixed and variable parts of the tariff respectively.[161] While several commentators argued that CTC's comfortable returns on equity in the mid-1990s (see Figure 7.2 above) revealed that the market for fixed local telephony was insufficiently competitive and that price regulation was too lax,[162] CTC's return on equity figures have plummeted in recent years (see Figure 7.4 below). With about

[158] See Jorge Rosenblut, 'Telecommunications in Chile: Success and Post-Deregulatory Challenges in a Rapidly Emerging Economy' (1998) 51 *J of Intl Affairs* 7.

[159] See Section D.6 above.

[160] See 'Estadisticas Basicas del Sector de las Telecommunicaciones—April 2001' (n 150 above) 10.

[161] SUBTEL, 'Informe de Estadisticas Basicas del Sector de las Telecomunicaciones en Chile', Informe No 1, September 2000, 26, available at <http://www.subtel.cl/publicaciones/index.htm>.

[162] See, for example, Guash and Spiller (n 151 above) 116, and Eduardo Bitrán et al, 'Privatizing and Regulating Chile's Utilities, 1974–2000: Successes, Failures, and Outstanding Challenges' in

FIGURE 7.4. Return on equity of CTC

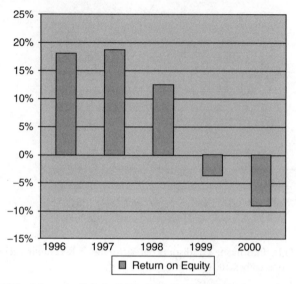

Source: CTC Chile, *Memoria Anual, 1997, 1998, 1999* and *2000*.

50 per cent of CTC's revenues generated by the provision of fixed local services,[163] the tighter price regulation of fixed local telephony introduced by SUBTEL in 1999 substantially contributed to this decline. The company estimates that the introduction of the new price regime reduced its revenues by close to 100,000 million pesos, ie about 11 per cent of its total revenues.[164]

The market for the provision of Internet services has expanded at a very fast pace in recent years (see Figure 7.5 below). In addition, the amount of time that Internet users are spending online is increasing at a faster rate than the number of users itself.[165] These developments are largely due to the price reductions imposed upon CTC in 1999 for the provision of local services and, in particular, for dial-up connection to local ISPs. While a metered price regime remains applicable to the provision of local services, these price reductions which, as mentioned above, decreased by 62 per cent the price charged for the use of the fixed local network to access the Internet, made Internet services affordable to more Chileans. Another important factor is the emergence of vigorous competition between ISPs. While ISPs affiliated to CTC

Guillermo Perry and Danny M Leipziger (eds), *Chile: Recent Policy Lessons and Emerging Challenges* (Washington, DC: WBI Development Studies, 1999) 337.

[163] See, CTC Chile, *Memoria Anual 2000* 31.

[164] ibid 43.

[165] See SUBTEL, 'Informe de Estadisticas del Sector de las Telecomunicaciones en Chile', Informe No 3, December 2001, 18, available at <http://www.subtel.cl/publicaciones/index.htm>.

FIGURE 7.5. Number of Internet users in Chile, 1998–2001

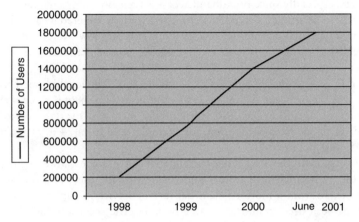

Source: SUBTEL, 'La Industria de Acceso a Internet en Chile' (May 2000) 10.

and ENTEL still dominate the market for Internet access services, SUBTEL had identified about 35 ISPs which were operating in Chile in March 2000.[166] Price competition between these operators is intense: in February 2000, Justice Telecom became the first ISP to offer free unlimited dial-up Internet access and SUBTEL identified three additional operators which were offering free unlimited access as well one month later.[167] While the PPP-based prices of Internet services remain substantially higher in Chile than in the other four countries studied here, Chilean prices expressed in current US$ are competitive with those of the other countries, at least for moderate Internet use (see Annex, Graphs 9a, 9b, 10a, and 10b). Finally, government initiatives aimed at making administrative services available online are contributing to increased Internet use as well: in 2000, about two thirds of all businesses, including many small and medium enterprises, filed their tax returns using the Internet.[168]

Broadband access offerings, on the other hand, remain limited. A few cable operators offer Internet access at relatively competitive rates.[169] However, cable penetration remains low in Chile. In addition, as mentioned above, while CTC is required to provide unbundled access to the local loop, no such unbundling agreements were in force at the end of 2000 and this has hindered the development of DSL services in Chile. As the GDP per capita continues to grow, however, the Chilean market—with its competitive environment and tested

[166] See SUBTEL, 'La Industria de Acceso a Internet en Chile' (May 2000) 7.
[167] ibid 11.
[168] See Bjorn Wellenius, 'Closing the Rural Communication Access Gap: Chile 1995–2002', The World Bank, Draft paper of 24 June 2001, 20, available at <http://www.infodev.org/library/work ing.htm>.
[169] The cable provider VTR, for example, offers one-way Internet access for US$47 per month and two-way access for US$54 per month. See Lucas Grave, 'Jupiter Communications—Latin America: Online Projections' vol 1, 7 March 2000 1.

regulatory framework—should prove promising for broadband access providers, especially since broadband access is typically unmetered and is therefore likely to be attractive to users seeking to avoid the metered local call regime associated with dial-up Internet access. While still very low overall, the number of broadband connections is in fact increasing exponentially at present: from 4370 connections in December 2000 to 24,394 in June 2001.[170]

Overall, service quality appears to be satisfactory. The local phone network, which was 37 per cent digital in 1987, has been fully digital since 1993.[171] Efficiency of operation has also substantially increased over the period: the number of phone lines per worker, for example, rose from 74 in 1987, to 235 in 1995, and 582 in 2000.[172]

Competition for the market has been introduced, in some market segments, to select the most efficient operators and ensure that the users and the Treasury would benefit from a more efficient delivery of services. Competitive auctions have thus been used to allocate scarce radio-electric spectrum and to channel public subsidies to universal service providers in charge of improving telecommunications access in poor urban and rural areas. This latter initiative was particularly successful. As of December 2000, five companies were operating rural concessions (one of these five companies is CTC; the other four are new entrants—distinct from the fourteen main providers of local fixed services mentioned above—established specifically to provide rural services). While about 15 per cent of the population had no access to a telephone in 1994, only about 1 per cent remains in that situation today. In addition, total subsidies committed by the Fund to establish public rural payphones amount only to US$21.8 million (or about 0.3 per cent of total telecommunications sector revenues over the 1995–2000 period), while private companies invested US$30 million in public payphones and an additional US$109 million for the provision of other telecommunications services in rural areas (mainly individual connections and value-added services for which no subsidies were received).[173] The results of the seven rounds of rural payphone auctions held since 1995 are summarized in Table 7.2 below.

A number of factors explain the success of the initiative. The bottom-up approach—involving local authorities, neighbourhood associations, etc—which was used to determine localities needing payphones, was effective at precisely identifying demand. The subsidies were collected from the national budget in a way which did not distort or prevent competition between operators. In addition, the subsidies were allocated in a competitive manner and the licences which were granted were not exclusive in order to maximize competitive pressures. The operators' obligations were limited and clear—mainly to install at least one public

    [170] See SUBTEL, 'Estadisticas Basicas del Sector de las Telecomunicaciones—December 2001' (n 165 above) 19.
    [171] See Guash and Spiller (n 151 above) 112.
    [172] ibid. See also, CTC Chile, *Memoria Anual 2000* 4.
    [173] See Wellenius (n 168 above) 5–7.

TABLE 7.2. Chile—Telecommunications Development Funds 1995–2000

	No of Localities/ Tel	Total Subsidy (US$ m)	Total Number of Beneficiary Inhabitants (m)	Subsidy per Telephone (US$)	Subsidy per Inhabitant (US$)
1995 (1st set of projects)	726	2.01	0.24	2,769	8
1996 (2nd set of projects)	1,632	0.87	0.76	533	1
1997 (3rd and 4th sets of projects)	2,146	7.28	0.77	3,392	9
1998 (5th set of projects)	858	5.19	0.23	6,049	23
1999 (6th set of projects)	554	4.58	0.15	8,267	31
2000 (7th set of projects)	143	1.82	0.04	12,727	45
Total	6,059	21.8	2.2	3,598 (on average)	10 (on average)

Source: Bjorn Wellenius, 'Closing the Rural Communication Access Gap: Chile 1995–2002', Draft Paper (The World Bank, 24 June 2001).

phone in each locality of the franchise territory—and the operators remained largely free to choose the technology and project design which would prove most cost-effective. Price controls were limited—they applied to local calls from payphones and to interconnection charges only—and they were set in a way which reflected the high costs of establishing and operating a rural network (as mentioned above, the prices of local calls were capped at a level about 50 per cent higher for rural payphones than for urban payphones, and access charges to be paid to rural operators were significantly higher than those paid to urban companies). The operators received all or at least a large part of their subsidy in lump sums, without indexation, after the facilities were completed, which gave them clear incentives to ensure that the telephones would become operational as soon as possible. Finally, commitment by senior government officials who conceived the Fund and shepherded enabling legislation as well as competent implementation by SUBTEL were key success factors.[174]

As Table 7.2 above shows, the average subsidy which the Government had to pay per phone as well as per inhabitant increased over the 1995–2000 period. One reason for this is that the projects became progressively more costly as they encompassed ever poorer and more isolated localities. Another reason, however,

[174] ibid 8–9.

is that competition between operators for the award of concessions tended to decline over time as operators focused on consolidating their market presence in regions where they were already dominant: while up to five operators bid for new projects in early rounds, there were seldom more than two bidders per project in later rounds. This evolving strategy of the operators explains why the subsidies requested increased over time beyond what can be explained by higher net costs alone.[175] In spite of this, it is clear that the competitive selection of private service providers remains a far more efficient way to increase telecommunications access than the non-competitive publicly funded and publicly implemented programme which was in place before. In the 1980s, when the network was far less extended and localities without phones easier to connect, the Government paid US$6 million to the incumbent operator to install only 300 rural phones, an average cost of US$20,000 per phone.[176] By comparison, the average subsidy per phone for the seven sets of projects auctioned so far is only US$3,598 and, as pointed out above, public subsidies of US$21.8 million leveraged private investments of about US$139 million.[177]

Some commentators have argued that allowing companies to operate in different segments of the telecommunications market, as is currently the case in Chile, might promote anti-competitive behaviours and hinder the development of truly competitive markets, especially when some companies operate both in regulated and in unregulated market segments. The promotion by CTC of its 'super phones' and the launch of its 'calling party pays plus' system, for example, have been presented as examples of such anti-competitive behaviours whereby CTC tried to use its market power in the local segment of the market to eliminate competition in mobile services.[178] CTC's refusals to enter into unbundling agreements with its competitors might, for their part, constitute examples of anti-competitive behaviours aimed at restricting entry into the local market itself.[179]

While such problems are real, the fact that CTC and ENTEL have been able to launch activities into each other's markets has probably accelerated the introduction of effective competition for the provision of some services as both companies were well established and well known by potential customers.[180] Overall, the option adopted by Chilean authorities—ie to let companies operate in different segments of the market but only if they set up separate subsidiaries, and to prohibit cross-subsidization between regulated and unregulated activities[181]—appears to be working reasonably well, as demonstrated by the level of competition present in most segments of the market. In the local

---

[175] ibid 10.

[176] See Bjorn Wellenius, 'Extending Telecommunications Service to Rural Areas: The Chilean Experience' *Public Policy for the Private Sector*, Note 105, The World Bank (1997) 4.

[177] See text accompanying n 173 above.

[178] See Eduardo Bitrán and Pablo Serra, 'Regulation of Privatized Utilities: The Chilean Experience' (1998) 20 *World Development* 945, 954.

[179] See text accompanying n 158 above.

[180] See text accompanying nn 111–113 above.

[181] See text accompanying n 42 above.

market, however, the incumbent still retains a very dominant position. These factors would tend to suggest that re-imposing a separation between the local market and other segments of the market might not be justified, but that it may be worth exploring the pros and cons of separating CTC's provision of local infrastructure and access services on the one hand, from the provision of local retail services on the other hand.

2. Specificity versus Coherence

The regulatory framework of the first part of the 1980s emphasized, overall, coherence over specificity. A sector-specific regulator had been in place since 1977 and the 1982 Telecommunications Law did provide for the award of telecommunications licences and for the imposition of technical standards upon all licensees, but few other sector-specific features existed. The 1982 Law opened all market segments to competition. Interconnection prices were to be negotiated between operators, which had to turn to the antitrust authorities in case of disputes. In addition, it stated that the types of services to be subjected to price regulation would be identified by economy-wide antitrust authorities. Very little was said about the regulated price regime except that it had to be cost-based. Finally, general antitrust rules were applicable to all telecommunications activities and appeals against regulatory decisions could be presented before the courts.[182] This regulatory framework proved ill-suited to foster effective competition and efficiency in telecommunications. As noted above, numerous interconnection disputes between CTC and new operators had to be resolved by the antitrust commissions and that process was clearly much too slow; abuses of monopoly power tended to remain unpunished; and the prices which needed to be regulated because of the lack of effective competition were set at inefficient levels.[183] By the mid-1980s, it had become clear that additional rules were needed and the 1987 and 1994 Laws introduced a detailed telecommunications-specific price regime applicable to fixed telephony services provided in insufficiently competitive markets and to interconnection.[184] Similarly, it appeared in the late 1980s and early 1990s that the antitrust authorities were very slow in determining exactly which operators could compete in the long-distance market and under what conditions. Once again, the situation was clarified by law when legislative provisions were introduced in 1994 to specify the conditions under which local service providers could enter the long-distance market and to launch the multi-carrier system.[185]

---

[182] See text accompanying nn 22–26, 93 and 101–102 above.

[183] See text accompanying nn 104–106 above.

[184] See Luis Guash and Pablo Spiller, *Managing the Regulatory Process: Design, Concepts, Issues and the Latin America and Caribbean Story* (Washington, DC: The World Bank, 1999) 122.

[185] ibid.

It would be wrong, however, to construe these changes as simply reflecting a shift away from cross-sector consistency toward telecommunications specificity. Indeed, the new legislative provisions were instrumental in fostering competition in almost all segments of the telecommunications market, inter alia because they provided a firm basis for establishing interconnection prices (first for linking fixed networks; and later on for linking fixed and mobile networks—thereby enabling the introduction of the 'calling party pays' system). This in turn, made it possible progressively to reduce the number of services subject to the telecommunications-specific price regime (as indicated above, the provision of long-distance services was deregulated first in 1994, and the provision of local services by non-dominant operators was deregulated later, in 1999).[186] In the Chilean case, it can thus be argued that the adoption of some specific rules did, in fact, reduce rather than increase the extent of sector-specific regulation. In addition, while the role of antitrust authorities in determining interconnection prices or conditions to be met by companies entering new markets has, fortunately, been much reduced, economy-wide antitrust and judicial authorities do retain the other very important functions allocated to them by the 1982 Law.[187]

Overall, it can be argued that the Chilean model, as it stands today, represents a rather good compromise between coherence and specificity. Conferring upon the antitrust authorities the task of reviewing the scope of specific price regulations in particular, is very useful—especially given the existence of a sector-specific regulator—to ensure that specific rules can be eliminated when they are no longer needed.[188] One could argue, however, that the system might still be too sector-specific in some respects. For example, application of the 1987 price-setting regime could be extended to other infrastructure activities characterized by increasing returns to scale and limited competition. The fact that specific exemptions to a series of norms—particularly technical standards—had to be adopted to facilitate operation of rural telecommunications companies would tend to indicate that the general framework was, in fact, too specific; at the very least, the need for sector-specific norms and technical standards could be reassessed when services are provided under competitive conditions. Also, the need for a telecommunications-specific regulator could be reviewed with a view to determine whether an infrastructure-wide regulator could be set up instead, or whether all economic regulation in telecommunications could be left to economy-wide authorities such as the antitrust authorities.[189] On the other hand, telecommunications-specific rules on number portability, for example, should probably be added to the regulatory framework, as well as more precise procedural rules to examine requests for changing the location of rural payphones.[190]

---

[186] See text accompanying nn 116 and 129 above.
[187] See text accompanying nn 62–69, 73–79, 93 and 101 above.
[188] See text accompanying n 93 above.
[189] Such an option could probably be envisaged only if antitrust bodies were substantially strengthened, as explained below. See text accompanying n 210 below.
[190] See text accompanying nn 140 and 159 above.

3. Flexibility versus Certainty

The Chilean model, as it currently stands, certainly puts strong emphasis on the certainty of the regulatory framework. At first, as noted above, operators and antitrust authorities were granted wide discretion to determine interconnection prices and the Government, SUBTEL, and the two main operators also had wide latitude to determine the prices of telecommunications services.[191] Starting in the late 1980s, the situation progressively changed, however. First, the price-setting mechanism adopted in 1987 is very sophisticated and extremely specific, leaving little room for discretion to the regulator. For example, as noted above, it determines the price of each regulated service individually and it states that pricing formulas must remain in place for a full five years.[192] Second, the specific conditions under which competition is allowed in the long-distance market have been specified through the provisions of the 1994 amendments to the Telecommunications Law.[193] Third, those detailed rules are embedded in laws which tend to be difficult to modify, particularly in Chile where presidents might not necessarily be backed by a majority in Parliament and where the need for compromises between the executive and legislative branches might therefore make it rather difficult to amend the legislative framework.[194] Fourth, the decision to transfer a certain percentage of CTC's and of ENTEL's shares to the companies' employees and to the public at large, particularly through the holdings of the pension funds, was taken to foster popular support for the privatization of the utilities and to make a future reversal of the reforms unlikely.[195]

Overall, increased certainty—in particular with respect to the price regime—played a part in prompting CTC to expand and modernize its network after 1989,[196] along with other factors such as the imposition of universal service obligations by the 1987 law, the increased financial resources which the company possessed following its privatization, and increasing competitive pressures. A substantial acceleration of the rate of network expansion can be observed after 1989. While the number of lines in service had increased by about 3 per cent a year from 1972 to 1982, and by about 8 per cent a year from 1982 to 1989, it increased by close to 20 per cent a year from 1989 to 1997 (see Figure 7.6 below). After 1997, the rate of network expansion was reduced as solvent demand was being satisfied. At the end of 2000, there were 22 main lines per 100 inhabitants.

The number of pending requests for a telephone line remained relatively stable from 1972 to 1982 and actually tended to increase from 1982 until 1992 even

---

[191] See text accompanying nn 104–106 above.

[192] See text accompanying nn 29–35 above.

[193] See text accompanying nn 39–44 above.

[194] See Ahmed Galal, 'Regulation and Commitment in the Development of Telecommunications in Chile', Policy Research Working Paper No 1278 (Washington, DC: The World Bank, 1994) 28.

[195] See Brian Levy and Pablo Spiller, *Regulation, Institutions and Commitment* (Cambridge: Cambridge University Press, 1996) 21.

[196] See Guash and Spiller (n 184 above) 115.

FIGURE 7.6. Chile—Number of fixed lines in service

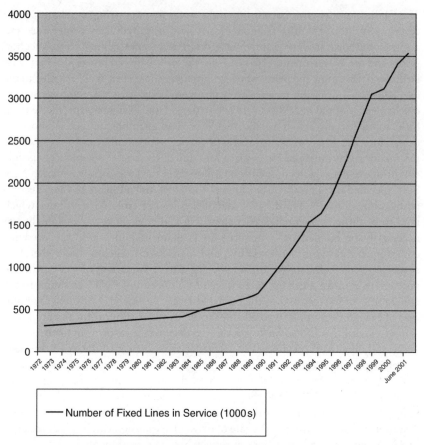

Sources: Ahmed Galal, 'Regulation and Commitment in the Development of Telecommunications in Chile', Policy Research Working Paper (Washington, DC: The World Bank, 1994) 14; and SUBTEL, 'Informe de Estadisticas del Sector de las Telecomunicaciones en Chile', Informe no 3 (April 2001) 8.

though the network was expanding, reflecting increasing purchasing power as well as higher expectation by consumers of getting a telephone installed.[197] The number of pending requests did, however, drop very rapidly after 1992 (see Figure 7.7 below).

While emphasis has been put on limiting regulatory uncertainty, it would be inaccurate to assume that no effort has been made to provide at least some measure of flexibility. For example, the scope of telecommunications services subject to price regulation can be reviewed at any time by the Resolutive

[197] See Galal (n 194 above) 13.

FIGURE 7.7. Chile—Number of pending requests, 1972–2000

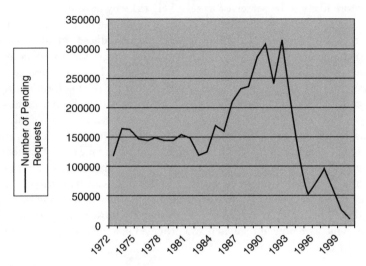

Source: Figures obtained from CTC.

Commission as mentioned above,[198] and the prices which are regulated are maximum prices, thus leaving regulated companies flexibility to adjust prices downward if technological or market conditions warrant it.[199] Also, providers of universal access are completely free to choose the technology they will use to meet the service standards set out in their licences, and some changes were progressively brought to the regulatory framework applicable to rural telephony to increase flexibility with regard to technical standards and location of payphones, for example.[200] Finally, the fact that the prices of regulated services are calculated by assessing the costs of a benchmark efficient firm does leave a certain degree of discretion to the regulator.

One could even argue that, in some respects, the regulatory framework does not offer sufficient guarantees against the misuse of regulatory discretion. For example, the fact that the Executive directly exercises some regulatory functions—for example, the Minister of Transport and Telecommunications formally grants licences,[201] and the Ministers of Telecommunications and Economy formally adopt the pricing formulas applicable to regulated services[202]—introduces a small, but unwarranted, degree of uncertainty in the regulatory process.

It can be argued that the strong emphasis which is put, overall, on limiting discretionary power and on ensuring a high degree of regulatory stability is justified in a country such as Chile, whose regulatory institutions are far from perfect (this point will be developed below) and whose main objective has been to attract private operators and investors to promote competition and network

---

[198] See text accompanying n 93 above.
[199] See text accompanying n 32 above.
[200] See text accompanying nn 138 and 140 above.
[201] See text accompanying n 80 above.
[202] See text accompanying n 82 above.

development in an environment which is that of a developing country, and which is therefore likely to be perceived as relatively risky by most investors.

In order to increase yet further the certainty of the regulatory framework, the direct regulatory powers of the Executive could be reduced. In addition, some limited changes could be made, which would increase flexibility without jeopardizing the stability of the regulatory framework. Thus, for example, while defining the price regime by law and requiring that the pricing formulas remain in place for five years is probably wise both to provide sufficient certainty to investors and to give them strong incentives to limit costs, price caps could be set for baskets of services rather than for individual services in order to provide increased pricing flexibility which is an important advantage in the fast-changing telecommunications sector.[203] Similarly, while the elaboration and monitoring of technical standards might be justified under price-cap regulation to ensure that regulated companies do not lower quality in order to decrease their costs, there should be room, as argued above, to simplify those rules, particularly for services which are now unregulated and provided in a fully competitive environment.[204]

4. Regulatory Competence and Ability to Resist Undue Pressure

Several commentators have pointed out that SUBTEL has difficulty retaining its best staff because its budget is rather limited and because the remuneration of its staff is set at civil service levels.[205] The office of the National Economic Attorney-General has the same problem for similar reasons.[206] As pointed out above, the regulated price regime that SUBTEL has to administer is very complex (for example, calculating the costs of an 'efficient' firm is a particularly difficult task when the regulated firm has no equivalent in the country—as is still very much the case in the fixed local segment of the market—so that comparisons can only be made with foreign firms operating in environments which might be substantially different from that of the regulated firm).[207] In addition, like any regulator, SUBTEL suffers from some degree of informational disadvantage vis-à-vis the regulated industry. In these conditions, any shortcomings regarding the technical capacity of SUBTEL's staff should be a serious cause for concern. The risk is that the regulator might not always be able properly to evaluate the tariff proposals submitted by the operators and might, at times, be unduly influenced by potentially better qualified experts hired by the regulated companies. The fact that there is no specific sanction for denying information to the regulator only

---

[203] See Chapter 2, Section D. 3.

[204] See text accompanying n 189 above.

[205] See Eduardo Bitrán et al, 'Privatizing and Regulating Chile's Utilities, 1974–2000: Successes, Failures, and Outstanding Challenges' in Guillermo Perry and Danny M Leipziger (eds), *Chile: Recent Policy Lessons and Emerging Challenges* (Washington, DC: WBI Development Studies, 1999) 339.

[206] ibid 340.

[207] Leroy Jones, *Appropriate Regulatory Technology: The Interplay of Economic and Institutional Conditions*, Annual Bank Conference on Development Economics, 1993, at 20.

makes matters worse.[208] Finally, it is widely agreed that SUBTEL has been slow to define and allocate spectrum frequency during the last decade, a problem which might also be caused, at least in part, by SUBTEL's lack of resources.[209]

Competence is a problem as well for the antitrust commissions, but for slightly different reasons. While the members of the commissions are not paid, they hold other offices and are, in some cases, highly trained professionals. This is particularly true of the Resolutive Commission which is made up of a Supreme Court Justice, academics, and high-ranking civil servants. The problem, however, is that since their regulatory mandate is non-remunerated and comes in addition to their 'main' functions, commissioners tend to have insufficient time to devote to their regulatory responsibilities. In addition, the short duration of their mandate—two years only as mentioned above—leaves them little time to acquire expertise in the most difficult and specific aspects of their job. Also, while the Resolutive Commission is made up of highly trained people, the same cannot necessarily be said of the Regional Preventive Commissions, and, to a lesser extent, of the Central Preventive Commission (it is unclear why representatives of neighbourhood committees are members of such commissions, for example).[210] Finally, the courts, which play an important role on appeal in the regulatory process, are staffed with lawyers who are usually considered competent but who lack the experience and qualifications required to solve highly technical issues of economic regulation.[211]

Protection against undue influence by industry and by political authorities appears to be a problematic issue as well. As mentioned above, any serious discrepancy between the regulator's and the companies' competency increases the risk that the former might be influenced by the latter. This risk is compounded in Chile by the fact that wages are much higher in the industry than in SUBTEL and that there are no provisions to limit the ability of SUBTEL's staff to seek employment in regulated companies. As a result, there is evidence that after a relatively short time with SUBTEL the agency's best people tend to work for the operators, which spawns the risk of industry capture.[212] The Executive is also in a position to exert direct pressures upon SUBTEL, since SUBTEL is part of the Ministry of Transport and Telecommunications and since the head of the regulatory agency is designated, and can be removed at will, by the Executive.[213] In addition, an agency headed by a single person is arguably more at risk of industry or government capture than agencies headed by several commissioners.

---

[208] See Bitrán et al (n 205 above) 365.

[209] See, for example, Pyramid Research Perspective, *Chile: Antimonopoly Commission Suspends Tender for FWA Concessions*, 16 May 2000, at 1.

[210] See Pablo Serra, 'La Politica de Competencia en Chile' (1995) 10 *Revista de Análisis Económico* 74.

[211] ibid 75.

[212] See Luis Guash and Pablo Spiller, *Managing the Regulatory Process: Design, Concepts, Issues and the Latin America and Caribbean Story* (Washington, DC: The World Bank, 1999) 115.

[213] See text accompanying nn 58–59 above.

Finally, there is some room for direct regulatory decision-making by the Executive, as pointed out above.[214]

The direct and indirect power that the Government retains with respect to regulation also creates additional risks of industry capture. While the privatization of CTC and ENTEL has promoted a clearer separation between operational and regulatory responsibilities, the operators still have incentives to try to influence the regulatory process through the pressures they can bring to bear on the Executive. Thus, some operators have invited politicians and other influential public figures to join their board of administrators.[215] In some cases, they have launched high-visibility campaigns on important regulatory issues in the hope that it would induce political authorities to influence the regulatory process. After the 1994 price-setting exercise, for example, CTC claimed— wrongly as it later turned out—that its profitability would be severely affected by the new price regime. As a result, the company's stock price fell abruptly and the Securities Commission had to suspend trading of CTC's shares for a few days.[216]

While the risks that SUBTEL might be unduly influenced by the Executive or the operators are undoubtedly very real, they are, however, somewhat mitigated by the fact that the main rules, which are embodied in laws, are hard to change and leave relatively little discretion to the regulators. In addition, while SUBTEL has been accused of being insufficiently strict with regard to CTC in the past, its willingness to impose sharp price reductions upon CTC in 1999 appears to demonstrate that, during the last round of price reviews at least, the regulator was not captured by the incumbent operator. This has prompted Pyramid Research to revise its regulator ranking for Latin America, giving SUBTEL— along with the Brazilian regulator—the highest mark for autonomy among Latin American telecommunications regulators.[217]

Other regulatory players appear better able to resist undue pressures. The antitrust commissions are better protected against both industry and political pressures because they have multiple members who are designated by different authorities, who are much less likely than SUBTEL's staff to end up working for telecommunications operators, and some of whom, at least, have a reputation of independence (the Supreme Court Justice and the academics, for example). The judiciary also has established a reputation of independence in Chile.[218]

---

[214] See text accompanying nn 80–84 above.

[215] See Serra (n 210 above) 79.

[216] See Eduardo Bitrán and Pablo Serra, 'Regulation of Privatized Utilities: The Chilean Experience' (1998) 20 *World Development* 960, 961.

[217] See Pyramid Research Perspective, *Chile: Telefónica CTC Faces Poor Results and a Stricter Regulator*, 9 May 2001, 2.

[218] The Supreme Court, for example, insisted that the seizure of several factories by their workers was illegal, in spite of the assertion by the Allende administration that those seizures were valid. See Ahmed Galal, 'Regulation and Commitment in the Development of Telecommunications in Chile', Policy Research Working Paper No 1278 (Washington, DC: The World Bank, 1994) 28–29.

Much could be done to strengthen the regulatory institutions. Reducing the direct regulatory powers of the Government would be a step in the right direction, as already suggested.[219] Exempting SUBTEL from civil service salary rules and preventing its staff from accepting jobs in the telecommunications industry for some time after they leave the agency would help enhance SUBTEL's technical capacity and protect it against industry pressures. Conferring regulatory responsibility on a cross-sector or economy-wide body, headed by a commission rather than a single individual, and designing nomination and removal processes for commission members which reduce the scope for arbitrary intervention by the Government could also contribute to increased regulatory capacity and to protect regulators against both industry and political capture. The composition of the Preventive Commissions could also be reviewed to ensure that all their members are qualified to exercise antitrust functions. With some of these measures in place to bolster the credibility of other regulatory institutions, the role of the courts, on appeal, could be limited to a review of purely legal rather than substantive issues, as the judges would be better qualified to handle this more limited role.

5. Regulatory Accountability and Stakeholder Participation

Allowing appeals against regulatory decisions to be introduced before the courts undoubtedly contributes to making regulatory institutions accountable, especially given the generally positive reputation of the judiciary in Chile. One can argue, however, that limiting the role of the courts to a review of legal rather than substantive issues, as suggested above, would not unduly compromise regulatory accountability.

If regulatory functions in telecommunications were to be carried out by a body truly autonomous from the Government, some procedures would need to be devised to ensure that such a body reports to the Executive on its activities and accounts for the use of its financial resources. The issue does not arise in the present context, however, given SUBTEL's integration within the Ministry of Transport and Telecommunications.

Other accountability issues which could, however, have been addressed in the regulatory framework seem to have been left aside. The legislation is basically mute on the need for the regulators to prepare publicly available reports of their activities, to ensure the transparency of regulatory processes, and to let interested parties—and particularly users—present their views. Thus, for example, just before the last rate-setting process in 1999, the Chilean Association of Internet Users expressed fears that its voice would not be heard during that process.[220] In recent years, some steps have been taken to fill these gaps. For instance, in 1998, SUBTEL started publishing an annual report of its activities which is available on

[219] See text accompanying n 203 above.
[220] See Revista Mouse, *Chile: Tarifas telefónicas en la polémica*, 13 October 1998, available at <http://www.noticias.com/noticias/1998/9810/n98101410.htm>.

the Internet.[221] As mentioned above, a draft law under preparation would introduce measures designed to enable users of telecommunications services to participate in the price-setting process.[222] Finally, a Telecommunications Consultative Committee, grouping service providers and makers of telecommunications equipment has been established at SUBTEL's initiative to facilitate discussions of technical and administrative issues.[223]

6. Regulatory Costs

The direct costs of regulation are relatively limited in Chile. As indicated above, the budgets of SUBTEL and of the Office of the National Economic Attorney-General are small, while the mandates of the various antitrust commissioners are not remunerated. While additional financial resources would arguably be needed to enable SUBTEL and the Office of the National Economic Attorney-General to retain their best staff, the financial resources needed to regulate the telecommunications sector adequately could still remain relatively modest. Indeed, the body of sector-specific rules is limited and could even be narrower if technical regulation was kept to a minimum in the segments of the market where competition has been effectively introduced. In addition, the cost of the Telecommunications Development Fund—approximately 0.3 per cent of total sector revenue as pointed out above—makes it one of the most cost-effective telecommunications support programmes worldwide.[224]

Indirect regulatory costs might, however, arise because of regulatory mistakes. As pointed out above, the Chilean pricing formulas are complex, they must be applied to each individual service, and concerns exist with respect to SUBTEL's ability to retain its best performing staff. In addition, at least four other categories of indirect regulatory costs have existed, or still exist, in Chile. First, uncertainties in the 1982 Telecommunications Law gave rise to complex antitrust disputes which were costly for the parties involved and produced pro-competition outcomes only after long delays. Second, the wide degree of latitude left to the parties to lodge appeals before the courts against the decisions of the regulators and to obtain, at least in some cases, a suspension of the implementation of those decisions, also led to a large number of judicial proceedings. The problem has been recently addressed, at least in part, by requiring hefty deposits to discourage frivolous complaints (limiting the grounds for appeal, as suggested above, would help in this respect

---

[221] See SUBTEL, 'Informe de Gestion 1998', available at <http://www.subtel.cl/publicaciones/index.htm>.

[222] See text accompanying n 142 above.

[223] See SUBTEL, 'Informe de Gestion 2000', 22, available at <http://www.subtel.cl/publicaciones/index.htm>.

[224] See Bjorn Wellenius, 'Closing the Rural Communication Access Gap: Chile 1995–2002', The World Bank, Draft paper of 24 June 2001, 5, available at <http://www.infodev.org/library/working.htm>.

as well).[225] Third, the influence which the Executive retains over the regulatory process induces operators to spend substantial resources on lobbying activities.[226] Fourth, as mentioned above, SUBTEL has been slow in defining spectrum rights and the ensuing delays in spectrum allocation have had high opportunity costs in a market as dynamic as that for mobile telecommunications services.[227]

7. Allocation of Regulatory Responsibilities

As pointed out above, given the weakness of many regulatory bodies and the extent of the regulatory powers left to the Executive, it was certainly wise to regulate by law and in great detail some important issues, such as pricing, and thus limit the discretionary powers of those in charge of implementing the regulatory framework. This state of affairs also justifies relying on the antitrust authorities and on the courts to exercise some functions, such as the imposition of pecuniary penalties on telecommunications operators and the determination as to whether specific telecommunications activities are provided in a sufficiently competitive environment to be deregulated. The fact that this latter role was given to antitrust authorities—rather than to a sector-specific regulator—is a particularly attractive feature of the Chilean model. Indeed, antitrust authorities are arguably best qualified to determine the intensity of competition which exists in a market, and they are certainly better placed than SUBTEL to determine whether sector-specific regulation remains needed as deregulation does, in fact, reduce the extent of SUBTEL's powers.

The main drawback of the Chilean model, on the other hand, relates to the excessive regulatory role and influence which the Executive can exercise.[228] In addition, as argued above, the powers given to the courts on appeal are excessive and could be limited to a review of purely legal issues, especially if the credibility of the telecommunications regulator was increased through reforms aimed at improving its level of competency and autonomy.[229] Finally, some commentators have argued that the repeated interventions of the Resolutive Commission in spectrum allocation processes conducted by SUBTEL have slowed things down and created an incentive for the operators to try to influence auctions by claiming that the chosen frameworks violate antitrust rules.[230] As the interventions of the antitrust authorities are widely seen as having made auction

---

[225] See Bjorn Wellenius, 'Regulating the Telecommunications Sector: The Experience of Latin America', Conference on Regulation in Post-Privatization Environment, Buenos Aires, 21–22 May 1998.

[226] See text accompanying nn 215–216 above.

[227] See Pyramid Research Perspective, *Chile: Antimonopoly Commission Suspends Tender for FWA Concessions*, 16 May 2000, 1.

[228] See text accompanying nn 213–315 above.

[229] See Section E.4 above.

[230] See Pyramid Research Perspective, *Chile: Disappointing Turnout for WLL Licenses Generates Doubts about Increased Competition in the Local Loop*, 24 May 2001, 3.

processes more competitive,[231] the most appropriate solution might not be to reduce their role in that area but, on the contrary, to consider entrusting broader regulatory responsibilities to economy-wide antitrust authorities, rather than to a sector-specific agency such as SUBTEL.

---

[231] See Pyramid Research Perspective, *Chile: Revised WLL Bidding Rules and New 3G Frequencies*, 2 October 2000, 2.

8

Australia

Full liberalization of telecommunications is still relatively recent in Australia, and Australian policy-makers closely studied the experience of other countries—especially that of New Zealand—before opting for the specific framework which is in place today. The Australian model is particularly interesting, inter alia because, unlike the other models discussed in this book, it is characterized by the integration of the main sector-specific rules within the antitrust legislation, and by the fact that it is the antitrust regulator which is in charge of applying both general antitrust and sector-specific rules.

A. Origins of the present regulatory framework

The three decades which followed the end of the Second World War witnessed a steady expansion of the role of the State in Australia, with a strong commitment by the Government to guarantee full employment and to implement the macro- and micro-economic policies required to meet that objective.[1] In Australia, as in many other OECD countries, infrastructure industries were in public hands. In the telecommunications sector, domestic services were provided by the Post-Master General's Department while international services were provided, since 1946, by the Overseas Telecommunications Commission (OTC).

In 1975, domestic telecommunications were separated from postal services and entrusted to Telecom Australia, a new, distinct entity. In 1981, the Government established a new publicly-owned operator, Aussat, to operate a domestic satellite system. Aussat started commercial operations in 1985 when the first satellite was launched. During the 1980s, the three telecommunications operators—Telecom Australia, OTC, and Aussat—were progressively run in a manner more similar to that of private firms. However, there was almost no competition in the telecommunications sector, except for the marketing of some terminal equipment and the provision of some services, such as radio paging, unrelated to traditional voice telephony. In addition, Telecom Australia continued to assume important regulatory duties in addition to operational responsibilities. This severely restricted the scope for effective competition, even for the sale of telecommunications equipment, as Telecom Australia had the right to

---

[1] On the post-war policies of the Australian Government, see, for example, John Quiggin, *Great Expectations—Microeconomic Reform and Australia* (St Leonards, NSW: Allen & Unwin, 1996) 23–25.

approve all equipment attaching to the network. As a result, users—particularly business users—were dissatisfied with the speed at which new services were being introduced.[2]

Following a review of the telecommunications sector, the Minister for Transport and Communications issued a statement in May 1988 recognizing the need to separate regulatory and operational functions and to introduce additional competition in the sector.[3] Following the adoption of the Telecommunications Act 1989, the markets for value-added services and for customer premise equipment were liberalized and a new sector-specific agency—AUSTEL—was established to implement the regulatory aspects of the new regime.[4]

Financial problems with Aussat led to a second wave of telecommunications reforms implemented shortly thereafter.[5] Telecom Australia and OTC were merged as the Australian and Overseas Telecommunications Corporation (AOTC), renamed Telstra Corporation Ltd in 1993, a 100 per cent public operator providing the whole range of telecommunications services. A second general licence, for the provision of fixed as well as mobile services, was awarded to a private competitor, Optus, which also bought Aussat. A third mobile licence was issued to Arena GSM (now Vodafone) in 1992.[6]

The basic policy premise underlying the reforms was that competition for the provision of fixed infrastructure should be limited to a duopoly until 30 June 1997, in order to enable Optus to develop into an effective rival for Telstra, and that, for similar reasons, the number of Telstra's competitors for the provision of public mobile services should be limited to two (Optus and Vodafone) over the same period.[7] The provision of other telecommunications services was fully opened to competition.

The Telecommunications Act 1991 contained the regulatory principles applicable to the new regime. One of its main objectives was to foster competition between Telstra, Optus, and Vodafone. Given the market power of the incumbent, strong competitive safeguards were deemed necessary.[8] A telecommunications-specific access regime was established whereby conditions of

---

[2] See Department of Communications, Information Technology, and the Arts, 'Liberalisation of the Telecommunications Sector: Australia's Experience' (June 2000) 3–4, available at <http://www.dcita .gov.au>.

[3] See Stephen King and Rodney Maddock, *Unlocking the Infrastructure—The Reform of Public Utilities in Australia* (St Leonards, NSW: Allen & Unwin, 1996) 137.

[4] Henry Ergas, 'Telecommunications Across the Tasman: A Comparison of Economic Approaches and Economic Outcomes in Australia and New Zealand', paper prepared for the International Institute of Communications (May 1996) 4.

[5] Marina C van der Vlies, 'The Transition from Monopoly to Competition in Australian Telecommunications' (1996) 20 *Telecommunications Policy* 323.

[6] See Deena Shiff, 'Australian Telecoms Regulation' (July/August 1995) *Intl Business Lawyer* 316.

[7] See Peter G Leonard, 'Australia', in Colin D Long (ed), *Telecommunications Law and Practice* (London: Sweet & Maxwell, 1995) 300.

[8] See G Taperell, 'Misuse of Market Power in Telecommunications—The Legislative Safeguards' in Stephen G Corones (ed), *Competition Policy in Telecommunications and Aviation* (Sydney: Federation Press in association with the Centre for Commercial and Property Law, Queensland University of Technology, 1992) 179. See also J Holmes, 'The Telecommunications Act 1991 and its Meaning for Consumers and Competition' in Corones (above) 228.

access to another operator's network were to be determined either through negotiation or through arbitration by AUSTEL.[9] In addition, dialling parity, for example, was imposed upon the incumbent to help Optus gain market shares in the long-distance segment.[10]

During the period 1991–97, a certain number of factors contributed to shape government decisions regarding the form which the post-1997 telecommunications sector should take. First, there was a gradual realization that the duopoly regime might not be the most conducive to vigorous competition as it facilitated co-ordination between the two competitors.[11] In addition, some argued that a regime of administered competition such as the one established in 1991 carried the risk that regulatory authorities would focus too much on the protection of competitors rather than on the promotion of competition itself.[12] Some estimates put the cost of insufficient competition and regulatory inefficiencies during this period at about AU$ 400 million per year.[13]

Second, at the request of the Prime Minister, an independent inquiry was conducted on competition policy issues in 1992–93. The Hilmer Report, as it is known, was published in 1993 and contained several recommendations which were to have a profound influence on the policies to be adopted regarding the post-1997 telecommunications sector.[14] The authors argued that to the extent possible, competition should be strongly promoted in infrastructure sectors and that many existing barriers to entry should be removed in those sectors.[15] They considered that infrastructure sectors should be regulated by an economy-wide regulator rather than by various sector-specific agencies such as AUSTEL.[16] Finally, they recommended the adoption of a cross-sector access regime to enable firms to gain access to certain essential facilities on fair and reasonable terms.[17]

The third major influence on the post-1997 regime stems from the New Zealand experience in telecommunications, which was closely studied in Australia.[18] An analysis of the dispute between Clear and Telecom over conditions of interconnection convinced most Australian observers that courts applying general antitrust rules were unable to come to specific decisions on technically

[9] Telecommunications Act 1991, s 137(3)(b).

[10] See James R Green and David J Teece, 'Four Approaches to Telecommunications Deregulation and Competition: The US, UK, Australia, and New Zealand' 11, available at <http://groups.haas.berkeley.edu/imio/crtp/publications/workingpapers/wp49.PDF>.

[11] See Ergas (n 4 above) 23.

[12] See van der Vlies (n 5 above) 323.

[13] See Network Economics Consulting Group, 'Assessment of the Telecommunications Regulatory Regime in Australia' (March 2000) 7.

[14] Frederick Hilmer et al, 'National Competition Policy—Report by the Independent Committee on Inquiry' (1993).

[15] ibid 201.

[16] ibid 325–328.

[17] ibid 242–249. For a description of the access regime proposed in the Hilmer Report, see Warren Pengilley, 'Hilmer and Essential Facilities' (1994) 17 *U of New South Wales L J* 1.

[18] The Hilmer Report, for example, bases its recommendations for the regulation of infrastructure sectors partly on an analysis of the New Zealand experience in telecommunications. See Hilmer et al (n 14 above) 245.

complex telecommunications matters and that they were ill-suited to exercise the continual supervision of regulatory arrangements which might, at times, be required.[19]

These various factors prompted the authorities to open all segments of the telecommunications sector to competition on 1 July 1997 and to rely on a specialized, but economy-wide, institution to regulate telecommunications. In addition, as will be discussed below, the cross-sector access regime called for by the Hilmer Report was adopted as well.

B. THE MAIN RULES

We turn first to the general antitrust rules. The telecommunications-specific rules are examined thereafter.

1. Antitrust Rules

The main antitrust rules, applicable to the Australian economy as a whole, are included in Part IV of the Trade Practices Act. As of 1 July 1997, the exemption from the application of Part IV of the Act that telecommunications operators had enjoyed was discontinued.[20] Part IV prohibits contracts, arrangements or understandings which contain exclusionary provisions,[21] fix prices,[22] hinder the supply or acquisition of goods or services,[23] or otherwise have the purpose or the effect of substantially lessening competition.[24] Part IV also prohibits exclusive dealings[25] and retail price maintenance.[26]

Additional provisions prohibit a corporation that has a substantial degree of power in a market from taking advantage of that power for the purpose of eliminating a competitor or preventing the emergence of a competitor.[27] Finally, a corporation is prohibited from acquiring shares or assets of another business if, as a result, the corporation would be in a position to dominate a market for goods or services or to substantially strengthen its power to dominate a market.[28]

---

[19] See Warren Pengilley, 'Access to Essential Facilities: A Unique Experiment in Australia' (1998) XLIII *The Antitrust Bulletin* 519, 525.

[20] Department of Communications and the Arts, 'Australia's Open Telecommunications Market: The New Framework' (hereafter, 'Australia's Open Telecommunications Market') (Melbourne, 1998) 25.

[21] Trade Practices Act 1974, s 45(1)(a).

[22] ibid s 45A.   [23] ibid s 45E.   [24] ibid s 45(1)(b).

[25] ibid s 47. 'Exclusive dealing' is defined by reference to specific vertical restraint practices such as supplying goods or services on condition that the purchaser does not acquire goods or services from a competitor of the supplier.

[26] Trade Practices Act 1974, s 48. 'Retail price maintenance' refers to practices such as attempting to induce a person not to sell a supplier's products below a price specified by the supplier.

[27] ibid s 46.   [28] ibid s 50.

In line with the recommendations of the Hilmer Report, a cross-sector access regime was adopted in 1995; it is contained in the Trade Practices Act, Part IIIA.[29] This regime is more sophisticated than the telecommunications-specific access rules of the Telecommunications Act 1991. Under Part IIIA, services can be 'declared' by the relevant Minister when the Minister considers that access should be granted to the facilities required to provide the service. A service can only be declared when all the following conditions are met:

(i) access to the service would promote competition;
(ii) it would be uneconomical for anyone to develop another facility to provide the service;
(iii) the facility is of national significance;
(iv) access to the service can be provided without undue risk to human health and safety;
(v) an effective access regime is not already in place; and
(vi) access to the service is not contrary to the public interest.[30]

Declarations must be given an expiry date.[31] Once a service is declared, terms of access are determined either through commercial agreement between the access provider and the access seeker or through arbitration by the antitrust regulator, the Australian Competition and Consumer Commission (ACCC—see Section C below). Alternatively, providers of non-declared services may give to the ACCC a written undertaking setting out the terms and conditions under which access to the services will be granted. Industry bodies can also submit to the ACCC written codes setting out the rules of access to a given service applicable to all operators.[32] Once an undertaking is accepted by the ACCC, access is governed totally by the terms of that undertaking.[33]

2. Telecommunications-specific Rules

The Telecommunications Act 1997 established a regime of open entry into all segments of the telecommunications market. The authorities considered, however, that Parts IV and IIIA of the Trade Practices Act would be insufficient, on their own, to foster competition in the telecommunications market and, in 1997, specific provisions were therefore introduced in the Trade Practices Act to regulate anti-competitive conduct (Part XIB of the Trade Practices Act) and access to bottleneck services (Part XIC of the Trade Practices Act) in the

[29] On Part IIIA, see National Competition Council, 'The National Access Regime—A Draft Guide to Part IIIA of the Trade Practices Act' (August 1996).
[30] See Trade Practices Act 1974, s 44G.
[31] ibid s 44I.
[32] ibid ss 44ZZA and 44ZZAA.
[33] For an excellent description of the workings of Part IIIA provisions, see Warren Pengilley, 'Hilmer and Essential Facilities' (1994) 17 *U of New South Wales L J* 1, 528.

telecommunications sector.[34] Additional pro-competition provisions are included, inter alia, in the Telecommunications Act 1997 and in the Radiocommunications Act 1992. Finally, a 1999 piece of legislation is devoted to universal obligations and other consumer protection requirements. These different provisions are examined below.

2.1 Open Entry (Telecommunications Act 1997)

The Telecommunications Act 1997 removed all restrictions placed by the 1991 Act upon entry into the various segments of the telecommunications market. Operators are free to provide telecommunications services and to establish telecommunications networks in Australia. Licences are required only from owners of telecommunications networks wishing to provide services to the public.[35] Licences are available on application with no technical or financial entry hurdles and no limit on the number of infrastructure providers.[36] There are, however, standard licence conditions with which licensed operators must comply. These include, inter alia, an obligation for these operators to comply with the Act,[37] to produce a business development plan (called an industry development plan),[38] and to enable other infrastructure providers to gain access to their facilities and to obtain information on their networks.[39]

2.2 Prohibition of Anti-Competitive Conduct (Trade Practices Act, Part XIB)

Two types of behaviour are deemed anti-competitive under Part XIB. First, s 151AJ(2) prohibits a telecommunications operator which holds a substantial degree of power in a telecommunications market from taking advantage of that power with the effect, or likely effect, of substantially lessening competition in that or any other telecommunications market. Second, s 151AJ(3) prohibits a telecommunications operator from engaging in conducts which violate some of the provisions of Part IV such as: concluding contracts, arrangements, or understandings that affect competition;[40] misusing market power;[41] engaging in exclusive dealings;[42] or engaging in resale price maintenance.[43]

---

[34] See the Trade Practices Amendment (Telecommunications) Act 1997. The explanatory memorandum to the draft text—Memorandum to the Trade Practices Amendment (Telecommunications) Bill 1996—states, on p 6: 'Telecommunications is an extremely complex, horizontally and vertically integrated industry and competition is not established in some telecommunications markets. There is considerable scope for incumbents to engage in anti-competitive conduct because competitors in downstream markets depend on access to network facilities controlled by the incumbent. (...) Anti-competitive behaviour in telecommunications could cause particularly rapid damage to competition because of the volatile state of the industry during the early stages of competition. Against this background, Part IV alone may prove insufficient to deal with anti-competitive behaviour in telecommunications at this time.'

[35] See Telecommunications Act 1997, s 42.

[36] See Department of Communications and the Arts, 'Australia's Open Telecommunications Market' (Melbourne, 1998) 12.

[37] See Telecommunications Act 1997, Sch 1 Part 1.

[38] ibid Sch 1 Part 2.

[39] ibid Sch 1 Parts 3 and 4.

[40] See Trade Practices Act 1974, s 45.   [41] ibid s 46.   [42] ibid s 47.   [43] ibid s 48.

Section 151AJ provides for a stricter antitrust regime in the telecommunications sector than would be possible under Part IV. Thus, for example, misusing market power is prohibited under Part IV only when an anti-competitive purpose can be established.[44] Under s 151AJ(2), on the other hand, the conduct at issue is prohibited independently of purpose as long as it has the effect, or likely effect, of substantially lessening competition in telecommunications. In addition, under Part XIB, the onus of proof might, in some cases, be reversed with the telecommunications operator having to prove that it did not engage in an anti-competitive conduct (this point will be explored further under Section C below). Finally, the penalties which can be imposed for violations of Part XIB provisions are more severe than those which can be imposed for violations of Part IV provisions.[45]

The Minister responsible for telecommunications must arrange for a review of the operation of Part XIB of the Trade Practices Act before 1 July 2000. The objective of the review is to determine whether any or all of the provisions of Part XIB should be repealed or amended. The report of the review is required to be tabled in both Houses of Parliament.[46]

2.3 Access Regime (Trade Practices Act, Part XIC)

Part XIC establishes, for its part, a regulatory regime which is derived from Part IIIA and which is aimed at facilitating the access of all competitors to certain bottleneck services in the telecommunications sector. Its primary object is to promote the long-term interests of end-users (LTIE), as defined under s 152AB. Section 152AL provides for the 'declaration' by the ACCC of certain telecommunications services which constitute bottlenecks. In order to determine whether such a declaration would be in the LTIE, regard must be given to: (i) promoting competition; (ii) achieving any-to-any connectivity; and (iii) encouraging efficient use of, and efficient investment in, the infrastructure.[47] Unlike under Part IIIA, declarations granted under Part XIC of the Act do not have an expiry date.

Providers of declared services are subject to standard access obligations. Such obligations include the obligation to supply the declared services and permit interconnection of their facilities under conditions equivalent to those which they reserve for themselves, to provide billing information associated with the declared services, and to enable other operators to access customer equipment required to use the bottleneck facilities (such equipment could, for example, be the set-top boxes used for the supply of pay television).[48] As to the specific terms

---

[44] ibid s 46(1) (a) (b) and (c).

[45] Up to AU$10 million plus AU$1 million for each day during which the violation continues. See Stephen Corones, 'Anti-competitive Conduct in Telecommunications' (1998) 26 *Australian Business L Rev* 151, 153.

[46] Trade Practices Act 1974, s 151CN.   [47] ibid s 152AB.

[48] See Department of Communications and the Arts, 'Australia's Open Telecommunications Market' (Melbourne, 1998) 37.

and conditions with which access providers must comply under standard access obligations, they may be determined in three ways: (i) through commercial agreements between access providers and access seekers; (ii) through arbitration if the parties cannot agree; and (iii) through implementation of 'access undertakings', which constitute commitments on the part of access providers regarding the conditions under which they are to provide access.[49] Access undertakings themselves are of two types: code undertakings which adopt model terms and conditions;[50] and individual undertakings in which individual access providers specify particular terms and conditions applying to one or more declared services.[51]

2.4 Additional Pro-Competition Provisions (Telecommunications Act 1997 and Radiocommunications Act 1992)

A certain number of additional measures have been adopted to promote competition in the telecommunications sector. For example, the Telecommunications Act 1997 states that regulatory authorities may require providers of standard telephone services[52] to enable their subscribers to pre-select their preferred providers of other types of services (such as long-distance and international services, for example) and to select alternative providers of such services on a call-by-call basis using override dial codes.[53] The Telecommunications Act 1997 also provides for the preparation of a numbering plan which may set out rules about the portability of numbers.[54] In addition, the Act provides for the elaboration of Rules of Conduct to govern dealings between telecommunications operators providing international services in Australia and their partners outside Australia.[55] These Rules of Conduct would address concerns that foreign operators which enjoy a monopoly position in their home country could abuse their market power and distort the Australian telecommunications market either through direct intervention in that market or through alliances with Australian operators which would then derive an unfair advantage from such alliances.[56] Finally, the Radiocommunications Act 1992 provides for the competitive auctioning of spectrum licences.[57]

2.5 Universal Service Obligations and Price Control Measures (Telecommunications (Consumer Protection and Service Standards) Act 1999)

Universal service and consumer protection provisions are now included in a new piece of legislation adopted in 1999. As far as the definition of universal service

---

[49] See Trade Practices Act 1974, s 152AY.   [50] ibid Part XIC, Division 4.   [51] ibid s 152BV.

[52] The standard telephone service is defined in the Telecommunications (Consumer Protection and Service Standards) Act 1999, s 6, as voice telephony or an equivalent service for a person with a disability.

[53] Telecommunications Act 1997, ss 349 and 350.

[54] ibid s 455.

[55] ibid s 367.

[56] See Department of Communications and the Arts, 'Australia's Open Telecommunications Market' (Melbourne, 1998) 80.

[57] See Radiocommunications Act 1992, s 60.

obligations is concerned, the Act mostly re-enacts provisions of the Telecommunications Act 1997 but adds digital data service provision to the concept of universal service obligations. Thus, under the new definition of universal service obligations, standard telephone services (ie voice telephony or its equivalent for disabled people), payphones, and digital data services (ie services comparable to that provided by a 64Kbp/s basic rate ISDN service) must now be reasonably accessible to all people in Australia on an equitable basis.[58] The law allows the Minister responsible for telecommunications to design a selection system whereby different universal service providers would be designated in different areas or for the provision of different services in the same area.[59] The law identifies various principles according to which the costs of universal service obligations and each operator's share of these costs are to be calculated.[60] The Telecommunications (Consumer Protection and Service Standards) Act 1999 also re-enacts the price control provisions which the Telstra Corporation Act 1991 imposed on Telstra, as well as provisions of the Telecommunications Act 1997 introduced to ensure that unmetered local call options would remain available.[61]

The law was modified in 2000 to provide for:

(i) the launch of an auction to select an operator responsible for meeting unmetered local call and other universal service obligations outside the main cities;

(ii) pilot schemes to be implemented on a regional basis, whereby new operators could be authorized to compete with Telstra for the—subsidized—provision of universal services;

(iii) changes in the way in which the costs of universal service obligations are estimated; and

(iv) a broadening, by the Minister, of the definition of operators required to contribute to the costs of universal service obligations.[62]

C. The main institutions

The Minister responsible for telecommunications retains important regulatory powers in Australia. In addition, in line with the recommendations of the Hilmer Report, the main industry-specific regulator, AUSTEL, was eliminated and its competition policy functions were transferred to the economy-wide antitrust authority, the ACCC. AUSTEL's technical functions were, for their part, transferred to a new regulatory body, the Australian Communications Authority (ACA). Other entities with regulatory responsibilities in the telecommunications sector include the Australian Competition Tribunal (ACT), the

---

[58] See Telecommunications (Consumer Protection and Service Standards) Act 1999, ss 19 and 19A.
[59] ibid ss 22–26.   [60] ibid ss 57 and 67.   [61] ibid Part 4.
[62] See Telecommunications (Consumer Protection and Service Standards) Amendment Acts (No 1 and No 2).

Telecommunications Industry Ombudsman (TIO), and some industry bodies with specific responsibilities regarding access conditions and technical standards. The main characteristics of these different entities are discussed below.

1. The Minister Responsible for Telecommunications

As mentioned above, it is the Minister who declares services of national significance under the cross-sector access regime set out in Part IIIA of the Trade Practices Act. The Minister is responsible for determining the way in which providers of universal telecommunications services are to be selected, for specifying the price controls which can be imposed upon them, for regulating Telstra's prices, and for implementing the provisions of the Telecommunications (Consumer Protection and Service Standards) Act 1999 which deal with the evaluation and allocation of universal service costs.[63] The Minister may also set out principles determining how standard access obligations are to be priced.[64]

It is the Minister who directs the ACA to develop performance standards and to modify them when it feels it is necessary.[65] The Minister can also give directions to the ACA regarding the allocation of spectrum licences.[66] It is the Minister who has the power to issue the Rules of Conduct aimed at protecting the Australian telecommunications market from distortions caused by international operators.[67] Finally, the Telecommunications (Consumer Protection and Service Standards) Act 1999, Part 10, gives new, and very broad, powers to the Minister to direct Telstra to take specific action to ensure that it complies with the requirements of the Act. The Minister must, however, consult with Telstra before making such a direction.

2. The Australian Competition and Consumer Commission

The ACCC was established by the Competition Policy Reform Act of 1995. It is responsible for administering the antitrust and consumer protection provisions of the Trade Practices Act and, in 1997, it assumed responsibility for administering the new telecommunications-specific antitrust rules introduced under Part XIB and Part XIC of the Act. The ACCC currently comprises seven full-time commissioners and a number of part-time associate commissioners (see Figure 8.1 below).[68] The ACCC has recently established a Telecommunications Group comprising about thirty staff and one of the commissioners has been appointed to assist in managing the ACCC's telecommunications responsibilities. The 2000 budget of the ACCC's Telecommunications Group is about AU$3.2 million.

---

63 Telecommunications (Consumer Protection and Service Standards) Act 1999, ss 57(6) and 67(3).
64 ibid s 152CH.
65 ibid ss 114, 115 and 125.
66 See Radiocommunications Act 1992, s 60.
67 See Telecommunications Act 1997, Part 20.
68 See ACCC Annual Report, 1999–2000 16, available at <http://www.aca.gov.au/publications/annual/index.htm>.

FIGURE 8.1. ACCC organizational chart

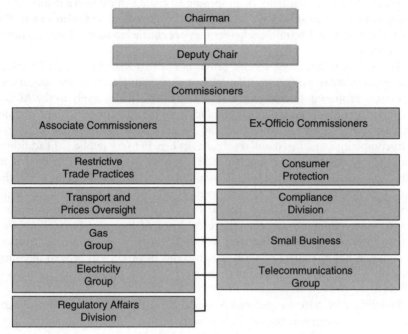

Source: <http://www.accc.gov.au/resources/org_chart.htm>.

Members of the Commission are appointed by the Governor-General.[69] They must be chosen among people whom the Minister responsible for trade practices recognises as being qualified by virtue of their knowledge of industry, commerce, economics, law, public administration, or consumer protection.[70] Grounds for terminating the appointment of a commissioner are precisely specified and enumerated.[71] Conflicts of interests rules are in place to force commissioners to disclose interests which could conflict with the proper exercise of their functions and to prevent commissioners from participating in the determination of specific cases when such conflicts of interests arise.[72] Finally, as in New Zealand, the Government may give directions to the Commission. No directions can however be given in relation to Parts IIIA, IV, XIB or XIC of the Trade Practices Act.[73]

The Commission can initiate proceedings before the Federal Court to obtain that penalties be imposed to punish anti-competitive conducts prohibited by Part IV provisions. The Commission can also authorize contracts, arrangements, and understandings, as well as acquisition of shares or assets, which fall within the

---

[69] The Governor-General is the representative of the Commonwealth in Australia. Decisions requiring the signature of the Governor-General are, in practice, taken by the Government.

[70] See Trade Practices Act 1974, s 7.

[71] ibid s 13.   [72] ibid s 17.   [73] ibid s 29.

scope of Part IV of the Act when it considers that they would be beneficial to the public.[74] Businesses engaging or proposing to engage in exclusive dealing conducts which would otherwise breach Part IV provisions can also notify the ACCC which then determines whether they are entitled to benefit from statutory protection.[75]

The telecommunications-specific provisions of Part XIB of the Trade Practices Act grant similar powers to the ACCC. For example, telecommunications operators proposing to engage in a given conduct can also apply to the ACCC to obtain an order exempting that conduct from the anti-competitive provisions of Part XIB.[76] Such an exemption can be granted when the conduct is not anti-competitive or when it will result in a net benefit to the public.[77] In addition, Part XIB provisions grant supplementary powers to the ACCC to deal with anti-competitive conducts in the telecommunications sector. Thus, in 1997, the ACCC was given the right to issue competition notices, explaining in detail how operators were violating specific Part XIB provisions. The competition notice was considered as prima facie evidence of the matters in the notice in any proceedings under the Act; in other words, as mentioned in Section B above, it had the effect of reversing the onus of proof.[78] If proven in court, violations of Part XIB provisions can carry severe penalties as mentioned above.[79]

In 1999, Part XIB was amended by the Telecommunications Amendment Act 1999 to strengthen the ACCC's powers further. The Telecommunications Amendment Act 1999 introduced a distinction between two types of competition notices: Part A notices, which do not need to define the alleged violation in great detail, and Part B notices which can be issued after Part A notices and need to be as detailed as the notices issued under the previous regime.[80] Only Part B notices have the effect of reversing the onus of proof before the Court.[81] Additional daily penalties for continued violation of Part XIB provisions, however, might be due as soon as a Part A notice comes into force.[82] In addition, in order to reduce the incentives of a recipient of a competition notice to seek judicial review of the ACCC's decision to issue the notice, the Telecommunications Amendment Act 1999 introduced in the Trade Practices Act a provision stating that the ACCC's decision would stand during such judicial review.[83]

---

[74] ibid ss 88–91.   [75] ibid s 93.   [76] Trade Practices Act 1974, s 151AS.

[77] ibid s 151BC.

[78] See Stephen Corones, 'Anti-competitive Conduct in Telecommunications' (1998) 26 *Australian Business L Rev* 151, 153.

[79] See n 45 above.

[80] See Trade Practices Act 1974, ss 151AKA and 151AL.

[81] ibid s 151AN.

[82] See Network Economics Consulting Group, 'Assessment of the Telecommunications Regulatory Regime in Australia' (March 2000) 50.

[83] See Trade Practices Act 1974, s 151AQA. See also Diane Staats, *Competition Law—Competition Law and Access Rules Get More Teeth* (Sydney: Freehils, 1999) 2–3.

With respect to the cross-sector access regime established under Part IIIA, the Commission plays three main roles. First, it arbitrates disputes between access providers and access seekers which relate to a facility which has been declared by the Minister.[84] Second, it reviews individual access undertakings submitted by providers of non-declared services or code undertakings submitted by the industry and it accepts or rejects such undertakings.[85] Finally, it can register access contracts concluded between parties, which has the effect of making the agreement enforceable before the courts.[86]

The ACCC also plays a major role with respect to the access regime established under Part XIC. As is the case under Part IIIA, the ACCC is the arbitrator of disputes between access seekers and access providers,[87] it determines whether access undertakings are acceptable,[88] and it registers access agreements.[89] Furthermore, under Part XIC, it is the ACCC (rather than the Minister as is the case under Part IIIA) which 'declares' the services to which standard access obligations apply, and the ACCC is entitled to exempt providers of declared services from standard access obligations if the ACCC is satisfied that it will promote the LTIE.[90] The ACCC must, however, hold public inquiries before it can declare a service on its own initiative.

The Telecommunications Amendment Act 1999 strengthened the ACCC's powers under Part XIC as well. The ACCC may give directions to a party negotiating an access agreement if it is requested to do so by one of the parties.[91] The ACCC may also attend or mediate at access negotiations if jointly requested to do so by the parties.[92] Finally, some amendments have been introduced to discourage parties from initiating procedures aimed at delaying the arbitration process. The ACCC can make final determinations retroactive in their application, and it can issue an interim determination which remains in force even if the Australian Competition Tribunal stays a final determination pending its review of that final determination.[93]

Section 87B, which was introduced in the Trade Practices Act in 1993, states that the ACCC may accept written undertakings related to matters over which the Commission has power or functions under the Act. Such undertakings can only be changed or withdrawn with the consent of the Commission. Section 87B considerably strengthens the powers of the Commission. When it believes that a violation of the Trade Practices Act is taking place, the Commission can refrain from initiating judicial action if the concerned party commits, under the terms of a s 87B undertaking, to adopt a specific behaviour compatible with the provisions of the Act. If the violation continues after approval of the undertaking, the

---

[84] Trade Practices Act 1974, s 44V.   [85] ibid ss 44ZZA and 44ZZAA.   [86] ibid s 44ZW.
[87] See Trade Practices Act 1974, Part XIC, Division 8, Subdivision D.
[88] ibid Part XIC, Division 5.
[89] ibid s 152ED.
[90] ibid Part XIC, Division 3.
[91] ibid s 152BBA.   [92] ibid s 152BBC.   [93] ibid Part XIC, Division 8, Subdivision E.

Commission can seek an order from the courts directing the party to comply with the undertaking, to pay penalties, or to compensate other parties for the damage they might have suffered as a result of the breach.[94]

The ACCC has important responsibilities in the area of price regulation. It intervenes with respect to access prices through the exercise of its functions under Part XIC of the Trade Practices Act (including arbitration of access disputes and review of access undertakings). In addition, the Telecommunications (Consumer Protection and Service Standards) Act 1999 states that the Minister may determine that modifications of charges subject to price controls, proposed by Telstra or universal service providers, can only come into force if approved by the ACCC.[95]

Finally, the ACCC has broad information-gathering powers. It can, in particular, require a person to provide information which would be relevant to the performance of the ACCC's functions under the Telecommunications Act 1997, Parts XIB and XIC of the Trade Practices Act, and the Telecommunications (Consumer Protection and Service Standards) Act 1999.[96] The ACCC can also direct telecommunications operators to file tariff information with the ACCC if it is satisfied that those operators have a substantial degree of power in a telecommunications market.[97] It has the power to require telecommunications operators to retain records when access to such records would facilitate execution of the ACCC's tasks.[98] The Telecommunications Amendment Act 1999 gave the ACCC the additional power to require operators to prepare reports based on the information contained in those records.[99] The ACCC can also make these reports available to the public if it is satisfied that such disclosure would promote competition.[100] The ACCC can, in addition, conduct public inquiries, either at its own initiative or at the initiative of the Minister responsible for telecommunications.[101] Each financial year, the ACCC must report to the Government on competition matters and on telecommunications prices.[102]

3. The Australian Communications Authority

The ACA was established in 1997 by the Australian Communications Authority Act.[103] It is a body corporate consisting of a Chairman, a Deputy Chairman, and between one and three other members appointed by the Governor-General.[104] The ACA has about 420 staff and a budget of about AU$56 million (year 2000–2001), covered for the most part by licence fees and other charges.[105]

---

[94] See Trade Practices Act 1974, s 87B(4).
[95] See Telecommunications (Consumer Protection and Service Standards) Act 1999, ss 44 and 156.
[96] See Trade Practices Act 1974, s 155.
[97] ibid s 151BK.   [98] ibid s 151BU.   [99] ibid s 151BU(1).   [100] ibid s 151BUA.
[101] See Telecommunications Act 1997, Part 25.
[102] See Trade Practices Act 1974, ss 151CL and 151CM.
[103] See Australian Communications Authority Act, s 14.   [104] ibid ss 15 and 16.
[105] See ACA, 'Annual Report 2000–2001', available at <http://www.aca.gov.au/publications/annual/index.htm>.

The ACA is responsible for technical aspects of telecommunications regulation under the Telecommunications Act 1997, the Telecommunications (Consumer Protection and Service Standards) Act 1999, and the Radiocommunications Act 1992. Thus, for example, under the Telecommunications Act 1997, the ACA is responsible for issuing licences, for ensuring that codes of technical standards are developed, for ensuring that operators provide pre-selection services (and that users can override their pre-selected choice of carrier on a call-by-call basis), and for preparing the numbering plan.[106] Under the Telecommunications (Consumer Protection and Service Standards) Act 1999, the ACA must, when directed to do so by the Minister, develop and monitor performance standards applicable to telecommunications operators and design a schedule of damages to punish violations of such standards.[107] The ACA must also provide advice to the Minister on the evaluation and allocation of universal service costs.[108] It must, in addition, select the universal service providers allowed to compete with Telstra under the regional pilot schemes.[109] Finally, the Radiocommunications Act 1992 entrusts the ACA with the task of managing the radio frequency spectrum and issuing spectrum licences.[110]

As is the case for the ACCC, the ACA can conduct public inquiries.[111] It can obtain information and documents from telecommunications operators in connection with the exercise of any of its functions.[112] It may also order telecommunications operators to retain records on matters relating to their performance or the provision of universal service.[113] The ACA must report to the Government, each financial year, on all significant matters relating to the performance of telecommunications operators with particular reference to consumer satisfaction, consumer benefits, and quality of service.[114]

Because of the close links which exist between antitrust and technical regulations, the Australian legislation provides for a degree of co-ordination between the ACCC and the ACA. For example, the ACCC may direct the ACA to set technical standards for interconnection[115] and to include rules for number portability in its numbering plan.[116] The ACA must in addition consult the ACCC on a variety of technical matters on which it is the ACA which is taking the lead including, for example, operator pre-selection and override dial codes.[117] In addition, to further reduce the risks of conflicts or overlaps between the two institutions, the Chairperson of the ACA is currently an associate member of the ACCC, while a member of the ACCC is an associate member of the ACA.[118]

---

[106] See Telecommunications Act 1997, ss 117–125, 348 and 455.

[107] See Telecommunications (Consumer Protection and Service Standards) Act 1999, ss 115, 117, 118, 124 and 125.   [108] ibid ss 16A and 20F.   [109] See text accompanying n 62 above.

[110] See Radiocommunications Act 1992, s 60.   [111] See Telecommunications Act 1997, Part 25.

[112] ibid ss 521 and 522.   [113] ibid s 529.   [114] ibid s 105.   [115] ibid s 384.

[116] ibid ss 460–461.   [117] ibid ss 349–350.

[118] See OECD, 'Relationship Between Regulators and Competition Authorities' DAFFE/CLP(99)8 (June 1999) 110, available at <http://www1.oecd.org/daf/clp/roundtables/relations.pdf>.

4. The Australian Competition Tribunal

The ACT was established under the Trade Practices Act (1965) and currently operates under the Trade Practices Act (1974). It is a non-judicial body made up of Federal Court judges and of people with experience in industry, commerce, public administration, or economics. A Federal Court judge presides over the tribunal which comprises two other members, an economist and a business person.[119] Most of the ACCC decisions can be appealed to the ACT, which can review all aspects of the ACCC's decision.[120] The main exception to this rule concerns the service declarations made by the ACCC under Part XIC of the Trade Practices Act, which are not subject to a merit review by the ACT and can only be appealed to the Federal Court on questions of law.[121] Decisions of the ACT, in turn, can be appealed before the Federal Court on questions of law only.[122]

5. The Telecommunications Industry Ombudsman

The TIO is a body set up to settle unresolved complaints made by residential and small business customers about telecommunications services. The TIO scheme comprises a Council, a Board of Directors, and the Ombudsman. The Council which is responsible, inter alia, for maintaining the independence of the Ombudsman is composed of equal numbers of industry representatives and of consumer and community representatives. The Board of Directors, composed of industry representatives, is responsible for the formal administration of the scheme and supervises its financial affairs. The Ombudsman, who must be an independent person not associated with the industry, is appointed by the Board upon recommendation of the Council.

All telecommunications operators which provide telephone services or Internet access to residential and small business users must be registered as members of the TIO scheme and they must comply with any TIO determinations or directions unless they are exempted from entering into the TIO scheme by the ACA.[123] The TIO is an industry-funded scheme, deriving its income from members who are charged fees for complaint resolution services provided by the TIO. Its budget for the year 2000–2001 was about AU$5 million.[124]

---

[119] See Trade Practices Act 1974, Parts III and IX. See also Warren Pengilley, 'Hilmer and Essential Facilities' (1994) 17 *U of New South Wales L J* 1, 523 and Network Economics Consulting Group, 'Assessment of the Telecommunications Regulatory Regime in Australia' (March 2000) 13.

[120] See Department of Communications, Information Technology, and the Arts, 'Liberalisation of the Telecommunications Sector: Australia's Experience' (June 2000), 31, available at <http://www.dcita.gov.au>.

[121] See Network Economics Consulting Group (n 119 above) 13.

[122] See, for example, Trade Practices Act 1974, s 152DQ.

[123] See Telecommunications (Consumer Protection and Service Standards) Act 1999, s 129.

[124] See Telecommunications Industry Ombudsman, 'Annual report 2001' 64, available at <http://www.tio.com.au/publications/annual_reports/annual_2001.download.htm>.

The TIO is empowered to investigate and make determinations or directions relating to the quality of telecommunications services provided to end-users. The TIO does not investigate complaints about the levels at which tariffs are set or about the content of a content service,[125] and it cannot compel production of relevant documents or information.[126]

6. The Main Industry Bodies

Two of the most important industry bodies with specific responsibilities in the field of telecommunications are the Telecommunications Access Forum (TAF) and the Australian Communications Industry Forum (ACIF). The TAF is an association designated by the ACCC.[127] The association must be open to all telecommunications infrastructure providers. It has two main roles under the access regime of Part XIC. First, it recommends to the ACCC the declaration of services[128] (the ACCC may also declare a service on its own initiative after having held a public enquiry on the matter).[129] Second, it may submit an access code to be approved as a code undertaking by the ACCC[130] (the ACCC is also empowered to design an access code if the TAF fails to deliver).[131] The TAF's decisions must be taken unanimously by its members.[132]

The ACIF is a body which is owned, operated, and funded by various stakeholders in the telecommunications industry; its members include telecommunications operators, equipment vendors, industry associations, and consumer groups. It is primarily responsible for developing technical and operational standards.[133] The ACIF cannot mandate standards; it can only encourage industry participants to sign up to these standards. The ACIF works in conjunction with other regulatory agencies, especially the ACA. The ACA may, for example, request that the ACIF develop industry standards, it can register those standards, and, if necessary, make them mandatory.[134] Because the ACIF has a very broad membership base and because it cannot impose its standards upon industry participants, it was decided that the ACIF's decisions would not need to be unanimous.[135]

---

[125] See Telecommunications (Consumer Protection and Service Standards) Act 1999, s 129.

[126] See Telecommunications Industry Ombudsman (n 124 above) 24.

[127] The ACCC designated the Australian Communications Access Forum Inc, an association of telecommunications operators, as the TAF in May 1997 in accordance with the Trade Practices Act 1974, s 152AI. See Network Economics Consulting Group (n 119 above) 58.

[128] See Trade Practices Act 1974, s 152AL(2).

[129] ibid s 152AL(3).

[130] ibid ss 152BH and 152BF.

[131] ibid s 152BJ.

[132] See Network Economics Consulting Group, 'Assessment of the Telecommunications Regulatory Regime in Australia' (March 2000) 59.

[133] See the ACIF website at <http://www.acif.org.au>.

[134] See Network Economics Consulting Group (n 132 above) 59–60.

[135] ibid 60.

D. Implementation of the regulatory framework

Much has happened in Australia since the full liberalization of the telecommunications market in 1997. The main developments, which we review below, include:

(i) the publication by the ACCC of a number of principles and guidelines specifying the way in which it would exercise some of its most important functions;

(ii) the declaration of a number of services by the ACCC;

(iii) the ACCC's review of access undertakings and the ACCC's conduct of arbitration processes with respect to a number of access disputes;

(iv) the ACCC's issuance of several competition notices against Telstra;

(v) the ACCC's review of several proposed mergers and acquisitions;

(vi) the imposition of price caps on Telstra's services;

(vii) the adoption by the ACA of decisions on a range of technical issues;

(viii) the development of a controversy related to universal service obligations; and

(ix) the latest review of the regulatory framework mandated by law.

1. ACCC's Principles and Guidelines

The ACCC has published principles and guidelines on the way it intended to tackle a number of important questions. For example, as required by the Trade Practices Act, the Commission issued written guidelines before 1 July 1997 on the way it intended to proceed to determine whether or not to issue a competition notice.[136] In early August 1999, these guidelines were replaced by new ones designed to accommodate the new distinction between Part A and Part B notices.[137] The ACCC has indicated that when it concludes that a complaint is justified, it would strive to issue a competition notice no more than five months after receiving the complaint.[138]

In July 1997, the ACCC published access pricing principles which it intended to use when deciding to approve or reject access undertakings or when arbitrating access disputes.[139] The ACCC focused on four main principles:

(i) access prices should be cost based;

(ii) they should be non-discriminatory;

---

[136] See Australian Competition and Consumer Commission, 'Competition Notice Guideline Issues Pursuant to s 151AP of the Trade Practices Act 1974' (27 June 1997) available at <http://www.accc.gov.au/docs/draft1/telecomm.htm>.

[137] See Clayton Utz, 'New Telecommunications Legislation' (October 1999) *Communications Issues* 2.

[138] See Diane Staats, *Competition Law—Competition Law and Access Rules Get More Teeth* (Sydney: Freehils, 1999) 3.

[139] Australian Competition and Consumer Commission, 'Access Pricing Principles—Telecommunications' (July 1997).

(iii) they should not be inflated to reduce competition in dependent markets; and

(iv) they should not be predatory (ie they should cover at least incremental costs).

The ACCC announced that the model it would generally use to determine the adequacy of proposed access prices would be the total service long-run incremental cost model (TSLRIC).[140] TSLRIC is a form of forward-looking long-run incremental cost model very similar to the US TELRIC model.[141]

In the next three years, the ACCC published a number of reports specifying in greater detail how it would calculate access prices for some particular services.[142] In line with its 1997 principles, the ACCC generally opted for a TSLRIC methodology. One exception to this rule concerns the recently declared local carriage services (ie resale of local call services). The ACCC, like the FCC, opted in that instance for the 'retail price minus avoidable costs' model (often called retail minus model).[143] As pointed out in the US Chapter, the retail minus model is very similar to the ECPR model.

The ACCC has also produced a discussion paper on the way it would assess the concept of LTIE, mentioned, as indicated above, under the Trade Practices Act (1974), s 152AB.[144] Finally, the ACCC has published guidelines on the way it would determine whether or not to declare a particular service and on the length of time which declaration inquiries should take.[145]

2. Declaration of Services

The Telecommunications (Transitional Provisions and Consequential Amendments) Act 1997 carried forward as declared services, as of 1 July 1997, the services supplied, prior to 1 July, under an AUSTEL-registered inter-operator access agreement.[146] These services included, inter alia, PSTN originating and

---

[140] For a discussion of the access pricing principles, see Peter Waters, 'LRICal Access: The ACCC's Pricing Principles' (Gilbert & Tobin, October 1997) available at <http://www.gtlaw.com.au/gt/pubs>.

[141] TSLRIC refers to the forward-looking LRIC of access to a given service, while TELRIC, as mentioned above, refers to the forward-looking LRIC of access to a specific element of the access provider's infrastructure under an unbundled access scheme. See J Gregory Sidak and Daniel F Spulberg, *Deregulatory Takings and the Regulatory Contract—The Competitive Transformation of the Network Industries in the United States* (Cambridge: Cambridge University Press, 1997) 403–404.

[142] See, for example, the following ACCC publications, available at <http://www.accc.gov.au/telco/fs-telecom.htm>: 'Pricing of Unconditioned Local Loop Services (ULLS) and Review of Telstra's Proposed ULLS Charges' (August 2000); 'Access Pricing Paper—Local Carriage Service' (November 2000); 'Pricing Guidelines for Access Prices of PSTN Terminating and Originating Access Services Provided by Non-Dominant or Smaller Fixed Networks' (March 2001); 'Pricing Methodology for the GSM Termination Service' (July 2001).

[143] See ACCC, 'Access Pricing Paper—Local Carriage Service' Final Report (November 2000).

[144] For a discussion of the concept of LTIE, see Anne Peters, 'Competition in Telecommunications: Promoting the Long Term Interests of End-Users' (1998) 5 *Competition and Consumer L J* 272.

[145] See ACCC, 'Telecommunications Services—Declaration Provisions' (July 1999) available at <http://www.accc.gov.au/fs-pubs.htm>.

[146] See Peter G Leonard, 'A Hostile Land: Competition Regulation and Australian Telecommunications, 1997–2000' (Gilbert & Tobin, 19 September 2000) 6, available at <http://www.gtlaw.com.au/pubs>.

terminating services (ie provision of originating or terminating services to enable calls to be carried on other carriers' long-distance networks), originating and terminating services for mobile (GSM) calls, as well as transmission service at 2.048Mbit/s capacity between certain cities, except on particular routes where different operators had already established transmission facilities.[147]

As the TAF has not been able to reach a consensus on which additional services it should recommend that the ACCC declare, the ACCC has decided to hold a series of public inquiries. The first inquiry which it completed was on roaming. Given the fact that new entrants could enter into negotiations with any one of the three incumbents (Telstra, Optus, and Vodafone), the ACCC decided not to declare roaming.[148] It also concluded, for similar reasons, that GSM long-distance transmission did not need to be declared. However, since July 1997, a certain number of additional services have been declared by the ACCC, including ISDN originating and terminating services,[149] local PSTN originating and terminating services (ie provision of local originating or terminating services to enable competition in the local market), local carriage services (ie resale of local call services), unconditioned local loop services (ie unbundled access to the local loop), and analogue Pay-TV broadcast carriage services.[150] As the unconditioned local loop had already been duplicated in certain areas, the ACCC announced that it would review this declaration in 2004.[151]

In May 2001, the ACCC decided to remove access regulation on transmission service between cities, arguing that this market was now sufficiently competitive to be left unregulated.[152] Today, a total of twelve services have been declared, the majority of which focus on fixed services.

On average, it took about a year for the ACCC to decide whether or not to declare a service. Decisions not to declare a service took less time on average and decisions to declare services took longer. In fact, all decisions to declare services

---

[147] See ACCC, 'Annual Report 1999–2000' 85, available at <http://www.aca.gov.au/publications/annual/index.htm>.

[148] Rod Shogren, 'How Light-Handed Can you Get?—A Report on Telecommunications Regulation in Australia', paper distributed at the TUANZ Competition Symposium, Wellington, New Zealand, 7–8 April 1998, 10.

[149] 'ISDN' means Integrated Services Digital Network (a switched network providing digital connectivity for simultaneous transmission of voice and/or data)—ISDN services were declared in November 1998, see Network Economics Consulting Group, 'Assessment of the Telecommunications Regulatory Regime in Australia' (March 2000) 87.

[150] See ACCC, 'Declaration of Local Telecommunications Services' (July 1999), available at <http://www.accc.gov>.

[151] See Productivity Commission, 'Telecommunications Competition Regulation', Report No 16 (Canberra: AusInfo, September 2001) 228, available at <http://www.pc.gov.au/inquiry/telecommunications/index.html>.

[152] See Australian Competition and Consumer Commission, 'ACCC Issues Final Decision to Deregulate Intercapital Telecommunications Transmission', media release, 30 May 2001, available at <http://www.accc.gov.au/media/mediar.htm>.

except one took longer than the seven months (or ten months for complex inquiries) which the ACCC had indicated the process would take.[153]

3. A Review of Access Undertakings and Arbitration Processes

Four access undertakings have, so far, been submitted to the ACCC. On 7 November 1997, Telstra submitted to the ACCC three undertakings specifying the conditions under which it proposed to supply originating and terminating access to its fixed, digital mobile (GSM), and analogue mobile (AMPS) networks. The ACCC rejected these proposals in the summer of 1999. It concluded that the proposed non-price conditions for both fixed and mobile access services were unacceptable and that the price for fixed access services should be halved.[154] Telstra submitted a new undertaking concerning the supply of originating and terminating access to its fixed network in September 1999. This proposal was, once again, rejected by the ACCC which considered that the proposed access prices were still too high.[155]

In addition, the ACCC has conducted arbitration processes with respect to a number of access disputes. As of August 2001, forty three arbitration requests had been lodged with the ACCC, which had made seventeen interim arbitrations, five of which have now proceeded to final arbitration (two of the final arbitrations are currently under appeal).[156] Most of the disputes are between new entrants and Telstra. Almost all of them focus on the price conditions which the access provider seeks to impose upon the access seeker.[157] Seven operators, for example, sought arbitration to force Telstra to lower the prices at which it would grant unbundled access to the local loop. Preliminary ACCC findings suggested that Telstra's proposed prices should be lowered by more than 40 per cent.[158] Public documents reveal that, on average, ACCC prices have been about 50 per cent lower than prices offered commercially, with the gap between arbitration and commercially offered prices narrowing over time.[159]

On the whole, reviews of undertakings and arbitration appear to be rather lengthy processes. It has taken the ACCC around one and a half years to evaluate undertakings and some final assessments were made after initial terms and

[153] See Productivity Commission (n 151 above) 229.

[154] See Australian Competition and Consumer Commission, 'ACCC Rejects Telstra's Interconnect Proposal: Concludes Prices Should be Halved', media release, 19 January 1999, available at <http://www.accc.gov.au/media/mr4–99.html;> and 'ACCC Rejects Telstra's Undertakings For Mobile Service', media release, 23 August 1999, available at <http://www.accc.gov.au/media/mr016–99.html>.

[155] See Australian Competition and Consumer Commission, '$250 Million Win for Telecommunications Consumers', media release, 27 April 2000, available at <http://www.accc.gov.au/media/mr2000/mr-79–00.htm>. See also 'Annual Report 1999–2000' (n 147 above) 87.

[156] See Productivity Commission (n 151 above) 217.   [157] ibid 236.

[158] See International Telecommunication Union, 'Case Study: Broadband, the Case of Australia' (hereafter 'Broadband, the Case of Australia'), Regulatory Implications of Broadband Workshop, 2–4 May 2001, 25, available at <http://www.itu.int/osg/spu/ni/broadband/workshop/Australiafinal.doc>.

[159] See Productivity Commission (n 151 above) 217.

conditions had expired. As pointed out above, of the thirty nine arbitrations conducted by the ACCC, only four have progressed to final determinations, three of which took over eighteen months to finalize. Twenty-five arbitrations currently remain pending.[160]

The modifications to Part XIC provisions—introduced by the Telecommunications Legislation Amendment Act 1999—which gave to the ACCC the power to intervene in access negotiations, to make final determinations retroactive, and to issue interim determinations which cannot be suspended through requests for judicial review were aimed both at reducing the number of negotiations which would need to be arbitrated and to make arbitration more effective. The additional powers which the ACCC was granted to obtain and disseminate information was also aimed, inter alia, at facilitating negotiations between parties. These amendments do not seem, so far, to have had exactly the intended effects as the number of arbitration requests has in fact tended to increase in recent months. Some commentators argue that it is due to the fact that the arbitration process is more appealing to access seekers since the ACCC can issue interim determinations which remain in force during appeal processes.[161]

4. Competition Notices

The ACCC has issued several competition notices against Telstra under the Trade Practices Act, Part XIB. Six of these notices relate to the process by which Telstra transferred users who had chosen to subscribe to the services offered by competing local service providers. The ACCC considered that Telstra's transfer process was anti-competitive for several reasons. For example, Telstra required that operators benefiting from the transfer either assume responsibility for the users' unpaid bills vis-à-vis Telstra, or pay AU$15 to Telstra per transferred line, without offering quantity discount for transfers of services comprising several lines. The ACCC claimed that such requirements imposed undue costs upon Telstra's competitors and hindered their ability to compete with Telstra in the local telephony market.[162] The ACCC initiated proceedings in court based on the claims contained in these notices. These proceedings were discontinued in February 2000 after some changes were made in Telstra's transfer process and after Telstra agreed to contribute AU$4.5 million to a fund, administered by the ACCC, to help other operators upgrade their technical capacity to deal with the transfer process.[163]

---

[160] ibid 239.

[161] See Network Economics Consulting Group, 'Assessment of the Telecommunications Regulatory Regime in Australia' (March 2000) 36–37.

[162] See Australian Competition and Consumer Commission, 'ACCC Institutes Proceedings Against Telstra', media release, 24 December 1998, available at <http://www.accc.gov.au/media/mr1998/mr243%2D98.html>.

[163] See Australian Competition and Consumer Commission, 'ACCC and Telstra Reach Agreement on Commercial Churn', media release, 23 February 2000, available at <http://www.accc.gov.au/media/mr2000/mr%2D30%2D00.htm>.

In two other notices, the ACCC claimed that Telstra was violating the provisions of Part XIB because it charged other operators for provision of Internet data transmission services over its network, but did not pay when it received similar services from these other operators. The ACCC suggested that Telstra should enter into peering arrangements with the three operators which had lodged a complaint. Ultimately, the notices did not come into effect as Telstra complied by concluding peering arrangements with Cable & Wireless Optus and two of the larger ISPs.[164]

In September 2001, the ACCC issued a competition notice arguing that Telstra was failing to provide a true wholesale broadband service which would enable other operators to compete with Telstra's own ISP, BigPond, for the provision of ADSL high-speed Internet services. The ACCC considered, in particular, that Telstra's wholesale prices prevented other operators from competing with Big-Pond's retail prices and that the wholesale service was configured in a way which made it impossible for competitors to offer different services or a different quality of service from that offered by BigPond.[165]

In all cases, it took more than a year for the ACCC to issue a competition notice after it had received complaints regarding a particular behaviour. In addition, Telstra contended, in several instances, that the ACCC had not described the alleged anti-competitive conducts in sufficient detail in the notices. At the same time, when notices did contain a detailed description of the behaviour at issue, Telstra was able to side-step application of the notices by partially modifying the conduct as particularized.[166] The introduction, through the Telecommunications Legislation Amendment Act 1999, of Part A notices (which can contain relatively few details), of provisions ensuring that requests for judicial review could not be used to suspend such notices, and of additional information gathering powers to the ACCC, was aimed precisely at facilitating the issuance of competition notices and at reducing the scope for procedural challenges. Only one competition notice has been dealt with under the new regime.[167]

[164] See Henry Ergas, *Internet Peering: A Case Study of the ACCC's Use of its Power Under Part XIB of the Trade Practices Act 1974*, Mimeo, 8 May 1999 1; Bernadette Jew and Rob Nicholls, 'Internet Connectivity: Open Competition In the face of Commercial Expansion' (Gilbert & Tobin) 19, available at <http://www.gtlaw.com.au/pubs/opencompetition.html>.

[165] See Australian Competition and Consumer Commission, 'ACCC Believes Telstra Holding Back Competition for High Speed Internet to the Home', media release, 7 September 2001, available at <http://www.accc.gov.au/media/mediar.htm>.

[166] See Diane Staats, *Competition Law—Competition Law and Access Rules Get More Teeth* (Sydney: Freehils, 1999) 1. See also Peter Leonard, 'A Hostile Land: Competition Regulation and Australian Telecommunications, 1997–2000' (Gilbert & Tobin, 19 September 2000) 10, available at <http://www.gtlaw.com.au/pubs>.

[167] See Productivity Commission, 'Telecommunications Competition Regulation', Report No 16 (Canberra: AusInfo, September 2001) 170, available at <http://www.pc.gov.au/inquiry/telecommunications/index.html>.

5. A Review of Proposed Mergers and Acquisitions

In 1999, Cable & Wireless Optus, Australia's second largest carrier, announced its intention to acquire the third largest carrier, AAPT Ltd. Before Cable & Wireless put a formal offer to shareholders, the ACCC began an investigation of the potential impact of that acquisition on competition. At the end of this review, the ACCC announced that it was concerned the acquisition would have the effect or likely effect of substantially lessening competition in some whole-sale markets, such as the market for transmission services, and in some retail markets, such as the markets for the provision of Internet services and local call access. The ACCC communicated this opinion to Cable & Wireless Optus in May 1999 and Cable & Wireless withdrew its offer the same month.[168]

In January 2000, Telstra announced that it had entered into an agreement to purchase OzEmail's residential customer base. At the time, Telstra's BigPond was Australia's largest ISP with around 500,000 customers and OzEmail was the second largest with about 400,000 customers. Once again, the ACCC launched an investigation and concluded that the agreement would likely breach Part IV of the Trade Practices Act. Telstra was made aware of that view in February 2000 and announced that it would withdraw from the agreement.[169]

Other proposed acquisitions were brought to the ACCC's attention, including proposed mergers between ISPs and acquisitions of spectrum suitable for GSM telephony. In those cases, the ACCC considered that competition would not be reduced in the relevant markets, and it decided not to intervene.[170]

6. Price Caps Imposed Upon Telstra's Services

Telstra has been subject to a price-cap regime since 1989. These price control arrangements have tended to be revised every one to two years. From July 2000 to June 2001, a CPI minus 5.5 per cent cap was imposed upon a broad basket comprising the main services provided by Telstra while less demanding price caps (of CPI minus 0 per cent or CPI minus 1 per cent) were imposed on baskets comprising narrower sets of services (in particular some residential services).[171] For the period after June 2001, the ACCC proposed to scale back the scope of the price controls imposed upon Telstra: a price-cap of CPI minus 5 per cent would be imposed for a period of three years over a basket of services comprising many, but not all, of the services previously subject to the CPI minus 5.5 per cent cap (the ACCC considered that the provision of leased lines and of certain types of mobile services was now sufficiently competitive to be removed from the

[168] See Australian Competition and Consumer Commission, 'Infrastructure Industries—Telecommunications' (May 2001) 23–24, available at <http://www.accc.gov.au/fs-pubs.htm>.
[169] ibid 25–26.   [170] ibid 26.
[171] See Australian Competition and Consumer Commission, 'Review of Price Control Arrangements—An ACCC Discussion Paper' (September 2000) 7–8, available at <http://www.accc.gov.au/fs-search.htm>.

basket); the other price caps imposed on narrow sets of services would be dropped; and the local call parity requirement, which forced Telstra to charge broadly the same for local calls in metropolitan and in non-metropolitan areas, would be eliminated as well in order to maintain incentives for investment and new entry in rural areas.[172]

7. The ACA's Main Decisions

Since 1997, the ACA has been called upon to take decisions on a series of important issues. At the request of the Minister, the ACA developed standards regarding, for example, the time required to connect new customers, the speed at which faults needed to be rectified, and the keeping of appointments to meet customers. These standards were introduced on 1 January 1998. They were replaced, on 7 July 2000, by a new set of somewhat more demanding standards.[173]

The ACA has conducted eleven spectrum auctions since 1 July 1997.[174] These auctions included a tender, conducted in March 2001, for the allocation of spectrum suitable for the provision of 3G mobile services. No bidder could acquire more than 25 per cent of the available 3G spectrum. Six companies acquired portions of the spectrum, including two new entrants into the Australian mobile market. The auction of 3G spectrum generated revenues of about AU$1.2 billion. The eleven auctions together generated about AU$3.2 billion in total.[175] The auctions were conducted, in each case, according to a simultaneous ascending auction system inspired by the one used by the FCC. Licences are for a fixed term of up to fifteen years. They are technology-neutral (ie licensees are free to offer any type of communication services within their spectrum band) and tradable. They can be aggregated or subdivided to form new licences.[176]

In February 2000, the ACA registered a new industry code on pre-selection prepared by the ACIF. This code expands the basket of pre-selectable services to include fixed to mobile calls, in addition to other services such as long-distance and international calls included in a previous code.[177] At present, users can

---

[172] See Australian Competition and Consumer Commission, 'Review of Price Control Arrangements' (February 2001) xiii–xv and 89–90, available at <http://www.accc.gov.au/telco/Review_Price_Control_Arrangements.PDF>.

[173] See Department of Communications, Information Technology, and the Arts, 'Connecting Australia—Report of the Telecommunications Service Inquiry' (hereafter, 'Connecting Australia') (2000) 30–31, available at <http://www.telinquiry.gov.au/final_report.html>.

[174] An additional auction for the 500 MHz band was conducted just before the reforms, in February–March 1997. See Ian Hayne, 'Spectrum Property Rights and Practical Auction Design: The Australian Experience', 1997 Industry Economics Conference 190.

[175] See ACA, 'Annual Report 2000–2001', available at <http://www.aca.gov.au/publications/annual/index.htm>.

[176] See ACA, 'Introduction to Spectrum Licensing' (June 1998), available at <http://www.aca.gov.au/licence/spectrum/index.htm>.

[177] See ACA, 'New Pre-selection Industry Code' (9 February 2000), available at <http://www.aca.gov.au/media/2000/04–00.htm>.

pre-select the company which will provide them with the whole set of services included in the basket of pre-selectable services. The ACA has announced that it is considering the introduction of multi-basket pre-selection, which would enable users to pre-select different companies for different baskets of pre-selectable services.[178]

Finally, since 1997, the ACCC has required the ACA to ensure number portability with respect to local services (ie for calls to one fixed location), freephone and local rate services (ie for calls which are free or charged at local rates to the caller), as well as mobile services. Limited local number portability—limited because the service available to users with ported numbers might be of lesser quality—has been available since 1 May 1998. Full local number portability was introduced on 1 January 2000 (but with exemptions granted to some operators). Number portability for freephone and local rate services was implemented on 30 November 2000. And lastly, mobile number portability was implemented on 25 September 2001.[179] The ACA reported that over 90,000 users ported their mobile numbers over the next two months.[180]

8. Recent Developments Related to Universal Service Obligations

Costs incurred by Telstra through the provision of universal services have traditionally been evaluated on the basis of particular cost models rather than on the basis of competitive auctions to allocate the required subsidies. In 1998, a change in the design of the model resulted in a seven-fold increase in Telstra's estimate of the costs associated with universal service provision in 1997–98. In order to reduce uncertainty, the Government felt compelled to cap Telstra's claim for the year 1997–98, and for the years 1998–1999 and 1999–2000 as well (see Box 8.1 below).

Box 8.1: Contradictory Estimates of the Costs of Universal Service Obligations in Australia

For several years prior to the enactment of the 1997 Act, the cost to Telstra of fulfilling its universal service obligations was assessed using a model developed in the late 1980s by the Bureau of Transport and Communications Economics. After enactment of the 1997 Act, a new costing model was developed to reflect the requirements of the new legislative regime and it was used for the first time to calculate the cost of universal service obligations for the financial year 1997–98. Whereas, in previous years, Telstra's claim had averaged around AU$250 million, it filed a claim for the 1997–98 year for more than AU$1.8 billion. Unsurprisingly, the magnitude of the change

(continuous)

---

[178] See 'Annual Report 2000–2001' (n 175 above)   [179] ibid.
[180] See ACA, '90,000 Customers Have Moved Their Mobile Number', media release, 26 November 2001, available at <http://www.aca.gov.au/media/2001/01–62.htm>.

(continued)
created a high degree of uncertainty with respect to the actual level of costs incurred by Telstra as the universal service provider.

The Government reacted by enacting the Telecommunications Laws Amendment (Universal Service Cap) Act 1999, which capped Telstra's claim for 1997–98 at AU$253.32 million and for the years 1998–99 and 1999–2000 at AU$253.32 million plus CPI, while leaving to the Minister the power to determine other amounts if appropriate. The Government also requested that the ACA review Telstra's 1.8 billion claim. The ACA considered that the costs effectively incurred by Telstra were about AU$548 million. The difference between Telstra's original claim and the ACA's assessment was due to various factors including: (i) different estimates of the cost of capital; (ii) different depreciation figures; (iii) differing views about the set of technologies which could be used to provide universal services at least cost; and (iv) differing assumptions about the size of the geographic area over which the provision of universal services entailed a loss for the service provider.

The cap of AU$253.32 million was maintained for the year 1997–98. For the years 1998–99 and 1999–2000, Telstra then suggested an evaluation of universal service costs based on the ACA's 1997–98 assessment of AU$548 million. The final figures, set by the Minister, were about AU$280 million for each of these two years.

Sources: Caroline Lovell, *The Future of the Australian Universal Service Obligation*, Paper presented at the International Telecommunications Society, XIII Biennial Conference, 2–5 July 2000, Buenos Aires, Argentina; and Productivity Commission, 'Telecommunications Competition Regulation', Report No. 16 (Canberra: AusInfo, September 2001) 565.

This episode prompted the Government to undertake a complete review of the system. As a result, changes were brought, in 2000, to the Telecommunications (Consumer Protection and Service Standards) Act 1999. As pointed out above, these changes were aimed, inter alia, at introducing some degree of competition for the provision of universal services.[181] Thus, the Government indicated that it would organize a competitive tender to select the operator which would gain access to a AU$150 million fund earmarked to enable provision of untimed local calls and other services to inhabitants living outside the main cities. A 'beauty contest' was launched in October 2000 to select the operator which would become the universal service provider in those areas and be eligible for exclusive universal service obligations subsidies for three years. The Government invited seven companies to present a bid and Telstra was ultimately selected as the preferred tenderer.[182] The Government also decided to launch two regional

[181] See text accompanying n 62 above.
[182] See International Telecommunication Union, 'Case Study: Broadband, the Case of Australia' (hereafter, 'Broadband, the Case of Australia'), Regulatory Implications of Broadband Workshop, 2–4 May 2001, 24, available at <http://www.itu.int/osg/spu/ni/broadband/workshop/Australiafinal.doc>.

pilot schemes whereby operators will be able to apply to the ACA for approval as competing universal service providers and thus have access to subsidies ear-marked for the provision of loss-making services. Approvals by the ACA rely on the adequacy of the operators' policy statements and marketing plans. Telstra is required to continue operating as the primary universal service provider in these areas and customers will thus be able to choose their service provider among the primary and competing universal service providers.[183]

A recent report communicated to the Government on 30 September 2000 by the Telecommunications Service Inquiry supports the introduction of competition in the market for the provision of universal services. In line with a previous Government commitment, the Inquiry was set up to conduct an independent assessment of service levels prior to any sale of the State's current (50.1 per cent) majority ownership in Telstra (the Government, which had sold one third of its equity stake in Telstra in 1996, sold a further 16.6 per cent in 1999).[184] The Inquiry concludes that Australians are generally satisfied with the quality of telecommunications services but that levels of dissatisfaction are somewhat higher in rural areas, in particular with regard to the timely installation and repair of basic telephone services, coverage of mobile services, and access to Internet over standard telephone lines. It strongly supports the introduction of competitive universal service obligation arrangements to promote market entry and greater innovation in rural service provision and it recommends, inter alia, that service standards be applied only to universal service providers in order to encourage competition from other operators for the provision of services in remote areas.[185]

9. A Review of the Regulatory Framework

The Productivity Commission—an independent agency in charge of advising the Government on microeconomic policy and regulation—completed in September 2001 the review of the operation of the Trade Practices Act, Part XIB which, as mentioned above, was mandated by the provisions of the Act itself. The review covered, in fact, not only Part XIB but also, inter alia, Part XIC of the Trade Practices Act.

The Productivity Commission considered that the ACCC should continue to perform its regulatory role in the telecommunications sector.[186] It also considered that, for the time being, the telecommunications-specific provisions dealing with anti-competitive conduct in the Trade Practices Act, Part XIB

---

[183] See Clayton Utz, 'New Telecommunications Legislation' (October 1999) *Communications Issues* 8.

[184] See 'Connecting Australia' (n 173 above) 9.   [185] ibid 176–177.

[186] See Productivity Commission, 'Telecommunications Competition Regulation', Report No 16 (Canberra: AusInfo, September 2001), 308, available at <http://www.pc.gov.au/inquiry/telecommunications/index.html>.

should be maintained.[187] It stressed, however, that Part XIB should only be a transitional measure adopted to compensate for insufficient competition in the telecommunications sector and that the need for the anti-competitive provisions under Part XIB should be re-assessed in three to five years.[188]

The Productivity Commission also recommended the retention of provisions for a telecommunications-specific access regime as it judged that without such a regime, Telstra would be able to leverage its market power in the local market to distort competition in other segments of the market. It judged, however, that the current provisions of Part XIC have deficiencies which tend to increase uncertainty and could lead to reduced investment in telecommunications infrastructure with adverse long-run consequences for Australia's economy. It considered, in particular, that the declaration criteria and access pricing rules of Part XIC leave excessive discretion to the ACCC, that arbitration procedures tend to be lengthy, and that there are some inconsistencies between Part XIC and Part IIIA. It also argued that the Minister possesses excessive discretionary powers. The Productivity Commission, therefore, made the following specific recommendations:

(i) The declaration criteria mentioned under Part XIC of the Act should be more specific and aligned with those mentioned under Part IIIA.[189]

(ii) Sunset provisions should be introduced for declarations under Part XIC. This would help align the regime of Part XIC more closely with that of Part IIIA which requires expiry dates for declarations as pointed out above, and it would help prevent undue persistence of specific access regimes.[190]

(iii) A number of access pricing principles should be incorporated in Part XIC. Such principles should, inter alia, ensure: that prices cover the long-run costs of providing access, including a return on investment commensurate with the risks involved; that a vertically integrated access provider cannot discriminate in favour of its own downstream operations; and that access providers have incentives to reduce costs or otherwise improve productivity. Legislating such principles would, in the Productivity Commission's view, reduce uncertainty as well as the risk of regulatory error.[191]

(iv) A group of access seekers should have the capacity to rely on class arbitration—rather than on a series of bilateral negotiations—to determine prices jointly for all members of the group[192] and binding time limits should be defined for arbitration.[193] These various measures, among others, are required, in the Productivity Commission's view, to speed up the arbitration process.

(v) The discretionary powers of the Minister responsible for telecommunications should be reduced by ensuring that the Minister does not retain the power to determine how standard access obligations are to be priced.[194]

---

[187] ibid 151.   [188] ibid 202.   [189] ibid 282–283.   [190] ibid 301.
[191] ibid 390–391.   [192] ibid 327–328.   [193] ibid 334.   [194] ibid 312.

E. A CRITICAL APPRAISAL OF THE REGULATORY FRAMEWORK

The Australian model, like the UK and Chilean models, constitutes, in many ways, a compromise between the more 'radical' and sharply contrasted approaches of the United States and New Zealand. The Australian model presents, however, very specific features which make it an interesting object of comparison. For example, unlike the other countries considered here, Australia chose to integrate the main telecommunications-specific rules into its antitrust legislation and to give responsibility to apply both general and telecommunications-specific rules to the economy-wide antitrust regulator. While the Australian framework has been in place for a relatively limited period only, enough has already taken place to at least begin to shed some light on the respective advantages and disadvantages of the system.

1. Competition and Other Incentives to Generate and Share Efficiency Gains

A broad array of measures have been adopted, in Australia, to promote competition in telecommunications. All segments of the sector were opened to full competition in 1997 and licences, required only from network owners wishing to provide services to the public, are supposed to be available without restrictions.[195] In addition, general antitrust law was made applicable to telecommunications. To complement these measures, a sophisticated set of access rules was adopted. Those rules, contained for the most part in the Trade Practices Act, Part XIC, mandate access to some facilities,[196] give priority to negotiated solutions,[197] and provide for regulatory intervention when such solutions cannot be found.[198] Finally, additional sector-specific provisions relating, for example, to number portability, operator pre-selection, and override dial codes, have been designed to ease the process of switching from one service provider to another.[199]

Overall, these efforts appear to have been broadly successful. While there were three licensed network operators in 1997, 77 licences had been issued by the end of June 2001.[200] In addition, there is vigorous competition between these network operators to serve the providers of resale and value-added services which have entered the market since 1997.[201] More than 1,000 such providers are

---

[195] In fact, it is not clear in that context why new entrants should be forced to publish a development plan in order to obtain a licence. See text accompanying n 38 above.

[196] See text accompanying n 48 above.　　　　[197] See text accompanying n 49 above.

[198] ibid.　　　　[199] See text accompanying nn 53–54 above.

[200] See Productivity Commission (n 186 above) 69.

[201] See Peter Waters, David Stewart and Andrew Simpson, 'Regulation of Telecommunications Liberalisation: Lesson From Australian Experience' (Gilbert & Tobin, 2 June 1999) 1–2, available at <http://www.gtlaw.com.au/pubs>.

currently registered with the TIO.[202] The market shares of new entrants have also substantially increased since the 1997 reforms in all segments of the market (see Table 8.1 below).

Competition is especially intense in mobile services. As of September 2001, four main operators were offering both wholesale and retail services and additional companies are operating as resellers of retail services. Telstra's market share is now below 50 per cent as mentioned in Table 8.1 below. The mobile penetration rate of about 60 per cent in mid-2001 is one of the highest in the world, fuelled by price reductions over the 1997–2000 period of about 19 per cent.[203] The price comparisons presented in the Annex tend to confirm the competitiveness of the Australian mobile prices: PPP-based prices are the second or third cheapest, depending upon the volume of calls (see Graphs 11b and 12b). An increasing range of product offerings provides another indication that the market is effectively competitive.[204]

TABLE 8.1. Evolution of market revenue shares of Telstra's competitors between 1997 and 2001 in Australia

	December, 1997	June, 2001
Local	0.5%	19%
National long-distance	19%	25%*
International long-distance	31%	52%*
Mobile	38%	60%*

*June 2000
Source: Network Economics Consulting Group, 'Assessment of the Telecommunications Regulatory Regime in Australia' (March 2000) 36; and Productivity Commission, 'Telecommunications Competition Regulation' Report No. 16, (Canberra: AusInfo, September 2001) ch 4.

Mobile number portability has certainly helped to foster competitive pressures and such pressures might be further increased following the auction of 3G spectrum in 2001 since it might promote the entry of new operators into the

[202] See Department of Communications, Information Technology, and the Arts, 'Liberalisation of the Telecommunications Sector: Australia's Experience' (June 2000) available at <http://www.dcita. gov.au>.

[203] See Global Information Inc, '2001/2002 Voice and Data Australia', available at <http://www.gii. co.jp/english/pa7758_2000_2001_voice.html>; and Australian Competition and Consumer Commission, 'Changes in the Prices Paid for Telecommunications Services in Australia 1996–97 to 1999–2000' (hereafter, 'Changes in the Prices Paid for Telecommunications Services' (April 2001) 4, available at <http://www.accc.gov.au/pubs/Publications/Utilities/Telecommunications/telcocharges2001.pdf>.

[204] See Productivity Commission, 'Telecommunications Competition Regulation', Report No 16 (Canberra: AusInfo, September 2001) 132, available at <http://www.pc.gov.au/inquiry/ telecommunications/index.html>.

market. Just after the auction closed, Optus Mobile, for example, announced an aggressive timetable with provision of commercial services by October 2002.[205] The use of simultaneous auctions, and of technology-neutral, tradable, licences should help ensure that spectrum is allocated efficiently (even though the auction of spectrum management rights, as conducted in New Zealand and envisaged in the United States, might ensure even greater flexibility and efficiency in the spectrum reallocation process).

The market for international services appears very competitive as well. Telstra's revenue share fell from about 60 to about 48 per cent from 1998 to 2000. Interestingly, the share of Cable & Wireless Optus fell as well from about 23 to 18 per cent, while the share of new entrants substantially increased from 17 to 34 per cent.[206] Prices have decreased by about 53 per cent between 1997 and 2000.[207] Australian international prices are the lowest of our sample in current US$ and the second lowest when based on PPPs. The price of calls from Australia to the United States is also substantially cheaper than the price of calls in the other direction (see Annex, Graphs 5a, 5b, 6a, 6b, 7a, 7b, 8a, and 8b).

Competition appears to be intense as well in the market for dial-up Internet services. There are about 5.6 million Internet users in Australia (or about 30 per cent of the population) and more than 700 ISPs.[208] Telstra's ISP, BigPond, remained the largest ISP in mid-2000, but with a market share of less than 25 per cent, and average ISP prices for unlimited access declined by more than 40 per cent from 2000 to 2001 with a growing number of ISPs offering free Internet access.[209] Data collected by the Telecommunications Service Inquiry suggest that Australian prices of dial-up Internet services are among the lowest in the world.[210] This appears to be confirmed by the price comparisons presented in the Annex which show that Australian prices expressed in current US$ are the lowest of our sample, and that Australian prices based on PPPs are only slightly above those in the United States and lower than those in the other three countries (see Graphs 9a, 9b, 10a, and 10b).

Several factors are contributing to these positive developments. First, the existence of an unmetered local call regime lowers dial-up costs and fosters Internet penetration. Second, there are four main backbone networks, largely replicating each other in terms of geographic scope and population coverage,

---

[205] See Clayton Utz, 'New Telecommunications Legislation' (October 1999) *Communications Issues* 10.

[206] See Productivity Commission (n 204 above) 122.

[207] See 'Changes in the Prices Paid for Telecommunications Services' (n 203 above) 5.

[208] See CyberAtlas, 'The World's Online Populations', available at <http://cyberatlas.internet.com/big_picture/article/0,1323,5911_151151,00.html>.

[209] See Productivity Commission (n 204 above) 135–136.

[210] See Department of Communications, Information Technology, and the Arts, 'Connecting Australia—Report of the Telecommunications Service Inquiry' 111, available at <http://www.telinquiry.gov.au/final-report.html>.

with very substantial spare capacity.[211] This gives ISPs a choice of providers of backbone services.[212] Third, the ACCC has been successful in preventing anti-competitive mergers in the ISP market. Thus, the ACCC's intervention to prevent Telstra from acquiring OzEmail prompted the sale of OzEmail's dial-up business to another ISP. Faced with the threat of more intense competition, Telstra then announced major reductions in ISP charges in the following weeks.[213]

Finally, there are positive developments in the market for broadband services as well. During the past two years, a large number of operators have started to deploy local access networks—mainly in the central business districts of large cities, but in some cases in other cities or even in rural areas—using a range of technologies including DSL, optic fibre, microwave, and satellites.[214] The ACCC's declaration of unbundled access to the local loop in particular, has prompted established carriers and a host of new entrants to start deploying DSL networks. It is estimated that about fifteen operators will invest close to AU$2 billion in their DSL networks over the 2001–2003 period.[215] Telstra itself started to offer ADSL services in August 2000 at the same time as it was forced to provide its competitors with unbundled access to the local loop.[216] As mentioned above, the ACCC also declared the provision of analogue Pay-TV broadcast carriage services and some commentators argue that an important open access principle has thus been set which may be applied—with potential competitive benefits—to other broadband networks in the future.[217]

This is not to say that all segments of the telecommunications market are equally competitive or that the pro-competition measures adopted in 1997 have all worked exactly as intended. Telstra's local network, for example, still accounts for about 95 per cent of the total number of connections. However, the recent introduction of full number portability and the declaration of several fixed local services (including local call resale and local loop unbundling) combined

---

[211] The Australian Government conducted a national bandwidth inquiry in 2000 which found that usage is generally less than 1 per cent of current bandwidth capacity. See Minister for Communications, Information Technology, and the Arts, 'National Bandwidth Inquiry', 5 April 2000, 75, available at <http://www.noie.gov.au/projects/information_economy/bandwidth/index.htm# Publications>.

[212] See Australian Competition and Consumer Commission, 'Internet Interconnection: Factors Affecting Commercial Arrangements Between Network Operators in Australia' discussion paper (February 2000) 7, available at <http://www.accc.gov.au?telco/fs-telecom.htm>.

[213] See OECD, *Local Access Pricing and E-Commerce*, DSTI/ICCP/TISP(2000)1/FINAL, 27 June 2000, 37, available at <http://www.olis.oecd.org/olis/2000doc.nsf/linkto/dsti-iccp-tisp(2000)1–final>.

[214] See BIS Shrapnel, 'Telecommunication Infrastructures in Australia 2001—A Research Report Prepared for ACCC' (July 2001) 13–15, available at <http://www.accc.gov.au/fs-pubs.htm>.

[215] ibid 56–57.

[216] See Australian Competition and Consumer Commission, 'Telstra Commits to Unbundling its Local Loop at the Same Time as Offering its Own High-Speed Services', media release, 22 March 2000, available at <http://www.accc.gov.au/media/mediar.htm>.

[217] See 'Broadband, the Case of Australia' (n 182 above) 25.

with increasing investments in local networks is expected to foster competitive pressures in the local market. In fact, Telstra's revenue share in the local retail market has fallen sharply in recent years to around 81 per cent (it was still around 88.5 per cent in mid-2000). This is due, mainly, to the presence of resellers of Telstra's local telephony services, who have captured around 14 per cent of revenues (up from 8.5 per cent in mid-2000), while Cable & Wireless Optus' own network accounts for another 5 per cent of revenues (up from 3 per cent in mid-2000).[218]

The national long-distance market remains rather concentrated as well, with Telstra still accounting for around 75 per cent of revenues in 2000, while the three largest providers (Telstra, Cable & Wireless Optus, and AAPT) account for about 97 per cent. While prices decreased by about 23.5 per cent in the national long-distance market between 1997 and 2000,[219] they seem to remain relatively high by international standards: the price comparisons in the Annex show that Australian national long-distance prices are the highest of our sample when expressed in current US$ and the second highest, just behind those of New Zealand, when based on PPPs (see Graphs 4a and 4b). Competitive pressures are, however, likely to intensify in the future. The entry of facilities-based operators on major backbone routes will increase competition in the market for long-haul transmission services and should contribute to further reduce prices at the retail level. In addition, increased competition in the local market is likely to reduce Telstra's share of the long-distance market as well, as customers who change their local service provider tend to choose the same provider for long-distance services also.[220]

While substantial investments in broadband networks are now being carried out, such developments are recent and the vast majority of broadband capacity is still owned and controlled by Telstra.[221] New entry has been delayed because of disputes between Telstra and its competitors regarding the conditions imposed by the incumbent for the provision of wholesale ADSL services and unbundled local loop access. Broadband services remain relatively expensive, existing fibre optic cable networks pass by only about 30 per cent of Australian households, and the number of broadband users—estimated at 122,800 by the ACCC as of 31 July 2001—is low by international standards.[222]

As is the case in the United States, some commentators have argued that the existence of a regime of mandated access through resale of local call services and unbundling of the local loop has limited facilities-based competition and

---

[218] See Productivity Commission, 'Telecommunications Competition Regulation', Report No 16 (Canberra: AusInfo, September 2001) 113–114, available at <http://www.pc.gov.au/inquiry/telecom munications/index.html>.

[219] See 'Changes in the Prices Paid for Telecommunications Services' 5, available at <http://www.accc.gov.au/pubs/Publications/Utilities/Telecommunications/telcocharges2001.pdf>.

[220] See Productivity Commission (n 218 above) 122.

[221] See 'Broadband, the Case of Australia' (n 182 above) 9.

[222] ibid 32 and Australian Competition and Consumer Commission, 'Snapshot of Broadband Deployment as at 31 July 2001', available at <http://www.accc.gov.au/telco/fs-telecom.htm>.

therefore the overall intensity of competition in the Australian telecommunications sector.[223] The existing data do not seem to support that argument, however. As mentioned above, a variety of networks are currently being deployed by Telstra's competitors. The Productivity Commission, for its part, has indicated that while the gap between arbitration and commercially negotiated access prices seems to be narrowing over time, a regime of mandated access still appears necessary to prevent Telstra from using its dominant position in the local loop to hinder the operations of its competitors.[224] Finally, as discussed in previous chapters, while a regime of mandated access may reduce the level of facilities-based competition, this may not necessarily be a problem. When access prices and conditions are adequately set, it may be possible to strike a welfare-enhancing balance between the key objectives of limiting unnecessary duplication of infrastructure, preserving the incumbent's incentives to invest, and enhancing competition.

A separate question is whether the specific regime of mandated access adopted in Australia is adequate. One problem, recognized by a majority of commentators, is that service declarations, reviews of proposed undertakings, and arbitration processes, all tend to be cumbersome and slow. As pointed out above, declarations have, on average, taken longer than the indicative time limits published by the ACCC itself; all four undertakings submitted by Telstra have been rejected after lengthy procedures; and a majority of the arbitration processes which have been initiated remain pending. While the 1999 amendments of Part XIC brought some improvements—for example, the new powers of the ACCC to issue interim determinations in arbitration processes were viewed favourably by most industry participants—delay remains a problem in the administration of the access regime.[225] A second issue is more controversial. The Productivity Commission considers that the access regime leaves excessive discretion to the ACCC and that access prices might in some cases be set too low to ensure sufficient remuneration of the facilities' owner—two factors which could hamper investment in core telecommunications infrastructure.[226] While investment in broadband networks by Telstra's competitors may have been delayed, as argued above, the Productivity Commission itself recognizes, however, that investment levels appear to be on the rise in the industry. Telstra and Cable & Wireless have both increased investments in recent years, and various operators are now undertaking substantial deployment of customer access networks.[227]

The adoption of an ECPR-type methodology to calculate adequate prices for the resale of local services could, for its part, induce Telstra to engage in

[223] See, for example, Rodney Maddock and Anthony Marshall, 'Access Regulation: The New Australian Model' (1997) 6 *Utilities Policy* 73; and David Boles de Boer et al, 'The Internet Service Provider (ISP) Markets of Australia and New Zealand' (May 2000) 14, available at <http://www.iscr.org.nz/research.html>.

[224] See Productivity Commission (n 218 above) 253.   [225] ibid 229.

[226] ibid 282–283 and 404.   [227] ibid 88–97.

managerial or accounting cross-subsidization. Indeed, Telstra could potentially increase interconnection payments by allocating to the bottleneck segment some of the costs incurred in the competitive segments.[228] Telstra has argued, however, that the price-cap regime in place in the retail local market did in fact force it to provide local services to end-users below costs, and that with a negative opportunity cost of providing retail services, ECPR-based resale prices would not cover the costs of access provision.[229] Telstra's argument has some credibility, given that all its competitors have indicated a preference for the ECPR methodology, while Telstra has, for its part, indicated that, in this situation, it would in fact prefer a TSLRIC regime (even though—as discussed in Chapter 3—TSLRIC might not enable the incumbent to cover all its costs).[230] In practice, the incentive properties of the access regime will depend upon the way in which the price methodology which is chosen is interpreted and applied. And once again, the risk of deterring investment in infrastructure through the imposition of insufficient access prices has to be balanced with the potential dynamic efficiency benefits which can be obtained through the imposition of tough price controls upon an incumbent which is only now beginning to face some degree of competition for market share in the local market from resellers.[231]

Some issues also arise with respect to the price-cap regime applied to a variety of Telstra's services. First, the fact that Telstra's price caps are reviewed every one or two years reduces the company's incentives to cut costs (the ACCC's recent decision to impose a new cap for a period of three years marks a progress in that respect). Second, as argued above, local charges might be set too low to ensure cost recovery. Third, such low, and unmetered, local call charges combined with free Internet service provision might increase congestion problems in the local network as Internet usage keeps growing. Fourth, the focus on price caps, combined with insufficient competition in the local market, might have led the incumbent to lower service quality, particularly in rural areas, as mentioned above. In that respect, the report of the Telecommunications Service Inquiry is rather convincing when it argues that imposing detailed quality standards on all operators risks being less effective than encouraging competition for the provision of universal services. Indeed, unless it faces competition, an incumbent has incentives to skimp on quality in a price-cap environment, and exclusive reliance on enforcing quality standards—even when combined with extensive monitoring and quality control—might prove insufficient to ensure that quality is maintained.

The ACCC's decision to eliminate the local call parity requirement could help increase the commercial viability of rural service provision and therefore enable more competition in that market which could, in turn, improve service quality. The two pilot schemes under which operators will compete directly with Telstra

---

[228] See Chapter 3, Section B 3.   [229] ibid.

[230] See ACCC, 'Access Pricing Paper—Local Carriage Service' Final Report (November 2000) 2.

[231] See Chapter 3, Section C.

to gain access to subsidies earmarked to promote the provision of otherwise non-profitable services could have similar positive impacts. As to the Government's decision to auction the right to provide universal services outside the main cities, it could also contribute to raise service quality by forcing the winning bidder to commit to high standards to gain access to the AU$150 million subsidy. Some commentators have pointed out that this latter scheme could also have improved quality standards through the introduction of some degree of yardstick competition between operators. In order to really increase the scope for yardstick competition, however, it might in fact have been preferable to launch not one, but several auctions to select different universal service providers in different—and relatively comparable—rural areas. In any case, whatever potential for yardstick competition existed under the present scheme will not be realized, at least in the short term, as Telstra was selected as the winning bidder.

The introduction of some degree of competition in the provision of universal services may also help address, to some extent, the highly contested issues related to the estimation of the costs of universal service obligations. Two distinct types of issues arise in this respect. First, the discrepancy between Telstra's claim and the ACA's analysis shows that disagreements exist about how to compute the total costs actually incurred by Telstra. Second, there are questions about whether Telstra's costs, whatever they are, reflect efficient operations and sufficient service quality levels. The different types of 'beauty contests' organized in Australia to select universal service providers can help ensure that the subsidies earmarked by the Government are used efficiently by the operators and therefore yield the highest possible quality of service that can be 'bought' for that amount. Such contests do not, however, directly reduce the overall costs of universal service provision as a set level of subsidy is earmarked in advance. As to the Government's cap on Telstra's claim for the years 1997–98, 1998–99, and 1999–2000, it has rather arbitrarily limited those claims at just above 1 per cent of total sector revenues (as mentioned above, the ACA's estimate was about twice as high and Telstra's estimate was about seven times higher), which is low if compared to the costs in the United States but high if compared to those in Chile for example. The Productivity Commission argued, for its part, that consideration should be given to a system similar to the Chilean model, whereby the right to provide a pre-determined level of service would be auctioned to the bidder requiring the lowest level of subsidy.[232]

Finally, some authors also argue that, as in New Zealand, insufficient attention was paid in Australia to the need for structural reforms in the telecommunications sector.[233] Some consider that the merger of Australia Telecom and OTC

---

[232] See Productivity Commission, 'Telecommunications Competition Regulation' Report No 16 (Canberra: AusInfo, September 2001) 578, available at <http://www.pc.gov.au/inquiry/telecommuni cations/index.html>.

[233] See, for example, Peter Waters, 'The Mystery of the Missing Ring Fence—Regulation of Vertically Integrated Telecommunications Operators' (Gilbert & Tobin, April 1998), available at <http://www.gtlaw.com.au/gt/pubs>; see also Henry Ergas, 'Telecommunications Across the Tasman:

strengthened the market power of the dominant player, thus making the tele-communications market less competitive and complicating to this day the task of the regulator.[234] On the one hand, the resources that a vertically integrated incumbent can use to hinder the emergence of competition in the telecommuni-cations sector should certainly not be underestimated, and there is evidence that Telstra did successfully resort to some delaying tactics and hampered the intro-duction of new services by its competitors in some cases. On the other hand, since the adoption of the Telecommunications Legislation Amendment Act 1999, the regulator appears to be better equipped to handle interconnection disputes and competition is clearly emerging in most segments of the market. The notable exception is the fixed local market, but low retail prices are likely to be part of the problem there, at least as much as structural obstacles to competition.

As always, the merits of imposing a separation between different activities depend, inter alia, upon the extent to which economies of scope would be lost. A recent development presents some interesting clues in that regard. The utility which provides Canberra with electricity and water is currently deploying an advanced broadband network in the city. TransACT, the company set up for this purpose, has decided to act as a pure infrastructure provider (except for the provision of phone services), thus voluntarily implementing a radical form of vertical separation between infrastructure and advanced service provision. Other operators have reached agreement with TransACT to use its network to provide a range of services including, for example, permanent high-speed con-nections to the Internet, video-on-demand, and Pay-TV services.[235] TransACT's business strategy could indicate that, in this case at least, the economies of scope between the provision of access services and the provision of retail services might be limited, and some commentators are advocating the imposition of a similar type of separation between Telstra's local network and wholesale business on the one hand and its local retail business on the other.[236]

2. Specificity versus Coherence

While establishing the telecommunications-specific rules needed to promote competition (for example, rules on operator pre-selection, number portability, and conditions of access), the Australian Government has tried to take into account the growing similarities between telecommunications and other economic activities. Thus, in Australia, general antitrust rules (such as the

A Comparison of Economic Approaches and Economic Outcomes in Australia and New Zealand', paper prepared for the International Institute of Communications (May 1996) 3.

[234] ibid 5.
[235] See 'Broadband, the Case of Australia' (n 182 above) 15.
[236] See Tristan Gilbertson, 'Telecommunications-Specific Competition Regulation in Australia: What Next?' (Gilbert & Tobin, April 2001) 25, available at <http://www.gtlaw.com.au/binaries/pdf/publications/telecomspecific.pdf>.

provisions of the Trade Practices Act, Part IV, on anti-competitive conduct) are applicable to telecommunications. In addition, many sector-specific rules have been integrated into the Trade Practices Act to reflect a general policy of bringing the regulation of competition in telecommunications more closely in line with the general antitrust regime.[237] Also, telecommunications-specific antitrust rules are administered by an economy-wide regulator to ensure a consistency of approach to the administration of antitrust laws across all industry sectors.[238]

Reviews of existing regulations are also conducted to assess whether the existence of telecommunications-specific rules is still justified. As mentioned above, review of Part XIB provisions is mandated by the Trade Practices Act itself and the review which has been conducted by the Productivity Commission covered, in fact, a broader set of telecommunications-specific rules. The ACCC's decisions to review some of its declarations (eg declaration of transmission services between certain cities which was recently repealed; or declaration of unconditioned local loop services to be reviewed in 2004), as well as the price controls imposed upon Telstra, pursue the same objective.

In spite of the Government's efforts to align the antitrust regime applicable in telecommunications with the regime applicable in the rest of the economy, one could, however, argue that there are still too many different rules potentially applicable to the same issues. Problems of interconnection could, for example, be tackled through the application of general antitrust rules such as s 46 of Part IV of the Trade Practices Act, of telecommunications-specific antitrust rules such as ss 151AJ(2) and (3) of Part XIB, of the infrastructure-wide access rules of Part IIIA, or of the telecommunications-specific access regime of Part XIC. The complexity of this regulatory framework suggests that the need for some sector-specific rules has been exaggerated.[239] For example, it is not clear why there should be two slightly different definitions of the concept of misuse of market power, one for telecommunications only under s 151AJ(2) (under Part XIB) and one for all economic activities under s 46 (under Part IV). A similar point can be made with respect to Part IIIA and Part XIC: if the access regime under Part XIC improves upon the one established under Part IIIA, why not adopt a unique access regime for all sectors based upon Part XIC rules? Under such conditions, the Productivity Commission's proposal to review the need for Part XIB provisions in three to five years, and to align more closely the provisions of Part IIIA and of Part XIC would seem to be a step in the right direction. One may even wonder whether the telecommunications-specific provisions of Part XIB should not be repealed sooner, as the Productivity Commission had originally proposed in its Draft Inquiry Report.[240]

[237] See Section B.2 above.

[238] See 'Liberalisation of the Telecommunications Sector: Australia's Experience' 10, available at <http://www.dcita.gov.au>.

[239] See Geoff Taperell and Richard Dammery, 'Anti-Competitive Conduct in Telecommunications: Are Supplementary Rules Required?' (1996) 4 *Competition and Consumer L J* 63.

[240] See Productivity Commission, 'Telecommunications Competition Regulation', Draft Report (2001) 5.42.

Some commentators have also argued that the ACCC has been prone to regulatory overreach. They consider, for example, that the regulator declared too many services, intervening, for instance, with respect to some services which, in their views, were already supplied in a competitive manner or were too technology-specific.[241] The ACCC itself points out, however, that it seeks to narrow the scope of existing regulation to reflect increasing competition in the telecommunications market. And it appears that, in some cases at least, ACCC reviews did narrow the scope of sector-specific rules. As pointed out above, transmission services between cities have recently been deregulated and the scope of the price controls imposed upon Telstra has been reduced.[242] Whatever the merit of these different arguments, introducing sunset clauses for declarations—as proposed by the Productivity Commission—would appear to be a sound policy prescription.

3. Flexibility versus Certainty

The Australian approach constitutes an interesting attempt to combine flexibility and certainty. On the one hand, the regulatory framework leaves broad discretionary powers to the ACCC on a wide range of issues, including, for example, access matters which have to be assessed on the basis of the rather vague LTIE test.[243] On the other hand, the ACCC produced guidelines on the issuance of competition notices, on access pricing, and on service declaration for example, to provide information about the way in which it would exercise those powers. The general approach adopted in Australia has merit when the regulator has the legitimacy, the capacity, and the degree of independence required to design and apply adequate rules—a question which will be discussed further under Section 4 below.

Some aspects of the Australian regime are clearly sub-optimal however. For example, as mentioned under Section C above, the Minister responsible for telecommunications can exercise broad powers in particular with respect to the regulation of universal service pricing, the regulation of Telstra's tariffs, the adoption of performance standards, the design of rules aimed at preventing market distortions caused by international operators, the monitoring of Telstra's compliance with the provisions of the Telecommunications (Consumer Protection and Service Standards) Act 1999, and the pricing of standard access obligations. Such rules, which leave a large degree of discretionary power to a political authority on issues which can have an enormous impact on the profitability of telecommunications operators, are likely to raise private investors' concerns. The fact that the Government remains one of Telstra's shareholders is likely to

---

[241] See, for example, Network Economics Consulting Group, 'Submission to New Zealand Telecommunications Inquiry' (July 2000) 3, available at <http://www.necg.com.au/pappub/papers-submission-to-NZ-telecom-inquiry-july00.pdf>.

[242] See text accompanying n 152 above.   [243] See text accompanying n 47 above.

heighten such concerns as there are clear conflicts of interests between the ownership and the regulatory functions exercised by the Government.[244]

In addition, the existence, within the Trade Practices Act, of multiple rules potentially applicable to the same issues introduces a degree of uncertainty as operators might be unsure about which rules will be applied to a particular case and as the application of different rules to similar issues could potentially lead to incoherent decisions. Some commentators have argued, for example, that it was not clear why the competition notices relating to Internet peering were issued on the basis of Part XIB rather than Part XIC provisions.[245]

For its part, the Productivity Commission considers, as mentioned above, that the declaration criteria and access pricing rules of Part XIC leave excessive discretion to the ACCC and that this, in turn, unnecessarily increases uncertainty in the sector. In the face of sustained investment in the telecommunications sector, the point is debatable. Whether current provisions create a high degree of uncertainty or not however, the Productivity Commission's recommendation that clear, but relatively general, access pricing principles be incorporated in the legislation rather than in guidelines issued by the regulator itself appears to be a sound policy prescription as it could enhance certainty without unduly constraining the discretion of the regulator.

On the other hand, it can be argued that, in some cases, detailed regulations do introduce an excessive degree of rigidity in the regulatory framework at present. This might well be the case with the imposition of detailed performance standards upon all operators for example. The Telecommunications Service Inquiry argued in this respect that with the prospect of new entrants offering alternative services using network technologies substantially different from those of Telstra, there must be some questions regarding the appropriateness of applying common performance standards across all service providers.[246]

4. Regulatory Competence and Ability to Resist Undue Pressure

The ACCC is staffed, for the most part, with specialists in matters of economic regulation. The cross-sector nature of the institution enables the staff to gain expertise from work across sectors, while the establishment of a Telecommunications Group within the ACCC helps to ensure that in-depth knowledge of the telecommunications sector is developed within the institution. Most commentators agree that the combination of general and industry-specific responsibilities within a single agency is a strength of the Australian model.[247]

---

[244] See Peter G Leonard, 'A Hostile Land: Competition Regulation and Australian Telecommunications, 1997–2000' (Gilbert & Tobin, 19 September 2000) 19, available at <http://www.gtlaw.com.au/pubs>.

[245] See Network Economics Consulting Group (n 161 above) 54.

[246] See 'Connecting Australia' (n 173 above) 75.

[247] See, for example, Peter Waters, David Stewart and Andrew Simpson, 'Regulation of Telecommunications Liberalisation: Lesson from Australian Experience' (Gilbert & Tobin, 2 June 1999) 4, available at <http://www.gtlaw.com.au/pubs>.

This is not to say, however, that the ACCC's performance is absolutely flawless. The ACCC's position with respect to the access dispute between Telstra and other Internet service providers has been widely criticized (see Box 8.2 below). In addition, some have argued, as pointed out above, that the ACCC has declared too many services and that this, in turn, is slowing the arbitration process as it forces the regulator to arbitrate an unduly high number of access disputes.[248] On the other hand, if the number of declared services is not excessive, then the problem might be insufficient ACCC resources to exercise the arbitration function speedily.

The ACT and the Federal Court, for their part, appear well suited to play their respective roles. The ACT, which is the main appeal body empowered to evaluate all aspects of the ACCC decisions which it is called upon to review, comprises at least two members (out of three) competent in economic and commercial matters. The Federal Court, on the other hand, comprises judges only but can only review decisions on questions of law.

Box 8.2: The Internet Peering Competition Notices—A Regulatory Mistake?

As mentioned in Section D above, in 1998 the ACCC issued competition notices stating that Telstra was violating the provisions of the Trade Practices Act, Part XIB because it charged other operators for the provision of Internet data transmission services over its network, but did not pay when it received similar services from these other operators. The ACCC suggested that Telstra should enter into peering arrangements with the three operators—Cable & Wireless Optus and two ISPs—which had lodged a complaint. Cable & Wireless Optus had constructed a national Internet backbone, it had acquired substantial international capacity, and traffic levels between its network and that of Telstra were roughly balanced. Traffic between Telstra and the other two operators was unbalanced, however, and in such situations a strong case can be made against the conclusion of peering arrangements for the reasons discussed under Chapter 3, Section B.4.

Some commentators stressed that point, arguing that the arrangement between Telstra and the two ISPs did not reflect an abuse of market power but rather the application of sound economic principles. Telstra was providing other operators with backbone transmission services between places in Australia and between Australia and overseas, and Telstra transferred more data to these other operators than it received from them. In those conditions, performing a compensation and agreeing on a price to be paid by the other operators on the basis of the volume of traffic they received from Telstra is efficient. In addition, it provides socially desirable incentives as it encourages the operators which tend to be net recipients of transmission services to economize on their use of international transmission. It is also less vulnerable

(continuous)

---

[248] See Network Economics Consulting Group (n 241 above) 3.

(continued)

to abuse than two-way payments because small operators can easily generate dummy traffic toward a larger network in an effort to increase the payments due to them, whereas the reverse is less easy: flows of dummy traffic towards the smaller networks would run more quickly into capacity constraints and would also be detected more easily.

Sources: See Henry Ergas, *Internet Peering: A Case Study of the ACCC's Use of its Power Under Part XIB of the Trade Practices Act 1974*, Mimeo, 8 May 1999; and Bernadette Jew and Rob Nicholls, 'Internet Connectivity: Open Competition In the face of Commercial Expansion' (Gilbert & Tobin) 18–20.

Certain measures have also been taken to ensure the independence of the ACCC from industry players. While the commissioners are designated by the Government, professional requirements and protection against arbitrary dismissal provide the ACCC with some degree of autonomy vis-à-vis political authorities. The fact that the ACCC operates across all sectors of the economy also tends to reduce the risks of regulatory capture by both industry and government.

However, as it gives important powers to the Minister responsible for telecommunications, the regulatory model does leave some room for politically motivated interventions in the regulatory process. These concerns are heightened, to a certain extent, by the Government's continued participation in Telstra's capital. Some commentators also consider that particular characteristics of the TIO scheme should be modified to strengthen its independence vis-à-vis the industry. It has been argued, for example, that as several members of the Council are industry representatives, the Council is in fact unable to ensure the independence of the Ombudsman. Some also consider that this problem is compounded by the fact that it is the Board of Directors, composed of industry representatives, which supervises the financial affairs of the Council.[249]

5. Regulatory Accountability and Stakeholder Participation

Every year, the ACCC must report to the Minister responsible for trade practices on its activities.[250] The ACA, for its part, must report in a similar fashion to the Minister responsible for telecommunications.[251] The ACCC and the ACA both fulfil their obligations through the publication of very comprehensive annual reports. The possibility to lodge appeals against the decisions of the ACCC before the ACT, on factual as well as legal grounds (except for declarations),[252]

---

[249] See Anita Stuhmcke, 'The Corporatisation and Privatisation of the Australian Telecommunications Industry: The Role of the Telecommunications Industry Ombudsman' (1998) *U of New South Wales L J* 807, 823–825.

[250] See Trade Practices Act 1974, s 290.

[251] See Telecommunications Act 1997, s 105.

[252] See text accompanying nn 120–121 above.

and before the Federal Court on legal grounds only, also contributes to make the regulator accountable.

The Australian regulatory model is also characterized by the scope that it leaves for industry participation in the regulatory process. Thus for example, the TAF can recommend services to be declared by the ACCC[253] as well as develop access codes specifying terms and conditions of access[254] and the ACIF is responsible for developing codes of technical standards to be registered by the ACA.[255] Individual operators have an important role as well as they can submit individual access undertakings[256] while regulatory intervention in interconnection disputes takes place only if the parties are unable to come to an agreement on their own.[257]

Some provisions on industry participation have not worked as expected, however. As mentioned above, the TAF, for example, has been unable to agree on services to recommend for declaration, beyond those declared on 1 July 1997. This is due, in large part, to the unanimity principle by which TAF members must abide. This has meant, in practice, that access providers have been able to veto recommendations of service declarations.[258] Some observers consider that the TAF has, in fact, played a useful role as a technical advisor to the ACCC on declaration issues; others perceive it as irrelevant or even a source of delay.[259] The ACIF, for its part, appears to have worked well. By drawing on its members' technical expertise, it developed various technical and operational standards which could be implemented with minimum controversy.[260] Twelve ACIF-sponsored industry codes have been registered by the ACA so far, six of which deal with consumer protection matters.[261]

While industry participation has been encouraged, backstop measures have also been adopted to avoid gridlock when operators are unable to come to an agreement. The ACCC has the mandate to intervene to ensure, for example, that services can be declared.[262] The ACCC can also require that access codes be developed even if the industry representative does not take action and it arbitrates disputes when parties fail to come to a negotiated solution.[263]

Other provisions are designed to ensure adequate consultation of the general public. Thus for example, as mentioned above, both the ACCC and the ACA are free to launch public inquiries or reviews aimed at facilitating the exercise of their regulatory functions in telecommunications.[264] The ACCC must, in fact,

---

[253] See text accompanying n 128 above.   [254] See text accompanying n 130 above.

[255] See text accompanying nn 133–134 above.   [256] See text accompanying n 49 above.

[257] See text accompanying nn 91–92 above.

[258] See Network Economics Consulting Group, 'Assessment of the Telecommunications Regulatory Regime in Australia' (March 2000) 61.

[259] See, for example, Network Economics Consulting Group ibid 61; and Productivity Commission (n 151 above) 314.

[260] See Network Economics Consulting Group (n 258 above) 60–61.

[261] See ACA, 'Annual Report 2000–2001', available at <http://www.aca.gov.au/publications/annual/index.htm>.

[262] See text accompanying n 129 above.   [263] See text accompanying nn 87 and 131 above.

[264] See text accompanying nn 101 and 111 above.

hold public inquiries before it can declare a service on its own initiative, and it must also invite public submissions before it can accept an individual undertaking on access terms and conditions.[265] When they decide to conduct a public inquiry, the ACCC and the ACA must take a number of steps to ensure that the public is made aware of the existence and nature of the inquiry and that people can make submissions about the issues at stake.[266] In addition, a Consumer Consultative Forum, comprising representatives of a broad range of consumer interests, provides a formal mechanism for bi-annual consultations with the ACA to ensure that consumers' interests are adequately considered by the ACA.[267] Finally, the existence of the TIO scheme—whatever its possible flaws—should also help to ensure that users' complaints are heard and taken into account.[268]

6. Regulatory Costs

Efforts have been deployed in Australia to limit regulatory costs in telecommunications. For example, conferring the main regulatory responsibilities on an economy-wide body such as the ACCC is generally more cost-efficient than setting up a variety of distinct sector-specific regulatory agencies.[269] The resources spent by the ACCC on telecommunications regulation—about thirty staff and a telecommunications-related budget of AU$3.2 million per year—are indeed very limited. As mentioned above, the TIO's budget was, for its part, about AU$5 million in 2000–2001—a relatively limited amount also. The cost of the ACA—420 staff and a budget of about AU$56 million—appears a lot more substantial, however, and one might wonder whether there is not a discrepancy between the amount of resources allocated, on the one hand, to the technical, and, on the other hand, to the economic aspects of telecommunications regulation.

As already pointed out, a series of measures have been adopted in an attempt to speed up the regulatory process: the Trade Practices Act, s 87B, for example, enables the Commission to act without necessarily having to initiate costly judicial proceedings; legislative provisions have been adopted in 1999 to reduce the scope for procedural tactics aimed at slowing down the implementation of arbitration determinations and the processing of competition notices; and the ACCC has published indicative time limits for the conduct of declaration inquiries and the issuance of competition notices.

Regulatory delays are still an issue, however. Arbitration processes in particular appear to remain relatively cumbersome and costly for the parties. The measures proposed by the Productivity Commission to accelerate the arbitration process—such as the introduction of class arbitration and of binding time limits—may help. As to the measures introduced in 1999 to deter operators

---

[265] Trade Practices Act 1974, s 152AL.   [266] See Telecommunications Act 1997, ss 485–505.
[267] See ACA 'Annual Report 1999–2000', 80, available at <http://www.aca/gov.au/publications/annual/index.htm>.
[268] See text accompanying n 123 above.
[269] See discussion of the sixth criterion in Chapter 2, Section D above.

from seeking judicial review of competition notices, their effectiveness remains to be tested as only one competition notice has yet been issued under the new regime.[270]

Finally, some individual decisions of the ACCC have been criticized and mistakes appear to have been made—for example with respect to Internet peering as discussed above. On the whole, however, there is broad consensus that regulatory staff are generally competent and that they possess the required sector-specific expertise—which does limit to some extent the risks, and the costs, of regulatory mistakes.

7. The Allocation of Regulatory Responsibilities

The allocation of responsibilities with respect to the economic regulation of telecommunications appears to be reasonably clear in Australia. The way regulatory responsibilities have been allocated presents a number of additional positive features which have already been pointed out: for example, the allocation of the main responsibilities for the economic regulation of the sector to a specialized cross-sector regulator with a telecommunications-specific department; or the presence, within the ACT, of two members specialized in commercial and economic matters.

One source of concern, already mentioned above, relates to the scope of the powers which have been left to the Minister responsible for telecommunications. Some observers, as has been pointed out above as well, have claimed that the discretionary powers of the ACCC are excessive also. While the claim may have some merit (eg with respect to the lack of any legislative guidelines on access pricing principles), it seems reasonable to submit that, generally speaking, the ACCC appears to possess the competency, autonomy, and legitimacy required to be entrusted with a relatively high level of discretionary power.

On the other hand, the ACCC appears to have been unable, in some cases, to prevent operators from delaying the regulatory process by imposing judicial reviews of the ACCC's decisions. Some measures have been taken in that respect—such as the introduction of s 87B in the Trade Practices Act which enables the ACCC to get violators of competition provisions to commit to a change of behaviour without having to go to the courts; and the design of new competition notices which decrease the scope for judicial challenges—but more could arguably be done. For example, the ACCC does not have the power to impose fines for breaches of regulatory obligations and a strong case can be made for filling that gap because it would eliminate the need to institute court proceedings each time fines need to be imposed and because it would increase the deterrence of the regulatory regime.[271]

---

[270] See text accompanying n 167 above.
[271] See Tristan Gilbertson (n 236 above).

Other issues stem from the way responsibilities are shared between the ACCC and the ACA. First, leadership responsibility might not always have been granted to the agency best equipped to handle it. For example, the ACCC may direct the ACA to take action on interconnection standards and number portability, while it is the ACA which takes the lead with respect to pre-selection. Because of the competitive implications of decisions in this latter area, it would appear desirable that the ACCC take the lead there as well and determine which services should be subject to pre-selection.[272] A second issue concerns overall co-ordination between the two agencies, independently of which agency makes the first move. For example, while it is the ACCC which administers the price control regime which applies to the provision of universal service[273] or to access charges,[274] the ACA, on the other hand, is in charge of developing performance standards and of monitoring the performance of telecommunications operators.[275] The ACCC's and ACA's responsibilities are therefore closely interrelated since a modification of performance standards will affect the operators' costs and therefore the prices at which they can maintain the same level of profitability. The close links which exist between the ACCC's and the ACA's responsibilities with respect to interconnection standards, number portability, and pre-selection raise similar issues. While bringing both economic and technical expertise to bear on these issues is undoubtedly useful, it remains to be seen whether the co-ordination mechanisms which exist between the ACCC and the ACA will be sufficient to prevent incoherent decision-making processes.

Some commentators have also argued that since the TAF's role, in practice, has been limited to that of advisor to the ACCC on technical aspects of service declaration, there is some overlap with the ACIF which is in charge of developing technical standards related, inter alia, to service declaration.[276] The Productivity Commission considered, for its part, that the TAF serves no useful role and should be eliminated.[277]

[272] See Productivity Commission, 'Telecommunications Competition Regulation', Report No 16 (Canberra: AusInfo, September 2001) 481, available at <http://www.pc.gov.au/inquiry/telecommuni cations/index.html>.
[273] See Department of Communications, Information Technology, and the Arts, 'Liberalisation of the Telecommunications Sector: Australia's Experience' (June 2000) 58, available at <http://www.dci ta.gov.au>.
[274] See text accompanying n 95 above.
[275] See text accompanying n 65 above.
[276] See Network Economics Consulting Group, 'Assessment of the Telecommunications Regulatory Regime in Australia' (March 2000) 61.
[277] See Productivity Commission (n 272 above) 314.

9

Comparative Analysis

This chapter seeks to compare the experiences of the United States, New Zealand, Chile, the United Kingdom, and Australia in an attempt to draw some lessons on how to design, and balance the relative importance of, the different components of the regulatory framework in order to ensure that the seven objectives identified in Chapter 2 are met to the largest possible extent.

As already pointed out, the five countries examined have relied to a different extent on economy-wide rules and institutions and sector-specific ones as a way to control market power in liberalized telecommunications markets. The United States adopted in 1996 a very detailed set of telecommunications-specific regulations and gave a large implementing role to a sector-specific regulator (the FCC). By contrast, New Zealand put until recently great emphasis on economy-wide antitrust rules implemented by economy-wide institutions (ie the Commerce Commission and the courts). To some extent, the Australian, Chilean and British models represent compromises between the radical New Zealand and US approaches. These three countries adopted more specific rules than New Zealand, but the regulatory regimes they put in place are less specific than the US 1996 Telecommunications Act. A key difference between the Chilean and the British models, on the one hand, and the Australian model, on the other hand, is that while Chile and the United Kingdom adopted a specific telecommunications law and established a sector-specific regulator, Australia chose to integrate many of the telecommunications-specific rules into its antitrust legislation and to give responsibility to apply these rules to the economy-wide antitrust regulator (the ACCC).

As indicated in the introduction, particular country circumstances will determine to some extent the way in which different components of the regulatory framework should be designed and balanced. The objective of the present chapter is therefore not to identify a single overall best model, but rather to discuss what works best in what circumstances. While this discussion should help to draw lessons applicable beyond the five countries studied here, it is important to remember that circumstances in other countries may be so fundamentally different from those examined in this book that very different recommendations should apply.

A. Competition and other incentives to generate and share efficiency gains

All five countries have now established what are some of the most competitive telecommunications markets in the world. In each case, all explicit legal barriers to entry into any segment of the telecommunications market have been removed and the market is fully open to competition. Moreover, in all the countries, general antitrust rules are fully applicable to the telecommunications sector, thereby prohibiting operators from engaging in anti-competitive behaviours and excessive market consolidation. Beyond that, however, the options chosen to generate and share efficiency gains in telecommunications differ in substantial ways among the five countries.

The following topics will be examined in turn:

(i) main tools used in the five countries to promote competition in the various segments of the telecommunications market;
(ii) retail pricing regulation;
(iii) use of spectrum allocation mechanisms to maximize efficiency and competition in the mobile market;
(iv) universal service obligations arrangements;
(v) overall competitiveness of service provision in the various segments of the telecommunications markets in the five countries; and
(vi) pros and cons of imposing vertical separation between the various segments of the telecommunications markets in the five countries.

1. The Main Tools Used to Promote Competition

We will focus here on a limited number of areas which are important for the promotion of competition in telecommunications and which are of particular relevance because, in these areas, the balance between sector-specific and economy-wide regulation has been set quite differently in the five countries and has, in some cases, shifted over time within a single country.

As far as interconnection is concerned, New Zealand decided at first not to adopt any specific rules on interconnection. The Government considered that, to the extent they arise, interconnection disputes could be adequately solved through the application of the antitrust rules. Similarly, Chile had only relatively vague rules on interconnection in the first few years following liberalization. On the other hand, the United States, the United Kingdom and Australia adopted at the outset a more detailed interconnection regime to be implemented by a specialized regulatory entity.

New Zealand's light-handed approach left much to be desired as operators often proved unable to reach negotiated agreements while the courts were unable to formulate specific decisions on the level of interconnection prices, even after very long judicial proceedings. Recently, interconnection agreements have been renegotiated in the local market and 'bill and keep' arrangements have been concluded without recourse to the courts. This might indicate that negotiated agreements become progressively easier to reach as parties gain experience and as the incumbent is subjected to more intense competitive pressures. A Ministerial Inquiry conducted in 2000 concluded, however, that New Zealand would benefit from more specific rules concerning inter alia interconnection. Such rules have now been adopted and are to be implemented by a specialized Telecommunications Commissioner within the Commerce Commission. Chile had a somewhat similar experience as interconnection disputes failed to be adequately solved until a much more detailed interconnection regime, to be applied by a specialized regulator, was adopted in 1987 and 1994. In the other three countries, implementation of a more detailed sector-specific interconnection regime has not been without its difficulties: for example, BT has modified its pricing methods several times and access arbitration has been slow in Australia. However there are no moves in those countries toward reliance on much more general rules with respect to interconnection (on the contrary, the Australian Productivity Commission is arguing for more specific rules which would reduce regulatory discretion in that area). In view of these experiences, it may be advisable, at least for a certain period after the liberalization of the various segments of the telecommunications market, to adopt a detailed interconnection regime and to confer responsibility for implementing such a regime on a specialized regulatory entity.

As far as the calculation of interconnection rates is concerned, in the absence of negotiated agreements between the parties, such rates are currently supposed to be calculated on the basis of the forward-looking incremental costs of providing the service (LRIC) in the United States, the United Kingdom, Australia, and Chile, and, since the adoption of the Telecommunications Act 2001, in New Zealand as well. As we have seen in Chapter 3, all main pricing methods used to calculate interconnection rates (LRIC, ECPR, etc) have pros and cons. Hence, the selection of a method in any given country should depend on the policy goals the government seeks to achieve (for example, we have seen that, unless the incumbent makes a loss on the provision of retail services, LRIC tends to be more favourable to new entrants and thus more likely to stimulate competition than ECPR), as well as on the specifics of the relevant telecommunications market and, in particular, the degree of market power which the incumbent is able to exercise (for example, when the incumbent retains a strong degree of market power and potential competition for the market remains limited, tight control of interconnection prices might be warranted) and the level regulatory capacity (for example, as LRIC is a complex methodology and as it gives incentives to incumbents to resist entry, it thus requires strong regulatory capacity).

Seen in that light, the choice of an LRIC methodology seems consistent with the overriding goal of telecommunications policy reforms in the five countries, which is to promote competition. The choice of LRIC seems to be further justified by the fact that, as will be seen below, the incumbents continue to retain strong market power in the provision of local exchange services in all the countries examined (with no exception, the local incumbent continues to own most of the local lines, has a strong brand name, and has deep pockets). Finally, while the difficulty of properly implementing LRIC pricing methodologies should not be underestimated, the regulator in charge of calculating access pricing regimes in the United States, the United Kingdom and Australia seems at least to be able to bring a high level of technical capacity to bear on that task. The new institutional framework adopted in New Zealand, and in particular the setting up of a Telecommunications Commissioner, should also help in the implementation of the LRIC-based interconnection regime. More concerns can, however, be expressed over the capacity of the Chilean regulator to implement a complex LRIC regime. Besides a strengthening of SUBTEL's regulatory capacity, a solution which could be explored by the Chileans would be to rely on a pricing mechanism inspired by the one recently adopted in New Zealand. In the two-step process adopted in New Zealand, the initial determination is to be derived in most cases from benchmarking of similar prices in comparable countries. Reliance on benchmarking—as an alternative to cost-based methods or as a check to be used in parallel with cost-based methods—may simplify the task of the regulator. It is thus an attractive strategy to help implement complex pricing models in most situations, in particular when the regulator enjoys only limited resources.

Besides granting interconnection rights to new entrants, competition can also be promoted by mandating incumbents to provide competitors with access to unbundled elements of their local networks, as well as by regulating the conditions under which resellers can purchase services from other operators.

In some countries which have adopted regulations in these areas—for example in the United States and in Australia—commentators have argued that mandating resale services and local loop unbundling should always be prohibited because they discourage new entrants from deploying additional facilities and therefore limit overall competition in the telecommunications market. As argued in previous chapters, however, there are conditions under which resale and local loop unbundling would promote rather than hinder competition. The key question is whether access is granted under conditions which are indeed conducive to enhancing competitive pressures.

Four of the five countries examined have mandated unbundling of the local loop (New Zealand remaining the exception). Unbundling presents advantages when it comes to introducing competition in sectors characterized by high entry barriers such as the local segment. It might also be an advisable strategy in countries where there is little or no competition in the local loop and a growing demand for high-bandwidth services. The four countries which have opted for an unbundling strategy appear to be in this situation, even the United Kingdom where the Government and the regulator have strongly promoted facilities-based competition. When justifying its decision to amend BT's licence to mandate the incumbent to unbundle its local network, OFTEL considered that the cable network, whose development had been promoted through asymmetric regulation, did not offer the same degree of functionality or ubiquity as the incumbent's network and that, therefore, the unbundling of BT's local network was necessary.

While unbundling is, in theory, a valid pro-competition strategy, its successful implementation requires complex regulatory assessments on the part of the regulator. A first difficult task for the regulator is to define the individual network components to which access must be granted by the local loop owner. As we have seen, this issue has raised a great deal of controversy in the United States where the list, initially drawn by the FCC, of network elements that had to be made available was rejected by the Supreme Court as it violated statutory requirements. Moreover, unbundling requires an access price regime to be designed. The United States, the United Kingdom, Chile, and Australia have opted for an LRIC-based pricing methodology comparable to the one they use for interconnection. However, compared with interconnection pricing, a specific difficulty of unbundled access pricing is that it requires an appropriate price to be established for access to each specific network component, thereby placing further demands on the regulator. Finally, implementing unbundling may require additional intervention by the regulator to ensure, for instance, that space within the (hundreds of existing) local exchanges is adequately shared between the incumbent and the access seekers. In the United Kingdom, OFTEL was severely criticized by BT's competitors for failing to act sufficiently swiftly on this space allocation issue.[1] Local loop unbundling is thus a strategy which places a heavy burden on the regulator. As mentioned with respect to interconnection pricing, relying on international benchmarking might be an attractive option, especially when regulatory resources and expertise are limited.

All the countries examined in this study are now regulating the price at which resellers can purchase services from the incumbent. In all cases, regulators have used a retail price minus avoidable costs model to determine the appropriate prices for the resale of local services, although the UK regulator has recently proposed that resellers be entitled to purchase wholesale services at a price based on BT's costs instead of BT's retail prices. As we have seen above, the retail minus model is an ECPR-type methodology as the price paid by resellers includes the incumbent's forgone profit (only avoidable costs are deducted from the retail price).

A potential problem with this approach is that ECPR maintains the monopoly profits of the incumbent (when they exist) and therefore tends to set resale prices too high for new entrants. Conversely, the ECPR methodology can be unduly harsh for the incumbent when retail prices are set below costs (eg because tariffs have not yet been sufficiently rebalanced). As illustrated by the Australian experience, the incumbent might then prefer that an LRIC-based methodology be applied to calculate wholesale prices even though this strategy might not

---

[1] See 'Leaving the Opposition Out of the Loop', *Financial Times*, 20 September 2000, 15.

allow it to recover all its costs. This may, however, result in wholesale prices being higher than retail prices, thereby removing any possibility of resale entry. Another potential problem with the ECPR methodology is that it might induce the incumbent to engage in managerial or accounting cross-subsidization by allocating to the services regulated under ECPR some of the costs actually incurred under services which are left unregulated or which are regulated under price caps. This problem can, however, be mitigated when, as is the case in the United States, the regulator administratively sets the discount to be deducted from the retail price.

Competition can be further enhanced by adopting regulatory requirements mandating number portability or carrier pre-selection. Such requirements are designed to lower switching costs and thus facilitate entry into the markets concerned. Four of the five countries have now adopted rules requiring number portability (the United States, the United Kingdom, Australia and New Zealand). In New Zealand, prior to the adoption of the Telecommunications Act 2001, number portability was commercially negotiated by the operators. As in the case of interconnection, negotiations between operators took a very long time and pressure had to be applied by both the Commerce Commission (which declared that those parties which would adopt 'unreasonable positions' on that issue would be potentially violating the Commerce Act) and the Minister of Communications before an agreement was eventually reached. No number portability requirements have so far been mandated by regulation or commercially negotiated in Chile, a factor which has been mentioned by observers as hindering competition. The New Zealand and Chilean experiences suggest that, as in the case of interconnection, adoption of specific rules might be the better approach.

All five countries have now imposed carrier pre-selection. As we have seen, this allows end-users to nominate their carrier of choice in advance so that calls are automatically used via this carrier without the need for dialling any special code. In Chile, users can not only 'pre-select' the operator of their choice, but also select carriers on a call-by-call basis, an arrangement which has proved particularly effective at promoting competition in the long-distance market. In New Zealand, the Telecommunications Act 2001 mandates carrier pre-selection only in some market segments (ie Telecom's fixed network to mobile carrier pre-selection) where operators had failed to reach an agreement (see Table 9.1 below which summarizes the main sector-specific rules adopted in the five countries).

Even when sector-specific rules have been adopted on the issues mentioned above, general antitrust rules remain essential for the economic regulation of telecommunications.

First, antitrust rules are needed—and indeed are best suited—to deal with a range of issues of economic regulation which are not addressed by the few sector-specific rules discussed above. Merger control is a key example. We have seen, for example, that the, US DoJ recently blocked the planned merger between MCI–WorldCom and Sprint and that, in Australia, the ACCC blocked proposed

TABLE 9.1. Main sector-specific rules adopted in the five countries (including the pricing methodology used when relevant)

	United States	New Zealand	United Kingdom	Chile	Australia
Interconnection	Yes, TELRIC	No (Since Telecommunications Act 2001: Yes, TSLRIC or bill-and-keep or combination of both)	Yes, LRIC	Yes, LRIC	Yes, TSLRIC
Unbundling of the local loop	Yes, TELRIC	No (Since Telecommunications Act 2001: Commerce Commission to report to Minister within two years)	Yes, LRIC	Yes, LRIC	Yes, TSLRIC
Resale	Yes, retail minus	No (Since Telecommunications Act 2001: Yes, retail minus)	Yes, retail minus[a]	Yes, retail minus	Yes, retail minus
Number portability	Yes	No (Since Telecommunications Act 2001: Yes)	Yes	No	Yes
Carrier pre-selection	Yes	No (Since Telecommunications Act 2001: Yes)	Yes	Yes, plus selection on call-by-call basis	Yes

Source: Authors' compilations.

[a]In its 2000 Price Control Review, OFTEL proposed to enable resellers to purchase wholesale services from BT at charges based on BT's costs instead of BT's retail prices.

mergers between Cable & Wireless Optus and AAPT Ltd, as well as betweenTelstra and OzEmail. Antitrust rules have also been used repeatedly to try to ensure that spectrum allocation processes would enhance competition in the mobile services market. The Chilean antitrust authorities, for example, intervened to ensure that spectrum allocation processes themselves would be more competitive, while, in New Zealand, antitrust authorities examined the legality of Telecom's acquisition of certain spectrum bands suitable for the provision of mobile services.

Various practices intended to make it more difficult for users to switch from one service provider to another have also been declared incompatible with antitrust rules in some of the countries examined here. For example, in the *I4free v Telecom* case, the New Zealand antitrust authorities considered that Telecom's attempts to prevent ISPs from subscribing to the service offered by competing telecommunications operators were anti-competitive, while, in Australia, the ACCC considered that the payments that Telstra required from its competitors when subscribers decided to leave Telstra for these competitors were incompatible with antitrust law. A range of additional practices have also been reviewed and sometimes condemned under antitrust provisions, such as CTC's 'calling party pays plus' system, which exempted CTC's mobile phone users from any payments for calls received from subscribers to CTC's fixed network, and which was viewed by the Chilean antitrust authorities as creating an anti-competitive cross-subsidy from CTC's regulated fixed activities to CTC's unregulated mobile activities.

Second, antitrust rules may play a residual role and fill gaps which might exist in sector-specific regulatory regimes. While recourse to antitrust law will often be sub-optimal in those cases, it does at least provide a tool to tackle problems which would remain completely unaddressed otherwise. This is particularly obvious in a country like New Zealand which had until recently decided to adopt very few sector-specific rules. A host of interconnection issues, for example, had to be tackled through antitrust law in New Zealand and while this proved inefficient in many cases, a few specific issues were in fact tackled satisfactorily in that way. Thus, Telecom's attempts to impose an access code upon Clear's customers and to impose the same access charge upon Clear as the one imposed upon its own large customers were swiftly found to be anti-competitive. The obligation imposed upon the mobile operator BellSouth to obtain Telecom's authorization prior to concluding interconnection agreements with third parties was considered anti-competitive too. In other countries, antitrust law was also used to address some interconnection or resale issues, particularly in the Internet service market which has so far remained largely exempt from sector-specific regulation. Thus, in the United States, the FTC subjected its approval of the AOL/Time Warner merger to the adoption of a series of steps by the merged entity to ensure that subscribers would have access to a range of competing cable ISPs. And in Australia, the ACCC issued competition notices against Telstra for failing to enter into peering arrangements with certain ISPs as well as for failing to provide a true wholesale broadband service which would enable other operators to compete with Telstra's own ISP for the provision of ADSL high-speed Internet services.

Given the almost complete absence of sector-specific regulation in New Zealand, other issues often addressed through sector-specific rules in other countries were also tackled through antitrust law in New Zealand. Thus, for example, the Commerce Commission warned that parties who would adopt 'unreasonable positions' on number portability could potentially be violating antitrust rules.

Finally, antitrust rules might be used to impose structural remedies when appropriate specific rules appear to be lacking on this topic. The break-up of AT&T in the early 1980s, which was imposed more than a decade before the full liberalization of all segments of the US telecommunications market, constitutes a well-known example of reliance on antitrust rules to implement structural reforms in the telecommunications market. Another example, this time in an already fully liberalized market, is provided by the Chilean Supreme Court rulings that Telefonica, which had become a major shareholder of both CTC and ENTEL, had to sell its participation in one of the two companies and that the two companies could then enter each other's markets under certain conditions.

2. Retail Pricing Regulation

All the countries covered in this study are regulating the prices of some end-user services through a system of price-caps.[2] Price-caps provide strong cost-cutting incentives on the part of the operators and, thus, tend to generate efficiency gains. Combined with the LRIC methodology used for interconnection and unbundled access pricing (ie a methodology pursuant to which prices are based on the costs of a benchmark efficient firm and not the costs actually incurred by the incumbent), a price-cap regime for retail services reduces the risk of managerial and accounting cross-subsidies between different activities as it ensures that most telecommunications services are regulated in ways which provide similar incentives to cut costs to the operators.

On the other hand, some features of the price-cap regimes adopted in the countries under study create problems. First, frequent revisions of the price-caps in some of the countries after two years in some cases in the United Kingdom (1989–91 and 1991–93) and even after one year in Australia reduce the operators' incentives to cut costs, thereby undermining the efficiency-enhancing feature of the price-cap mechanism. Second, evidence suggests that, in some of the countries examined, price-caps might have been set too high, thereby allowing the operator to realize substantial profits. For instance, the 3 per cent 'X' factor set by OFTEL for the period 1984–89 allowed BT to realize what OFTEL later considered an 'excessive' return. The regulator thus tightened the efficiency factor to 4.5 per cent for the period 1989–91, 6.5 per cent for the period 1991–93, and 7.5 per cent for the period 1993–97. A similar trend (of price control being initially set at a level favourable to the incumbent and then tightened by the regulator) could be seen in Chile where CTC's comfortable returns on equity in the mid-1990s have plummeted following the adoption of tighter price regulation of fixed local services in 1999. Moreover, there have been concerns in some of the countries examined about the impact of price-cap induced cost reductions on the quality of service. For instance, in the late 1980s, OFTEL had to intervene to force BT to improve its quality of service and, in the United States, US West was accused of lowering the quality of service following the adoption of a price-cap regime. The New Zealand experience, however, points to a different direction as quality of service seems to have been maintained and has even improved recently in some respects in spite of the price-cap imposed upon residential services through the Kiwi share obligations.

More generally, while implementing a price-cap regime might certainly be an efficiency-inducing strategy to control the prices of telecommunications services, it should not be forgotten that competition remains the best way to impose continuous pressure on the prices of such services. This is well demonstrated, for example, by the drastic price reductions which were observed when Chile

---

[2] As we have seen, in the United States, price control was traditionally based on a rate-of-return regime, but in more recent years a growing number of state-level regulators have decided to rely on price caps.

switched from a regime of price regulation to a regime of unhindered competition in the national and international long-distance market. As competition spread in new segments of the telecommunications market, several of the countries examined here have progressively reassessed the scope of their price control regime—a point to which we return in Section B below.

3. Spectrum Allocation

Today, the most common way of allocating spectrum in the five countries under study is to organize simultaneous, ascending, multiple-round auctions. Other methods were used at first in some countries but problems arose which convinced the authorities to switch to simultaneous auctions (for example, the sealed bid, second price auctions used in New Zealand to award frequencies suitable for cellular telephony in 1990 yielded politically unpalatable results when it appeared that while the highest prices offered for two distinct bands were similar, the second prices—which determined the prices actually paid by the winners—were very different, with a large gap between the first and the second price for one of the bands). Overall, as discussed in Chapter 3, simultaneous auctions appear to be well suited to the allocation of multiple sets of resources (such as various spectrum bands) whose individual values, for a bidder, depend upon the number and identity of the sets that the bidder can acquire.

The use of simultaneous auctions to allocate 3G licences has been criticized, in particular in the United Kingdom, on the ground that bidders had paid too much for the licences and that the process would ultimately result in higher consumer prices and slower roll-out of networks. As pointed out in Chapter 3, however, such criticism appears to be misguided: after all, telecommunications operators are best placed to estimate the value of the licences, and once it is paid, the price of the licence is a sunk cost which should not, in most cases, affect future roll-out and price decisions.

Some of the countries examined have tried to introduce further flexibility into the use of spectrum through a variety of means. For instance, whereas spectrum rights allocated through auctions are generally very precisely defined and specify the type of technology to be used, New Zealand and Australia have developed technology neutral allocation systems which do not specify the exact use to which the frequencies have to be put and which allow the resale of spectrum rights. An important difference between these two countries, however, is that in New Zealand spectrum can be traded by spectrum managers—ie operators whose commercial activity is to subdivide the spectrum they acquire through auctions in the manner they consider appropriate and lease it to third party users—whereas this possibility does not exist in Australia.

In the United States and the United Kingdom, administrative obstacles currently impede the development of secondary markets in spectrum. In the United States, the FCC has, however, recently unveiled plans to stimulate the development of secondary markets. Among the options that the FCC plans to explore to stimulate such markets is the reliance on spectrum managers, an approach with which it has already experimented for a small part of the spectrum. Similarly, in May 1999, the British Government mandated the UK Radiocommunications Agency to develop detailed proposals to introduce spectrum trading. In its consultation paper initially released in 1998, the Radiocommunications Agency indicated that reliance on intermediaries who would be permitted to acquire blocks of spectrum for resale could be envisaged since such intermediaries could add depth to, and facilitate the functioning of, the market.

In sum, there is a trend in many of the countries examined here towards the development of spectrum trading. Two of those countries have in fact provided for the creation of spectrum managers. One advantage of relying on spectrum managers is that, since these operators derive their revenues from leasing their spectrum to other operators, they have every incentive to use the spectrum they own in the most effective fashion. From the point of view of spectrum users, the presence of spectrum managers may also reduce search costs and provide more flexibility to obtain access to the amount of spectrum that suits their need. The New Zealand experience suggests, however, that the successful development of such secondary markets does not only depend upon the design of the licensing regime, but also on local circumstances. In this country, the communications market may have been too small to support a successful resale market, a factor which may explain why such resale did not take place.

Recent spectrum auctions have also been successfully designed in many cases to promote new entry into the mobile market. In May 2000, for example, the UK Government reserved the largest 3G licence for a new entrant. In Australia and New Zealand, the latest 3G auctions imposed limits on the amount of spectrum which could be acquired by a single bidder in order to ensure that new entrants would be allocated part of the spectrum. And in Chile, the antitrust authorities have forced SUBTEL to increase the number of PCS licences on offer and to reduce the deposit guarantees required from the operators in order to facilitate new entry into the market for wireless local loop services.

4. Universal Service Obligations

Competitive mechanisms are also increasingly being used to allocate universal service subsidies. It is the Chilean experiment which has, so far, produced the most impressive results. In Chile, a system of competitive bidding has been used to allocate the public subsidies made available to improve telecommunications access in poor and rural areas. Besides the fact that it introduces competition *for* the market (thereby lowering the amount of subsidies needed to provide universal service), the system has other attractive features. For example, rural concessions have been granted to several distinct operators, thereby providing for some degree of benchmarking across regions. The operators' obligations are limited and clear, price controls reflect the high costs of rural telephony and selected operators remain largely free to choose the technology and project design which would prove most effective. The operators receive a large part of their subsidy in lump sums without indexation and only after the service is actually provided in order to give them strong incentives to become operational as soon as possible. Furthermore, the licences are not exclusive in order to leave the door open to the introduction of some degree of competition not only for, but also in, the market.

A reform of universal service has also been launched in the United States following the adoption of the 1996 Act. In order to ensure an adequate provision of telecommunications services in high cost areas in a more transparent manner than under the existing regime of implicit subsidies, the FCC set up a system whereby carriers offering services to customers located in such areas receive an 'explicit' subsidy, the amount of which is set by the FCC. Such subsidies are, however, portable so that competing carriers can pocket the subsidy by luring subsidized customers. Compared with the bidding system put in place in Chile, the main disadvantage of the US system is that the level of the subsidy is set administratively on the basis of a cost model developed by the FCC. Evaluating the costs of universal service is a notoriously difficult task for regulators and, as illustrated by the Australian experience (before a new system was put in place in 2000; see below), changes in the chosen cost model can suddenly entail large differences in the estimate of the amount of subsidy needed. There is thus a risk that the subsidy provided be too low or too high for the level of universal services required, though the forward-looking cost model chosen by the FCC will allow efficiency considerations to be taken into account. On the other hand, one advantage of the US system is that it places all operators on an equal footing and, thus, stimulates competition between them. Competitive pressures should in turn create incentives for operators to offer a high quality of service and have a downward effect on the overall prices of telecommunications services.[3]

Like Chile and the United States, Australia has, since 2000, introduced contestability in the provision of universal services. Until the adoption of this regime, Telstra had been designated *ex ante* as the only universal service provider and the costs of universal service obligations were calculated on the basis of an administratively set cost model, the modification of which led to much contention about the actual costs of universal service obligations from 1997 to 2000. Pursuant to the new regime, competition in universal service provision is introduced in two main ways.

First, a competitive tender was organized in October 2000 to select the operator which would gain access to a AU$150 million fund for the infrastructure upgrades necessary to enable the provision of unmetered local calls and related services outside the main cities. The successful bidder would also become the exclusive universal service provider in the areas concerned and would be eligible for the exclusive universal service obligation subsidies for a period of

---

[3] See Peter K Pitsch, 'Reforming Universal Service: Competitive Bidding or Consumer Choice?', Cato Institute Briefing Paper No 29, 7 May 1997.

three years. Like the Chilean regime, this new system introduces a degree of competition *for* the market. However, this system appears to have weaknesses. First, unlike in Chile, only one operator will be chosen to provide the service outside the main cities. This prevents any form of benchmarking between regions. Second, the tendering process does not bear on the level of subsidy required to provide the service, but on other, more qualitative, factors. The selection of a provider on the basis of these other factors does not directly promote a reduction of the overall cost of universal service provision (as the level of subsidy is determined in advance). This weakness has been identified by the Productivity Commission which, in its recent review of the Australian telecommunications regime, has argued in favour of adopting a system similar to the Chilean model, whereby the right to provide a pre-determined level of service would be auctioned to the bidder requiring the lowest subsidies.

In addition, two pilot schemes have been put into place to promote competition in the delivery of universal services in regional areas. Pursuant to such schemes, carriers designated by the ACA are entitled to compete with Telstra for the provision of universal services to 'subsidized' customers. These pilot schemes share some common features with the US regime discussed above as they rely on a system of portable subsidies. As we have seen, the downside of such an approach is that evaluating the level of the subsidy might not be an easy task, while the upside is that it promotes competition in the market between universal service providers.

The reform of universal service is less advanced in New Zealand and the United Kingdom. The regime in place in New Zealand until December 2001 could give rise to serious distortions of competition. A single operator (ie Telecom) was chosen *ex ante* to provide universal service and there did not seem to be any guarantee that the fees indirectly levied upon all operators through the interconnection price to compensate the universal service provider were adequately calibrated to cover the true costs of the service. Following the agreement reached between the Government and Telecom in December 2001, Telecom will remain the universal service provider, but the payments made by the operators to contribute to the costs of universal service will be paid directly to Telecom rather than indirectly through the interconnection price. Though this approach should increase the transparency of the system, it offers no guarantee that the compensation paid to Telecom will be adequate. In this regard, a competitive bidding system such as the one in place in Chile would have been preferable, but the Government has expressly rejected this approach, arguing that it would be too complex.

The UK situation shares similarities with that of New Zealand since BT has also been chosen *ex ante* as the country's sole universal service provider (with the small exception of the Hull area where universal service is provided by Kingston). However, unlike Telecom, BT does not receive any form of compensation for its universal mission since OFTEL considers that BT derives sufficient benefits from being a universal service provider. There is no guarantee, however, that this system is fair to all operators as it is not entirely clear that the costs that BT incurs to provide universal service are exactly compensated by the commercial advantages it supposedly derives from its status of universal service provider. Here again, one of the merits of establishing a competitive bidding system is that it would provide much more precise information about the true costs of providing universal service.

To illustrate the foregoing analysis, it is interesting to compare the net cost of universal service obligations as a percentage of total sector revenues in the five countries examined. Table 9.2 below shows that this percentage is relatively high in Australia, New Zealand, and the United States, but remarkably low in Chile and the United Kingdom.[4] Of course, this percentage will not only be determined by the efficiency of the mechanisms used to provide universal service, but also by the scope of universal service obligations, by the level of development of the telecommunications market and by geographical and other factors. Chile, for example, may benefit from a narrow definition of universal service obligations (based on one public phone per rural community rather than individual phones). But, on the other hand, it is clearly 'penalized' by the fact that the level of development of the telecommunications market (and therefore total telecommunications revenues) is certainly lower than in the other countries in our sample.

All in all, Chile appears to be a remarkable success with respect to universal service, both when compared to the other four countries and when the present situation in Chile is compared with the situation prior to the launch of competitive auctions (see figures mentioned in Chapter 7).

TABLE 9.2. Net cost of universal service obligations

Country	Percentage of total sector revenues
Australia	2.0%
Chile	0.2%
New Zealand	3.85%
United Kingdom	0.2%–0.3%
United States	5.0%

Sources: Bjorn Wellenius, 'Extending Telecommunications Beyond the Market—Toward Universal Service in Competitive Environments', 206 (2000) Viewpoint 7; Telecom Corporation of New Zealand Ltd, Telecommunications (Information Disclosure) Regulations 1999—Kiwi Share Obligation Loss Estimate, 31 March 2001.

[4] The figures in Table 9.2 do not take into account the recent modifications of the universal service regimes in Australia and the United States.

5. Overall Competitiveness of Service Provision in the Different Segments of the Market

On the whole, the market for fixed local service remains, in the five countries, the segment of the telecommunications market where effective competition has yet to be fully introduced. Several reasons can be advanced to explain this state of affairs. First, in some countries, such as the United States and Australia, the rates for residential services have traditionally been maintained at very low levels for political reasons and, in recent years, rate rebalancing has been slow. Such low rates might discourage entry or even make it impossible. Second, competition in the local market may have been hampered in some countries by the absence of specific rules in certain areas. As mentioned above, New Zealand, for example, has arguably suffered from the absence, until December 2001, of regulation pertaining to interconnection, unbundling, resale, and number portability, and the same may be true for Chile as far as number portability is concerned. Third, in the United States, the United Kingdom, Chile and Australia, regulations pertaining to interconnection and—even more so—to unbundling, have proven challenging to implement. In particular, the LRIC methodology which was chosen to price interconnection and unbundling services has given the incumbents incentives to adopt exclusionary behaviours to resist new entry into the local market and regulators have clearly had difficulties preventing such behaviours. In addition, in the United States, for instance, the implementation of unbundling requirements has been delayed by complex litigation between the FCC, the state utility commissions, and the Bell operators. In the United Kingdom, implementation has also been described as slow due to BT's foot-dragging and the lack of intervention by the regulator on issues such as space allocation in exchanges. In Australia, dispute resolution on price conditions for unbundled access to the local loop is proceeding very slowly. Finally, in Chile, no unbundling agreement has yet been reached between CTC and its competitors. Fourth, we have seen that in the United States, by conditioning the entry of the Bell operators into the long-distance market on the meeting of their interconnection obligations, the 1996 Telecommunications Act may in fact have contributed to delay, rather than accelerate, competition in local services.

Overall, the market share gained by new entrants, in both 'connections' and 'calls' markets, remains modest. As far as the connections market is concerned, incumbents' shares remain generally very high (eg Telstra still accounts for 95 per cent of connections in Australia and, in the United States, 91.5 per cent of exchange lines are still provided by the local incumbents). The fact that Telecom NZ retains 96 per cent of connections suggests that the absence of regulation on unbundling does not necessarily lead to intense facilities-based competition in the local market, even though such competition is now apparently starting to develop in New Zealand with the launch of residential services by Saturn in

Wellington and Christchurch. In Chile, on the other hand, where there were no pricing rules applicable to unbundling and resale until 1999, new entrants have managed to capture an 18 per cent share of the connections market. New entrants in the United Kingdom have also captured about 18 per cent of the connections market. This may be due in part to the Government's strategy of promoting facilities-based competition, which heavily relied on asymmetric regulation, and the presence of cable operators which already owned some local infrastructures may have enabled new entrants to acquire a higher share of the connections market. Still, the fact that the cable operators' share of the connections market is still limited to 18 per cent as in Chile suggests that facilities-based competition is not an easy strategy to implement.

New entrants have generally managed to capture a higher share of the calls market than of the connections market, though their shares of local calls revenues remain generally limited, with the exception of the United Kingdom where they reach 25 per cent for residential users and slightly over 30 per cent for business users. The difference between the calls and the connections market can be explained by the competition brought about by operators that did not establish their own facilities, such as resellers. In Australia, for instance, resellers have captured 14 per cent of local market revenues. As we have noted, the prices at which wholesale services are sold will determine the margins of the operators and, thus, their ability to enter the market and capture market shares. Finally, it should be noted that competition in the local market, where it exists, has so far been limited to the main urban areas, mostly the central business districts of the larger cities. Chile is in fact the only country where the incumbent does not have a monopoly or a quasi-monopoly over rural areas, but even in Chile, there is no competition in the market in rural areas.

The national long-distance market has generally been much more competitive than the local market in each of the five countries. The provision of fixed long-distance services appears to be the most competitive in the United Kingdom, the United States, and in Chile. The price comparisons presented in the Annex confirm the competitiveness of these three markets, which are the cheapest in prices based on PPPs (see Graphs 4a and 4b).

In the United States, the markets for local and long-distance services remained separated until 1996 but strong competition had, by that time, developed between different long-distance providers. As we have seen, the impact of the provisions of the 1996 Act aimed at letting the Bell operators enter the long-distance market has been fairly limited so far, as only a few such operators have been allowed to provide long-distance services from their local market since the adoption of the Act. Some observers have argued that a quicker entry of the Bell operators in the long-distance market would have introduced further competition in the market with corresponding reductions in prices. In recent months, long-distance prices have, however, been rapidly falling due to over-capacity in the sector and it is not clear whether the entry of BOCs would lead to further significant price reductions. In Chile, the local and long-distance markets remained quasi-separate as well until 1994 and, unlike in the United States, were each monopolized by one dominant operator. From 1994 onward, the multi-carrier system, and the strength of the local operator's challenge in the long-distance market, quickly introduced a substantial degree of competition in the provision of long-distance services. As early as 1995, ENTEL's market share had fallen below 50 per cent. In the United Kingdom, a distinction must be made between the individual household market (still dominated by BT) and the business users' market which is increasingly competitive (with BT's market share falling below 50 per cent) due to the presence of companies (such as Mercury) especially targeting such users.

New Zealand and Australia might have been somewhat handicapped by the presence of a dominant company operating in both the local and the long-distance markets, though this factor was also present in the United Kingdom. In New Zealand, besides the presence of an integrated operator, the introduction of strong competition in long-distance has likely been hampered by the lack of clear interconnection rules until December 2001. As far as Australia is concerned, the rather disappointing performance with respect to national long-distance services might also be explained by the fact that this market remained a duopoly until 1997. Commentators predict, however, that the entry of facilities-based operators on major backbone routes and increasing competition in the local market are likely to bring about more intense competition in the Australian national long-distance market in the near future.

Competition is even more intense in the market for international, rather than national, services, with the incumbent's market revenue share well below 50 per cent in all five countries. The relative strengths and weaknesses of each country in the international market are relatively similar to those that they exhibit in the national long-distance market. The main difference concerns Australia which appears to be a lot more competitive in the international market according to the price comparisons presented in the Annex, while it is the prices of New Zealand and Chile which appear to be the highest, at least when based on PPPs (see Graphs 5a and 5b, and 6a and 6b).

Competition in mobile services is now fierce in four of the five countries (Australia, Chile, the United States and the United Kingdom) and in these four countries prices have decreased sharply. In Australia, four operators are competing with each other and the market share of Telstra is now below 50 per cent. The sharp price reductions that took place during the 1997–2000 period have promoted a rapid increase in mobile services penetration, which is now among the highest in the world. In the United Kingdom, little competition took place during the duopoly period which lasted until 1993. The two incumbents, Cellnet and Vodafone, adopted parallel pricing and sought to restrict competition in the retail market by tying a maximum of independent service providers to their network. The entry into the market of One2One and Orange in 1993 and 1994 respectively has led to sharp price reductions which make UK mobile services among the cheapest in the world (our price comparisons in the Annex show that UK mobile prices based on PPPs are the cheapest of the five countries—see Graphs 11a and 11b, and 12a and 12b).

Similarly, in the United States and Chile, prices substantially decreased only after at least three operators started to operate in most geographic areas. The Chilean mobile market now comprises six operators and we have seen that in the United States the vast majority of metropolitan areas have at least five wireless providers. In the United States, the penetration rate of wireless services is, however, lower than one would anticipate. This relatively low penetration rate (32 per cent nationwide) is essentially due to the fact that most states continue to keep fixed telephony residential rates low, thereby reducing the incentives for consumers to substitute wireless for wireline services, and to the lack of a 'calling-party-pays' tariff scheme, which acts as a disincentive for consumers to use wireless phones as a way to receive incoming calls.

In New Zealand, on the other hand, the price of cellular services remains relatively high and, until recently, the penetration rate of wireless services was quite low. The price comparisons provided in the Annex show that the prices of cellular services both in current US dollars and in prices based on PPPs are higher in New Zealand than in the other four countries (see Graphs 11a, 11b, 12a and 12b). As in the case of spectrum resale, New Zealand might suffer from the small size of its market and from the fact that only two operators, including the local incumbent Telecom, have so far been active in that market. In recent months, penetration rates have, however, improved and the market share of the incumbent's competitor (Vodafone) is increasing fast. As pointed out in Chapter 5, this more vibrant market might be due to the fact that the two operators are preparing for a more competitive environment following the recent auction of 3G licences which will promote the entry of additional competitors into the mobile market.

Internet penetration has grown very rapidly these last few years in each of the five countries. As far as residential users are concerned, the cost of using the Internet, which in turn drives the growth of Internet use, essentially depends upon the local telephone charges (most residential users rely on dial-up access) and the fees charged by the ISPs. Regarding telephone rates, Australia, New Zealand and the United States have unmetered local telephone charges, a pricing regime which is conducive to the growth of Internet use as users do not feel constrained about the amount of time they spend online. Furthermore, price competition between ISPs has contributed to keep the prices of using the Internet low and, in these three countries, ISPs now offer unmetered Internet access pricing regimes. It should therefore come as no surprise that Australia, New Zealand and the United States figure among the six OECD countries that have greater than average penetration of both Internet hosts and servers (see Figure 9.1 below).

In the United Kingdom, local telephone operators have traditionally offered metered services, a factor which may help explain why the United Kingdom has lagged behind Australia, New Zealand and the United States in terms of Internet

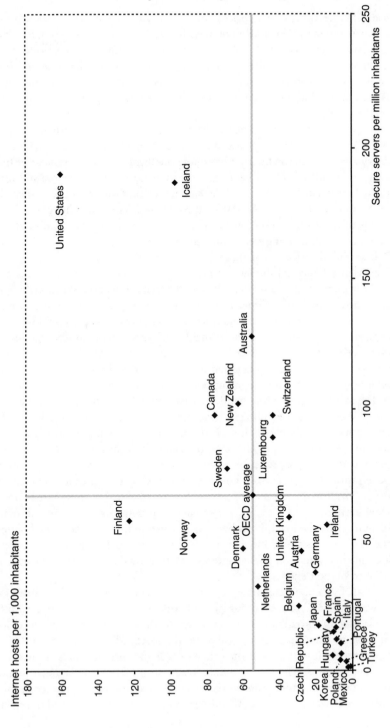

FIGURE 9.1. Penetration of Internet Hosts and Secure Servers in OECD Countries

Source: OECD, Local Access Pricing and E-Commerce, DSTI/ICCP/PSIP (2000) 1/Final, July 2000, 32.

use. On the other hand, prices for ISP services have been driven down by competition in the United Kingdom with several companies offering free Internet access as early as 1999. Moreover, some operators are now offering fully unmetered Internet services, comprising both the local telephone and Internet access charges (one such scheme, the unmetered FRIACO scheme offered by BT, is used for the Internet price comparisons presented in the Annex, Graphs 9a, 9b, 10a, and 10b).

However, a metered regime for the pricing of local services remains applicable in Chile and, while drastic cuts in the price charged for the use of the fixed local network to access the Internet has made the local access component of Internet usage more affordable to Chileans, this metered local call regime still tends to make Internet costs higher in Chile than in the other four countries, especially for heavy Internet users (see Annex, Graphs 9a, 9b). As in the other countries, price competition between ISPs has been particularly intense lately and in 2000 four operators were offering free unlimited Internet access.

It seems, therefore, that there is a broad trend in the five countries towards increased reliance on unmetered pricing regimes both for local access charges and for Internet access services. While this trend will certainly contribute to the sustained growth of Internet use, some observers have expressed concern that reliance on unmetered price regimes will inevitably create congestion in the local network. However, given the difficulty of establishing price regimes which effectively reflect congestion levels (see Chapter 3), the best way to address congestion, as we have suggested above, may well be to provide an enabling environment for the development of alternatives to dial-up access.

The availability of broadband Internet access is growing in all five countries, yet at a slower rate than might have been anticipated. There is still insufficient competition in the market for ADSL services which remains largely dominated by the local incumbent. This lack of competition has generally prevented the introduction of low prices for ADSL services and has, in turn, slowed down the penetration of such services. One key reason why competition has failed to take off is certainly the absence of unbundling of the local loop requirements (as in New Zealand until now) or, where such requirements exist, their slow implementation by the local incumbent (as in Australia, Chile, the United States and the United Kingdom). In each of the latter countries, disputes arose between incumbents and companies interested in providing ADSL services, which delayed market entry.

In all five countries, some degree of competition in broadband services is, however, being brought about by cable operators, which have started offering cable modem broadband Internet access to their consumers. The development of cable modem Internet access has been particularly spectacular in the United States where it is at present the prime broadband Internet access technology for residential users. The United States and Australia are also playing a pioneering role on the regulatory front in that area. As mentioned in Chapter 4, the FTC authorized the AOL/Time Warner merger subject to the condition that the merged entity make available to subscribers some non-affiliated broadband ISP services on Time Warner's cable—a decision which is widely seen by commentators as a first step toward the imposition of broader open access requirements upon cable operators. In Australia, the ACC's declaration of analogue Pay-TV broadcast carriage services is also seen by some commentators as an important open access principle which could be applied to other broadband networks in the future. However, except in the United States, cable suffers from network coverage limitation, especially in Chile where cable penetration is limited to 42 subscribers per 1,000 inhabitants.

The foregoing analysis shows the existence of broadly consistent trends in the development of competition in telecommunications in the five countries examined here. First, with some limited variations, a relatively high degree of competition has now been introduced in the markets for international and national long-distance, mobile and Internet services. Competition in such market segments has been facilitated by the presence of a range of sector-specific requirements, including rules over interconnection, number portability, resale, and carrier pre-selection for example. By contrast, there is still a flagrant lack of competition in the local segment of the market with the incumbent operators still controlling the vast majority of the fixed access lines. Due to the high costs involved, facilities-based competition has so far been limited (even in countries, such as the United Kingdom where it has been promoted through asymmetric regulation) and regulatory requirements designed to facilitate entry into the local segment through resale or—even more so—through unbundling requirements have so far proven very difficult to implement in large part due to the regulators' inability to prevent local incumbents from resorting to exclusionary tactics.

6. Vertical Integration or Vertical Separation?

A question which has been raised in all five countries is whether, when the various segments of the telecommunications market are open to competition, operators should be allowed to remain vertically integrated. There is indeed a clear incentive for a vertically integrated operator of bottleneck facilities (ie the local exchange segment) to distort competition in other market segments (for example, by providing more favourable interconnection conditions to itself than to its competitors) or in the bottleneck segment itself (for example, by preventing resale or unbundled access in order to maintain its dominance over this segment).

With regard to the risk that competition be distorted in non-bottleneck segments, a distinction can be made here between the countries in which a vertical separation existed between the local market and other markets at the time of liberalization (ie Chile and the United States) and those in which vertically integrated companies were present (ie the United Kingdom, New Zealand and Australia). Interestingly, none of the last three countries decided to get rid of these vertically integrated companies as a way to prevent anti-competitive behaviours in the newly liberalized markets. In the United Kingdom, there was a strong belief on the part of the UK Government and the telecommunications regulator that their strategy of facilities-based competition would soon create competition in the local loop, thereby preventing BT from leveraging its market power in that segment to distort competition in other segments of the telecommunications market.[5] In New Zealand, the Government was satisfied with the incumbent's undertaking that it would restructure the company so as to entrust local, long-distance, and mobile services to different subsidiaries dealing with each other on an arm's length basis. And in Australia, the authorities trusted that the sophisticated access regime put in place at the time of liberalization would facilitate competition in the long-distance and mobile markets. In Chile and the United States, the restrictions on the local exchange operator to provide long-distance services were lifted following liberalization (in both cases subject to conditions).

The above observations raise two questions. The first is whether Chile and the United States were wrong to have introduced a separation between the local and long-distance segments in the 1980s. The response is probably negative for two reasons. First, as shown by the US experience, in the absence of a detailed interconnection regime, the separation between the local and the long-distance segment permitted a rapid, unimpeded development of competition in long-distance services. Second, as illustrated by the case of Chile, the separation between the two segments permitted the development of strong companies in both sectors which, once the vertical separation was removed, could strongly challenge each other in their respective markets.

The second question is whether vertical separation could be usefully introduced today in some of the five countries as a way to strengthen competition in the long-distance and mobile segments of the telecommunications market. Once again, it is suggested that the answer is likely to be negative, mainly because competition is clearly taking hold in these segments in all five countries. In four of the five countries examined, the ability of vertically integrated companies to use their control of the local infrastructure to discriminate against long-distance or mobile competitors is constrained by the imposition of detailed interconnection regimes. The successful adoption of 'non-structural' regulatory safeguards has thus reduced the need for structural solutions. The only exception is New Zealand where the absence of interconnection rules initially made it more difficult for new entrants to obtain access to the incumbent's local infrastructure. A number of interconnection agreements have, however, now been concluded and specific interconnection rules have been adopted. On balance, it thus seems that the introduction of a vertical separation no longer seems justified in the five countries to prevent local exchange operators from using their control of bottleneck facilities to impede competition in the other segments of the market.

---

[5] We have also seen that another factor contributing to the UK Government's decision to maintain BT intact was to avoid delays in the firm's privatization process.

The situation in the local market is, however, markedly different. As seen above, the local market is still largely dominated by the incumbents and regulators have found it very difficult to force these companies to implement the unbundling requirements that are now contained in all five countries' regulatory frameworks. Given the lack of effectiveness of the regulatory approach, some observers have suggested the need for structural solutions, and in particular for introducing a separation between the incumbents' local infrastructure and wholesale activities on the one hand, and their local retail activities on the other hand. As we have seen in Chapter 3, one of the potential weaknesses of structural solutions is that they might generate a loss of economies of scope. However, the fact that large telecommunications conglomerates such as BT and AT&T, as well as new operators such as TransACT in Australia, are voluntarily separating previously integrated activities into distinct companies tends to suggest that the economies of scope which result from integration are probably lower than previously anticipated. Unlike a few years ago where mega-mergers were raging, today's marketplace seems to favour specialist companies competing within their fields of expertise.[6]

Overall, structural measures seem to be particularly warranted when the following conditions are present:

(i) competition in the local loop is limited;
(ii) unbundling is either not required or difficult to implement;
(iii) there is no specialized telecommunications regulator or this regulator is weak and, thus, appears unable to enforce non-structural safeguards; and
(iv) there seems to be few competitors strong enough to enter the local market and mount a strong challenge to the incumbent.

While some of these conditions—and in particular the first two—apply to all five countries, it could be argued that structural reforms might deserve particularly close consideration in Chile, because of some concerns regarding regulatory independence and capacity, and in New Zealand, because the new regulatory framework is still untested and because of the particularly strong dominance that Telecom still exercises in the local market.

Summary

1. Simply removing formal barriers to entry into the various segments of the telecommunications market is insufficient, per se, to promote competition effectively in all segments of the market. The most important additional measure that is needed is to provide for clear rules on interconnection—and in particular on interconnection pricing—to be implemented by a specialized regulator.

(continuous)

---

[6] See, eg, 'When Big is No Longer Beautiful', *The Economist*, 16 December 2000, 91.

(continued)

2. Specific rules on number portability and carrier pre-selection (and, even better, selection on a call-by-call basis) may be useful as well, to promote competition.

3. Given the costs and economies of scale involved in deploying fixed local telecommunications networks, clear rules on interconnection and number portability are likely to be insufficient to enable effective competition in the local market. Additional rules mandating access to the incumbent's network through resale or unbundling may help. Rules on unbundled access to the local loop are, however, particularly difficult to implement and require sophisticated regulatory capacity.

4. All methods used to calculate the price of wholesale services (LRIC, ECPR, etc) have pros and cons. Hence, the selection of a method in any given country should depend on the policy goals which the government seeks to achieve, as well as on the specifics of the telecommunications market in question, and, in particular, on the degree of market power which the incumbent is able to exercise and the level of regulatory capacity. International benchmarking of wholesale prices should be considered, especially when regulatory resources are limited, as an alternative to, or as a check on, the use of cost-based models.

5. Introducing effective competition in the market is a far more efficient way of imposing downward pressure on retail prices than imposing direct controls on such prices. Retail price regulation does remain necessary, however, as long as competition cannot be relied upon to introduce sufficient market discipline on the provision of certain services.

6. To the extent that retail prices need to be regulated, a price-cap regime has the advantage, over a rate-of-return regime, of promoting efficiency on the part of the operators. To really promote efficiency, however, it is essential that caps be set for rather long periods and that, when rates are modified, the regulator refrain from attempting to claw back past profits. As a price-cap regime generates more risks for investors than a rate-of-return regime, successful implementation of a price-cap regime requires sufficient regulatory capacity and credibility. When a price-cap regime is adopted, measures should also be taken to ensure that cost savings do not translate into lower quality.

7. The telephone rate structure should be rebalanced as soon as possible since below-cost tariffs introduce distortions of competition and might prevent entry into market segments where prices are maintained artificially low (a frequent problem in the local market, for example).

8. Unmetered local telephone charges are an effective way to promote Internet penetration. In order to avoid congestion of the local network, however, an enabling environment should be provided for the development of alternatives to dial-up access.

(continuous)

(continued)

9. Spectrum should be allocated through competitive auctions. When regulatory capacity is sufficient and when different bands are to be allocated, the value of which would depend, for a bidder, on the number and identity of the bands which that bidder does acquire, simultaneous, multiple round auctions should generally be preferred. Auctions should also be designed to promote sufficient entry to ensure an adequate level of competition in the market.

10. Public authorities should ensure maximum flexibility in the use of spectrum and should give consideration to introducing technology-neutral, tradable, spectrum management rights, which leave the spectrum manager complete freedom to determine how the spectrum is to be subdivided and used.

11. Competitive pressures should also be brought to bear on the provision of universal services. One possibility is to select USO providers on the basis of the lowest subsidy requested, with different providers operating in different geographical areas so as to establish the conditions for some yardstick competition. A second possibility is to promote direct competition between providers by designing a system of portable subsidies which enables users to choose among competing providers.

12. Given the difficulty of introducing substantial competition in the local market, even when the telephone rate structure has been rebalanced and when appropriate rules on interconnection, carrier pre-selection, number portability, resale, and local loop unbundling are in place, it may be advisable to give serious consideration to imposing separation between the deployment of local infrastructure and the provision of local wholesale services on the one hand, and local retail activities on the other hand.

13. In addition to the sector-specific rules mentioned above, general antitrust rules remain essential for the economic regulation of telecommunications. Antitrust rules are needed—and indeed are best suited—to deal with a range of issues of economic regulation which are not addressed by sector-specific rules. While recourse to antitrust law will often be sub-optimal to address issues which should be tackled through sector-specific regulation, antitrust rules may play a useful residual role and fill gaps which might exist in sector-specific regulatory regimes.

B. Specificity versus coherence

The balance between specificity and coherence was originally set in a significantly different manner in the five countries under study, although we will see that four of the five countries appear to be converging toward a similar balance.

First, a contrast can be drawn between the 'light-handed' regulatory approach originally adopted in New Zealand, on the one hand, and the 'heavy-handed' regulatory approach adopted in the United States and in the United Kingdom, on the other hand. As we have seen, New Zealand has, until December 2001, essentially relied on general antitrust rules to regulate telecommunications. The advantage of this approach is that it ensures some coherence in the way market power is controlled in different network industries and across the economy in general. The New Zealand experience, however, also reveals the shortcomings of general antitrust rules. First, those rules seem insufficiently precise to adequately solve interconnection, number portability, and carrier pre-selection issues. In addition, the absence of specific rules on local service resale and local loop unbundling appears to hinder new entry into the local market (especially for the provision of advanced services such as xDSL services). Moreover, antitrust rules fail to distinguish between regulatory solutions which are relatively easy or very difficult to apply in practice. For instance, we have seen that, when assessing the legality of an ECPR-based interconnection price under s 36, the Privy Council assumed that it did not have to consider the practical difficulties involved with reliance on such a methodology. Finally, several commentators have noted that, as antitrust rules are usually designed to prevent distortions of competition, they may be ill-suited to introducing competition in markets where no competition existed before and they could lead in some cases to sub-optimal vertical deintegration (in order to be able to charge high interconnection charges without being accused of distorting competition, the monopolist may simply decide to operate only in the bottleneck market and not in the downstream competitive market even if economies of scale or scope would dictate vertical integration). Such problems are compounded, in New Zealand, by the lack of a specialized regulator.

As we have seen, the shortcomings of this 'light-handed' approach have led the Government to launch reforms leading to the adoption of sector-specific rules covering, inter alia, interconnection, number portability, and local service resale, to be implemented by a specialized regulator. Such reforms introduce a better balance between specificity and coherence. Indeed, while such reforms inevitably increase the specificity of the New Zealand regulatory regime, the overall coherence of this regime does not appear to be seriously threatened as the number of specific rules remains limited, efforts have been made to ensure that these rules would not be overly specific or overly complicated (eg through reliance on benchmarking to set interconnection prices as pointed out above) and it is a Commissioner located within the economy-wide Commerce Commission who is in charge of implementing these rules.

An opposite approach has been followed in the United States and in the United Kingdom where great emphasis has been placed on the adoption of detailed, highly prescriptive rules (in the United States these rules are inserted in congressional acts and administrative orders and in the United Kingdom in the operators' licences) to be implemented by a sector-specific regulator. As far as the regulators are concerned, a distinction can be made between the United States and the United Kingdom. While OFTEL is only competent to regulate the telecommunications industry, the FCC also has the ability to regulate the broadcasting industry. This difference might, however, have little practical significance and seems set to disappear. On the one hand, the FCC has been criticized for being structured along rigid sectional lines with different bureaus taking care of different industries.[7] On the other hand, we have seen that the UK Government is planning to dismantle OFTEL and replace it with a communications-wide regulator, which would be competent to deal with both telecommunications and broadcasting. Some observers also make a distinction between the US and the UK regimes on the ground that the former imposes heavier requirements on the local incumbents (especially in terms of access to the local network) than the latter.[8] Overall, both regimes are, however, highly specific and thus could arguably be criticized for losing sight of the growing similarities which are developing between telecommunications and other sectors of the economy. In the case of the United Kingdom, several factors tend to suggest that the telecommunications regulatory regime should gain in coherence in the years to come. In recent policy documents, OFTEL clearly indicated that it would increasingly rely in the future on the prohibitions in the Competition Act 1998 to control market power in telecommunications. OFTEL also indicated that, to the extent that some specific rules need to be applied to supplement competition rules, these rules should be generic in order to promote regulatory consistency.

The Chilean and Australian models both attempt to strike a balance between the more extreme approaches initially adopted in New Zealand, on the one hand, and in the United States and the United Kingdom, on the other hand. Both models seek to add to general antitrust rules where needed without establishing an unduly specific regulatory regime. In Chile, the regime adopted in 1982 provided insufficient clarity on a number of specific issues, in particular on interconnection conditions, and, as in New Zealand, reliance on antitrust rules and institutions to solve those issues proved unsatisfactory. Additional rules on retail and wholesale prices, as well as on carrier selection, greatly helped to introduce much stronger competitive pressures in the telecommunications market. At this stage, some steps could be considered to strengthen the overall coherence of the regulatory framework, such as entrusting the main regulatory functions to an infrastructure-wide regulator or limiting the application of sector-specific norms and technical standards to services provided in non-competitive markets. On the other hand, more specific rules would be needed on number portability.

In Australia, efforts have been made to ensure the overall coherence of the regulatory framework by incorporating sector-specific rules within the

[7] See Adam D Thierer, 'A 10-Point Agenda for Comprehensive Telecom Reform', Cato Institute Briefing Paper No 63, 8 May 2001, 4.

[8] See NERA, 'Costs of Telecommunications Competition Policies', report prepared for Telecom New Zealand, 9 May 2000.

economy-wide antitrust legislation and by conferring responsibility for implementing those rules on a single economy-wide antitrust authority.

Another particularly interesting feature of the Australian model, which can also be found in Chile and in the United States, is that the need for some sector-specific rules is to be reassessed by the authorities. In Australia, the Productivity Commission was called upon to assess whether some telecommunications-specific rules were still justified and the ACCC also reviews some of its service declarations at regular intervals. In Chile, antitrust authorities are in charge of determining the range of services to which the pricing rules apply (entrusting such a task to an economy-wide authority is a wise decision, as noted above, since a sector-specific regulator would probably have built-in incentives to maximize the scope of sector-specific regulation). In the United States, the 1996 Act authorizes the FCC to forbear from applying provisions of the Act if it determines that such forbearance 'will promote competitive market conditions'. The FCC is also required by the Act to review every two years all of its rules that apply to telecommunications service providers and to repeal or modify those rules that are no longer necessary in the public interest. This is a very positive step since many sector-specific rules are likely to be needed during a transition period only. Indeed, while general antitrust rules might be ill-suited to deal with markets where no competition exists or to provide specific solutions to new technical issues, they might suffice when competition has developed and information has been generated on how to tackle particular technical issues.

Thus, in Australia, the ACCC has recently deregulated transmission services between cities and the scope of price controls imposed upon Telstra has been reduced. In Chile, as competition spread, a growing number of services have been exempted from the application of telecommunications-specific pricing regimes. In the United States, the FCC has used its forbearance power to deregulate domestic long-distance services and international exchange services. Nor is the trend likely to stop there. We noted, for example, that in Australia, the gap between ACCC-determined access prices and commercially offered prices was narrowing over time, while it appears that interconnection negotiations are progressively becoming easier in the New Zealand local market—two pieces of evidence that the need for detailed sector-specific rules is likely to decrease over time.

As mentioned above, and as is the case in Chile, still more could arguably be done in Australia to align the regime applicable to the economic regulation of telecommunications with the one adopted in other sectors of the economy. Some sector-specific rules either do not seem to add much to economy-wide or infrastructure-wide rules, or could be used as a basis for establishing a single set of better designed rules applicable to the whole economy or at least to multiple sectors. In this regard, the Productivity Commission's proposal to review the need for telecommunications-specific provisions of Part XIB in three to five years, and to align more closely the provisions of Part IIIA and Part XIC would seem to be a step in the right direction as we have indicated above.

FIGURE 9.2. Specificity vs coherence

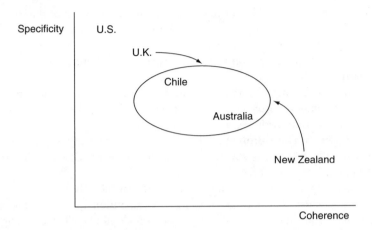

Overall, as illustrated in Figure 9.2 above, four of the five regulatory regimes analysed in this book (Australia, Chile, New Zealand, and the United Kingdom) seem to be progressively converging towards a balance between specificity and coherence. Progressive shifts of emphasis are particularly noticeable in New Zealand (where the regime gained in specificity through the adoption of some sector-specific rules implemented by a specialized body within the Commerce Commission) and in the United Kingdom (where the regulatory framework will gain in coherence through increased reliance on competition rules and the creation of a communications-wide regulatory body). This 'middle of the road' approach seems to be particularly well suited to a context where the telecommunications industry is progressively converging with other industries (both within the communications sector and beyond), but where the need for specific rules might still remain for some time. Only the United States, where rules continue to be extremely detailed and specific, seems not to be converging towards the same balance. Changes in the leadership of the FCC following the election of President George W Bush suggest that this institution might, however, adopt a more deregulatory stance in the months and years to come.[9]

Summary

1. As mentioned in Section A, a set of sector-specific rules on interconnection, number portability, operator pre-selection (or selection on a call-by-call basis), resale, local loop unbundling, as well as some retail price regulation in non-competitive market segments, and, in some cases perhaps, vertical separation between local infrastructure and local retail activities, still appear to be useful to enable and deepen competition in the various segments of the

(continuous)

[9] See Randolph May, 'A Reform Agenda for the New FCC', 5 (2001) *Info* 407.

(continued)

telecommunications market at the present stage of evolution of that market in the five countries under study. To the extent that adoption of sector-specific rules does remain necessary, the number as well as the degree of specificity and sophistication of such rules should be kept to the minimum required.

2. One way to ensure a greater degree of coherence between telecommunications and other industry sectors, is to integrate telecommunications-specific rules into economy-wide regulatory frameworks.

3. Another way to promote coherence is to entrust implementation of sector-specific rules to a specialized economy-wide regulator with strong telecommunications expertise.

4. Sector-specific rules should be reviewed periodically with a view to eliminating those that become obsolete as competition spreads in the telecommunications market. Such a review process should be carried out by an economy-wide body rather than a sector-specific agency whose *raison d'être* might depend on the existence of such rules.

C. Flexibility versus certainty

The UK and the Chilean models are arguably the ones that put the strongest emphasis on regulatory certainty. Making a policy reversal by a future Labour Government impossible was a key objective of the ruling Conservative Party when it decided to privatize BT and to liberalize the telecommunications market in the mid-1980s. With this objective in mind, the British Government opted for a system of detailed licences that could only be modified through a complex procedure. Highly detailed and hard-to-modify licences clarify the rights and obligations of each operator and reduce the amount of discretion left to the regulator. In this regard, one benefit of the British model is that it led to comparatively less litigation over the interpretation of rules than regulatory models adopted in other countries. The highly specific nature of the licences and the fact that they are hard to modify tend, however, to make it difficult to adapt the regulatory framework to new market circumstances and, thus, introduce an excessive amount of rigidity in the system. The imposition of price-caps on baskets of services—rather than on individual services—provides, on the other hand, some flexibility to the operators. The streamlining of the regulatory framework that is envisaged by the British Government notably through the use of less intrusive regulatory mechanisms such as self-regulation or co-regulation, as well as OFTEL's greater reliance on the powers it holds under the Competition Act 1998, should also introduce a greater degree of flexibility into the British regulatory regime in the future.

As modified by the 1987 and 1994 amendments to the General Telecommunications Law, the Chilean model also places great emphasis on regulatory certainty: the price regime is very precise, conditions of entry into various segments of the markets are set out in detail, and the overall regime is particularly difficult to modify because numerous regulatory details are embedded in laws whose modification generally requires difficult compromises between the legislative and executive branches and because the transfer of shares of the privatized companies to a wide range of stakeholders makes a reversal of the reforms unlikely. As argued above, the direct regulatory powers that are retained by the Executive introduce a small but unnecessary degree of uncertainty, and they could therefore be reduced. In addition, imposing price-caps on baskets of services rather than on individual services and limiting the scope of quality standards could probably increase flexibility without introducing much additional uncertainty. Overall, however, the Chilean regime, as it stands, appears to have served the interests of the country rather well, as it has convinced numerous private investors and operators to get involved in the telecommunications market and to contribute to the investments which increased phone penetration rates at a fast pace during the late 1980s and 1990s, in spite of the risks normally associated with developing economies.

By relying on general antitrust rules to be enforced by court decisions, New Zealand, on the other hand, opted until December 2001 for the most flexible of the five regulatory models. However, such an approach arguably introduced too much uncertainty in the regulatory process. Contradictory decisions over fundamental issues such as interconnection pricing, for example, have been rendered by different courts. The fact that the courts intervened *ex-post* and the very long periods of time required to reach final decisions also contributed to increase uncertainty. In addition, the reliance on government intervention to secure certain agreements between operators and the existence of a price-control regime which—although it has not been used so far—gives broad powers to the Government could certainly cause concern among investors as it opens the door to politically motivated and unpredictable regulatory decisions. The New Zealand experiment with respect to spectrum rights allocation, on the other hand, appears well designed to increase flexibility without introducing unwarranted uncertainty. The reforms recently adopted should help reduce, to a large extent, the level of uncertainty which existed in the sector.

The United States and Australia, have, for their part, striven to accommodate both flexibility and certainty requirements in more equal measures. In the United States, the risks of excess rigidity often associated with the adoption of a large set of specific rules have been reduced, inter alia, through the use of a broad public interest standard which leaves relatively wide discretion to the FCC and through the power which is given to the FCC to forbear from applying some provisions of the 1996 Telecommunications Act when certain conditions are met. Some observers have criticized the public interest standard as granting excessive power to the FCC.[10] However, as the FCC is generally recognized as a reasonably competent and independent institution, it does not appear misguided to give it broad latitude to tailor decisions to the evolving circumstances. The US regulatory regime is not, however, free from unnecessary uncertainty, in particular due to insufficient statutory guidance on some critical issues, such as the allocation of competencies between federal and state regulators.

In Australia, flexibility comes, in a somewhat similar fashion as in the United States, from the discretion that is given to the ACCC through the application of the broad long-term interests of end-users (LTIE) test. Certainty is enhanced, however, through publication, by the ACCC, of guidelines and discussion papers on the way the regulatory agency intends to perform its functions. As argued with respect to the FCC above, one can submit that the competence and legitimacy of the ACCC does justify the degree of discretionary power that it has been granted. The overall framework could, however, still be improved if some sources of uncertainty were eliminated. For example, the broad regulatory powers left to the Minister for Communications and the Arts with respect inter alia to the adoption of industry development plans, the regulation of pricing of universal services, the regulation of the incumbent's tariffs, and the adoption of performance standards give an excessively wide degree of discretionary power to a political authority and may, thus, raise private investors' concerns, especially since the Government remains one of the incumbent operator's shareholders. In addition, the existence, within the Trade Practices Act of multiple rules potentially applicable to the same issues (we have seen, for example, that abuses of a dominant position with respect to interconnection could potentially be tackled by four distinct sets of rules), introduces an unwarranted degree of uncertainty in the regulatory framework. Finally, the Productivity Commission has argued that access pricing principles should be incorporated in the legislation in order to enhance regulatory certainty.

Summary

1. The balance between flexibility and certainty should vary depending on a number of factors, such as the degree of confidence one can have in the overall predictability of the regulatory regime and the competence and independence of all entities entrusted with regulatory authority. The greater the predictability of the regulatory regime and the competence and independence of the regulator, the wider the scope for introducing flexibility in the system.

2. The nature of the regulatory instruments will determine, to some extent, the degree of flexibility of the regulatory regime. Different instruments will, however, yield different degrees of flexibility in different institutional contexts and the choice of instruments should therefore depend upon the institutional

(continuous)

---

[10] See, eg Thierer (n 7 above) 7.

(continued)

characteristics of the relevant country. Laws, for example, can generally be modified through co-operation between the executive and the legislative branches. Modifications will thus be easier in systems that require that the executive have the support of a majority in parliament than in systems where different political forces may dominate those two types of institutions.

3. Governments should not be given broad discretionary powers over key regulatory issues as this may cause concerns among investors about politically motivated and unpredictable regulatory decisions. Such concerns will usually be heightened when the government retains ownership of telecommunications operators.

4. Antitrust authorities and courts should not be relied upon to take decisions on untested, complex, telecommunications-specific issues, on the basis of general antitrust rules. The fact that those authorities tend to intervene *ex-post*, that judicial proceedings are likely to be long, and that contradictory decisions may be taken by different bodies is likely to raise uncertainty to unacceptable levels.

5. The insertion of public interest-type standards into regulatory regimes is a valid way of introducing flexibility into the system when the regulator in charge of applying such standards is sufficiently competent and independent. Requiring that the regulator publish guidelines on the way it will exercise its powers may increase certainty without unduly limiting the flexibility of the regulatory regime.

6. Applying price-caps to baskets of services instead of individual services is another way of introducing some flexibility without unduly increasing uncertainty.

7. Adoption of multiple rules applicable to the same issues should be avoided as it creates uncertainty as to which rules will be applied in a specific case.

8. On the other hand, the lack of any rule on certain key issues—such as the allocation of powers between federal and state entities for example—also creates unnecessary uncertainty.

D. REGULATORY COMPETENCE AND ABILITY TO RESIST UNDUE PRESSURE

As pointed out in Chapter 2, the need for highly competent regulators can be mitigated to some extent through reliance on competition rather than regulation to ensure that operators provide the telecommunications services that users want at the highest possible quality–price ratio. Reliance on clear and simple rules can also reduce the need for regulatory capacity. Similarly, the requirement that the regulator be able to resist undue pressure can be somewhat mitigated through the design of a regulatory framework which leaves little discretionary power to regulatory authorities. As pointed out under Sections A and B, above, some of the countries under study have taken clear steps to rely more on competitive pressures and less on regulatory interventions. The examples of Australia, where transmission services between cities have recently been deregulated as competition increased, and of Chile, where a growing number of services have been exempted from the application of telecommunications-specific pricing regimes, come to mind. Some efforts have also been made to keep specific rules relatively simple (for example, by relying on international benchmarking to calculate interconnection prices as provided for by the Telecommunications Act 2001 in New Zealand). Finally, the scope for discretion has been limited in some instances where the independence and capacity of regulatory authorities were in doubt (as mentioned above, this is, at least in part, what explains the choice made in Chile to insert specific regulatory provisions in hard-to-modify laws). At the present stage of evolution of the telecommunications markets in the five countries under study, regulatory competence and autonomy remain paramount, however, as there are still a range of difficult regulatory issues which call for sophisticated regulatory analysis and the unavoidable use of some degree of regulatory discretion.

The level of competence of the authorities in charge of controlling market power in telecommunications tends to vary considerably among the five countries. In the United Kingdom, the United States, and Australia, the specialized regulatory bodies focusing on the economic regulation of telecommunications (OFTEL, the FCC, and the ACCC) strive to recruit high-calibre specialists and are generally recognized as competent institutions (although, as will be seen below, their decisions are sometimes contested and they are not immune from making mistakes). The ACCC, in particular, has both economy-wide competencies (which should favour cross-fertilization of experiences across sectors) and a department specializing in telecommunications (which should facilitate the acquisition of in-depth sector-specific knowledge), a combination which appears well suited to ensure a high level of expertise. In the United States and the United Kingdom, the existence of separate sector-specific regulators and antitrust authorities (the FCC, the DoJ, and the FTC in the US case, and OFTEL, the OFT, and the Competition Commission in the United Kingdom's case) means that knowledge tends to be more segmented and cross-fertilization of experiences more difficult. The individuals working for these bodies tend to be highly qualified however, though it seems that OFTEL has suffered from high levels of staff turnover, many of its employees being on secondment from other public bodies, law firms, and consulting companies.

By contrast, the level of competence of the regulatory authorities in Chile and, until recently, in New Zealand, is less satisfactory. In Chile, SUBTEL, the sector-specific regulator, has limited financial resources and therefore experiences difficulties retaining its most qualified staff, a particularly serious problem given the degree of complexity of some aspects of the regulatory regime, such as the pricing provisions. Chilean antitrust regulators, for their part, exercise their regulatory functions on a part-time basis only and their mandates are of short duration, two factors that make it difficult for them to develop the level of expertise required for the regulation of telecommunications. It is, however, arguably in New Zealand that the level of competence of the institutions in charge of enforcing the economic regulation of telecommunications has raised most concerns. As we have seen, the New Zealand model gave, until the recent reforms of December 2001, the major role to judges (the Commerce Commission's main role being to refer matters to the courts), who have limited expertise in the telecommunications sector, and appear to be ill-qualified to deal with the complex technical and economic issues pertaining to the regulation of the telecommunications sector. With the Telecommunications Act 2001, the New Zealand Government has, however, opted for an institutional model that closely resembles the system in place in Australia. This should significantly improve the quality of economic regulation in the telecommunications sector in New Zealand.

The importance of attempting to ensure a sufficient degree of autonomy for those entrusted with the task of regulating telecommunications has been recognized, to some extent, in the United States, New Zealand and Australia, and at least some measures are in place, in those three countries, to protect the regulators against undue pressures, both from political authorities and from the regulated industry. The US system seems to contain adequate protection mechanisms against the capture of the regulator including, for example, a nomination process which involves both the executive and the legislative branches, staggered terms for the commissioners, and conflicts of interests rules. However, the US system seems quite vulnerable to another form of capture that we call 'legislative capture'. As we have seen, Congressional debates over the extremely complex provisions of the 1996 Act were largely influenced by lobbyists acting on behalf of telecommunications operators. Thus, while detailed legislative provisions might reduce the risks of regulatory capture, they may also increase the risk that telecommunications operators invest large resources to influence the legislative process. The New Zealand system prior to the recent reforms, for its part, presented good guarantees against the risks of regulatory capture as judges enjoy protection against undue pressures from the Government and are independent from industry. Members of the Commerce Commission also enjoy protection against undue government pressure and are independent from the industry as well: criteria for recruiting Commission members include specific capacity requirements; the grounds for terminating the appointment of Commissioners are limited by law; the Commission's budget is determined by Parliament; and conflicts of interests rules are in place to ensure the independence of the Commission from industry. Moreover, as noted above, the fact that both the Commerce Commission and the courts are competent across the economy and act on a case-by-case basis tends to further limit the risk of capture by both industry and the Government. These positive features remain in place under the new regime adopted in December 2001. In Australia, as in New Zealand, members of the ACCC must be chosen among people who meet pre-determined professional qualifications, grounds for terminating the appointment of Commissioners are limited and conflicts of interests rules are in place. In addition, the economy-wide competence of the ACCC also tends to limit the risks of capture. Drawbacks, however, include the fact that the Government may, as in New Zealand, give directions to the Commission (albeit not with regard to the main legislative provisions relevant for telecommunications), that industry representatives play a large role in the administrative and financial supervision of the Telecommunications Industry Ombudsman scheme; and that the minister responsible for telecommunications retains important powers, which raises the risk of politically motivated interventions in the regulatory process. As noted above, this latter risk is exacerbated by the fact that the Australian Government remains a shareholder of the incumbent operator.

The Chilean model, for its part, is the one where the risks that the regulatory process might be captured by the industry or by the Executive are highest. First, there are no provisions to limit the ability of SUBTEL's staff to seek employment in regulated companies. The Executive is also in a position to exert pressures upon SUBTEL, since SUBTEL is part of the Ministry of Transport and Telecommunications and since the Head of the regulatory agency can be removed at will by the Executive. Furthermore, SUBTEL is headed by a single individual, a factor that increases the risk of capture. Finally, there is room for direct regulatory decision making by the Executive as pointed out above. While other regulatory players, such as the antitrust commissions and the courts appear better able to resist both industry and government pressures, and while SUBTEL's lack of autonomy is somewhat compensated by the fact that the agency has limited discretionary powers, there is little doubt that much could be gained by better protecting SUBTEL's staff from undue influences.

As far as the United Kingdom is concerned, the main weakness of the regulatory regime comes from the system of 'regulation by bargaining' that has progressively taken place between BT and the regulator. BT's influence on the regulatory process stems from the fact that it is very difficult for OFTEL to modify BT's licence without its consent. The fact that many OFTEL employees decide, after a period of employment with the agency, to work for telecommunications operators also increases the risks of capture. The entry into force of the Competition Act 1998 should, however, decrease BT's influence on the regulatory process by reducing the importance of licence modifications as a regulatory tool. It should also better protect OFTEL from political influence from the Department of Trade and Industry since the Secretary of State has no role to play in the competition enforcement process. Finally, we have noted that the presence of a single regulator (the DGT) instead of a board of commissioners may also increase the risks of capture. This problem should also be corrected with the establishment of OFCOM (in place of OFTEL and the several broadcasting regulators) which, as announced by the UK Government, should no longer be governed by a single individual but by a board.

Summary

1. Reliance on competition rather than regulation and—when rules are required—on clear and simple rather than overly complicated rules can mitigate, to some extent, the need for sophisticated regulatory capacity. Similarly, limiting regulatory discretion minimizes the potentially negative impact of insufficient regulatory autonomy. Both regulatory competence and regulatory autonomy remain crucial however, as complex issues arise in telecommunications which require thorough analysis and the unavoidable exercise of regulatory discretion.

2. Regulatory functions in telecommunications should be entrusted to specialized bodies. Steps which can be taken to ensure that regulatory authorities possess a high level of expertise include: offering working conditions which are geared to attracting and retaining qualified staff; appointing regulators on a full-time basis and for sufficiently long periods of time; and providing regulatory staff with opportunities to improve their skills. Bodies which combine economy-wide competencies and specialized knowledge of telecommunications (eg an antitrust authority with a telecommunications unit) are well designed to ensure a high level of expertise.

3. Economy-wide regulatory bodies are also well designed to maintain arm's-length relationships with political authorities (since they do not have to establish particularly close working relationships with any sector-specific ministry) and to remain independent from industry (since they interact with a wide group of companies). Other measures which can promote regulatory autonomy from both government and industry include, for example: entrusting regulatory authority on a plurality of commissioners rather than on a single regulator; limiting the discretionary powers of the regulatory authority; and ensuring that the revenues of the regulatory authority cannot be arbitrarily blocked or reduced either by the executive or by industry.

4. Additional steps which can be taken to ensure arm's length relationships between political and regulatory authorities include: ensuring that recruitment criteria are objective and clearly spelled out; involving more than one branch of government in nominating regulators; staggering the terms of the regulators so that not all of them can be removed by a single government; protecting regulators from arbitrary dismissals; and preventing the Executive from giving policy directions to the regulator.

5. Additional steps which can be taken to ensure the independence of the regulator from industry include: preventing regulators and members of their families from holding financial interests in any regulated companies; ensuring that regulated companies do not have the power to block regulatory processes and to force the regulator to engage in "regulatory bargaining"; and preventing regulators from seeking employment within any regulated companies for some years after the expiration of their mandates.

E. REGULATORY ACCOUNTABILITY AND STAKEHOLDER PARTICIPATION

In each of the five countries, the requirement that regulatory decisions be reasoned, the possibility to lodge appeals against the decisions of the regulators before the courts, and the publication of reports of activities by the regulators (whether mandated by law or not) provide for some degree of regulatory accountability. In the United Kingdom and Chile judges have, up to now, been competent to rule on both legal and substantive aspects of regulatory decisions. This was true in New Zealand as well until December 2001 but the Telecommunications Act 2001 now states that appeals against regulatory decisions can be brought before the courts on legal grounds only. Providing for judicial review on factual grounds is probably not desirable. As we have noted, the New Zealand experience prior to December 2001 showed that judges were ill-equipped to tackle complex issues of regulation, such as interconnection pricing.[11] While allowing judges to rule on factual issues may offer broader avenues to telecommunications operators to obtain legal redress against the decisions they consider inadequate, it may also generate some regulatory mistakes and unpredictability. Under the new Telecommunications Bill, the courts in New Zealand will review appeals on questions of law only.

Beyond this, Australia has adopted a range of interesting measures to promote stakeholder participation in the regulatory process, including, for example, the launch of public inquiries on a variety of regulatory topics, as well as the establishment of a Consumer Consultation Forum and of the TIO scheme. The Australian system also leaves a relatively wide scope for industry participation in the regulatory process, notably through the TAF, which can inter alia recommend services to be declared by the ACCC, and the ACIF, which is responsible for developing codes of technical standards to be registered by the ACA, as well as the submission of access undertakings by operators. This system of industry participation is not always ideally structured. For instance, the requirement that decisions be taken at unanimity within the TAF has made it unable to agree on services to recommend for declaration. Backstop measures have, however, been taken to avoid gridlock when operators are unable to come to an agreement.

While the UK telecommunications regulator has had a reputation of secrecy, it also adopted in recent years a range of measures to ensure greater public involvement in its regulatory work. As we have seen, for all important regulatory matters, OFTEL issues consultation documents, invites representations on these, calls meetings of representatives of industry and other interested parties, publishes the representations made, and makes public the advice provided to the Secretary of State. These procedures now generally make the British system

---

[11] On the limits of judicial intervention as a way to ensure regulatory accountability, see Robert Baldwin and Martin Cave, *Understanding Regulation: Theory, Strategy, and Practice* (Oxford: Oxford University Press, 1999) 302.

very transparent. In the United States, stakeholder participation is also ensured in FCC proceedings which offer ample room for public consultation. The main downside of such proceedings is that they tend to be very burdensome. There is also a risk that they be used by telecommunications operators to slow down the implementation of reforms that go against their interests.

On the other hand, in New Zealand, reliance on traditional court proceedings until the adoption of the Telecommunications Act 2001 might not have provided the best vehicle to ensure that the opinions of stakeholders who were not necessarily parties to the disputes, such as end-users for example, were heard and taken into account. As pointed out in Chapter 5, the new regulatory framework, which confers the main regulatory responsibilities on a special regulator, does provide for a greater degree of stakeholders' involvement. Finally, in Chile, the regulatory framework contains very few measures to ensure the transparency of regulatory processes and to enable interested parties to present their views.

Summary

1. Providing for the publication of reports of activities by the regulators, requiring that regulatory decisions be reasoned, and ensuring that appeals can be lodged against regulatory decisions are minimum accountability requirements.

2. Appeals against regulatory decisions can be lodged before the courts when the latter are reasonably competent and efficient. As judges will, however, generally lack expertise on complex telecommunications-specific issues, judicial reviews of regulatory decisions should generally be conducted on legal grounds only.

3. Public inquiries, publication of consultation documents and of the comments received on such documents, as well as establishment of an ombudsman-type entity to which users can turn to present unaddressed grievances can help ensure appropriate user representation in the regulatory process.

4. Adequate forms of co-regulation or self-regulation, combined with backstop measures to enable the regulator to act on its own when operators are unable to come to an agreement, deserve consideration as they promote participation of industry representatives in the regulatory process.

5. Regulatory proceedings conducted before specialized regulatory bodies appear, in general, to leave more scope for stakeholder participation than proceedings conducted before the courts.

F. REGULATORY COSTS

Given the existence of two levels of regulatory institutions (the FCC at the federal level and the public utility commissions at the state level), the reliance on sector-specific regulation at the federal level, and the extremely detailed nature of the telecommunications statutes and regulations themselves, the direct costs of establishing regulatory institutions and of complying with existing rules are higher in the United States than in the other four countries. With very few telecommunications specialists within the economy-wide Commerce Commission and very few detailed rules, New Zealand, for its part, kept such costs to a minimum prior to December 2001. Greater regulatory costs will, however, be generated under the new regime. The United Kingdom, Chile, and Australia are somewhere between the US model and the New Zealand model prior to the reforms. UK rules tend to be almost as detailed and complex as US rules and, thus, tend to generate relatively high compliance costs but OFTEL, however, has a much smaller staff and operating budget than the FCC. It is true that OFTEL's competencies are also more limited than those of the FCC since it does not regulate spectrum issues, which have to be dealt with by the Radiocommunications Agency. Nevertheless, compared with the size of the British market, OFTEL appears to be a rather cost-effective regulator. Chile has a sector-specific regulator (albeit with a small budget) and the complex price regime in place imposes non-negligible compliance costs on the operators. Australia, for its part, has limited the costs of the economic regulation of telecommunications by entrusting it to the economy-wide antitrust regulator. The Australian regulatory regime also involves lower compliance costs than the US or UK regimes as the rules that it contains are less complex and detailed while only limited resources are spent, within the ACCC, on the regulation of telecommunications. On the other hand, the costs of the ACA appear high and, as pointed out above, one may wonder whether there is not a discrepancy between the amount of resources allocated, on the one hand, to the technical, and, on the other hand, to the economic aspects of telecommunications regulation.

When the costs of judicial proceedings and regulatory delays are taken into account, comparisons between the five models might yield somewhat different results. The US model certainly remains by far the most expensive, inter alia because of the long and costly judicial procedures that proved necessary to define the limits of the regulatory competencies of the FCC and state utility commissions. The other legal challenges launched against the orders adopted by the FCC to implement the 1996 Act further increased regulatory costs for stakeholders. Some substantial costs were incurred in New Zealand as well because of long judicial processes. Long judicial processes have been avoided in the United Kingdom, in part, because operators cannot easily challenge OFTEL's decisions in court, though, as has been noted above, there will be greater avenues to litigate in the future. In Chile, the number of appeals lodged against the decisions of the regulator (at least before relatively high deposits were required to discourage frivolous complaints) and the incentives which the operators have to lobby the Executive in the hope of influencing the regulatory process entail costs as well. Finally, in Australia, the main problem comes from the delays involved in the regulatory processes. Arbitration proceedings, in particular, appear to be relatively cumbersome and costly for the parties. The measures proposed by the Productivity Commission (eg the introduction of class arbitration and of binding time limits) should, however, help to reduce such costs and delays.

Finally, the results of the comparison between the five countries might be further modified if one adds the costs of regulatory mistakes. The New Zealand system prior to the reforms was probably the one most prone to regulatory mistakes as it relied heavily on court decisions drafted by judges who may have had little understanding of specific economic issues pertaining to telecommunications regulation. The reforms that were recently adopted by the Government should, however, entrust the economic regulation of telecommunications to better qualified individuals and should, thus, reduce the risks of regulatory mistakes. The lack of resources allocated to regulatory authorities and the difficulty that such authorities have in attracting or retaining qualified staff makes the Chilean regime also prone to regulatory mistakes. The US and UK systems appear generally well equipped to avoid such mistakes as their regulators have sufficient resources and have competent staff. In the United States, regulatory inefficiencies stem, however, from the provisions of the 1996 Act. We have seen, for instance, that by conditioning the entry of the Bell operators into the long-distance market on the meeting of their interconnection obligations, the 1996 Act may in fact have contributed to delay local competition, hence reducing welfare. UK regulatory processes have not been immune from mistakes either. Such mistakes might have resulted, in part, from BT's ability to influence the regulatory process (an influence which might have contributed to the adoption of much-criticized measures, such as the inclusion of access deficit contributions in the interconnection charges in 1993). Finally, as we have seen above, the Australian regime seems well equipped to provide for a high level of expertise. A question may be raised, however, as to whether the resources allocated by the ACCC to the regulation of the telecommunications sector are sufficient, and some of the ACCC's decisions have been criticized, such as the decision to force the incumbent to enter into peering agreements for Internet data transmission services with three other operators, two of which received far more data from the incumbent than the incumbent received from them.

Summary

1. Entrusting the economic regulation of telecommunications and other network industries to an economy-wide regulator contributes to limit direct regulatory costs.

2. Telecommunications-specific rules should be limited to what is truly required to enable effective competition in all market segments (see Section B above). In addition, unnecessarily complex regulatory provisions should be avoided as they might encourage lobbying during the adoption process ('legislative capture') and raise compliance costs.

(continuous)

(continued)

3. Entrusting specialized authorities with the task of regulating the telecommunications sector and limiting judicial processes to appeals on legal grounds only, limiting the number of sector-specific rules and keeping them as simple as possible, discouraging delaying tactics, streamlining procedures and adopting time-limits, can all help to reduce the length and costs of regulatory processes.

4. Finally, ensuring that the regulatory framework is as clear and simple as possible and adopting the measures listed under Section D, above, to maximize the competence of regulatory authorities will help to reduce the risks and costs of regulatory mistakes.

G. ALLOCATION OF REGULATORY RESPONSIBILITIES

Potential problems appear to exist in each of the five countries with respect to the allocation of responsibilities for economic regulation in the telecommunications sector.

As discussed in Chapter 2, allocation of regulatory responsibilities should, first and foremost, be clear, with no gaps and no unnecessary overlaps. The most serious problems in this regard are found in the United States and in the United Kingdom. In the United States, the allocation of responsibilities between the FCC and the state utility commissions which results from the 1996 Act is not clear, and the way responsibilities have been divided between the FCC and the DoJ with respect to mergers might lead to concurrent and inconsistent decisions. In the United Kingdom, the main problem comes from the concurrent powers that have been granted to the OFT and the sector-specific regulators to enforce the prohibitions of the Competition Act of 1998. Several arguments have been advanced in favour of concurrent competencies (eg the fact that sector-specific regulators have developed high expertise in their sector and that granting antitrust powers to sector-specific regulators might make these more willing to streamline the regulatory regime). However, the arguments against concurrent competencies and in particular the risk that concurrent powers lead to an inconsistent application of antitrust law appear stronger.

A second objective is to ensure that regulatory responsibilities are allocated to the authorities best suited to handle them. A first source of concern here is that the Executive retains excessive regulatory powers particularly in Australia and Chile. Second, judges also appear to have been granted too much power in some cases. Prior to December 2001, this was particularly true in New Zealand where judges played the most important role. In addition, as argued under Section 5, it would be preferable to limit the appeal responsibilities of judges on questions of law only in the United Kingdom and Chile (in New Zealand, under the new regime, the Court of Appeal is allowed to review the decisions of the Telecommunications Commissioner on legal grounds only). Third, specialized regulatory bodies lack sufficient powers in some instances. Once again, this was particularly true in New Zealand where the responsibilities of the Commerce Commission were interpreted very narrowly by the courts. Also, while the FCC has the power to impose sanctions, including financial penalties, on operators which violate the telecommunications regulatory framework, OFTEL, the New Zealand Commerce Commission, the ACCC, and SUBTEL are completely dependent on the courts to impose formal sanctions. Some observers have argued that, at least in the United Kingdom and Australia (and perhaps in New Zealand as well even though the regulatory regime remains to be tested), regulators should be entrusted with formal powers to sanction. This would enhance the deterrence effect of the regulatory regime and would reduce the temptation for regulators to negotiate compliance with the operators (thereby giving the operators an opportunity to extract concessions) in order to avoid costly and unpredictable court proceedings. The situation might be somewhat different in Chile as it could be argued that conferring the power to sanction on the courts only was a wise decision in a country where the credibility, independence, and trust enjoyed by the judiciary were probably superior to those enjoyed by SUBTEL. Finally, in a few specific cases where two distinct authorities are supposed to intervene on some issues with one of these authorities taking the lead, it appears that the leading role has not necessarily been entrusted to the institution best equipped to handle it. Thus, in the United States, it may have been preferable to give to the DoJ, rather than to the FCC, final authority to rule on the BOCs' applications to enter the long-distance market, as the antitrust authorities are arguably better placed than a sector-specific regulator to assess the degree of competition which exists in telecommunications (as argued above, the decision of the Chilean authorities to entrust the antitrust regulator, rather than SUBTEL, with the task of assessing whether the provision of various telecommunications services can be deregulated is very sound in that respect). In Australia, the ACA is competent to take decisions over carrier pre-selection whereas the competitive implications of decisions in this area would have made it preferable to let the ACCC take the lead there.

A third objective is to ensure that closely interrelated issues are regulated by a single entity or—when different entities are involved—that at least there is very close co-ordination between those entities. As mentioned above, some concerns may arise in this respect in Australia because the ACCC has primary responsibility to regulate prices while the ACA is responsible for quality regulation (even though efforts have been made to facilitate co-ordination between the two agencies).

Summary

1. Allocation of regulatory responsibilities should be clear, with no gaps and no unnecessary overlaps.

2. Regulatory responsibilities should be allocated to the authorities best suited to handle them. This means, inter alia, that:

(continuous)

(continued)

(i) the regulatory powers of the executive should be strictly limited;

(ii) when the courts are considered trustworthy, judges should be able to review the decisions of specialized regulatory bodies but in general only on legal rather than factual grounds;

(iii) the scope of the powers of specialized regulatory bodies should be commensurate with their capacity to perform their functions adequately and the trust that they enjoy—when such capacity and trust are high, specialized regulatory bodies should have the authority to impose sanctions upon telecommunications operators when the latter are in breach of their regulatory obligations;

(iv) the assessment of the degree of competitiveness of various segments of the telecommunications market and the implementation of provisions which have important competitive effects should ideally be left to economy-wide antitrust, rather than telecommunications-specific, authorities.

3. Closely interrelated issues (such as price and quality regulation, for example) should be regulated by a single entity or, if different entities are involved, there should be very close co-ordination between those different entities.

10

Conclusions

A central objective of this book has been to examine the respective roles that should be played by sector-specific rules and institutions, on the one hand, and antitrust rules and institutions, on the other hand, to control market power in telecommunications.

Our analysis and comparison of five different regulatory regimes suggest the following conclusions:

Our first conclusion is that the adoption of some sector-specific rules is desirable when a country engages in market opening reforms. For instance, adoption of a default interconnection regime is an essential tool to prevent the local exchange incumbent from blocking entry into the local market and extending its market power in the provision of local exchange services to other services, such as long-distance or mobile telephony. While antitrust rules can be relied upon by new entrants to force incumbents to grant them interconnection rights, the adoption of a specific interconnection regime will generally avoid much of the delays, costs, and uncertainties—and the potentially inconclusive outcomes—associated with antitrust litigation in that area. Besides interconnection, a range of other regulatory requirements including rules mandating unbundling of the local loop, removing restrictions on resale, ensuring number portability and carrier pre-selection (or, even better, selection on a call-by-call basis), or imposing vertical separation between different activities, such as retail and wholesale activities in the local loop for example, are additional tools that may be needed to control market power and promote competition in telecommunications. Moreover, while effective competition in the market is a far more efficient way of controlling market power in telecommunications than the adoption of retail price regulation, price controls may be needed to protect end-users as long as competitive pressures remain insufficient. Finally, specific rules are also required to deal with matters such as the definition of universal service obligations and the allocation of scarce resources.

Our second conclusion is that, even when sector-specific rules have been adopted, antitrust rules remain essential for the economic regulation of telecommunications. First, antitrust rules are needed—and indeed are best suited—to deal with a range of issues of economic regulation which are not addressed by the sector-specific rules discussed above. In the five countries examined here, antitrust rules have, for instance, been used to review mergers between telecommunications operators, prohibit collusive practices between competitors, and prevent anti-competitive cross-subsidies from regulated to unregulated activities. Second, antitrust rules may play a residual role and fill gaps that might exist in sector-specific regulatory regimes. Recourse to antitrust law will generally be a second-best solution when needed sector-specific rules are missing, but it does at least provide a way to deal with some issues that would otherwise remain completely unaddressed. Antitrust rules might, for example, be used to impose structural remedies when appropriate specific rules appear to be lacking in this respect.

Our third conclusion is that implementation arrangements, and in particular the institutional choices made in that regard, are central determinants of the effectiveness of the regulatory regime. The experiences of the five countries under study strongly suggest that specialized entities are needed to deal with some of the most complex issues that require regulatory intervention in telecommunications. Interconnection and unbundling of the local loop are cases in point. While such issues can be addressed by a telecommunications-specific authority or an entity with a broader mandate such as an antitrust authority, economy-wide regulatory bodies present some distinct advantages, at least when they combine breadth of competencies with sufficiently in-depth knowledge of telecommunications-specific issues. First, the existence of cross-sector regulatory bodies increases the likelihood that consistent principles will be applied in different sectors. Second, since their *raison d'être* does not depend upon the existence of sector-specific rules, cross-sector bodies are better equipped than their sector-specific counterparts to perform the very important task of determining, at regular intervals, whether sector-specific rules are still needed or whether they should be replaced by rules applicable across sectors. Finally, since they deal with a variety of ministries and regulated industries, cross-sector regulators are less prone to political and industry capture than sector-specific regulators.

Our fourth conclusion is that there is a growing degree of convergence between countries towards adoption of some of the best practices of economic regulation outlined above. At the time when they had just completed the full liberalization of their telecommunications markets, the five countries had substantially different regulatory frameworks, and different good—and bad—practices could be identified in each of these countries. Today, following, perhaps, a process of regulatory emulation among the early reformers, some best practices appear to be spreading. For example, with some limited exceptions, the sector-specific regulatory requirements discussed above, such as rules on interconnection, local loop unbundling, number portability and carrier pre-selection, are now in place in the five countries examined. Furthermore, the five countries now rely on auctions to allocate spectrum and a majority of these countries have established (New Zealand and the United States), or are planning to establish (the United Kingdom and Australia), secondary markets for licences with the objective of fostering the efficiency-enhancing properties of auctions. Convergence towards best practices can also be observed with respect to institutional issues. Following the latest reforms in New Zealand, a specialized regulatory authority is now in place in all five countries. With perhaps the exception of Chile, the five countries have also adopted mechanisms to ensure the independence of the regulatory authority, as well as to facilitate public participation in regulatory processes.

While predicting the future is a perilous exercise, progressive convergence towards this set of best practices is likely to continue in the future. For instance, one can already witness a progressive evolution away from sector-specific regulators. New Zealand has decided to imitate Australia in establishing a telecommunications regulatory capability within the economy-wide antitrust authority. Similarly, the United Kingdom seems set to imitate the American model with its plan to move away from a telecommunications regulator only (OFTEL) and to set up a communications-wide authority (OFCOM). Greater reliance on competitive mechanisms to allocate universal service subsidies (which can already be observed in Chile, the United States, and Australia) is another example of anticipated convergence towards best practices.

In addition, with the spread of new, price-competitive, mobile technology among other technological developments, one can expect to see increasing competition in the local segment of the telecommunications market in the five countries. This in turn is likely to allow for the progressive relaxation of sector-specific regulation. We have seen that at the time of liberalization, adoption of sector-specific rules is desirable to control the market power that the incumbent is able to exercise thanks to its control of the local network. However, as competition takes place in the local loop due to the anticipated arrival of alternative networks, some of these rules may no longer be desirable. In the presence of a local bottleneck, a default interconnection regime is necessary as the local incumbent has few incentives to conclude interconnection agreements with the operators with which it competes in other markets. The arrival of competition in the local loop and the resulting losses of subscribers for the incumbent should, however, increase its incentives to interconnect with its competitors and, thus, progressively reduce or even suppress the need for mandating interconnection. Competition in the local loop should also suppress the need for rules mandating unbundling or resale (as non-facilities-based competitors will be able to negotiate with a range of network operators), as well as the need for vertical separation between the provision of local and wholesale retail services. Whatever the degree of competition in the market, some specific rules will, however, be needed to deal with universal service issues and the allocation of scarce resources. Nevertheless, local loop competition would shift the appropriate balance between telecommunications-specific and economy-wide rules toward the latter and would strengthen the case for entrusting a specialized, economy-wide, regulator with the task of controlling market power in telecommunications.

It is important, finally, to repeat a note of caution that has already been sounded. While further adoption of best practices is likely and while increased competition in the local loop could indeed bring about the regulatory shift mentioned in the previous paragraph, the five countries on which we have been focusing will not—and in fact should not—adopt absolutely identical regulatory frameworks. For one thing, the objectives to be pursued through implementation of the regulatory framework will vary from country to country. For example, some may prefer to minimize the burden of universal service provision on tax-payers by auctioning the right to provide a minimum set of services to the operators requiring the lowest subsidy, while others may want to encourage innovation and the highest service quality possible by designing a, potentially more expensive, system of portable subsidies. Another reason why regulatory frameworks are likely to differ is that, even when similar objectives are being pursued, such frameworks need to be tailored to specific country circumstances. We have noted, for example, that the five countries are, to some extent, charac-terized by differing levels of regulatory capacity and unequal abilities to protect regulatory institutions from undue influences and that this justified striking a different balance between flexibility and certainty.

The same reasons which justify opting for different regulatory solutions in the five countries that we have been studying apply, of course, with even greater strength when one enlarges the sample of countries under consideration. While many of the best practices identified above may be relevant for different coun-tries and while the arguments which have been mentioned in favour or against specific regulatory choices should be taken into account while determining the appropriate role of sector-specific and economy-wide instruments in different contexts, specific solutions will need to be carefully tailored to specific country circumstances and policy objectives.

Annex: Price Comparisons Among the Five Countries for Different Baskets of Services

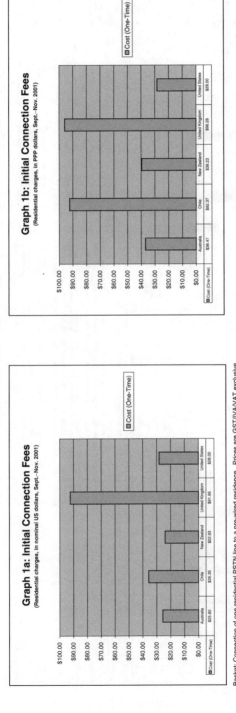

Graph 1a: Initial Connection Fees
(Residential charges, in nominal US dollars, Sept.–Nov. 2001)

	Australia	Chile	New Zealand	United Kingdom	United States
■ Cost (One-Time)	$25.80	$35.35	$22.93	$91.95	$28.00

■ Cost (One-Time)

Graph 1b: Initial Connection Fees
(Residential charges, in PPP dollars, Sept.–Nov. 2001)

	Australia	Chile	New Zealand	United Kingdom	United States
■ Cost (One-Time)	$36.47	$92.37	$39.23	$98.28	$28.00

■ Cost (One-Time)

Basket: Connection of one residential PSTN line to a pre-wired residence. Prices are GST/IVA/VAT exclusive.

Country	Company	Notes	Source	Date
Australia	Telstra	Prices quoted in Telstra's Standard Form of Agreement	http://www.telstra.com.au/sfoa/docs/psts.doc	November-01
Chile	CTC	Prices given by e-mail inquiry	http://800ventas2@atentochile.cl	November-01
New Zealand	Telecom New Zealand	Prices quoted in Telecom's List of Prices	http://www2.telecom.co.nz/pdf/tloctelephone_services.pdf	September-01
United Kingdom	British Telecom	Prices quoted in British Telecom's Price List	http://www.serviceview.bt.com/list/current/zdocs/Exchange_Lines.tar.gz	November-01
United States	Verizon DC	Price quoted in the tariff filed with the local regulatory commission	http://www.bellatlantic.com/tariffs_info/intra/efftar/dc203/pdf/e_sec3.pdf	November-01

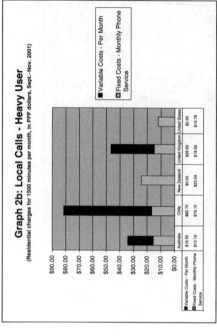

Graph 2a: Local Calls - Heavy User
(Residential charges for 1500 minutes per month, in nominal US dollars, Sept.–Nov. 2001)

- Variable Costs - Per Month
- Fixed Costs - Monthly Phone Service

	Australia	Chile	New Zealand	United Kingdom	United States
Variable Costs - Per Month	$13.83	$23.99	$0.00	$27.55	$0.00
Fixed Costs - Monthly Phone Service	$9.34	$7.33	$13.46	$17.78	$12.78

Graph 2b: Local Calls - Heavy User
(Residential charges for 1500 minutes per month, in PPP dollars, Sept.–Nov. 2001)

- Variable Costs - Per Month
- Fixed Costs - Monthly Phone Service

	Australia	Chile	New Zealand	United Kingdom	United States
Variable Costs - Per Month	$19.55	$62.70	$0.00	$28.85	$0.00
Fixed Costs - Monthly Phone Service	$13.19	$19.15	$23.04	$18.62	$12.78

Basket: 75 10-minute calls made during weekdays day-time and 75 10-minute calls made at night, all to PSTN phones on the same network. Fixed costs are monthly charges for basic phone service. Variable costs are per-minute or per-call charges where they apply. Calls made during weekdays day-time are made between 9am and 6pm. Calls made at night are made between 8pm and 8am. All prices are GST/IVA/VAT exclusive.

Country	Company	Notes	Source	Date
Australia	Telstra	Prices quoted in Telstra's Standard Form of Agreement for HomeLine Complete Plan. Variable cost includes a single charge per call. This charge is differentiated between neighbourhood (within the same exchange) and local (within the local calling area, about 50km) calls. Basket includes 1/3 neighbourhood calls, 2/3 local calls.	http://www.telstra.com.au/sfoa/docs/psts.doc	November-01
Chile	CTC	Prices quoted on CTC's web page for standard phone service in Santiago. Variable cost includes a rate per second, differentiated between on-peak (weekday day-time and Saturday mornings) and off-peak (weekday & Saturday night-time, Sundays) calls. Rates multiplied by 100/118 to subtract 18% IVA.	http://www.ctc.cl/contactenos/informacion/index_tarifas.html	November-01
New Zealand	Telecom New Zealand	Prices quoted in Telecom's List of Prices for standard phone service. Variable cost does not exist because fixed price includes unlimited untimed calls.	http://www2.telecom.co.nz/pdf/tloctelephone_services.pdf	September-01
United Kingdom	British Telecom	Prices quoted in British Telecom Price List for BT Talk Together Plan. Variable cost includes a rate per minute, differentiated between on-peak (weekday day-time) and off-peak (weekday night-time, weekends) calls.	http://www.serviceview.bt.com/list/current/zdocs/Customer_Opti ons.tar.gz	November-01
United States	Verizon DC	Prices quoted in Verizon's tariff filed with the D.C. Public Service Commission for Flat Rate Service. Variable cost does not exist because fixed price includes unlimited untimed calls.	http://www.bellatlantic.com/tariffs_info/intra/efftar/dc/dc202/pdf/e_sec2.pdf	November-01

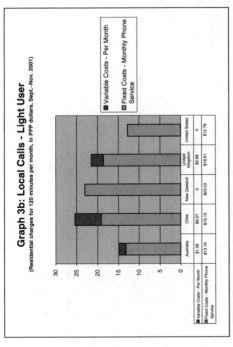

Graph 3b: Local Calls - Light User
(Residential charges for 120 minutes per month, in PPP dollars, Sept.–Nov. 2001)

Legend: ■ Variable Costs - Per Month ■ Fixed Costs - Monthly Phone Service

	Australia	Chile	New Zealand	United Kingdom	United States
Variable Costs - Per Month	$1.56	$6.27	0	$2.88	0
Fixed Costs - Monthly Phone Service	$13.19	$19.15	$23.03	$18.61	$12.78

Graph 3a: Local Calls - Light User
(Residential charges for 120 minutes per month, in nominal US dollars, Sept.–Nov. 2001)

Legend: ■ Variable Costs - Per Month ■ Fixed Costs - Monthly Phone Service

	Australia	Chile	New Zealand	United Kingdom	United States
Variable Costs - Per Month	$1.10	$2.39	0	$2.75	0
Fixed Costs - Monthly Phone Service	$9.33	$7.32	$13.46	$17.77	$12.78

Service Basket: 6 10-minute calls made during weekdays day-time and 6 10-minute calls made at night, all to PSTN phones on the same network. Fixed costs are monthly charges for basic phone service. Variable costs are per-minute or per-call charges where they apply. Calls made during weekdays day-time are made between 8am and 6pm. Calls made at night are made between 8pm and 6am. All prices are GST/IVA/VAT exclusive.

Country	Company	Notes	Source	Date
Australia	Telstra	Prices quoted in Telstra's Standard Form of Agreement for HomeLine Complete Plan. Variable cost includes a single charge per call. This charge is differentiated between neighbourhood (within the same exchange) and local (within the local calling area, about 50km) calls. Basket includes 1/3 neighbourhood calls, 2/3 local calls.	http://www.telstra.com.au/sfoa/docs/psts.doc	November-01
Chile	CTC	Prices quoted on CTC's web page for standard phone service in Santiago. Variable cost includes a rate per second, differentiated between on-peak (weekday day-time and Saturday mornings) and off-peak (weekday & Saturday night-time, Sundays) calls. Rates multiplied by 100/118 to subtract 18% IVA.	http://www.ctc.cl/contactenos/informacion/index_tarifas.html	November-01
New Zealand	Telecom New Zealand	Prices quoted in Telecom's List of Prices for standard phone service. Variable cost does not exist because fixed price includes unlimited untimed calls.	http://www2.telecom.co.nz/pdf/tloctelephone_services.pdf	September-01
United Kingdom	British Telecom	Prices quoted in British Telecom Price List for BT Talk Together Plan. Variable cost includes a rate per minute, differentiated between on-peak (weekday day-time) and off-peak (weekday night-time, weekends) calls.	http://www.serviceview.bt.com/list/current/zdocs/Customer_Options.tar.gz	November-01
United States	Verizon DC	Prices quoted in Verizon's tariff filed with the D.C. Public Service Commission for Flat Rate Service. Variable cost does not exist because fixed price includes unlimited untimed calls.	http://www.bellatlantic.com/tariffs_info/intra/efftar/dc/dc202/pdf/e_sec2.pdf	November-01

Graph 4a: National Long-Distance Calls
(Residential charges for 600 minutes per month, nominal US dollars, Sept.-Nov. 2001)

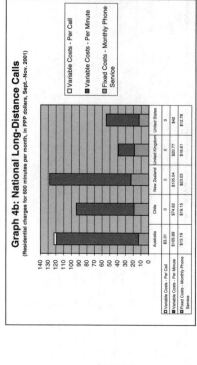

Legend:
- Variable Costs - Per Call
- Variable Costs - Per Minute
- Fixed Costs - Monthly Phone Service

	Australia	Chile	New Zealand	United Kingdom	United States
Variable Costs - Per Call	$2.34	0	0	0	0
Variable Costs - Per Minute	$74.92	$28.55	$61.39	$19.83	$42
Fixed Costs - Monthly Phone Service	$9.33	$7.32	$13.46	$17.77	$12.78

Graph 4b: National Long-Distance Calls
(Residential charges for 600 minutes per month, in PPP dollars, Sept.-Nov. 2001)

Legend:
- Variable Costs - Per Call
- Variable Costs - Per Minute
- Fixed Costs - Monthly Phone Service

	Australia	Chile	New Zealand	United Kingdom	United States
Variable Costs - Per Call	$3.31	0	0	0	0
Variable Costs - Per Minute	$105.89	$74.62	$105.04	$20.77	$42
Fixed Costs - Monthly Phone Service	$13.19	$19.15	$23.03	$16.61	$12.78

Service Basket: 10 30-minute calls made during weekdays day-time and 10 30-minute calls made at night. All calls to distances over 50km, using no-monthly-charge distance-independent discount plans available in each country. All calls are to PSTN phones on the same network. Prices include 'fixed cost of monthly phone service and 'variable cost of phone calls. Fixed costs are monthly charges for basic phone service. Variable costs are per-minute or per-call charges where they apply. Calls made during weekdays day-time are made between 9am and 6pm. Calls made at night are made between 8pm and 6am. All prices are GST/IVA/VAT exclusive.

Country	Company	Notes	Source (source of fixed cost is same as for local calls)	Date
Australia	Telstra	Prices quoted in Telstra's Standard Form of Agreement for Wide Area Calling Plan. Variable cost includes two components: (a) a AUD 0.2273 charge per call and (b) a per-minute rate, differentiated between on-peak (weekday) and off-peak (weekend) calls. Calls between 7 pm and midnight Sun – Fri and between 4 pm and midnight Sat are capped at AUD 2.70 per call. In this basket, all night-time calls are capped.	http://www.telstra.com.au/sfoa/docs/psts.doc	November-01
Chile	Entel	Prices quoted on Entel's website for Plan 123 Nacional Plano. Variable cost includes a rate per second not differentiated between on-peak and off-peak calls. Price does not include CLP 1244.15 one-time fee for initiation of long distance service plan. Rates multiplied by 100/118 to subtract 18% IVA.	http://www.entel.cl/todopersonas/FrameArea.asp?cod=10&i=det alle&cod_cont=217	November-01
New Zealand	Telecom New Zealand	Prices quoted in Telecom's List of Prices for 2.67 Nights and Weekend Plan. Variable cost includes a rate for the first minute plus a similar rate per subsequent second differentiated between on-peak (weekday) and off-peak (weekend and weeknight) calls. Off-peak calls are capped at NZD 2.67 per call for the first 6 hours of each call and charged at standard off-peak rates thereafter. In this basket, all off-peak calls are capped.	http://www2.telecom.co.nz/pdf/flloccall_tariffs.pdf	September-01
United Kingdom	British Telecom	Prices quoted in British Telecom Price List for BT Talk Together Plan combined with the Friends & Family Plan. Variable cost includes prices to call 11 pre-nominated numbers charged at a rate per minute, differentiated between on-peak (weekday day-time) and off-peak (weekday night-time, weekends) calls.	http://www.serviceview.bt.com/list/current/zdocs/Customer_Opt ions.tar.g	November-01
United States	AT&T	Prices quoted in AT&T Service Guide for $0.05 Nights Plan. Variable cost includes a rate per minute differentiated between on-peak (daytime) and off-peak (night-time) calls. This calling plan requires billing to be conducted over the internet.	http://serviceguide.att.com/ACS/ext/od.cfm?OID=420	November-01

Graph 5a: International Long-Distance Calls - Heavy User
(Residential charges for 960 minutes per month, in nominal US dollars, Sept.–Nov. 2001)

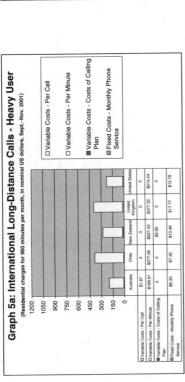

Legend:
- ☐ Variable Costs - Per Call
- ☐ Variable Costs - Per Minute
- ■ Variable Costs - Costs of Calling Plan
- ■ Fixed Costs - Monthly Phone Service

	Australia	Chile	New Zealand	United Kingdom	United States
☐ Variable Costs - Per Call	$1.87	0	0	$377.33	$214.24
☐ Variable Costs - Per Minute	$189.91	$377.43	$257.43	0	0
■ Variable Costs - Costs of Calling Plan	0	$7.32	$5.55	0	0
■ Fixed Costs - Monthly Phone Service	$9.33	$13.46	$13.46	$17.77	$12.78

Graph 5b: International Long-Distance Calls - Heavy User
(Residential charges for 960 minutes per month, in PPP dollars, Sept.–Nov. 2001)

Legend:
- ☐ Variable Costs - Per Call
- ☐ Variable Costs - Per Minute
- ■ Variable Costs - Costs of Calling Plan
- ■ Fixed Costs - Monthly Phone Service

	Australia	Chile	New Zealand	United Kingdom	United States
☐ Variable Costs - Per Call	$2.65	0	0	$395.10	$214.24
☐ Variable Costs - Per Minute	$268.41	$985.43	$440.45	0	0
■ Variable Costs - Costs of Calling Plan	0	$19.15	$9.50	0	0
■ Fixed Costs - Monthly Phone Service	$13.19		$23.03	$18.61	$12.78

Service Basket: Two 1-hour calls made during weekdays day-time and two 1-hour calls made at night to a country in four different continents based on high-usage calling plans. Calls are made to four to five countries depending upon country of origin: Australia, Chile, Japan, UK, US. Fixed costs are monthly charges for basic phone service. Variable costs are per-minute or per-call charges where they apply. Calls made during weekdays day-time are made between 9am and 6pm. Calls made at night are made between 8pm and 6am. All prices are GST/IVA/VAT exclusive.

Country	Company	Notes	Source (source of fixed cost is same as for local calls)	Date
Australia	Telstra	Prices quoted in Telstra's Standard Form of Agreement based on 0018 1/2 Hour Call Plan. Variable cost includes two components: (a) a AUD 0.2273 charge per call, and (b) prices of calls made to Chile, Japan, the United Kingdom, and the United States, differentiated between on-peak or off-peak calls. For 0018 1/2 Hour Call Plan, calls are charged in increments of a half hour. For increments less than a half hour, a higher rate per minute is charged.	http://www.telstra.com.au/sfoa/docs/psts.doc	November-01
Chile	Entel	Prices quoted on Entel's website for Plan 123 Nacional Plano. Variable cost includes prices of calls made to Australia, Japan, the United Kingdom, and the United States, charged at a rate per minute not differentiated between on-peak or off-peak calls. Rates were multiplied by 100/118 to subtract 18% IVA.	http://www.entel.cl/todopersonas/FrameArea.asp?cod=108&det alle&cod_cont=217	November-01
New Zealand	Telecom New Zealand	Prices for calls to Chile quoted in Telecom's List of Prices. Prices for calls to Japan, the United Kingdom and the United States quoted on Telecom's website for Personalised International Offers - Super Low Rate Option. Variable cost includes two components (a) a NZD5.00 charge per month per country for discounted calls to Chile, Japan, the United Kingdom and the United States, unavailable for Chile, and (b) prices of calls made to Chile, Japan, the United Kingdom, and the United States, charged at a rate for the initial minute and a rate per subsequent second, differentiated between on-peak (weekday) and off-peak (weeknight and weekend) calls for Chile, not differentiated between on-peak and off-peak calls for Japan, the United Kingdom and the United States. Rates for Japan, the United Kingdom and the United States were multiplied by 100/112.5 to subtract 12.5% GST (rates for Chile were given without GST).	For calls to Chile: http://www2.telecom.co.nz/pdf/tlocall_tariffs.pdf For calls to Japan, United States and United Kingdom: http://www.telecom.co.nz/content/0,2502,100471-1031,00.html	September-01
United Kingdom	British Telecom	Prices quoted in British Telecom Price List for BT Talk Together combined with Friends & Family International. Variable cost includes prices of calls made to Australia, Japan, Chile, and the United States to 5 pre-nominated numbers, charged a rate per minute, differentiated between on-peak (weekday) and off-peak (weeknight and weekend) calls.	http://www.serviceview.bt.com/list/current/zdocs/Customer_Opti ons.tar.g	November-01
United States	AT&T	Prices quoted in AT&T Service Guide for AT&T Savings Plus. Variable cost includes prices of calls made to Australia, Japan, Chile, and the United Kingdom charged at a rate for the first minute and a lower rate per subsequent minute not differentiated between on-peak and off-peak calls.	http://serviceguide.att.com/ACS/ext/Documents.cfm?DID=1388	November-01

Graph 6a: International Long-Distance Calls - Light User

(Residential charges for 40 minutes per month, in nominal US dollars, Sept.–Nov. 2001)

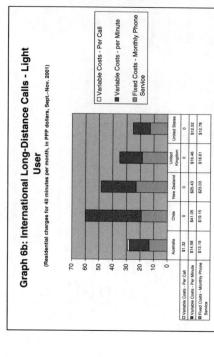

Legend:
- ☐ Variable Costs - Per Call
- ■ Variable Costs - Per Minute
- ▨ Fixed Costs - Monthly Phone Service

	Australia	Chile	New Zealand	United Kingdom	United States
Variable Costs - Per Call	$0.93	0	0	0	0
Variable Costs - Per Minute	$10.32	$15.71	$14.86	$15.72	$12.52
Fixed Costs - Monthly Phone Service	$9.33	$7.32	$13.46	$17.77	$12.78

Graph 6b: International Long-Distance Calls - Light User

(Residential charges for 40 minutes per month, in PPP dollars, Sept.–Nov. 2001)

Legend:
- ☐ Variable Costs - Per Call
- ■ Variable Costs - per Minute
- ▨ Fixed Costs - Monthly Phone Service

	Australia	Chile	New Zealand	United Kingdom	United States
Variable Costs - Per Call	$1.32	0	0	0	0
Variable Costs - Per Minute	$14.58	$41.05	$25.43	$18.46	$12.52
Fixed Costs - Monthly Phone Service	$13.19	$19.15	$23.03	$18.61	$12.78

Service Basket: One 5-minute call made during weekdays day-time and one 5-minute call made at night to a country in four different continents based on low-usage calling plans. Calls are made to four of the following five countries depending upon country of origin: Australia, Chile, Japan, UK, US. Fixed costs are monthly charges for basic phone service. Variable costs are per-minute or per-call charges where they apply. Calls made during weekdays day-time are made between 9am and 6pm. Calls made at night are made between 8pm and 6am. All prices are GST/IVA/VAT exclusive.

Country	Company	Notes	Source (source of fixed cost is same as for local calls)	Date
Australia	Telstra	Prices quoted in Telstra's Standard Form of Agreement based on 0011 Direct Dialed Minutes Plan. Variable cost includes two components: (a) a AUD 0.2273 charge per call, and (b) prices of calls made to Chile, Japan, the United Kingdom, and the United States, charged at a rate per minute, not differentiated between on-peak or off-peak calls.	http://www.telstra.com.au/sfoa/docs/psts.doc	November-01
Chile	Entel	Prices quoted on Entel's website for Plan 123 Nacional Plano. Variable cost includes calls made to Australia, Japan, the United Kingdom, and the United States, charged at a rate per minute not differentiated between on-peak or off-peak calls. Rates were multiplied by 100/118 to subtract 18% IVA.	http://www.entel.cl/nodopersonas/FrameArea.asp?cod=10&t=det alle&cod_cont=217	November-01
New Zealand	Telecom New Zealand	Prices quoted in Telecom's List of Prices. Variable cost includes prices of calls made to Chile, Japan, the United Kingdom, and the United States, charged at a rate for the first minute and a rate per subsequent second, differentiated between on-peak (weekday) and off-peak (weeknight and weekend) calls.	http://www2.telecom.co.nz/pdf/ltocall_tariffs.pdf	September-01
United Kingdom	British Telecom	Prices quoted in British Telecom Price List for BT Talk Together combined with Friends & Family International. Variable cost includes prices of calls made to Australia, Japan, Chile, and the United States to 5 pre-nominated numbers, charged a rate per minute, differentiated between on-peak (weekday) and off-peak (weeknight and weekend) calls.	http://www.serviceview.bt.com/list/current/zdocs/Customer_Opt ions.tar.gz	November-01
United States	AT&T	Prices quoted in AT&T Service Guide for AT&T Savings Plus. Variable cost includes prices of calls made to Australia, Japan, Chile, and the United Kingdom charged at a rate for the first minute and a lower rate per subsequent minute not differentiated between on-peak and off-peak calls.	http://serviceguide.att.com/ACS/ext/Documents.cfm?DID=1388	November-01

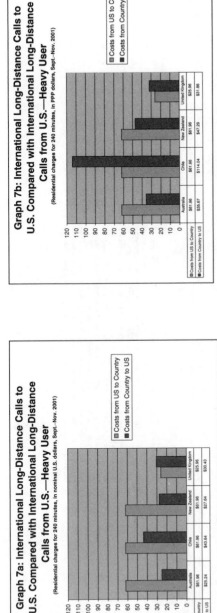

Graph 7a: International Long-Distance Calls to U.S. Compared with International Long-Distance Calls from U.S.—Heavy User

(Residential charges for 240 minutes, in nominal U.S. dollars, Sept.–Nov. 2001)

Legend: Costs from US to Country; Costs from Country to US

	Australia	Chile	New Zealand	United Kingdom
Costs from US to Country	$61.96	$61.96	$61.96	$25.96
Costs from Country to US	$25.24	$43.64	$27.64	$30.43

Graph 7b: International Long-Distance Calls to U.S. Compared with International Long-Distance Calls from U.S.—Heavy User

(Residential charges for 240 minutes, in PPP dollars, Sept.–Nov. 2001)

Legend: Costs from US to Country; Costs from Country to US

	Australia	Chile	New Zealand	United Kingdom
Costs from US to Country	$61.96	$61.96	$61.96	$25.96
Costs from Country to US	$38.67	$114.04	$47.29	$31.86

Service Basket: Two 1-hour calls made during weekdays day-time and two 1-hour calls made at night from country to U.S. / from U.S. to country, based on high-usage calling plans. Calls made during weekdays day-time are made between 9am and 6pm. Calls made at night are made between 8pm and 6am. All prices are GST/IVA/VAT exclusive.

Country	Company	Notes	Source (source of fixed cost is same as for local calls)	Date
Australia	Telstra	Prices quoted in Telstra's Standard Form of Agreement based on 0018 1/2 Hour Call Plan. Cost includes two components: (a) a AUD 0.2273 charge per call , and (b) prices of calls made to the United States, charged at a rate per half hour, not differentiated between on-peak or off-peak calls. For 0018 1/2 Hour Call Plan, calls are charged in increments of a half hour. For increments less than a half hour, a higher rate per minute is charged.	http://www.telstra.com.au/sfoa/docs/psts.doc	November-01
Chile	Entel	Prices quoted on Entel's website for Plan 123 Nacional Plano. Cost includes prices of calls made to the United States, charged at a rate per minute not differentiated between on-peak or off-peak calls. Rates were multiplied by 100/118 to subtract 18% IVA.	http://www.entel.cl/todopersonas/FrameArea.asp?cod=10&t=det alle&cod_cont=217	November-01
New Zealand	Telecom New Zealand	Prices for calls to the United States quoted on Telecom's website for Personalised International Offers - Super Low Rate Option. Cost includes two components: (a) price of calls made to the United States, charged at a rate for the initial minute and a rate per subsequent second, not differentiated between on-peak and off-peak calls and (b) a NZD 5.00 charge per month for the calling plan. Rates were multiplied by 100/112.5 to subtract 12.5% GST.	http://www.telecom.co.nz/content/0,2502,100471-1031,00.html	September-01
United Kingdom	British Telecom	Prices quoted in British Telecom Price List for BT Talk Together combined with Friends & Family International. Cost includes prices of calls made to 5 pre-nominated numbers in the United States charged a rate per minute, differentiated between on-peak (weekday) and off-peak (weeknight and weekend) calls.	http://www.serviceview.bt.com/list/current/zdocs/Customer_Opt ions.tar.g	November-01

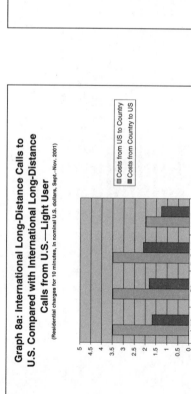

Graph 8a: International Long-Distance Calls to U.S. Compared with International Long-Distance Calls from U.S.—Light User

(Residential charges for 10 minutes, in nominal U.S. dollars, Sept.–Nov. 2001)

☐ Costs from US to Country
■ Costs from Country to US

	Australia	Chile	New Zealand	United Kingdom
☐ Costs from US to Country	$3.48	$3.48	$3.48	$1.98
■ Costs from Country to US	$1.67	$1.81	$2.09	$1.25

Graph 8b: International Long-Distance Calls to U.S. Compared with International Long-Distance Calls from U.S.—Light User

(Residential charges for 10 minutes, in PPP dollars, Sept.–Nov. 2001)

☐ Costs from US to Country
■ Costs from Country to US

	Australia	Chile	New Zealand	United Kingdom
☐ Costs from US to Country	$3.48	$3.48	$3.48	$1.98
■ Costs from Country to US	$2.37	$4.75	$3.58	$1.32

Service Basket: Two 5-minute calls made during weekdays day-time and two 5-minute calls made at night from country to U.S. / from U.S. to country. Calls made during weekdays day-time are made between 9am and 6pm. Calls made at night are made between 8pm and 6am. All prices are GST/IVA/VAT exclusive.

Country	Company	Notes	Source (source of fixed cost is same as for local calls)	Date
Australia	Telstra	Prices quoted in Telstra's Standard Form of Agreement based on 0011 Direct Dialed Minutes Plan. Cost includes two components: (a) a AUD 0.2273 charge per call ; and (b) prices of calls made to the United States, charged at a rate per minute, not differentiated between on-peak or off-peak calls.	http://www.telstra.com.au/sfoa/docs/psts.doc	November-01
Chile	Entel	Prices quoted on Entel's website for Plan 123 Nacional Plano. Cost includes prices of calls made to the United States, charged at a rate per minute not differentiated between on-peak or off-peak calls. Rates were multiplied by 100/118 to subtract 18% IVA.	http://www.entel.cl/todopersonas/FrameArea.asp?cod=10&t=det alle&cod_cont=217	November-01
New Zealand	Telecom New Zealand	Prices quoted in Telecom's List of Prices. Cost includes prices of calls made to the United States, charged at a rate for the first minute and a rate per subsequent second, differentiated between on-peak (weekday) and off-peak (weeknight and weekend) calls.	http://www2.telecom.co.nz/pdf/tloccall_tariffs.pdf	September-01
United Kingdom	British Telecom	Prices quoted in British Telecom Price List for BT Talk Together combined with Friends & Family International. Cost includes prices of calls to 5 pre-nominated numbers in the United States charged a rate per minute, differentiated between on-peak (weekday) and off-peak (weeknight and weekend) calls.	http://www.serviceview.bt.com/list/current/zdocs/Customer_Opt ions.tar.g	November-01

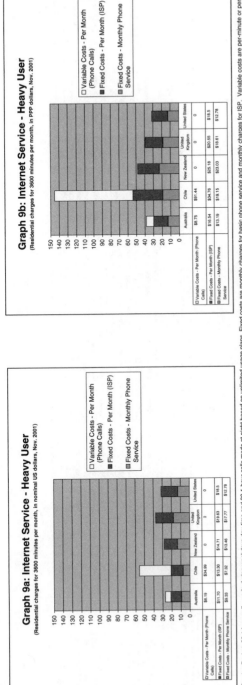

Graph 9a: Internet Service - Heavy User
(Residential charges for 3600 minutes per month, in nominal US dollars, Nov. 2001)

☐ Variable Costs - Per Month (Phone Calls)
■ Fixed Costs - Per Month (ISP)
▨ Fixed Costs - Monthly Phone Service

	Australia	Chile	New Zealand	United Kingdom	United States
☐Variable Costs - Per Month (Phone Calls)	$6.19	$34.99	0	0	0
■Fixed Costs - Per Month (ISP)	$11.70	$13.30	$14.71	$19.63	$18.5
▨Fixed Costs - Monthly Phone Service	$9.33	$7.32	$13.46	$17.77	$12.78

Graph 9b: Internet Service - Heavy User
(Residential charges for 3600 minutes per month, in PPP dollars, Nov. 2001)

☐ Variable Costs - Per Month (Phone Calls)
■ Fixed Costs - Per Month (ISP)
▨ Fixed Costs - Monthly Phone Service

	Australia	Chile	New Zealand	United Kingdom	United States
☐Variable Costs - Per Month (Phone Calls)	$8.75	$91.44	0	0	0
■Fixed Costs - Per Month (ISP)	$16.54	$34.76	$25.18	$20.55	$18.5
▨Fixed Costs - Monthly Phone Service	$13.19	$19.15	$23.03	$19.61	$12.78

Service Basket: 30 1-hour calls made during weekdays day-time and 30 1-hour calls made at night based on unlimited usage plans. Fixed costs are monthly charges for basic phone service and monthly charges for ISP. Variable costs are per-minute or per-call charges where they apply. Calls made during weekdays day-time are made between 9am and 6pm. Calls made at night are made between 8pm and 6am. All prices are GST/IVA/VAT exclusive.

Country	Company	Notes	Source (source of fixed and variable costs for phone service is same as for local calls)	Date
Australia	Telstra	Prices quoted on BigPond's (Telstra affiliate) website. Variable cost includes price of calls made to access ISP, charged per call. All calls to access ISP are local calls. Rates multiplied by 100/110 to subtract 10% GST. Assumes less than 10Mb downloaded per day.	http://www.bigpond.com/Home/Products/Access/essential.asp	November-01
Chile	Entel	Prices quoted on Entel's website. Variable cost includes price of calls made to access ISP, charged at a special negotiated rate, calculated per second, differentiated between on-peak (weekday, Saturday morning) and off-peak (weeknight, weekend) calls. Rates multiplied by 100/118 to subtract 18% IVA	http://www.entel.cl/todopersonas/mainsec.asp?opcion=subsec &cod_subsec=17	November-01
New Zealand	Telecom New Zealand	Prices quoted in Telecom's List of Prices. Variable cost does not exist because calls to access ISP are included in fixed price for monthly phone service.	http://www2.telecom.co.nz/pdf/tlcspecialservices.pdf	November-01
United Kingdom	British Telecom	Prices quoted on BTInternet's (British Telecom Affiliate) website. Variable cost does not exist because calls to access ISP are free under FRIACO scheme. Rates multiplied by 100/110 to subtract 10% VAT.	https://register.btinternet.com/cgi-bin/pageserve/register/global/payment_plan_option.html	November-01
United States	AT&T	Prices quoted on Prodigy's website. Variable cost does not exist because calls to access ISP are included in fixed price for monthly phone service. Assumes one year contract for service.	http://myhome.prodigy.net/pserv/connect/dial/price_plans.html	November-01

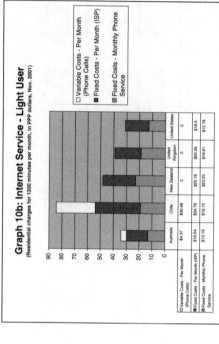

Graph 10a: Internet Service - Light User
(Residential charges for 1200 minutes per month, in nominal US dollars, Nov. 2001)

Legend:
- ☐ Variable Costs - Per Month (Phone Calls)
- ■ Fixed Costs - Per Month (ISP)
- ▨ Fixed Costs - Monthly Phone Service

	Australia	Chile	New Zealand	United Kingdom	United States
Variable Costs - Per Month (Phone Calls)	$3.09	$11.66	0	0	0
Fixed Costs - Per Month (ISP)	$11.70	$13.30	$14.71	$19.63	$18.5
Fixed Costs - Monthly Phone Service	$9.33	$7.32	$13.46	$17.77	$12.78

Graph 10b: Internet Service - Light User
(Residential charges for 1200 minutes per month, in PPP dollars, Nov. 2001)

Legend:
- ☐ Variable Costs - Per Month (Phone Calls)
- ■ Fixed Costs - Per Month (ISP)
- ▨ Fixed Costs - Monthly Phone Service

	Australia	Chile	New Zealand	United Kingdom	United States
Variable Costs - Per Month (Phone Calls)	$4.37	$30.48	0	0	0
Fixed Costs - Per Month (ISP)	$16.54	$34.76	$25.18	$20.55	$18.5
Fixed Costs - Monthly Phone Service	$13.19	$19.15	$23.03	$18.61	$12.78

Service Basket: 15 40-minute calls made during weekdays day-time and 15 40-minute calls made at night based on unlimited usage plans. Fixed costs are monthly charges for basic phone service and monthly charges for ISP. Variable costs are per-minute or per-call charges where they apply. Calls made during weekdays day-time are made between 9am and 6pm. Calls made at night are made between 8pm and 6am. All prices are GST/IVA/VAT exclusive.

Country	Company	Notes	Source (source of fixed and variable costs for phone service is same as for local calls)	Date
Australia	Telstra	Prices quoted on BigPond's (Telstra affiliate) website. Variable cost includes price of calls made to access ISP, charged per call. All calls to access ISP are local calls. Rates multiplied by 100/110 to subtract 10% GST. Assumes less than 10Mb downloaded per day.	http://www.bigpond.com/Home/Products/Access/essential.asp	November-01
Chile	Entel	Prices quoted on Entel's website. Variable cost includes price of calls made to access ISP, charged at a special negotiated rate, calculated per second, differentiated between on-peak (weekday, Saturday morning) and off-peak (weeknight, weekend) calls. Rates multiplied by 100/118 to subtract 18% IVA.	http://www.entel.cl/todopersonas/mainsec.asp?opcion=subsec&cod_subsec=17	November-01
New Zealand	Telecom New Zealand	Prices quoted in Telecom's List of prices. Variable cost does not exist because calls to access ISP are included in fixed price for monthly phone service.	http://www2.telecom.co.nz/pdf/tlocspecialservices.pdf	November-01
United Kingdom	British Telecom	Prices quoted on BTinternet's (British Telecom Affiliate) website. Variable cost does not exist because calls to access ISP are free under FRIACO scheme. Rates multiplied by 100/110 to subtract 10% VAT.	https://register.btinternet.com/cgi-bin/pageserve/register/global/payment_plan_option.html	November-01
United States	AT&T	Prices quoted on Prodigy's website. Variable cost does not exist because calls to access ISP are included in fixed price for monthly phone service. Assumes one year contract for service.	http://myhome.prodigy.net/pserv/connect/dial/price_plans.html	November-01

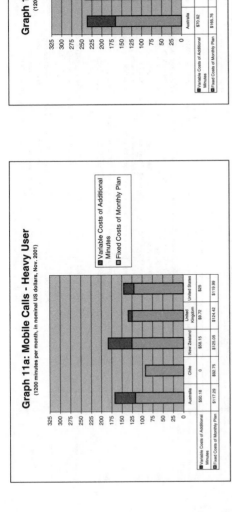

Graph 11a: Mobile Calls - Heavy User
(1200 minutes per month, in nominal US dollars, Nov. 2001)

Legend: ■ Variable Costs of Additional Minutes ▨ Fixed Costs of Monthly Plan

	Australia	Chile	New Zealand	United Kingdom	United States
Variable Costs of Additional Minutes	$50.18	0	$50.15	$9.72	$25
Fixed Costs of Monthly Plan	$117.29	$92.75	$125.05	$124.42	$119.99

Graph 11b: Mobile Calls - Heavy User
(1200 minutes per month, in PPP dollars, Nov. 2001)

Legend: ■ Variable Costs of Additional Minutes ▨ Fixed Costs of Monthly Plan

	Australia	Chile	New Zealand	United Kingdom	United States
Variable Costs of Additional Minutes	$70.92	0	$99.49	$10.118	$25
Fixed Costs of Monthly Plan	$165.76	$242.38	$213.96	$130.28	$119.99

Service Basket: 30 20-minute calls made during weekdays day-time and 30 20-minute calls made at night to domestic PSTN numbers, based on high-usage plans. Calls made during weekdays day-time are made between 9am and 6pm. Calls made at night are made between 8pm and 6am. Fixed costs include cost of calling plan. Variable costs include cost of additional minutes. All prices are GST/IVA/VAT exclusive.

Country	Company	Notes	Source	Date
Australia	Telstra	Prices quoted in Telstra's Standard Form of Agreement for Flexible Plan 250 plus an additional AUD 97.24 for the total basket. Variable cost for additional minutes, which includes a per-call charge of AUD 0.22727 per call and a rate given in 30 second increments differentiated between on-peak (weekday and mid-day Saturday) and off-peak (night-time and Sunday) calls. Does not include connection cost.	http://www.telstra.com.au/sfoa/docs/pmtsb.doc	November-01
Chile	BellSouth	Prices quoted on BellSouth's website for FullTimePlus 1200 Plan, which includes 1200 minutes that can be used any time. Rates were multiplied by 100/118 to subtract 18% IVA. Does not include connection cost.	http://www.bellsouth.cl/telefonia/planes/planes.htm	November-01
New Zealand	Telecom New Zealand	Prices quoted on Telecom's website for Anytime 750 Plan which includes 750 minutes that can be used any time. Variable cost includes price of 225 additional mid-day minutes and 225 additional night-time minutes, charged at a per-minute rate that differentiates between on-peak (weekday) and off-peak (weekend) calls. Does not include connection cost.	http://www.telecom.co.nz/content/0,2502,100404-1054,00.html	November-01
United Kingdom	Vodafone	Prices quoted on Vodafone's website for Vodafone 1100 Plan which includes 1100 minutes that can be used any time. Variable cost includes price of 50 additional mid-day minutes and 50 additional night-time minutes, charged at a per-minute rate that differentiates between on-peak (weekday) and off-peak (night-time and weekend) calls. Rates were multiplied by 100/110 to subtract 10% VAT. Does not include connection cost.	http://www.vodafone.co.uk/cgi-bin/COUK/priceplanoverview.jsp?category=phonesandpriceplans+priceplans+paymonthly+standard&channel=Phones+%26+Price+Plans&menupath=1,6,1,1&BV_SessionID=@@@@10809 13688.1005233404@@@@&BV_EngineID=fadccghkdeembekgcgjcifdnj,0	November-01
United States	AT&T Wireless	Prices quoted on AT&T Wireless's website for Digital One-Rate Plan for 20037 zip-code, which includes 1100 minutes that can be used any time. Variable cost includes price of 100 additional minutes that can be used any time, charged at a per-minute rate that does not differentiate between on-peak and off-peak calls. Does not include connection cost.	http://www.attws.com/personal/ps/select_plan_minutes.jhtml?offerType=DOR	November-01

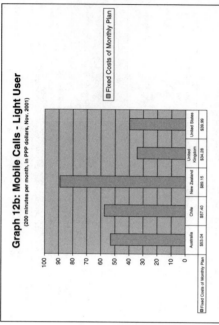

Graph 12a: Mobile Calls - Light User
(200 minutes per month, in nominal US dollars, Nov. 2001)

■ Fixed Costs of Monthly Plan

	Australia	Chile	New Zealand	United Kingdom	United States
■ Fixed Costs of Monthly Plan	$37.53	$21.96	$52.10	$32.74	$39.99

Graph 12b: Mobile Calls - Light User
(200 minutes per month, in PPP dollars, Nov. 2001)

■ Fixed Costs of Monthly Plan

	Australia	Chile	New Zealand	United Kingdom	United States
■ Fixed Costs of Monthly Plan	$53.04	$57.40	$86.15	$34.28	$39.99

Service Basket: Ten 10-minute calls made during weekdays day-time and ten 10-minute calls made at night to regional PSTN numbers, based on low-usage plans. Calls made during weekdays day-time are made between 9am and 6pm. Calls made at night are made between 8pm and 6am. Fixed costs include cost of calling plan. Variable costs include cost of additional minutes. All prices are GST/IVA/VAT exclusive.

Notes

Country Company	Source	Date
Australia Telstra	Prices quoted in Telstra's Standard Form of Agreement, for Flexible Plan 80, which includes over 100 on-peak and 100 off-peak minutes. Fixed price includes monthly call allowance of AUD 72.73 applicable to any type of call charged at AUD 0.22727 per call in addition to rates per 30-second increment that are specific to Flexible Plan 80, differentiated by on-peak (weekdays and Saturday mid-day) and off-peak (nights and Sunday) calls. Does not include connection cost. http://www.telstra.com.au/sfoa/docs/pmtsb.doc	November-01
Chile BellSouth	Prices quoted on BellSouth's website for FullTime 200 Plan, which includes 200 minutes that can be used any time. Rates were multiplied by 100/118 to subtract 18% IVA. Does not include connection cost. http://www.bellsouth.cl/telefonia/planes/planes.htm	November-01
New Zealand Telecom New Zealand	Prices quoted on Telecom's website for Anytime 200 Plan which includes 200 minutes that can be used any time. Does not include connection cost. http://www.telecom.co.nz/content/0,2502,100404-1054,00.html	November-01
United Kingdom Vodafone	Prices quoted on Vodafone's website for Vodafone 200 Plan which includes 200 minutes that can be used any time. Rates multiplied by 100/110 to subtract 10% VAT. Does not include connection cost. http://www.vodafone.co.uk/cgi-bin/COUK/priceplanoverview.jsp?category=phonesandpriceplans +priceplans+paymonthly+standard&channel=Phones+%26+ Price+Plans&menupath=1,6,1,1&BV_SessionID=@@@@10809 13688.1005233404@@@&BV_EngineID=ladcoghkdeembek gcgjcfgdnj,0	November-01
United States AT&T Wireless	Prices quoted on AT&T Wireless's website for Regional One-Rate Plan for users in 20037 zip code, which includes 200 minutes that can be used any-time. Calls can be made to numbers in: Virginia, Washington, D.C., Maryland, Delaware, Pennsylvania, New Jersey, Massachusetts, and parts of New York, West Virginia, Connecticut, Rhode Island, Vermont, New Hampshire, and Maine. Does not include connection cost. http://www.attws.com/personal/ps/select_plan_minutes.jhtml? offerType=RA	November-01

Exchange Rate Calculations

Local currency - US dollars: Nominal currency exchange rates are given by the Integrated Controllers System of the World Bank. The ICS takes data from Reuters and calculates a 1-month average. The 1-month average is for November 1 - November 30, 2001. (Nominal prices in local currency are November, 2001 prices.)

Local currency - PPP dollars: Base PPP Rates are given by the World Development Indicators (World Bank) for 1999. To calculate 2000 PPP rates, 1999 PPP rates were multiplied by (1 + Consumer Price Index Change in 2000 in Local Country / 1 + Consumer Price Index Change in 2000 in the United States) To Calculate 2001 PPP rates, the derived 2000 PPP rates were multiplied by (1 + Estimated Consumer Price Index Change in 2001 in Local Country / 1 + Estimated Consumer Price Index Change in 2001 in the United States). Consumer Price Index Changes for 2000 and Estimated Consumer Price Index Change for 2001 are given by the World Economic Outlook of October 2001 by the International Monetary Fund

Exchange Rates

Country	Nominal	PPP
Australia	0.516085	0.729395207
Chile	0.001440080	0.003763309
New Zealand	0.4168583	0.713202884
United Kingdom	1.440765	1.508601603
United States	1	1

Bibliography

Adler, Aimee M, 'Competition in Telephony: Perception or Reality? Current Barriers to the Telecommunications Act of 1996' (1999) 7 *J of L and Policy* 571.

Afualo, Valeen, and John McMillan, 'Auctions of Rights to Public Property' in Peter Newman, *The New Palgrave Dictionary of Economics and the Law* vol 1 (London: Macmillan, 1998) 125.

Ahdar, Rex J, 'Battles in New Zealand's Deregulated Telecommunications Industry' (1995) 23 *Australian Business L Rev* 78.

Alexander, Georges J, 'Antitrust and the Telephone Industry after the Telecommunications Act of 1996' (1996) 12 *Santa Clara Computer and High Technology L J* 227.

Alger, Dan, and Joanne Leung, *The Relative Costs of Local Telephony Across Five Countries* (Wellington: New Zealand Institute for the Study of Competition and Regulation (NZISCR), March 1999).

Allport, Peter, 'Natural Monopoly Regulation in New Zealand', Institute of Public Affairs Deregulation Conference, Melbourne, 24 July 1998.

Armstrong, Mark, 'Competition in Telecommunications' (1997) 13 *Oxford Rev of Economic Policy* 64.

Armstrong, Mark, Chris Doyle and John Vickers, 'The Access Pricing Problem: A Synthesis' (1996) 44 *J of Industrial Economics* 131.

Armstrong, Mark, et al, *Regulatory Reform: Economic Analysis and British Experience* (Cambridge, Mass., and London: MIT Press, 1994).

Areeda, Philip, *Antitrust Analysis—Problems, Text and Cases* (Boston, Mass., Toronto, London: Little Brown and Company, 1981).

Areeda, Philip, 'Essential Facilities: An Epithet in Need of Limiting Principles' (1990) 58 *Antitrust L J* 841.

Averch, Harvey, and Leland L Johnson, 'Behaviour of the Firm under Regulatory Constraint' (1962) 92 *American Economic Rev* 1052.

Baldwin, Robert, and Martin Cave, *Understanding Regulation: Theory, Strategy, and Practice* (Oxford: Oxford University Press, 1999).

Baldwin, Thomas F et al, *Convergence: Integrating Media, Information and Communication* (Thousand Oaks, Cal.: Sage Publications, 1996).

Baumol, William J, et al, *Contestable Markets and the Theory of Industry Structure* (New York: Harcourt Brace Jovanovich, 1982).

Baumol, William J, and J Gregory Sidak, 'The Pricing of Inputs Sold To Competitors' (1994) 11 *Yale J on Regulation* 171.

Beca, Raimundo, 'Privatization, Deregulation, and Beyond: Trends in Telecommunications in Some Latin American Countries' in Meheroo Jussawalla (ed), *Global Telecommunications Policies: The Challenge of Change* (Westport, Conn.: Greenwood Press, 1993) 134.

Bellamy, Christopher, and Graham Child, *Common Market Law of Competition* (3rd edn, London: Sweet & Maxwell, 1993).

Bishop, Simon, and Mike Walker, *The Economics of EC Competition Law* (London: Sweet & Maxwell, 1999).

Bitrán, Eduardo, and Raúl Sáez, 'Privatization and Regulation in Chile' in Barry P Bosworth et al (eds), *The Chilean Economy: Policy Lessons and Challenges* (Washington, DC: The Brookings Institution, 1994) 365.

Bitrán, Eduardo, and Pablo Serra, 'Regulation of Privatized Utilities: The Chilean Experience' (1998) 20 *World Development* 945.

Bitrán, Eduardo, et al, 'Privatizing and Regulating Chile's Utilities, 1974–2000: Successes, Failures, and Outstanding Challenges' in Guillermo Perry and Danny M Leipziger (eds), *Chile: Recent Policy Lessons and Emerging Challenges* (Washington, DC: WBI Development Studies, 1999) 340.

Blackman, Colin, 'Editorial: Spectrum Auctions—Who's Screwing Whom?' (2000) 2 *Info* 339.

Blanchard, Carl, 'Telecommunications Regulation in New Zealand—How Effective is Light-Handed Regulation?' (1994) 18 *Telecommunications Policy* 154.

Blanchard, Carl, 'Telecommunications Regulation in New Zealand—The Court of Appeal's Decision in Clear Communications v. Telecom Corporation' (1994) 18 *Telecommunications Policy* 725.

Blanchard, Carl, 'Telecommunications Regulation in New Zealand—Light-Handed Regulation and the Privy Council's Judgment' (1995) 19 *Telecommunications Policy* 465.

Bloom, Margareth, 'A UK Perspective on the Europeanisation of National Competition Law', speech delivered at the Conference 'Modernisation and Decentralisation: The New Relationship between Community and National Competition Law', University College London, 17 September 1999.

Bloom, Margareth, 'The Impact of the Competition Bill' in Christopher McCrudden (ed), *Regulation and Deregulation: Policy and Practice in the Utilities and Financial Services Industries (Oxford Law Colloquium)* (Oxford: Clarendon Press, 1999).

Blumenfeld, Jeffrey, and Christy C Kunin, 'United States' in Colin Long (ed), *Telecommunications Law and Practice* (London: Sweet & Maxwell, 1995) 649.

Boles de Boer, David, and Lewis Evans, 'The Economic Efficiency of Telecommunications in a Deregulated Market: The Case of New Zealand' *The Economic Record*, March 1996, 25.

Boles de Boer David, Lewis Evans and Bronwyn Howell, 'The State of e-New Zealand' (September 2000), available at <http://www.iscr.org.nz/navigation/research.html>.

Boles de Boer David, Christina Enright and Lewis Evans, 'The Internet Service Provider (ISP) Markets of Australia and New Zealand' (May 2000), available at <http://www.iscr.org.nz/navigation/research.html>.

Bollard, Alan, and Rae Ellingham, 'Regulation in New Zealand Telecommunications: The Regulatory Body's Perspective', AIC Conference, Competition, Customer Care and Retention in New Zealand Telecommunications, Stamford Plaza, Auckland, 28 October 1997.

Bollard, Allan, and Michael Pickford, *Utility Regulation in New Zealand*, Institute of Economic Affairs, Lectures on Regulation, London, 1996.

Bond, James, 'Telecommunications is Dead, Long Live Networking', Public Policy for the Private Sector, Note 199 (The World Bank, July 1997).

Brennan, Timothy J, 'Regulated Firms in Unregulated Markets: Understanding the Divestiture in US v. AT&T' (1987) 32 *Antitrust Bulletin* 741.

Breyer, Stephen, *Regulation and Its Reform* (Cambridge, Mass.: Harvard University Press, 1982).

Brock, Gerald W, *Telecommunication Policy for the Information Age* (Cambridge, Mass.: Harvard University Press, 1994).

Campbell, Angela J, 'Universal Service Provisions: The "Ugly Duckling" of the 1996 Act' (1996) 29 *Connecticut L Rev* 187.

Campbell, Dennis (ed), *International Communications Law* (Washington, DC: BNA International Inc, 2000).

Carter, Michael, and Julian Wright, 'Bargaining over Interconnection: The Clear–Telecom Dispute', Center for Research in Network Economics and Communications, University of Auckland, Working Paper 13, 1997.

Cave, Martin, and Tommaso Valletti, 'Are Spectrum Auctions Ruining our Grandchildren's Future?' (2000) 2 *Info* 349.

Cave, Martin, and Peter Williamson, 'Entry, Competition, and Regulation in UK Telecommunications' (1996) 12 *Oxford Rev of Economic Policy* 113.

Chen, Jim, 'TELRIC in Turmoil, Telecommunications in Transition: A Note on The Iowa Board Litigation' (1998) 33 *Wake Forest L Rev* 51.

Coase, Ronald H, 'The Federal Communications Commission' (1959) 2 *J of L and Economics* 1.

Coase, Ronald H, 'The Nature of the Firm' *Economica* 4 (November) 386–405, reprinted in R H Coase, *The Firm, the Market and the Law* (Chicago, Ill.: University of Chicago Press, 1988).

Cole, Marion, *Introduction to Telecommunications—Voice, Data and the Internet* (Upper Saddle River, NJ: Prentice-Hall, 2000).

Coleman, Martin, and Michael Grenfell, *The Competition Act 1998: Law and Practice* (Oxford: Oxford University Press, 1999).

Cook, John, and Christopher Kerse, *EC Merger Control* (3rd edn, London: Sweet & Maxwell, 2000).

Cramton, Peter, 'The FCC Spectrum Auctions: An Early Assessment' (1997) 6 *J of Economics and Management Strategy* 431.

Cramton, Peter, 'The Efficiency of FCC Spectrum Auctions' (1998) 41 *J of L and Economics* 727.

Crandall, Robert W, 'New Zealand Spectrum Policy: A Model for the United States?' (1998) XLI *J of L and Economics* 837.

Crandall, Robert W, 'An Assessment of the Competitive Local Exchange Carriers Five Years After the Passage of the Telecommunications Act' (June 2001), available at <www.usta.org/on_the_hill/HR1542/crandall.pdf>.

Crandall, Robert W, and Jerry A Hausman, 'Competition in U.S. Telecommunications Services: Effects of the 1996 Legislation' in Sam Peltzman and Clifford Winston (eds), *Deregulation of Network Industries: What Next?* (Washington, DC: AEI–Brookings Joint Center for Regulatory Studies, 2000) 73.

Cribbett, Peter, 'Population Distribution and Telecommunication Costs', Productivity Commission Staff Research Paper (Canberra: AusInfo, August 2000) 27.

Curien, Nicolas, 'The Theory and Measure of Cross-Subsidies: An Application to the Telecommunications Industry' (1991) 9 *Intl J of Industrial Organization* 73.

Daniels, Alex, 'Competitors Hope to Take Verizon to the Chopping Block', *Techway Washington* (15 October 2001), document available at <http://washtech.com/washtech-way/2_20/ techcap/12957–1.html>.

Dippon, Christian M, 'Local Loop Unbundling: Flaws of the Cost Proxy Model' (2001) 3 *Info* 159.

Director, Mark D, *Restructuring and Expanding National Telecommunications Markets: A Primer on Competition, Regulation and Development for East and Central European Regulators* (The Annenberg Washington Program), ch 2 available at <http://www.annenberg.nwu.edu/pubs/telmar/telmar02.htm>.

Dnes, Antony, 'Post-Privatization Performance—Regulating Telecommunications in the UK' *Viewpoint* (Washington, DC: The World Bank, October 1995).

Doern, G Bruce, and Stephen Wilks, *Comparative Competition Policy: National Institutions in a Global Market* (Oxford: Clarendon Press, 1996).

Donahue, Hugh Carter, 'Opening the Broadband Cable Market: A New Kingsbury Commitment' (2001) 3 *Info* 111.

Donegan, Michelle, 'Operators Target BT's Network', *Communications Week Intl* (21 May 2001).

Donegan, Michelle, 'Telcos Pressured to Split Up', *Communications Week Intl* (8 October 2001).

Economides, Nicholas, 'The Economics of Networks' (1996) 16 *Intl Journal of Industrial Organization* 673.

Economides, Nicholas, 'The Telecommunications Act of 1996 and Its Impact' (September 1998), available at <http://raven.stern.nyu.edu/networks/telco96.html>.

Edmonds, David, 'OFCOM: What Are We Worried About?' (11 October 2001), available at <http://www.oftel.gov.uk/publications/about_oftel/strat100.htm>.

Ergas, Henry, 'Competition Policy in Deregulated Industries' (July/August 1995) *Intl Business Lawyer* 305.

Ergas, Henry, 'Telecommunications Across the Tasman: A Comparison of Economic Approaches and Economic Outcomes in Australia and New Zealand', paper prepared for the International Institute of Communications (May 1996) 4.

Ergas, Henry, *Internet Peering: A Case Study of the ACCC's Use of its Power Under Part XIB of the Trade Practices Act 1974*, Mimeo, 8 May 1999.

Falhauber, Gerald, 'Pricing Internet: The Efficient Subsidy' in Brian Kahin (ed), *Building Information Infrastructure* (New York, Toronto, London: McGraw-Hill, 1992).

Flood, Colleen, 'Regulation of Telecommunications in New Zealand—Faith in Competition Law and the Kiwi Share' (1995) 3 *Competition and Consumer L J* 214.

Foster, Christopher, *Privatization, Public Ownership and Regulation of Natural Monopoly* (Oxford: Basil Blackwell, 1993).

Fried, Lisa I, 'Curbing FCC Powers: Agency's Role in Telecom Mergers Questioned' 221 *New York L J* 5.

Frieden, Rob, *Managing Internet Driven Change in International Telecommunications* (Boston, Mass., and London: Artech House, 2001).

Frieden, Robert M, 'The Computer Inquiries: Mapping the Communications/Information Processing Terrain' (1981) 33 *Federal Communications L J* 55.

Frieden, Robert M, 'The Third Computer Inquiry: A Deregulatory Dilemma' (1987) 38 *Federal Communications L J* 383.

Frieden, Robert M, 'The Telecommunications Act of 1996: Predicting the Winners and Losers' (1997) 20 *Hastings Communications & Entertainment L J* 11.

Frieden, Robert M, 'Last Days of the Free Ride? The Consequences of Settlement-Based Interconnection for the Internet' (1999) 1 *Info* 225.

Frieden, Robert M, 'Does a Hierarchical Internet Necessitate Multilateral Intervention?' (2001) 26 *North Carolina J of Intl L and Commercial Regulation* 361.

Gabel, David, and David I Rosenbaum, 'Who's Taking Whom?: Some Comments and Evidence on the Constitutionality of TELRIC' (2000) 52 *Federal Communications L J* 239.

Galal, Ahmed, 'Regulation and Commitment in the Development of Telecommunications in Chile', Policy Research Working Paper 1278 (Washington, DC: The World Bank, 1994).

Galal, Ahmed, et al, *Welfare Consequences of Selling Public Enterprises—An Empirical Analysis* (Oxford: Oxford University Press, 1994).

Gallo, Michael L, 'AT&T Corp v. Iowa Utilities Board' (2000) 15 *Berkeley Technology L J* 417.

Gellhorn, Ernest, and William E Kovacic, *Antitrust Law and Economics in a Nutshell* (St Paul, Minn.: 4th edn, West Publishing, 1994).

Geradin, Damien, 'Institutional Aspects of EU Regulatory Reforms in the Telecommunications Sector: An Analysis of the Role of National Regulatory Authorities' (2000) 1 *J of Network Industries* 5.

Geradin, Damien, 'Regulatory Issues Raised by Network Convergence: The Case of Multi-Utilities' (2001) 2 *J of Network Industries* 113.

Geradin, Damien, and Christophe Humpe, 'Regulatory Issues in Establishment and Management of Communications Infrastructure: The Impact of Network Convergence' (2002) 3 *J of Network Industries* 99.

Green, James R, and David J Teece, 'Four Approaches to Telecommunications Deregulation and Competition: The US, UK, Australia, and New Zealand', available at <http://groups.haas.berkeley.edu/imio/crtp/publications/workingpapers/wp49.pdf>.

Green, Laurence, 'The UK Approach to Spectrum Pricing and Auctions', paper presented at the IDEE Telecom Conference (11 June 1999), available at <http://www.radio.gov.uk/topics/spectrum-price/documents/idee.htm>.

Green, Richard, 'Checks and Balances in Utility Regulation—The UK Experience', Public Policy for the Private Sector, Note No 185 (Washington, DC: The World Bank, May 1999).

Grice, Corey, and Evan Hansen, 'FTC Decision: A Broadband Portent', *ZDNet News*, 14 December 2000.

Guash, Luis, and Pablo Spiller, *Managing the Regulatory Process: Design, Concepts, Issues and the Latin America and Caribbean Story* (Washington, DC: The World Bank, 1999).

Guislain, Pierre, *The Privatization Challenge: A Strategic, Legal and Institutional Analysis of International Experience* (Washington, DC: The World Bank, 1997).

Hachette, Dominique, and Rolph Luders, *Privatization in Chile: An Economic Appraisal* (Oakland, Cal.: International Center for Economic Growth, 1993).

Hahn, Robert, *Improving Regulatory Accountability* (Washington, DC: AEI Press, 1996).

Hall, Clare, et al, *Telecommunications Regulation—Culture, Chaos and Interdependence Inside the Regulatory Process* (London and New York: Routledge, 2000).

Hall, Thomas J, 'The FCC and the Telecom Act of 1996: Necessary Steps to Achieve Substantial Deregulation' (1998) 11 *Harvard J of L and Technology* 797.

Hammond, Allen S, 'Universal Service in the Digital Age: The Telecommunications Act of 1996: Codifying the Digital Divide' (1997) 50 *Federal Communications L J* 179.

Harmer, David, and Grant Hannis, 'The Commerce Act—What Must Change?', paper distributed at the TUANZ Competition Symposium, Wellington, New Zealand, 7–8 April 1998.

Harrington, David, 'Access for All? Spectrum Auctions in the Local Loop' (2000) 2 *Info* 351.

Hausman, Jerry A, et al, 'Cable Modem and DSL: Broadband Internet Access for Residential Customers' (2001) 91 *AEA Papers and Proceedings* 302.

Hausman, Jerry A, et al, 'The Consumer-Welfare Benefits from Bell Company Entry into Long-Distance Telecommunications: Empirical Evidence from New York and Texas', document available at <http://papers.ssrn.com/sol3/cf_dev/AbsByAuth.cfm?per_id =206474>.

Hay, George A, 'Reflections on Clear' (1996) 3 *Competition and Consumer L J* 231.

Helm, Dieter, 'British Utility Regulation: Theory, Practice and Reform' (1994) 10 *Oxford Rev of Economic Policy* 17.

Hewitt, Patricia, '3G Licence Allocation—Why an Auction was Best for the UK' (2000) 2 *Info* 341.

Hilmer, Frederick, et al, 'National Competition Policy—Report by the Independent Committee on Inquiry' (Canberra: Australian Government Publishing Services, 1993).

Hoe, E Sanderson, and Stephen Ruscus, 'Taking Aim at the Takings Argument: Using Forward-Looking Pricing Methodologies to Price Unbundled Network Elements' (1997) 5 *CommLaw Conspectus* 231.

Holmes, J, 'The Telecommunications Act 1991 and its Meaning for Consumers and Competition' in Stephen G Corones, *Competition Policy in Telecommunications and Aviation* (Sydney: Federation Press, 1992) 228.

Holson, Laura M, and Seth Schiesel, 'MCI Worldcom to Acquire Sprint in Stock Swap Valued at $108 Billion' *New York Times*, 5 October 1999.

Hovenkamp, Herbert, *Federal Antitrust Policy: The Law of Competition and its Practice* (St Paul, Minn.: West Publishing, 1994).

Huber, Peter H, et al, *Federal Telecommunications Law* (2nd edn, New York: Aspen Law & Business, 1999).

Hulsink, Willem, *Privatisation and Liberalisation in European Telecommunications—Comparing Britain, the Netherlands and France* (London and New York: Routledge, 1998).

Huntley, John AK, 'Competition and the Provision of a Universal Telecommunications Service' (1994) 17 *World Competition* 7.

Huntley, John AK, et al, 'Laboratories of De-Regulation? Implications for Europe of American State Telecommunications Policy' 1997 (1) *J of Information, L and Technology*, available at <http://elj.warwick.ac.uk/jilt/telecoms/97_1hunt/default.htm>.

Intven, Hank (ed), *Telecommunications Regulation Handbook* (Washington, DC: The World Bank, 2000) B-14–B-18.

Jones, Christopher, and Enrique Gonzalez-Diaz, *The EEC Merger Regulation* (London: Sweet & Maxwell, 1992).

Jorde, Thomas M, et al, 'Innovation, Investment and Unbundling' (2000) 17 *Yale J on Regulation* 1.

Joseph, Richard A, 'The Politics of Telecommunications Reform: A Comparative Study of Australia and New Zealand', University of Wollongong, Science and Technology Analysis Research Programme, Working Paper No 12 (July 1993).

Kahn, Alfred E, *The Economics of Regulation—Principles and Institutions* (Cambridge, Mass., and London: MIT Press, 1998).

Kahn, Alfred E, *Whom the Gods Would Destroy or How Not to Deregulate* (Washington, DC: AEI–Brookings Joint Center for Regulatory Studies, 2001).

Kahn, Alfred E, and William E Taylor, 'The Pricing of Inputs Sold To Competitors: A Comment' (1994) 11 *Yale J on Regulation* 225.

Katz, Michael L, and Carl Shapiro, 'Network Externalities, Competition, and Compatibility' (1985) 75 *American Economic Rev* 424.

Kearney, Joseph D, 'From the Fall of the Bell System to the Telecommunications Act: Regulation of Telecommunications Under Judge Greene' (1999) 50 *Hastings L J* 1395.

Kearney, Joseph D, and Thomas W Merrill, 'The Great Transformation of Regulated Industries Law' (1998) 98 *Columbia L Rev* 1323.

Kende, Michael, 'The Digital Handshake: Connecting Internet Backbones', OPP Working Paper No 32, Federal Communications Commission (September 2000).

Kerf, Michel, and Damien Geradin, 'Controlling Market Power in Telecommunications: Antitrust vs. Sector-specific Regulation—An Assessment of the United States, New Zealand and Australian Experiences' (1999) 14 *Berkeley Technology LJ* 919.

Kerf, Michel, and Damien Geradin, 'Post-liberalization Challenges in Telecommunications: Balancing Antitrust and Sector-specific Regulation—Tentative Lessons from the Experiences of the United States, New Zealand, Chile and Australia' (2000) 23(2) *J of World Competition* 27.

Kerf, Michel, et al, 'Concessions for Infrastructure: A Guide to their Design and Award' World Bank Technical Paper No 399 (Washington, DC: The World Bank, 1998).

Kerr, Roger, and Bryce Wilkinson, 'The Regulation of Monopoly in New Zealand', paper distributed at the TUANZ Competition Symposium, Wellington, New Zealand, 7–8 April 1998.

Kezsbom, Allen, and Alan Goldman, 'No Shortcut to Antitrust Analysis: The Twisted Journey of the "Essential Facilities" Doctrine' (1996) *Columbia Business L Rev* 1.

Khemani, R Shyam, 'Competition Law—Some Guidelines for Implementation' FPD Note No 14 (Washington, DC: The World Bank, July 1994).

King, Stephen, and Rodney Maddock, *Unlocking the Infrastructure—The Reform of Public Utilities in Australia* (St Leonards, NSW: Allen & Unwin, 1996).

Kirk, Robert G, 'Wireless Mobile Communications' in Leon T Knauer et al (eds), *Beyond the Telecommunications Act—A Domestic and International Perspective for Business* (Rockville, Mld.: Government Institutes, 1998), 74.

Klein, Joseph A, 'Antitrust Law as a Regulator of the Rapidly Transforming Telecommunications Market' (1998) 23 *Communications & Strategies* 209.

Klein, Michael, 'Bidding for Concessions—The Impact of Contract Design' 158 *Public Policy for the Private Sector* (Washington, DC: The World Bank, 1998).

Klein, Michael, 'Designing Auctions for Concessions—Guessing the Right Value to Bid and the Winner's Curse' 160 *Public Policy for the Private Sector* (Washington, DC: The World Bank, 1998).

Korah, Valentine, 'Charges for Inter-Connection to a Telecommunications Network' (1995) 2 *Competition and Consumer L J* 213.

Krasnow, Erwin G, and Jack N Goodman, 'The 'Public Interest' Standard: The Search for the Holy Grail' (1998) 50 *Federal Communications L J* 605.

Krattenmaker, Thomas G, 'The Telecommunications Act of 1996' (1996) 29 *Connecticut L Rev* 123.

Krattenmaker, Thomas G, *Telecommunications Law and Policy* (2nd edn, Durham, NC: Carolina Academic Press, 1998).

Labaton, Stephen, 'FCC to Promote a Trading System to Sell Airwaves', *New York Times*, 13 March 2000.

Labaton, Stephen, 'Communications Lobby Puts Full-Court Press on Congress', *New York Times*, 24 October 2000.

Laffont, Jean-Jacques, and Jean Tirole, *Competition in Telecommunications* (Cambridge, Mass., and London: MIT Press, 2000).

Laffont, Jean-Jacques, and Jean Tirole, 'Access Pricing and Competition' (1994) 38 *European Economic Rev* 1673.

Laffont, Jean-Jacques, and Jean Tirole, 'Creating Competition Through Interconnection: Theory and Practice' (1996) 10 *J of Regulatory Economics* 227.

Lapointe, Mackenzy, 'Universal Service and the Digital Revolution: Beyond the Telecommunications Act of 1996' (1999) 25 *Rutgers Computer and Technology L J* 61.

Larouche, Pierre, *Competition Law and Regulation in European Telecommunications* (Oxford and Portland, Ore.: Hart Publishing, 2000).

Larson, Alexander C and Douglas R Mudd, 'The Telecommunications Act of 1996 and Competition Policy: An Economic View in Hindsight' (1999) 4 *Virginia J of L and Technology* 1.

Lehr, William, and Martin Weiss, 'The Political Economy of Congestion Charges and Settlements in Packet Networks' (1996) 20 *Telecommunications Policy* 219.

Lemley, Mark A, and Lawrence Lessig, 'Open Access to Cable Modems' (2000) 22 *Whittier L Rev* 3.

Lemley, Mark A, and Lawrence Lessig, 'The End of End-to-End: Preserving the Architecture of the Internet in the Broadband Era' (2001) 48 *UCLA L Rev* 925.

Lemley, Mark A, and David McGowan, 'Legal Implications of Network Economic Effects' (1998) 86 *California L Rev* 479.

Leonard, Peter, 'A Hostile Land: Competition Regulation and Australian Telecommunications, 1997–2000' (Gilbert & Tobin, 19 September 2000), available at <www.gtlaw.com.au/pubs>.

Leroy, Jones, 'Appropriate Regulatory Technology: The Interplay of Economic and Institutional Conditions', Annual Bank Conference on Development Economic, 1993.

Levy, Brian, and Pablo Spiller, *Regulation, Institutions and Commitment* (Cambridge: Cambridge University Press, 1996).

Lipschitz, Benjamin, 'Regulatory Treatment of Network Convergence: Opportunities and Challenge in the Digital Era' (1998) 7 *Media L and Policy* 14.

Lipsky, Abbott B, and Gregory J Sidak, 'Essential Facilities' (1999) 51 *Stanford L Rev* 1187.

Litan, Robert E, and Roger G Noll, 'Unleashing Telecommunications: The Case for Competition', Policy Brief No 39 (Washingdon, DC: The Brookings Institution, November 1998) 1.

Lojkine Susan, 'Competition Litigation in the High Court', Materials for Third Annual Workshop, Competition Law and Policy Institute of New Zealand, vol II (August 1991).

Long, Colin D, *Telecommunications Law and Practice* (2nd edn, London: Sweet & Maxwell, 1995).

Long, Colin D, 'Whether and How to Regulate Convergence' (1999) *Computer and Telecommunications L Rev* 3.

Lovell, Caroline, 'The Future of the Australian Universal Service Obligation', paper presented at the International Telecommunications Society, XIII Biennial Conference, Buenos Aires, Argentina 2–5 July 2000, available at <http://www.its2000.org.ar/conference/lovell.pdf>.

MacAvoy, Paul W, and Kenneth Robinson, 'Winning by Losing: The AT&T Settlement and its Impact on Telecommunications' (1983) 1 *Yale J on Regulation* 1.

MacKie-Mason, Jeffrey K, and Hal Varian, 'Economic FAQs About the Internet' (1994), available at <http://www.virtualschool.edu/mon/Economics/VarianInternet Economics.html>.

MacKie-Mason, Jeffrey, and Hal R Varian, 'Pricing the Internet' in Brian Kahin and James Keller, *Public Access to the Internet* (Cambridge, Mass., and London: MIT Press, 1995) 269.

MacKie-Mason, Jeffrey, and Hal R Varian, 'Pricing Congestible Network Resources' (1995) 13 *IEEE Journal* 1141.

Maddock, Rodney, and Anthony Marshall, 'Access Regulation: The New Australian Model' (1997) 6 *Utilities Policy* 73.

Mankiw, N Gregory, *Principles of Economics* (Fort Worth, Tex.: Dryden Press, 1997).

May, Randolph J, 'An Agency for Bill and Al' *Legal Times*, 5 June 2000, 75.

May, Randolph J, 'A Reform Agenda for the New FCC' (2001) 5 *Info* 407.

Mayton, William T, 'The Illegitimacy of the Public Interest Standard at the FCC' (1989) 38 *Emory L J* 715.

McAfee, Preston, and John McMillan, 'Auctions and Bidding' (1987) 25 *J of Economic Literature* 699.

McLaughlin, Duane, 'FCC Jurisdiction Over Local Telephone Under the 1996 Act: Fenced Off?' (1997) 97 *Columbia L Rev* 2210.

McMillan, John, 'Selling Spectrum Rights' (1994) 8 *J of Economic Perspectives* 145.

Melamed, Douglas, 'Antitrust: The New Regulation' (1995) 10 *Antitrust* 13.

Melo, José Ricardo, 'Liberalization and Privatization in Chile' in Bjorn Wellenius and Peter A Stern (eds), *Implementing Reforms in the Telecommunications Sector: Lessons from Experience* (Washington, DC: The World Bank, 1994) 145.

Melody, William H, 'On the Meaning and Importance of "Independence" in Telecom Reform' (1997) 21 *Telecommunications Policy* 195.

Meyerson, Michael I, 'Ideas of the Marketplace: A Guide to the 1996 Telecommunications Act' (1997) 49 *Federal Communications L J* 252.

Millard, Nicole M, 'Universal Service, Section 254 of the Telecommunications Act of 1996: A Hidden Tax?' (1997) 50 *Federal Communications L J* 265.

Mini, Frederico, 'The Role and Incentives for Opening Monopoly Markets: Comparing GTE and RBOC Cooperation with Local Entrants' Georgetown University, Department of Economics, Working Paper 00-09, July 1999.

Molano, Walter T, *The Logic of Privatization: The Case of Telecommunications in the Southern Cone of Latin America* (Westport, Conn.: Greenwood Press, 1997).

Morris, Derek, 'A New Dawn for Competition Policy in the UK', IBC Conference, 24 November 1999, available at <http://www.competition-commission.org.uk/inquiries/ibcspeech.htm>.

Morris, Roy L, 'A Proposal to Promote Telephone Competition: The LoopCo Plan' (Jan/Feb 1998) *CCH Power and Telecom L* 35.

Mueller, Milton, *Universal Service: Competition, Interconnection and Monopoly in the Making of the American System* (Washington, DC: AEI Press, 1997).

Mueller, Milton, 'On the Frontier of Deregulation: New Zealand Telecommunications and the Problem of Interconnecting Competing Networks' in David Gabel and David F Weiman (eds), *Opening Networks to Competition, The Regulation of Pricing and Access* (Boston, Mass., and Dordrecht: Kluwer Academic Publishers, 1998) 115.

Munoz, Oscar (ed), *Despues de las Privatizaciones: Hacia el Estado Regulador* (Santiago de Chile: CEPLAN, 1993).

Naftel, Mark, and Lawrence J Spiwak, *The Telecoms Trade War* (Oxford and Portland, Ore.: Hart Publishing, 2000).

NERA, 'Costs of Telecommunications Competition Policies' report prepared for Telecom New Zealand, 9 May 2000.

Neu, Werner, and Ulrich Stumpf, 'Evaluating Compensation Requirements by Telecommunications Universal Service Providers: A New Challenge to Regulators' (1997) 26 *Communications and Strategies* 165.

Newbery, David M, *Privatization, Restructuring, and Regulation of Network Utilities* (Cambridge, Mass., and London: MIT Press, 2000).

Noam, Eli M, Seisuke Komatsuzaki, and Douglas A Conn (eds), *Telecommunications in the Pacific Basin: an Evolutionary Approach* (Oxford: Oxford University Press, 1994).

Noam, Eli M, 'Toward a Common Law of Telecom' (1996), available at: <http://www.columbia.edu/dlc/wp/citi/citinoam19.html>.

Noam, Eli M, 'Will Universal Service and Common Carriage Survive the Telecommunications Act of 1996?' (1997) 97 *Columbia L Rev* 955.

Noam, Eli M, *Interconnecting the Network of Networks* (Cambridge, Mass., and London: MIT Press, 2001).

Noll, Roger G, 'The Role of Antitrust in Telecommunications' (Fall 1995) *Antitrust Bulletin*, 501.

Noll, Roger G, 'Telecommunications Reforms in Developing Countries' AEI–Brookings Joint Center for Regulatory Studies, Working Paper 99-10 (November 1999).

Nowicki, Elizabeth A, 'Competition in the Local Telecommunications Market: Legislate or Litigate?' (1996) 9 *Harvard J of L and Technology* 353.

Oberst, Gerald, 'European Telecommunications Licensing' (1997) 5 *Computer and Telecommunications L Rev* 216.

Ogus, Anthony, *Regulation: Legal Form and Economic Theory* (Oxford: Clarendon Press, 1994).

Oxman, Jason, 'The FCC and the Unregulation of the Internet' OPP Working Paper No 31, Federal Communications Commission (July 1999).

Parkes, Sarah, 'Competition in the Last Mile Remains Elusive' *Financial Times Special Survey on Telecoms*, 18 July 2000, IV.

Patterson, Ross, 'Light-Handed Regulation in New Zealand Ten Years On: Stimulus to Competition or Monopolist's Charter?', paper distributed at the TUANZ Competition Symposium, Wellington, New Zealand, 7–8 April, 1998.

Peltzman, Sam, 'Toward a More General Theory of Regulation' (1976) 19 *J of L and Economics* 211.

Pengilley, Warren, 'Hilmer and Essential Facilities' (1994) 17 *U of New South Wales L J* 1.

Pengilley, Warren, 'The Privy Council Speaks on Essential Facilities Access in New Zealand: What are the Australasian Lessons?' (1995) 3 *Competition and Consumer L J* 28.

Pengilley, Warren, 'Access to Essential Facilities: A Unique Antitrust Experiment in Australia' (1998) XLIII *The Antitrust Bulletin* 519.

Piraino, Thomas A, 'A Proposed Antitrust Analysis of Telecommunications Joint Ventures' (1997) *Wisconsin L Rev* 639.

Pitsch, Peter K, 'Reforming Universal Service: Competitive Bidding or Consumer Choice?' Cato Institute Briefing Paper No 29 (7 May 1997), available at <http://www.cato.org/pubs/briefs/bp-029es.html>.

Pitt, Edward, 'Telecommunications Regulation: Is It Realistic to Rely on Competition Law to Do the Job?' (1999) *European Competition L Rev* 245.

Posner, Richard A, 'Theories of Economic Regulation' (1974) 5 *Bell J of Economic Regulation* 335.

Posner, Richard A, *Antitrust Law: An Economic Perspective* (Chicago, Ill.: University of Chicago Press, 1978).

Posner, Richard A, *Natural Monopoly and Its Regulation* (30th edn, Washington, DC: Cato Institute, 1999).

Prosser, Tony, *Law and The Regulator* (Oxford: Clarendon Press, 1997).

Quiggin, John, *Great Expectations—Microeconomic Reform and Australia* (St Leonards, NSW: Allen & Unwin, 1996).

Read, William H, and Ronald Alan Weiner, 'FCC Reform: Governing Requires a New Standard' (1998) 49 *Federal Communications L J* 293.

Rill, James F, et al, 'Institutional Responsibilities Affecting Competition in the Telecommunications Industry' in Claus Dieter Ehlermann and Louisa Gosling, *European Competition Law Annual 1998: Regulating Communications Markets* (Oxford and Portland, Ore.: Hart Publishing, 2000) 667.

Romero, Simon, 'Wireless is Getting a Cool Reception in US' *New York Times*, 29 January 2001.

Rosenblum, Mark C, 'The Antitrust Rationale for the MFJ's Line-of-Business Restrictions and a Policy Proposal for Removing Them' (1996) 25 *Southwestern U L Rev* 605.

Rosenblut, Jorge, 'Telecommunications in Chile: Success and Post-Deregulatory Challenges in a Rapidly Emerging Economy' (1998) 51 *J of Intl Affairs* 8.

Rosston, Gregory L, and Jeffrey S Steinberg, 'Using Market-Based Spectrum Policy to Promote the Public Interest' (1997) 50 *Federal Communications L J* 1.

Rosston, Gregory L, and Bradley S Wimmer, 'The ABC's of Universal Service: Arbitrage, Big Bucks, and Competition' (1999) 50 *Hastings L J* 1585.

Ryan, Michael, 'United Kingdom Policy on Equal Access and the Promotion of Network Competition' (1998) *Computer and Telecommunications L Rev* 7.

Sandbach, Jonathan, 'Levering Open the Local Loop: Shaping BT for Broadband Competition' (2001) 3 *Info* 195.

Scherer, Frederic M, *Competition Policies for an Integrated World Economy* (Washington, DC: Institute for International Economics, 1994).

Schiesel, Seth, 'For Local Phone Users, Choice Isn't an Option' *New York Times*, 21 November 2000.

Schiesel, Seth, 'Phone Mergers that May Help Competition' *New York Times*, 27 November 2000.

Schiesel, Seth, 'Rules for AOL–Time Warner Have a Narrow Impact' *New York Times*, 18 December 2000.

Schuler, Joseph F, 'Will the Sun Set on PUCs?' *Public Utilities Fortnightly*, 15 July 1998, 28.

Schwartz, Marius, 'Conditioning the Bells' Entry Into Long Distance: Anticompetitive Regulation or Promoting Competition?', paper presented at the Robert Schuman Center of the European University Institute, Florence, 9 September 1999.

Schwartz, Marius, 'The Economic Logic for Conditioning Bell Entry into Long Distance on the Prior Opening of Local Markets', AEI–Brookings Joint Center for Regulatory Studies, Working Paper 00-4, April 2000.

Scott, Colin, 'Institutional Competition and Coordination in the Process of Telecommunications Liberalization' in Joseph McCahery et al, *International Regulatory Competition and Regulatory Coordination: Perspectives on Economic Regulation in Europe and the United States* (Oxford: Clarendon Press, 1996) 383.

Scott, Colin, 'Accountability and the Regulatory State' (2000) 27 *J of L and Society* 38.

Serra, Pablo, 'La Politica de Competencia en Chile' (1995) 10 *Revista de Análisis Económico* 72.

Sharkey, William W, *The Theory of Natural Monopoly* (Cambridge: Cambridge University Press, 1982).

Shelansky, Howard, and Peter Huber, 'Administrative Creation of Property Rights to Radio Spectrum' (1998) 41 *J of L and Economics* 581.

Shogren, Rod, 'How Light-Handed Can you Get?—A Report on Telecommunications Regulation in Australia', paper distributed at the TUANZ Competition Symposium, Wellington, New Zealand, 7–8 April 1998.

Sidak, J Gregory, and Daniel F Spulber, *Deregulatory Takings and the Regulatory Contract: The Competitive Transformation of Competitive Industries in the United States* (Cambridge: Cambridge University Press, 1997).

Sidak, J Gregory, and Daniel F Spulber, 'Givings, Takings and the Fallacy of Forward-Looking Costs' (1997) 72 *New York U L Rev* 1068.

Sidak, J Gregory, and Daniel F Spulber, 'The Tragedy of the Telecommons: Government Pricing of Unbundled Network Elements Under the Telecommunications Act of 1996' (1997) 97 *Columbia L Rev* 1081.

Sidak, J Gregory, and Daniel F Spulber, 'Cyberjam: The Law and Economics of Internet Congestion of the Telephone Network' (1998) 21 *Harvard J of L and Public Policy* 327.

Sloan, Tim, 'Creating Better Incentives through Regulation: Section 271 of the Communications Act of 1934 and the Promotion of Local Exchange Competition' (1998) 50 *Federal Communications L J* 312.

Small, John P, 'Light Handed Regulation of Network Industries in New Zealand', paper distributed at the TUANZ Competition Symposium, Wellington, New Zealand, 7–8 April 1998.

Smith, Peter, 'Subscribing to Monopoly, The Telecom Monopolist's Lexicon—Revisited' Public Policy for the Private Sector, The World Bank, Note No 53 (September 1995).

Smith, Warrick, 'Utility Regulators—The Independence Debate' *Viewpoint*, No 127 (Washington, DC: The World Bank, October 1997).

Smith, Warrick, 'Utility Regulators—Roles and Responsibilities' *Viewpoint*, No 128 (Washington, DC: The World Bank, October 1997).

Smith, Warrick, *Regulatory Institutions for Utilities and Competition*, Mimeo, The World Bank, Private Sector Development, February 1998.

Speta, James B, 'Handicapping the Race for the Last Mile?: A Critique of Open Access Rules for Broadband Platforms' (2000) 17 *Yale J on Regulation* 39.

Speta, James B, 'The Vertical Dimension of Cable Open Access' (2000) 71 *U of Colorado L Rev* 975.

Spiller, Pablo, and Carlo Cardilli, 'Towards a Property Rights Approach to Communications Spectrum' (1999) 16 *Yale J on Regulation* 1.

Spulber, Daniel F, 'Deregulating Telecommunications' (1995) 12 *Yale J on Regulation* 25.

Staats, Diane, *Competition Law—Competition Law and Access Rules Get More Teeth* (Sydney: Freehils, 1999).

Steinberg, Tom, 'Open Networks: A Solution to Britain's Broadband Problems?' (Institute of Economic Affairs, February 2001).

Stewart-Smith, Martin C, 'Industry Structure and Regulation' Policy Research Working Paper No 1419 (Washington, DC: The World Bank, February 1995).

Stigler, Georges, 'The Theory of Economic Regulation' (1971) 2 *Bell J of Economic Regulation* 3.

Stuhmcke, Anita, 'The Corporatisation and Privatisation of the Australian Telecommunications Industry: The Role of the Telecommunications Industry Ombudsman' (1998) *U of New South Wales L J* 807.

Su, Wang, 'FCC Preemption Power' (1998) 13 *Berkeley Technology L J* 435.

Taperell, Geoff, 'Misuse of Market Power in Telecommunications—The Legislative Safeguards' in Stephen G Corones (ed), *Competition Policy in Telecommunications and Aviation* (Sydney: Federation Press, 1992) 179.

Taperell, Geoff, and Richard Dammery, 'Anti-Competitive Conduct in Telecommunications: Are Supplementary Rules Required?' (1996) 4 *Competition and Consumer L J* 63.

Tardiff, Timothy J, 'New Technologies and Convergence of Markets: Implications for Telecommunications Regulation' (2000) 1 *J of Network Industries* 447.

Thierer, Adam, 'A 10-Point Agenda for Comprehensive Telecom Reform' Cato Institute Briefing Papers No 63 (May 2001).

Tomlinson, Melissa, *Latin American Telecommunications: A Study of Deregulation and Privatization in Argentina, Chile and Mexico* (Alexandria, Vir.: Telecom Publishing Group, 1995).

Tramont, Bryan N, 'Too Much Power, Too Little Restraint: How the FCC Expands Its Reach through Unenforceable and Unwieldy "Voluntary Agreements"' (2000) 53 *Federal Communications L J* 49.

Trinchero, Mark P, and Holly Rachel Smith, 'Federal Preemption of State Universal Service Regulations Under the Telecommunications Act of 1996' (1998) 51 *Federal Communications L J* 303.

Turestky, David, 'Bell Operating Company Interlata Entry Under Section 271 of the Telecommunications Act 1996: Some Thoughts', remarks before the Communications Committee NARUC Summer Meeting, 22 July 1996, available at <http://www.usdoj.gov/atr/public/speeches/turetsky796.html>.

Tye, William B, and Carlos Lapuerta, 'The Economics of Pricing Network Interconnection: Theory and Application to the Market for Telecommunications in New Zealand' (1996) 13 *Yale J on Regulation* 419.

Utz, Clayton, *New Telecommunications Legislation* (October 1999) *Communications Issues*.

Vachris, Michelle A, and James Thomas, 'International Price Comparisons Based on Power Purchasing Parity' (October 1999) *Monthly Labor Rev* 3.

Valletti, Tommaso, 'The Practice of Access Pricing—Telecommunications in the United Kingdom' Policy Research Working Paper No 2063, The World Bank, Economic Development Institute (February 1999).

Valletti, Tommaso, and Martin Cave, 'Competition Policy in UK Mobile Communications' (1998) 22 *Telecommunications Policy* 109.

Van Siclen, Sally, 'Privatization and Deregulation of Regulated Industries, and Competition Policy', paper prepared for the 5th International Workshop on Competition Policy, Seoul, Korea, 8 November 2000.

Vautier, Kerrin M, and Allan E Bollard, 'Competition Policy in New Zealand' in Carl J Green and Douglas E Rosenthal, *Competition Regulation in the Pacific Rim* (New York: Oceana Publications Inc, 1996) 390.

Vickers, John, and Michael Waterson, 'Vertical Relationships: An Introduction' (1991) 39 *J of Industrial Economics* 445.

Viscusi, W Kip, et al, *Economics of Regulation and Antitrust* (2nd edn, Cambridge, Mass., and London: MIT Press, 1998).

Vogel, Steven K, *Freer Market, More Rules—Regulatory Reforms in Advanced Industrial Countries* (Ithaca, NY: Cornell University Press, 1996).

Vogelsang, Ingo, and Bridget M Mitchell, *Telecommunications Competition—The Last Ten Miles* (Washington, DC: The AEI Press and, Cambridge, Mass., and London: MIT Press, 1997).

Wakefield, Jane, 'UK Slow to Take Up Broadband, Says Report' *ZDUKNet News*, 18 October 2000, available at <http://zdnet.com.com/2100-11-524888.html>.

Waters, Peter, 'The Mystery of the Missing Ring Fence—Regulation of Vertically Integrated Telecommunications Operators' (Gilbert & Tobin, April 1998), available at <http://www.gtlaw.com.au/gt/pubs>.

Watson, Chris, and Anne M Connaty, 'BT and Unbundling of the Local Loop' (2000) *Computer and Telecommunications L Rev* 7.

Webb, Malcom, and Martyn Taylor, 'Light-Handed Regulation of Telecommunications in New Zealand: Is Generic Competition Law Sufficient?' (Winter 1998/99) 2 *Intl J of Telecommunications L and Policy* 11.

Webbink, Douglas W, 'Frequency Spectrum Deregulation Alternatives' Federal Communications Commission, Office of Plans and Policy Working Paper No 2 (1980).

Weiss, James R, and Martin L Stern, 'Serving Two Masters: The Dual Jurisdiction of the FCC and the Justice Department Over Telecommunications Transactions' (1998) 6 *Communications L Conspectus* 195.

Wellenius, Bjorn, 'Extending Telecommunications Beyond the Market—Toward Universal Service in Competitive Environments' *Viewpoint,* Note 206, The World Bank, 2000.

Wellenius, Bjorn, 'Extending Telecommunications Service to Rural Areas: The Chilean Experience', Public Policy for the Private Sector, Note No 105, The World Bank (February 1997).

Wellenius, Bjorn, 'Regulating the Telecommunications Sector: The Experience of Latin America', Conference on Regulation in Post-Privatization Environment, Buenos Aires, Argentina, 21–22 May 1998.

Wellenius, Bjorn, 'Closing the Rural Communication Access Gap: Chile 1995–2002', The World Bank, draft paper of 24 June 2001, available at <http://www.infodev.org/library/working.htm>.

Wellenius, Bjorn, and Peter A Stern (eds), *Implementing Reforms in the Telecommunications Sector, Lessons from Experience* (Washington, DC: The World Bank, 1994).

Weller, Dennis, 'Auctions for Universal Service Obligations' (1999) 23 *Telecommunications Policy* 645.

World Bank and OECD, *A Framework for the Design and Implementation of Competition Law and Policy* (Washington, DC: World Bank and Paris: OECD, 1998).

Young, Alison, *The Politics of Regulation—Privatized Utilities in Britain* (London: Palgrave, 2001).

Ypsilanti, Dimitry, and Patrick Xavier, 'Towards Next Generation Regulation' (1998) 22 *Telecommunications Policy* 643.

Index